See inside for an illustration of

THE
CRIMINAL
JUSTICE
SYSTEM

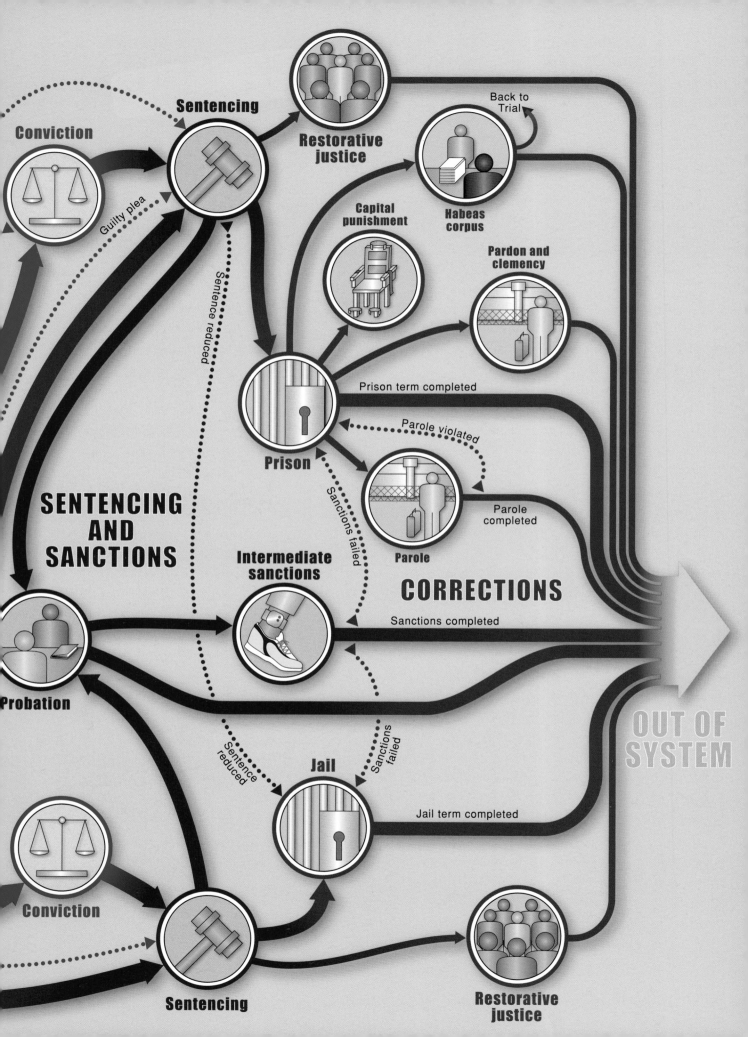

Conviction

Sentencing

Restorative justice

Back to Trial

Guilty plea

Capital punishment

Habeas corpus

Pardon and clemency

Sentence reduced

SENTENCING AND SANCTIONS

Prison term completed

Parole violated

Prison

Parole completed

Sanctions failed

Intermediate sanctions

Parole

CORRECTIONS

Sanctions completed

Probation

OUT OF SYSTEM

Sentence reduced

Jail

Sanctions failed

Jail term completed

Conviction

Sentencing

Restorative justice

THE CRIMINAL JUSTICE SYSTEM

CRIME

ENTRY INTO THE SYSTEM

Reported and observed crime

Investigation

Arrest

Charges filed

Released without prosecution

Released without prosecution

Unsolved crime or no arrest

Initial appearance

PROSECUTION AND PRETRIAL SERVICES

Charges dropped or dismissed

Bail or detention hearing

Charges dropped or dismissed

Grand jury

Refusal to indict

Charge dismissed

Felonies

Misdemeanors

Gather information

Gather information

Preliminary hearing

Arraignment

ADJUDICATION

Reduction of charge

Appeal rejected

Appeal filed

Appeal

New trial granted

Acquitted

Found guilty

Guilty plea

Trial

Plea bargain

Preliminary hearing

Arraignment

Charge dismissed

Plea bargain

Acquitted

Found guilty

Trial

Guilty plea

CRIMINAL JUSTICE
IN AMERICA

CRIMINAL JUSTICE IN AMERICA

EDITION 6

GEORGE F. COLE
UNIVERSITY OF CONNECTICUT

CHRISTOPHER E. SMITH
MICHIGAN STATE UNIVERSITY

WADSWORTH
CENGAGE Learning™

Australia • Brazil • Japan • Korea • Mexico • Singapore • Spain • United Kingdom • United States

Criminal Justice in America, Sixth Edition
George F. Cole, Christopher E. Smith

Senior Publisher: Linda Schreiber

Senior Acquisitions Editor: Carolyn Henderson
Meier

Development Editor: Shelley Murphy

Assistant Editor: Megan Power

Editorial Assistant: John Chell

Media Editor: Ting Jian Yap

Senior Marketing Manager: Michelle Williams

Marketing Assistant: Jillian Myers

Senior Marketing Communications Manager:
Tami Strang

Content Project Manager: Christy Frame

Creative Director: Rob Hugel

Senior Art Director: Maria Epes

Senior Print Buyer: Paula Vang

Rights Acquisitions Account Manager, Text:
Bob Kauser

Rights Acquisitions Account Manager, Images:
Leitha Etheridge-Sims

Production Service: Greg Hubit, Bookworks

Photo Editor: Sarah Evertson

Copy Editor: Molly Roth

Text Designer: Diane Beasley

Cover Designer: Riezebos Holzbaur Design
Group

Cover Image: Background, VEER/Daniel Smith;
prisoner, Getty Images; eagle, iStockphoto;
gavel, iStockphoto

Compositor: Pre-PressPMG

For product information and technology assistance, contact us at
Cengage Learning Customer & Sales Support, 1-800-354-9706

For permission to use material from this text or product,
submit all requests online at **www.cengage.com/permissions**
Further permissions questions can be emailed to
permissionrequest@cengage.com

Library of Congress Control Number: 2009930837

ISBN-13: 978-0-495-80982-1

ISBN-10: 0-495-80982-9

Wadsworth
20 Davis Drive
Belmont, CA 94002
USA

Cengage Learning is a leading provider of customized learning solutions with
office locations around the globe, including Singapore, the United Kingdom,
Australia, Mexico, Brazil, and Japan. Locate your local office at
www.cengage.com/global

Cengage Learning products are represented in Canada by Nelson Education, Ltd.

To learn more about Wadsworth, visit **www.cengage.com/wadsworth**

Purchase any of our products at your local college store or at our preferred
online store **www.cengagebrain.com**

Printed in the United States of America
2 3 4 5 6 7 15 14 13 12 11

3 Criminal Justice and the Rule of Law   67

PART II POLICE

4 Police 97

5 Twenty-First-Century Challenges in Policing 129

6 Police and Law   167

PART III　COURTS

7　Courts and Adjudication　199

8　Pretrial Procedures, Plea Bargaining, and the Criminal Trial　231

9 Punishment and Sentencing 261

PART IV CORRECTIONS

10 Corrections 293

11 Community Corrections: Probation and Intermediate Sanctions 325

12 Incarceration and Prison Society 343

PART V   CONTEMPORARY ISSUES IN CRIMINAL JUSTICE

13 Reentry into the Community   377

14 Technology and Criminal Justice   397

15 Juvenile Justice   433

CAREERS IN CRIMINAL JUSTICE

CLOSE UP

COMPARATIVE PERSPECTIVE

THE CRIMINAL JUSTICE PROCESS

INSIDE THE CRIMINAL JUSTICE SYSTEM AND BEYOND: ONE MAN'S JOURNEY

THE POLICY DEBATE

Criminal Justice in America, Sixth Edition, is designed for instructors seeking a textbook that thoroughly introduces students to the dynamics of the American system of criminal justice without overwhelming them. The text is an offspring of *The American System of Criminal Justice*, which has been used by more than half a million students over the course of its 12 editions. But much has changed in the 30 years since the first edition of *The American System of Criminal Justice* was published. And that is exactly why we created *Criminal Justice in America*—a briefer, more applied, student-centered introduction to the American system of criminal justice. In creating the new text, we did not merely drop a few chapters, combine others, and limit the graphic elements to reduce page count, however. We started from scratch. So, while *Criminal Justice in America* relies on the research and conceptual framework of the larger text, it is not overly theoretical; throughout the book, examples from today's headlines are used to link the concepts and information to real-life criminal justice situations. And while the focus of *Criminal Justice in America* is just as interdisciplinary as the comprehensive book's focus is, it is less encyclopedic and benefits from added career-based material, international and comparative coverage, skill-building writing exercises, and up-to-the-minute coverage of technology, terrorism, homeland security, cyber crime, and other current topics.

The Approach of This Text

Three key assumptions about the nature of American criminal justice as a discipline and the way the introductory course should be taught run throughout the book.

1. *Criminal justice involves public policies* that are developed within the political framework of the democratic process.

2. *The concept of social system is an essential tool* for explaining and analyzing the way criminal justice is administered and practiced.

3. *American values provide the foundation on which criminal justice is based.*

   With concerns about terrorism and civil liberties at the forefront of the national agenda, basic American values—individual liberty, equality, fairness, and the rule of law—need to be emphasized.

   This book's approach has met with a degree of acceptance and might be called the dominant paradigm in criminal justice education. Criminal justice is interdisciplinary, with criminology, sociology, law, history, psychology, and political science contributing to the field. The three themes of public policy, social system, and American values help place the research contributions of these disciplines in a context that allows students to understand better the dynamics of criminal justice.

New to the Sixth Edition

This edition encompasses important revisions in content and presentation. Users of the sixth edition will find many significant changes. In particular, the police chapters in Part 2 have been completely reorganized, and Chapter 14 is an entirely new chapter on technology in criminal justice. Throughout the book, we have increased our coverage of technology, terrorism, homeland security, and cyber crime, reflecting the growing importance of these subjects in the study of criminal justice. In addition, there is a new emphasis on informing students about the variety of careers in the field of criminal justice. The sixth edition takes a different approach to careers by profiling actual criminal justice professionals in order to illustrate the range of opportunities in different organizations connected to criminal justice. Even as some sectors of the American economy face a downturn, criminal justice remains a field with many opportunities, especially as more government resources are directed to issues related to homeland security.

The rest of this section outlines the major content changes in the book and then examines the new elements in each chapter.

Enhanced Coverage

- **Focus on the Public's Beliefs about Criminal Justice and How Those Beliefs Differ from Reality** Each chapter contains a new feature called "Criminal Justice: Myth and Reality" that examines a commonly held belief about criminal justice. Students will recognize many of the sentiments described as "common beliefs," such as the justice system not being tough enough on offenders, the availability of jury trials, the prominent role of the FBI, and the deterrence value of mandatory sentences. In some cases, the beliefs are shown to be incorrect. In others, students come to see a larger picture in which the commonly held belief might only apply to specific situations and limited contexts.

- **Expanded Coverage of Cyber Crime** The financial harms caused by rapidly expanding methods of cyber crime are imposing extraordinarily significant costs on governments, businesses, and individuals throughout the world. Students of criminal justice need to recognize the extent of these problems and the challenges of addressing forms of criminal behavior that are continuously shifting and adapting. This edition presents information on new topics such as cyber bullying and cooperative international law enforcement efforts to address computer crime.

- **Expanded Coverage of Criminal Justice and Homeland Security** The war on terrorism has brought about changes in the American criminal justice system. The creation of the Department of Homeland Security has brought about a reorganization of many federal law enforcement agencies. Private security is playing a much greater role than in the past in protecting people and property. The detection and detention of people who violate immigration laws in entering the United States raise additional issues related to homeland security. This edition also presents new information on the changing role of the FBI, fusion centers, and new laws.

- **The Role of Technology in Criminal Justice** Newly written, Chapter 14 focuses exclusively on technology in criminal justice. The chapter examines the use of technology in policing, courts, and corrections, as well as larger issues about the role of technology and beliefs that equate new science-based techniques and devices with progress.

Chapter-by-Chapter Changes

- **Chapter 1**, "The Criminal Justice System," opens with a new vignette concerning the prosecution of former New York Yankee baseball player Jim Leyritz. Leyritz was charged with manslaughter after an automobile collision in which the other driver was killed and Leyritz was reportedly under the influence of alcohol. The case illustrates the various stages of the justice process. This chapter's "Careers in Criminal Justice" feature presents a federal special agent in the U.S. Department of Agriculture who investigates food stamp fraud, dogfighting rings, food safety issues, and other matters that students may not realize come under the jurisdiction of an agency outside of the Justice Department. The new "Criminal Justice: Myth and Reality" features public perceptions that the American system does not impose tough punishments on criminal offenders. The chapter also expands discussion on racial disparities in the criminal justice system.

- **Chapter 2,** "Crime and Justice in America," begins with a new vignette concerning the shooting at Northern Illinois University that produced six deaths and 16 wounded victims. Such examples challenge students to consider the causes of crime and whether different kinds of causes may be at work for different crimes, situations, and offenders. "Careers in Criminal Justice" highlights the role of crime analysts who use data and statistical analyses to evaluate patterns and causes of crime in order to assist city police departments. "Criminal Justice: Myth and Reality" examines perceptions of sexual assault and victimization by strangers. The updated coverage of criminology gives new attention to feminist theories and integrated theories. The coverage of women and crime is now linked to life-course theories.

- **Chapter 3,** "Criminal Justice and the Rule of Law," opens with a new vignette describing the assault case of U.S. Navy Captain Lisa Nowak, the shuttle astronaut who was accused of attacking another female naval officer who was her rival for the attention of another shuttle astronaut. Because the insanity defense was raised, the case illuminates issues of criminal responsibility and legal defense. "Careers in Criminal Justice" examines the career of U.S. Supreme Court Justice Ruth Bader Ginsburg to illustrate the path to careers on appellate courts. "Criminal Justice: Myth and Reality" examines the contradiction between the Constitution's words about the availability of jury trials "in all criminal prosecutions" and the Supreme Court's interpretation of the Sixth Amendment that grants a limited right to jury trials. The right to counsel coverage includes the 2008 Supreme Court decisions in *Rothgery v. Gillespie* and *Indiana v. Edwards.*

- **Chapter 4,** "Police," describes the 2009 shootings of four Pittsburgh police officers in a new chapter-opening vignette to illustrate the unexpected dangers that law enforcement officers face when responding to seemingly routine domestic disturbance complaints. As part of the reorganization of the policing chapters, this initial chapter includes material on the recruitment, training, and socialization of police, with expanded details on qualifications, hiring, and salaries. The featured career is that of a police patrol officer in Illinois. "Criminal Justice: Myth and Reality" weighs the perception of the FBI's importance against the relatively narrow jurisdiction and small size of federal agencies.

- **Chapter 5,** "Twenty-First-Century Challenges in Policing," is a significantly reorganized chapter with coverage of the delivery of police services, issues in patrolling, police–community relations, homeland security, and private security management. The chapter's new opening vignette, concerning the highway bridge collapse in Minneapolis that killed 13 people, shows the first-responder duties of police and the need for interagency cooperation and coordination. The new "Careers in Criminal Justice" discusses the work of federal border patrol agents in the U.S. Bureau of Customs and Border Protection, an agency that actively recruits recent college students. "Criminal Justice: Myth and Reality" raises questions about the connection between police patrol and crime rates. There is extended coverage of the FBI's and law enforcement's role in homeland security. In addition, there is new coverage of legal controversies surrounding the USA Patriot Act and other homeland security measures. The chapter also discusses the government's use of private police and contracting for related private security services.

- **Chapter 6,** "Police and Law," reflects the restructuring of the policing topics by including coverage of police corruption, use of force, and accountability mechanisms as part of the examination of law's impact on the police. The chapter opens with the story of a married couple disagreeing about whether to grant police permission to search their house. The case eventually reached the U.S. Supreme Court and produced a controversial decision that limited police officers' opportunities for some kinds of consent searches (*Georgia v. Randolph,* 2006). The chapter discusses a 2009 case concerning the exclusionary rule (*Herring v. United States*) and also presents recent information on police shootings. The Careers feature focuses on an intelligence analyst working in a state center to process law enforcement intelligence, a new and expanding career opportunity for college graduates. "Criminal Justice: Myth and Reality" discusses police officers' authority to make determinations of probable cause, a task often thought to be reserved for judges.

- **Chapter 7,** "Courts and Adjudication," has a new opening vignette about a highly publicized murder case that illustrates the roles of prosecutors and defense attorneys. The Careers feature focuses on Detroit prosecutor Kym Worthy and provides a glimpse of the career path for an elected county prosecutor. "Criminal Justice: Myth and Reality" reveals that criminal defense attorneys are not required to have any special expertise or training in criminal law. This chapter also has new material on the impact of budget shortfalls on indigent criminal defense.

- **Chapter 8,** "Pretrial Procedures, Plea Bargaining, and the Criminal Trial," uses an opening scenario that focuses on the 2009 plea proceeding of Bernard Madoff, who stole billions of dollars from investors in an elaborate long-term fraud scheme. The new Comparative Perspective presents a description of the harsh circumstances of pretrial detention in the Philippines. The Careers feature highlights an experienced criminal defense attorney in private practice. Perceptions about plea bargaining producing insufficiently tough punishments are examined in "Criminal Justice: Myth and Reality."

- **Chapter 9,** "Punishment and Sentencing," begins with a new opening vignette, on the 2008 sentencing hearing of movie actor Wesley Snipes for failing to file federal tax returns. The maximum sentence imposed on Snipes, including serving his three sentences consecutively instead of concurrently, raises questions about whether Snipes was being punished for the tax evasion charges for which he was acquitted by the jury. The new Careers feature focuses on a state trial judge who must use his judgment and discretion in the sentencing process. The deterrence potential of long, mandatory sentences is examined in "Criminal Justice: Myth and Reality." There is extensive discussion of issues affecting capital punishment, including the Supreme Court ruling on the constitutionality of lethal injection (*Baze v. Rees,* 2008) and recent legislative action in several states to abolish the death penalty.

- **Chapter 10,** "Corrections," opens with a discussion of the 2008 Pew Center report documenting the troubling fact that one in 100 adult Americans are in prison or jail. The report starkly illustrates major debates in criminal justice: Do we overuse incarceration as a sanction? Can state and local governments afford the high costs associated with running prisons and jails? What are the alternatives? A new "Careers in Criminal Justice" focuses on a supervisory corrections officer in the residential unit of a secure prison. "Criminal Justice: Myth and Reality" examines the issue of permitting incarcerated offenders to enjoy the protections of constitutional rights. The chapter describes the recent development of using correctional settings to hold noncitizens suspected of violating immigration laws.

- **Chapter 11,** "Community Corrections: Probation and Intermediate Sanctions," supplements the extensive discussion of intermediate sanctions with a new "Careers in Criminal Justice" feature on a federal probation officer. The new opening vignette focuses on actress Lindsay Lohan and her multifaceted sentence involving probation, fines, community service, drug treatment, and a morgue visit. "Criminal Justice: Myth and Reality" examines whether community service should actually be regarded as punishment. The chapter talks about the growth of community corrections as it provides details about the various forms of punishment applied within the community.

- **Chapter 12,** "Incarceration and Prison Society," includes a new Careers feature about substance abuse counseling in correctional settings. Correctional officers' lack of coercive power and need for communication skills are discussed in "Criminal Justice: Myth and Reality." The chapter describes medical issues in correctional settings, including recent issues involving prison health care. There is new coverage of prison rape in the discussion of violence in corrections.

- **Chapter 13,** "Reentry into the Community," opens with a discussion of new programs intended to address the problems facing the large numbers of offenders returning to society each year. This issue will become more important as state budget deficits spur governors and legislators to find ways to reduce the size and costs of their corrections systems. "Careers in Criminal Justice" features an official at a unique reentry prison that is designed to prepare offenders for successful release into the community. The use of civil commitment to keep sex offenders in custody after the expiration of criminal sentences is the focus of "Criminal Justice: Myth and Reality."

- **Chapter 14,** "Technology and Criminal Justice," is an entirely new chapter examining technology in all phases of the criminal justice process. The chapter discusses how technology is used both by offenders, to commit new kinds of crimes or to increase their efficiency and success in traditional crimes, and by law enforcement officials, who seek their own improvements in fighting crime. Cyber crime and counterfeiting are examined as developing crimes that use technology. The chapter presents the history of the electric chair to raise questions about the consequences of new technology. The chapter also examines the use of technology throughout the criminal justice system. Police, for example, use a wide range of devices and techniques, from computers in patrol cars to less-lethal weapons to forensic science in investigations. The courts have also employed new technology to increase efficiency in record keeping and improve the presentation of evidence. In corrections, technological developments include increased use of GPS tracking devices. The featured career is forensic scientist, a high-interest occupation for today's students who have spent many hours watching *CSI* shows on television. "Criminal Justice: Myth and Reality" challenges the assumption that forensic science is infallible. The chapter discusses databases, DNA, surveillance, the so-called "CSI effect," and other issues.

- **Chapter 15,** "Juvenile Justice," provides a new opening vignette that raises issues of prolonged detention and racial discrimination in the juvenile system. There is greater in-depth coverage of juvenile justice, including the problem of gangs, drug abuse, and adolescents' developmental maturity. Attention is directed at juvenile detention and waiver of juveniles into the adult system. The Career feature examines a juvenile court referee who makes important initial decisions about juveniles who are brought to court. "Criminal Justice: Myth and Reality" examines the belief that youths and adults have identical protections from the rights contained in the Constitution.

Study and Review Aids

To help students identify and master core concepts, *Criminal Justice in America* provides several study and review aids in each chapter:

- Chapter outlines preview the structure of each chapter.
- Opening vignettes introduce the chapter topic with a high-interest, real-life case or illustrative discussion of a major policy issue, enhancing the book's relevancy for today's student.

- *Learning Objectives* highlight the chapter's key topics and themes and serve as a road map for readers.
- *Checkpoints* throughout each chapter allow students to test themselves on content and get immediate feedback to help them assess their understanding of concepts as they progress through the chapter.
- End-of-chapter *Summaries* and *Questions for Review* reinforce key concepts and provide further checks on learning.
- *Key Terms and Cases* are listed at the end of each chapter; these are defined throughout the text in the margins and included in the Glossary.

Promoting Understanding

Aided by the features just described, diligent students can master the essential content of the introductory course. While such mastery is no small achievement, most instructors aim higher. They want students to complete this course with the ability to take a more thoughtful and critical approach to issues of crime and justice. *Criminal Justice in America*, Sixth Edition, provides several features that help students learn how to think about the field.

- **Close Ups and Other Real-Life Examples** Understanding criminal justice in a purely theoretical way does not give students a balanced understanding of the field. The wealth of examples in this book shows how theory plays out in practice and what the human implications of policies and procedures are. In addition to the many illustrations in the text, the "Close Up" features in each chapter draw on newspaper articles, court decisions, first-person accounts, and other current sources.

- **A Question of Ethics: Writing Assignment** In the criminal justice system, decisions must be made within the framework of law but also be consistent with the ethical norms of American society. At the end of each chapter, boxes entitled "A Question of Ethics: Writing Assignment" place students in the context of decision makers faced with a problem involving ethics. Students become aware of the many ethical dilemmas that criminal justice personnel must deal with and the types of questions they may have to answer if they assume a role in the system.

- **What Americans Think** Public opinion plays an important role in the policy-making process in a democracy. As such, we present the opinions of Americans on controversial criminal justice issues, as collected through surveys.

- **The Policy Debate** This edition includes boxes presenting important policy issues for student discussion and debate. In each, we describe an issue such as aggressive policing or the death penalty, outline its pros and cons, and then ask students to decide which policy they think the United States should adopt.

- **Careers in Criminal Justice** (Expanded for this edition) The topical focus on career opportunities is primarily intended to help students think about the wide range of occupational possibilities in criminal justice. As they examine the qualifications and career path of an actual criminal justice professional, students gain insights about who plays what roles in the criminal justice system. Each professional featured provides an insightful comment on the challenges of his or her particular occupation.

- **Criminal Justice: Myth and Reality** (New to this edition) Through the examination of widely held beliefs about criminal justice, students can look critically at the actual complexity or unexpected consequences of various policies and practices. By addressing viewpoints that many students themselves hold, students are encouraged to question assumptions and seek information before drawing conclusions.

- **Comparative Perspective** The globalization of crime and the need for international cooperation in criminal justice require that students be aware of criminal justice issues and institutions in other countries. Moreover, American students can gain additional perspective on their own system by contrasting the United States with other countries. The Comparative Perspective feature, included in each section of the text, presents such diverse topics as Islamic criminal law, police patrol in Japan, pretrial detention in the Philippines, and juvenile justice in Norway.

- **Inside the Criminal Justice System and Beyond** Many students have limited firsthand knowledge of what it is like to be "processed" by the criminal justice system. A hallmark of *Criminal Justice in America* is a serialized essay by Chuck Terry titled "Inside the Criminal Justice System and Beyond: One Man's Journey." Each part of the book concludes with a segment of Terry's moving story, providing a rare insider's look at the steps in the criminal justice process.

Supplements

An extensive package of supplemental aids accompanies this edition of *Criminal Justice in America*. They are available to qualified adopters. Please consult your local sales representative for details.

■ For the Instructor

Instructor's Resource Manual   Fully updated and revised by Christina DeJong of Michigan State University, the manual includes learning objectives, key terms, a detailed chapter outline, a chapter summary, discussion topics, student activities, and a test bank. Each chapter's test bank contains questions in multiple-choice, true-false, fill-in-the-blank, and essay formats, with a full answer key. The test bank is coded to the learning objectives that appear in the main text and includes the page numbers in the main text where the answers can be found. Finally, each question in the test bank has been carefully reviewed by experienced criminal justice instructors for quality, accuracy, and content coverage. Our Instructor Approved seal, which appears on the front cover, is our assurance that you are working with an assessment and grading resource of the highest caliber.

ExamView® Computerized Testing   The comprehensive *Instructor's Resource Manual* described above is backed up by ExamView, a computerized test bank available for IBM-PC compatibles and Macintosh computers. With ExamView you can create, deliver, and customize tests and study guides (both print and online) in minutes. You can easily edit and import your own questions and graphics, change test layouts, and reorganize questions. And using ExamView's complete word-processing capabilities, you can enter an unlimited number of new questions or edit existing questions.

JoinIn™ on TurningPoint®   Spark discussion and assess your students' comprehension of chapter concepts with interactive classroom quizzes and background polls developed specifically for use with this edition of *Criminal Justice in America*. Also available are polling/quiz questions that enable you to maximize the educational benefits of the ABC News video clips we custom selected to accompany this textbook. Cengage Wadsworth's exclusive agreement with TurningPoint software lets you run our tailor-made Microsoft® PowerPoint® slides in conjunction with the "clicker" hardware of your choice. Enhance how your students interact with you, your lecture, and each other. *For college and university adopters only. Contact your local Cengage representative to learn more.*

Cengage PowerLecture DVD   This instructor resource includes Microsoft PowerPoint lecture slides with graphics from the text, making it easy for you to assemble, edit, publish, and present custom lectures for your course. The PowerLecture DVD also includes video-based polling and quiz questions that can be used with the JoinIn on TurningPoint personal response system, and integrates ExamView testing software for customizing tests of up to 250 items that can be delivered in print or online. Finally, all of your media teaching resources in one place!

WebTutor™   Jumpstart your course with customizable, rich, text-specific content within your Course Management System. Whether you want to Web-enable your class or put an entire course online, WebTutor™ delivers. WebTutor™ offers a wide array of resources including media assets, test bank, practice quizzes and additional study aids. Visit webtutor.cengage.com to learn more.

The Wadsworth Criminal Justice Video Library   So many exciting new videos—so many great ways to enrich your lectures and spark discussion of the material in this text! A list of our unique and expansive video program follows. The library includes these selections and many others:

- *ABC Videos:* Featuring short, high-interest clips from current news events, and specially developed for courses in Introduction to Criminal Justice, Criminology, Corrections, Terrorism, and White-Collar Crime, these videos are perfect for use as discussion starters or lecture launchers to spark student interest. The brief video clips provide students with a new lens through which to view the past and present, one that will greatly enhance their knowledge and understanding of significant events and open up to them new dimensions in learning. Clips are drawn from such programs as *World News Tonight*, *Good Morning America*, *This Week*, *PrimeTime Live*, *20/20*, and *Nightline*, as well as numerous ABC News specials and material from the Associated Press Television News and British Movietone News collections.

- *The Wadsworth Custom Videos for Criminal Justice:* Produced by Wadsworth and Films for the Humanities, these videos include short (5- to 10-minute) segments that encourage classroom discussion. Topics include white-collar crime, domestic violence, forensics, suicide and the police officer, the court process, the history of corrections, prison society, and juvenile justice.

Classroom Activities for Criminal Justice   This valuable booklet, available to adopters of any Wadsworth criminal justice text, offers instructors the best of the best in criminal justice classroom activities. Containing both tried-and-true favorites and exciting new projects, its activities are drawn from across the spectrum of criminal justice subjects, including introduction to criminal justice, criminology, corrections, criminal law, policing, and juvenile justice, and can be customized to fit any course. Novice and seasoned instructors alike will find it a powerful tool to stimulate classroom engagement.

Internet Activities for Criminal Justice, Third Edition   This is the resource that no introductory criminal justice instructor should be without! The user-friendly booklet allows instructors to send their students far beyond the classroom, guiding them online to conduct research and retrieve information. Its URLs and virtual projects, drawn from all foundational criminal justice areas, have been completely revised and expanded.

The Wadsworth Criminal Justice Resource Center (www.cengage.com/criminal justice)   Designed with the instructor in mind, this website features information about Cengage Wadsworth's technology and teaching solutions, as well as several features created specifically for today's criminal justice student. Supreme Court updates, time lines, and hot-topic polling can all be used to supplement in-class assignments and discussions. You'll also find a wealth of links to careers and news in criminal justice, book-specific sites, and much more.

For the Student

CengageNOW™   This unique, interactive online resource is the most exciting assessment-centered student learning tool ever offered for this course. CengageNOW determines each student's unique study needs by having him take a chapter Pretest and then offers him a Personalized Study plan that focuses his study time on the concepts he needs to master. Personalized Study includes ABC News clips with questions, career profile videos, concept learning modules with assessments, integrated simulations, interactive diagrams, animations, lectures, topic reviews, an e-book, and more. Once the student has completed her Personalized Study plan, a Posttest evaluates her improved comprehension of chapter content. At any time the student can view her Pre-/Post-test scores, and all scores and gradable assignments flow directly into the instructor's grade book.

Study Guide   An extensive student guide has been developed and updated for this edition by Sameer Hinduja of Florida Atlantic University. Because students learn in different ways, the guide includes a variety of pedagogical aids. Each chapter is outlined and summarized, major terms and figures are defined, and worksheets and self-tests are provided.

Lesson Plans   The instructor-created Lesson Plans bring accessible, masterful suggestions to every lesson. The Lesson Plan includes a sample syllabus, learning objectives, lecture notes, discussion topics, in-class activities, a detailed lecture outline, and assignments. Lesson Plans are available on the PowerLecture resource and the instructor website, or by emailing your local representative and asking for a download of the eBank files.

Companion Website (www.cengage.com/criminaljustice/cole)   The companion website provides many chapter-specific resources, including chapter outlines, learning objectives, glossary, flash cards, crossword puzzles, web links, and tutorial quizzing.

Careers in Criminal Justice Website (www.cengage.com/login)   This unique website helps students investigate the criminal justice career choices that are right for them, offering several important tools:

- *Career Profiles:* Video testimonials from a variety of practicing professionals in the field as well as information on many criminal justice careers, including job descriptions, requirements, training, salary and benefits, and the application process.
- *Interest Assessment:* Self-assessment tool to help students decide which careers suit their personalities and interests.
- *Career Planner:* Résumé-writing tips and worksheets, interviewing techniques, and successful job-search strategies.
- *Links for Reference:* Direct links to federal, state, and local agencies where students can get contact information and learn more about current job opportunities.

Wadsworth's Guide to Careers in Criminal Justice, Third Edition   This handy guide, compiled by Caridad Sanchez-Leguelinel of John Jay College of Criminal Justice, gives students information on a wide variety of career paths, including requirements, salaries, training, contact information for key agencies, and employment outlooks.

Writing and Communicating for Criminal Justice   This book contains articles on writing skills—along with a basic grammar review and a survey of verbal communication on the job—that will give students an introduction to academic, professional, and research writing in criminal justice. The voices of professionals who have used these techniques on the job will help students see the relevance of these skills to their future careers.

Handbook of Selected Supreme Court Cases, Third Edition   This supplementary handbook covers almost 40 landmark cases, each of which includes a full case citation, an introduction, a summary from WestLaw, excerpts from the case, and the decision. The updated edition includes *Hamdi v. Rumsfeld, Roper v. Simmons, Ring v. Arizona, Atkins v. Virginia, Illinois v. Caballes*, and much more.

Current Perspectives: Readings from InfoTrac® College Edition   These readers, designed to give students a deeper taste of special topics in criminal justice, include free access to InfoTrac College Edition. The timely articles are selected by experts in each topic from within InfoTrac College Edition and are available for free when bundled with the text. Topics include

- Terrorism and Homeland Security
- Juvenile Justice
- Public Policy and Criminal Justice
- Crisis Management and National Emergency Response
- Racial Profiling
- New Technologies and Criminal Justice
- White-Collar Crime

Terrorism: An Interdisciplinary Perspective   Available for bundling with each copy of *Criminal Justice in America*, Sixth Edition, this 80-page booklet discusses terrorism in general and the issues surrounding the events of September 11, 2001. This information-packed booklet examines the origins of terrorism in the Middle East, focusing on Osama bin Laden in particular, as well as issues involving bioterrorism, the specific role played by religion in Middle Eastern terrorism, globalization as it relates to terrorism, and the reactions and repercussions of terrorist attacks.

Crime Scenes 2.0: An Interactive Criminal Justice CD-ROM   Recipient of several *New Media Magazine* Invision Awards, this interactive CD-ROM allows your students to take on the roles of investigating officer, lawyer, parole officer, and judge in excitingly realistic scenarios. Available free when bundled with every copy of *Criminal Justice in America*, Sixth Edition. An online instructor's manual for the CD-ROM is also available.

Internet Guide for Criminal Justice, Second Edition   Intended for the novice user, this guide provides students with the background and vocabulary necessary to navigate and understand the Web, then provides them with a wealth of criminal justice websites and Internet project ideas.

A Group Effort

No one can be an expert on every aspect of the criminal justice system. Authors need help in covering new developments and ensuring that research findings are correctly interpreted. The many criminal justice students and instructors who have used previous editions of *Criminal Justice in America* have contributed abundantly to this edition. Their comments provided crucial practical feedback. Others gave us their comments personally when we lectured in criminal justice classes around the country.

Many others have helped us as well. Chief among them was Senior Acquisitions Editor Carolyn Henderson Meier, who is very supportive of our efforts. Developmental Editor Shelley Murphy contributed invaluable ideas and tremendous organizational skills as we revised the book. The project has benefited much from the attention of Project Manager Christy Frame. Christina DeJong contributed to the content in the chapters on criminology and juvenile justice and was invaluable in helping us develop the supplements. Molly Roth prevented us from committing egregious errors in the use of English. As always, Greg Hubit used his managerial skills to oversee the project from manuscript submission to bound books. Diane Beasley designed the interior of the book. Finally, the following reviewers for this edition contributed valuable comments:

Matthew S. Crow, University of West Florida
Rhonda R. Dobbs, University of Texas at Arlington
James N. Gilbert, University of Nebraska–Kearney
Linda M. Merola, George Mason University
Melody L. Rayl, Johnson County Community College
Chief John H. Ward, Ret., Cape Fear Community College
Richard G. Wright, Bridgewater State College

Ultimately, however, the full responsibility for the book is ours alone. We hope you will benefit from it, and we welcome your comments.

George F. Cole
gcole281@earthlink.net

Christopher E. Smith
smithc28@msu.edu

About the Authors

George F. Cole (right) is Professor Emeritus of Political Science at the University of Connecticut. A specialist in the administration of criminal justice, he has published extensively on such topics as prosecution, courts, and corrections. George Cole is also co-author with Christopher Smith of The American System of Criminal Justice, co-author with Todd Clear and Michael Reisig of American Corrections, and co-author with Marc Gertz and Amy Bunger of The Criminal Justice System: Politics and Policies. He developed and directed the graduate corrections program at the University of Connecticut and was a Fellow at the National Institute of Justice (1988). Among his other accomplishments, he has been granted two awards under the Fulbright-Hays Program to conduct criminal justice research in England and the former Yugoslavia. In 1995 he was named a Fellow of the Academy of Criminal Justice Sciences for distinguished teaching and research.

Trained as a lawyer and social scientist, Christopher E. Smith, J.D., Ph.D., is Professor of Criminal Justice at Michigan State University, where he teaches courses on criminal justice policy, courts, corrections, and law. In addition to writing more than 100 scholarly articles, he is the author of 20 books, including several other titles with Wadsworth: Criminal Procedure; Law and Contemporary Corrections; Courts, Politics, and the Judicial Process; The Changing Supreme Court: Constitutional Rights and Liberties with Thomas R. Hensley and Joyce A. Baugh; Courts and Public Policy; Politics in Constitutional Law; and Courts and the Poor.

CRIMINAL JUSTICE
IN AMERICA

COURTROOM

6870

The Criminal Justice System

JIM LEYRITZ, a retired Major League Baseball player who helped the New York Yankees win the World Series twice, looked somber as he appeared before Judge Ilona Holmes in a Broward County, Florida, courtroom. His appearance in court on February 23, 2009, was not a new experience for him. He had come to court on many occasions for bail hearings and other preliminary matters since his arrest for DUI manslaughter on December 28, 2007. His blood alcohol level was reportedly 0.14, even several hours after witnesses claimed that he ran a red light and crashed his sport utility vehicle into another car (Wright, 2009). Under Florida law, any driver whose blood alcohol level exceeds 0.08 is guilty of "DUI"—driving under the influence. Tragically, the driver of the other vehicle died. She was Fredia Veitch, the 30-year-old married mother of two children, who was working her final week as a late-shift bartender prior to reducing her hours in order to spend more time at home raising her children (ESPN.com, 2008). Leyritz faced up to 15 years in prison if convicted.

At the February 2009 hearing, Leyritz waited to hear if Judge Holmes would revoke his bail. After his arrest, a judge had determined at a bail hearing that Leyritz must pay $11,000 to the court as bail money in order to gain release from jail. If he were to violate the conditions of bail or fail to show up for a hearing, the court would keep the money, rearrest Leyritz, and jail him until his trial. One of the bail conditions for Leyritz was regular alcohol testing. In April 2008, the alcohol testing switched from in-home tests to a device attached to the ignition of Leyritz's car. He had to breathe into the device, which would show whether he had consumed alcohol; if he had, the vehicle would not start. Prosecutors alleged that Leyritz failed this test on four occasions over a six-month period; as such, they wanted his bail revoked so that he could be held in jail until his trial. However, Leyritz's attorney argued that Leyritz had not been clearly told that he could never drink alcohol while out on bail.

The judge believed him, permitting Leyritz to remain free. She warned him, though, that he could neither consume nor use any product with alcohol, including cough medicines and mouthwash (Wright, 2009). As she said, "I don't care if it's Listerine." She added, in a comment to a justice system official, that if Leyritz was found to consume any alcohol at all, "Give me the [arrest] warrant and I am signing it and [Leyritz] will be in Broward County Jail." The judge also ordered Leyritz to report to the court four times each week, as well as undergo random urine tests. Leyritz walked out of the courtroom—still free, but at risk of losing his freedom for further mistakes. That freedom would be challenged again in September 2009, when he was to stand trial for the death of Veitch. However, additional delays might again postpone the start of a trial that had originally been scheduled for November 2008 (K. Thomas, 2008).

The case against Jim Leyritz illustrates many elements of the criminal justice system. As this chapter will discuss, cases are processed through a series of steps in which justice system officials make decisions about whether a case will move forward or leave the system. Police officers decided to test Leyritz for alcohol consumption at the scene of the collision. They decided to believe witnesses who said that Leyritz had run a red light. If the officers had decided otherwise at either time, then no case against Leyritz would have gone forward. Similarly, a prosecutor decided what charges to pursue, and judges made decisions about whether Leyritz could remain free while awaiting the start of his trial. Many of these court decisions depended on the arguments formulated and presented by the defense attorneys representing Leyritz. As a prominent individual, Leyritz could gather the necessary resources to hire effective, experienced attorneys.

Think about the key factors in the Leyritz story: discretionary decisions by justice system officials; a sequence of steps; interactions among attorneys, prosecutors, and judges; long delays for defendants who wait for the attorneys to prepare evidence and arguments for trial. These elements affect criminal cases throughout the United States and reflect many essential characteristics of the justice system.

In this chapter, we examine the goals of the criminal justice system and how American criminal justice operates as a system. Moreover, we shall see how that system's processes are shaped by scarce resources, individual decision makers, and other factors that can lead to divergent treatment for similar criminal cases. In the United States, our history has taught us the importance of knowing that differences in the treatment of suspects, defendants, and offenders may be related to issues of race, ethnicity, and social class as these demographic factors interact with the criminal justice system's processes. Anyone in the United States, including law-abiding college students, can be drawn into the criminal justice system in a variety of roles: victim, witness, juror, defendant. Thus, all Americans need to gain an understanding of the system, how it operates, and how it affects people's lives.

The Goals of Criminal Justice

To begin our study of the criminal justice system, we must ask the following: What goals does the system serve? Although these goals may seem straightforward as ideas, saying exactly what they mean in practice can be difficult.

In 1967 the U.S. President's Commission on Law Enforcement and Administration of Justice described the criminal justice system as the means that society uses to "enforce the standards of conduct necessary to protect individuals and the community" (U.S. President's Commission, 1967:7). This statement provides the basis of our discussion of the goals of the system. Although there is much debate about the purposes of criminal justice, most people agree that the system has three goals: (1) doing justice, (2) controlling crime, and (3) preventing crime.

■ Doing Justice

Doing justice forms the basis for the rules, procedures, and institutions of the criminal justice system. Without the principle of justice, little difference would exist between criminal justice in the United States and that in authoritarian countries. Fairness is essential. Americans want to have fair laws, and they want to investigate, judge, and punish fairly. Doing justice also requires upholding the rights of individuals and punishing those who violate the law. Thus, the goal of doing justice embodies three principles: (1) offenders will be held fully accountable for their actions, (2) the rights of persons who have contact with the system will be protected, and (3) like offenses will be treated alike and officials will take into account relevant differences among offenders and offenses (DiIulio, 1993:10).

Doing justice successfully is a tall order. We can easily identify situations in which criminal justice agencies and processes fall short of this ideal. In authoritarian political systems, criminal justice primarily serves the interests of those in power, but in a democracy people can try to improve the capacity of their institutions to do justice. Thus, however imperfect they may be, criminal justice institutions and processes can enjoy public support. In a democracy, a system that makes doing justice a key goal is viewed as legitimate and can therefore pursue the secondary goals of controlling and preventing crime.

Thousands of St. Louis residents participated in a unity march against crime in June 2008. Their theme of a "call to oneness" was intended to make people think about social problems and crime in their communities. How can the interest and energy generated by such public events be translated into concrete actions to prevent crime?

AP Images/Jeff Robertson

■ Controlling Crime

The criminal justice system is designed to control crime by arresting, prosecuting, convicting, and punishing those who disobey the law. A major constraint on the system, however, is that efforts to control crime must be carried out within the framework of law. Criminal law not only defines what is illegal but also outlines the rights of citizens and the procedures officials must use to achieve the system's goals.

In every city and town, the goal of crime control is actively pursued: Police officers walk a beat, patrol cars race down dark streets, lawyers speak before a judge, probation officers visit clients, and guards patrol the grounds of a prison. Taking action against wrongdoers helps control crime, but the system must also attempt to prevent crimes from happening.

■ Preventing Crime

Crime can be prevented in various ways. Perhaps most important is the deterrent effect of the actions of police, courts, and corrections. These actions not only punish those who violate the law, they also provide examples that will likely keep others from committing wrongful acts. For example, a racing patrol car responding to a crime scene also serves as a warning that law enforcement is at hand. Technological advances also deter crime, but sometimes at a cost to privacy and personal liberty with new kinds of surveillance and searches.

Crime prevention depends on the actions of criminal justice officials and citizens. Unfortunately, many people do not take the simple steps necessary to protect themselves and their property. For example, they leave their homes and cars unlocked, forgo alarm systems, and walk in dangerous areas.

Citizens do not have the authority to enforce the law; society has assigned that responsibility to the criminal justice system. Thus, citizens must rely on the police to stop criminals; they cannot take the law into their own hands. Still, they can and must be actively engaged in preventing crime.

The ways in which American institutions have evolved to achieve the goals of doing justice, controlling crime, and preventing crime lead to a series of choices. Decisions must be made that reflect legal, political, social, and moral values. As we study the system, we need to be aware of the possible conflicts among these values and the implications of choosing one value over another. The tasks assigned to the criminal justice system could be much easier to perform if they were clearly defined so that citizens and officials could act with precise knowledge of their duties.

CHECKPOINT

ANSWERS

❶ *What are the three goals of the criminal justice system?*

❶ Doing justice, controlling crime, preventing crime.

❷ *What is meant by "doing justice"?*

❷ Offenders are held fully accountable for their actions, the rights of persons who have contact with the system will be protected, like offenses will be treated alike, and officials will take into account relevant differences among offenders and offenses.

Criminal Justice in a Federal System

■ **federalism** A system of government in which power is divided between a central (national) government and regional (state) governments.

Criminal justice, like other aspects of American government, is based on the concept of **federalism**, in which power is divided between a central (national) government and regional (state) governments. States have a great deal of authority over their own affairs, but the federal government handles matters of national concern. Because of federalism, no single level of government is solely responsible for the administration of criminal justice.

The U.S. government's structure was created in 1789 with the ratification of the U.S. Constitution. The Constitution gave the national government certain powers, including raising an army, coining money, and making treaties with foreign countries. But the states retained all other powers, including police power. No national police force with broad powers may be established in the United States.

The Constitution does not include criminal justice among the federal government's specific powers. However, the United States government is involved in criminal justice in many ways. The Federal Bureau of Investigation (FBI) is a national law enforcement agency. Federal criminal cases are tried in U.S. district courts, which are federal courts, and there are federal prisons throughout the nation. Most criminal justice activity, however, occurs at the state level, and the vast majority of cases are handled by state and local police, state courts, and state correctional agencies.

■ Two Justice Systems

Both the national and state systems of criminal justice enforce laws, try criminal cases, and punish offenders, but their activities differ in scope and purpose. Most criminal laws are written by state legislatures and enforced by state agencies. However, a variety of national criminal laws have been enacted by Congress and are enforced by the FBI, the Drug Enforcement Administration, the Secret Service, and other federal agencies.

Except in the case of federal drug offenses, relatively few offenders break federal criminal laws, compared with the large numbers who break state criminal laws. For example, only small numbers of people violate the federal laws against counterfeiting and espionage, whereas large numbers violate state laws against assault, larceny, and drunken driving. Even in the case of drug offenses, which during the 1980s and 1990s swept large numbers of offenders into federal prisons, many drug violators end up in state corrections systems because such crimes violate both state and federal laws (Black, 2007).

Federal law enforcement agencies bear a special responsibility for certain crimes, such as antiterrorism investigations, bank robberies, and drug trafficking. Federal agencies also provide expert assistance for the investigation of crimes that rely on scientific evidence, such as arson. Here, FBI agents assist local police in the search for a missing eight-year-old girl in California whose body was later found in a submerged suitcase in a pond. Would law enforcement nationwide be more effective if all police officers worked under a single federal agency rather than thousands of different state and local agencies?

■ Expansion of Federal Involvement

Since the 1960s the federal government has expanded its role in dealing with crime, a policy area that has traditionally been the responsibility of state and local governments. As Willard Oliver notes, the federal role has become much more active in "legislating criminal activity, expanding [the] federal law enforcement bureaucracy, widening the reach and scope of the federal courts, and building more federal prisons" (Oliver, 2002:1).

The report of the U.S. President's Commission on Law Enforcement and Administration of Justice (1967:613) emphasized the need for greater federal involvement in crime control at the local level and urged that federal grants be directed to the states to support criminal justice initiatives. Since then, Congress has allocated billions of dollars for crime control efforts and passed legislation, national in scope, to deal with street crime, the "war on drugs," violent crime, terrorism, and juvenile delinquency. Although most criminal justice expenditures and personnel are found at the local level, over the past 40 years the federal government has increased its role in fighting street crime (Oliver, 2002; Scheingold, 1995).

© Contra Costa Times/MCT/Landov

CAREERS IN CRIMINAL JUSTICE

Special Agent

MIKE PARRISH, SPECIAL AGENT/CRIMINAL INVESTIGATOR—U.S. DEPARTMENT OF AGRICULTURE, OFFICE OF INSPECTOR GENERAL (USDA-OIG), CHICAGO, IL

SPECIAL AGENTS conduct investigations relating to alleged or suspected violations of fraud, waste, and abuse in the programs and operations of the Department of Agriculture. Examples of criminal activities that must be investigated include food stamp fraud, animal fighting (dogfighting, for example), employee threats, food safety violations, preventable animal and plant disease incidents that threaten human health, and fraud related to farmers and government subsidy payments. Investigations involve obtaining physical evidence and documentary evidence, interviewing witnesses and subjects, examining files and records, and performing undercover and surveillance work. Investigative reports are used to assist U.S. attorneys and prosecutors on the state and local levels.

Special agents can also be assigned to an emergency response team (ERT). The ERT may be called upon in a variety of urgent situations, such as significant animal and plant disease outbreaks, food safety matters involving serious injuries or fatalities, threats or attacks related to USDA programs and facilities, or natural disasters that potentially affect the food supply.

Special Agent Parrish earned an undergraduate degree in psychology and a graduate degree in criminal justice with an emphasis on security management. During graduate school, he completed two law enforcement internships, one with a state police agency and the other with the USDA Office of Inspector General. The second internship gave him the appropriate experience and performance evaluations to be hired full-time with the same agency. He underwent federal law enforcement training after passing physical fitness tests and background investigations required for employment as a special agent.

Most people do not recognize the important and varied responsibilities of a special agent in the USDA. Each day is a new learning experience. I can be in the inner city of Chicago investigating food stamp fraud or dogfighting one day and the next day I'll be on a farm in Wisconsin investigating a farmer for fraud.

Because many crimes span state borders, we no longer think of some crimes as being committed at a single location within a single state. For example, crime syndicates and gangs deal with drugs, pornography, and gambling on a national level. Thus, Congress expanded the powers of the FBI and other federal agencies to investigate criminal activities for which the states had formerly taken responsibility.

Congress also passed laws designed to allow the FBI to investigate situations in which local police forces are likely to be less effective. Under the National Stolen Property Act, for example, the FBI may investigate thefts valuing more than $5,000 when the stolen property is likely to have been transported across state lines. As a national agency, the FBI can pursue criminal investigations across state borders better than any state agency can.

Disputes over jurisdiction may occur when an offense violates both state and federal laws. If the FBI and local agencies do not cooperate, they might each seek to catch the same criminals. This can have major implications if the agency that makes the arrest determines the court to which the case is brought. Usually, however, law enforcement officials at all levels of government seek to cooperate and to coordinate their efforts.

After the September 11, 2001, attacks on the World Trade Center and the Pentagon, the FBI and other federal law enforcement agencies focused their resources and efforts on investigating and preventing terrorist threats against the United States. As a result, the role of the FBI as a law enforcement agency has changed. One month after the attacks, 4,000 of the agency's 11,500 agents were dedicating their efforts to the aftermath of September 11. So many FBI agents were switched from their traditional law enforcement activities to antiterror initiatives that some observers claimed that other federal crimes were no longer being vigorously investigated (Kampeas,

2001). For example, the number of FBI agents assigned to drug investigations dropped from 1,400 to 800 between 2001 and 2003 as more agents focused on antiterrorism (*New York Times,* 2003). An examination of FBI statistics in 2006 found that white-collar crime and drug prosecutions based on FBI investigations declined by more than 40 percent in the years after 2001 (Willing, 2006). The federal government's response to potential threats to national security may ultimately diminish the federal role in traditional law enforcement and thereby effectively transfer responsibility for many criminal investigations to state and local officials.

The reorientation of the FBI's priorities is just one of many changes made in federal criminal justice agencies to address the issues of national security and terrorism. Congress and President George W. Bush sought to increase the government's effectiveness by creating new federal agencies and reorganizing existing agencies. The most significant expansion of the federal government occurred with the creation of a new Department of Homeland Security (DHS) through the consolidation of border security, intelligence, and emergency response agencies from other departments of government (see Table 1.1). The Transportation Security Administration (TSA), a new agency within DHS, assumed responsibility for protecting travelers and interstate commerce. Most importantly, federal employees of TSA took over the screening of passengers and their luggage at airports throughout the country. In light of the ease with which the September 11 hijackers brought box cutters on board commercial airliners, there were grave concerns that employees of private security agencies were neither adequately trained nor sufficiently vigilant to protect the traveling public.

Law enforcement officers work in a variety of federal government agencies, not just the FBI, DHS, Secret Service, and others that are well known for their roles in the justice system. As you read "Careers in Criminal Justice," about the law enforcement role of special agents in the U.S. Department of Agriculture, consider how law

TABLE 1.1   Department of Homeland Security

Congress approved legislation to create a new federal agency dedicated to protecting the United States from terrorism. The legislation merges 22 agencies and nearly 170,000 government workers.

	Agencies Moved to the Department of Homeland Security	Previous Department or Agency
Border and Transportation Security	Immigration and Naturalization Service enforcement functions	Justice Department
	Transportation Security Administration	Transportation Department
	Customs Service	Treasury Department
	Federal Protective Services	General Services Administration
	Animal and Plant Health Inspection Service (parts)	Agriculture Department
Emergency Preparedness and Response	Federal Emergency Management Agency	(Independent Agency)
	Chemical, biological, radiological and nuclear response units	Health and Human Services Department
	Nuclear Incident Response Teams	Energy Department
	National Domestic Preparedness Office	FBI
	Office of Domestic Preparedness	Justice Department
	Domestic Emergency Support Teams	(From various departments and agencies)
Science and Technology	Civilian biodefense research program	Health and Human Services Department
	Plum Island Animal Disease Center	Agriculture Department
	Lawrence Livermore National Laboratory (parts)	Energy Department
Information Analysis and Infrastructure Protection	National Communications System	Defense Department
	National Infrastructure Protection Center	FBI
	Critical Infrastructure Assurance Office	Commerce Department
	National Infrastructure Simulation and Analysis Center	Energy Department
	Federal Computer Incident Response Center	General Services Administration
Secret Service	Secret Service including presidential protection units	Treasury Department
Coast Guard	Coast Guard	Transportation Department

Source: *New York Times,* November 20, 2002, p. A12.

FIGURE 1.1

Percentage (rounded) of criminal justice employees at each level of government, 2001

The administration of criminal justice in the United States is very much a local affair, as these employment figures show. Only in corrections do states employ a greater percentage of workers than do municipalities.

Source: Bureau of Justice Statistics, *Sourcebook of Criminal Justice Statistics, 2003* (Washington, DC: U.S. Government Printing Office, 2004), Table 1.15.

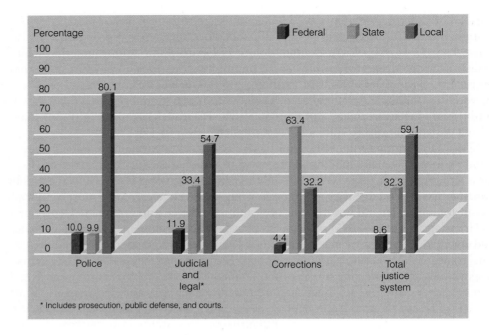

enforcement officers might play important roles in the U.S. Postal Service, U.S. Department of Education, and other agencies not typically regarded as performing criminal justice functions.

Although federal involvement in criminal justice has expanded, laws are enforced and offenders are brought to justice mainly in the states, counties, and cities (see Figure 1.1). As a result, local traditions, values, and practices shape the way criminal justice agencies operate. Local leaders, whether members of the city council or influential citizens, can help set law enforcement priorities by putting pressure on the police. Will the city's police officers crack down on illegal gambling? Will juvenile offenders be turned over to their parents with stern warnings, or will they be sent to state institutions? The answers to these and other important questions vary from city to city.

CHECKPOINT

ANSWERS

3 What is the key feature of federalism?

3 A division of power between a central (national) government and regional (state) governments.

4 What powers does the national government have in the area of criminal justice?

4 Enforcement of federal criminal laws.

5 What factors have caused federal involvement in criminal justice to expand?

5 The expansion of criminal activities across state borders; the war on terrorism.

Criminal Justice as a Social System

To achieve the goals of criminal justice, many kinds of organizations—police, prosecution, courts, corrections—have been formed. Each has its own functions and personnel. We might assume that criminal justice is an orderly process in which a variety of professionals act on each case on behalf of society. To know how the system really works, however, we must look beyond its formal organizational structure. In doing so, we can use the concept of a **system**: a complex whole made up of interdependent parts whose actions are directed toward goals and influenced by the environment in which they function.

The criminal justice system comprises several parts or subsystems. The subsystems—police, courts, corrections—have their own goals and needs but are also interdependent. When one unit changes its policies, practices, or resources, other units will be affected. An increase in the number of people arrested by the police, for example, will affect not only the judicial subsystem but also the probation and correctional subsystems. For criminal justice to achieve its goals, each part must make its own contribution; each must also have some contact with at least one other part of the system.

Although understanding the nature of the entire criminal justice system and its subsystems is important, we must also see how individual actors play their roles. The criminal justice system is made up of a great many people doing specific jobs. Some, such as police officers and judges, are well known to the public. Others, such as bail bondsmen and probation officers, are less well known. A key concept here is **exchange**, meaning the mutual transfer of resources among individual actors, each of whom has goals that he or she cannot accomplish alone. Each needs to gain the cooperation and assistance of other individuals by helping them achieve their own goals. The concept of exchange allows interpersonal behavior to be seen as the result of individual decisions about the costs and benefits of different courses of action.

Many kinds of exchange relationships exist in the criminal justice system, some more visible than others. Probably the most obvious example is the **plea bargain**, in which the defense attorney and the prosecutor reach an agreement: The defendant agrees to plead guilty in exchange for a reduction of charges or for a lighter sentence. As a result of this exchange, the prosecutor gains a quick, sure conviction; the defendant achieves a shorter sentence, and the defense attorney can move on to the next case. Thus, the cooperation underlying the exchange promotes the goals of each participant.

The concept of exchange serves as a reminder that decisions are the products of interactions among individuals and that the subsystems of the criminal justice system are tied together by the actions of individual decision makers. Figure 1.2 presents selected exchange relationships between a prosecutor and other individuals and agencies involved in the criminal justice process.

The systems perspective emphasizes that criminal justice is made up of parts or subsystems, including police, courts, and corrections. Here, Judge Orlando Houston confers with prosecutors and defense attorneys during the Durham, North Carolina, trial of Michael Peterson, who was convicted of murdering his wife, Kathleen. Each participant brings his or her own perspective to the system.

■ **system** A complex whole consisting of interdependent parts whose actions are directed toward goals and are influenced by the environment within which they function.

■ **exchange** A mutual transfer of resources: a balance of benefits and deficits that flow from behavior based on decisions about the values and costs of alternatives.

■ **plea bargain** A defendant's plea of guilty to a criminal charge with the reasonable expectation of receiving some consideration from the state for doing so, usually a reduction of the charge. The defendant's ultimate goal is a penalty lighter than the one formally warranted by the charged offense.

FIGURE 1.2
Exchange relationships between prosecutors and others
The prosecutor's decisions are influenced by relationships with other agencies and members of the community.

CHECKPOINT

ANSWERS

6 *What is a system?*

6 A complex whole made up of interdependent parts whose actions are directed toward goals and influenced by the environment within which they function.

7 *What are the subsystems of the criminal justice system?*

7 Police, courts, corrections.

8 *What is one example of an exchange relationship?*

8 Plea bargaining.

Characteristics of the Criminal Justice System

The workings of the criminal justice system have four major characteristics: (1) discretion, (2) resource dependence, (3) sequential tasks, and (4) filtering.

■ Discretion

■ **discretion** The authority to make decisions without reference to specific rules or facts, using instead one's own judgment; allows for individualization and informality in the administration of justice.

All levels of the justice process reflect a high degree of **discretion**. This term refers to officials' freedom to act according to their own judgment and conscience (see Table 1.2). For example, police officers decide how to handle a crime situation, prosecutors decide which charges to file, judges decide how long a sentence will be, and parole boards decide when an offender may be released from prison.

The extent of such discretion may seem odd, given that the United States is ruled by law and has created procedures to ensure that decisions are made in accordance with law. However, instead of a mechanical system in which decisions are dominated by law, criminal justice is a system in which actors may take many factors into account and exercise many options as they dispose of a case.

Two arguments are often made to justify discretion in the criminal justice system. First, discretion is needed because the system lacks the resources to treat every case the same way. If every violation of the law were pursued from investigation through trial, the costs would be immense. Second, many officials believe that discretion permits them to achieve greater justice than rigid rules would produce.

■ Resource Dependence

Criminal justice agencies do not generate their own resources but depend on other agencies for funding. Therefore, actors in the system must cultivate and maintain good relations with those who allocate

TABLE 1.2	**Who Exercises Discretion?**

Discretion is exercised by various actors throughout the criminal justice system.

These Criminal Justice Officials . . .	Must Often Decide Whether or How to . . .
Police	Enforce specific laws
	Investigate specific crimes
	Search people, vicinities, buildings
	Arrest or detain people
Prosecutors	File charges or petitions for adjudication
	Seek indictments
	Drop cases
	Reduce charges
Judges or Magistrates	Set bail or conditions for release
	Accept pleas
	Determine delinquency
	Dismiss charges
	Impose sentence
	Revoke probation
Correctional Officials	Assign to [which] type of correctional facility
	Award privileges
	Punish for infractions of rules
	Determine date and conditions of parole
	Revoke parole

Source: Bureau of Justice Statistics, *Report to the Nation on Crime and Justice,* 2nd ed. (Washington, DC: U.S. Government Printing Office, 1988), 59.

resources—that is, political decision makers, such as legislators, mayors, and city council members. Some police departments gain revenue through traffic fines and property forfeitures, but these sources cannot sustain their budgets.

Because budget decisions are made by elected officials who seek to please the public, criminal justice officials must also maintain a positive image and good relations with voters. If the police have strong public support, for example, the mayor will be reluctant to reduce the law enforcement budget. Criminal justice officials also seek positive coverage from the news media. Because the media often provide a crucial link between government agencies and the public, criminal justice officials may announce notable achievements while trying to limit publicity about controversial cases and decisions.

■ Sequential Tasks

Decisions in the criminal justice system are made in a specific sequence. The police must arrest a person before the case is passed to the prosecutor to determine if charges should be brought. The prosecutor's decisions influence the nature of the court's workload. Officials cannot achieve their goals by acting out of sequence. For example, prosecutors and judges cannot bypass the police by making arrests, and correctional officials cannot punish anyone who has not passed through the earlier stages of the process.

The sequential nature of the system is key to the exchange relationships among the justice system's decision makers, who depend on one another to achieve their goals. In other words, the system is highly interdependent partially because it is sequential.

■ Filtering

We can see the criminal justice system as a **filtering process**. At each stage some defendants are sent on to the next stage, while others are either released or processed under changed conditions. As shown in Figure 1.3, people who have been arrested may be filtered out of the system at various points. Note that relatively few suspects who are arrested are then prosecuted, tried, and convicted. Some go free because the police decide that a crime has not been committed or that the evidence is not sound. The prosecutor may decide that justice would be better served by sending the suspect to a substance abuse clinic. Many defendants will plead guilty, the judge may dismiss charges against others, and the jury may acquit a few defendants. Most of the offenders who are actually tried, however, will be convicted. Thus, the criminal justice system is often described as a funnel—many cases enter it, but only a few result in conviction and punishment. Some people look at how few people end up in prison and conclude that the system is not tough enough on criminal offenders. Consider this idea as you read "Criminal Justice: Myth and Reality."

To summarize, the criminal justice system is composed of a set of interdependent parts (subsystems). This system has four key attributes: (1) discretion, (2) resource dependence, (3) sequential tasks, and (4) filtering. Using this framework, we look next at the operations of criminal justice agencies and then examine the flow of cases through the system.

> ■ **filtering process** A screening operation; a process by which criminal justice officials screen out some cases while advancing others to the next level of decision making.

CHECKPOINT

ANSWER

9 *What are the major characteristics of the criminal justice system?*

9 Discretion, resource dependence, sequential tasks, filtering.

FIGURE 1.3

Criminal justice as a filtering process

Decisions at each point in the system result in some cases being dropped while others are passed to the next point. Are you surprised by the small portion of cases that remain?

Source: Bureau of Justice Statistics, *Sourcebook of Criminal Justice Statistics, 2003* (Washington, DC: U.S. Government Printing Office, 2004), Table 1.15.

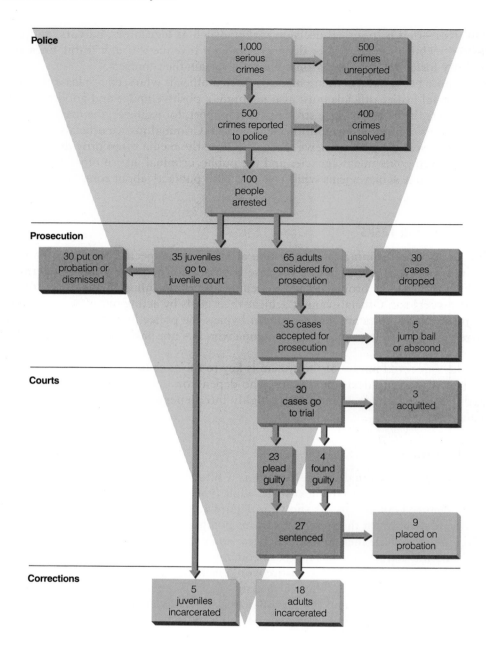

Operations of Criminal Justice Agencies

The criminal justice system has been formed to deal with people who are accused of violating the criminal law. Its subsystems consist of more than 60,000 public and private agencies with an annual budget of more than $200 billion and more than 2.3 million employees (BJS, 2008e; Hughes, 2006). Here we review the main parts of the criminal justice system and their functions.

■ Police

We usually think of the police as being on the "front line" in controlling crime. The term *police*, however, does not refer to a single agency or type of agency, but to many agencies at each level of government. The complexity of the criminal justice system can be seen in the large number of organizations engaged in law enforcement. There are only 50 federal law enforcement agencies in the United States, whereas 17,876 state and local law enforcement agencies operate. Forty-nine of these are state agencies (Hawaii has no state police). The remaining agencies are found in counties, cities, and towns, reflecting the fact that local governments dominate the police function. At the state and local levels, these agencies have more than one million full-time employees and a total annual budget that exceeds $68 billion (Hughes, 2006).

Police agencies have four major duties:

1. *Keeping the peace.* This broad and important mandate involves the protection of rights and persons in situations ranging from street-corner brawls to domestic quarrels.

2. *Apprehending violators and combating crime.* This is the task that the public most often associates with police work, although it accounts for only a small portion of police time and resources.

3. *Preventing crime.* By educating the public about the threat of crime and by reducing the number of situations in which crimes are likely to be committed, the police can lower the rate of crime.

4. *Providing social services.* Police officers recover stolen property, direct traffic, give emergency medical aid, help people who have locked themselves out of their homes, and provide other social services.

Courts

The United States has a **dual court system** that consists of a separate judicial system for each state in addition to a national system. Each system has its own series of courts; the U.S. Supreme Court is responsible for correcting certain errors made in all other court systems. Although the Supreme Court can review cases from both the state and federal courts, it will hear only cases involving federal law or constitutional rights.

With a dual court system, the law may be interpreted differently in various states. Although the wording of laws may be similar, none of the state courts interprets the laws the same way as the others. To some extent, these variations reflect different social and political conditions. The dominant values of citizens and judges may differ from one region to another. Differences in interpretation may also be due to attempts by state courts to solve similar problems by different means. For example, before the Supreme Court ruled that evidence the police obtained in illegal ways should usually be excluded at trials, some states had already established rules barring the use of such evidence.

Courts are responsible for **adjudication**—determining whether or not a defendant is guilty. In so doing, they must use fair procedures that will produce just, reliable decisions. Courts must also impose sentences that are appropriate to the behavior being punished. Certain cases or offenders, such as drug cases or juvenile offenders, may be sent to specialized courts that focus on specific matters.

Corrections

On any given day, nearly seven million American adults (one of every 31) are under the supervision of state and federal corrections systems. There is no "typical" correctional agency or official. Instead, a variety of agencies and programs are provided by private and public organizations—including federal, state, and local governments—and carried out in many different community and closed settings.

Criminal Justice: MYTH AND REALITY

COMMON BELIEF: The American criminal justice system is obviously not tough enough on criminal offenders, since so many of them go free and so few of them end up in prison.

The filtering of people out of the justice system does not mean that the American system is not tough on offenders. In fact, the United States incarcerates more people and keeps them locked up for longer periods than do comparable democracies. The biggest challenge for police is gathering enough evidence to identify a suspect and justify making an arrest. This difficulty accounts for the largest gap between reported crimes and prosecutions. After a suspect is arrested, filtering occurs for a variety of reasons. Officials need proper evidence to prove guilt in order to move forward with cases. Sometimes the wrong person is arrested and further investigation leads to a release. In other cases, if they do not yet have enough evidence, then they are likely to filter the suspect out of the system— but the person could be rearrested later if more incriminating evidence is found. The system also has limited resources. There are only so many police officers to investigate cases, prosecutors to prepare cases, courtrooms to process cases, and cells to hold detainees in jail and convicted offenders in prison. Discretionary decisions must inevitably be made to use the system's limited resources to the greatest effect. Thus, prosecutors focus their sustained attention on the most serious cases and consider ways to speed the processing of lesser cases and first offenders through plea bargaining. As indicated in Figure 1.3, when prosecutors have sufficient evidence and therefore move forward with a prosecution, they see very high conviction rates.

■ **dual court system** A system consisting of a separate judicial system for each state in addition to a national system. Each case is tried in a court of the same jurisdiction as that of the law or laws broken.

■ **adjudication** The process of determining whether the defendant is guilty.

Two witnesses are led away from a disturbing scene in Nampa, Idaho, after the head of a decapitated murder victim was found at the scene of an automobile collision. As part of law enforcement responsibilities, the police must deal with a wide range of witnesses and victims in emotionally charged situations. What skills and personal qualities are required to respond to emergencies? What skills do officers need to deal one-on-one with traumatized victims and witnesses?

AP Images/Idaho Press-Tribune, Mike Vogt

Although prisons provide the most familiar image of corrections, in fact two-thirds of offenders are in the community on probation, community-based sanctions, or parole. Do you ever notice the presence of convicted offenders serving their sentences in the community, or do they cause few problems that attract attention from the public?

© Ed Quinn/CORBIS

Although the average citizen may equate corrections with prisons, less than 30 percent of convicted offenders are in prisons and jails; the rest are being supervised in the community. Probation and parole have long been important aspects of corrections, as have community-based halfway houses, work release programs, and supervised activities.

The federal government, all the states, most counties, and all but the smallest cities engage in corrections. Nonprofit private organizations such as the Young Men's Christian Association (YMCA) have also contracted with governments to perform correctional services. In recent years, for-profit businesses have also entered into contracts with governments to build and operate correctional institutions.

The police, courts, and corrections are the main agencies of criminal justice. Each is a part, or subsystem, of the criminal justice system. Each is linked to the other two subsystems, and the actions of each affect the others. These effects can be seen as we examine the flow of decision making within the criminal justice system.

CHECKPOINT

ANSWERS

10 *What are the four main duties of police?*

10 Keeping the peace, apprehending violators and combating crime, preventing crime, providing social services.

11 *What is a dual court system?*

11 A separate judicial system for each state in addition to a national system.

12 *What are the major types of state and local correctional facilities and programs? What types of organizations operate them?*

12 Prisons, jails, probation, parole, intermediate sanctions. Public, nonprofit, and for-profit agencies carry out these programs.

The Flow of Decision Making in the Criminal Justice System

The processing of cases in the criminal justice system involves a series of decisions by police officers, prosecutors, judges, probation officers, wardens, and parole board members. At each stage in the process, they decide whether a case will move on to the next stage or be dropped from the system. Although the flowchart shown in Figure 1.4 appears streamlined, with cases entering at the top and moving swiftly toward the bottom, the actual route taken may be quite long and may involve many detours. At each step, officials have the discretion to decide what happens next. Many cases are filtered out of the system, others are sent to the next decision maker, and still others are dealt with informally.

Moreover, the flowchart does not show the influences of social relations or the political environment. In 2006, a retired FBI agent was charged with providing inside

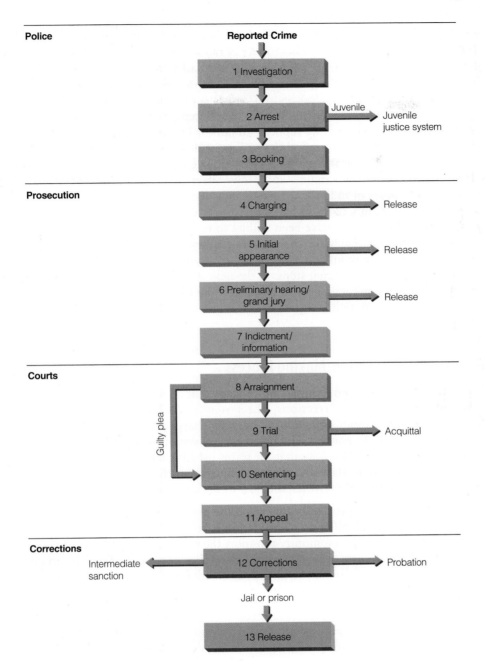

FIGURE 1.4
The flow of decision making in the criminal justice system
Each agency is responsible for a part of the decision-making process. Thus, the police, prosecution, courts, and corrections are bound together through a series of exchange relationships.

information to organized-crime figures so that informants could be murdered. It was then discovered that 30 years earlier this agent had been caught illegally selling unlicensed handguns to undercover agents of the U.S. Bureau of Alcohol, Tobacco, and Firearms. If the FBI agent had been prosecuted for the handgun sales, his career in the FBI would have been over and he never would have ended up in a high-level position that later allegedly allowed him to assist mobsters. However, according to one former federal prosecutor involved in the handgun case in 1976, a high official in the U.S. Justice Department used his discretion to drop the gun charges. According to the former prosecutor, the high official "expressed no other reason not to prosecute the guy except the guy was a cop—and he didn't want to embarrass the [FBI]" (Feuer, 2006). The flowchart does not take into account that someone in authority might exercise discretion unfairly in favor of certain people, such as those with wealth or political connections.

Another example shows how social relations and official discretion can create specific situations that make potential prosecutions more difficult. In 2004, Colorado prosecutors dropped rape charges against basketball star Kobe Bryant after the alleged victim changed her mind about her willingness to testify against him (T. R. Reid, 2004). Instead, the alleged victim reportedly accepted an undisclosed sum of money from Bryant to settle a lawsuit that she had filed against him (Sarche, 2005). The prosecutors chose not to pursue this case without the victim's cooperation.

On the other hand, prosecutors and judges sometimes pressure witnesses to testify, even jailing some reluctant witnesses for contempt of court. In 2005, for example, a federal judge sent a news reporter to jail for initially failing to disclose sources concerning an investigation to find the government officials who revealed the identity of a CIA officer. Thus, it is important to recognize that political influence, personal relationships, and specific circumstances may affect how officials' decisions shape the paths and outcomes of individual cases. Might Kobe Bryant have been convicted of rape if prosecutors in Colorado had chosen to exert more pressure on the reluctant witness? Would the victim have been willing to testify if Bryant, a millionaire athlete, had not paid her the money she sought in her lawsuit against him? There is no way to know. Such factors may influence decisions in ways that are not reflected in a simple description of decision-making steps. In the next section, as we follow the 13 steps of the criminal justice process, bear in mind that the formal procedures do not hold in every case. Discretion, political pressure, and other factors can alter the outcome for different individuals.

■ Steps in the Decision-Making Process

The criminal justice system consists of 13 steps that cover the stages of law enforcement, adjudication, and corrections. The system looks like an assembly line where decisions are made about *defendants*—persons charged with crimes. As these steps are described, recall the concepts discussed earlier: system, discretion, sequential tasks, filtering, and exchange. Be aware that the terms used for different stages in the process may differ from state to state and that the sequence of the steps differs in some parts of the country. In general, however, the flow of decision making follows this pattern:

1. *Investigation.* The process begins when the police believe that a crime has been committed. At this point an investigation is begun. The police normally depend on a member of the community to report the offense. Except for traffic and public order offenses, it is unusual for the police to observe illegal behavior themselves. Most crimes have already been committed and offenders have left the scene before the police arrive, placing the police at a disadvantage in quickly finding and arresting the offenders.

2. *Arrest.* If the police find enough evidence showing that a particular person has committed a crime, an arrest may be made. An **arrest** involves physically taking a person into custody pending a court proceeding. This action not only restricts the suspect's freedom but also is the first step toward prosecution.

   Under some conditions, arrests may be made on the basis of a **warrant**—a court order issued by a judge authorizing police officers to take certain actions, such as arresting suspects or searching premises. In practice, most arrests are made without warrants. In some states, police officers may issue a summons or citation that orders a person to appear in court on a certain date. This avoids the need to hold the suspect physically until decisions are made about the case.

3. *Booking.* After an arrest, the suspect is usually transported to a police station for booking, in which a record is made of the arrest. When booked, the suspect may be fingerprinted, photographed, questioned, and placed in a lineup to be identified by the victim or witnesses. Before being questioned, all suspects in custody must also be warned that they have the right to counsel, that they may remain silent, and that any statement they make may be used against them later. Bail may be set so that the suspect learns what amount of money must be paid or what other conditions must be met to gain release from custody until the case is processed.

■ **arrest** The physical taking of a person into custody on the grounds that there is reason to believe that he or she has committed a criminal offense. Police may use only reasonable physical force in making an arrest. The purpose of the arrest is to hold the accused for a court proceeding.

■ **warrant** A court order authorizing police officers to take certain actions, for example, to arrest suspects or to search premises.

4. *Charging.* Prosecuting attorneys are the key link between the police and the courts. They must consider the facts of the case and decide whether there is reasonable cause to believe that an offense was committed and that the suspect committed the offense. The decision to charge is crucial because it sets in motion the adjudication of the case.

5. *Initial appearance.* Within a reasonable time after arrest, the suspect must be brought before a judge. At this point, suspects are given formal notice of the charge(s) for which they are being held, advised of their rights, and, if approved by the judge, given a chance to post bail. At this stage, the judge decides whether there is enough evidence to hold the suspect for further criminal processing. If enough evidence has not been produced, the judge will dismiss the case.

   The purpose of bail is to permit the accused to be released while awaiting trial and to ensure that he or she will show up in court at the appointed time. Bail requires the accused to provide or arrange a surety (or pledge), usually in the form of money or a bond. The amount of bail is based mainly on the judge's view of the seriousness of the crime and the defendant's prior criminal record. Suspects may also be released on their own recognizance (also known as ROR)—a promise to appear in court at a later date without the posting of bail. In a few cases, bail may be denied and the accused held because he or she is viewed as a threat to the community.

6. *Preliminary hearing/grand jury.* After suspects have been arrested, booked, and brought to court to be informed of the charges against them and advised of their rights, a decision must be made as to whether there is enough evidence to proceed. The preliminary hearing, used in about half the states, allows a judge to decide whether there is probable cause to believe that a crime has been committed and that the accused person committed it. If the judge does not find probable cause, the case is dismissed. If there is enough evidence, the accused is bound over for arraignment on an **information**—a document charging a person with a specific crime.

   In the federal system and in some states, the prosecutor appears before a grand jury, which decides whether there is enough evidence to file an **indictment** or "true bill" charging the suspect with a specific crime. The preliminary hearing and grand jury are designed to prevent hasty and malicious prosecutions, to protect people from mistakenly being humiliated in public, and to decide whether there are grounds for prosecution.

7. *Indictment/information.* If the preliminary hearing leads to an information or the grand jury vote leads to an indictment, the prosecutor prepares the formal charging document and presents it to the court.

8. *Arraignment.* The accused person appears in court to hear the indictment or information read by a judge and to enter a plea. Accused persons may plead guilty or not guilty, or in some states, stand mute. If the accused pleads guilty, the judge must decide whether the plea is made voluntarily and whether the person has full knowledge of the consequences. When a guilty plea is accepted as "knowing" and voluntary, there is no need for a trial and the judge imposes a sentence.

   Plea bargaining may take place at any time in the criminal justice process, but it is likely to be completed just before or soon after arraignment. Very few criminal cases proceed to trial. Most move from the entry of the guilty plea to the sentencing phase.

9. *Trial.* For the small percentage of defendants who plead not guilty, the right to a trial by an impartial jury is guaranteed by the Sixth Amendment if the charges are serious enough to warrant incarceration for more than six months. In many jurisdictions, lesser charges do not entail the right to a jury trial. Most trials are summary or bench trials; that is, they are conducted without a jury. Because the

■ **information**   A document charging an individual with a specific crime. It is prepared by a prosecuting attorney and presented to a court at a preliminary hearing.

■ **indictment**   A document returned by a grand jury as a "true bill" charging an individual with a specific crime on the basis of a determination of probable cause as presented by a prosecuting attorney.

defendant pleads guilty in most criminal cases, only about 10 to 15 percent of cases go to trial and only about 5 percent are heard by juries. Whether a criminal trial is held before a judge alone or before a judge and jury, the procedures are similar and are set out by state law and U.S. Supreme Court rulings. A defendant shall be found guilty only if the evidence proves beyond a reasonable doubt that he or she committed the offense.

10. *Sentencing.* Judges are responsible for imposing sentences. The intent is to make the sentence suitable to the offender and the offense within the limits set by the law. Although criminal codes place limits on sentences, the judge still typically has leeway. Among the judge's options are a suspended sentence, probation, imprisonment, or other sanctions such as fines and community service.

11. *Appeal.* Defendants who are found guilty may appeal convictions to a higher court. An appeal may be based on the claim that the trial court failed to follow the proper procedures or that constitutional rights were violated by the actions of police, prosecutors, defense attorneys, or judges. The number of appeals is small compared with the total number of convictions; further, in about 80 percent of appeals, trial judges and other officials are ruled to have acted properly. Even defendants who win appeals do not go free right away. Normally, the defendant is given a second trial, which may result in an acquittal, a second conviction, or a plea bargain to lesser charges.

12. *Corrections.* The court's sentence is carried out by the correctional subsystem. Probation, intermediate sanctions such as fines and community service, and incarceration are the sanctions most often imposed. Probation allows offenders to serve their sentences in the community under supervision. Youthful offenders, first offenders, and those convicted of minor violations are most likely to be sentenced to probation rather than incarceration. The conditions of probation may require offenders to observe certain rules—to be employed, maintain an orderly life, or attend school—and to report to their supervising officer from time to time. If these requirements are not met, the judge may revoke the probation and impose a prison sentence.

   Many new types of sanctions have been used in recent years. These intermediate sanctions are more restrictive than probation but less restrictive than incarceration. They include fines, intensive supervision probation, boot camp, home confinement, and community service.

   Whatever the reasons used to justify them, prisons exist mainly to separate criminals from the rest of society. Those convicted of misdemeanors usually serve their time in city or county jails, whereas felons serve time in state prisons. Isolation from the community is one of the most painful aspects of incarceration. Not only are letters and visits restricted, but supervision and censorship are ever present. In order to maintain security, prison officials make unannounced searches of inmates and subject them to strict discipline.

13. *Release.* Release may occur when the offender has served the full sentence imposed by the court, but most offenders are returned to the community under the supervision of a parole officer. Parole continues for the duration of the sentence or for a period specified by law. Parole may be revoked and the offender returned to prison if the conditions of parole are not met or if the parolee commits another crime.

To see the criminal justice process in action, read the story of Christopher Jones, who was arrested, charged, and convicted of serious crimes arising from the police investigation of a series of robberies. The story is located just after this chapter.

■ The Criminal Justice Wedding Cake

Although the flowchart shown in Figure 1.4 is helpful, recall that not all cases are treated equally. The process applied to a given case, as well as its outcome, is shaped

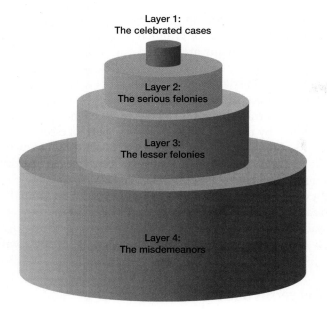

Layer 1:
The celebrated cases

Layer 2:
The serious felonies

Layer 3:
The lesser felonies

Layer 4:
The misdemeanors

FIGURE 1.5
The criminal justice wedding cake
This figure shows that different cases are treated in different ways. Only a very few cases are played out as "high drama"; most are handled through plea bargaining and dismissals.

Source: Drawn from Samuel Walker, *Sense and Nonsense about Crime and* Drugs, 4th ed. (Belmont, CA: Wadsworth, 1998), 30–37.

by many factors, including the importance of the case to decision makers, the seriousness of the charge, and the defendant's resources.

Some cases are highly visible either because of the notoriety of the defendant or victim or because of the shocking nature of the crime. At the other extreme are "run-of-the-mill cases" involving unknown persons charged with minor crimes.

As shown in Figure 1.5, the criminal justice process can be compared to a wedding cake. This model shows clearly how different cases receive different kinds of treatment in the justice process.

Layer 1 of the "cake" consists of "celebrated" cases that are highly unusual, receive much public attention, result in a jury trial, and often drag on through many appeals. These cases embody the ideal of an adversarial system of justice in which each side actively fights against the other, either because the defendant faces a stiff sentence or because the defendant has the financial resources to pay for a strong defense. The highly publicized child pornography trial of celebrity pop singer R. Kelly in 2008 serves as an example. Not all cases in Layer 1 receive national attention, however. From time to time, local crimes, especially cases of murder and rape, are treated in this way.

These cases serve as morality plays. The carefully crafted arguments of the prosecution and defense are seen as expressing key issues in our society or tragic flaws in individuals. Too often, however, the public concludes that all criminal cases follow this model.

Layer 2 consists of **felonies** that are considered serious by officials. Here we see violent crimes committed by persons with long criminal records against victims unknown to them. Police and prosecutors speak of serious felonies as "heavy" cases that should result in "tough" sentences. In such cases the defendant has little reason to plead guilty and the defense attorney must prepare for trial.

Layer 3 also consists of felonies, but the crimes and the offenders are seen as less important than those in Layer 2. The offenses may be the same as in Layer 2, but the offender

■ **felonies** Serious crimes usually carrying a penalty of death or of incarceration for more than one year.

The trial and acquittal of singer R. Kelly on child pornography charges in 2008 had all of the earmarks of a Layer 1 case. These cases embody the ideal of the due process model: with each side's attorneys battling in front of the jury in a lengthy trial. Should society devote enough resources to the justice system so that all defendants—rich or poor—can have Layer 1, adversarial trials?

© George McGinn/Getty Images

may have no record, and the victim may have had a prior relationship with the accused, for example. The main goal of criminal justice officials is to dispose of such cases quickly. For this reason, many are filtered out of the system, often through plea bargaining.

Layer 4 is made up of **misdemeanors**. About 90 percent of all cases fall into this category. They concern such offenses as public drunkenness, shoplifting, prostitution, disturbing the peace, and traffic violations. Looked on as the "garbage" of the system, these cases are handled by the lower courts, where speed is essential. Prosecutors use their discretion to reduce charges or recommend probation as a way to encourage defendants to plead guilty quickly. Trials are rare, processes are informal, and fines, probation, or short jail sentences result.

The wedding cake model is a useful way of viewing the criminal justice system. Cases are not treated equally; some are seen as very important, others as merely part of a large caseload that must be processed. When one knows the nature of a case, one can predict fairly well how it will be handled and what its outcome will be.

■ Crime Control versus Due Process

Models are simplified representations that illustrate important aspects of a system. As we saw in discussing the wedding cake model, they permit generalized statements and comparisons even though no one model necessarily portrays precisely the complex reality of specific situations. We now look at two more models to expand our picture of how the criminal justice system really operates.

In one of the most important contributions to systematic thought about the administration of justice, Herbert Packer (1968) described two competing models of the administration of criminal justice: the **crime control model** and the **due process model**. These are opposing ways of looking at the goals and procedures of the criminal justice system. The crime control model is much like an assembly line, whereas the due process model is like an obstacle course.

In reality, no one official or agency functions according to one model or the other. Elements of both models are found throughout the system. However, the two models reveal key tensions within the criminal justice process, as well as the gap between how the system is described and the way most cases are actually processed. Table 1.3 presents the major elements of each model

Crime Control: Order as a Value   The crime control model assumes that every effort must be made to repress crime. It emphasizes efficiency and the capacity to catch, try, convict, and punish a high proportion of offenders; it also stresses speed and finality. This model places the goal of controlling crime uppermost, putting less emphasis on protecting individuals' rights. As Packer points out, in order to achieve liberty for all citizens, the crime control model calls for efficiency in screening suspects, determining guilt, and applying sanctions to the convicted. Because of high rates of crime and the limited resources of law enforcement, speed and finality are necessary. All these elements depend on informality, uniformity, and few challenges by defense attorneys or defendants.

■ misdemeanors Offenses less serious than felonies and usually punishable by incarceration of no more than a year, probation, or intermediate sanction.

■ crime control model A model of the criminal justice system that assumes freedom is so important that every effort must be made to repress crime; it emphasizes efficiency, speed, finality, and the capacity to apprehend, try, convict, and dispose of a high proportion of offenders.

■ due process model A model of the criminal justice system that assumes freedom is so important that every effort must be made to ensure that criminal justice decisions are based on reliable information; it emphasizes the adversarial process, the rights of defendants, and formal decision-making procedures.

TABLE 1.3	Due Process and Crime Control Models Compared

What other comparisons can be made between the two models?

	Goal	Value	Process	Major Decision Point	Basis of Decision Making
Due Process Model	Preserve individual liberties	Reliability	Adversarial	Courtroom	Law
Crime Control Model	Repress crime	Efficiency	Administrative	Police pretrial processes	Discretion

In this model, police and prosecutors decide early on how likely the suspect is to be found guilty. If a case is unlikely to end in conviction, the prosecutor may drop the charges. At each stage, from arrest to preliminary hearing, arraignment, and trial, established procedures are used to determine whether the accused should be passed on to the next stage. Instead of stressing the combative aspects of the courtroom, this model promotes bargaining between the state and the accused. Nearly all cases are disposed of through such bargaining, and they typically end with the defendant pleading guilty. Packer's description of this model as an assembly-line process conveys the idea of quick, efficient decisions by actors at fixed stations that turn out the intended product—guilty pleas and closed cases

Due Process: Law as a Value   If the crime control model looks like an assembly line, the due process model looks more like an obstacle course. This model assumes that freedom is so important that every effort must be made to ensure that criminal justice decisions are based on reliable information. It stresses the adversarial process, the rights of defendants, and formal decision-making procedures. For example, because people are poor observers of disturbing events, police and prosecutors may be wrong in presuming a defendant to be guilty. Thus, people should be labeled as criminals only on the basis of conclusive evidence. To reduce error, the government must be forced to prove beyond a reasonable doubt that the defendant is guilty of the crime. Therefore, the process must give the defense every opportunity to show that the evidence is not conclusive, and the outcome must be decided by an impartial judge and jury. According to Packer, the assumption that the defendant is innocent until proved guilty has a far-reaching impact on the criminal justice system.

In the due process model, the state must prove that the person is guilty of the crime as charged. Prosecutors must prove their cases while obeying rules dealing with such matters as the admissibility of evidence and respect for defendants' constitutional rights. Forcing the state to prove its case in a trial protects citizens from wrongful convictions. Thus, the due process model emphasizes particular aspects of the goal of doing justice. It protects the rights of individuals and reserves punishment for those who unquestionably deserve it. These values are stressed even though some guilty defendants may go free because the evidence against them is not conclusive enough. By contrast, the crime control model values efficient case processing and punishment over the possibility that innocent people might be swept up in the process.

CHECKPOINT

ANSWERS

⓭ *What are the steps of the criminal justice process?*

⓭ (1) Investigation, (2) arrest, (3) booking, (4) charging, (5) initial appearance, (6) preliminary hearing/grand jury, (7) indictment/information, (8) arraignment, (9) trial, (10) sentencing, (11) appeal, (12) corrections, (13) release.

⓮ *What is the purpose of the wedding cake model?*

⓮ To show that not all cases are treated equally and processed in an identical fashion.

⓯ *What are the main features of the crime control model and the due process model?*

⓯ Crime control: Every effort must be made to repress crime through efficiency, speed, and finality. Due process: Every effort must be made to ensure that criminal justice decisions are based on reliable information; it stresses the adversarial process, the rights of defendants, and formal decision-making procedures.

Crime and Justice in a Multicultural Society

One important aspect of American values is the principle of equal treatment. This value is prominently displayed in important national documents such as the Declaration of Independence and the Fourteenth Amendment to the Constitution, which guarantees the right to "equal protection." Critics of the criminal justice system argue that discretionary decisions and other factors produce racial discrimination. Discrimination calls into question the country's success in fulfilling the values that it claims to regard as supremely important. As such, it is good to look closely at whether or not discrimination exists in various criminal justice settings.

■ Disparity and Discrimination

African Americans, Hispanics, and other minorities are subjected to the criminal justice system at much higher rates than are the white majority (BJS, 2008e; T. H. Cohen and Reaves, 2006; Cole, 1999:4–5; Engel and Calnon, 2004; J. A. Fox and Zawitz, 2007; J. Hagan and Peterson, 1995:14; Rand, 2008; West and Sabol, 2009). For example:

- African Americans account for 40 percent of felony defendants in the nation's 75 largest counties despite comprising only 15 percent of the population of those counties.

- A study of traffic stops found that, despite the greater likelihood of white drivers carrying drugs or guns, Hispanic drivers were 3.6 times more likely to be searched and 2.3 times more likely to be arrested by the police.

- The per capita incarceration rate for African Americans is nearly seven times greater than that for whites.

- Since 1980, the proportion of Hispanics among all inmates in U.S. prisons has risen from 7.7 percent to nearly 20 percent.

- The rate of unfounded arrests of Hispanics in California is double that of whites.

- Among 100,000 African American men aged 18–24, 102 will die as the result of a homicide, compared with about 12 among 100,000 white men in the same age group.

- The robbery victimization rate for African Americans is 2.5 times greater than that for whites.

■ **disparity** A difference between groups that may either be explained by legitimate factors or indicate discrimination.

■ **discrimination** Differential treatment of individuals or groups based on race, ethnicity, gender, sexual orientation, or economic status, instead of on their behavior or qualifications.

The experiences of minority group members with the criminal justice system may contribute to differences in their views about the system's fulfillment of the goal of equal treatment (Lundman and Kaufman, 2003). Many young men, in particular, can describe multiple incidents when they were followed by officers, temporarily taken into custody, forced by police to hand over money and property, or subjected to physical force for no reason other than walking down the street (Brunson, 2007). See "What Americans Think" for more on this.

A central question is whether racial and ethnic disparities like those just listed are the result of discrimination (Mann, 1993:vii–xiv; Wilbanks, 1987). A **disparity** is simply a difference between groups. Such differences can often be explained by legitimate factors. For example, the fact that 18- to 24-year-old men are arrested out of proportion to their numbers in the general population is a disparity explained by the fact that they commit more crime. It is not thought to be the result of public policy of singling out young men for arrest. **Discrimination** occurs when groups are differentially treated without regard to their behavior or qualifications, for example, if people of color are routinely sentenced to prison regardless of their criminal history. Thus, a disparity could result from either fair or unfair practices.

Young African American and Hispanic men contend that they are frequently hassled by the police. Is this racism or effective police work?

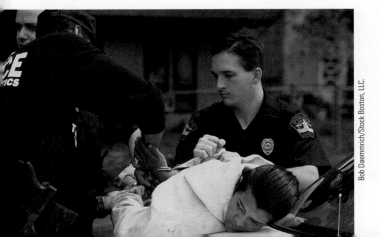

Bob Daemmrich/Stock Boston, LLC.

■ Explaining Disparities

Racial disparities in criminal justice are often explained in one of three ways: (1) people of color commit more crimes, (2) the criminal justice system is racist, with the result that people of color are treated more harshly, or (3) the criminal justice system expresses the racism found in society as a whole. We consider each of these views in turn.

Explanation 1: People of Color Commit More Crimes   Nobody denies that the proportion of minorities arrested and placed under correctional supervision (probation, jail, prison, parole) is greater than their proportion to the general population. However, people disagree over whether racial bias is responsible for the disparity.

Disparities in arrests and sentences might be due to legitimate factors. For example, prosecutors and judges are supposed to take into account differences between serious and petty offenses, and between repeat and first-time offenders. It follows that more people of color will end up in the courts and prisons if they are more likely to commit a greater number of serious crimes and have more-serious prior records than do whites.

But why would minorities commit more crimes? The most extreme argument is that they are more predisposed to criminality. This assumes that people of color are a "criminal class." The available evidence does not support this view. Behavior that violates criminal laws is prevalent throughout all segments of society. Indeed, nearly every adult American has committed an act for which he or she could be jailed. For example, studies of illicit drug use find that young adults, men, whites, and those with less than a high school education are more likely to use drugs than are others. As General Barry McCaffrey, the former director of the U.S. Office of National Drug Control Policy, has said, "The typical drug user is not poor and unemployed" (*New York Times,* September 9, 1999:A14). The 2004 *National Survey on Drug Use and Health* found that the percentage of white teens who used illicit drugs was higher than that of African American and Hispanic teens, but lower than that of Native Americans (U.S. Department of Health and Human Services, 2005). Furthermore, self-report studies, in which people are asked to report on their own criminal behavior, have shown that nearly everyone has committed a crime, although most are never caught. Indeed, both former President George W. Bush and former Vice President Dick Cheney have had drunken-driving convictions; further, in secretly taped conversations released in 2005, President Bush indicated that he had used marijuana and said, "I haven't denied anything" with respect to questions about whether he had used cocaine (Kirkpatrick, 2005).

Many of these kinds of crimes are difficult to detect or are low priorities for law enforcement agencies. In other instances, affluent perpetrators are better positioned to gain dismissals because of their status within the community, social networks, or access to high-quality legal representation.

In evaluating theories about possible links between race and crime, we must be aware that many commentators may be focusing only on crimes that resulted in prosecutions. Such limitations can distort an accurate understanding of this important issue. Race itself is not a cause of criminal behavior. Instead, any apparent associations between crime and race relate only to subcategories of people within racial and ethnic groups, such as poor, young men, as well as certain categories of crimes that are commonly investigated and prosecuted. Research links crime to social contexts, not to race (Bruce, 2003).

Crime problems evolve and change over time. Identity theft and computer crime, for example, cause economic losses in the billions of dollars, yet no one has claimed a link between these crimes and race. Even if we look at developments affecting "street crimes," we can see that factors other than race appear to create the contexts for criminal behavior. For example, one of the most significant crime problems to hit the United States at the dawn of the twenty-first century is the "meth crisis": the spread

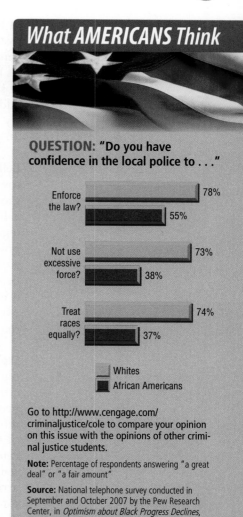

What AMERICANS Think

QUESTION: "Do you have confidence in the local police to . . ."

Enforce the law? — 78% / 55%

Not use excessive force? — 73% / 38%

Treat races equally? — 74% / 37%

■ Whites
■ African Americans

Go to http://www.cengage.com/criminaljustice/cole to compare your opinion on this issue with the opinions of other criminal justice students.

Note: Percentage of respondents answering "a great deal" or "a fair amount"

Source: National telephone survey conducted in September and October 2007 by the Pew Research Center, in *Optimism about Black Progress Declines,* (Washington, DC: Pew Research Center, 2007), 37.

of highly addictive methamphetamine that can be "cooked" in homemade labs using over-the-counter medicines and readily available chemicals. Americans use this inexpensive, dangerous drug more often than crack cocaine or heroin. Moreover, the "crisis has spread among white, often poor, usually rural Americans . . . [and] is rampant in small communities" (Bonne, 2001). According to U.S. Senator Tom Harkin, meth addiction accounts for up to 50 percent of thefts and burglaries in Iowa, as addicts try to support their habits; further, methamphetamine played a role in the crimes of 26 percent of that state's prison population (Harkin, 2005).

The link between crime and economic disadvantage is significant (McNulty and Bellair, 2003). The meth crisis has spread among poor whites in rural areas and small towns. Other kinds of crime prevail among the poor in urban areas. Further, minority groups suffer greatly from poverty and unemployment. If poor people seek to steal, it is likely to be through available means, whether burglaries at farmhouses or carjacking and shoplifting in urban areas. These sorts of crimes receive more attention from police than do crimes such as tax cheating, employee theft, and illegal stock transactions, which are associated with economic advantage. In light of the associations between race and poverty and between economic status and criminal opportunities, it is not surprising to find Native Americans, Hispanics, and African Americans to be overrepresented among perpetrators of certain categories of crimes, especially those that are the focus of police attention (Beckett, Nyrop, and Pfingst, 2006).

Explanation 2: The Criminal Justice System Is Racist   Racial disparities may result if people who commit similar offenses are treated differently by decision makers in the criminal justice system because of their race or ethnicity. In this view, the fact that people of color are arrested more often than whites does not mean that they are more crime prone. For example, although one report found that only 13 percent of monthly drug users are African American, these same people represent 35 percent of drug possession arrests, 55 percent of convictions, and 74 percent of prison sentences (Butterfield, 1995). Another study found that the police make unfounded arrests of African Americans four times as often as of whites (Donziger, 1996:109). *Racial profiling,* as described in the Close Up box, is an example of what many people believe is a racist activity by police. Evidence of its existence has led to new laws and policies that require police to keep records about their traffic-law enforcement patterns (Engel, Calnon, and Bernard, 2002).

Despite efforts to monitor and prevent such activities, evidence that some police officers use race as the basis for stopping, searching, and arresting individuals persists. Obviously, racial profiling activities—or the lack thereof—can vary from officer to officer and police department to police department (P. Warren et al., 2006). A 2005 study of Texas law enforcement agencies reported, for example, that the Houston Police Department searched 12 percent of African American drivers and 9 percent of Hispanic drivers stopped by its officers but searched only 3.7 percent of white drivers who were pulled over (Steward and Totman, 2005). A national study of traffic stops found that the odds of being searched were 50 percent higher for African American drivers and 42 percent higher for Hispanic drivers than for white drivers (Durose, Schmitt, and Langan, 2005; Engel and Calnon, 2004).

Is the criminal justice system racist? White Americans are less likely than African Americans to attribute the overrepresentation of minorities to biased decision making. A study published in 2008 found that 71 percent of African Americans believe that police bias is a "big reason" why minorities are disproportionately convicted of crimes and imprisoned, but only 37 percent of whites share this view (Unnever, 2008). Yet, the arrest rate of minority citizens is greater than their offense rates justify. According to data from the Bureau of Justice Statistics for 2005, victims of aggravated assaults identified their assailants as African Americans in 25 percent of cases, yet African Americans made up 34 percent of suspects arrested for aggravated assault (BJS, 2006b). With respect to sentencing, research indicates that African American and Hispanic men are less likely than white men to receive the benefit of prosecutors' discretionary recommendations for lesser sentences in federal cocaine prosecutions

Crime and Justice in America

FOR THE 100 STUDENTS IN THE LECTURE HALL, it was business as usual. Instructor Joseph Peterson illustrated his geosciences lecture with PowerPoint slides as they took notes and glanced at the clock, awaiting the approaching end of the class period. Then the first shot rang out. Nightmarish chaos erupted as a man jumped out from behind the curtain on the stage and began firing into the auditorium. "He's got a gun!" "Call 911!" Dozens of students screamed and ran for the exits, while others dove to the floor, desperately trying to hide beneath their seats. Just as quickly, the auditorium became eerily silent, except for the sound of the black-clad gunman firing randomly into the audience, reloading, and then emptying his guns again (Saulny and Davey, 2008).

The police at Northern Illinois University (NIU) arrived at the Cole Hall auditorium within two minutes. They found the gunman dead of a self-inflicted gunshot wound. He had brought a shotgun into the building in a guitar case, along with three handguns. The police counted six empty shotgun shells and 48 shell casings for handgun ammunition scattered around the body. They also found themselves in the middle of an urgent medical emergency, as dead and wounded students lay scattered among the seats. The tragic tally for the brief event was five dead and 16 wounded—plus the death of the perpetrator, Steven Kazmierczak, a former honors student at NIU who had received awards for his criminal justice research (Heinzmann and St. Clair, 2008).

The event was highly publicized because the nature of the crime and location of the incident differed so greatly from those of most crimes, which involve the loss of property or some other less dramatic event. The case embodies one of the worst fears of Americans: that they or their children will be trapped within the sights of a suicidal gunman, intent on killing as many people as possible without caring at all about the suffering of others or the consequences for himself. Despite the fact that the NIU campus shooting did not represent a "typical crime," the case raises key questions that shape the subject of crime victimization.

For example, who are the crime victims in this case? Obviously, the students who were killed and wounded. But what about their families? Aren't they also victims of this crime, having suffered psychological and emotional harm? What about the university? Has its reputation as a safe place to attend college been destroyed? What about members of the victims' hometown communities throughout Illinois? They lost relatives, friends, and neighbors while churches lost parishioners—and society lost future educated citizens who might have made significant contributions to the well-being of their communities, the nation, or the world. Would it be proper to say that all people in society are also victims of the crime? Members of the public may feel less safe as a result of hearing about this shocking crime, which could have happened to anyone. Does that make each of us—individually—a victim? We might feel as if we have lost a bit of our security and liberty if this event enhances our fears, nervousness, and discomfort when we wonder if any strangers around us—at the movies, at the ballpark, or in the mall—might turn out to have similar murderous plans.

These are important questions to consider, because how we answer them will define the scope of the subject of criminal victimization. In other words, when we talk about the victimizing consequences of crime, should we only talk about the individuals most directly harmed by a crime, or should we also consider people who suffer less direct, but equally real, consequences? These questions actually have practical consequences under circumstances in which we speak of "victims' rights," such as crime victims being entitled to compensation. We need to define what we mean by a "victim" before we can implement any such policy.

Another important question looms in this and every other criminal case: Why did the perpetrator do what he or she did? Criminal behavior is the main cause of criminal victimization. Scholars, policy makers, and the public have long pondered questions such as "What causes crime?" and "Why do criminal offenders cause harm to other human beings?" These questions have significant implications for theories about crime causation, which often influence government policies for controlling and punishing violations of criminal laws.

In considering this subject, we need to bear in mind that no single theory can explain all crimes. Remember that "crimes" are whatever actions a legislature defines as deserving punishment at a particular moment in history. Thus, we should not assume that a corporate official who employs deceptive accounting practices in order to skim off millions of dollars in business profits has the same motives as the man who shot the students at NIU. The fact that crime has many causes, however, does not mean that all proposed theories about crime causation are equally useful or valid. We need to look closely at theories about crime and evaluate what evidence supports them.

In order to understand the criminal justice system, we must understand the nature of crime and all of the people affected by it. Chapter 1 introduced you to decision makers in the system, such as police and prosecutors, as well as processes for handling criminal cases. Here you will consider other key individuals: criminal offenders and their victims. You will also examine the nature and extent of crime—the key elements that tell us how many offenders and victims will likely cause or be affected by crime in a given year.

Defining Crime

Why does the law label some types of behavior as criminal and not others? For example, why is it a crime to use marijuana when it is legal to drink alcohol, a substance that also has serious intoxicating, addictive, and harmful health affects?

The criminal law is defined by elected representatives in state legislatures and Congress, who make choices about the behaviors that the government will punish. Some of these choices reflect broad agreement in society that certain actions, such as rape and murder, are so harmful that they must be punished. Such crimes have traditionally been called **mala in se**—wrong in themselves.

However, legislatures may decide that certain actions are criminal even though people in society may disagree about the harmfulness of those actions. These crimes are called **mala prohibita**—they are crimes because they are prohibited by the government and not because they are wrong in themselves. Everyone does not agree, for example, that gambling, prostitution, and drug use should be punished.

The definitions of crimes do not necessarily remain fixed over time. Legislators can change the definitions as society's values change. For example, lotteries and casino gambling were illegal in most states during the first half of the twentieth century. In the second half of the century, however, states decided that they could profit from gambling; they began to sponsor state lotteries and, over time, approve various forms of casino gambling. Presumably, the moral value and social risks from gambling did not change over the decades. Instead, attitudes toward gambling changed and legislators enacted laws to reflect those changes in public policy.

Changes in the definitions of crimes can also occur when court decisions declare that the criminalization of specific actions violates people's constitutional rights. Court decisions ended the criminalization of early-term abortions (*Roe v. Wade*, 1973) and the private sexual conduct of adult gays and lesbians (*Lawrence v. Texas*, 2003).

■ **mala in se** Offenses that are wrong by their very nature.

■ **mala prohibita** Offenses prohibited by law but not wrong in themselves.

CHECKPOINT

ANSWER

❶ *What is the difference between* mala in se *offenses and* mala prohibita *offenses?*

❶ *Mala in se*—offenses that are wrong in themselves (murder, rape, assault).
Mala prohibita—acts that are crimes because they are prohibited (gambling, drug use).

Types of Crime

Crimes can be classified in various ways. As we have seen, scholars often use the distinction between *mala in se* and *mala prohibita*. Crimes can also be classified as either felonies or misdemeanors, depending on whether the prescribed punishment is more or less than one year in prison. A third scheme classifies crimes by the nature of the act. This approach has traditionally yielded five types of crime: visible crime, occupational crime, organized crime, victimless crime, and political crime. Each type has its own level of risk and reward, each arouses varying degrees of public disapproval, and each is committed by a certain kind of offender. New types of crime emerge as society changes. Cyber crimes committed through the use of computers and the Internet are becoming a major global problem.

■ Visible Crime

■ **visible crime** An offense against persons or property, committed primarily by members of the lower class. Often referred to as "street crime" or "ordinary crime," this type of offense is the one most upsetting to the public.

Visible crime, often called "street crime" or "ordinary crime," ranges from shoplifting to homicide. For offenders, such crimes are the least profitable and, because they are visible, the hardest to hide. These are the acts that the public regards as "criminal." The majority of law enforcement resources are employed to deal with them. We can divide visible crimes into three categories: violent crimes, property crimes, and public order crimes.

Violent Crimes   Acts against people in which death or physical injury results are *violent crimes*. These include criminal homicide, assault, rape, and robbery. The criminal justice system treats them as the most serious offenses and punishes them accordingly. Although the public is most fearful of violence by strangers, many of these offenses are committed by people who know their victim.

Property Crimes   *Property crime*s are acts that threaten property held by individuals or by the state. Many types of crimes fall under this category, including theft, larceny, shoplifting, embezzlement, and burglary. Some property offenders are amateurs who occasionally commit these crimes because of situational factors such as financial need or peer pressure. In contrast, professional criminals make a significant portion of their livelihood from committing property offenses.

Public Order Crimes   Acts that threaten the general well-being of society and challenge accepted moral principles are defined as *public order crimes*. They include public drunkenness, aggressive panhandling, vandalism, and disorderly conduct. Although the police tend to treat these behaviors as minor offenses, some scholars argue that this type of disorderly behavior instills fear in citizens, leads to more-serious crimes, and hastens urban decay (Kelling and Coles, 1996). The definition and enforcement of such behaviors as crimes highlight the tensions between different interpretations of American values. Many people see such behavior as simply representing the liberty that adults enjoy in a free society to engage in offensive and self-destructive behavior that causes no concrete harm to other people. By contrast, other people see their own liberty limited by the need to be wary and fearful of actions by people who are drunk or out of control.

Those charged with visible crimes tend to be young men. Further, in many communities, members of minority groups tend to be overrepresented among those arrested and prosecuted for such offenses. Some argue that this is due to the class bias of a society that has singled out visible crimes for priority

Multimillionaire Conrad Black, owner of many media businesses, leaves the Chicago federal courthouse in December 2007 after being sentenced to 6.5 years in prison for swindling investors out of millions of dollars. Do Americans view such occupational crimes as serious matters that deserve the attention of police and prosecutors?

AP Images/Jerry Lai

enforcement. They note that we do not focus as much police and prosecutorial attention on white-collar crimes, such as fraud and other acts committed by office workers and business owners, as we do on street crimes.

▪ Occupational Crime

Occupational crimes are committed in the context of a legal business or profession. Often viewed as shrewd business practices rather than illegal acts, they are crimes that, if "done right," are never discovered. Such crimes are often committed by respectable, well-to-do people taking advantage of opportunities arising from business dealings. Such crimes impose huge costs on society. Although there are no precise figures on the cost of occupational crime to American society, the Association of Certified Fraud Examiners estimates that occupational fraud may cost American businesses as much as $994 billion annually (Association of Certified Fraud Examiners, 2008). By contrast, the FBI calculates that the direct financial losses from street crimes involving the theft of property, such as burglary, robbery, and larceny, are about $15 billion annually (FBI, 2008a).

▪ **occupational crimes** Criminal offenses committed through opportunities created in a legal business or occupation.

▪ Organized Crime

Rather than referring to criminal acts per se, the term **organized crime** refers to the framework within which such acts are committed. A crime syndicate has an organizational structure, rules, a division of labor, and the capacity for ruthless violence and for corrupting law enforcement, labor and business leaders, and politicians (Jacobs and Panarella, 1998:160). Organized criminals provide goods and services to millions of people. They engage in any activity that provides a minimum of risk and a maximum of profit. Thus, organized crime involves a network of activities, usually cutting across state and national borders, that range from legitimate businesses to shady deals with labor unions to providing "goods"—such as drugs, sex, and pornography—that cannot be obtained legally. In recent years, organized crime has been involved in new services such as commercial arson, illegal disposal of toxic wastes, and **money laundering**. Few organized criminals are arrested and prosecuted.

▪ **organized crime** A framework for the perpetuation of criminal acts—usually in fields such as gambling, drugs, and prostitution—providing illegal services that are in great demand.

Although the public often associates organized crime with Italian Americans—indeed, the federal government indicted 73 members of the Genovese New York crime "family" in 2001 (Worth, 2001)—other ethnic groups have dominated at various times. Thirty-five years ago, one scholar noted the strangeness of America's "ladder of social mobility," in which each new immigrant group uses organized crime as one of the first rungs of the climb (Bell, 1967:150). However, debate about this notion continues, because not all immigrant groups have engaged in organized crime (Kenney and Finckenauer, 1995:38).

▪ **money laundering** Moving the proceeds of criminal activities through a maze of businesses, banks, and brokerage accounts so as to disguise their origin.

Over the last few decades, law enforcement efforts have greatly weakened the Italian American Mafia. An aging leadership, lack of interest by younger family members, and pressures from new immigrant groups have also contributed to the fall of the Mafia. Today African Americans, Hispanics, Russians, and Asians have formed organized-crime groups. Drug dealing has brought Colombian and Mexican crime groups to U.S. shores, and groups led by Vietnamese, Chinese, and Japanese have formed in California. Because these new groups do not fit the Mafia pattern, law enforcement agencies have had to find new ways to deal with them (Kleinknecht, 1996).

Just as multinational corporations have emerged during the past 20 years, organized crime has also developed global networks. Increasingly transnational criminal groups "live and operate in a borderless world" (Zagaris, 1998:1402). In the aftermath of the events of September 11, American law enforcement and intelligence

Sex workers such as this prostitute provide a service that is in demand but illegal. Are these willing and private exchanges truly "victimless"? Why should this be considered a criminal activity?

Douglas Engle/The New York Times/Redux

■ **crimes without victims** Offenses involving a willing and private exchange of illegal goods or services that are in strong demand. Participants do not feel they are being harmed, but these crimes are prosecuted on the ground that society as a whole is being injured.

■ **political crime** An act, usually done for ideological purposes, that constitutes a threat against the state (such as treason, sedition, or espionage); also describes a criminal act by the state.

officials increased their efforts to monitor and thwart international organizations that seek to attack the United States and its citizens. Many of these organizations use criminal activities, such as drug smuggling and stolen credit card numbers, to fund their efforts.

■ Crimes without Victims

Crimes without victims involve a willing and private exchange of goods or services that are in strong demand but illegal—in other words, offenses against morality. Examples include prostitution, gambling, and drug sales and use. These are called "victimless" crimes because those involved do not feel that they are being harmed. Prosecution for these offenses is justified on the ground that society as a whole is harmed because the moral fabric of the community is threatened. However, using the law to enforce moral standards is costly. The system is swamped by these cases, which often require the use of police informers and thus open the door for payoffs and other kinds of corruption.

The war on drugs is the most obvious example of policies against one type of victimless crime. Possession and sale of drugs—marijuana, heroin, cocaine, opium, amphetamines—have been illegal in the United States for over a hundred years. Especially during the past 40 years, all levels of government have applied extensive resources to enforce these laws and punish offenders.

The crime-fighting duties of police patrol officers typically focus on visible crimes and crimes without victims. As we shall see in later chapters, police officers also fulfill other functions, such as order maintenance and public service.

■ Political Crime

Political crime refers to criminal acts either by the government or against the government that are carried out for ideological purposes (F. E. Hagan, 1997:2). Political criminals believe they are following a morality that is above the law. Examples include James Kopp—arrested for the murder of Dr. Barnett Slepian near Buffalo, New York, and other doctors who performed abortions—and Eric Rudolph, convicted for the bombing of abortion clinics in Atlanta and Birmingham and the pipe bomb explosion at the Atlanta Olympics. Similarly, shocking acts of violence that are labeled as terrorism, including the 1995 bombing of the Federal Building in Oklahoma City by Timothy McVeigh and the 2001 attacks on the World Trade Center and Pentagon, spring from political motivations.

In some authoritarian states, merely criticizing the government is a crime that can lead to prosecution and imprisonment. In Western democracies today, there are few political crimes other than treason, which is rare. For example, in 2009 a retired employee of the U.S. State Department and his wife were charged with being spies for Cuba. They reportedly stole government documents because of their ideological admiration for the Cuban government and hostile feelings toward the U.S. government, not because they were seeking financial payments from Cuba (G. Thompson, 2009). Many illegal acts, such as the World Trade Center and Oklahoma City bombings, can be traced to political motives, but they are prosecuted as visible crimes under laws against bombing, arson, and murder rather than as political crimes per se.

■ Cyber Crime

Cyber crimes involve the use of computers and the Internet to commit acts against people, property, public order, or morality. Thus, cyber criminals have learned "new ways to do old tricks." Some use computers to steal information, resources, or funds. In 2007, the federal government's Internet Crime Complaint Center (IC3) received nearly 207,000 complaints about cyber crime, which had caused financial losses of over $239 million (Internet Crime Complaint Center, 2008). Other criminals use the Internet to disseminate child pornography, to advertise sexual services, or to stalk the unsuspecting. The more sophisticated "hackers" create and distribute viruses designed to destroy computer programs or gain control of computers from unsuspecting individuals. In 2003, a man in Great Britain was acquitted of child pornography charges when he argued successfully that an unknown individual had used a virus to hijack his computer and use it to download and disseminate child pornography (Schwartz, 2003). You will read more about cyber crime in the discussion of criminal justice and technology in Chapter 14.

Which of these main types of crime is of greatest concern to you? If you are like most people, it is visible crime. Thus, as a nation, we devote most of our criminal justice resources to dealing with such crimes. To develop policies to address these crimes, however, we need to know more about the amount of crime and all the types of crimes that occur in the United States. One of the most disturbing crimes, which has gained much attention lately, is hate crime; see the Close Up box for more.

■ **cyber crimes** Offenses that involve the use of one or more computers.

New Jersey state police officers check websites for child pornography. Cyber crime is a growing problem that costs American businesses and individuals millions of dollars each year. Law enforcement officials work diligently to keep up with the criminals' computer expertise, technology, and methods of deception. How can American police effectively combat the evolving and spreading threat of cyber crime, especially when so many cyber criminals are located in other countries?

AP Images/Daniel Hulshizer

CHECKPOINT

ANSWERS

❷ *What are the six main types of crime?*

❷ Visible crime, occupational crime, organized crime, crimes without victims, political crime, cyber crime.

❸ *What is the function of organized crime?*

❸ Organized crime usually provides goods and services that are in high demand but are illegal.

❹ *What is meant by the term crimes without victims?*

❹ These are crimes against morality in which the people involved do not believe that anyone has been victimized.

CLOSE UP

Hate Crimes: A New Category of Personal Violence

BLACK CHURCHES are set afire in the Southeast; the home of the mayor of West Hartford, Connecticut, is defaced by swastikas and anti-Semitic graffiti; gay Wyoming student Matthew Shepard is murdered; a black woman in Maryland is beaten and doused with lighter fluid in a race-based attack. These are just a few of the more than 7,500 hate crimes reported to the police each year. The U.S. Department of Justice said that threats, assaults, and acts of vandalism against Arab Americans and people of South Asian ancestry increased in the months following the events of September 11. Crimes based on the victims' ethnicity may become more diversified as Americans react to their anger and fear about the threat of terrorism from foreign organizations.

Hate crimes have been added to the penal codes of 45 states and the District of Columbia (Anti-Defamation League, 2008). The FBI's annual report on hate crimes defined them as bias-motivated offenses that target people for their race, religion, sexual orientation, ethnicity, or disability (FBI, 2007). Some states also include crimes based on gender discrimination. In 2009, the administration of President Barack Obama proposed expanding federal law to cover hate crimes based on gender or sexual orientation. The laws also make it a crime to vandalize religious buildings and cemeteries or to intimidate another person out of bias. Although the Ku Klux Klan, the World Church of the Creator, and Nazi-style "skinhead" groups represent the most visible perpetrators, most hate crimes are committed by individuals acting alone. For example, analysts believe that a single individual sent threatening letters to African American actor Taye Diggs and his wife, white Broadway actress Idina Menzel, in 2004. In 2008, an Ohio man was arrested by the FBI for sending threatening letters to Supreme Court Justice Clarence Thomas and other African American men who are married to white women.

Hate crime laws have been challenged on the ground that they violate the right of free speech. Some argue that racial and religious slurs must be allowed on this basis. In response, supporters of hate crime laws say that limits must be placed on freedom of speech and that some words are so hateful that they fall outside the free speech protection of the First Amendment.

In *Wisconsin v. Mitchell* (1993), the Supreme Court upheld a law providing for a severer sentence in cases in which the offender "intentionally selects the person against whom the crime [is committed] because of the race, religion, color, disability, sexual orientation, national origin or ancestry of that person." In a later case on a related issue, the Court decided that states can make it a crime to burn a cross with an intent to intimidate people. They rejected the argument that cross burning, a traditional ritual act by the Ku Klux Klan, a white supremacist organization with a violent history, constituted a protected form of free expression (*Virginia v. Black,* 2003).

In a society that is becoming more diverse, hate crimes arguably hurt not only their victims but the social fabric itself. Democracy depends on people sharing common ideals and working together. Under this view, when groups are pitted against one another, the entire community suffers.

RESEARCHING THE INTERNET

To see the American Psychological Association's analysis of hate crimes, go to the corresponding site listed on the Cole/Smith Criminal Justice in America Companion Website: http://www.cengage.com/criminaljustice/cole.

FOR CRITICAL ANALYSIS

Is criminal law the way to attack the problem of expressions of racial hatred?

Sources: Drawn from Federal Bureau of Investigation, *Hate Crime Statistics, 2006* (Washington, DC: U.S. Department of Justice, 2007); A. Fuller, "Republication Senators Question Need for Hate Crime Bill," *New York Times*, June 25, 2009, http://www.nytimes.com; J. Jacobs, "Should Hate Be a Crime?" *The Public Interest*, Fall 1993, pp. 1–14; C. Newton, "Crimes against Arabs, South Asians Up," *Washington Post*, June 26, 2002, http://www.washingtonpost.com; "Ohio Man Accused of Threat to Justice," *New York Times*, April 10, 2008, http://www.nytimes.com.

How Much Crime Is There?

Many Americans believe that the crime rate is rising, even though it has generally declined since the 1980s (see "What Americans Think"). For example, the rate of violent crime decreased by 37 percent from 1998 to 2007, including a 2 percent drop from 2005 to 2007. According to the Bureau of Justice Statistics, "The rates for every major violent and property crime measured by [our survey] in 2007 were at or near the lowest levels recorded since 1973, the first year that such data were available" (Rand, 2008:1).

In January 2009 the FBI released preliminary crime statistics for 2008. The initial analysis showed a 3.5 percent decrease in violent crime. From June 2007 to June 2008, all types of violent crime decreased, with murder and aggravated assault down by about 4 percent. The largest decrease in violent crime occurred in the Midwest (6 percent), while the South and Northeast demonstrated the least amount of change (FBI, 2009b). Some scholars and law enforcement professionals were concerned when crime rates increased modestly from 2004 to 2005; however, the increase was small and crime rates still remain low compared with the rates from two decades ago.

Much of the discussion in the section concerns national crime data and trends that affect the United States as a whole. Individual cities and their police departments, however, need to be keenly aware of patterns of crime within their own neighborhoods. By monitoring crime rates and trends, they can decide how to deploy their officers and what strategies to employ. Many cities employ their own crime analysts to help identify and track crime problems. As you read "Careers in Criminal Justice," consider whether you would like to develop the knowledge and skills necessary to become a crime analyst.

One of the frustrations in studying criminal justice is the lack of accurate means of knowing the amount of crime. Surveys reveal that much more crime occurs than is reported to the police. This is referred to as the **dark figure of crime**.

Most homicides and auto thefts are reported to the police. In the case of a homicide, a body must be accounted for, and insurance companies require a police report before they will pay for a stolen car. But about 43 percent of rape victims do not report the attack; almost 56 percent of victims of simple assault do not do so. Figure 2.1 shows the percentage of victimizations not reported to the police.

Until 1972, the only crimes counted by government were those that were known to the police and that made their way into the Federal Bureau of Investigation's Uniform Crime Reports (UCR). Since then, the Department of Justice has sponsored the National Crime Victimization Surveys (NCVS), which survey the public to find out how much victimization has occurred. One might hope that the data from these two sources would give us a clear picture of the amount of crime, crime trends, and the characteristics of offenders. However, the picture is blurred, perhaps even distorted, because of differences in the way crime is measured by the UCR and the NCVS.

The Uniform Crime Reports

Issued each year by the FBI, the **Uniform Crime Reports (UCR)** are a statistical summary of crimes reported to the police. At the urging of the International Association of Chiefs of Police, Congress in 1930 authorized this system for compiling crime data (Rosen, 1995). The UCR data come from a voluntary national network of some 16,000 local, state, and federal law enforcement agencies, policing 98 percent of the U.S. population.

With the sharp drop in crime in recent years, new pressures have been placed on police executives to show that their cities are following the national trend. Some officials have even falsified their crime statistics as promotions, pay raises,

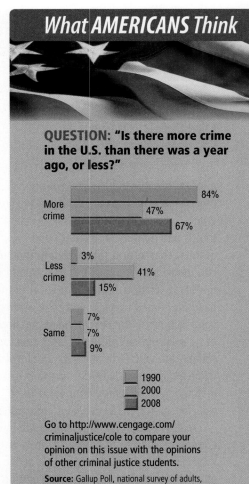

What AMERICANS Think

QUESTION: "Is there more crime in the U.S. than there was a year ago, or less?"

More crime — 84% / 47% / 67%

Less crime — 3% / 41% / 15%

Same — 7% / 7% / 9%

■ 1990
□ 2000
■ 2008

Go to http://www.cengage.com/criminaljustice/cole to compare your opinion on this issue with the opinions of other criminal justice students.

Source: Gallup Poll, national survey of adults, reported December 3, 2008, as adapted by Bureau of Justice Statistics, *Sourcebook of Criminal Justice Statistics, 2008* (Washington, DC: U.S. Government Printing Office, 2008), Table 2.33.2008.

■ **dark figure of crime** A metaphor that emphasizes the dangerous dimension of crimes that are never reported to the police.

■ **Uniform Crime Reports (UCR)** An annually published statistical summary of crimes reported to the police, based on voluntary reports to the FBI by local, state, and federal law enforcement agencies.

FIGURE 2.1
Percentage of victimizations not reported to the police
Why do some people not report crimes to the police? What can be done to encourage reporting?

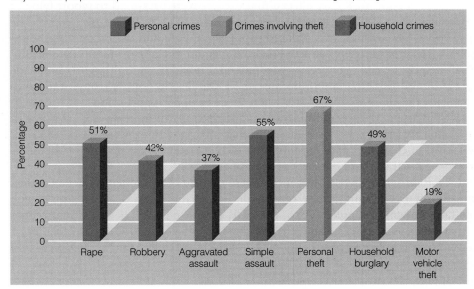

Personal crimes Crimes involving theft Household crimes

	Percentage
Rape	51%
Robbery	42%
Aggravated assault	37%
Simple assault	55%
Personal theft	67%
Household burglary	49%
Motor vehicle theft	19%

Source: Bureau of Justice Statistics, *Criminal Victimization in the United States, 2006 Statistical Tables* (Washington, DC: U.S. Government Printing Office, 2007), Table 91.

CAREERS IN CRIMINAL JUSTICE

Crime Analyst

MARK BRIDGE, CRIME ANALYST
CITY OF FREDERICK, MARYLAND

THE PRIMARY RESPONSIBILITIES of the crime analyst's job include the following: conducting preliminary and advanced statistical analysis; compiling crime, arrest, and calls-for-service data; identifying trends and patterns in the data and generating maps, graphs, charts, and tables; briefing members of the command staff on crime patterns and intelligence matters; writing crime and intelligence analysis bulletins related to ongoing trends; making substantial contributions to the development and implementation of new analytical methods; and developing ways to collaborate with federal, state, and local agencies. Data used in crime analysis are derived from many resources, including record management systems (reports, incidents, arrests, and so forth), calls for service, field interviews, and probation and parole data.

A crime analyst must keep the police chief and shift commanders informed about trends in crime rates in various locations within a community. This allows those investing in law enforcement to see what they are getting for their dollar. It also allows for the budgeting and planning of future resources, such

as the number of officers needed, which can be based on population growth, calls for service, crime rates, and other factors. Tactical analysis enables patrol and special details to focus on areas where their efforts are most needed. By analyzing data, crime analysts provide the peak days, times, and locations for crime problems within a community. Given a series of incidents that may involve the same suspect or suspects, the analyst can use forecasting techniques based on data from previous crimes to project the most likely dates, times, and places of the next crime.

Mark Bridge earned an undergraduate degree and a master's degree in criminal justice. He studied statistics, research methods, theories of crime, policing, and the operations of the criminal justice system. Prior to becoming a crime analyst, he worked in state government analyzing operations of the court system.

The biggest challenge of being a crime analyst is turning raw data into timely and useful information. There are a lot of sources to obtain information from, and you, as the analyst, must decide what to use and how to use it.

and departmental budgets have become increasingly dependent on positive data. For example, an audit of the Atlanta police released in 2004 found that they had underreported crimes as part of an effort to make the city appear safer when it was competing to be the host city for the 1996 Summer Olympics (Niesse, 2004). In 2005, leaders of police unions in New York City alleged that officers were pressured to report felonies as misdemeanors in order to help the city show favorable results (Moses, 2005). The Detroit Police Department was accused of misclassifying and undercounting homicides. Newspaper reporters conducted their own count and alleged that the police undercount helped the city avoid acknowledging that it had the nation's worst homicide rate (LeDuff and Esparza, 2009). Because the FBI relies on reports from local police departments, the UCR are inaccurate when agencies underreport crime.

The UCR use standard definitions to ensure uniform data on the 29 types of crimes listed in Table 2.1. For 8 major crimes—Part I (Index Offenses)—the data show factors such as age, race, and number of reported crimes solved. For the other 21 crimes—Part II (Other Offenses)—the data are less complete.

The UCR provide a useful but incomplete picture of crime levels. Because they cover only reported crimes, these reports do not include data on crimes for which people failed to call the police. Also, the UCR do not measure occupational crimes and other offenses that are not included in the 29 types covered. And because reporting is voluntary, police departments may not take the time to make complete and careful reports.

In response to criticisms of the UCR, the FBI has made some changes in the program that are now being implemented nationwide. Some offenses have been redefined,

TABLE 2.1	**Uniform Crime Report Offenses**

The UCR present data on 8 index offenses and 21 other crimes for which there is less information. A limitation of the UCR is that they tabulate only crimes that are reported to the police.

Part I (Index Offenses)	Part II (Other Offenses)
1. Criminal homicide	9. Simple assaults
2. Forcible rape	10. Forgery and counterfeiting
3. Robbery	11. Fraud
4. Aggravated assault	12. Embezzlement
5. Burglary	13. Buying, receiving or possessing stolen property
6. Larceny/theft	14. Vandalism
7. Auto theft	15. Weapons (carrying, possession, etc.)
8. Arson	16. Prostitution and commercialized vice
	17. Sex offenses
	18. Violation of narcotic drug laws
	19. Gambling
	20. Offenses against the family and children
	21. Driving under the influence
	22. Violation of liquor laws
	23. Drunkenness
	24. Disorderly conduct
	25. Vagrancy
	26. All other offenses (excluding traffic)
	27. Suspicion
	28. Curfew and loitering (juvenile)
	29. Juvenile runaways

Source: Federal Bureau of Investigation, *Crime in the United States, 2000* (Washington, DC: U.S. Government Printing Office, 2001)

and police agencies are being asked to report more details about crime events. Using the **National Incident-Based Reporting System (NIBRS)**, police agencies are to report all crimes committed during an incident, not just the most serious one, as well as data on offenders, victims, and the places where they interact. While the UCR now count incidents and arrests for the 8 index offenses and count arrests for other crimes, the NIBRS provides detailed incident data on 46 offenses in 22 crime categories. The NIBRS distinguishes between attempted and completed crimes as well.

How is the NIBRS different from the UCR? In addition to including more types of crime than the UCR, NIBRS data are *disaggregated*—that is, rather than police departments reporting counts of crime to the FBI (as in the UCR), many jurisdictions now report information on individual crimes. Thanks to advances in technology and data transfer, police departments can now transfer more data easily than when the UCR began collecting data from police departments in 1929. However, the reporting process is more difficult for NIBRS, and all agencies must adopt the same format for reporting data. These difficulties mean that not all states currently participate in the NIBRS system. As of December 2003, only 7 states reported NIBRS data for every one of their jurisdictions (Delaware, Idaho, Iowa, South Carolina, Tennessee, Virginia, and West Virginia). Another 16 states reported incident-level data to the FBI from at least one jurisdiction, while the remaining 27 states either did not participate or were in training to provide NIBRS data in the future (BJS, 2004c).

■ **National Incident-Based Reporting System (NIBRS)** A reporting system in which the police describe each offense in a crime incident, together with data describing the offender, victim, and property.

■ The National Crime Victimization Surveys

A second source of crime data is the **National Crime Victimization Surveys (NCVS)**. Since 1972 the Census Bureau has done surveys to find out the extent and nature of crime victimization. Thus, data have been gathered on unreported as well as reported crimes.

■ **National Crime Victimization Surveys (NCVS)** Interviews of samples of the U.S. population conducted by the Bureau of Justice Statistics to determine the number and types of criminal victimizations and thus the extent of unreported as well as reported crime.

Interviews are conducted twice each year with a national probability sample of approximately 76,000 people in 43,000 households. The same people are interviewed twice a year for three years and asked if they have been victimized in the last six months.

Each person is asked a set of "screening" questions (for example, "Did anyone beat you up, attack you, or hit you with something such as a rock or a bottle?") to determine whether he or she has been victimized. The person is then asked questions designed to elicit specific facts about the event, the offender, and any financial losses or physical injuries caused by the crime.

Besides the household interviews, surveys are carried out in the nation's 26 largest cities; separate studies are done to find out about the victimization of businesses. These data allow us to estimate how many crimes have occurred, learn more about the offenders, and note demographic patterns. The results show that for the crimes measured (rape, robbery, assault, burglary, theft) there were 22.8 million victimizations in 2007 (down from 43 million in 1973) (Rand, 2008). This number is much higher than the number of crimes actually reported to the police.

Although the NCVS provide a more complete picture of the nature and extent of crime than do the UCR, they too have flaws. Because government employees administer the surveys, the people interviewed are unlikely to report crimes in which they or members of their family took part. They also may not want to admit that a family member engages in crime, or they may be too embarrassed to admit that they have allowed themselves to be victimized more than once. In addition, the survey covers a limited range of crimes, and the relatively small sample of interviewees may lead to erroneous conclusions about crime trends for an entire country of nearly 300 million people (Mosher, Miethe and Phillips, 2002).

The NCVS are also imperfect because they depend on the victim's *perception* of an event. The theft of a child's lunch money by a bully may be reported as a crime by one person but not mentioned by another. People may say that their property was stolen when in fact they lost it. Moreover, people's memories of dates may fade, and they may misreport the year in which a crime occurred even though they remember the event itself clearly. In 1993 the Bureau of Justice Statistics made some changes in the NCVS to improve their accuracy and detail.

The next time you hear or read about crime rates, take into account the source of the data and its possible limitations. Table 2.2 compares the Uniform Crime Reports and the National Crime Victimization Surveys.

▪ Trends in Crime

Experts agree that, contrary to public opinion and the claims of politicians, crime rates have not been steadily rising. The NCVS show that the victimization rate peaked in 1981 and has declined since then. The greatest declines are in property crimes, but crimes of violence have also dropped, especially since 1993. The violent crime victimization rate fell by 43 percent from 1998 through 2007. Property crimes also saw declines over the same period, with a 30 percent drop in household burglaries and a 24 percent drop in motor vehicle thefts (Rand, 2008). The UCR show similar results, revealing a rapid rise in crime rates beginning in 1964 and continuing until 1980, when the rates began to level off or decline. The overall crime rate rose slightly in 2001 because of an increase in property crimes, but it subsequently resumed modest annual declines (BJS, 2007c: Table 3.106.2007).

Figure 2.2 displays four measures of violent crime, adjusted for changes made in the NCVS in 1992. The top two measures are based on the victimization survey; crimes recorded by the police and arrests are from the UCR and are presented below these. Remember that the differences in the trends indicated by the NCVS and the UCR are explained in part by the different data sources and different populations on which their tabulations are based.

What explains the drop in both violent and property crime well below the 1973 levels? Among the reasons given by analysts are the aging of the baby boom population,

TABLE 2.2   The UCR and the NCVS

Compare the data sources. Remember that the UCR tabulate only crimes reported to the police, whereas the NCVS are based on interviews with victims.

	Uniform Crime Reports	National Crime Victimization Survey
Offenses Measured	Homicide Rape Robbery (personal and commercial) Assault (aggravated) Burglary (commercial and household) Larceny (commercial and household) Motor vehicle theft Arson	Rape Robbery (personal) Assault (aggravated and simple) Household burglary Larceny (personal and household) Motor vehicle theft
Scope	Crimes reported to the police in most jurisdictions; considerable flexibility in developing small-area data	Crimes both reported and not reported to police; all data are for the nation as a whole; some data are available for a few large geographic areas
Collection Method	Police department reports to Federal Bureau of Investigation	Survey interviews: periodically measures the total number of crimes committed by asking a national sample of 43,000 households representing 76,000 people over the age of 12 about their experiences as victims of crime during a specific period
Kinds of Information	In addition to offense counts, provides information on crime clearances, persons arrested, persons charged, law enforcement officers killed and assaulted, and characteristics of homicide victims	Provides details about victims (such as age, race, sex, education, income, and whether the victim and offender were related) and about crimes (such as time and place of occurrence, whether or not reported to police, use of weapons, occurrence of injury, and economic consequences)
Sponsor	Department of Justice's Federal Bureau of Investigation	Department of Justice's Bureau of Justice Statistics

the increased use of security systems, aggressive police efforts to keep handguns off the streets, and the dramatic decline in the use of crack cocaine. Other factors may include the booming economy of the 1990s and the quadrupling of the number of people incarcerated since 1970. Let us look more closely at two factors—age and crack cocaine—as a means of assessing future crime levels.

Age   Changes in the age makeup of the population are a key factor in the analysis of crime trends. It has long been known that men aged 16 to 24 are the most crime-prone group. The rise in crime in the 1970s has been blamed on the post–World War II baby boom. By the 1970s the "boomers" had entered the high-risk crime group

FIGURE 2.2
Four measures of serious violent crime

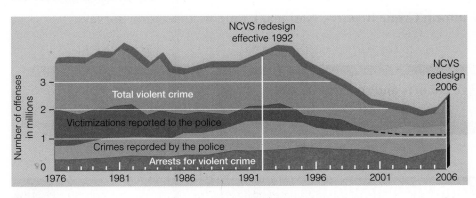

Note: The violent crimes included are rape, robbery, aggravated assault, and homicide. The shaded area at 1992 indicates that, because of changes made to the victimization survey, data prior to 1992 are adjusted to make them comparable to data collected under the redesigned methodology. Questions about homicides are not included in the NCVS, so the data here include the assumption that the 6,268 homicides in 2003 were reported to the police.

Sources: Michael Rand and Shannan Catalano, "Criminal Victimization, 2006," Bureau of Justice Statistics *Bulletin*, December 2007; FBI, *Crime in the United States, 2006* [Uniform Crime Reports], http://www.fbi.gov.

of 16- to 24-year-olds. They made up a much larger portion of the U.S. population than ever before. Between 40 and 50 percent of the total arrests during that decade could have been expected as a result of the growth in the total population and in the size of the crime-prone age group. Likewise, the decline in most crime rates that began during the 1980s has been attributed to the maturing of the post–World War II generation. During the 1990s the 16- to 24-year age cohort was smaller than it had been at any time since the early 1960s, and many people believe that this contributed to the decline in crime.

In 1994 a small but influential group of criminologists predicted that by the year 2000 the number of young men in the 14- to 24-year-old cohort would greatly increase. It was argued that the decline in crime experienced in the 1990s was merely the "lull before the storm" (Steinberg, 1999:4WK). However, the predicted rise in violent crime has not occurred. In fact, after the homicide rate for young people peaked in 1993, it dropped to a new low in 2000 and has remained relatively stable (Puzzanchera and Kang, 2008).

Crack Cocaine   The huge increase in violent crime, especially homicide, in the late 1980s and early 1990s is now generally attributed to killings by people aged 24 and under. These killings were driven by the spread of crack cocaine and the greater use of high-powered semiautomatic handguns by young people in that market (A. Blumstein, 1996; Butterfield, 1998a). During this period, hundreds of thousands of unskilled, unemployed young men from poor urban neighborhoods became street vendors of crack. To protect themselves, because they were carrying valuable merchandise—drugs and money—they were armed. They felt they needed this protection, because drug dealers cannot call for police assistance if threatened. As shootings increased among sellers engaged in turf battles over drug sales, other people began to arm themselves, and the resulting violence continued to skyrocket (A. Blumstein, 1996). The sharp drop in violent crime in the 1990s followed the sudden decline in the use of crack as more and more people saw the devastation that the drug brought (T. Egan, 1999:A1).

Government efforts to attack the drug problem led to increases in prison sentences for crack offenders and other lawbreakers. As a result, prison populations soared, and many people argue today that tough sentencing policies are actually a major factor in the falling crime rates. "The Policy Debate" examines the pros and cons of such policies.

CHECKPOINT

ANSWERS

5 *What are the two main sources of crime data?*

5 Uniform Crime Reports; National Crime Victimization Surveys.

6 *What are key factors in crime trends?*

6 Age cohorts and social conditions.

Crime Victimization

■ **victimology** A field of criminology that examines the role the victim plays in precipitating a criminal incident and also examines the impact of crimes on victims.

Until the past few decades, researchers paid little attention to crime victims. The field of **victimology**, which emerged in the 1950s, focuses attention on four questions: (1) Who is victimized? (2) What is the impact of crime? (3) What happens to victims in the criminal justice system? (4) What role do victims play in causing the crimes they suffer?

THE POLICY DEBATE

Have Tough Crime-Control Policies Caused a Decline in Crime?

THERE'S GOOD NEWS and there's bad news. The good news is that the amount of crime in the United States has been decreasing in recent years. Significant decreases have been seen in every type of violent and property crime, and virtually every demographic group has experienced drops in violent victimization.

Any reduction in crime is welcome, but the bad news is that experts do not agree on the causes for the decline in crime. Have the tough crime-control policies of the past 20 years really reduced crime? Or have crime rates declined because of factors unrelated to anything police, prosecution, courts, and corrections have done?

Some experts point out that there are more police officers on the streets, sentences are longer, and the probability upon conviction of going to prison is greater. They say the police have been more aggressive in dealing with public order offenses, the waiting period for handgun purchases has been effective, and more than a million Americans are already in prison and off the streets. In other words, the police and other agencies of criminal justice have made the difference.

Other experts question the impact of tough policies. They point out that the number of men in the crime-prone age group is relatively low compared with that age group's percentage of the national population from the 1960s to the 1980s. Many also say that the tough crime policies, instead of reducing crime, have devastated minority communities and diverted resources from dealing with the poverty that underlies crime. They urge policies that "put justice back in criminal justice."

Although crime rates have been falling, fear of crime is rising. Some opinion surveys find that Americans rank crime among the nation's most prominent problems after the economy, wars, and terrorism. Arguably, crime should rank much lower, given the fall in victimizations. Because views of crime are shaped more by television news than by statistics, Americans have an unrealistic picture of the crime problem. Grisly coverage of a murder scene on the evening news sticks in the mind in a way that the results of crime studies can never do.

Drugs and crime are perennially popular issues in U.S. politics. Legislators respond easily to pressures to "do something about crime." Who can argue with that? They usually act by coming up with new laws mandating stiffer sentences and allocating more money for police and corrections. But is this the best direction for public policy?

For Tough Crime Control

Supporters of tough crime-control policies say that crime, especially violent crime, is a serious problem. Even though rates have declined, they argue, violence is still many times higher here than in other developed democracies. We must continue to pursue criminals through strict law enforcement, aggressive prosecutions, and the sentencing of career criminals to long prison terms. To take the pressure off now will pave the way for problems in the future.

Here is a summary of the arguments for tough crime-control policies:

- The United States has a serious crime problem. It must ensure that offenders receive strict and certain penalties.

- Crime is not caused by poverty, unemployment, and other socioeconomic factors. Instead, crime causes poverty.

- The expansion of the prison population has taken hardened criminals out of the community, thus contributing to the drop in crime.

- The police must have the resources and legal backing to pursue criminals.

Against Tough Crime Control

Opponents of the get-tough approach believe that better ways are available to deal with crime. They argue that crime is no more effectively controlled today than it was in the early 1970s and that in many respects the problem has worsened, especially in the poorest neighborhoods. Neither the war on crime nor the war on drugs has stopped the downward spiral of livability in these neighborhoods. Another price of the tough crime-control policies has been an erosion of civil rights and liberties—especially for racial and ethnic minorities. What is needed is an infusion of justice into the system.

Here is a summary of the arguments against tough crime-control policies:

- The get-tough policies have not significantly reduced crime.

- Resources should be diverted from the criminal justice system to get to the underlying causes of criminal behavior—poor housing, unemployment, and racial injustice.

- Tough incarceration policies have devastated poor communities. With large numbers of young men in prison, families live in poverty, and children grow up without guidance from their fathers and older brothers.

- Crime policies emphasizing community policing, alternatives to incarceration, and community assistance programs will do more to promote justice than will the failed get-tough policies of the past.

What Should U.S. Policy Be?

The justice system costs about $200 billion a year. Advocates of tough crime-control policies say that the high cost is worth the price—cutting back would cost much more to crime victims and society as a whole. The crime rate is lower because of the more aggressive and punitive policies of the past two decades.

Opponents of these policies respond that the police, courts, and corrections have had little impact on crime. Other factors, such as the booming economy of the 1990s and the smaller number of men in the crime-prone age cohort, have been responsible for the reduction. The diversion of resources—both money and people—to fighting crime has limited government programs that could improve conditions in poor neighborhoods where crime flourishes.

Even though they are told that crime has gone down, Americans remain fearful. Their opinions translate into support for politicians who advocate the tough approach. No candidate for public office wants to be labeled "soft on crime." What would be the costs—economic and human—of continuing the get-tough policies? Would that same fearful public be affected?

RESEARCHING THE INTERNET

To see a 2009 public opinion study about alternatives to imprisonment as a policy for addressing crime, see the corresponding website listed on the Cole/Smith Criminal Justice in America Companion Website: http://www.cengage.com/criminaljustice/cole.

FOR CRITICAL ANALYSIS

How can we determine which factors have caused the declines in crime rates? Are there ways to experiment with our public policies that might tell us which factors are most influential in affecting contemporary crime rates? Should the declining crime rates cause us to create any new policies, shift our allocation of resources, or give less attention to crime as a policy issue?

■ Who Is Victimized?

Not everyone has an equal chance of being a crime victim. Moreover, people who are victimized by crime in one year are also more likely to be victimized by crime in a subsequent year (Menard, 2000). Research also shows that members of certain demographic groups are more likely to be victimized than others. Puzzling over this fact, victimologists have come up with several answers (Karmen, 2001:87). One explanation is that demographic factors (age, gender, income) affect lifestyle—people's routine activities, such as work, home life, and recreation. Lifestyles, in turn, affect people's exposure to dangerous places, times, and people (Varano et al., 2004). Thus, differences in lifestyles lead to varying degrees of exposure to risks (Meier and Miethe, 1993:466). Figure 2.3 shows the links among the factors used in the lifestyle-exposure model of personal victimization. Using this model, think of people whose lifestyle includes going to nightclubs in a "shady" part of town. Such people run the risk of being robbed if they walk alone through a dark high-crime area at two in the morning to their luxury car. By contrast, older individuals who watch television at night in their small-town home have a very low chance of being robbed. But these cases do not tell the entire story. What other factors make victims more vulnerable than nonvictims?

According to the lifestyle-exposure model, demographic factors (age, gender, income) and exposure to dangerous places, times, and people influence the probability of being victimized. Based on this model, how would you assess your own risk of victimization?

© Syracuse Newspapers/J. Commentucci/The Image Works

Men, Youths, Nonwhites   The lifestyle-exposure model and survey data shed light on the links between personal characteristics and the chance that one will become a victim. Figure 2.4 shows the influence of gender, age, and race on the risk of being victimized by a violent crime, such as rape, robbery, or assault. If we apply these findings to the lifestyle-exposure model, we see that male African American teenagers are most likely to be victimized because of where they live (urban, high-crime areas), how they may spend their time (on the streets late at night), and the people with whom they may associate (violence-prone youths) (Lauritsen, Laub, and Sampson, 1992). Lifestyle factors may also explain why elderly white women are least likely to be victimized by a violent crime. Perhaps it is because they do not go out at night, do not associate with people who are prone to crime, carry few valuables, and take precautions such as locking their doors. Thus, lifestyle choices directly affect the chances of victimization.

Race is a key factor in exposure to crime. African Americans and other minorities are more likely than whites to be raped, robbed, and assaulted. The rate of violent crime victimization for whites is 23.9 per 1,000 people, compared with 32.9 per 1,000 for African Americans (BJS, 2008c: Table 6). For Hispanics, the rate is 28.4 per 1,000 (BJS, 2008c: Table 7).

FIGURE 2.3
Lifestyle-exposure model of victimization
Demographic and subcultural factors determine personal lifestyles, which in turn influence exposure to victimization.

Source: Adapted with permission from Robert F. Meier and Terance D. Miethe, "Understanding Theories of Criminal Victimization," in *Crime and Justice: A Review of Research,* ed. Michael Tonry (Chicago: University of Chicago Press, 1993), 467.

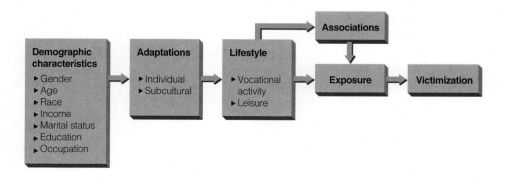

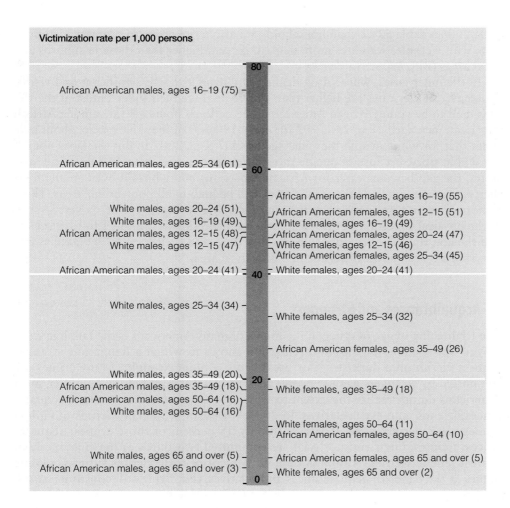

Victimization rate per 1,000 persons

African American males, ages 16–19 (75)
African American males, ages 25–34 (61)
African American females, ages 16–19 (55)
White males, ages 20–24 (51)
African American females, ages 12–15 (51)
White males, ages 16–19 (49)
White females, ages 16–19 (49)
African American males, ages 12–15 (48)
African American females, ages 20–24 (47)
White males, ages 12–15 (47)
White females, ages 12–15 (46)
African American females, ages 25–34 (45)
African American males, ages 20–24 (41)
White females, ages 20–24 (41)
White males, ages 25–34 (34)
White females, ages 25–34 (32)
African American females, ages 35–49 (26)
White males, ages 35–49 (20)
African American males, ages 35–49 (18)
White females, ages 35–49 (18)
African American males, ages 50–64 (16)
White males, ages 50–64 (16)
White females, ages 50–64 (11)
African American females, ages 50–64 (10)
White males, ages 65 and over (5)
African American females, ages 65 and over (5)
African American males, ages 65 and over (3)
White females, ages 65 and over (2)

FIGURE 2.4
Victimization rates for violent crime
Male African American teenagers aged 16–19 have the highest victimization rate for violent crimes. Why are they more likely than other age, gender, and racial groups to be robbed or assaulted?

Source: Bureau of Justice Statistics, *Criminal Victimization in the United States, 2006 Statistical Tables* (Washington, DC: U.S. Department of Justice, 2008), Table 10—Violent Crimes, 2006 (see also http://www.ojp.usdoj.gov/bjs/).

White Americans are fearful of being victimized by African American strangers (Skogan, 1995:59). However, most violent crime is intraracial: More than two-thirds of victims are of the same race as the attacker (BJS, 2008c: Table 42). These numbers simply reflect that African Americans and whites often live in separate neighborhoods. Most of their daily contacts are with people who share their demographic characteristics. And, most importantly, African American neighborhoods are much more likely to experience what scholars call "high levels of socioeconomic disadvantage" with respect to unemployment, quality of schools, quality of housing, and other factors associated with income and wealth (Lauritsen and White, 2001:53). These factors are often associated with higher levels of street crime, although obviously other kinds of crime, such as occupational crime and computer crime, occur in other settings.

Low-Income City Dwellers   Income is also closely linked to exposure to crime. Americans with incomes below $15,000 annually experienced a victimization rate of over 38 violent crimes per 1,000 people. By contrast, those with incomes in excess of $75,000 experienced only 15 violent crimes per 1,000 people (BJS, 2008c: Table 14). Economic factors largely determine where people live, work, and seek recreation. For low-income people, these choices are limited. Some have to live in crime-prone areas, lack security devices to protect their homes, cannot avoid contact with people who are prone to crime, or cannot spend their leisure time in safe areas. Poor people and minorities have a greater risk of being victimized, because they are likely to live in inner-city zones with high rates of street crime. People with higher incomes have more lifestyle-exposure choices open to them and can avoid risky situations (Meier and Miethe, 1993:468).

Living in a city is, in fact, a key factor in victimization. Violent crime occurs mainly in large cities, where the violent crime and personal theft victimization rate is 31 per 1,000 people, compared with 19 per 1,000 in suburbs and 17 per 1,000 in rural areas

(BJS, 2006c: Table 52). Urban households are also more prone to property victimization, with victimization rates more than 50 percent higher than those in suburbs and rural areas (BJS, 2006c: Table 53).

In the inner cities, where drug dealing and drug use pose significant and visible problems, murder rates are higher than elsewhere. Like their killers, most of the victims tend to be young African Americans. The national homicide rate among African American men aged 18 to 24 is 102 for every 100,000 of the same group, about nine times that for white men in the same age bracket (BJS, 2007d). But this does not tell the whole story, because homicide rates differ by city and state. In some cities and states, the gap between rates for African Americans and whites is even greater. Further, we cannot conclude that crime rates will be high in all poor urban areas. There is more crime in some poor areas than in others. Many factors besides poverty—such as the physical condition of the neighborhood, the residents' attitudes toward society and the law, the extent of opportunities for crime, and social control by families and government—can affect the crime rate of a given area.

■ Acquaintances and Strangers

The frightening image of crime in the minds of many Americans is the familiar scene played out in many movies and television shows in which a dangerous stranger grabs a victim on a dark street or breaks into a home at night. Many crimes are committed by strangers against people they have never seen before. However, most Americans do not realize the extent to which violent crimes occur among acquaintances, friends, and even relatives. In 2004, for example, female victims of violent crimes were victimized by strangers in only 35 percent of those crimes; acquaintances, spouses, boyfriends, or relatives committed two-thirds of the violent crimes against female victims. Although only 42 percent of male victims suffered violent crimes at the hands of acquaintances and relatives, that figure still constitutes a significant percentage of violent crimes (BJS, 2008c: Table 29). As you read "Criminal Justice: Myth and Reality," consider how you evaluate your risk of victimization in different situations.

Although Americans often fear violent victimization at the hands of strangers, most violence against women is perpetrated by those with whom they are intimate—husbands, boyfriends, and former lovers. What policies could address this problem?

© James Wiedel Photolibrary/Alamy

The kind of crime a victim suffers tends to depend on whether strangers or nonstrangers are the perpetrators. Most robberies are committed by strangers to the victim, but sexual assault victims are more likely to be victimized by someone they know. These differences reflect, in part, the contexts in which these crimes occur. In robberies, valuables are taken from an individual by force and then the robber typically runs away. Thus, the scenario fits situations in which the robber hopes to escape without being caught or identified. This result is much more difficult for a robber who is known to the victim. By contrast, sexual assaults often take place in isolated or private locations. People are most likely to place themselves in isolated or private locations, such as inside a house or apartment, with someone they know.

People may be reluctant to report crimes committed by relatives, such as the theft of their own valuables by a relative with a substance abuse problem. They may be upset about losing their valuables, but they do not want to see their son, daughter, or cousin arrested and sent to prison. If the perpetrators of such crimes know that their relatives will not report them, they may feel encouraged to victimize these people further in order to support a drug habit. Thus, the prior relationships among people may facilitate some crimes and keep victims from seeking police assistance.

The lifestyle-exposure model helps us understand some of the factors that increase or decrease the risk of being victimized, but what is the impact of crime on the nation and on individuals? We turn to this question in the next section.

■ The Impact of Crime

Crime affects not only the victim but all members of society. We all pay for crime through higher taxes, higher prices, and fear. These factors impinge on key American values such as individual liberty and protection of private property and personal wealth.

Costs of Crime   Crime has many kinds of costs: (1) the economic costs—lost property, lower productivity, and medical expenses; (2) the psychological and emotional costs—pain, trauma, and diminished quality of life; and (3) the costs of operating the criminal justice system.

A Justice Department study from the mid-1990s estimated the total annual cost of tangible losses from crime (medical expenses, damaged or lost property, work time) at $105 billion. The intangible costs (pain, trauma, lost quality of life) to victims were estimated at $450 billion (NIJ, 1996). Operating the criminal justice system costs taxpayers more than $204 billion a year to pay for police, courts, and corrections (BJS, 2008e: Table 1.2.2005). Government costs also increased in the aftermath of the September 11 tragedy as more money was spent on airport security, border patrols, and counterterrorist activities. These figures do not include the costs to consumers of occupational and organized crime. Businesses' losses from hackers' attacks on their computers stood at $600 million in 2003 (McGuire, 2004). Overall losses from economic crimes alone were $200 billion in 2000, and private businesses spent more than $103 billion on consultants, services, and products to combat these economic crimes (Security Industry Association, 2000). In 2006, an annual survey of 150 corporate retail chains by Professor Richard Hollinger of the University of Florida found that retailers had more than $40 billion in annual losses from theft. Employee theft accounted for $19 billion, shoplifting caused $13 billion in losses, and the rest was from vendor fraud ("Survey Estimates," 2007). In addition, individual citizens who install locks and alarms or employ guards and security patrols incur crime-related costs.

Fear of Crime   One impact of crime is fear. Fear limits freedom. Because they are fearful, many people limit their activities to "safe" areas at "safe" times. Fear also creates anxieties that affect physiological and psychological well-being. Ironically, the very people who have the least chance of being victimized, such as women and the elderly, are often the most fearful (Miethe, 1995:14). Not all Americans experience the same fears (M. S. Lee and Ulmer, 2000), but some people adjust their daily activities to prevent being victimized.

Since 1965, public opinion polls have asked Americans whether they "feel more uneasy" or "fear to walk the streets at night." When people are afraid to walk near their homes, their freedom is limited. From 1972 to 1993, more than 40 percent of respondents indicated that fear of crime affected their nighttime activities in their neighborhoods. Coinciding with the declining crimes rates during the 1990s, the percentage of respondents who were fearful of walking near their homes dropped to 30 percent in 2001. However, as indicated in "What Americans Think," the percentage moved up to 37 percent in 2008—barely less than the percentages in some years with much higher national crime rates. Thus, a significant segment of the American public remains fearful despite the significant drop in crime rates over the past 20 years (BJS, 2008e: Table 2.37.2008).

Although crime rates are down, Americans' fears seem to exceed actual victimization risks. As we have seen, people do not have a clear picture of the true risk of crime in their lives. They gain perceptions about crime from talk at their workplace and from politicians' statements and campaign promises. Their views about crime also seem to be shaped more by what they see on television than by reality (Chiricos, Padgett, and Gertz, 2000). Although fewer than 8 percent of victimizations are due to violent crime, such crimes are the ones most frequently reported by the media.

Criminal Justice: MYTH AND REALITY

COMMON BELIEF: Women are more likely to be raped by a stranger than by someone they know.

Most women take protective measures to avoid being attacked by strangers. They avoid walking alone at night, park their cars in well-lighted areas, or even carry weapons such as pepper spray. The "stranger in the bushes" stereotype of rape certainly does occur, but women are significantly more likely to be raped by a friend or acquaintance than a stranger. At least two-thirds of sexual assaults are perpetrated by someone the victim knows, whether an acquaintance, friend, or intimate partner (Ullman, 2007). This misperception about the risk of sexual assault can lead to women taking the wrong kinds of action to protect themselves from rape. For example, a college student drinking at a bar might fear walking alone at night and ask a male student she knows from one of her classes to walk her home. While this action has reduced her risk of being raped by a stranger, it may actually increase her risk of victimization by placing her alone in the company of an acquaintance.

What AMERICANS Think

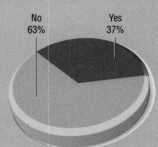

QUESTION: "Is there any area near where you live—that is, within a mile—where you would be afraid to walk alone at night?"

No 63%	Yes 37%

Go to http://www.cengage.com/criminaljustice/cole to compare your opinion on this issue with the opinions of other criminal justice students.

Source: Bureau of Justice Statistics, *Sourcebook of Criminal Justice Statistics Online*, Table 2.37, http://www.albany.edu/sourcebook/.

■ The Experience of Victims within the Criminal Justice System

After a crime has occurred, the victim is often forgotten. Victims may have suffered physical, psychological, and economic losses, yet the criminal justice system focuses on finding and prosecuting the offender.

Too often the system is not sensitive to the needs of victims. For example, defense attorneys may ask them hostile questions and attempt to paint them, rather than the defendant, as having caused the crime to occur. Similarly, whereas victims are a key source of evidence, the police may question them closely—and in a hostile fashion—to find out if they are telling the truth. Often the victim never hears the outcome of a case. Sometimes a victim comes face-to-face with the assailant who is out on bail or on probation. This can be quite a shock, especially if the victim assumed that the offender was in prison.

Victims may be forced to miss work and lose pay in order to appear at judicial proceedings. They may be summoned to court again and again, only to learn that the arraignment or trial has been postponed. Any recovered property may be held by the court for months as the case winds its way through the system. In short, after cases have been completed, victims may feel that they have been victimized twice, once by the offender and once by the criminal justice system.

During the past three decades, justice agencies have become more sensitive to the interests of crime victims. This has happened partly because victims often are the only witnesses to the crime and their help is needed. Many victims are not willing to provide such help if it involves economic and emotional costs. Some research indicates that victims are more likely to cooperate with the prosecutor if victim assistance workers meet with them to provide comfort as well as information about how the court system operates (Dawson and Dinovitzer, 2001).

Various laws adopted in recent years provide funds to counsel victims and give financial compensation for injuries, although victims often do not receive enough timely information to take advantage of these programs (Sims, Yost, and Abbott, 2005). In addition, victims' rights statutes in many states permit crime victims to speak at sentencing and parole hearings and receive information about any impending release of the offender who victimized them. The Justice for All Act passed by Congress in 2004 mandates such rights for victims in criminal cases processed in the federal courts.

Victims' assistance laws raise questions about which individuals or family members can receive benefits as "victims" (Trulson, 2005). Questions about fairness may arise if some individuals receive different benefits than do other people. Read "A Question of Ethics" at the end of the chapter to consider whether the families of crime victims in general are treated fairly, compared with the families of 9/11 victims.

■ The Role of Victims in Crime

Victimologists study the role victims play in some crimes. Researchers have found that many victims behave in ways that facilitate the acts committed against them. This does not mean that it is the victim's fault that the crime occurred. It means instead that the victim's behavior may have led to the crime through consent, provocation, enticement, risk taking, or carelessness with property.

What do studies tell us about these situations? First, some people do not take proper precautions to protect themselves. For example, they leave keys in their cars or fail to lock their doors and windows at night. They seem to lack the "common sense" of understanding the price of living safely in modern society. Second, some victims provoke or entice another person to commit a crime. Arguing with a stranger at a bar can lead to criminal assaults. Third, some victims of nonstrangers are not willing to help with the investigation and prosecution. These behaviors do not excuse criminal acts, but they do force us to think about other aspects of the crime situation.

CHECKPOINT

ANSWERS

7 What are the main elements of the life-style-exposure model?

7 Demographic characteristics, adaptations, lifestyle, associations, exposure.

8 What are some of the impacts of crime?

8 Fear, financial costs, emotional costs, lifestyle restrictions.

9 Why do some crime victims feel mistreated by the criminal justice system?

9 The system focuses on finding and punishing the offender; police and lawyers often question victims closely, in an unsympathetic manner; victims do not always receive assistance that covers their medical expenses and other losses.

Causes of Crime

Whenever news of a crime hits the headlines, whether the crime is a grisly murder or a complex bank fraud, the first question is "Why did he (or she) do it?" Do people commit crimes because they are poor, greedy, mentally ill, or just plain stupid? Do any of these explanations apply to the Northern Illinois University shooter discussed at the beginning of the chapter?

Various theories about the root causes of criminal behavior have been developed, and scholarly research regularly tests these theories. When substantiated, these theories can provide the basis for new public policies aimed at preventing crime.

Criminology is concerned mainly with learning about criminal behavior, the nature of offenders, and how crime can be prevented. Research focuses mainly on the offender. Fewer questions are asked about how factors such as the economy, government policy, family, and education affect crime (Messner and Rosenfeld, 1994:45–47). In this section we look at the two major schools of criminological thought—classical and positivist. We then review biological, psychological, sociological, life course, and integrated theories of the causes of criminal behavior. Finally, we look at women's criminal behavior and provide an overall assessment of the theories in this section.

Classical and Positivist Theories

Two major schools of criminological thought are the classical and positivist schools. Each was pioneered by scholars who were influenced by the dominant intellectual ideas of their times.

The Classical School Until the eighteenth century, most Europeans explained criminal behavior in supernatural terms. Those who did wrong were "possessed" by the devil. Some Christians believed that all humanity had fallen with Adam and had remained in a state of total depravity ever since. Indictments often began, "[John Doe], not having the fear of God before his eyes but being moved and seduced by the instigation of the devil, did commit [a certain crime]." Before the eighteenth century, defendants had few rights. The accused had little chance to put forth a defense, confessions were obtained through torture, and the penalty for most offenses was physical punishment or death.

In 1764 Cesare Beccaria published his *Essays on Crime and Punishments*. This was the first attempt to explain crime in secular, or worldly, terms, as opposed to religious terms. The book also pointed to injustices in the administration of criminal laws. Beccaria's ideas prompted reformers to try to make criminal law and procedures

■ **classical criminology** A school of criminology that views behavior as stemming from free will, demands responsibility and accountability of all perpetrators, and stresses the need for punishments severe enough to deter others.

more rational and consistent. From this movement came **classical criminology**, whose main principles are as follows:

1. Criminal behavior is rational, and most people have the potential to engage in such behavior.
2. People may choose to commit a crime after weighing the costs and benefits of their actions.
3. Fear of punishment is what keeps most people in check. Therefore, the severity, certainty, and speed of punishment affects the level of crime.
4. The punishment should fit the crime rather than the person who committed it.
5. The criminal justice system must be predictable, with laws and punishments known to the public.

Classical ideas declined in the nineteenth century, partly because of the rise of science and partly because its principles did not take into account differences among individuals or the way the crime was committed.

Neoclassical Criminology   After remaining dormant for almost a hundred years, classical ideas took on new life in the 1980s, when America became more conservative. Some scholars argue that crimes may result from the rational choice of people who have weighed the benefits to be gained from the crime against the costs of being caught and punished. But they also recognize that criminal law must take into account the differences among individuals. To a large extent, sentencing reform, criticisms of rehabilitation, and greater use of incarceration stem from a renewed interest in classical ideas. However, the positivist school of thought is what has dominated American criminology since the start of the twentieth century.

■ **positivist criminology** A school of criminology that views behavior as stemming from social, biological, and psychological factors. It argues that punishment should be tailored to the individual needs of the offender.

Positivist Criminology   By the middle of the nineteenth century, as the scientific method began to take hold, the ideas of the classical school seemed old-fashioned. Instead, **positivist criminology** used science to study the body, mind, and environment of the offender. Science could help reveal why offenders committed crimes and how they could be rehabilitated. Here are the key features of this approach:

1. Human behavior is controlled by physical, mental, and social factors, not by free will.
2. Criminals are different from noncriminals.
3. Science can be used to discover the causes of crime and to treat deviants.

Understanding the main theories of crime causation is important because they affect how laws are enforced, guilt is determined, and crimes are punished. As we describe each of the theories, consider its implications for crime policies. For example, if biological theories are viewed as sound, then the authorities might try to identify potential offenders through genetic analysis and then segregate or supervise them. On the other hand, the acceptance of sociological theories might lead to efforts to end poverty, improve education, and provide job training.

■ Biological Explanations

The medical training of Cesare Lombroso (1836–1909) led him to suppose that physical traits distinguish criminals from law-abiding citizens. He believed that some people are at a more primitive state of evolution and hence are born criminal. These "throwbacks" have trouble adjusting to modern society. Lombroso's ideas can be summarized as follows (Lombroso, 1912/1968):

■ **criminogenic** Having factors thought to bring about criminal behavior in an individual.

1. Certain people are **criminogenic**, that is, they are born criminals.
2. They have primitive physical traits such as strong canine teeth, huge jaws, and high cheekbones.
3. These traits are acquired through heredity or through alcoholism, epilepsy, or syphilis.

Early biological studies traced the generations of specific families to count how many people in each violated criminal laws. These early studies may no longer seem credible to us, but they were taken seriously in their time and affected criminal justice for decades. For example, many states passed laws that required repeat offenders to be sterilized. It was assumed that crime could be controlled if criminal traits were not passed from parents to children. Not until 1942 did the U.S. Supreme Court declare required sterilization unconstitutional (*Skinner v. Oklahoma*).

Although **biological explanations** of crime were ignored or condemned as racist after World War II, they have attracted renewed interest. *Crime and Human Nature,* by James Wilson and Richard Herrnstein (1985), reviews the research on this subject. Unlike the early positivists, the authors do not claim that any one factor explains criminality. Instead, they argue that biological factors predispose some individuals to a crime. Genetic makeup, body type, and IQ may outweigh social factors as predictors of criminality. The findings of research on nutrition, neurology, genetics, and endocrinology give some support to the view that these factors may contribute to violent behavior in some people (Brennan, Mednick, and Volavka, 1995:65). Other researchers have identified physiological factors associated with antisocial behavior, an association they see as a step toward considering a possible link between biology and offending (Cauffman, Steinberg, and Piquero, 2005).

■ **biological explanations** Explanations of crime that emphasize physiological and neurological factors that may predispose a person to commit crimes.

These new findings have given biological explanations a renewed influence and have reduced the dominance of sociological and psychological explanations. Scientists are doing further research to see if they can find biological factors that make some people prone to violence and criminality (Fishbein, 1990:27). For example, a study published in 2002 found that a single gene can help predict which abused children will become violent or antisocial adults. Abused children with a specific gene identified in the study were twice as likely as other abused children to commit acts of violence (Hathaway, 2002). Other studies examine the role of nutrition, such as consumption of fish rich in omega-3 being associated with lower levels of hostility in young adults (Iribarren et al., 2004), and the impact of environmental lead, such as lead-based paint, on brain development and behavior (University of Pittsburgh Medical Center, 2005). Behavior may also be affected by head injuries, tumors in specific locations on the brain, and natural chemical imbalances within the body. These findings behind biology and behavior do not necessarily purport to seek a single explanation for crime. They merely demonstrate an increased recognition that biological factors influence certain kinds of behavior in some offenders.

A Los Angeles jury convicted legendary record producer Phil Spector of second-degree murder in 2009. An actress died of a gunshot wound to the head in Spector's home on the night that he met her at a nightclub. Five other women testified at the trial that Spector had threatened them with guns. Does criminological theory help us understand what motivated him to commit these acts?

AP Images/Nick Ut

■ Psychological Explanations

People have often viewed criminal behavior as being caused by a mental condition, a personality disturbance, or limited intellect. **Psychological explanations** of crime center on these ideas.

Sigmund Freud (1856–1939), now seen as one of the foremost thinkers of the twentieth century, proposed a psychoanalytic theory that crime is caused by unconscious forces and drives. Freud also claimed that early childhood experiences greatly affect personality development. Freud's followers expanded his theory, saying that the personality is made up of three parts: the id, ego, and superego. The id controls drives that are primarily sexual, the ego relates desires to behavior, and the superego (often referred to as the conscience) judges actions as either right or wrong. Psychoanalytic theory explains criminal behavior as resulting from either

■ **psychological explanations** Explanations of crime that emphasize mental processes and behavior.

an undeveloped or an overdeveloped superego. For example, a person who commits a violent sex crime is thought to have an undeveloped superego, because the urges cannot be controlled. Alternatively, a person with an overdeveloped superego may suffer from guilt and anxiety. To reduce the guilt, the person may commit a crime, knowing that punishment will follow. To ensure punishment, the offender will unconsciously leave clues at the crime scene. Psychoanalysts say this occurred in the famous Loeb-Leopold murder of Bobby Franks in 1924 (Regoli and Hewitt, 1994).

Psychiatrists have linked criminal behavior to such concepts as innate impulses, psychic conflict, and repression of personality. Such explanations propose that crime is a behavior that stems from abnormal urges and desires. Although the psychological approach takes many different forms, all are based on the idea that early personality development is a key factor in later behavior. The terms *psychopath, sociopath,* and *antisocial personality* refer to a person who is unable to control impulses, cannot learn from experience, and does not feel emotions, such as love. This kind of person is viewed as psychologically abnormal and may become a crazed killer or sex fiend.

Psychological theories have been widely criticized. Some critics point to the fact that it is hard to measure emotional factors and to identify people thought to be prone to crime. Others note the wide range of sometimes contradictory theories that take a psychological approach to crime.

■ Sociological Explanations

■ **sociological explanations** Explanations of crime that emphasize as causes of criminal behavior the social conditions that bear on the individual.

In contrast to psychological approaches, **sociological explanations** focus on the way that belonging to social groups shapes people's behavior. Sociologists believe that criminality is not inborn but caused by external factors. Thus, sociological theories of crime assume that contact with the social world, as well as such factors as race, age, gender, and income, mold the offender's personality and actions.

In the 1920s a group of researchers at the University of Chicago looked closely at aspects of urban life that seemed to be linked to crime: poverty, bad housing, broken families, and the problems faced by new immigrants. They found high levels of crime in those neighborhoods that had many opportunities for delinquent behavior and few legitimate means of earning a living.

From a sociological perspective, criminals are made, not born. Among the many theories stressing the influence of societal forces on criminal behavior, three types deserve special mention: social structure theories, social process theories, and critical theories.

■ **social structure theories** Theories that blame crime on the existence of a powerless lower class that lives with poverty and deprivation and often turns to crime in response.

Social Structure Theories   Social structure theories suggest that criminal behavior is related to social class. People in various social classes have quite different amounts of wealth, status, and power. Those in the lower class suffer from poverty, poor education, bad housing, and lack of political power. Therefore, members of the lower class, especially the younger members, are the most likely to engage in crime. Crime thus is created by the structure of society.

The sociologist Robert Merton drew from theories about the role of social change and urbanization on crime. He stressed that social change often leads to a state of **anomie,** in which the rules or norms that guide behavior have weakened or disappeared. People may become anomic when the rules are unclear or they cannot achieve their goals. Under such conditions, antisocial or deviant behavior may result.

■ **anomie** A breakdown or disappearance of the rules of social behavior.

It is said, for example, that U.S. society highly values success but makes it impossible for some of its members to succeed. It follows that those who are caught in this trap may use crime as a way out. Theorists believe that this type of situation has led some ethnic groups into organized crime. Others argue that social disorganization brings about conditions in which, among other things, family structure breaks down, alcohol or drug abuse becomes more common, and criminal behavior increases. They assert that poverty must be ended and the social structure reformed if crime is to be reduced (Sampson and Wilson, 1995).

Contemporary theorists have drawn from social structure concepts and Merton's anomie theory to develop certain theories of crime causation. Prominent among modern approaches is the general theory of strain. According to this approach, negative relationships can lead to negative emotions. These emotions, particularly anger, are expressed through crime and delinquency. Strain is produced by the failure to achieve valued goals, which may particularly affect poor people in a society that values financial success. Strain is also produced by negative experiences, including unemployment, child abuse, criminal victimization, and family problems, which also tend to prevail in poor communities. Under this theory, those who cannot cope with negative experiences may be predisposed to criminal behavior (Liska and Messner, 1999:36–37).

As these ideas have become more refined, they have also been used to explain white-collar crime. To achieve even higher levels of success in a structure that values ever-increasing wealth, individuals may break rules and violate laws in order to enhance their personal success. Poverty relative to others' wealth is what causes crime. Thus, structure theories have been used to explain the behavior of corporate leaders who manipulate stock prices and take other actions to add to their wealth despite already being millionaires (Liska and Messner, 1999:37).

Social Process Theories   Despite such arguments, many criminologists believe that the social structure approach does not adequately explain criminality by middle-class and affluent people. More importantly, they fear that a focus on social structure erroneously emphasizes crime as primarily a problem of the poor. **Social process theories**, which date from the 1930s but did not gain recognition until the 1960s and 1970s, assume that any person, regardless of education, class, or upbringing, has the potential to become a criminal. However, some people are likely to commit criminal acts because of the circumstances of their lives. Thus, these theories try to explain the processes by which certain people become criminals.

There are three main types of social process theories: learning theories, control theories, and labeling theories.

Learning theories hold that criminal activity is learned behavior. Through social relations, some people learn how to be a criminal and acquire the values associated with that way of life. This view assumes that people imitate and learn from one another. Thus, family members and peers are viewed as major influences on a person's development.

In 1939 Edwin Sutherland proposed a type of learning theory called the **theory of differential association**, which states that behavior is learned through interactions with others, especially family members (Sutherland, 1947). Criminal behavior occurs when a person encounters others who are more favorable to crime than opposed to it. If a boy grows up in a family in which, say, an older brother is involved in crime, he is likely to learn criminal behavior. If people in the family, neighborhood, and gang believe that illegal activity is nothing to be ashamed of, this belief increases the chance that the young person will engage in crime.

Control theories hold that social links keep people in line with accepted norms (Gottfredson and Hirschi, 1990; Hirschi, 1969). In other words, all members of society have the potential to commit crime, but most are restrained by their ties to family, church, school, and peer groups. Thus, sensitivity to the opinion of others, commitment to a conventional lifestyle, and belief in the standards or values shared by friends all influence a person to abide by the law. A person who lacks one or more of these influences may engage in crime.

Finally, **labeling theories** stress the social process through which certain acts and people are labeled as deviant. As Howard Becker noted, society creates deviance—and, hence, criminality—"by making the rules whose infraction constitutes deviance, and by applying those rules to particular people and labeling them outsiders" (Becker, 1963). Decisions that result in the imposition of labels do not necessarily affect all individuals in the same way. Thus, researchers are exploring the association between labels and specific categories of people labeled as offenders (Chiricos et al., 2007).

According to labeling theories, social control agencies, such as the police, courts, and corrections, are created to label certain people as outside the normal, law-abiding community. When they have been labeled, those people come to believe that the label is true. They take on a deviant identity and start acting in deviant ways. Labeling

■ **social process theories** Theories that see criminality as normal behavior. Everyone has the potential to become a criminal, depending on (1) the influences that impel one toward or away from crime and (2) how one is regarded by others.

■ **learning theories** Theories that see criminal behavior as learned, just as legal behavior is learned.

■ **theory of differential association** The theory that people become criminals because they encounter more influences that view criminal behavior as normal and acceptable than influences that are hostile to criminal behavior.

■ **control theories** Theories holding that criminal behavior occurs when the bonds that tie an individual to society are broken or weakened.

■ **labeling theories** Theories emphasizing that the causes of criminal behavior are not found in the individual but in the social process that labels certain acts as deviant or criminal.

theory suggests the justice system creates criminals by labeling people in order to serve its own bureaucratic and political ends. Those who support this view call for decriminalization of drug use, gambling, and prostitution.

Critical Theories   In the mid-1960s, the reigning biological, psychological, and sociological explanations of criminal behavior were challenged by scholars who developed theories known as **critical criminology**. These theories assume that criminal law and the justice system are designed by those in power, whose purpose is to oppress those who are not in power (particularly, the poor, women, and minorities). The powerful commit as many crimes as do the less powerful, it is argued, but unempowered individuals are more likely to be caught and punished. Those in power use the law to impose their version of morality on society in order to protect their property and safety. They also use their power to change the definitions of crime to cover acts they view as threatening.

Several different theories can be said to fall under the umbrella of critical criminology. **Social conflict theories** posit that crime is the result of conflict within societies. One type of social conflict theory has been proposed by critical, radical, or Marxist criminologists. It holds that the class structure causes certain groups to be labeled as deviant. In this view, "deviance is a status imputed to groups who share certain structural characteristics (e.g., powerlessness)" (Spitzer, 1975:639). Thus, the criminal law is aimed at the behavior of specific groups or classes. One result is that the poor are deeply hostile toward the social order, and this hostility is one factor in criminal behavior. Moreover, when the status quo is threatened, legal definitions of crime are changed in order to trap those who challenge the system. For example, vagrancy laws have been used to arrest labor union organizers, civil rights workers, and peace activists when those in power believed that their interests were threatened by these groups.

Feminist theories of crime are based on the idea that traditional theory centers on male criminality and ignores female offending. While this idea is adopted by all feminist theorists, some adopt less critical perspectives that integrate recognition of women's experiences into social process theories, psychological theories, and other existing approaches. Others, such as radical, Marxist, and socialist feminists, take a more critical view toward traditional, mainstream theories of crime. Recent feminist theorists underscore the need to integrate race and class issues with gender for a full understanding of crime (Chesney-Lind, 2006).

Like other theories about the causes of criminal behavior, sociological theories have been criticized. Critics argue that these theories are imprecise, unsupported by evidence, and based on ideology. Even so, sociological theories have served as the basis for many attempts to prevent crime and rehabilitate offenders.

■ Life Course Theories

Life course theories seek to identify factors that shape criminal careers, in order to explain when and why offenders begin to commit crimes and to see what factors lead individuals to stop their participation in crimes. Studies in this area often try to follow individuals from childhood through adulthood in order to identify the factors associated with beginning, avoiding, continuing, or ceasing criminal behavior. Criminal careers often begin at an early age; people who eventually become involved with crime often exhibit disruptive behavior, lack family support, and experiment with drinking and drugs as youths. Some theorists discuss *pathways* into crime, which may begin with minor habits of lying and stealing that lead to more-serious offenses. However, pathways into crime are not identical for all kinds of offenders (Maxwell and Maxwell, 2000). For example, those youths who engage in bullying and fighting may begin a pathway toward different kinds of crimes than do those who start out using drugs.

As identified by life course theorists, the factors that can impact criminal careers overlap with factors discussed in psychological, social structure, and social process theories, such as unemployment, failure in school, impulsiveness, and unstable families. In other words, life course theorists' ideas about factors associated with criminal behavior are consistent with factors identified in other theories. However, these theorists study criminal behavior from a broader perspective.

■ critical criminology Theories that assume criminal law and the criminal justice system are primarily a means of controlling the lower classes, women, and minorities.

■ social conflict theories Theories that view crime as the result of conflict in society, such as conflict between economic classes caused by elites using law as a means to maintain power.

■ feminist theories Theories that criticize existing theories for ignoring or undervaluing women's experiences as offenders, victims, and people subjected to decision making by criminal justice officials. These theories seek to incorporate an understanding of differences between the experiences and treatment of men and women while also integrating consideration of other factors, such as race and social class.

■ life course theories Theories that identify factors affecting the start, duration, nature, and end of criminal behavior over the life of an offender.

The research of Robert Sampson and John Laub is among the most influential in examining the life course and criminal careers (Laub and Sampson, 2003; Sampson and Laub, 1993). They reanalyzed and built on the famous studies of Sheldon and Eleanor Glueck that had followed the lives of 1,000 Boston-area boys from 1940 through the 1960s (Glueck and Glueck, 1950). Sampson and Laub gathered data on the same men in the 1990s, by which time the surviving "boys" from the original study were senior citizens.

Using their research, Sampson and Laub discuss informal and formal social controls over the life course. Unlike some researchers, who see youthful criminality as setting behavior patterns that continue into adulthood, Sampson and Laub emphasize *turning points* in life that move individuals away from criminal careers. For example, their study showed that military service, employment, and marriage served as particularly important factors leading away from criminal careers. By contrast, incarceration and alcohol abuse were associated with continued lawbreaking. Researchers have also sought to test other factors, such as the development of religiosity, but further studies are needed to see if such factors generate turning points away from crime (Giordano et al., 2008).

Life course explanations do not seek to identify a single or primary factor as the cause of criminal behavior. Instead, they try to identify and evaluate the timing, interaction, and results of complex factors that affect people's lives.

■ Integrated Theories

As the number of theoretical perspectives has grown, researchers have called for the development of **integrated theories** drawn from different disciplines—that is, theories that merge several perspectives on crime. In 1979, a group of researchers created a new theory from components of strain, social control, and social learning theories (D. S. Elliott, Ageton, and Cantor, 1979). From their data, they concluded that some juveniles enter delinquency through a combination of weak commitment to conventional norms (control theory) and vulnerability to delinquent peers (social learning theory). Others were more likely to become delinquent after forming strong commitments to conventional society (control theory), which are later weakened by their inability to achieve goals (strain theory). These weakened bonds lead to relationships with delinquent peers (social learning theory).

■ **integrated theories** Theories that combine differing theoretical perspectives into a larger model.

While the integration of theories makes sense, given the large array of factors that affect human behavior, there has been much debate about whether multiple theories can be integrated at all. For example, some theorists, such as Lombroso, believe that humans are inherently criminal and that positive social forces are needed to keep people from offending, while other theorists believe that people are generally not prone to criminal behavior but that negative forces can lure them into committing crime (Henry and Lanier, 2006). These issues are currently being debated by modern criminologists in an attempt to construct valid, integrated theories of crime.

■ Women and Crime

As mentioned earlier in this section, theories about causes of crime are almost all based on observations of men. That women commit crime less often than do men (and that most criminologists have historically been male) helps explain this fact (D. Klein, 1973). Traditionally, many people assumed that most women, because of their nurturing and dependent nature, could not commit serious crimes. Those who did commit crimes were labeled as "bad" or "fallen" women. Unlike male criminals, then, female criminals were viewed as moral offenders.

Most traditional theories of crime cannot explain two important facts about gender and offending. First, a theory must explain why women are less likely to commit crime than are men (the "gender gap"). Women accounted for approximately 24 percent of all arrests in 2007, with men responsible for the remaining 76 percent (FBI, 2008a: Table 4.8.2007). Second, a theory must explain why women commit different kinds of crime than do men—women are less likely to be arrested for violent crimes than are men, and women are more likely to be arrested for crimes such as embezzlement and prostitution (FBI, 2008a: Table 4.8.2007).

A Miami police officer arrests Josephine Martinez in 2008 as part of a crackdown on mortgage fraud scams. How has women's participation in crime changed in recent decades?

© Jim Raedle/Getty Images

Female suspects are less likely than male suspects to be arrested for any type of offense. For example, in 2006, 89 percent of arrested murder suspects, and the same percentage of arrested robbery suspects, were men (FBI, 2007). In addition, women are mostly likely to be arrested for larceny/theft than any other offense although they constituted only 40 percent of all arrestees for this offense.

Two books published in 1975 attempted to explain these facts about female offending. Rita Simon's *Women and Crime* and Freda Adler's *Sisters in Crime* both hypothesized that women's liberation would result in increases in female offending. While Adler and Simon disagreed about how the *types* of crime committed by women would be affected by women's liberation, both predicted the gender gap would be reduced significantly. Although there are still significant differences in patterns of criminal behavior by men and women, these books helped alert scholars to societal changes that affect women's status, self-image, behavior, and opportunities to commit crimes.

Beginning in the 1990s, theorists recognized the importance of *social structure* in explaining female criminality. These theorists posit three things: that our society is structured in such a way as to create different opportunities for men and women in the workforce, that power differentials exist between men and women, and that important differences in sexuality shape the behavior of men and women (Messerschmidt, 1993).

Recent developments related to women and crime include life course theories, which focus on the paths taken by individuals through life and identify important turning points in people lives. Recall that these "transitions" can affect individual behavior and lead people either to or away from criminal activity (Sampson and Laub, 1990). To explain gender and crime, feminist pathways researchers focus on the impact of critical life events, such as victimization, to determine why some women engage in criminal behavior. It is well known, for example, that many women working as prostitutes were sexually abused as children (Widom, 1995).

As the status of women changes and as more women pursue careers in business and industry, some scholars believe that women will commit more economic and occupational crimes, such as embezzlement and fraud. However, research continues to show that arrested women, like male offenders, tend to come from poor families in which physical and substance abuse are present (Rosenbaum, 1989:31). Other researchers believe that the higher crime rates among women are due in part to a greater willingness of police and prosecutors to treat them like men. Thus far, the findings of research on gender differences in crime are not conclusive (Decker and Wright, 1993).

■ Assessing Theories of Criminality

Scholars have presented evidence to support aspects of each theory of crime (see Table 2.3). This does not mean, however, that the strength of supporting evidence is the same for each theory. In addition, some research may provide evidence for more than one theory. For example, research about the impact of neighborhoods may have implications for both social structure and social process theories (Kurbrin and Stewart, 2006). When criminologists theorize that a recent rise in murders among young people in Boston is attributable, in part, to a "street culture" in which lethal violence is used to preserve reputations and respect (Llana, 2006), does that reflect social structure, social process, or some other theory? As yet, no theory is accurate enough to predict criminality or establish a specific cause for an offender's behavior.

The theories are limited in other ways as well. They tend to focus on visible crimes and the poor. They have less to say about upper-class or organized crime.

TABLE 2.3 | Major Theories of Criminality and Their Policy Implications

Scholars and the public support various types of policies. We know little about the real causes of crime, but note how many people think they have the answers!

Theory	Major Premise	Policy Implications	Policy Implementation
Biological	Genetic, biochemical, or neurological defects cause some people to commit crime.	Identification and treatment or control of persons with crime-producing biological factors. Selective incapacitation, intensive supervision.	1 Use of drugs to inhibit biological urges of sex offenders. 2 Use of controlled diet to reduce levels of antisocial behavior caused by biochemical imbalances. 3 Identification of neurological defects through CAT scans. Use of drugs to suppress violent impulses. 4 Special education for those with learning disabilities.
Psychological	Personality and learning factors cause some people to commit crime.	Treatment of those with personality disorders to achieve mental health. Those whose illegal behavior stems from learning should have their behavior punished so they will realize that crime is not rewarded.	1 Psychotherapy and counseling to treat personality disorders. 2 Behavior modification strategies, such as electric shock and other negative impulses, to change learned behavior. 3 Counseling to enhance moral development. 4 Intensive individual and group therapies.
Social Structure	Crime is the result of underlying social conditions such as poverty, inequality, and unemployment.	Actions taken to reform social conditions that breed crime.	1 Education and job-training programs. 2 Urban redevelopment to improve housing, education, and health care. 3 Community development to provide economic opportunities.
Social Process	Crime is normal learned behavior and is subject to either social control or labeling effects.	Individuals to be treated in groups, with emphasis on building conventional bonds and avoiding stigmatization.	1 Youth programs that emphasize positive role models. 2 Community organizing to establish neighborhood institutions and bonds that emphasize following society's norms. 3 Programs designed to promote family stability.
Critical	Criminal definitions and punishments are used by some groups to control other groups.	Fundamental changes in the political and social systems to reduce class conflict.	1 Development of programs to remove injustice in society. 2 Provision of resources to assist women, minorities, and the poor in dealing with the criminal justice system and other government agencies. 3 Modification of criminal justice to deal similarly with crimes committed by upper-class members and crimes committed by lower-class members.
Life Course	Offenders have criminal careers that often begin with pathways into youth crime but can change and end through turning points in life.	Foster positive turning points such as marriage and stable employment.	1 Policies to reduce entry pathways associated with youth incarceration and substance abuse. 2 Policies to promote educational success, full employment, successful marriages, and stable families.

Most of the theories also focus on male behavior. What is missing, and truly needed, is a theory that merges these disparate ideas about the causes of crime. Once we have a complete and testable account of what causes crime, we can develop better policies to deal with it.

CHECKPOINT

ANSWERS

10 What were the main assumptions of the classical school of criminology?

10 Criminal behavior is rational, and the fear of punishment keeps people from committing crimes.

11 What are the different kinds of sociological theories?

11 Social structure theories; social process theories; critical theories, including social conflict theory.

12 What are potential turning points for criminal careers in life course theories?

12 Military service, employment, marriage.

structure theories, social process theories, and critical theories, including social conflict theories.

▸ Feminist theories call attention to scholars' neglect of women's criminal behavior. Such theories often take a

some argue that, as society increasingly treats women and men as equals, the number of crimes committed by women will increase.

▸ Theories of criminality are criticized for focusing too exclusively on lower-class and male perpetrators.

Questions for Review

1. What are the six types of crimes?
2. What are the positive and negative attributes of the two major sources of crime data?
3. Who is most likely to be victimized by crime?
4. What are the costs of crime?
5. How does the criminal justice system treat victims?
6. What are the major theories of criminality?
7. What have scholars learned about the criminal behavior of women?

Key Terms and Cases

anomie (p. 58)
biological explanations (p. 57)
classical criminology (p. 56)
control theories (p. 59)
crimes without victims (p. 40)
criminogenic (p. 56)
critical criminology (p. 60)
cyber crimes (p. 41)
dark figure of crime (p. 43)
feminist theories (p. 60)
integrated theories (p. 61)
labeling theories (p. 59)

learning theories (p. 59)
life course theories (p. 60)
mala in se (p. 37)
mala prohibita (p. 37)
money laundering (p. 39)
National Crime Victimization Surveys (NCVS) (p. 45)
National Incident-Based Reporting System (NIBRS) (p. 45)
occupational crimes (p. 39)
organized crime (p. 39)
political crime (p. 40)

positivist criminology (p. 56)
psychological explanations (p. 57)
social conflict theories (p. 60)
social process theories (p. 59)
social structure theories (p. 58)
sociological explanations (p. 58)
theory of differential association (p. 59)
Uniform Crime Reports (UCR) (p. 43)
victimology (p. 48)
visible crime (p. 38)

A QUESTION OF ETHICS: WRITING ASSIGNMENT

Imagine the following scenarios: Two women, who live in different cities, arise early one morning to prepare to leave for their jobs at different insurance companies. As single parents, they both bear the responsibility of providing financial support as well as parental guidance to their children. After one woman parks in the underground garage next to her office building, an unfamiliar man sneaks up behind her, places a handgun against her face, and demands her purse and the keys to her car. Because she is startled and frightened, she drops her keys and reflexively bends to retrieve them. When she moves, the gun goes off and she is killed. In the other city, the woman is sitting at her desk in her office tower when suddenly her entire office suite bursts into flames in an explosion. She is killed instantly. The date is September 11, 2001. One woman has been killed in a parking garage in the Midwest and the other has died in the hijackers' attack on the World Trade Center in New York City.

In the aftermath of the September 11 tragedy, Congress enacted legislation to compensate victims with financial awards that exceed those of victim compensation programs and instead match the kinds of significant awards that someone might win in a wrongful death lawsuit. Thus, the family of the woman killed at the World Trade Center would be eligible for significant financial support from the federal government to replace the income that she would have provided for her family. By contrast, the family of the woman killed in the parking garage would receive very little. If the state's law provided for compensation, it would probably be a modest amount that might not even cover the cost of the funeral. Both women were killed during sudden attacks by strangers. Both women left behind children who had relied on them for financial support as well as emotional support and parental guidance.

WRITING ASSIGNMENT

Is it ethical for the federal government to provide financial support for one victim's family but not for the other? Are there any persuasive reasons to treat the two families differently? Imagine that you are the advisor to a commission that must propose a policy concerning compensation for future crime victims as well as future victims of terrorist attacks. Write a memo explaining how you would treat these two groups for purposes of government compensation. Be sure to explain the reasons for your recommendation.

Summary

Understand the legal definitions of crime

◗ Criminal laws are made by elected representatives in state legislatures and Congress.

◗ *Mala in se* crimes are wrongs in themselves, such as murder, while *mala prohibita* offenses are acts prohibited by government but not necessarily inherently wrongful acts, such as gambling.

Categorize crimes by their type

◗ There are six broad categories of crime: visible crime, occupational crime, organized crime, crimes without victims, political crime, and cyber crime.

◗ Each type of crime has its own level of risk and profitability, each arouses varying degrees of public disapproval, and each has its own group of offenders with

Understand why some people are at higher risk of victimization than others

◗ Young male residents of lower-income communities are among those most likely to be victimized by crime.

◗ Because of the connection between race and social status in the United States, African Americans are more frequently victimized by crime than are whites.

◗ A significant percentage of crimes, especially those against women, are committed by acquaintances and relatives of victims.

Recognize the negative consequences of victimization

◗ Crime significantly affects all of society through financial and other costs.

◗ Financial costs from white-collar crime, employee

Criminal Justice and the Rule of Law

3

AFTER A LATE-NIGHT FLIGHT IN FEBRUARY 2007, U.S. Navy Captain Colleen Shipman hurried toward her car in the parking lot of the Orlando, Florida, airport. When she became aware that someone was following her, she rushed to her car and locked the door. A woman standing outside her car tapped on her window and asked for a ride. Shipman said she told the woman that she would send someone to help her. When the woman began to cry, Shipman rolled down the window a few inches—when suddenly the woman pulled out a canister and sprayed Shipman with pepper spray. Shipman quickly drove away and notified police about the attack (CNN, 2007).

Police quickly found the alleged attacker, who had thrown a wig and a BB gun into a nearby trash container. The police also found a steel mallet, a folding knife, and rubber tubing. Further investigation revealed latex gloves and driving directions from Houston to the Orlando airport. These items aroused suspicions that a crime more significant than a mere assault had been planned (CNN, 2007). Was it an attempted kidnapping? Might the perpetrator have even intended to kill the victim?

Normally, an assault with minor injuries would attract attention only from the local news media. In this case, however, the event triggered weeks of national news coverage when the suspect was identified as U.S. Navy Captain Lisa Nowak, an astronaut who had orbited the earth on the space shuttle. Her arrest in this case came just a few short months after her professional high point, when the space shuttle *Discovery* landed smoothly at Cape Canaveral, Florida, in July 2006 and NASA officials celebrated the mission's success. Among the smiling heroes welcomed home was Nowak, who had operated the shuttle's robot arm during space walks in order to transfer tons of cargo from the *Discovery* to the International Space Station that orbits the earth (Schwartz, 2006).

According to news reports, Nowak had been in an affair with another shuttle astronaut, who had subsequently dropped Nowak and begun to date Shipman. When questioned by the police, Nowak reportedly said that she drove from Houston to Orlando just to find Shipman and talk to her. Her use of pepper spray as well as the other items found in her possession at the airport led law enforcement officials to conclude that she had instead intended to harm Shipman. Thus, Nowak was charged with assault, kidnapping, and attempted murder (Schwartz, 2007b).

As the case worked its way through preliminary hearings in the Florida courts, Nowak's attorney submitted a document to inform the judge and the prosecutor that

LEARNING OBJECTIVES

▶ Recognize the bases and sources of American criminal law

▶ Understand how substantive criminal law defines a crime and the legal responsibility of the accused

▶ Understand how procedural criminal law defines the rights of the accused and the processes for dealing with a case

▶ Recognize the U.S. Supreme Court's role in interpreting the criminal justice amendments to the Constitution

Nowak would be asserting the insanity defense at trial. According to Donald Lykkebak, Nowak's defense attorney, she suffered from manic-depressive disorder, obsessive-compulsive disorder, and other serious psychological problems (Schwartz, 2007a). By making a claim of insanity, Nowak hoped to avoid any finding of guilt or imposition of punishment for her actions. In April 2009, after several pretrial hearings concerning the admissibility of evidence found in Nowak's car, the trial judge ordered that she be examined by two psychiatrists prior to beginning the trial later in the summer or fall (Lundy, 2009).

A criminal defendant's claim of insanity raises difficult questions for the justice system. Two psychiatrists reportedly planned to testify that Nowak was legally insane at the time she committed the assault. In such cases, however, the psychiatrists' testimony does not decide the issue. Prosecutors typically present other psychiatrists who testify that the defendant was not insane. Moreover, the judge or jury must apply the law that defines insanity and reach their own conclusions about the conflicting testimony and evidence.

Claims of insanity frequently cause observers to question whether such a defense should be available to permit people to avoid **legal responsibility** and punishment for their criminal acts. In this case, can we avoid wondering how a military officer could claim to be insane after having undergone careful psychological screening in order to become an astronaut? Could a U.S. Naval Academy graduate with advanced degrees in engineering, who recently played a key role in the success of a space shuttle mission, really be insane? Moreover, how can someone claim to be insane when she has carefully planned the details of a trip from Houston to Orlando in order to confront, if not physically harm, someone toward whom she felt anger and jealousy? Criminal law must address difficult questions such as these, for which easy answers rarely come.

In this chapter, we shall examine the primary components of criminal law. Substantive criminal law is developed through statutes enacted by the American people's elected representatives in state legislatures and Congress. It addresses the specific acts for which people will be punished as well as the circumstances in which people may not be held fully responsible for their actions. We shall also introduce procedural criminal law, which defines the procedures used in legal processes and the rights possessed by criminal suspects and defendants. Even though Nowak acknowledged that she attacked Shipman with pepper spray, she was still entitled to a trial and representation by an attorney as she attempted to show why she should not be held fully responsible for her actions. The right to counsel and the right to trial by jury are two of the elements provided by procedural criminal law. The precise nature of individuals' rights under procedural criminal law is determined by judges' interpretations of the U.S. Constitution, state constitutions, and relevant statutes enacted by Congress and state legislatures.

Foundations of Criminal Law
Substantive Criminal Law
Seven Principles of Criminal Law
Elements of a Crime
Statutory Definitions of Crimes
Responsibility for Criminal Acts
Procedural Criminal Law
The Bill of Rights and the Fourteenth Amendment
The Fourteenth Amendment and Due Process
The Due Process Revolution

The Fourth Amendment: Protection against
    Unreasonable Searches and Seizures
The Fifth Amendment: Protection against
    Self-Incrimination and Double Jeopardy
The Sixth Amendment: The Right to Counsel
    and a Fair Trial
The Eighth Amendment: Protection against
    Excessive Bail, Excessive Fines, and Cruel
    and Unusual Punishment

Constitutional Rights and Criminal Justice Professionals

Foundations of Criminal Law

legal responsibility The accountability of an individual for a crime because of the perpetrator's characteristics and the circumstances of the illegal act.

Like most Americans, you are probably aware that law and legal procedures are key elements of the criminal justice system. Americans are fond of saying that "we have a government of laws, not of men (and women)." According to our American values, we do not have a system based on the decisions of a king or dictator. In the United States, even our most powerful leaders have to make decisions within limits imposed by law. The government can seek to punish only people who violate defined laws, and their guilt has to be determined through procedures established by law. Since the tragic events of September 11, however, some commentators have expressed fears that the federal government has moved away from traditional constitutional values by jailing suspected terrorists without charging them with crimes or presenting evidence to prove their involvement in wrongdoing (Turley, 2002). Thus, we find ourselves entering a new era in which the government's actions against terrorism clash with traditional American values and functions of law.

Laws tell citizens what they can and cannot do. Laws also tell government officials when they can seek to punish citizens for violations and how they must go about it. Government officials, including the President of the United States, who take actions according to their own preferences run the risk that judges will order them to take different actions that comply with the law. Government officials are expected to follow and enforce the law. Thus, in a democracy, laws are major tools for preventing government officials from seizing too much power or using power improperly.

Criminal law is only one category of law. Peoples' lives and actions are also affected by **civil law**, which governs business deals, contracts, real estate, and the like. For example, if you damage other people's property or harm them in an accident, they may sue you to pay for the damage or harm. By contrast, the key feature of criminal law is the government's power to punish people for damage they have done to society.

civil law Law regulating the relationships between or among individuals, usually involving property, contracts, or business disputes.

Among the two categories of criminal law, **substantive criminal law** defines actions that the government can punish. It also defines the punishments for such offenses. Often called the "penal code," substantive law answers the question "What is illegal?" Elected officials in Congress, state legislatures, and city councils write the substantive criminal laws. These legislators decide which kinds of behaviors are so harmful that they deserve to be punished. They also decide whether each violation should be punished by imprisonment, a fine, probation, or another kind of punishment. When questions arise about the meaning of substantive criminal laws, judges interpret the laws by seeking to fulfill the legislators' intentions.

substantive criminal law Law that defines acts that are subject to punishment and specifies the punishments for such offenses.

By contrast, **procedural criminal law** defines the rules that govern how the laws will be enforced. It protects the constitutional rights of defendants and provides the rules that officials must follow in all areas of the criminal justice system. Many aspects of procedural criminal law are defined by legislatures, such as how bail will be set and which kind of preliminary hearing will take place before a trial. However, the U.S. Supreme Court and state supreme courts also play a key role in defining procedural criminal law. These courts define the meaning of constitutional rights in the U.S. Constitution and in state constitutions. Their interpretations of constitutional provisions create rules on issues such as when and how police officers can question suspects and when defendants can receive advice from their attorneys.

procedural criminal law Law defining the procedures that criminal justice officials must follow in enforcement, adjudication, and corrections.

CHECKPOINT

ANSWERS

1 *What is contained in a state's penal code?*

1 Penal codes contain substantive criminal law that defines crimes and also punishments for those crimes.

2 *What is the purpose of procedural criminal law?*

2 Procedural criminal law specifies the defendants' rights and tells justice system officials how they can investigate and process cases.

Substantive Criminal Law

Substantive criminal law defines acts that are subject to punishment and specifies the punishments. It is based on the doctrine that no one may be convicted of or punished for an offense unless the offense has been defined by the law. In short, people must know in advance what is required of them. Thus, no act can be regarded as illegal until it has been defined as punishable under the criminal law. While this sounds like a simple notion, the language of law is often confusing and ambiguous. As a result, judges must become involved in interpreting the law so that the meaning intended by the legislature can be understood.

The Draconian Code promulgated in classical Greece in the seventh century B.C. is one of the earliest substantive criminal laws. It defined acts that were illegal and specified punishments for each offense. Are there additional criminal laws that contemporary legislators should create for your state?

© Getty/Hulton/Archive Photos

■ Seven Principles of Criminal Law

The major principles of Western criminal law were summarized in a single statement by legal scholar Jerome Hall (1947). To convict a defendant of a crime, prosecutors must prove that all seven principles have been fulfilled (see Figure 3.1).

1. *Legality.* There must be a law that defines the specific action as a crime. Offensive and harmful behavior is not illegal unless it has been prohibited by law before it was committed. The U.S. Constitution forbids *ex post facto laws,* or laws written and applied after the fact. Thus, when the legislature defines a new crime, people can be prosecuted only for violations that occur after the new law has been passed.

2. *Actus reus.* Criminal laws are aimed at human acts, including acts that a person failed to undertake. The U.S. Supreme Court has ruled that people may not be convicted of a crime simply because of their status. Under this *actus reus* requirement, for a crime to occur there must be an act of either commission or omission by the accused. In *Robinson v. California* (1962), for example, the Supreme Court struck down a California law that made being addicted to drugs a crime. States can prosecute people for using, possessing, selling, or transporting drugs when they catch them performing these acts, but states cannot prosecute them for the mere status of being addicted to drugs.

3. *Causation.* For a crime to have been committed, there must be a causal relationship between an act and the harm suffered. In Ohio, for example, a prosecutor tried to convict a burglary suspect on a manslaughter charge when a victim, asleep in his house, was killed by a stray bullet as officers fired at the unarmed, fleeing suspect. The burglar was acquitted on the homicide charge because his actions in committing the burglary and running away from the police were not the direct cause of the victim's death (Bandy, 1991).

4. *Harm.* To be a crime, an act must cause harm to some legally protected value. The harm can be to a person, property, or some other object that a legislature deems valuable enough to deserve protection through the government's power to punish. This principle is often questioned by those who feel that they are not committing a crime, because they may be

FIGURE 3.1
The seven principles of criminal law
These principles of Western law provide the basis for defining acts as criminal and the conditions required for successful prosecution.

A crime is	
1 legally proscribed	(legality)
2 human conduct	(*actus reus*)
3 causative	(causation)
4 of a given harm	(harm)
5 which conduct coincides	(concurrence)
6 with a blameworthy frame of mind	(*mens rea*)
7 and is subject to punishment	(punishment)

causing harm only to themselves. Laws that require motorcyclists to wear helmets have been challenged on this ground. Such laws, however, have been written because legislatures see enough forms of harm to require protective laws. These forms of harm include injuries to helmetless riders, tragedy and loss for families of injured cyclists, and the medical costs imposed on society for head injuries that could have been prevented.

An act can be deemed criminal if it could do harm that the law seeks to prevent; this is called an **inchoate offense**. Thus, the criminal law includes conspiracies and attempts, even when the lawbreaker does not complete the intended crime (Cahill, 2007a). For example, people can be prosecuted for planning to murder someone or hiring a "hit man" to kill someone. The potential for grave harm from such acts justifies the application of the government's power to punish.

■ **inchoate offense** Conduct that is criminal even though the harm that the law seeks to prevent has not been done but merely planned or attempted.

5. *Concurrence.* For an act to be considered a crime, the intent and the act must be present at the same time (J. Hall, 1947:85). Let us imagine that Joe is planning to murder his archenemy, Bill. He spends days planning how he will abduct Bill and carry out the murder. While driving home from work one day, Joe accidentally hits and kills a jogger who suddenly—and foolishly—runs across the busy street without looking. The jogger turns out to be Bill. Although Joe had planned to kill Bill, he is not guilty of murder, because the accidental killing was not connected to Joe's intent to carry out a killing.

6. *Mens rea.* The commission of an act is not a crime unless it is accompanied by a guilty state of mind. This concept is related to intent. It seeks to distinguish between harm-causing accidents, which generally are not subject to criminal punishment, and harm-causing crimes, in which some level of intent is present. Certain crimes require a specific level of intent; examples include first-degree murder, which is normally a planned, intentional killing, and larceny, which involves the intent to deprive an owner of his or her property permanently and unlawfully. Later in this chapter we examine several defenses, such as necessity and insanity, that can be used to assert that a person did not have *mens rea*—"guilty mind" or blameworthy state of mind—and hence should not be held responsible for a criminal offense. The element of *mens rea* becomes problematic when there are questions about an offender's capacity to understand or plan harmful activities, as when the perpetrator is mentally ill or a child. The defense attorneys in shuttle astronaut Lisa Nowak's case, described at the beginning of the chapter, sought to attack the *mens rea* element by claiming she was legally insane at the time that the crime was committed.

■ **mens rea** "Guilty mind" or blameworthy state of mind, necessary for legal responsibility for a criminal offense; criminal intent, as distinguished from innocent intent.

Exceptions to the concept of *mens rea* are strict liability offenses involving health and safety, in which it is not necessary to show intent. Legislatures have criminalized certain kinds of offenses in order to protect the public. For example, a business owner may be held responsible for violations of a toxic waste law whether or not the owner actually knew that his employees were dumping polluting substances into a river. Other laws may apply strict liability to the sale of alcoholic beverages to minors. The purpose of such laws is to put pressure on business owners to make sure that their employees obey regulations designed to protect the health and safety of the public. Courts often limit the application of such laws to situations in which recklessness or indifference is present.

7. *Punishment.* There must be a provision in the law calling for punishment of those found guilty of violating the law. The punishment is enforced by the government and may carry with it social stigma, a criminal record, loss of freedom, and loss of rights.

The seven principles of substantive criminal law allow authorities to define certain acts as being against the law and provide the accused with a basis for mounting a defense against the charges. During a criminal trial, defense attorneys will often try to show that one of the seven elements either is unproved or can be explained in a way that is acceptable under the law.

Elements of a Crime

Legislatures define certain acts as crimes when they fulfill the seven principles under specific "attendant circumstances" while the offender has a certain state of mind. These three factors—the act (*actus reus*), the attendant circumstances, and the state of mind (*mens rea*)—are together called the *elements* of a crime. They can be seen in the following section from a state penal code:

> Section 3502. Burglary 1 Offense defined: A person is guilty of burglary if he enters a building or occupied structure, or separately secured or occupied portion thereof, with intent to commit a crime therein, unless the premises are at the time open to the public or the actor is licensed or privileged to enter.

The elements of burglary are, therefore, entering a building or occupied structure (*actus reus*) with the intent to commit a crime therein (*mens rea*) at a time when the premises are not open to the public and the actor is not invited or otherwise entitled to enter (attendant circumstances). For an act to be a burglary, all three elements must be present.

Statutory Definitions of Crimes

Federal and state penal codes often define criminal acts somewhat differently. To find out how a state defines an offense, one must read its penal code; this will give a general idea of which acts are illegal. To understand the court's interpretations of the code, one must analyze the judicial opinions that have sought to clarify the law.

The classification of criminal acts becomes complicated when statutes divide related acts, such as taking a person's life, into different offenses. For example, the definition of criminal homicide has been subdivided into degrees of murder and voluntary and involuntary manslaughter. In addition, some states have created new categories, such as reckless homicide, negligent homicide, and vehicular homicide. Each of these definitions involves slight variations in the *actus reus* and the *mens rea*. Table 3.1 defines these offenses according to the Uniform Crime Reports, which count murder and nonnegligent manslaughter as index offenses.

In legal language, the phrase *malice aforethought* is used to distinguish murder from manslaughter. This phrase indicates that the crime of murder is a deliberate, premeditated, and willful killing of another human being. Most states extend the definition of murder to these two circumstances: (1) defendants knew their behavior had a strong chance of causing death, showed indifference to life, and thus recklessly engaged in conduct that caused death or (2) defendants' behavior caused death while they were committing a felony. Mitigating circumstances, such as "the heat of passion" or extreme provocation, would reduce the offense to manslaughter, because the requirement of malice aforethought would be absent or reduced. Similarly, manslaughter would include a death resulting from an attempt to defend oneself that was not fully excused as self-defense. It might also include a death resulting from recklessness or negligence.

Police officers must carefully gather evidence at crime scenes in order to identify the proper suspect and then prove that the suspect actually committed the crime. They seek evidence relevant to each element in the definition of the specific law that was broken. For which crimes do you believe police have the hardest time gathering sufficient evidence for proving a suspect's guilt?

AP Images/David Adame

TABLE 3.1	Definitions of Offenses in the Uniform Crime Reports (Part I)

The exact descriptions of offenses differ from one state to another, but these UCR definitions provide a national standard that helps us distinguish among criminal acts.

1 Criminal homicide:
 a. Murder and nonnegligent manslaughter: the willful (nonnegligent) killing of one human being by another. Deaths caused by negligence, attempts to kill, assaults to kill, suicides, accidental deaths and justifiable homicides are excluded. Justifiable homicides are limited to (1) the killing of a felon by a law enforcement officer in the line of duty and (2) the killing of a felon by a private citizen.
 b. Manslaughter by negligence: the killing of another person through gross negligence. Excludes traffic fatalities. While manslaughter by negligence is a Part I crime, it is not included in the crime index.

2 Forcible rape:
 The carnal knowledge of a female forcibly and against her will. Included are rapes by force and attempts or assaults to rape. Statutory offenses (no force used—victim under age of consent) are excluded.

3 Robbery:
 The taking or attempting to take anything of value from the care, custody, or control of a person or persons by force or threat of force of violence and/or by putting the victim in fear.

4 Aggravated assault:
 An unlawful attack by one person upon another for the purpose of inflicting severe or aggravated bodily injury. This type of assault usually is accompanied by the use of a weapon or by means likely to produce death or great bodily harm. Simple assaults are excluded.

5 Burglary—breaking or entering:
 The unlawful entry of a structure to commit a felony or a theft. Attempted forcible entry is included.

6 Larceny/theft (except motor vehicle theft):
 The unlawful taking, carrying, leading, or riding away of property from the possession or constructive possession of another. Examples are thefts of bicycles or automobile accessories, shoplifting, pocket picking, or the stealing of any property or article that is not taken by force and violence or by fraud. Attempted larcenies are included. Embezzlement, "con" games, forgery, worthless checks, and so on, are excluded.

7 Motor vehicle theft:
 The theft or attempted theft of a motor vehicle. A motor vehicle is self-propelled and runs on the surface and not on rails. Specifically excluded from this category are motorboats, construction equipment, airplanes, and farming equipment.

8 Arson:
 Any willful or malicious burning or attempt to burn, with or without intent to defraud, a dwelling house, a public building, a motor vehicle or an aircraft, the personal property of another, and so on.

Source: Federal Bureau of Investigation. *Crime in the United States, 2001* (Washington, DC: U.S. Government Printing Office, 2007).

The definitions of crimes and required proof in the American system differ from those in other systems, as such definitions reflect the values of a particular system of justice. An act committed in one country may not be a crime, yet if that same act were committed elsewhere, it might be punished harshly. The Comparative Perspective on traditional Islamic criminal law provides examples of approaches that differ from those in the United States. These traditional approaches are not advocated by all Muslims and are not followed in all countries in which Muslims constitute a majority of the population. However, these approaches operate in several locations around the world. They are advocated by many fundamentalists who seek to have their interpretation of Islam control law and government.

■ Responsibility for Criminal Acts

Of the seven principles of criminal law, *mens rea* is crucial in establishing responsibility for the act. To obtain a conviction, the prosecution must show that the offender not only committed the illegal act but also did so in a state of mind that makes it appropriate to hold him or her responsible for the act. In 2002, two Florida brothers pleaded guilty and accepted 8-year prison sentences for killing their sleeping father with a baseball bat when they were 12 and 13 years of age, despite their mother's claim that they did not understand the charges and the plea agreement (Kaczor, 2002). Were these young boys old enough to plan their crimes and understand the consequences of their actions? Is a child capable of forming the same intent to commit a crime that an adult can form? The analysis of *mens rea*

COMPARATIVE PERSPECTIVE

ISLAMIC Criminal Law

THE RISE OF FUNDAMENTAL-IST *Islamic thought throughout the world has made Americans aware of great cultural differences between American legal traditions and those of the segment of Muslims who seek to have their governments run according to their interpretations of religious rules. Islamic criminal law, in particular, differs significantly from justice as it is administered in the Western democracies. Countries that define their crimes and punishments according to* Shari'a, *the law of Islam, appear harsh in the eyes of many Americans. Bear in mind, however, that there are different Islamic sects and differing perspectives on religious-based commands. Therefore, not all Muslim countries interpret and apply* Shari'a *in the same way. What are some of the major differences that exist between the American system and the elements of Islamic law described here?*

The U.S. State Department, the federal government agency responsible for foreign affairs, publishes annual reports on human rights in countries around the world. The 2007 report on Saudi Arabia provided a glimpse of stark differences between that country's approach to crime and punishment and the approach taken in the United States. According to the Country Reports on Human Rights Practices (U.S. Department of State, 2008):

> There are two types of courts: Shari'a and special. The legal system is based on the government's interpretation of Islamic law in all courts. . . . During the year according to Human Rights Watch (HRW), the press reported 153 beheadings of individuals who were convicted of murder, narcotics-related offenses, and armed robbery, as well as rape, sorcery, and adultery. The government also punished persons for various offenses with amputations for theft and lashings, including for alcohol-related offenses or for being alone in the company of an unrelated person of the opposite sex. . . . In a Shari'a court, the testimony of one man equals that of two women. Under the Hanbali interpretation of Shari'a, judges may discount the testimony of persons who are nonpracticing Muslims or who do not adhere to the Hanbali doctrine.

Very few countries actually follow Islamic law to define their crimes and punishments. Although Saudia Arabia and Sudan do, for example, Iran suspended the religion-based use of amputation and execution by stoning in December 2002, although the government can still enforce crimes defined by Islamic law. In 2008, there were reports that officials in a region of southern Iran were, in fact, using amputation as criminal punishment for robbers. Pakistan defines some crimes and punishments according to the *Shari'a*, but over the past 20 years it has emphasized ordinary punishments, such as imprisonment, rather than amputation and other religious punishments. However, in following religious laws, Pakistan can create difficult issues concerning proof of a crime. For example, when a Pakistani court overturned a rape conviction, the case drew international attention and outrage. As described by one *New York Times* reporter: "In Pakistan, if a woman reports a rape, four Muslim men must generally act as witnesses before she can prove her case. Otherwise, she risks being charged with fornication or adultery and suffering a public whipping and long imprisonment" (Kristof, 2005). In 2006, the Pakistani government pushed the national legislature to reform the rape law and move such cases from Islamic courts to criminal courts.

Despite its infrequent use by national governments, local villages in places such as Pakistan and Afghanistan may apply Islamic law. In various other countries, including Nigeria and Iraq, advocates are pushing for its use throughout society, although many of the Islamic-dominated states of northern Nigeria moderated their enforcement of Islamic law in 2007. Because the use of Islamic law is one focal point for activists seeking to turn these countries into religion-based governments, it is useful to compare aspects of *Shari'a* with those of the American approach.

Such practices as stoning for adultery and amputation for theft give Americans the perception that Islamic law is exceptionally harsh. What most Americans do not realize is that there are judicial and evidentiary safeguards within the *Shari'a*. One reason that the national government of Pakistan has not imposed punishments from the *Shari'a* is that conviction for these crimes requires the presentation of specific evidence and a higher standard of proof than in nonreligious systems. Islamic criminal law is concerned with (1) the safety of the public from physical attack, insult, and humiliation; (2) the stability of the family; (3) the protection of property against theft, destruction, or unauthorized interference; and (4) the protection of the government and the Islamic faith against subversion.

Criminal acts are divided into three categories. *Hudud* offenses are crimes against God, and punishment is specified in the Koran and the Sunna, a compilation of Muhammad's statements. *Quesas* and *Tesars* are crimes against others such as those that threaten a family's livelihood, including physical assault and murder, which are punishable by retaliation "the return of life for a life in case of murder." As shown here for the seven *Hudud* offenses, the Koran defines the crime, specifies the elements of proof required, and sets the punishment.

is difficult because the court must inquire into the defendant's mental state at the time the offense was committed. It is not easy to know what someone was thinking when he or she performed an act. Moreover, as discussed in the Close Up box, factors such as age, the effects of medications, and specific medical conditions can complicate the task of deciding whether someone acted with the intent necessary to deserve criminal punishment.

Although many defendants admit that they committed the harmful act, they may still plead not guilty. They may do so not only because they know that the state must prove them guilty but also because they—or their attorneys—believe that *mens rea* was not present. Accidents are the clearest examples of such situations: The defendant argues that it was an accident that the pedestrian suddenly crossed into the path of the car.

COMPARATIVE PERSPECTIVE (continued)

Theft

Theft is the taking of property belonging to another, the value of which is equal to or exceeds a prescribed amount, usually set at ten dirhams or about 75 cents. The property must be taken from the custody of another person in a secret manner, and the thief must obtain full possession of the property. "Custody" requires that the property should have been under guard or in a place of safekeeping.

By contrast, American criminal law focuses on ownership rather than custody, so that stealing something left in the open, including items sitting unattended in public places, clearly falls under laws against theft if the offender intends to take items known to be owned by others.

Extramarital Sexual Activity

Sexual relations outside marriage are believed to undermine marriage and lead to family conflict, jealousy, divorce, litigation, and the spread of disease.

Some American states continue to criminalize adultery and premarital cohabitation through old laws that remain on the books. However, these laws are rarely enforced, and many prosecutors doubt whether juries will convict people of such offenses, because society has become more tolerant of such commonplace behavior.

Defamation

In addition to false accusations of fornication, this offense includes impugning the legitimacy of a woman's child. Defamation by a husband of his wife leads to divorce and is not subject to punishment.

Defamation under American law can lead to civil lawsuits concerning harmful falsehoods spoken or written about a person that significantly harm that person's reputation.

Highway Robbery

This crime interferes with commerce and creates fear among travelers and is therefore subject to punishment.

American robbery statutes typically apply in all contexts and do not focus on travelers. The primary exception is carjacking statutes enacted by Congress and state legislatures in response to highly publicized incidents of drivers being killed and injured by robbers who forcibly stole their vehicles as they sat at traffic lights or stop signs.

Use of Alcohol

Drinking wine and other intoxicating beverages is prohibited because it brings about indolence and inattention to religious duties.

By contrast, alcoholic beverages are legal in the United States, subject to regulations concerning the legal drinking age and criminal statutes concerning the operation of vehicles while a person is under the influence of alcohol.

Apostasy

This is the voluntary renunciation of Islam. The offense is committed by any Muslim who converts to another faith, worships idols, or rejects any of the tenets of Islam. Enforcement varies by country. For example, in 2008 an Egyptian court ruled that Christians who converted to Islam in order more easily to obtain a divorce were permitted to convert back to Christianity later.

In the United States, the First Amendment protections for freedom of religion and freedom of speech permit people to change religions and to criticize the religions of others without fear of criminal prosecution.

Rebellion

Rebellion is the intentional, forceful overthrow or attempted overthrow of the legitimate leader of the Islamic state.

In the United States, the government can change only through the process of democratic elections. Any effort to use force as the means to overthrow the government will result in criminal prosecution.

Sources: Articles from the *New York Times* (http://www.nytimes.com): Nadim Audi, "Egyptian Court Allows Return to Christianity," February 11, 2008; Nazila Fathi, "Spate of Executions and Amputations in Iran," January 11, 2008; Noah Feldman, "Why Shariah?" March 16, 2008; Nicholas D. Kristof, "When Rapists Walk Free," March 5, 2005; Salman Masood, "Pakistan Moves toward Altering Rape Law," November 16, 2006; Lydia Polgreen, "Nigeria Turns from Harsher Side of Islamic Law," December 1, 2007. Other sources: U.S. Department of State, *Country Reports on Human Rights Practices, 2007,* http://www.state.gov; Council of Foreign Relations, Governing under Sharia, March 14, 2003, http://www.cfr.org. Portions are excerpts from the following: *Islamic Criminal Law and Procedure: An Introduction,* by M. Lippman, S. McConville, and M.Yerushalmi, 42–43. Copyright © 1988 by Praeger Publishers. Reprinted by permission of Greenwood Publishing Group, Inc., Westport, CT; A. A. Mansour, "Hudud Crimes," in *The Islamic Criminal Justice System,* ed. M. C. Bassiouni (Dobbs Ferry, NY: Oceana, 1982), 195. Copyright © 1982 by Oceana Publications. Reprinted by permission.

The absence of *mens rea*, as we have seen, does not guarantee a verdict of not guilty in every case. In most cases, however, it relieves defendants of responsibility for acts that would be labeled criminal if they had been intentional. Besides the defense of accidents, there are eight defenses based on lack of criminal intent: entrapment, self-defense, necessity, duress (coercion), immaturity, mistake of fact, intoxication, and insanity.

Entrapment **Entrapment** is a defense that can be used to show lack of intent. The law excuses a defendant when it is shown that government agents have induced the person to commit the offense. That does not mean the police may not use undercover agents to set a trap for criminals, nor does it mean the police may not provide ordinary opportunities for the commission of a crime. But the entrapment defense may be used when the police have acted so as to induce the criminal act.

Entrapment raises tough questions for judges, who must decide whether the police went too far toward making a crime occur that otherwise would not have happened

■ entrapment The defense that the individual was induced by the police to commit the criminal act.

CLOSE UP

Criminal Intent and the Appropriateness of Punishment

IN 2009, AN 18-YEAR-OLD IN OHIO was accused of beating his mother so badly that she died a few days later from internal injuries. Is this a clear-cut case of criminal responsibility? The suspect is an adult whose intentional violent actions caused a death. In this case, however, the suspect has autism. He has a limited ability to communicate, using specific words and phrases that only his mother understood. In his jail cell, the deputies positioned a television set just outside the bars and played recordings of *The Price Is Right* over and over again because watching his favorite show kept him calm. Friends and relatives were permitted to bring barbecue potato chips, McDonald's Happy Meals, and items from his bedroom at home as jail officials, lawyers, and judges tried to determine how best to detain him safely as judicial processes moved forward to decide whether he was competent to stand trial.

In Arizona in 2008, an eight-year-old boy shot his father and another man at point-blank range with a hunting rifle that his father had given him for his birthday. He stopped and reloaded as he shot each victim at least four times. He was charged with premeditated murder. Some news reports indicated that the boy was tired of being spanked by his father. Was this an intentional act of homicide? Apparently, yes. But should a child so young be held criminally responsible in the same manner as an adult?

In South Carolina, a 12-year-old boy walked into his grandparents' bedroom one night and killed them with two blasts of a shotgun as they slept. He was a troubled boy who came to live with his grandparents because he had been abandoned by his mother and had serious conflicts with his father. At the time, he was taking an antidepressant medication prescribed by doctors—but one that cannot be prescribed for teenagers in some other countries because it is known to affect thinking and behavior, including the risk of suicide. Could the medication have affected his thinking so that he actually did not have the requisite intent to commit the crime? Did he really know what he was doing that night?

All three of these examples raise serious questions about how we evaluate *mens rea* and determine whether someone is capable of forming criminal intent. Advances in modern science affect such situations. For example, the development and use of new medications may lead to unintended consequences for people's clarity of thought and control over their own actions. In addition, greater understanding of mental conditions and neuroscience—the science of the brain and thinking—may help us analyze the capabilities

of people with specific medical conditions. Yet there will always be difficult decisions to be made.

In Ohio, a judge ordered the autistic homicide suspect be moved from the jail to a state residential facility for developmentally disabled people while the court system decided whether he should stand trial. The boy in Arizona was eventually permitted to plead guilty to one count of negligent homicide instead of facing trial on two counts of first-degree murder. He was ordered to remain under the custody and supervision of the state until age 18, with further determinations to be made about whether he should live in a juvenile detention facility, sent to a treatment facility, placed with foster parents, or permitted to live with his mother. If he stayed out of trouble until age 18, his record would be expunged. By contrast, the South Carolina boy was unsuccessful in challenging the *mens rea* element of the crime by pointing to the effects of his medication. Christopher Pittman was sentenced to 30 years in prison for murder. The U.S. Supreme Court declined to hear his appeal.

RESEARCHING THE INTERNET

To read about other cases that raise issues concerning *mens rea*, including cases such as Lisa Nowak's that use the insanity defense, go to the corresponding site listed on the Cole/Smith Criminal Justice in America Companion Website: http://www.cengage.com/criminaljustice/cole.

FOR CRITICAL ANALYSIS

What rule could we formulate that would guide us in determining which individuals were capable of forming criminal intent and are deserving of punishment? Alternatively, how could we use a case-by-case approach effectively to analyze the capability of each defendant? Would we advance the goal of justice by thinking about appropriate treatment instead of punishment when such questions arise about a defendant? What would you decide about each of the three defendants profiled here?

Sources: Associated Press, "Autistic Murder Defendant Poses Challenges," March 19, 2009, http://www.msnbc.com; "Son of Late KSU Professor Sent to State Facility," *Akron Beacon Journal*, March 27, 2009, http://www.ohio.com. Articles from the *New York Times*, ht\tp://www.nytimes.com: S. Dewan and B. Meier, "Boy Who Took Antidepressants Is Convicted in Killings," February 15, 2005; J. Dougherty and A. O'Connor, "Prosecutors Say Boy Methodically Shot His Father," November 11, 2008; S. Moore, "Boy, 9, Enters a Guilty Plea in 2 Killings in Arizona," February 20, 2009.

(Carlon, 2007). The key question is the predisposition of the defendant. In 1992 the Supreme Court stressed that the prosecutor must show beyond a reasonable doubt that a defendant was predisposed to break the law before he or she was approached by government agents. The Court's decision invalidated the conviction of a Nebraska farmer who purchased child pornography after receiving multiple solicitation letters from law enforcement officials pretending to be pen pals and bookstore operators (*United States v. Jacobson*).

Self-Defense   A person who feels that he or she is in immediate danger of being harmed by another person may ward off the attack in *self-defense*. The laws of most states also recognize the right to defend others from attack, to protect property, and to prevent a crime. For example, in August 2002, T. J. Duckett, an African American football player for the NFL's Seattle Seahawks, was attacked by three white men who also yelled racial slurs at him as he walked toward his car after a concert. After Duckett lost a tooth and suffered a cut that required four stitches when he was struck with a bottle in the surprise attack, the 250-pound running back defended himself. He knocked one attacker unconscious and caused a second attacker to be hospitalized with injuries. The third attacker ran away. The attackers received the most serious injuries, yet they faced criminal charges because Duckett was entitled to defend himself with reasonable force against an unprovoked criminal assault (Winkeljohn, 2002).

The level of force used in self-defense cannot exceed the person's reasonable perception of the threat (Simons, 2008). Thus, a person may be justified in shooting a robber who is holding a gun to her head and threatening to kill her, but homeowners generally are not justified in shooting an unarmed burglar who has left the house and is running across the lawn.

In 2007, a New Jersey court found Denise Volpicelli "not guilty by reason of insanity" for first-degree murder charges after she suffocated her 12-year-old son and then repeatedly stabbed herself. The judge ordered that she be committed to a secure psychiatric facility. Should severe mental problems enable people who kill others to avoid prison sentences?

Star-Ledger Photographs © The Star-Ledger, Newark, NJ

Necessity   Unlike self-defense, in which a defendant feels that he or she must harm an aggressor to ward off an attack, the *necessity* defense is used when people break the law in order to save themselves or prevent some greater harm. A person who speeds through a red light to get an injured child to the hospital or breaks into a building to seek refuge from a hurricane could claim to be violating the law out of necessity.

The English case *The Queen v. Dudley and Stephens* (1884) is a famous example of necessity. After their ship sank, four sailors were adrift in the ocean without food or water. Twenty days later, two of the sailors, Thomas Dudley and Edwin Stephens, killed the youngest sailor, the cabin boy, and ate his flesh. Four days later they were rescued by a passing ship. When they returned to England, they were tried and convicted for murder because the court did not accept their claim of necessity. However, their sentences were later reduced from the death penalty to 6 months in prison.

Duress (Coercion)   The defense of *duress* arises when someone commits a crime because he or she is coerced by another person. During a bank robbery, for instance, if an armed robber forces one of the bank's customers at gunpoint to drive the getaway car, the customer would be able to claim duress. However, courts generally are not willing to accept this defense if people do not try to escape from the situation.

Immaturity   Anglo American law excuses criminal acts by children under age seven on the grounds of their *immaturity* and lack of responsibility for their actions—*mens rea* is not present. Common law has presumed that children aged 7–14 are not liable for their criminal acts; however, prosecutors have been able to present evidence of a child's mental capacity to form *mens rea*. Juries can assume the presence of a guilty mind if it can be shown, for example, that the child hid evidence or tried to bribe a witness. As a child grows older, the assumption of immaturity weakens. Since the development of juvenile courts in the 1890s, children generally have been tried by different rules than are adults. In some situations, however, children may be tried as adults—if, for example, they are repeat offenders or are charged with a particularly heinous crime. Because of the public's concerns about violent crimes by young people, in the 1990s it became increasingly common to see prosecutors seek to hold children responsible for serious crimes in the same manner that adults are held responsible. In 2008, as discussed in the Close Up, the U.S. Supreme Court declined to hear an appeal from Christopher Pittman, who as a 12-year-old killed his grandparents, was tried as an adult, and was sentenced to 30 years.

Mistake of Fact   The courts have generally upheld the view that ignorance of the law is no excuse for committing an illegal act. But what if there is a *mistake of fact*? If an accused person has made a mistake on some crucial fact, that may serve as a defense (Christopher, 1994). For example, suppose some teenagers ask your permission to grow sunflowers in a vacant lot behind your home. You help them weed the garden and water the plants. Then it turns out that they are growing marijuana. You were not aware of this because you have no idea what a marijuana plant looks like. Should you be convicted for growing an illegal drug on your property? The answer depends on the specific degree of knowledge and intent that the prosecution must prove for that offense. The success of such a defense may also depend on the extent to which jurors understand and sympathize with your mistake.

For example, in 2008 a college professor attending a professional baseball game bought his seven-year-old son a bottle of "lemonade." Because he and his family seldom watch television, however, he had no idea that "hard lemonade" even existed. Thus, he made a mistake of fact by purchasing an alcoholic beverage for his underage son. When police officers spotted the child drinking the beverage, the boy was taken from the custody of his parents for a few days until officials decided that it was an unintentional mistake. If prosecutors had pursued criminal charges against the professor, his fate would have depended on whether the jury believed his claim of making an ignorant mistake of fact in purchasing the alcoholic "lemonade" for a child (Dickerson, 2008).

Intoxication   The law does not relieve an individual of responsibility for acts performed while voluntarily intoxicated. There are, however, cases in which *intoxication* can be used as a defense, as when a person has been tricked into consuming a substance without knowing that it may cause intoxication. Christopher Pittman's attorney attempted unsuccessfully to use this defense by arguing that the boy's prescribed antidepressant drugs caused his violent behavior. Other complex cases arise in which the defendant must be shown to have had a specific, rather than a general, intent to commit a crime. For example, people may claim that they were too drunk to realize that they had left a restaurant without paying the bill. Drunkenness can also be used as a mitigating factor to reduce the seriousness of a charge.

In 1996, the U.S. Supreme Court narrowly approved a Montana law that barred the use of evidence of intoxication, even for defendants who claimed that their condition prevented them from forming the specific intent necessary to be guilty of a crime (*Montana v. Egelhoff*). Thus, states may enact laws that prevent the use of an intoxication defense.

Insanity   The defense of *insanity* has been a subject of heated debate. It is available in all but four states (Idaho, Montana, Nevada, and Utah). The public believes that many criminals "escape" punishment through the skillful use of psychiatric testimony. Yet, only about 1 percent of incarcerated offenders are held in mental hospitals because they were found "not guilty by reason of insanity." The insanity defense is rare and is generally used only in serious cases or where there is no other valid defense.

Over time, U.S. courts have used five tests of criminal responsibility involving insanity: the *M'Naghten* Rule, the Irresistible Impulse Test, the *Durham* Rule, the *Model Penal Code*'s Substantial Capacity Test, and the test defined in the federal Comprehensive Crime Control Act of 1984. These tests are summarized in Table 3.2.

M'NAGHTEN RULE   More than a dozen states use the *M'Naghten* Rule, which was developed in England in 1843. In that year Daniel M'Naghten was acquitted of killing Edward Drummond, a man he had thought was Sir Robert Peel, the prime minister of Great Britain. M'Naghten claimed that he had been delusional at the time of the killing. The British court developed a standard for determining criminal responsibility known as the "right-from-wrong test." It asks whether "at the time of the committing of the act, the party accused was laboring under such a defect of reason, from

TABLE 3.2	Insanity Defense Standards		

The standards for the insanity defense have evolved over time.

Test	Legal Standard Because of Mental Illness	Final Burden of Proof	Who Bears Burden of Proof
M'Naghten (1843)	"Didn't know what he was doing or didn't know it was wrong."	Varies from proof by a balance of probabilities on the defense to proof beyond a reasonable doubt on the prosecutor	
Irresistible Impulse (1897)	"Could not control his conduct."		
Durham (1954)	"The criminal act was caused by his mental illness."	Beyond a reasonable doubt	Prosecutor
Model Penal Code (1972)	"Lacks substantial capacity to appreciate the wrongfulness of his conduct or to control it."	Beyond a reasonable doubt	Prosecutor
Present federal law	"Lacks capacity to appreciate the wrongfulness of his conduct."	Clear and convincing evidence	Defense

Source: National Institute of Justice, *Crime File*, "Insanity Defense," a film prepared by Norval Morris (Washington, DC: U.S. Government Printing Office, n.d.).

disease of the mind, as not to know the nature and quality of the act he was doing, or if he did know it that he did not know he was doing what was wrong" (*M'Naghten's Case*, 1843).

IRRESISTIBLE IMPULSE TEST Four states supplemented the *M'Naghten* Rule with the Irresistible Impulse Test. Because psychiatrists argued that some people can feel compelled by their mental illness to commit criminal actions even though they recognize the wrongfulness of their conduct, the Irresistible Impulse Test was designed to bring the *M'Naghten* Rule in line with modern psychiatry. This test excuses defendants when a mental disease was controlling their behavior even though they knew that what they were doing was wrong.

DURHAM RULE The *Durham* Rule, originally developed in New Hampshire in 1871, was adopted by the Circuit Court of Appeals for the District of Columbia in 1954 in the case of *Durham v. United States*. Under this rule, the accused is not criminally responsible "if an unlawful act is the product of mental disease or mental defect."

MODEL PENAL CODE'S SUBSTANTIAL CAPACITY TEST It was argued that the *Durham* Rule offered no useful definition of "mental disease or defect." By 1972 (*United States v. Brawner*), the federal courts had overturned the *Durham* Rule in favor of a modified version of a test proposed in the *Model Penal Code* (a penal code developed by the American Bar Association as a model of what "should" be). By 1982, all federal courts and about half of the state courts had adopted the *Model Penal Code*'s Substantial Capacity Test, which states that a person is not responsible for criminal conduct "if at the time of such conduct as a result of mental disease or defect he lacks substantial capacity either to appreciate the criminality [wrongfulness] of his conduct or to conform his conduct to the requirements of law." The Substantial Capacity Test broadens and modifies the *M'Naghten* and Irresistible Impulse rules. By stressing "substantial capacity," the test does not require that a defendant be unable to distinguish right from wrong.

COMPREHENSIVE CRIME CONTROL ACT The Comprehensive Crime Control Act of 1984 changed the federal rules on the insanity defense by limiting it to those who are unable, as a result of severe mental disease or defect, to understand the nature or wrongfulness of their acts. This change means that the Irresistible Impulse Test cannot be used in the federal courts. It also shifts the burden of proof from the prosecutor to the defendant, who has to prove his or her insanity. Further, the act creates a new procedure whereby a person who is found not guilty only by reason of insanity must be committed to a mental hospital until he or she no longer poses a danger to society. These rules apply only in federal courts, but they are spreading to the states.

All of the insanity tests are difficult to apply. Moreover, deciding what to do with someone who has been found not guilty by reason of insanity poses significant difficulties. Finally, jurors' fears about seeing the offender turned loose might affect their decisions about whether the person was legally insane at the time of the crime.

John Hinckley's attempt to assassinate President Ronald Reagan in 1981 reopened the debate on the insanity defense. Television news footage showed that Hinckley had shot the president. Yet, with the help of psychiatrists, Hinckley's lawyers counteracted the prosecution's efforts to persuade the jury that Hinckley was sane. When Hinckley was acquitted, the public was outraged, and several states acted to limit or abolish the insanity defense. Twelve states introduced the defense of "guilty but mentally ill" (Klofas and Yandrasits, 1989:424). This defense allows a jury to find the accused guilty but requires that he or she be given psychiatric treatment while in prison (L. A. Callahan et al., 1992).

CHECKPOINT

ANSWERS

3 What are the seven principles of criminal law?

3 Legality, *actus reus*, causation, harm, concurrence, *mens rea*, punishment.

4 What are the defenses in substantive criminal law?

4 Entrapment, self-defense, necessity, duress (coercion), immaturity, mistake of fact, intoxication, insanity.

5 What are the tests of criminal responsibility used for the insanity defense?

5 *M'Naghten* Rule (right-from-wrong test), Irresistible Impulse Test, *Durham* Rule, *Model Penal Code*, Comprehensive Crime Control Act.

Procedural Criminal Law

Procedural law defines how the state must process cases. According to procedural due process, accused persons must be tried in accordance with legal procedures. The procedures include providing the rights granted by the Constitution to criminal defendants. As we saw in Chapter 1, the due process model is based on the premise that freedom is so valuable that efforts must be made to prevent erroneous decisions that would deprive an innocent person of his or her freedom. Rights are not only intended to prevent the innocent from being wrongly convicted. They also seek to prevent unfair police and prosecution practices aimed at guilty people, such as conducting improper searches, using violence to pressure people to confess, and denying defendants a fair trial.

The importance of procedural law has been evident throughout history. U.S. history contains many examples of police officers and prosecutors harassing and victimizing those who lack political power, including poor people, racial and ethnic minorities, and unpopular religious groups. The development of procedural safeguards through the decisions of the U.S. Supreme Court has helped protect citizens from such actions.

In these decisions, the Supreme Court may favor guilty people by ordering new trials or may even release them from custody because of the weight it places on protecting procedural rights and preventing police misconduct.

Individual rights and the protection against improper deprivations of liberty represent central elements of American values. Americans expect that their rights will be protected. At the same time, however, the protection of rights for the criminally accused can clash with competing American values that emphasize the control of crime as an important component of protecting all citizens' freedom of movement and sense of security. Because the rules of procedural criminal law can sometimes lead to the release of guilty people, some observers regard them as weighted too heavily in favor of American values emphasizing individual rights rather than equally valid American values that emphasize the protection of the community.

Public opinion does not always support the decisions by the Supreme Court and other courts that uphold the rights of criminal defendants and convicted offenders. Many Americans would prefer if other goals for society, such as stopping drugs and ensuring that guilty people are punished, took a higher priority over the protection of rights. Such opinions raise questions about Americans' commitment to the rights described in the Bill of Rights. Public opinion data indicate that most first-year college students believe that courts have placed too much emphasis on the rights of criminal defendants. This view, while reduced since 1998, remains stronger than in 1971. Although male and female students' support for rights differed in 1971, there is less difference between the two groups today (see "What Americans Think"). Do you agree that there are too many rights? Can you identify specific rights that give too much protection to criminal defendants? Would there be any risks from reducing the rights available in the criminal justice process?

Unlike substantive criminal law, which is defined by legislatures through statutes, procedural criminal law is defined by courts through judicial rulings. Judges interpret the provisions of the U.S. Constitution and state constitutions, and those interpretations establish the procedures that government officials must follow. Because it has the authority to review cases from state supreme courts as well as from federal courts, the U.S. Supreme Court has played a major role in defining procedural criminal law. The Supreme Court's influence stems from its power to define the meaning of the U.S. Constitution, especially the Bill of Rights—the first ten amendments to the Constitution, which list legal protections against actions of the government. Although public opinion may clash with Supreme Court rulings, the Supreme Court can make independent decisions because its members cannot be removed from office by the voters but only through impeachment for misconduct. How does someone get to be one of these important decision makers on the nation's highest court? Read the "Careers in Criminal Justice" box about Justice Ruth Bader Ginsburg to gain an understanding of the career path to the U.S. Supreme Court. Comparable professional training and experience are also typically necessary to gain judgeships on other federal and state appellate courts. In Chapter 9, you will read about a career path to a state trial court judgeship.

The Bill of Rights and the Fourteenth Amendment

The U.S. Constitution contained few references to criminal justice when it was ratified in 1788 and 1789. Because many people were concerned that the document did not set forth the rights of individuals in enough detail, ten amendments were added in 1791. These first ten amendments are known as the **Bill of Rights**. As you read the Bill of Rights, included here, note how many amendments focus on criminal justice. Although several amendments have implications for criminal justice, four of them directly concern procedural criminal law. The Fourth Amendment bars

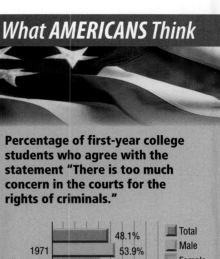

What AMERICANS Think

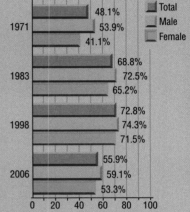

Percentage of first-year college students who agree with the statement "There is too much concern in the courts for the rights of criminals."

	Total	Male	Female
1971	48.1%	53.9%	41.1%
1983	68.8%	72.5%	65.2%
1998	72.8%	74.3%	71.5%
2006	55.9%	59.1%	53.3%

Go to http://www.cengage.com/criminaljustice/cole to compare your opinion on this issue with the opinions of other criminal justice students.

Source: Bureau of Justice Statistics, *Sourcebook of Criminal Justice Statistics Online*, http://www.albany.edu/sourcebook/, Table 2.92.2006.

■ **Bill of Rights** The first ten amendments added to the U.S. Constitution to provide specific rights for individuals, including criminal justice rights concerning searches, trials, and punishments.

The Magna Carta, signed by England's King John in 1215, is the first written guarantee of due process. It established the principle that people must be arrested and tried according to the processes outlined in the law. What might the American criminal justice system look like if it lacked procedural rights?

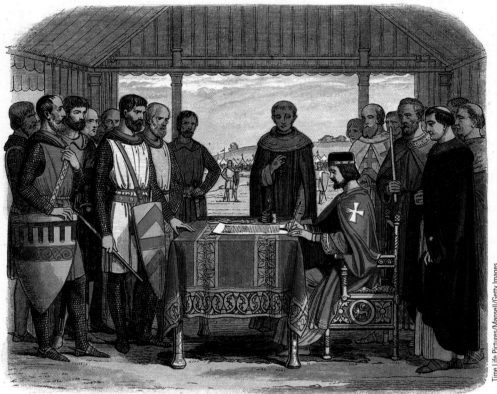

Time Life Pictures/Mansell/Getty Images

■ **self-incrimination** The act of exposing oneself to prosecution by being forced to respond to questions whose answers may reveal that one has committed a crime. The Fifth Amendment protects defendants against compelled self-incrimination.

■ **double jeopardy** The subjecting of a person to prosecution more than once in the same jurisdiction for the same offense; prohibited by the Fifth Amendment.

unreasonable searches and seizures. The Fifth Amendment outlines basic due process rights in criminal cases. For example, consistent with the assumption that the state must prove the defendant's guilt, protection against **self-incrimination** means that persons cannot be forced to respond to questions whose answers may reveal that they have committed a crime. The protection against **double jeopardy** means that a person may be subjected to only one prosecution or punishment for a single offense within the same jurisdiction. The Sixth Amendment provides for the right to a speedy, fair, and public trial by an impartial jury, as well as the right to counsel. The Eighth Amendment bars excessive bail, excessive fines, and cruel and unusual punishment.

Here are the Bill of Rights and the Fourteenth Amendment of the United States Constitution. The first ten were ratified on December 15, 1791; the Fourteenth Amendment was ratified on July 28, 1868. Refer back to these texts in the sections that follow.

First Amendment: Congress shall make no law respecting an establishment of religion, or prohibiting the free exercise thereof; or abridging the freedom of speech, or of the press; or the right of the people peaceably to assemble, and to petition the Government for redress of grievances.

Second Amendment: A well regulated Militia, being necessary for the security of a free State, the right of the people to keep and bear Arms, shall not be infringed.

Third Amendment: No Soldier shall, in time of peace, be quartered in any house, without the consent of the Owner, nor in time of war, but in a manner to be prescribed by law.

CAREERS IN CRIMINAL JUSTICE

Appellate Judges

RUTH BADER GINSBURG, U.S. SUPREME COURT JUSTICE
U.S. SUPREME COURT, WASHINGTON, D.C.

JUDGES ON APPELLATE COURTS read detailed written arguments submitted by lawyers and listen to oral arguments from lawyers in selected cases as they consider claims that specific errors occurred when a trial court processed a criminal or civil case. Appellate judges do not decide whether someone is guilty of a crime. They interpret statutes, constitutional provisions, and prior judicial decisions to clarify rules of law and provide guidance to judges and lawyers. In the course of making these decisions, they may expand or narrow the definition of rights for everyone. They may also identify a trial court or police error that requires permitting a criminal defendant to have a new trial.

AP Images/Ron Edmonds, File

Judges on appellate courts sit in groups as they hear and decide cases. Intermediate appellate courts typically sit in panels consisting of three judges. State supreme courts normally have either five or seven members, and the U.S. Supreme Court decides cases as a group of nine justices. They must discuss the cases and try to persuade each other about the appropriate outcomes. They must also write elaborate opinions explaining their decisions and justifying their interpretations of law. When in the majority, they may write the majority opinion that explains the decision and rule of law on behalf of the court. When they disagree with the court's decision, they may write dissenting opinions that describe in detail why they think the court's rule is incorrect. These dissenting opinions may persuade judges in future cases to move the law in a different direction. Thus, appellate judges must be able to deliberate carefully and write clearly in order to do their jobs effectively.

Justice Ruth Bader Ginsburg earned her undergraduate degree at Cornell University and then was an honor student at Harvard Law School before transferring to Columbia University Law School, where she graduated at the top of her class. She graduated from law school in the 1950s, a time when women faced tremendous discrimination in seeking employment as lawyers. Many law firms would not hire women as lawyers, and there were no antidiscrimination laws at that time to prevent such unfair treatment. After graduation, she worked as a researcher at Columbia University before gaining a position as a law professor, first at Rutgers University and later at Columbia. As she taught law school, Ginsburg also became active as a public interest lawyer, arguing cases concerning gender discrimination in front of the U.S. Supreme Court on behalf of the American Civil Liberties Union's Women's Rights Project. In her work as a lawyer, she made significant contributions to the development of judicial decisions that provided some protections against discrimination.

Because of Ginsberg's national prominence as a legal scholar and experienced public interest lawyer, President Jimmy Carter appointed Ginsburg to be a judge on the U.S. Court of Appeals for the District of Columbia Circuit. During her 12 years on the federal intermediate appellate court, she established a reputation as a careful, thoughtful judge. In 1993, President Bill Clinton appointed her to fill a vacancy on the U.S. Supreme Court; the U.S. Senate confirmed her appointment by an overwhelming vote of 96 to 3, showing support from both Republicans and Democrats.

My experience teaches that there is nothing better than an impressive dissent to improve an opinion for the Court. A well reasoned dissent will lead the author of the majority opinion to refine and clarify her initial [draft]. . . . On rare occasions, a [draft] dissent will be so persuasive that it attracts the votes necessary to become the opinion of the Court. . . . I will continue to give voice to my dissent if, in my judgment, the Court veers in the wrong direction when important matters are at stake.

Sources: Ruth Bader Ginsburg, "The Role of Dissenting Opinions," Eizenstat Memorial Lecture, October 21, 2007, Atlanta, Georgia, http://www.supremecourtus.gov/publicinfo/speeches/sp_10-21-07.html.

Fourth Amendment: The right of the people to be secure in their persons, houses, papers, and effects, against unreasonable searches and seizures, shall not be violated, and no Warrants shall issue, but upon probable cause, supported by Oath or affirmation, and particularly describing the place to be searched, and the persons or things to be seized.

Fifth Amendment: No person shall be held to answer for a capital or otherwise infamous crime, unless on a presentment or indictment of a Grand Jury, except in cases arising in the land or naval forces, or in the Militia, when in actual service in time of War or public danger; nor shall any person be subject for the same offence to be twice put in jeopardy of life or limb; nor shall be compelled in any criminal case to be a witness against himself, nor be deprived of life, liberty, or property, without due process of law; nor shall private property be taken for public use, without just compensation.

Sixth Amendment: In all criminal prosecutions, the accused shall enjoy the right to a speedy and public trial, by an impartial jury of the State and district wherein the crime shall have been committed, which district shall have been previously ascertained by law, and to be informed of the nature and cause of the accusation; to be confronted with the witnesses against him; to have compulsory process for obtaining witnesses in his favor, and to have the Assistance of Counsel for his defense.

Seventh Amendment: In Suits at common law, where the value in controversy shall exceed twenty dollars, the right of trial by jury shall be preserved, and no fact tried by a jury, shall be otherwise re-examined in any Court of the United States, than according to the rules of the common law.

Eighth Amendment: Excessive bail shall not be required, nor excessive fines imposed, nor cruel and unusual punishments inflicted.

Ninth Amendment: The enumeration in the Constitution, of certain rights, shall not be construed to deny or disparage others retained by the people.

Tenth Amendment: The powers not delegated to the United States by the Constitution, nor prohibited by it to the States, are reserved to the States respectively, or to the people.

Fourteenth Amendment: Section 1. All persons born or naturalized in the United States, and subject to the jurisdiction thereof, are citizens of the United States and of the State wherein they reside. No State shall make or enforce any law which shall abridge the privileges or immunities of citizens of the United States; nor shall any State deprive any person of life, liberty, or property, without due process of law; nor deny to any person within its jurisdiction the equal protection of the laws. . . .

Section 5. The Congress shall have the power to enforce, by appropriate legislation, the provisions of this article.

For most of American history, the Bill of Rights did not apply to most criminal cases, because it was designed to protect people from abusive actions by the federal government. It did not seek to protect people from state and local officials, who handled nearly all criminal cases. This view was upheld by the U.S. Supreme Court in the 1833 case of *Barron v. Baltimore*. However, as we shall see shortly, this view gradually changed in the late nineteenth and early twentieth centuries.

■ *Barron v. Baltimore* (1833) The protections of the Bill of Rights apply only to actions of the federal government.

■ The Fourteenth Amendment and Due Process

After the Civil War, three amendments were added to the Constitution. These amendments were designed to protect individuals' rights against infringement by state and local government officials. The Thirteenth Amendment abolished slavery and the Fifteenth Amendment attempted to prohibit racial discrimination in voting; these had little impact on criminal justice. However, the Fourteenth Amendment profoundly affected it by barring states from violating people's right to due process of law. It says that "no State shall . . . deprive any person of life, liberty, or property, without due process of law; nor deny to any person within its jurisdiction the equal protection of the laws." These rights to due process and equal protection served as a basis for protecting individuals from abusive actions by local criminal justice officials. However, the terms *due process* and *equal protection* are so vague that it was left to the U.S. Supreme Court to decide if and how these new rights applied to the criminal justice process.

For example, in *Powell v. Alabama* (1932), the Supreme Court ruled that the due process clause required states to provide attorneys for poor defendants facing the death penalty. This decision stemmed from a notorious case in Alabama in which nine African American men, known as the "Scottsboro boys," were quickly convicted and condemned to death for allegedly raping two white women, even though one of the alleged victims later admitted that she had lied about the rape (Goodman, 1994).

In these early cases, the justices had not developed clear rules for deciding which specific rights applied to state and local officials as components of the due process clause of the Fourteenth Amendment. They implied that procedures must meet a standard of **fundamental fairness**. In essence, the justices simply reacted against brutal situations that shocked their consciences. In doing so, they showed the importance of procedural criminal law in protecting individuals from abusive and unjust actions by government officials.

The Due Process Revolution

From the 1930s to the 1960s, the fundamental fairness doctrine was supported by a majority of the Supreme Court justices. It was applied on a case-by-case basis, not always consistently. After Earl Warren became chief justice in 1953, he led the Supreme Court in a revolution that changed the meaning and scope of constitutional rights. Instead of requiring state and local officials merely to uphold fundamental fairness, the Court began to require them to abide by the specific provisions of the Bill of Rights (Marceau, 2008). Through the process of **incorporation**, the Supreme Court during the Warren Court era declared that elements of the Fourth, Fifth, Sixth, Eighth, and other amendments were part of the due process clause of the Fourteenth Amendment. Previously, states could design their own procedures so long as those procedures passed the fairness test. Under Warren's leadership, however, the Supreme Court's new approach imposed detailed procedural standards on the police and courts.

As it applied more and more constitutional rights against the states, the Court made decisions that favored the interests of many criminal defendants. These defendants had their convictions overturned and received new trials because the Court believed that it was more important to protect the values underlying criminal procedure than single-mindedly to seek convictions of criminal offenders. In the eyes of many legal scholars, the Warren Court's decisions made criminal justice processes consistent with the American values of liberty, rights, and limited government authority.

To critics, however, these decisions made the community more vulnerable to crime and thereby harmed American values by diminishing the overall sense of liberty and security in society. Warren and the other justices were strongly criticized by politicians, police chiefs, and members of the public. These critics believed that the Warren Court was rewriting constitutional law in a manner that gave too many legal protections to criminals who harm society. In addition, Warren and his colleagues were criticized for ignoring established precedents that defined rights in a limited fashion.

From 1962 to 1972, the Supreme Court, under Chief Justices Earl Warren (1953–1969) and Warren Burger (1969–1986), applied most criminal justice rights in the U.S. Constitution against

■ *Powell v. Alabama* (1932) An attorney must be provided to a poor defendant facing the death penalty.

■ **fundamental fairness** A legal doctrine supporting the idea that so long as a state's conduct maintains basic standards of fairness, the Constitution has not been violated.

■ **incorporation** The extension of the due process clause of the Fourteenth Amendment to make binding on state governments the rights guaranteed in the first ten amendments to the U.S. Constitution (the Bill of Rights).

Police need to conduct searches and examine people's property as part of criminal investigations. They also need to search in order to prevent crimes by people who might conceal weapons, drugs, or other illegal items at airports, borders, nightclubs, and stadiums. All searches must either be done with warrants or be "reasonable" under judges' interpretations of the Fourth Amendment. Have you had your clothes or property examined by police or security guards? Is every examination of property a "search" under the Fourth Amendment? Is this dog "searching" the luggage?

AP Images/Evan Vucci

the states. By the end of this period, the process of incorporation was nearly complete. Criminal justice officials at all levels—federal, state, and local—were obligated to respect the constitutional rights of suspects and defendants.

■ The Fourth Amendment: Protection against Unreasonable Searches and Seizures

The Fourth Amendment limits the ability of law enforcement officers to search a person or property in order to obtain evidence of criminal activity. It also limits the ability of the police to detain a person without justification (Perkins and Jamieson, 1995). When police take an individual into custody or prevent an individual from leaving a location, such detentions are considered to be "seizures" under the Fourth Amendment. As we shall examine in greater detail in Chapter 6, the Fourth Amendment does not prevent the police from conducting searches or making arrests; it merely protects people's privacy by barring "unreasonable" searches and arrests. It is up to the Supreme Court to define the situations in which a search or seizure is reasonable or unreasonable.

The justices also face challenges in defining such words as *searches* and *seizures*. For example, in 2005 the Supreme Court ruled that no issues concerning Fourth Amendment rights arose when a K-9 officer had a trained police dog sniff the exterior of a vehicle that was stopped for a traffic violation. The dog indicated to the officer that the car's trunk contained marijuana, and that discovery led to a criminal conviction. However, unlike a *search,* for which officers must have proper justifications, the use of the dog did not require any justification, because the dog's scent-based examination of the vehicle's exterior did not invade the driver's right to privacy (*Illinois v. Caballes*). Because different Supreme Court justices do not always agree on the Constitution's meaning, the definitions of these words and the rules for police searches can change as the makeup of the Court changes.

The wording of the Fourth Amendment makes clear that the authors of the Bill of Rights did not believe that law enforcement officials should have the power to pursue criminals at all costs. The Fourth Amendment's protections apply to suspects as well as law-abiding citizens. Police officers are supposed to follow the rules for obtaining search warrants, and they are not permitted to conduct unreasonable searches even when trying to catch dangerous criminals. As we shall see in Chapter 6, improper searches that lead to the discovery of criminal evidence can lead judges to bar police and prosecutors from using that evidence to prove the suspect's guilt. Thus, police officers need to be knowledgeable about the rules for searches and seizures and to follow those rules carefully in conducting criminal investigations.

Police face challenges in attempting to respect Fourth Amendment rights while also actively seeking to prevent crimes and catch offenders. Officers may be tempted to go too far in investigating crimes without an adequate basis for suspicion and thereby violate Fourth Amendment rights. The discussion of racial profiling in Chapter 1 illustrates one aspect of the risk that officers will, by conducting stops and searches without an appropriate basis, use their authority in ways that collide with the Fourth Amendment (Rudovsky, 2007).

■ The Fifth Amendment: Protection against Self-Incrimination and Double Jeopardy

The Fifth Amendment clearly states some key rights related to the investigation and prosecution of criminal suspects. For example, the protection against compelled self-incrimination seeks to prevent authorities from pressuring people into acting as witnesses against themselves. Presumably, this right also helps protect against torture or other rough treatment when police officers question criminal suspects. In Chapter 6, we shall discuss the Fifth Amendment rules that guide officers in questioning criminal suspects. Improper questioning can affect whether evidence obtained through that questioning can be used in court. For example, in the case of astronaut Lisa Nowak that opened this chapter, a Florida court determined that she was questioned improperly by police and therefore her statements made to the police could not be used against her in court (*State v. Nowak*, 2008).

Because of the right against double jeopardy imposed by the Fifth Amendment, a person charged with a criminal act may be subjected to only one prosecution or punishment for that offense in the same jurisdiction. The purpose of the right is to prevent the government from trying someone over and over again until a conviction is obtained. Generally, a person acquitted of a crime at trial cannot be tried again for that same crime. As interpreted by the Supreme Court, however, the right against double jeopardy does not prevent a person from facing two trials or receiving two sanctions from the government for the same criminal acts (Henning, 1993; Hickey, 1995; Lear, 1995). Because a single criminal act may violate both state and federal laws, for example, a person may be tried in both courts. Thus, when Los Angeles police officers were acquitted of assault charges in a state court after they had been videotaped beating motorist Rodney King, they were convicted in a federal court for violating King's civil rights. The Supreme Court further refined the meaning of double jeopardy in 1996 by ruling that prosecutors could employ both property forfeiture and criminal charges against someone who grew marijuana at his home. The Court did not see this as double jeopardy, because the property forfeiture was not a "punishment" (*United States v. Ursery*). In yet another case, the Supreme Court permitted Alabama to pursue kidnapping and murder charges against a man who had already been convicted for the same murder in Georgia, because the victim was kidnapped in one state and killed in the other (*Heath v. Alabama*, 1985). Thus, the protection against double jeopardy does not prevent two different trials based on the same criminal acts as long as the trials are in different jurisdictions and based on different charges, a violation of the Georgia murder law being a different charge than a violation of the Alabama murder law even when both charges concern the same killing.

One of the rights in the Fifth Amendment, the entitlement to indictment by a grand jury before being prosecuted for a serious crime, applies only in federal courts. This is one of the few rights in the Bill of Rights that the Supreme Court never applied to the states. A **grand jury** is a body of citizens drawn from the community to hear evidence from the prosecutor in order to determine whether there is a sufficient basis to move forward with a criminal prosecution (Washburn, 2008). Some states use grand juries by their own choice; they are not required to do so by the Fifth Amendment. Other states simply permit prosecutors to file charges directly against criminal suspects.

■ **grand jury** Body of citizens drawn from the community to hear evidence presented by the prosecutor in order to decide whether enough evidence exists to file charges against a defendant.

■ The Sixth Amendment: The Right to Counsel and a Fair Trial

The Sixth Amendment includes several provisions dealing with fairness in a criminal prosecution. These include the rights to counsel, to a speedy and public trial, and to an impartial jury.

The Right to Counsel   Although the right to counsel in a criminal case had prevailed in federal courts since 1938, not until the Supreme Court's landmark decision in *Gideon v. Wainwright* (1963) was this requirement made binding on the states. Many states already provided attorneys, but in this ruling the Court forced all of the states to meet Sixth Amendment standards. In previous cases, the Court, applying the doctrine of fundamental fairness, had ruled that states must provide poor people with counsel only when this was required by the special circumstances of the case. A defense attorney had to be provided when conviction could lead to the death penalty, when the issues were complex, or when a poor defendant was either very young or mentally handicapped.

■ *Gideon v. Wainwright* (1963) Indigent defendants have a right to counsel when charged with serious crimes for which they could face 6 or more months of incarceration.

Although the *Gideon* ruling directly affected only states that did not provide poor defendants with attorneys, it set in motion a series of cases that affected all the states by deciding how the right to counsel would be applied in various situations. Beginning in 1963, the Court extended the right to counsel to preliminary hearings, initial appeals, postindictment identification lineups, and children in juvenile court proceedings. Later, however, the Burger Court declared that attorneys need not be provided for discretionary appeals or for trials in which the only punishment is a fine (*Ross v. Moffitt*, 1974; *Scott v. Illinois*, 1979). Even in recent years, the Supreme Court has continued to clarify the extent of the right to counsel (McCall, McCall, and Smith, 2008b). In 2008, for example, the Court determined that counsel must be provided to indigent defendants at an early stage in the process during the initial appearance before a judge at a preliminary hearing (*Rothgery v. Gillespie*). The Court also declared that trial judges can require that mentally ill defendants be represented by defense attorneys, even when those defendants wish to represent themselves in court (*Indiana v. Edwards*, 2008).

Because defense attorneys are an important component of a legal process that uses an adversarial system to pursue the truth and protect rights, defendants' conversations and communications with attorneys are secret. Prosecutors are not entitled to know what defendants tell their attorneys, even if they admit their guilt. As part of the effort to combat terrorism, however, in the aftermath of 9/11 the federal government proposed that it should gain the authority to monitor conversations between jailed defendants and their attorneys. Others believe that defense attorneys should have an obligation to reveal information that might help to solve any crime. Do you think such proposals improperly weaken Sixth Amendment rights? See "What Americans Think" to compare your view with those of people surveyed in North Carolina on the topic.

The Right to a Speedy and Public Trial   The nation's founders were aware that, in other countries, accused people might often languish in jail awaiting trial and often were convicted in secret proceedings. At the time of the American Revolution, the right to a speedy and public trial was recognized in the common law and included in the constitutions of six of the original states. But the word *speedy* is vague, and the Supreme Court has recognized that the interest of quick processes may conflict with other interests of society (such as the need to collect evidence) as well as with interests of the defendant (such as the need for time to prepare a defense).

The right to a public trial is intended to protect the accused against arbitrary conviction. The Constitution assumes that judges and juries will act in accordance with the law if they must listen to evidence and announce their decisions in public. Again, the Supreme Court has recognized that there may be cases in which the need for a public trial must be balanced against other concerns. For example, the right to a public trial does not mean that *all* members of the public have the right to attend the trial. The courtroom's seating capacity and the interests of a fair trial, free of outbursts from the audience, may be considered. In hearings on sex crimes when the victim or witness is a minor, courts have barred the public in order to spare the child embarrassment. In some states, trials have become even more public than the authors of the Sixth Amendment ever imagined, because court proceedings are televised—some are even carried on national cable systems through COURT-TV.

The Right to an Impartial Jury   The right to a jury trial was well established in the American colonies at the time of the Revolution. In their charters, most of the colonies guaranteed trial by jury, and it was referred to in the First Continental Congress's debates in 1774, the Declaration of Independence, the

What AMERICANS Think

QUESTION: "Should lawyers be required to disclose what their clients told them in private when that information will help to solve crimes?"

Not sure:
20%

No: Lawyers should not disclose
32%

Yes: Lawyers should be required to disclose
48%

Go to http://www.cengage.com/criminaljustice/cole to compare your opinion on this issue with the opinions of other criminal justice students.

Note: Statewide poll of 600 North Carolina voters conducted in October 2005 by Research 2000.

Source: Matthew Eisley, "Nearly Half Favor Disclosure," *Raleigh News and Observer*, October 24, 2005, http://www.newsobserver.com.

constitutions of the thirteen original states, and the Sixth Amendment to the U.S. Constitution. Juries allow citizens to play a role in courts' decision making and to prevent prosecutions in cases in which there is not enough evidence. However, as discussed in "Criminal Justice: Myth and Reality," the right to trial by jury is not as widely available for criminal defendants as many Americans believe.

Several Supreme Court decisions have dealt with the composition of juries. The Court has held that the amendment requires selection procedures that create a jury pool made up of a cross section of the community. Most scholars believe that an impartial jury can best be achieved by drawing jurors at random from the broadest possible base (Levine, 1992; Vidmar and Hans, 2007). The jury is expected to represent the community, and the extent to which it does so is a central concern of jury administration (C. E. Smith, 1994).

■ The Eighth Amendment: Protection against Excessive Bail, Excessive Fines, and Cruel and Unusual Punishment

Although it is the briefest of the criminal justice amendments, the Eighth Amendment deals with the rights of defendants during the pretrial (bail) and correctional (fines, punishment) phases of the criminal justice system.

Release on Bail   The purpose of bail is to allow for the release of the accused while he or she is awaiting trial. The Eighth Amendment does not require that all defendants be released on bail, only that the amount of bail not be excessive. Many states do not allow bail for those charged with some offenses, such as murder, and there seem to be few limits on the amounts that can be required. In 1987 the Supreme Court, in *United States v. Salerno and Cafero*, upheld provisions of the Bail Reform Act of 1984 that allow federal judges to detain without bail suspects who are considered dangerous to the public.

Criminal Justice: MYTH AND REALITY

COMMON BELIEF: Because the Sixth Amendment clearly says, "In all criminal prosecutions, the accused shall enjoy the right to a speedy and public trial, by an impartial jury . . . ," all criminal defendants who decline to plead guilty and choose to go to trial are entitled to a trial by jury.

Despite the clear words of the Sixth Amendment, the U.S. Supreme Court has interpreted the constitutional right to trial by jury in a manner that limits the availability of jury trials. Although the justices did not specifically express concerns about the expense and time involved in jury trials, presumably such concerns were one unspoken aspect of their decision to limit the right to cases involving "serious" charges. In *Lewis v. United States* (1996), a majority of justices concluded that defendants charged with "petty" offenses, meaning those punishable by sentences of 6 months or less of jail time, are entitled only to a bench trial before a judge and not a jury trial under the Sixth Amendment. Ironically, someone charged with multiple petty offenses so that his total potential sentence could ultimately be many years in prison, if each offense led to a separate 6-month sentence to be served consecutively, would still not have a right to trial by jury. According to the Supreme Court, the right to trial by jury is triggered by the definition of each charge as "petty" (6 months or less) or "serious" (more than 6 months of imprisonment) rather than by the total sentence that could occur upon conviction of multiple petty offenses. A postal worker charged with 20 separate petty offenses of "obstructing the mail" for stealing 20 letters from the post office could end up with a cumulative sentence of 10 years in prison, yet have not have a right to trial by jury (C. E. Smith, 2004).

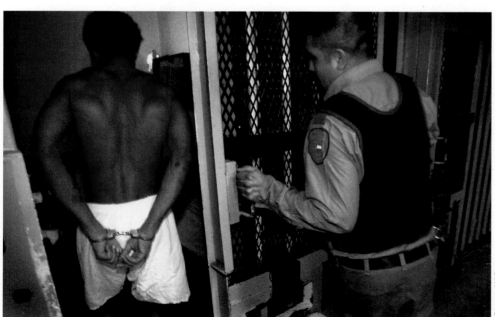

The Eighth Amendment protects offenders serving prison sentences. Under judges' interpretations of the Eighth Amendment, prisoners are entitled to food, shelter, sanitation facilities, and limited medical care. Is the maintenance of humane living conditions in prison an appropriate application of the protection against "cruel and unusual punishments"?

AP Images/LM Otero

Excessive Fines   The Supreme Court ruled in 1993 that the forfeiture of property related to a criminal case can be analyzed for possible violation of the excessive fines clause (*Austin v. United States*). In 1998 the Court declared for the first time that forfeiture constituted an impermissible excessive fine. In that case, a man failed to comply with the federal law requiring that travelers report if they are taking $10,000 or more in cash outside the country (C. E. Smith, 1999). There is no law against transporting any amount of cash. The law only concerns filing a report to the government concerning the transport of money. When one traveler at a Los Angeles airport failed to report the money detected in his suitcase by a cash-sniffing dog trained to identify people who might be transporting money for drug dealers, he was forced to forfeit all $357,000 that he carried in his luggage. Because there was no evidence that the money was obtained illegally and because the usual punishment for the offense would only be a fine of $5,000, a slim five-member majority on the Supreme Court ruled that the forfeiture of all the traveler's money constituted an excessive fine (*United States v. Bajakajian*, 1998). It remains to be seen

FIGURE 3.2
Protections of constitutional rights
The Bill of Rights and the Fourteenth Amendment protect defendants during various phases of the criminal justice process.

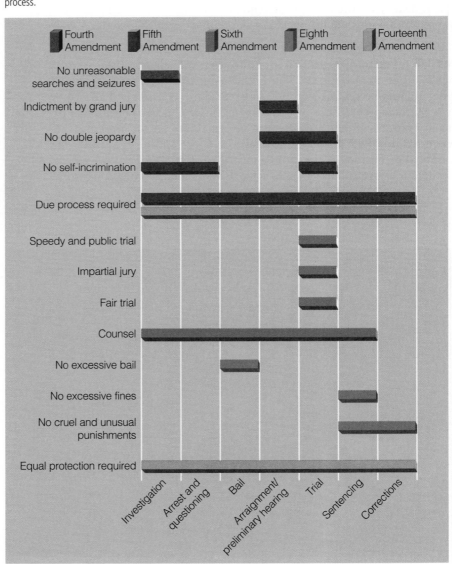

whether the Court's recent interest in violations of the excessive fines clause will limit law enforcement agencies' practices in forcing criminal defendants to forfeit cash and property.

Cruel and Unusual Punishment   The nation's founders were concerned about the barbaric punishments that had been inflicted in seventeenth- and eighteenth-century Europe, where offenders were sometimes burned alive or stoned to death—hence the ban on "cruel and unusual punishment." The Warren Court set the standard for judging issues of cruel and unusual punishment in a case dealing with a former soldier who was deprived of U.S. citizenship for deserting his post during World War II (*Trop v. Dulles,* 1958). Chief Justice Earl Warren declared that judges must use the values of contemporary society to determine whether a specific punishment is cruel and unusual.

Through the use of this test, punishments may be declared unconstitutional for being either disproportionate to the offense or comparable to a form of torture through the infliction of physical or psychological pain. In recent years, the Supreme Court has seldom regarded punishments other than the death penalty as disproportionate to any crime for which a legislature chooses to mandate it. The Court reinforced this view in 2003 by endorsing California's sentences of 25 years to life for offenders convicted of three felonies, even in a case when the third offense was merely shoplifting some children's videos from K-Mart (*Lockyer v. Andrade,* 2003).

The Court's test has been used in death penalty cases, but the justices have strongly disagreed over the values of American society on this issue. The Supreme Court's decisions in death penalty cases are extensively discussed in Chapter 9. (See also "A Question of Ethics" at the end of this chapter for a further discussion of capital punishment.)

Since the 1950s, the rights of defendants in state criminal trials have greatly expanded. The Supreme Court has incorporated most portions of the Fourth, Fifth, Sixth, and Eighth Amendments. Figure 3.2 shows the amendments that protect defendants at various stages of the criminal justice process.

CHECKPOINT

ANSWERS

6 *What is incorporation?*

6 Taking a right from the Bill of Rights and applying it against state and local officials by making it a component of the due process clause of the Fourteenth Amendment.

7 *Which Supreme Court era made the most significant expansion in the definitions of constitutional rights for criminal defendants?*

7 Warren Court era (1953–1969).

8 *What are the main criminal justice rights set forth in the Fourth, Fifth, Sixth, and Eighth Amendments?*

8 Fourth: the protection against unreasonable searches and seizures; Fifth: the right against compelled self-incrimination and against double jeopardy (also the right to due process); Sixth: the right to counsel, to a speedy and fair trial, to a jury trial (also to confrontation and compulsory process); Eighth: the right to protection against excessive bail, excessive fines, and cruel and unusual punishments.

Constitutional Rights and Criminal Justice Professionals

As a result of the Supreme Court's decisions, people in all states now enjoy the same minimum protections against illegal searches, improper police interrogations, and other violations of constitutional rights. In response to these decisions, police, prosecution, and correctional officers have had to develop policies and guidelines to inform criminal justice professionals about what they are and are not permitted to do while investigating, prosecuting, and punishing criminal offenders.

If you were a police officer, prosecutor, or correctional officer, how would you feel about the Supreme Court's decisions defining rights that benefit criminal defendants? Although you would recognize the desirability of upholding constitutional rights in order to maintain democratic freedoms, you might also feel frustrated when court decisions limited your ability to conduct searches and question suspects. In addition, you would be concerned about whether the Supreme Court's decisions give you clear guidance about what to do. You would not want to make an unintentional error that prevents an offender from being properly convicted of a crime.

Many people question whether the Supreme Court has struck the proper balance between the protection of constitutional rights and the ability of criminal justice officials to punish offenders (C. E. Smith and Baugh, 2000). Some people believe that criminal defendants' rights are too broad. Others believe that the Supreme Court favors law enforcement at the expense of constitutional rights. These debates are likely to continue even though the Supreme Court has moved consistently in one direction during the past two decades. In cases affecting criminal justice, the contemporary Supreme Court endorses the actions of police officers and prosecutors in more than two-thirds of cases (C. E. Smith, 2003).

In 2005, President George W. Bush appointed two new justices to the Supreme Court, Chief Justice John Roberts and Justice Samuel Alito. In their first terms on the Court, their decisions consistently reinforced the Court's support for broader police authority and more narrowly defined rights for criminal suspects and defendants (McCall, McCall, and Smith, 2008b). Observers predict that President Barack Obama, when given opportunities to appoint new justices, will likely select very different appointees who are more supportive of broad rights. In 2009, President Obama nominated Judge Sonia Sotomayor to replace the retiring Justice David Souter. After her nomination was confirmed by the U.S. Senate, observers watched closely to see if she endorsed broad protections for criminal suspects and defendants, as Souter did in many cases. The Court's oldest justices, Justices John Paul Stevens and Ruth Bader Ginsburg, were, respectively, 89 and 76 years old in 2009. If these justices also retire during the Obama presidency, their replacements will likely be equally liberal; therefore, the balance between liberals and conservatives on the Supreme Court would remain unchanged. If, however, a conservative justice retires in the near future, such as Justice Anthony Kennedy or Justice Antonin Scalia, who were both 73 in 2009, a new Obama appointee could tip the Court's composition in a new direction and change trends in decisions about criminal justice.

A QUESTION OF ETHICS: WRITING ASSIGNMENT

In executions by lethal injection, states typically use a combination of three drugs that, if administered improperly, merely paralyze the condemned convict without actually rendering him or her unconscious. This leads to the individual experiencing excruciating pain as a burning sensation in the veins and a slow process of suffocation. A medical study on postexecution examinations reported that as many as 43 percent of offenders executed in six states may have been subject to an excruciating death because of improperly administered or inadequate dosages of the drugs. Because of the infliction of needless pain, many states ban the use of these same drugs when veterinarians euthanize animals (put them "to sleep"). When the U.S. Supreme Court examined the issue, a majority of justices concluded that opponents of lethal injection had not proven that this method of execution violates the Eighth Amendment's prohibition on cruel and unusual punishments (*Baze v. Rees*, 2008). Thus, lethal injection remains as the primary method of execution.

As a result of the issues surrounding lethal injection, many doctors have refused to participate in executions. Indeed, the American Medical Association regards a physician's participation in an execution as a violation of doctors' ethical obligations and the oath to "do no harm." On the other hand, lethal injections are more likely to be botched if carried out by technicians and correctional officers who struggle to insert needles into proper veins and administer the drugs with appropriate dosages and timing.

WRITING ASSIGNMENT

If you were a doctor employed by a state's department of corrections, how would you respond if you were asked to participate in an execution? Is it unethical for trained healers to kill condemned offenders in a procedure that is legal under the U.S. Constitution? On the other hand, if trained medical personnel do not participate in executions, will the pain and injuries for condemned prisoners be even worse? Write a memo to the department of corrections as if you were a doctor responding to a request to administer the lethal injections for an execution.

Sources: Diane Jennings, "Lethal Injection Challenges Mount," *Dallas Morning News*, April 30, 2006, http://www.dallasnews.com; Nathan Thornburgh, "Legal Objection," *Time*, March 6, 2006, http://www.time.com.

Summary

Recognize the bases and sources of American criminal law

▶ Criminal law focuses on the prosecution and punishment of people who violate specific laws enacted by legislatures.

▶ Criminal law is divided into two parts: substantive law, which defines offenses and penalties, and procedural law, which defines individuals' rights and the processes that criminal justice officials must follow in handling cases.

Understand how substantive criminal law defines a crime and the legal responsibility of the accused

▶ Substantive criminal law involves seven important elements that must exist and be demonstrated by the prosecution in order to obtain a conviction: legality, *actus reus*, causation, harm, concurrence, *mens rea*, and punishment.

▶ The *mens rea* element, concerning intent or state of mind, can vary with different offenses, such as various degrees of murder.

▶ The values and goals of criminal law can differ according to a society's values, as illustrated by those countries that follow elements of religion-based Islamic law.

▶ Criminal law provides opportunities to present several defenses based on lack of criminal intent: entrapment, self-defense, necessity, duress (coercion), immaturity, mistake of fact, intoxication, and insanity.

▶ Standards for the insanity defense vary by jurisdiction, with various state and federal courts using several different tests: *M'Naghten* Rule, Irresistible Impulse Test, *Durham* Rule, *Model Penal Code*, and Comprehensive Crime Control Act.

Understand how procedural criminal law defines the rights of the accused and the processes for dealing with a case

▶ The provisions of the Bill of Rights were not made applicable to state and local officials by the U.S. Supreme Court until the mid-twentieth century, when the Court incorporated most of the Bill of Rights' specific provisions into the due process clause of the Fourteenth Amendment.

▶ The Fourth Amendment's prohibition on unreasonable searches and seizures seeks to impose limits on police authority to intrude on people's expectations of privacy with respect to their bodies, homes, and property.

▶ The Fifth Amendment provides protections against compelled self-incrimination and double jeopardy.

▶ The Sixth Amendment includes the right to counsel, the right to a speedy and public trial, and the right to an impartial jury.

▶ The Eighth Amendment includes protections against excessive bail, excessive fines, and cruel and unusual punishments. Supreme Court justices often disagree about whether aspects of the death penalty violate the prohibition on cruel and unusual punishments.

Recognize the U.S. Supreme Court's role in interpreting the criminal justice amendments to the Constitution

▶ Changes in the Supreme Court's composition may affect decisions concerning specific legal issues. Such changes occur when presidents replace retiring justices with appointees, who may interpret constitutional rights in new ways.

Questions for Review

1. What are the two major divisions within criminal law?

2. What are the seven principles of criminal law theory?

3. What is meant by *mens rea*? Give examples of defenses that may be used by defendants in which they deny that *mens rea* existed when the crime was committed.

4. What is meant by the incorporation of rights into the Fourteenth Amendment of the U.S. Constitution?

5. What rights are contained in the Fourth Amendment?

6. What rights are contained in the Fifth Amendment?

7. What rights are contained in the Sixth Amendment?

8. What rights are contained in the Eighth Amendment?

Key Terms and Cases

Bill of Rights (p. 81)
civil law (p. 69)
double jeopardy (p. 82)
entrapment (p. 75)
fundamental fairness (p. 85)
grand jury (p. 87)

inchoate offense (p. 71)
incorporation (p. 85)
legal responsibility (p. 68)
mens rea (p. 71)
procedural criminal law (p. 69)
self-incrimination (p. 82)

substantive criminal law (p. 69)
Barron v. Baltimore (1833) (p. 84)
Gideon v. Wainwright (1963) (p. 87)
Powell v. Alabama (1932) (p. 85)

My Affair with Heroin

Written by Chuck Terry

SELDOM DO WE HAVE the opportunity to view the criminal justice system through the eyes of a person who has experienced it. Chuck Terry is most unusual in that, after more than 20 years of heroin addiction, 12 of them incarcerated, he has "beaten the habit" and gained a Ph.D. and is now a university professor in criminal justice. The vivid chronicles of his journey, which conclude each part of this book, provide rare insights into the workings of "the system." His reflections should be thoughtfully considered by all students of criminal justice.

Tight handcuffs. Loud cellblocks. Racial tension. No women, kids, or pets. Violence. Road dogs (close friends). Iron bars. Concrete beds. Hate. Guard towers. Getting booked. Count times. Food lines. Parole boards. Judges. Degradation. District attorneys. Death. Cops. A.M.'s and P.M.'s—year in and year out. Monotony. Withdrawals. Preliminary hearings. The need to show no pain—ever. Release dates. Parole officers. Alienation. Hopelessness. Determinate sentencing. A guard on the way out of prison: "See you when you get back, Terry. Guys like you are job security for guys like me." A lot to deal with for a white, California-raised kid from middle-class suburbia. A lot for anybody.

From my first arrest in 1970 to my last discharge from parole in 1992, I became intimately familiar with all the components of the criminal justice system. Over the course of this twenty-plus-year "career," which included spending over twelve years inside state (prisons) and county (jails) "correctional" facilities for drug-related crimes, I experienced almost everything the system has to offer—except the death penalty or a sentence of life without possibility of parole.

These experiences have taught me that the way "criminals" are dealt with in America is anything but "fair" or "just." Rather, their fate is determined by who they are and how they are seen by system actors such as judges and prosecutors and by the general public. It is important to note that this "seeing" varies dramatically and is relative to an ever-changing social, economic, political, and historical context.

Crime today is politicized and a main focus of media attention. The "threat" posed by "criminals" is used to generate fear and legitimate spending of millions on more police, more prisons, and more mechanisms of social control. The reasons for this are complex and controversial. But it hasn't always been like this.

I was a kid in the 1960s, when the civil rights movement, protests against the Vietnam War, and an antiestablishment-oriented "counterculture" were in full swing. Instead of bombarding the public with visions of low-level street crime, the nightly news sent us images from the war, urban riots, and people getting beaten by police for participating in nonviolent sit-ins. Governmental policies and social inequality rather than addicts and "juvenile predators" were seen as "criminal" by a significant portion of the population. Rules and rule enforcers (like racial segregation policies, drug laws, government officials) were the targets of attention. In defiance of "the way things were," we grew our hair, spoke out against social norms, and got high.

My own drug use began in 1967 and escalated over time. Initially, I used whatever was available: alcohol, marijuana, reds, yellows, whites, LSD. In 1969 I used heroin for the first time.

Now, how could any sane person try heroin? Doesn't everyone know it's a "bad" thing to do? Though it was scary, I rationalized it as being OK. After all, I knew several people who used it. They seemed to be fine. Everything I had been told about all the other drugs I used had proved to be a lie; we were told that if we smoked pot we'd lie down on train tracks, and if we took LSD we'd jump out of tall buildings and lose our minds. So one night at a party I gave it a shot. Or, I should say, I stuck my arm out and a friend gave me a shot.

Turning points. Crossroads. Where do we go from here? The first thing I thought when I felt the effects of heroin was, "I can't believe I've been doing anything in life other than trying to use this stuff all the time." For the next twenty-plus years I did just that. Heroin made me feel "normal," like I fit, belonged, was not out of place. It is a powerfully enticing drug: Many first-time users instantly fall in love with it. I was one of those people. It provided me with a clear purpose in life and, though I didn't know it at first, a future that would involve spending a lot of time inside the various worlds of the criminal justice system.

Once I began using illegal drugs, I started seeing anyone affiliated with any type of legal authority as a potential enemy—especially police, whose job (in my mind) was to "catch" or "arrest" me. This distrustful outlook became magnified once I began using heroin. After all, heroin users are seen as "real" criminals.

The people in my life changed as my heroin habit took hold. Where I used to have friends who were about my age and white, now I frequently hung out with older people who were often a different color, brown or black. Their images remain. A 40-year-old hooker fixing (injecting narcotics), sores all over her body, pushing scabs on her arms out of the way with the needle in a desperate attempt to find a vein. A 65-year-old, jaundiced-eyed black man welcoming me into his home to share the joys of addiction. Trips into ethnic neighborhoods to buy dope where few, if any, white people were seen. Nodding. Throwing up. People getting arrested, disappearing, overdosing, dying. As my social circle changed, so did the way I saw the world and myself. Without realizing it I was "becoming" what society calls "criminal."

My love of heroin took me down a road that included many unplanned pit stops. I was investigated, arrested, booked more times than I care to recall. I appeared more than once at a preliminary hearing, still going through withdrawal—looking sickly and feeling weak as I interacted with bailiffs, public defenders, judges, and other prisoners. The road took me through cramped cell blocks, courtroom holding tanks, and jailhouse chow halls—to places where I witnessed alcoholics suffering from the DTs, epileptics and diabetics going into convulsions from a lack of medication, people jammed into cells with bullets still in their bodies, and more. From four different prison commitments came years behind walls, isolated from the world. My love of heroin took me down a path where I was either on the run, locked up, or on probation or parole for more than twenty years. The pieces that conclude each part of this book are scenes from that journey.

Police

4

AT 7:03 A.M. ON A SATURDAY MORNING, a Pittsburgh 911 operator received a call from Mrs. Poplawski on Fairfield Street. She wanted police officers to remove her 22-year-old son, Richard, from her home. She had just quarrelled with him after his dog had urinated on the floor. The operator heard Mrs. Poplawski call out to her son, "Are you moving or what? Or the police gotta come?" Then Mrs. Poplawski spoke to the operator again, "I'm requesting that he gets out. He came in last night when I was gone. . . . He stays, he comes and goes, but I want him out" (Silver, 2009).

"Does he have any weapons or anything?" the operator asked.

"Yes" came the answer, and then there was a long pause before the additional comment: "They're all legal."

"OK, but he's not threatening you with anything?" inquired the operator in response.

Mrs. Poplawski did not address the question. She simply said, "Look, I'm just waking up from a sleep. I want him gone."

"OK, we'll send 'em over, OK?," said the operator.

"Sounds good," said Mrs. Poplawski as she hung up the phone (Silver, 2009).

The 911 operator typed "no weapons" into the information that officers would receive from a dispatcher who directed them to respond to the call. The message was intended to convey that no weapons were involved in the domestic dispute. However, observers look back at that fateful morning of April 4, 2009, and wonder whether the officers might have misunderstood the message to mean that there were no weapons in the home at all (Silver, 2009). Might they have responded differently if they had known otherwise?

Police officers must react quickly to calls based on the information available to them. This information is often unavoidably incomplete. At the scene of an incident, officers must evaluate the situation and make fast decisions in order to protect public safety, maintain order, and enforce criminal laws. As Officers Paul J. Scuillo II and Stephen J. Mayhle were welcomed through the front door by Mrs. Poplawski, her son Richard opened fire on them with a rifle from 6 feet away in the living room. Mrs. Poplawski screamed, "What the hell have you done?" as she ran from the room (Schmitz and Balingit, 2009).

Officer Scuillo died from multiple gunshot wounds just inside the front door. A wounded Officer Mayhle fell to the ground outside the front stoop. Richard stepped

Opposite page: © REUTERS/JC Schisler–Tribune-Review/Landov

LEARNING OBJECTIVES

- Understand how policing evolved in the United States

- Recognize the main types of law enforcement agencies

- Identify why people become police officers and how they learn their job

- Understand the elements of the police officer's "working personality"

- Comprehend the functions of the police

- Understand the organization of the police

- Analyze influences on police policy and styles of policing

outside and executed the officer with additional shots to the head. Within minutes, other officers arrived. Richard, who was wearing a bulletproof vest and armed with multiple weapons, shot at them from the house. He fatally wounded Officer Eric Kelly, an off-duty officer who had come to the scene and radioed for assistance, and he also wounded Officer Timothy McManaway as he attempted to drag the seriously injured Officer Kelly to safety. Soon, dozens of officers surrounded the house. Richard continued to fire at them, maintaining a standoff for several hours. Eventually, after a police sniper on a rooftop shot Richard in the leg, he surrendered and was taken to the hospital. The next day he was formally charged with three counts of murder as he lay in his hospital bed (Schmitz and Balingit, 2009).

The Pittsburgh police officers who died that day did not predict the lethal danger that they would face in responding to the domestic dispute call. They had no information suggesting that a heavily armed man, who was consumed with conspiracy theories about the government's desire to take his guns away, was laying in wait and planning to shoot them. Of course, as veteran police officers, they were constantly aware of the possibility that their jobs might someday place them in extreme danger.

Indeed, they undoubtedly knew that only two weeks earlier a parolee in Oakland, California, had shot and killed four police officers, a tragic story that had received significant news coverage throughout the nation (T. Collins and Leff, 2009). Despite such knowledge, officers place themselves in potential danger every day. Officers Sciullo and Mayhle could not know the extent of the danger that awaited them, but after the shooting had started many of their fellow officers bravely risked their lives when they dodged gunfire in order to transport Officers Kelly and McManaway to the hospital (L. Thomas, 2009).

Who would choose a career that might entail life-threatening danger? What attracts people to a public service career that brings them into situations of conflict? Further, how do the police, on an individual as well as an organizational level, carry out their duties in the face of such risks?

In this chapter, we examine several aspects of policing. A brief history of the police precedes discussion of the types of law enforcement agencies in the United States. We also examine the recruitment and training of contemporary police officers, the police subculture, and the functions, organization, and policies of policing.

The Development of Police in the United States

Law and order is not a new concept; it has been a subject of debate since the first police force was formed in London in 1829. Looking back even farther, we find that the Magna Carta of 1215 placed limits on constables and bailiffs. Reading between the lines of that historic document reveals that the modern problems of police abuse, maintenance of order, and the rule of law also existed in thirteenth-century England. Further, current remedies—recruiting better-qualified people to serve as police, stiffening the penalties for official misconduct, creating a civilian board of control—were suggested even then to ensure that order was kept in accordance with the rule of law.

■ The English Roots of the American Police

The roots of American policing lie in the English legal tradition. Three major aspects of American policing evolved from that tradition: (1) limited authority, (2) local control, and (3) fragmented organization. Like the British police, but unlike police in continental Europe, the police in the United States have limited authority; their powers and duties are specifically defined by law. England, like the United States, has no national police force; instead, 43 regional authorities are headed by elected commissioners who appoint the chief constable. Above these local authorities is the home secretary of the national government, which provides funding and can intervene in cases of police corruption, mismanagement, and discipline. In the United States, policing is fragmented: There are many types of agencies—constable, county sheriff, city police, FBI—each with its own special jurisdiction and responsibilities.

Systems for protecting citizens and property existed before the thirteenth century. The **frankpledge** system required that groups of ten families, called *tithings*, agree to uphold the law, keep order, and bring violators to a court. By custom, every male person above the age of 12 was part of the system. When a man became aware that a crime had occurred, he was obliged to raise a "hue and cry" and to join others in his tithing to track down the offender. The tithing was fined if members did not perform their duties.

Over time, England developed a system in which individuals were chosen within each community to take charge of catching criminals. The Statute of Winchester, enacted in 1285, set up a parish constable system. Members of the community were still required to pursue criminals, just as they had been under the frankpledge system, but now a constable supervised those efforts. The constable was a man chosen from the parish to serve without pay as its law enforcement officer for one year. The constable had the power to call the entire community into action if a serious disturbance arose. Watchmen, who were appointed to help the constable, spent most of their time patrolling the town at night to ensure that "all's well" and to enforce the criminal law. They were also responsible for lighting street lamps and putting out fires.

Not until the eighteenth century did an organized police force evolve in England. With the growth of commerce and industry, cities expanded while farming declined as the main source of employment and the focus of community life. In the larger cities, these changes produced social disorder.

In the mid-eighteenth century, novelist Henry Fielding and his brother, Sir John Fielding, led efforts to improve law enforcement in London. They wrote newspaper articles to inform the public about crime, and they published flyers describing known offenders. After Henry Fielding became a magistrate in 1748, he organized a small group of "thief-takers" to pursue and arrest lawbreakers. The government was so impressed with Fielding's Bow Street Amateur Volunteer Force (known as the Bow Street Runners) that it paid the participants and attempted to form similar groups in other parts of London.

After Henry Fielding's death in 1754, these efforts declined. As time went by, however, many saw that the government needed to assert itself in enforcing laws and maintaining order. London, with its unruly mobs, had become an especially dangerous place. In the early 1800s, several attempts were made to create a centralized

■ **frankpledge** A system in old English law in which members of a *tithing* (a group of ten families) pledged to be responsible for keeping order and bringing violators of the law to court.

police force for London. While people saw the need for social order, some feared that a police force would threaten the freedom of citizens and lead to tyranny. Finally, in 1829 Sir Robert Peel, home secretary in the British Cabinet, pushed Parliament to pass the Metropolitan Police Act, which created the London police force.

This agency was organized like a military unit, with a thousand-man force commanded by two magistrates, later called "commissioners." The officers were called "bobbies" after Sir Robert Peel. In the British system, cabinet members who oversee government departments are chosen from the elected members of Parliament. Thus, because Peel supervised it, the first police force was under the control of democratically elected officials.

Under Peel's direction, the police had a four-part mandate:

1. To prevent crime without using repressive force and to avoid having to call on the military to control riots and other disturbances
2. To maintain public order by nonviolent means, using force only as a last resort to obtain compliance
3. To reduce conflict between the police and the public
4. To show efficiency through the absence of crime and disorder rather than through visible police actions (Manning, 1977:82)

In effect, this meant keeping a low profile while maintaining order. Because of fears that a national force would threaten civil liberties, political leaders made every effort to focus police activities at the local level. These concerns were transported to the United States.

■ Policing in the United States

As with other institutions and areas of public policy, the development of formal police organizations reflected the social conditions, politics, and problems of different eras of American history. The United States drew from England's experience but implemented policing in its own way.

The Colonial Era and the Early Republic   As settlers arrived in North America from Europe and eventually moved westward from the East Coast, they relied on each other for assistance and protection in all matters, from weather disasters to conflicts with Native Americans. They also needed to protect themselves and their neighbors from those who might cause harm through theft or other crimes.

Along the East Coast, the colonists drew from their experiences in England by adopting the English offices of constable, sheriff, and night watchman as the first positions with law enforcement responsibilities. Boston's watch system began before 1640. Such systems served to warn of dangers ranging from fires to crime. Each male citizen was required to be a member of the watch, but paid watchmen could be hired as replacements. Although the watch system originally operated at night, cities eventually began to have daytime watches, too. Over time, cities began to hire paid, uniformed watchmen to deal with public danger and crime (S. Walker, 1999).

In the South, slave patrols developed as organized forces to prevent slave revolts and catch runaway slaves. These patrols had full power to break into the homes of slaves who were suspected of keeping arms, to physically punish those who did not obey their orders, and to arrest runaways and return them to their masters. Under the watch system in northern cities, watchmen reacted to calls for help. By contrast, the mobility of slave patrols positioned them to operate in a proactive manner by looking for African Americans whom whites feared would disrupt society, especially the economic system of slavery. Samuel Walker (1999) describes the slave patrols as a distinctly American form of law enforcement and the first modern police force in the United States.

Beginning in the 1830s and continuing periodically for several decades, many American cities experienced violent riots. Ethnic conflicts, election controversies, hostility toward nonslave blacks and abolitionists, mob actions against banks during economic declines, and violence in settling questions of morality, such as the use of alcohol—all these factors contributed to fears that a stable democracy would not survive. The militia was called in to quell large-scale conflicts, because constables and watchmen proved ineffective in restoring order (Uchida, 2005). These disorders, along with perceptions of increased problems with serious crimes, helped push city governments to consider the creation of professional police forces.

American policing is often described in terms of three historical periods: the political era (1840–1920), the professional model era (1920–1970), and the community policing era (1970–present) (Kelling and Moore, 1988). This description has been criticized because it applies only to the urban areas of the Northeast and does not take into account the very different development of the police in rural areas of the South and West. Still, it remains a useful framework for exploring the organization of the police, the focus of police work, and the strategies employed by police (H. Williams and Murphy, 1990).

The Political Era: 1840–1920   The period from 1840 to 1920 is called the political era because of the close ties that were formed between the police and local political leaders at that time. In many cities, the police seemed to work for the mayor's political party rather than for the citizens. This relationship served both groups in that the political "machines" recruited and maintained the police while the police helped the machine leaders get out the vote for favored candidates. Ranks in the police force were often for sale to the highest bidder, and many officers took payoffs for not enforcing laws on drinking, gambling, and prostitution (S. Walker, 1999:26).

In the United States, as in England, the growth of cities led to pressures to modernize law enforcement. Around 1840 the large cities began to create police forces. In 1845 New York City established the first full-time, paid police force. Boston and Philadelphia were the first to add a daytime police force to supplement the night watchmen; other cities—Chicago, Cincinnati, New Orleans—quickly followed.

By 1850, most major cities had created police departments organized on the English model. A chief, appointed by the mayor and city council, headed each department. The city was divided into precincts, with full-time, paid patrolmen assigned to each. Early police forces sought to prevent crimes and keep order through the use of foot patrols. The officer on the beat dealt with crime, disorder, and other problems as they arose.

In addition to foot patrols, the police performed service functions, such as caring for derelicts, operating soup kitchens, regulating public health, and handling medical and social emergencies. In cities across the country, the police provided beds and food for homeless people. In station houses, overnight "lodgers" might sleep on the floor or sometimes in clean bunkrooms (Monkkonen, 1981:127). Because they were the only government agency that had close contact with life on the streets of the city, the police became general public servants as well as crime control officers. These close links with the community and service to it earned them the citizens' support (Monkkonen, 1992:554).

Police developed differently in the South because of the existence of slavery and the agrarian nature of that region. As noted previously, the first organized police agencies with full-time officers developed in cities with large numbers of slaves (Charleston, New Orleans, Richmond, and Savannah), where white owners feared slave uprisings (Rousey, 1984:41).

During the political era, the officer on a neighborhood beat dealt with crime and disorder as it arose. Police also performed various social services, such as providing beds and food for the homeless. Should today's police officers devote more time to providing social services for the public?

Culver Pictures

Westward expansion in the United States produced conditions quite different from those in either the urban East or the agricultural South. The frontier was settled before order could be established. Thus, those who wanted to maintain law and order often had to take matters into their own hands by forming vigilante groups.

One of the first official positions created in rural areas was that of sheriff. Although the sheriff had duties similar to those of the "shire reeves" of seventeenth-century England, the American sheriff was elected and had broad powers to enforce the law. As elected officers, sheriffs had close ties to local politics. They also depended on the men of the community for assistance. This is how the *posse comitatus* (Latin for "power of the county"), borrowed from fifteenth-century Europe, came into being. Local men above age 15 were required to respond to the sheriff's call for assistance, forming a body known as a posse.

After the Civil War, the federal government appointed U.S. marshals to help enforce the law in the western territories. Some of the best-known folk heroes of American policing were U.S. Marshals Wyatt Earp, Bat Masterson, and Wild Bill Hickok, who tried to bring law and order to the "Wild West" (Calhoun, 1990). While some marshals did extensive law enforcement work, most had mainly judicial duties, such as keeping order in the courtroom and holding prisoners for trial.

During the early twentieth century, much of the United States became more urban. This change blurred some of the regional differences that had helped define policing in the past. In addition, growing criticism of the influence of politics on the police led to efforts to reform the nature and organization of the police. Specifically, reformers sought to make police more professional and to reduce their ties to local politics.

The Professional Model Era: 1920–1970   American policing was greatly influenced by the Progressive movement. The Progressives were mainly upper middle-class, educated Americans with two goals: more-efficient government and more government services to assist the less fortunate. A related goal was to reduce the influence of party politics and patronage (favoritism in handing out jobs) on government. The Progressives saw a need for professional law enforcement officials who would use modern technology to benefit society as a whole, not just local politicians.

The key to the Progressives' concept of professional law enforcement is found in their slogan, "The police have to get out of politics, and politics has to get out of the police." August Vollmer, the chief of police of Berkeley, California, from 1909 to 1932, was a leading advocate of professional policing. He initiated the use of motorcycle units, handwriting analysis, and fingerprinting. With other police reformers, such as Leonhard Fuld, Raymond Fosdick, Bruce Smith, and O. W. Wilson, he urged that the police be made into a professional force, a nonpartisan agency of government committed to public service. This model of professional policing has six elements:

1. The force should stay out of politics.
2. Members should be well trained, well disciplined, and tightly organized.
3. Laws should be enforced equally.
4. The force should use new technology.
5. Personnel procedures should be based on merit.
6. The main task of the police should be fighting crime.

During the professional model era, the police saw themselves as crime fighters. Yet many inner-city residents saw them as a well-armed, occupying force that did not support efforts to advance civil rights and racial equality. If you looked out your window and saw these heavily armed Oklahoma City SWAT team members in your neighborhood, would you have any concerns about how your neighbors might perceive the dress, demeanor, and actions of these officers? Might you have a different reaction if you lived in your city's poorest neighborhood?

AP Images/The Oklahoman, Michael Dounes

Refocusing attention on crime control and away from maintaining order probably did more than anything else to change the nature of American policing. The narrow focus on crime fighting broke many of the ties that the police had formed with the communities they served. By the end of World War I, police departments had greatly reduced their involvement in social services. Instead, for the most part, cops became crime fighters.

O. W. Wilson, a student of Vollmer, was another leading advocate of professionalism. He earned a degree in criminology at the University of California in 1924 and became the chief of police of Wichita, Kansas, in 1928. By reorganizing the department and fighting police corruption, he came to national attention. He promoted the use of motorized patrols, efficient radio communication, and rapid response. He believed that one-officer patrols were the best way to use personnel and that the two-way radio, which allowed for supervision by commanders, made officers more efficient (Reiss, 1992:51). He rotated assignments so that officers on patrol would not become too familiar with people in the community (and thus prone to corruption). In 1960, Wilson became the superintendent of the Chicago Police Department with a mandate to end corruption there.

The new emphasis on professionalism had also spurred the formation of the International Association of Chiefs of Police (IACP) in 1902 and the Fraternal Order of Police (FOP) in 1915. Both organizations promoted training standards, the use of new technologies, and a code of ethics.

By the 1930s the police were using new technologies and methods to combat serious crimes. Officers became more effective against crimes such as murder, rape, and robbery—an important factor in gaining citizen support. By contrast, efforts to control victimless offenses and to maintain order often aroused citizen opposition. "The clean, bureaucratic model of policing put forth by the reformers could be sustained only if the scope of police responsibility was narrowed to 'crime fighting'" (M. Moore and Kelling, 1983:55).

In the 1960s, the civil rights and antiwar movements, urban riots, and rising crime rates challenged many of the assumptions of the professional model. In their attempts to maintain order during public demonstrations, the police in many cities seemed to be concerned mainly with maintaining the status quo. Thus, police officers found themselves enforcing laws that tended to discriminate against African Americans and the poor. The number of low-income racial minorities living in the inner cities was growing, and the professional style kept the police isolated from the communities they served. In the eyes of many inner-city residents, the police were an occupying army keeping them at the bottom of society, not public servants helping all citizens.

Although the police continued to portray themselves as crime fighters, citizens became aware that the police often were not effective in this role. Crime rates rose for many offenses, and the police could not change the perception that the quality of urban life was declining.

The Community Policing Era: 1970–Present

Beginning in the 1970s, calls were heard for a move away from the crime-fighting focus and toward greater emphasis on keeping order and providing services to the community. Research studies revealed the complex nature of police work and the extent to which day-to-day practices deviated from the professional ideal. The research also questioned the effectiveness of the police in catching and deterring criminals.

Community policing encourages personal contact between officers and citizens, especially interactions that facilitate citizens' cooperation with and support for the police. Is your own interest in criminal justice affected by your view of police officers and interactions with them?

© Syracuse Newspapers/Frank Ordo–ez/The Image Works

Three findings of this research are especially noteworthy:

1. Increasing the number of patrol officers in a neighborhood had little effect on the crime rate.

2. Rapid response to calls for service did not greatly increase the arrest rate.

3. Improving the percentage of crimes solved is difficult.

Such findings undermined acceptance of the professional crime-fighter model (M. Moore, 1992:99). Critics argued that the professional style isolated the police from the community and reduced their knowledge about the neighborhoods they served, especially when police patrolled in cars. Use of the patrol car prevented personal contacts with citizens. Instead, it was argued, police should get out of their cars and spend more time meeting and helping residents. Reformers hoped that closer contact with citizens would not only permit the police to help them in new ways but would also make citizens feel safer, knowing that the police were available and interested in their problems.

In a provocative article titled "Broken Windows: The Police and Neighborhood Safety," James Q. Wilson and George L. Kelling argued that policing should work more on "little problems" such as maintaining order, providing services to those in need, and adopting strategies to reduce the fear of crime (1982:29). They based their approach on three assumptions:

1. Neighborhood disorder creates fear. Areas with street people, youth gangs, prostitution, and drunks are high-crime areas.

2. Just as broken windows are a signal that nobody cares and can lead to worse vandalism, untended disorderly behavior is a signal that the community does not care. This also leads to worse disorder and crime.

3. If the police are to deal with disorder and thus reduce fear and crime, they must rely on citizens for assistance.

Advocates of the community policing approach urge greater use of foot patrols so that officers will become known to citizens, who in turn will cooperate with the police. They believe that through attention to little problems, the police may not only reduce disorder and fear but also improve public attitudes toward policing. When citizens respond positively to police efforts, the police will have "improved bases of community and political support, which in turn can be exploited to gain further cooperation from citizens in a wide variety of activities" (Kelling, 1985:299).

Closely related to the community policing concept is problem-oriented policing. Herman Goldstein, the originator of this approach, argued that instead of focusing on crime and disorder, the police should identify the underlying causes of problems such as noisy teenagers, battered spouses, and abandoned buildings used as drug houses. In doing so they could reduce disorder and fear of crime (Goldstein, 1979:236). Closer contacts between the police and the community might then reduce the hostility that has developed between officers and residents in many urban neighborhoods (Sparrow, Moore, and Kennedy, 1990).

In *Fixing Broken Windows*, written in response to the Wilson and Kelling article, George L. Kelling and Catherine Coles (1996) call for strategies to restore order and reduce crime in public spaces in U.S. communities. In Baltimore, New York, San Francisco, and Seattle, police are paying greater attention to "quality-of-life crimes" by arresting subway fare-beaters, rousting loiterers and panhandlers from parks, and aggressively dealing with those who are obstructing sidewalks, harassing others, and soliciting. By handling these "little crimes," the police not only help restore order but also often prevent worse crimes. In New York, for example, searching fare-beaters often yielded weapons, questioning a street vendor selling hot merchandise led to a fence specializing in stolen weapons, and arresting a person for urinating in a park resulted in the discovery of a cache of weapons.

Although reformers argue for a greater focus on order maintenance and service, they do not call for an end to the crime-fighting role. Instead, they want a shift of emphasis. The police should pay more attention to community needs and seek to understand the problems underlying crime, disorder, and incivility. These proposals have been adopted by police executives in many cities and by influential organizations such as the Police Foundation and the Police Executive Research Forum. The federal government created the Office of Community Oriented Policing Services, more commonly known as the "COPS Office," which provides grants for hiring new officers and developing community policing programs. Between 1995 and 2003, the COPS Office supplied nearly $7 billion to 13,000 state and local agencies to hire 118,000 new officers and implement training and other programs (Uchida, 2005). In 2009, the Obama administration provided $1 billion additional dollars to the COPS Office to fund the hiring of police officers around the nation as part of the stimulus program to revive the national economy (N. A. Lewis, 2009).

The call for a new focus for the police has not gone unchallenged (Reichers and Roberg, 1990:105). In the 1980s, for example, critics questioned whether the professional model really ever isolated police from community residents (S. Walker, 1984:88). Carl Klockars doubted that the police would give higher priority to maintaining order and wondered whether Americans wanted their police to be something other than crime fighters (1985:300). Others wondered whether the opportunity to receive federal money and hire new officers led departments to use the language of community policing in portraying their activities even though they never fully adopted the new methods.

Homeland Security: The Next Era of Policing?

After 9/11, homeland security and antiterrorist efforts became two of the highest priorities for the U.S. government. As we shall see in Chapter 5, this event shifted the federal government's funding priorities for law enforcement and led to a reorganization of federal agencies. According to Craig Uchida, "Priorities for training, equipment, strategies, and funding have transformed policing once again—this time focusing on homeland security" (2005:38). Instead of focusing funds on community policing, federal money moved toward supplying emergency preparedness training, hazardous materials gear, equipment for detecting bombs and other weapons of mass destruction, and the collection of intelligence data. In public comments, a few police officials have referred to "terrorist-oriented policing," but how such a concept or emphasis would be defined at the local level is not clear (Kerlikowske, 2004). Some observers believe that a shift toward homeland security may appeal to traditionalists in law enforcement who prefer to see themselves as heroically catching "bad guys" rather than solving problems within neighborhoods.

Community policing will not disappear. Many police executives remain committed to its purposes and principles. However, federal agencies have clearly made homeland security their top priority, and federal funding for local police departments has shifted in kind. Further development of a focus on homeland security throughout policing may depend on whether American cities suffer additional terror attacks.

CHECKPOINT

ANSWERS

1 What three main features of American policing were inherited from England?

1 Limited authority, local control, organizational fragmentation.

2 What are the historical periods of American policing?

2 Colonial era and early republic; political era, professional model era, community policing era.

3 What were the major recommendations of the Progressive reformers?

3 The police should be removed from politics, police should be well trained, the law should be enforced equally, technology should be used, merit should be the basis of personnel procedures, the crime-fighting role should be prominent.

Law Enforcement Agencies

As discussed in Chapter 1, the United States has a federal system of government with separate national and state structures, each with authority over certain functions. Police agencies at the national, state, county, and municipal levels are responsible for carrying out four functions: (1) enforcing the law, (2) maintaining order, (3) preventing crime, and (4) providing services to the community. They employ a total of more than one million sworn and unsworn personnel. Nearly 800,000 full-time sworn officers serve in state and local agencies, and an additional 88,000 sworn officers operate in federal agencies. Consider your own assumptions about the responsibilities of these agencies as you read "Criminal Justice: Myth and Reality."

Police agencies include the following (BJS, 2008e; Reaves, 2006):

- 12,766 municipal police departments
- 3,070 sheriff's departments
- 49 state police departments (all states except Hawaii)
- 135 Native American tribal police agencies
- 30 federal agencies that employ 100 or more full-time officers authorized to carry firearms and make arrests

In addition, there are 1,481 special police agencies (jurisdictions limited to transit systems, parks, schools, and so on) as well as additional federal agencies with fewer than 100 officers each.

This list shows both the fragmentation and the local orientation of American police. Seventy percent of expenditures for policing occur at the local level. Each level of the system has different responsibilities, either for different kinds of crimes, such as the federal authority over counterfeiting, or for different geographic areas, such as state police authority over major highways. Local units generally exercise the broadest authority.

■ Federal Agencies

Federal law enforcement agencies are part of the executive branch of the national government. They investigate a specific set of crimes defined by Congress. Recent federal efforts against drug trafficking, organized crime, insider stock trading, and terrorism have attracted attention to these agencies, even though they handle relatively few crimes and employ only 88,496 full-time officers authorized to make arrests.

The FBI   The Federal Bureau of Investigation (FBI) is an investigative agency within the U.S. Department of Justice (DOJ). It has the power to investigate all federal crimes not placed under the jurisdiction of other agencies. Established as the Bureau of Investigation in 1908, it came to national prominence under J. Edgar Hoover, its director from 1924 until his death in 1972. Hoover made major changes in the bureau (renamed the Federal Bureau of Investigation in 1935) to increase its professionalism. He sought to remove political factors from the selection of agents, established the national

Criminal Justice: MYTH AND REALITY

COMMON BELIEF: The FBI is the most important law enforcement agency in the United States.

As we shall see in this chapter and in Chapter 5, the FBI handles many important responsibilities. However, they pursue only a limited number of crimes. As a federal agency, they are authorized to investigate federal crimes, including bank robbery, kidnapping, and a variety of terrorism and espionage matters. These matters are undoubtedly quite important. But whether or not the FBI is the "most important" agency is debatable, especially if one considers the impact of law enforcement on the daily lives of Americans. The vast majority of crimes are investigated by local police departments and county sheriff's departments. Officers from these departments also make the vast majority of arrests. When people experience medical emergencies, hear a window break during the night, or seek resolution of a dispute between neighbors, they call the local police. These are the kinds of police-related matters that most frequently affect the daily lives of Americans. Although local police officers do not receive the same attention from the news media as do special agents of the FBI, there are strong reasons to argue that local police are the most important law enforcement officials in terms of their daily impact on the quality of life and safety in neighborhoods and communities.

FBI evidence technicians helped local police gather evidence when the remains of four dead babies were found at a home in Ocean City, Maryland, in July 2007. As the FBI increasingly devotes attention to counterterrorism efforts, will local police departments be able to investigate complex crimes effectively despite less assistance from FBI experts?

© Shawn Thew/epa/CORBIS

fingerprint filing system, and oversaw the development of the Uniform Crime Reporting System. Although Hoover has been criticized for many things, such as FBI spying on antiwar and civil rights activists during the 1960s, his role in improving police work and the FBI's effectiveness is widely recognized.

Within the United States, the FBI's 12,346 special agents work out of 56 field offices and 400 additional satellite offices known as "resident agencies." In 2002, the FBI announced a new list of priorities that describes its work (FBI, 2009a):

1. Protect the United States from terrorist attack.
2. Protect the United States against foreign intelligence operations and espionage.
3. Protect the United States against cyber-based attacks and high-technology crimes.
4. Combat public corruption at all levels.
5. Protect civil rights.
6. Combat transnational and national criminal organizations and enterprises.
7. Combat major white-collar crime.
8. Combat significant violent crime.
9. Support federal, state, county, municipal, and international partners.
10. Upgrade technology to successfully perform the FBI's mission.

As indicated by this list, the FBI has significant responsibilities for fighting terrorism and espionage against the United States. In addition, it continues its traditional mission of enforcing federal laws, such as those aimed at organized crime, corporate crime, corrupt government officials, and violators of civil rights laws. The bureau also provides valuable assistance to state and local law enforcement through its crime laboratory, training programs, and databases of fingerprints, stolen vehicles, and missing persons. With the growth of cyber crime, the FBI has become a leader in using technology to counteract crime as well as to prevent terrorism and espionage. The antiterrorist activities of the FBI will be discussed in greater detail in Chapter 5. In addition, Chapter 14 contains additional coverage of the FBI's role in fighting cyber crime.

Specialization in Federal Law Enforcement   The FBI is the federal government's general law enforcement agency. By contrast, other federal agencies enforce specific laws. Elsewhere within the Department of Justice is the semiautonomous Drug Enforcement Administration (DEA), which investigates the importation and sale of controlled drugs. The Internal Revenue Service (IRS) pursues violations of tax laws, and the Bureau of Alcohol, Tobacco, Firearms, and Explosives (ATF) deals with alcohol, tobacco, gun control, and bombings.

Some other agencies of the executive branch, such as the National Parks Service, have police powers related to their specific duties. The park officers need to enforce law and maintain order to protect people and property at national parks. In addition, few people realize that some law enforcement officers investigate crimes while working in agencies with responsibility for policy issues that are not traditionally viewed as connected to the justice system. For example, special agents in the U.S. Department of Education investigate student loan fraud, and similar officers in the U.S. Department of Health and Human Services investigate fraud in Medicare and Medicaid programs.

State Agencies

Throughout the United States, the American reluctance to centralize police power has generally kept state police forces from replacing local ones. Each state, except Hawaii, has a full-service police agency that patrols state highways or provides complete law enforcement services in rural areas. All state forces regulate traffic on main highways, and two-thirds of the states have also given them general police powers. In only about a dozen populous states—such as Massachusetts, Michigan, New Jersey, New York, and Pennsylvania—can these forces perform law enforcement tasks across the state. For the most part, they operate only in areas where no other form of police protection exists or where local officers ask for their help. In many states, the crime lab is run by the state police as a means of assisting local law enforcement agencies.

By contrast, Hawaii's Department of Public Safety has a "Sheriff's Division" with only limited responsibilities for transporting prisoners and protecting state facilities and the Honolulu airport. Thus, Hawaii is not considered to have a state police agency that is comparable to those in other states.

County Agencies

Sheriffs are found in almost every one of the 3,100 U.S. counties except in Alaska and Connecticut. Sheriffs' departments employ 175,018 full-time sworn officers. They are responsible for policing rural areas, but over time, especially in the Northeast, many of their criminal justice functions have been assumed by the state or local police. In parts of the South and West, however, the sheriff's department is a well-organized force. In more than 40 states, sheriffs are elected and hold the position of chief law enforcement officer in the county. Even when well organized, the sheriff's office may lack jurisdiction over cities and towns. In these situations, the sheriff and his or her deputies patrol unincorporated parts of the county or small towns that do not have police forces of their own.

In addition to performing law enforcement tasks, the sheriff often serves as an officer of the court; sheriffs may operate jails, serve court orders, and provide the bailiffs who maintain order in courtrooms. In many counties, law enforcement mixes with politics because sheriffs appoint their political supporters as deputies and bailiffs. In other places, such as Los Angeles County and Oregon's Multnomah County, the sheriff's department is staffed by professionals who are hired through competitive civil service processes.

Native American Tribal Police

Through treaties with the United States, Native American tribes are separate, sovereign nations and have a significant degree of legal autonomy. They have the power to enforce tribal criminal laws against everyone on their lands, including non-Native Americans (Mentzer, 1996). Traditionally, Native American reservations have been policed either by federal officers of the Bureau of Indian Affairs (BIA) or by their own tribal police. The Bureau of Justice Statistics identified 171 tribal law enforcement agencies with a total of 2,303 full-time sworn officers (Hickman, 2003). An additional 320 full-time sworn officers of the BIA provide law enforcement services on other reservations (Reaves, 2006).

Municipal Agencies

The police departments of cities and towns have general law enforcement authority. City police forces range in size from nearly 36,000 full-time sworn officers in the New York City Police Department to only one sworn officer in each of 561 small towns. Sworn personnel are officers with the power to make arrests. There are 446,974 full-time sworn municipal police officers nationwide. Nearly three-quarters of municipal police departments employ fewer than 25 sworn officers. The five largest police departments—New York City, Chicago, Los Angeles, Philadelphia, and Houston—together employ nearly 16 percent of all local police officers (Hickman and Reaves, 2006).

In a metropolitan area composed of a central city and many suburbs, policing is usually divided among agencies at all levels of government, giving rise to conflicts between jurisdictions that may interfere with efficient use of police resources. The city and each suburb buy their own equipment and deploy their officers without coordinating with those of nearby jurisdictions. In some areas with large populations, agreements have been made to enhance cooperation among jurisdictions.

CHECKPOINT

4 *What is the jurisdiction of federal law enforcement agencies?*

4 Enforcing the laws of the federal government.

5 *What are the functions of most state police agencies?*

5 All state police agencies have traffic law enforcement responsibilities, and in two-thirds of the states they exercise general police powers, especially in rural areas.

6 *Besides law enforcement, what functions do sheriffs perform?*

6 Operate jails, move prisoners, and provide court bailiffs.

Who Are the Police?

As they walk or drive on patrol, police officers never know what they might find around the next corner. What if they encounter an armed fugitive who surprises them with gunfire? Who would want to face such risks? What motivates someone to choose such a career? These questions are important because they help determine which people will be granted the authority to carry firearms and make discretionary decisions about arrests, searches, and even ending the lives of other human beings by pulling the trigger during the stressful, fast-moving events that confront police officers.

According to research, the biggest attraction of a career in policing is the variety of tasks that fill an officer's day. Instead of sitting in an office doing repetitive tasks, police officers are out on the streets doing a variety of activities that may change from day to day. Other factors that attract people to a career in policing include the opportunity to take on important responsibilities, an interest in serving the public, the possibility of adventure, and the prospect of having job security (Slater and Reiser, 1988).

Because policing is such an important occupation, society would obviously benefit from recruiting its most thoughtful, athletic, and dedicated citizens as police officers. Happily, many such individuals are attracted to this field. Yet many other people who would make fine law enforcement officers turn to other occupations because policing is such a difficult job. The modest salaries, significant job stress, and moments of danger involved in police work can deter some individuals from choosing this public service occupation. As you read "Careers in Criminal Justice," consider whether you would want to be a police officer.

The police are no longer exclusively made up of white men. Women and minorities now represent an increasing portion of the force, especially in urban areas. Are women or minority group members visible among the police officers that you see where you live?

© John Boykin/PhotoEdit

■ Recruitment

How can departments recruit well-rounded, dedicated public servants who will represent the diversity of contemporary America? Moreover, how can law enforcement agencies make sure that each individual is qualified to handle the wide array of responsibilities facing police officers? When considering applications, all agencies refer to a list of requirements regarding education, physical abilities, and background. Some federal agencies, including the FBI and Drug Enforcement Administration, seek additional skills, such as expertise in computers and accounting or fluency in a foreign

CAREERS IN CRIMINAL JUSTICE

Police Officer

MARY PETERSON, POLICE DEPARTMENT
GLENVIEW, ILLINOIS

POLICE OFFICERS conduct preventive patrol in an assigned beat area and provide the initial response to requests for police service. Officers investigate complaints, enforce state laws and local ordinances, prepare necessary reports, participate in the prosecution of criminal cases, and provide many public service activities. These responsibilities require a wide range of abilities, such as effective communication skills for interviewing witnesses and victims and physical skills for taking uncooperative arrestees into custody. Officers must be able to analyze situations quickly and accurately. They must also be able to function well during emergency situations.

Officer Peterson earned both undergraduate and graduate degrees in English. She worked in different jobs before securing city government employment working in the office of a police chief. From her position, she received a close and accurate view of the working lives of police officers. She found herself attracted to the variety of responsibilities involved in this public service career, as well as to the salary and pension benefits, including the possibility of early retirement. After undergoing the rigorous selection and training processes, she found that she really enjoyed "working the street."

The biggest challenge in police work is avoiding complacency. The major task of a genuine professional is to maintain officer survival skills learned early in training and initial experience while working in an atmosphere where those skills are not reinforced on a daily basis.

language. A typical list of basic requirements for a career in law enforcement includes the following (if you are interested in working for a particular agency, check for that agency's specific requirements):

- Be a U.S. citizen.
- Meet age requirements. The minimum age is normally 21, although some federal agencies place the minimum at 23. The maximum age for hiring in federal agencies ranges from 36 (FBI and DEA) to 39 (Border Patrol), depending on the agency.
- Have a high school diploma. Increasingly, state and local agencies require some college coursework (for instance, a four-year college degree is required for some federal agencies such as the FBI and DEA).
- Possess a valid driver's license.
- Have a healthy weight in proportion to height, body frame, and age.
- Pass a medical health examination, including a hearing test—reliance on a hearing aid can result in disqualification.
- Be in excellent physical condition. Recruits are typically required to pass a physical fitness exam administered by the agency or as part of a certification program in a police-training academy. For example, the U.S. Border Patrol requires 20 push-ups in one minute; 25 sit-ups in one minute; 30 steps-per-minute up and down a 1-foot step for 5 minutes; a 1.5-mile run in 13 minutes; a 220-yard dash in 46 seconds; and a timed obstacle course.
- Be able to lift and carry moderately heavy objects (45 to 60 pounds).
- Have vision correctable to 20/20 and uncorrected vision of at least 20/200; some agencies require normal color vision (the DEA, for example).
- Pass a background investigation, including a clean arrest record and credit check. Prior felony or serious misdemeanor convictions can disqualify an applicant, as can a misdemeanor conviction for domestic violence.

- Pass a polygraph examination (lie detector test).

- Take a urinalysis drug test. Often, recruits are also required to respond to written or interview questions about any prior use of illegal drugs.

- Take a written test to demonstrate literacy, basic math skills, and reasoning ability. Knowledge of the law and other subjects is also sometimes tested.

In addition, agencies increasingly require recruits to undergo psychological evaluations, because each officer will ultimately make important discretionary decisions, including those that determine life and death in stressful situations (Langworthy, Hughes, and Sanders, 1995:26).

Candidates for state and local enforcement positions must often obtain a certification for their state's law enforcement training agency, such as the Michigan Commission on Law Enforcement Standards. Many small towns and counties cannot afford to send their officer-applicants to a police academy program for this certification. Thus, they advertise job vacancies with the requirement that applicants have already obtained certification by attending a police academy, such as the 12- to 22-week non-degree classes offered through the criminal justice programs at many colleges. Paying to attend police academy programs imposes an extra expense on many individuals who seek a career in law enforcement. However, some of these programs can fulfill some of the requirements for associate or bachelor's degrees in criminal justice, depending on the college offering the program. Larger cities are more likely either to pay for their selected candidates to attend a police academy or to run their own academies to train their new hires. State police agencies also typically run their own training academies for new hires. The U.S. Marine Corps Base at Quantico, Virginia, is home to the training academies for new special agents in the DEA (16-week program) and the FBI (17-week program). New agents in the U.S. Secret Service, the ATF, and other federal law enforcement agencies attend 11-week training academies at the primary Federal Law Enforcement Training Center (FLETC) in Glynco, Georgia. These agencies subsequently provide new agents with additional specialized training, sometimes at the other FLETC training centers in Artesia, New Mexico; Charleston, South Carolina; and Cheltenham, Maryland.

Which agencies are the most attractive to people seeking careers in law enforcement? One factor in attracting recruits is the compensation that departments offer. In 2006, the average starting salary in local police departments was $38,569 per year; the average maximum salary for regular patrol officers was $53,811, a level that typically takes seven years to attain (BJS, 2008e: Table 1.69.2006). In the larger cities, with a population of 50,000 or more, salaries tend to be higher. Further, because supervisory personnel make higher salaries, many officers seek promotions to detective, sergeant, captain, and other ranks. The average annual salary for city police chiefs nationwide was $70,041; chiefs in cities with populations of 250,000 or more averaged over $100,000 per year (BJS, 2008e: Table 1.71.2006). Poor, rural counties may have a more difficult time competing for applicants. Such departments may recruit outstanding officers who want to live in a particular rural community, but more-attractive compensation packages in other agencies may also lure rural officers away.

Federal agencies, which offer higher salaries and better benefits than do many local departments, often attract large numbers of applicants. These positions also require higher levels of education and experience than do many local law enforcement agencies. Starting salaries for Border Patrol Agents are at least $33,000 per year (GS-5 level: four-year degree or one year of relevant professional experience) or at least $38,000 (GS-7 level: one year of graduate school or one year of law enforcement experience). FBI special agents begin at $43,441 (GS-10: four-year degree and special skill or law enforcement experience).

As indicated by these examples, federal agencies typically look for college graduates. By contrast, only 1 percent of local police departments require a four-year college degree, whereas 8 percent of departments require a two-year degree, and an additional 6 percent expect some college coursework (Hickman and Reaves, 2003). The number of departments requiring college classes for officers is steadily growing.

TABLE 4.1	Educational Requirements and Starting Salaries in Law Enforcement Careers (Selected Examples)		
Position	Agency	Education Required	Starting Salary
Local			
Police Officer	New York City Police Dept.	2 years college or 2 years military service	$43,062
Police Officer	Alamogorado, NM, Police Dept.	HS diploma and state law enforcement certification	$36,619
Deputy Sheriff	St. Mary's County, MD, Sheriff's Dept.	HS diploma	$40,976
Deputy Sheriff	Oneida Country, NY, Sheriff's Dept.	HS diploma	$34,638
State			
Trooper	Tennessee Highway Patrol	HS diploma	$32,676
Highway Patrol Officer	California Highway Patrol	HS diploma	$65,185
Federal (minimum salaries listed; higher salaries come with more education and skills)			
Special Agent	Drug Enforcement Administration	4-year college degree or substantial work experience	$49,746
Special Agent	U.S. Secret Service	4-year college degree or substantial work experience	$43,200
Special Agent	U.S. Department of Education	4-year college degree or substantial work experience	$45,510

Source: Websites of individual law enforcement agencies.

Even those departments that require only a high school diploma often prefer candidates with college coursework and encourage their officers to seek additional education. The idea that college-educated officers would make more effective officers helped to spur the creation of the federal Police Corps program that provided training and financial incentives for college graduates to work as local police officers (Gest, 2001). Although some researchers found that a college education makes little difference for police performance, other scholars have concluded that it reduces disciplinary problems and citizens' complaints while it improves report writing and other aspects of performance (Krimmel, 1996; Lersch and Kunzman, 2001). See Table 4.1 for examples of educational requirements and starting salaries for a variety of law enforcement positions.

■ The Changing Profile of the Police

For most of the nation's history, almost all police officers were white men. Today, women and minorities represent a growing percentage of police departments in many areas. The Equal Employment Opportunity Act of 1972 bars state and local governments from discriminating in their hiring practices. Pressured by state and federal agencies as well as by lawsuits, most city police forces have mounted campaigns to recruit more minority and female officers (Martin, 1991). Since the 1970s the percentage of minority group members and women working as police has doubled. More than 22 percent of officers nationwide belong to minority groups (see Figure 4.1). The percentage is even larger—38 percent—in the police departments of cities with populations greater than 500,000 (Hickman and Reaves, 2006).

Minority Police Officers Before the 1970s many police departments did not hire nonwhites. As this practice declined, the makeup of police departments changed, especially in large cities. A study of the nation's 62 local police departments serving a population of 250,000 or more found that from 1990 to 2000 the percentage of African American officers rose to 20 percent of the force, Hispanics rose to 14 percent, and Asian/Pacific Islander/Native Americans to 3.2 percent (Reaves and Hickman, 2002). There was an additional 7 percent increase in minority representation from 2002 to 2003. The fact that minority officers constitute 38 percent of these departments represents a dramatic change in staff composition over the past two decades (Hickman and Reaves, 2006).

As population and political power shift toward minorities in some U.S. cities, the makeup of their police forces reflects this change. Today, three-quarters of the people living in Detroit are African American; about 63 percent of the city's police

FIGURE 4.1

The changing profile of the American police officer

Today about one in ten officers is female and one in five belongs to a racial or ethnic minority.

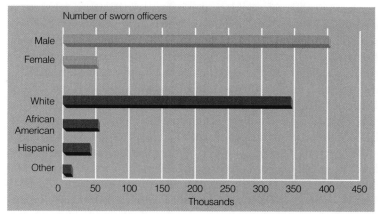

Source: Matthew J. Hickman and Brian A. Reaves, *Local Police Departments,* 2003 (Washington, DC: Bureau of Justice Statistics, U.S. Government Printing Office, 2006), 7.

officers are as well. In El Paso and San Antonio, Texas, which have large Hispanic populations, 72 percent and 42 percent of their police departments are Hispanic, respectively. The extent to which the police reflect the racial composition of a city is believed to affect police–community relations and thus the quality of law enforcement. A survey of Detroit residents found that African Americans held more favorable attitudes toward the police than did whites. As researchers note, "In Detroit, the people who perform the police function are not alien to African Americans; instead they represent an indigenous force" (Frank et al., 1996:332).

Women on the Force   Women have been police officers since 1905, when Lola Baldwin became an officer in Portland, Oregon. Prior to that time, many cities had "police matrons" to assist in handling women and children in jails but they did not have the power to arrest or engage in investigative and patrol activities (Horne, 2006). After Baldwin became the trailblazing first officer, the number of women officers remained small for most of the twentieth century because of the belief that policing was "men's work." This attitude changed as the result of federal and state laws against employment discrimination as well as court decisions enforcing those laws. Court decisions opened up police work for women by prohibiting job assignments by gender; changing minimum height, weight, and physical fitness requirements; and insisting that departments develop job classification and promotion criteria that were nondiscriminatory (*Blake v. Los Angeles,* 1979; *Griggs v. Duke Power Company,* 1971).

The percentage of female officers rose from 1.5 percent of sworn officers in 1970 to about 11 percent in 2003 (Hickman and Reaves, 2006). Interestingly, the larger the department, the higher the proportion of women as sworn officers. In cities of more than one million inhabitants, women make up 17 percent of officers, but in cities with fewer than 10,000 residents, women make up only 6 percent of officers, on average (Hickman and Reaves, 2006). In large police agencies, though, women hold less than 10 percent of the supervisory positions, and women hold only 7 percent of the top command spots (rank of captain or higher) (Horne, 2006).

Many male officers were upset by the entry of women into what they viewed as a male world. They complained that if their patrol partner was a woman, they could not be sure of her ability to provide necessary physical help in times of danger. The challenges for female officers from minority groups may be even more difficult if they perceive others as doubting their qualifications and ability because of their race as well as their gender (Dodge and Pogrebin, 2001).

Although some male police officers may still question whether women can handle dangerous situations and physical confrontations, most policewomen have easily met the expectations of their superiors. Studies done by the Police Foundation and other researchers have found that, in general, male and female officers perform in similar ways. Alissa Worden's research found few differences in the ways male and female officers viewed "their role, their clientele, or their departments" (Worden, 1993:203). Research has also found that most citizens have positive things to say about the work of policewomen (Bloch and Anderson, 1974; Grennan, 1987; Sichel, 1978; Worden, 1993). Some researchers believe that women have generally superior performance in avoiding excessive use of force and in interviewing crime victims, especially in cases of sexual assault and domestic violence (Prussel and Lonsway, 2001). Rape victims sometimes specifically request to be interviewed by a female officer, so gender diversity on a police force may be valuable in investigating specific types of crimes or dealing with certain kinds of victims and witnesses (Jordan, 2002). Despite these findings, women still have trouble breaking into police work. Cultural expectations of women often conflict with ideas about the proper behavior of officers.

According to Susan Martin, the statistics on women in policing provide both "good news and bad news . . . because the steady numerical and proportional gains [are counterbalanced] by the concentrat[ion] of women at the bottom of the police hierarchy" (Martin, 2005:352). In a few cities, such as Atlanta, Portland, Boston, and Detroit, a small number of women have risen to the top ranks of police departments. Elsewhere, employment discrimination lawsuits have helped open promotional opportunities for women. In many other departments, however, few women have gained supervisory jobs. Thus, male administrators are usually the ones who must identify and combat any remaining barriers to the recruitment, retention, and promotion of female officers (Lord and Friday, 2003; S. Walker and Turner, 1992).

◼ Training

The performance of the police is not based solely on the types of people recruited; it is also shaped by their training. As mentioned previously, aspiring officers may have to pay for their own police academy training if they are not hired by departments that pay for or provide the training. Police academy training courses range from two-week sessions that stress the handling of weapons to academic four-month programs followed by fieldwork. Recruits hear lectures on social relations, receive foreign-language training, and learn emergency medical treatment.

Formal training is needed to gain an understanding of legal rules, weapons use, and other aspects of the job. However, the police officer's job also demands social skills that cannot be learned from a lecture or a book. Much of the most important training of police officers takes place during a probationary period when new officers work with and learn from experienced ones. When new officers finish their classroom training and arrive for their first day of patrol duty, experienced officers may say, "Now, I want you to forget all that stuff you learned at the academy. You really learn your job on the streets." Many departments require newcomers to ride with an experienced training officer for a certain number of weeks or months before they can patrol on their own.

◼ **socialization** The process by which the rules, symbols, and values of a group or subculture are learned by its members.

The process of **socialization**—in which members learn the symbols, beliefs, and values of a group or subculture—includes learning the informal rather than the rule-book ways of law enforcement. New officers must learn how to look "productive," how to take shortcuts in filling out forms, how to keep themselves safe in dangerous situations, how to analyze conflicts so as to maintain order, and a host of other bits of wisdom, norms, and folklore that define the subculture of a particular department. Recruits learn that loyalty to other officers, esprit de corps, and respect for police authority are highly valued.

In police work, the success of the group depends on the cooperation of its members. All patrol officers are under direct supervision, and their performance is measured by their contribution to the group's work. Besides supervisors, the officers' colleagues also evaluate and influence them. Officers within a department may develop strong, shared views on the best way to "handle" various situations. How officers use their personal skills and judgment can mean the difference between defusing a conflict and making it worse so that it endangers citizens and other officers. In tackling their "impossible mandate," new recruits must learn the ways of the world from the other officers, who depend on them and on whom they depend.

CHECKPOINT

ANSWERS

7 What are the main requirements for becoming a police officer?

7 High school diploma, good physical condition, absence of a criminal record.

8 How has the profile of American police officers changed?

8 Better educated; more female and minority officers.

9 Where does socialization to police work take place?

9 On the job.

The Police Subculture

A **subculture** is made up of the symbols, beliefs, values, and attitudes shared by members of a subgroup within the larger society. The subculture of the police helps define the "cop's world" and each officer's role in it. Like the subculture of any occupational group that sees itself as distinct, police develop shared values that affect their view of human behavior and their role in society. As we just saw, the recruit learns the norms and values of the police subculture through a process of socialization. This begins at the training academy but really takes hold on the job through interactions with experienced officers. The characteristics of a subculture are not static, though; they change as new members join the group and as the surrounding environment changes. For example, the composition of the police has changed dramatically during the past 30 years in terms of race, gender, and education. We should thus expect these "new officers" to bring different attitudes and cultural values to the police subculture (S. Walker, 1999:332).

There are four key issues in our understanding of the police subculture: the concept of the "working personality," the role of police morality, the isolation of the police, and the stress involved in police work.

■ **subculture** The symbols, beliefs, values, and attitudes shared by members of a subgroup of the larger society.

■ The Working Personality

Social scientists have demonstrated that there is a relationship between one's occupational environment and the way one interprets events. The police subculture produces a **working personality**—that is, a set of emotional and behavioral characteristics developed by members of an occupational group in response to the work situation and environmental influences. The working personality of the police thus influences the way officers view and interpret their occupational world.

Two elements of police work define the working personality of the police: (1) the threat of danger and (2) the need to establish and maintain one's authority (Skolnick, 1966:44).

■ **working personality** A set of emotional and behavioral characteristics developed by members of an occupational group in response to the work situation and environmental influences.

New York City police had to be ready for any threat while providing security for a meeting of the city's mayor, the state's governor, and the U.S. Secretary of Homeland Security during a heightened terrorism alert in 2004. Do the danger and stress police officers face create a risk that they will overreact when citizens fail to cooperate with their requests and instructions?

© Jeff Zelevansky/Reuters/CORBIS

Danger Because they often face dangerous situations, officers are keenly aware of clues in people's behavior or in specific situations that indicate that violence and lawbreaking may be imminent. As they drive the streets, they notice things that seem amiss—a broken window, a person hiding something under a coat—anything that looks suspicious. As sworn officers, they are never off duty. People who know that they are officers will call on them for help at any time, day or night.

Throughout the socialization process, experienced officers warn recruits to be suspicious and cautious. Rookies are told about officers who were killed while writing a traffic ticket or trying to settle a family squabble (as in the case starting this chapter). The message is clear: Even minor offenses can escalate into extreme danger. Constantly pressured to recognize signs of crime and be alert to potential violence, officers may become suspicious of everyone, everywhere. Thus, police officers remain in a constant state of "high alert," always on the lookout and never letting down their guard.

Being surrounded by risks creates tension in officers' lives. They may feel constantly on edge and worried about possible attack. This concern with danger may affect their interactions with citizens and suspects. Citizens who come into contact with them may see their caution and suspicion as hostile, and such suspicion may generate hostile reactions from suspects. As a result, many on-the-street interrogations and arrests can lead to confrontations.

Authority The second aspect of the working personality is the need to exert authority. Unlike doctors, psychiatrists, lawyers, and other professionals whose clients recognize and defer to their authority, police officers must establish authority through their actions. The officer's uniform, badge, gun, and nightstick symbolize his or her position and power, but the officer's demeanor and behavior are what determine whether people will defer.

Victims are glad to see the police when they are performing their law enforcement function (Hawdon and Ryan, 2003), but the order maintenance function puts pressure on officers' authority. If they try too hard to exert authority in the face of hostile reactions, officers may cross the line and use excessive force.

Researchers have studied expressions of disrespect by officers toward members of the public and vice versa (Reisig et al., 2004). One finding indicates that police officers' own expressions of disrespect in encounters with citizens, such as name-calling and other kinds of derogatory statements, occur most often when those citizens have already shown disrespect to the officers (Mastrofski, Reisig, and McCluskey, 2002).

In sum, working personality and occupational environment are closely linked and constantly affect the daily work of the police. Procedural rules and the structure of policing are overshadowed by the need to exert authority in the face of potential danger in many contexts in which citizens are angry, disrespectful, or uncooperative.

■ Police Morality

In his field observations of Los Angeles patrol officers, Steve Herbert found a high sense of morality in the law enforcement subculture. He believes that three aspects of modern policing create dilemmas that their morality helps to overcome. These dilemmas include (1) the contradiction between the goal of preventing crime and the officers' inability to do so, (2) the fact that officers must use their discretion to "handle" situations in ways that do not strictly follow procedures, and (3) "the fact that they invariably act against at least one citizen's interest, often with recourse to coercive force that can maim or kill" (Herbert, 1996:799).

Herbert believes that justifying their actions in moral terms, such as upholding the law, protecting society, and chasing "bad guys," helps officers lessen the dilemmas of their work. Thus, they may condone use of force as necessary for ridding "evil from otherwise peaceable streets." It is the price we pay to cleanse society of the "punks," "crazies," or "terrorists." But police morality can also be applauded: Officers work long hours and are genuinely motivated to help people and improve their lives, often placing themselves at risk. Yet, to the extent that police morality crudely categorizes individuals and justifies insensitive treatment of some community members, it contributes to tension between police and citizens.

Police Isolation

Police officers' suspicion of and isolation from the public may stem in part from their belief that the public is hostile to them. Many officers feel that people look on them with suspicion, in part because they have the authority to use force to gain compliance. Public opinion polls have found that a majority of people have a high opinion of the police. However, as shown in "What Americans Think," various demographic groups can differ in their opinions regarding police officers' ethical standards.

Police officers' isolation from the public is made worse by the fact that many officers interact with the public mainly in moments of conflict, emotion, and crisis. Victims of crimes and accidents are often too hurt or distraught to thank the police. Citizens who are told to stop some activity when the police are trying to keep order may become angry at the police. Even something as minor as telling someone to turn down the volume on a stereo can make the police the "bad guy" in the eyes of people who believe that the officer's authority limits personal freedom.

Ironically, these problems may be worst in poor neighborhoods, where effective policing is needed most. There, pervasive mistrust of the police may keep citizens from reporting crimes and cooperating with investigations. Because they believe that the public is hostile to them and that the nature of their work makes the situation worse, the police tend to separate themselves from the public and to form strong in-group ties.

One result of the demands placed on the police is that officers often cannot separate their job from other aspects of their lives. From the time they receive badges and guns, they must always carry these symbols of the position—the "tools of the trade"—and be prepared to use them. Their obligation to remain vigilant even when off duty and to work at odd hours reinforces the values shared with other officers. Strengthening this bond is officers' tendency to socialize mainly with their families and other officers.

Job Stress

The work environment and police subculture contribute to the stress felt by officers. This stress can affect not only the way officers treat the citizens they encounter but also the officer's health (Anderson, Litzenberger, and Plecas, 2002). Stress also affects how officers interact with each other (Haarr and Morash, 1999). Further, scholars have found that work environment, work–family conflict, and individual coping mechanisms are the most significant predictors of stress for individual officers (Zhao, He, et al., 2003).

Police officers are always on alert, sometimes face grave danger, and feel unappreciated by a public they perceive to be hostile. That their physical and mental health suffers at times is not surprising. In fact, one study found police officers just behind coal miners as carrying out one of the most stressful occupations ("Most Stress,"

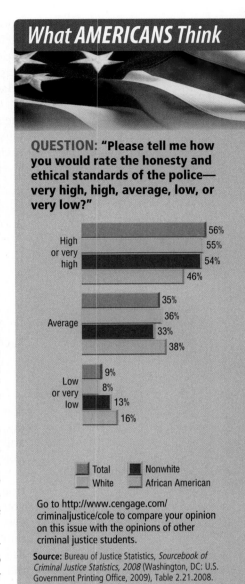

What AMERICANS Think

QUESTION: "Please tell me how you would rate the honesty and ethical standards of the police—very high, high, average, low, or very low?"

High or very high	56%
	55%
	54%
	46%
Average	35%
	36%
	33%
	38%
Low or very low	9%
	8%
	13%
	16%

Total   Nonwhite
White   African American

Go to http://www.cengage.com/criminaljustice/cole to compare your opinion on this issue with the opinions of other criminal justice students.

Source: Bureau of Justice Statistics, *Sourcebook of Criminal Justice Statistics, 2008* (Washington, DC: U.S. Government Printing Office, 2009), Table 2.21.2008.

2006). The effects of stress are compounded by the long hours many officers work, including double shifts that deprive them of sleep and make them work under conditions of severe fatigue (Vila and Kenney, 2002). The stress of police work may help explain why officer suicide poses a problem for some law enforcement agencies (Hackett and Violanti, 2003).

Only since the late 1970s have law enforcement officials become fully aware of the stress-related harms experienced by officers (Lumb and Breazeale, 2003). Psychologists have identified four kinds of stress that officers face and the factors that cause each (Cullen et al., 1985):

1. *External stress.* This is produced by real threats and dangers, such as the need to enter a dark and unfamiliar building, respond to "man with a gun" alarms, and chase lawbreakers at high speeds.

2. *Organizational stress.* This is produced by the nature of work in a paramilitary structure: constant adjustment to changing schedules, irregular work hours, and detailed rules and procedures.

3. *Personal stress.* This can be caused by an officer's racial or gender status among peers, which can create problems in getting along with other officers and adjusting to group-held values that differ from one's own. Social isolation and perceptions of bias also contribute to personal stress.

4. *Operational stress.* This reflects the total effect of dealing with thieves, derelicts, and the mentally ill; being lied to so often that all citizens become suspect; being required to face danger to protect a public that seems hostile; and always knowing that one may be held legally liable for one's actions.

Some departments now have programs centering on stress prevention, group counseling, liability insurance, and family involvement. Many states have more-liberal disability and retirement rules for police than for other public employees, because their jobs are more stressful (Goolkasian, Geddes, and DeJong, 1989).

As we have seen, police officers face special pressures that can affect their interactions with the public and even harm their physical and mental health. How would you react to the prospect of facing danger and being on the lookout for crime at every moment, even when you were not actually working? It seems understandable that police officers become a close-knit group, yet their isolation from society may decrease their understanding of other people. It may also strengthen their belief that the public is ungrateful and hostile. As a result, officers' actions toward members of the public may be gruff or even violent.

CHECKPOINT

ANSWERS

10 *What are the two key aspects of the police officer's working personality?*

10 Danger, authority.

11 *What are the four types of stress felt by the police?*

11 External stress, organizational stress, personal stress, operational stress.

Police Functions

The police are expected to maintain order, enforce the law, and prevent crime. However, they perform other tasks as well, many of them having little to do with crime and justice and more to do with community service. They direct traffic, handle accidents and illnesses, stop noisy parties, find missing persons, enforce licensing regulations, provide ambulance services, take disturbed people into protective custody, and so on. The list is long and varies from place to place. Some researchers have suggested that the police have more in common with social service agencies than with the criminal justice system.

How did the police gain such broad responsibilities? In many places, the police are the only public agency that is available 7 days a week, 24 hours a day to respond to calls for help. They are also best able to investigate many kinds of problems. Moreover, the power to use force when necessary allows them to intervene in problematic situations.

The functions of the police can be classified into three groups: (1) order maintenance, (2) law enforcement, and (3) service. Police agencies divide their resources among these functions on the basis of community need, citizen requests, and departmental policy.

■ Order Maintenance

The **order maintenance** function is a broad mandate to prevent behavior that either disturbs or threatens to disturb the peace or involves face-to-face conflict between two or more people. A domestic quarrel, a noisy drunk, loud music in the night, a beggar on the street, a tavern brawl—all are forms of disorder that may require action by the police.

Unlike most laws that define specific acts as illegal, laws regulating disorderly conduct deal with ambiguous situations that different police officers could view in different ways. For many crimes, determining when the law has been broken is easy. On the other hand, order maintenance requires officers to decide not only whether a law has been broken but also whether any action should be taken and, if so, who should be blamed. In a bar fight, for example, the officer must decide who started the fight, whether an arrest should be made for assault, and whether to arrest other people besides those who started the conflict.

Officers often must make judgments in order maintenance situations. They may be required to help people in trouble, manage crowds, supervise various kinds of services, and help people who are not fully accountable for what they do. The officers have a high degree of discretion and control over how such situations will develop. Patrol officers are not subject to direct control. They have the power to arrest, but they may also decide not to make an arrest. The order maintenance function is made more complex by the fact that the patrol officer is normally expected to "handle" a situation rather than to enforce the law, usually in an emotionally charged atmosphere. In controlling a crowd outside a rock concert, for example, the arrest of an unruly person may restore order by removing a troublemaker and also serving as a warning to others that they could be arrested if they do not cooperate. However, an arrest may cause the crowd to become hostile toward the officers, making things worse. Officers cannot always predict precisely how their discretionary decisions will promote or hinder order maintenance.

■ **order maintenance** The police function of preventing behavior that disturbs or threatens to disturb the public peace or that involves face-to-face conflict between two or more people. In such situations, the police exercise discretion in deciding whether a law has been broken.

■ **law enforcement** The police function of controlling crime by intervening in situations in which the law has clearly been violated and the police need to identify and apprehend the guilty person.

Police in East Lansing, Michigan, used tear gas and arrested more than 50 people in April 2008 when an outdoor party adjacent to Michigan State University's campus attracted several thousand participants and turned into a civil disturbance with bottle throwing and property damage. Police officers must control their own emotions and avoid escalating such conflicts, even when they risk injury from thrown objects. How can police be trained to handle conflicts to limit harm to public safety?

■ Law Enforcement

The **law enforcement** function applies to situations in which the law has been violated and the offender needs to be identified or located and then apprehended. Police officers who focus on law enforcement serve in specialized branches such as the vice squad and the burglary detail. Although the patrol officer may be the first officer at the scene of a crime, in serious cases a

© Kevin W. Fowler/Lansing State Journal

detective usually prepares the case for prosecution by bringing together all the evidence for the prosecuting attorney. When the offender is identified but not located, the detective conducts the search. If the offender is not identified, the detective must analyze clues to find out who committed the crime.

The police often portray themselves as enforcers of the law, but many factors interfere with how effectively they can do so. For example, when a property crime is committed, the perpetrator usually has some time to get away. This limits the ability of the police to identify, locate, and arrest the suspect. Burglaries, for instance, usually occur when people are away from home. The crime may not be discovered until hours or days have passed. The effectiveness of the police is also reduced when assault or robbery victims cannot identify the offender. Victims often delay in calling the police, reducing the chances that a suspect will be apprehended.

■ Service

■ **service** The police function of providing assistance to the public, usually in matters unrelated to crime.

Police perform a broad range of services, especially for lower-income citizens, that are not related to crime. This kind of **service**—providing first aid, rescuing animals, helping the disoriented, and so on—has become a major police function. Crime prevention has also become a major component of police services to the community. Through education and community organizing, the police can help the public take steps to prevent crime.

It may appear that valuable resources are being inappropriately diverted from law enforcement to services. However, performing service functions can help police control crime. Through the service function, officers gain knowledge about the community, and citizens come to trust the police. Checking the security of buildings clearly helps prevent crime, but other activities—dealing with runaways, drunks, and public quarrels—may help solve problems before they lead to criminal behavior.

■ Implementing the Mandate

Although most citizens depend most heavily on the order maintenance and service functions of the police, the public acts as though law enforcement—the catching of lawbreakers—is the most important function. According to public opinion polls, the crime-fighter image of the police is firmly rooted in citizens' minds and is the main function that recruits cite for attracting them to policing careers.

Public support for budgets is greatest when the crime-fighting function is stressed. This emphasis can be seen in the organization of big-city departments. The officers who perform this function, such as detectives, enjoy high status. The focus on crime leads to the creation of special units to deal with homicide, burglary, and auto theft. All other tasks fall to the patrol division. In some departments, this pattern creates morale problems, because extra resources are allocated and prestige devoted to a function that is concerned with a small percentage of the problems brought to the police. In essence, police are public servants who keep the peace, but their organization reinforces their own law enforcement image and the public's focus on crime fighting.

But do the police prevent crime? David Bayley claims that they do not. He says that "the experts know it, the police know it, but the public does not know it" (1994:3). He bases this claim on two facts. First, no link has been found between the number of police officers and crime rates. Second, the main strategies used by modern police have little or no effect on crime. Those strategies are street patrolling by uniformed officers, rapid response to emergency calls, and expert investigation of crime by detectives. Bayley says that the police believe these strategies are essential to protecting public safety, yet no evidence exists that they achieve this goal (1994:5).

CHECKPOINT

ANSWERS

12 What is the order maintenance function? What are officers expected to do in situations where they must maintain order?

12 Police have a broad mandate to prevent behavior that either disturbs or threatens to disturb the peace or involves face-to-face conflict between two or more people. Officers are expected to "handle" the situation.

13 How do law enforcement situations compare with order maintenance situations?

13 The police in order maintenance situations must first determine if a law has been broken. In law enforcement situations, that fact is already known; thus, officers must only find and apprehend the offender.

Organization of the Police

Most police agencies follow a military model of organization, with a structure of ranks and responsibilities. But police departments are also bureaucracies designed to achieve objectives efficiently. *Bureaucracies* are characterized by a division of labor, a chain of command with clear lines of authority, and rules to guide the activities of staff. Police organization differs somewhat from place to place depending on the size of jurisdiction, the characteristics of the population, and the nature of the local crime problems. However, all sizeable departments have the basic characteristics of a bureaucracy.

■ Bureaucratic Elements

The police department in Phoenix, Arizona, reveals the elements of bureaucracy in a typical urban police force. Figure 4.2 shows the Phoenix Police Department's organizational chart, which we refer to in the following discussion.

Division of Labor   The Phoenix department is divided into four divisions, marked in Figure 4.2 by different colors: Headquarters, Management and Support Services, Investigations, and Field Operations (patrol). Within the Management and Support Services Division and the Investigations Division, authority is further delegated to bureaus and units that have special functions (for example, property management, training, laboratory, organized crime). The Field Operations Divisions are further divided into geographic units for patrol in precincts and into specialized units to deal with traffic or special projects, for example.

The bureaucratic organization of an urban police department such as Phoenix's allows the allocation of resources and the supervision of personnel, taking into account the needs and problems of each district.

Chain and Unity of Command   The military character of police departments is illustrated by the chain of command according to ranks—officer, commander, sergeant, lieutenant, captain, major, and chief. These make clear the powers and duties of officers at each level. Each officer has an immediate supervisor who holds authority over and responsibility for the actions of those below. Relationships between superiors and

FIGURE 4.2

Organization of the Phoenix, Arizona, Police Department
This is a typical structure. Note the major divisions of headquarters, management, and support services, investigations, and field operations (patrol). Specialized and geographic divisions are found within these divisions.

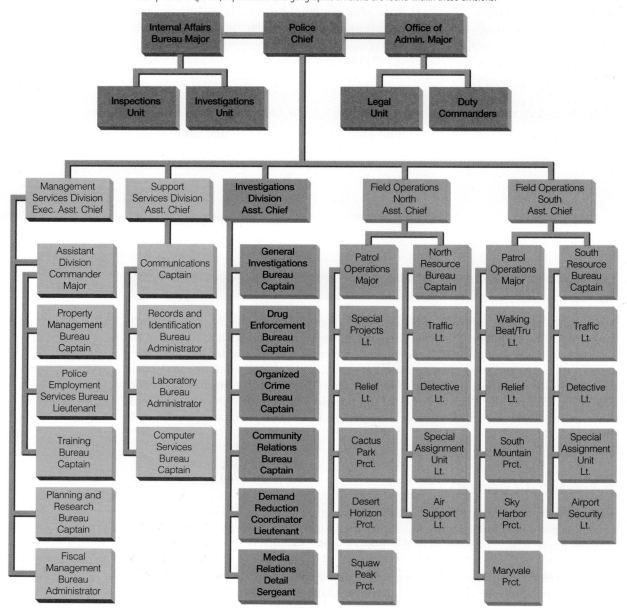

Source: City of Phoenix, Arizona, Police Department, *Annual Report*, 1990.

subordinates emphasize discipline, control, and accountability. These values help officers mobilize resources. They also help protect important legal rights; if police officers are accountable to their superiors, they are less likely to abuse their authority by needlessly interfering with the freedom and rights of citizens.

■ Operational Units

All but the smallest police departments assign officers to operational units that focus on specific functions: patrol, investigation, traffic, vice, and juvenile. These units perform the basic tasks of crime prevention and control. The patrol and investigation (detective) units form the core of the modern department. The patrol unit handles a wide range of functions, including preventing crime, catching suspects, mediating quarrels, helping the ill, and giving aid at accidents. The investigation unit identifies, apprehends, and collects evidence against lawbreakers who commit serious crimes. Because of their overlapping duties, the separation of patrol and investigation can cause problems. Whereas the investigation unit usually focuses on murder, rape, and major robberies, the patrol unit has joint responsibility for investigating those crimes but is also solely responsible for investigating the more numerous lesser crimes.

The extent to which departments create special units may depend on the size of the city. Many departments have traffic units, but only those in mid-size to large cities also have vice and juvenile units. As a result of the war on drugs, some cities have special units working only on this problem. Large departments usually have an internal affairs section to investigate charges of corruption against officers as well as other problems associated with the staff and officers. All special units depend on the patrol officers for information and assistance.

■ The Police Bureaucracy and the Criminal Justice System

The police play an important role as a bureaucracy within the broader criminal justice system. Three issues arise in the organizational context within which the police operate.

First, the police are the gateway through which information and individuals enter the justice system. Police have the discretion to determine which suspects will be arrested and moved into the system. Cases that are sent to the prosecutor for charging and then to the courts for adjudication begin with an officer's decision that there is probable cause for an arrest. The ultimate success of the prosecution depends on the care taken by the officer in making the arrest and collecting evidence. To a large extent, the outcome of the case hinges on the officer's judgment and evidence-gathering activities.

Second, police administration is influenced by the fact that the outcome of a case is largely in the hands of others. The police bring suspects into the criminal justice process, but they cannot control the decisions of prosecutors and judges. In some cases, the police officers feel that their efforts have been wasted. For example, the prosecutor sometimes agrees to a plea bargain that does not, in the eyes of the officer, adequately punish the offender. The potential for conflict between police and other decision makers in the system is increased by the difference in social status between police officers, who often do not have college degrees, and lawyers and judges, who have graduate degrees.

Third, as part of a bureaucracy, police officers are expected to observe rules and follow the orders of superiors while at the same time making independent, discretionary judgments. They must stay within the chain of command yet also make choices in response to events on the streets. These factors affect police behavior on a daily basis.

CHECKPOINT

ANSWERS

⓮ *What are three characteristics of a bureaucracy?*

⓮ Division of labor, chain and unity of command, rules and procedures.

⓯ *What are the five operational units of all but the smallest police departments?*

⓯ Patrol, investigation, traffic, vice, juvenile.

CLOSE UP

High-Speed Pursuit

THE SUSPECT'S pickup truck barreled across the Bridgeport, Connecticut, city line with a Trumbull police cruiser in hot pursuit. When the driver of the truck lost control, it slammed into a parked station wagon with two women inside. One, a mother of three, later died, and her sister was hospitalized for seven months. The truck continued on its way. Instead of stopping to assist the injured, the officer continued the pursuit.

Trumbull police say the pursuing officer followed departmental procedures. The suspect had broken into a house and stolen a microwave oven and other household goods. Critics say that the officer was so intent on making his collar that he never noticed others on the street.

National Highway and Traffic Safety Administration data show that about four hundred people die annually in police chases nationwide. About 1 to 3 percent of pursuits result in death. In Metro-Dade County, Florida, researchers found that 20 percent of pursuits resulted in injuries and 41 percent in accidents. Only 35 percent of pursuits were initiated to catch suspected felons, with nearly half for traffic violators.

Critics have called for strict rules banning high-speed chases, arguing that the risk to public safety is too great. Police organizations say that officers cannot be constrained too tightly or they will not be able to catch suspects. However, public pressure to restrict high-speed chases has come from accident victims and their families who, since 1980, have filed an increasing number of civil lawsuits. When a bicyclist was killed by a motorist being pursued by police in Kansas City in 2003, a citizens' committee worked with the police department to develop a restrictive policy and training program for pursuits.

Many states now require police departments to have written policies governing high-speed chases. Some departments have banned them completely. Others have guidelines requiring officers to consider such factors as driving conditions, the seriousness of the crime, and the danger the suspect poses to the community, before pursuing a suspect. Courts have consulted such departmental policies in considering the liability of officers for damages resulting from high-speed chases.

As in so much of police work, guidelines may exist, but it is still the officer, acting alone, who must analyze the situation and exercise discretion in a dangerous situation.

RESEARCHING THE INTERNET

To read more about police pursuit driving, read a 2004 report written for San Francisco's government officials that includes descriptions of differences in training and discretionary decision making authority for police officers in different cities. You can find the report at the corresponding website listed on the Cole/Smith Criminal Justice in America Companion Website: http://www.cengage.com/criminaljustice/cole.

FOR CRITICAL ANALYSIS

Should police simply let traffic violators and suspects in nonviolent crime cases escape because of a reluctance to engage in chases? Are there any new technologies that could be developed to address the problems associated with high-speed chases?

Sources: Geoffrey P. Alpert, "Pursuit Driving: Planning Policies and Action from Agency, Officer, and Public Information," *Police Forum 7* (January 1997): 3; "Bicyclists Request for Changes in KCMO Police Pursuit Policies Pays Off," *Missouri Bicycle News*, November 17, 2004, http://www.sfgov.org/site/bdsupvrs_page.asp?id=24020; *Hartford Courant*, September 12, 1997, p. 1; Jennifer Upshaw, "Marin, Other Police Agencies Follow Strict Vehicle Pursuit Policies," *Marin Independent Journal*, April 3, 2009, http://www.marinij.com.

Police Policy

The police cannot enforce every law and catch every lawbreaker. Legal rules limit the ways officers can investigate and pursue offenders. For example, the constitutional ban on unreasonable searches and seizures prevents police from investigating many crimes without a search warrant.

Because the police have limited resources, they cannot have officers on every street at all times of the day and night. This means that police executives must develop policies regarding how the members of their department will implement their mandate (W. Hicks, 2003). These policies guide officers as to which offenses will receive the most attention and which tactics will be used—for example, which neighborhoods to patrol and whether to patrol in cars or on foot. These policies also determine which people will be caught committing crimes and brought into the criminal justice system for prosecution and punishment. Changes in policy—such as increasing the size of the night patrol or tolerating prostitution and other public order offenses—affect the amount of crime that gets official attention and affect the system's ability to deal with offenders. Policies with regard to high-speed pursuit, a controversial tactic in most departments, are discussed in the Close Up box.

Police policies may reflect the preferences and values of police executives. However, choices about policies are also influenced by politics, public pressure, and social context. American cities differ in government, economic, and racial and ethnic characteristics as well as in their degree of urbanization. These factors can affect the style of policing expected by the community. In a classic study, James Q. Wilson found that citizen expectations regarding police behavior affect departments through the political process; specifically, chiefs who run their departments in ways that antagonize the community are not likely to stay in office very long. Wilson's key finding was that a city's political culture, which reflects its socioeconomic characteristics and its government organization, had a major impact on the style of policing found there. Wilson further described three different styles of policing—the watchman, legalistic, and service styles (Wilson, 1968).

Departments with a *watchman* style stress order maintenance. Patrol officers may ignore minor violations of the law, especially those

The styles of policing employed by police departments can vary by the characteristics of a community. Do you see evidence of the any of the three classic styles—watchman, legalistic, or service—in your hometown? Does the use of specific patrol methods, such as bicycles, tell you anything about the style of policing in a community?

© A. Ramey/PhotoEdit

involving traffic and juveniles, as long as there is order. The police exercise discretion and deal with many infractions in an informal way. Officers make arrests only for flagrant violations and when order cannot be maintained. The broad discretion exercised by officers can produce discrimination when officers do not treat members of different racial and ethnic groups in the same way.

In departments with a *legalistic* style, police work is marked by professionalism and an emphasis on law enforcement. Officers are expected to detain a high proportion of juvenile offenders, act vigorously against illicit enterprises, issue traffic tickets, and make a large number of misdemeanor arrests. They act as if there is a single standard of community conduct—that prescribed by the law—rather than different standards for juveniles, minorities, drunks, and other groups. Thus, although officers do not discriminate in making arrests and issuing citations, the strict enforcement of laws, including traffic laws, can seem overly harsh to some groups in the community.

Suburban middle-class communities often experience a *service* style. Residents feel that they deserve individual treatment and expect the police to provide service. Burglaries and assaults are taken seriously, whereas minor infractions tend to be dealt with by informal means such as stern warnings. The police are expected to deal with the misdeeds of local residents in a personal, nonpublic way so as to avoid embarrassment. See "A Question of Ethics" at the end of the chapter for a look at how policing styles can affect ethical decisions "down at the station."

In all cases, before officers investigate crimes or make arrests, each police chief decides on policies that will govern the level and type of enforcement in the community. Given that the police are the entry point to the criminal justice system, the decisions made by police officials affect all segments of the system. Just as community expectations shape decisions about enforcement goals and the allocation of police resources, they also shape the cases that will be handled by prosecutors and correctional officials.

Twenty-First-Century Challenges in Policing

5

MINNEAPOLIS, MINNESOTA: AUGUST 1, 2007. As their cars sped along I-35W, drivers felt the roadway shake beneath them as concrete and steel loudly groaned and cracked—before giving way. Some cars tumbled into the swiftly flowing Mississippi River. Others dropped straight down into the twisted remnants of the bridge that had collapsed. Because the shocking event occurred on a major highway, in broad daylight, and in the middle of a major city, the emergency call center instantly received dozens of 911 calls from witnesses and victims reporting the catastrophe. Police officers were on the scene within minutes. Officers immediately took charge of the rescue effort, including trying to ensure the safety of civilian bystanders who had jumped into the river and climbed through the wreckage in their own efforts to find survivors (Levy, 2007).

When emergencies occur, police officers serve as first responders. Along with firefighters and emergency medical personnel, law enforcement officers are expected to rush to the scene, restore order, and assist in rescue operations. The rescue and recovery effort in this case was coordinated by the Minneapolis Police Department and the Hennepin County Sheriff's Office. Other police agencies provided specialized assistance as well. The Federal Bureau of Investigation (FBI) sent its Evidence Response Team, which possessed special expertise in gathering information to help determine the cause of the bridge collapse. The FBI also sent its Underwater Search team with divers and underwater cameras to find any bodies submerged in the river. In addition, officers from the U.S. Marshals came to the scene to provide perimeter security and prevent onlookers from interfering or being endangered. Similarly, other local, state, and federal agencies sent personnel to assist in the initial rescue efforts as well as the subsequent recovery work. Although the tragic event took 13 lives and injured an additional 145 people, the federal government's report on the event in 2008 praised the cooperation and communication among the law enforcement officers, firefighters, and emergency medical personnel (Karnowski, 2008).

Before the terrorist attack on the World Trade Center on September 11, 2001, many Americans had had little reason to recognize the importance of law enforcement agencies at all levels of government in serving society in numerous ways. The courageous response of police officers and firefighters, many of whom lost their lives in the collapse of the twin towers, changed that. Today, as illustrated

LEARNING OBJECTIVES

▶ Understand the everyday actions of police

▶ Recognize the factors that affect police response

▶ Understand the main functions of police patrol, investigation, and special operations units

▶ Analyze patrol strategies that police departments employ

▶ Recognize the importance of connections between the police and the community

▶ Identify issues and problems that emerge from law enforcement agencies' increased attention to homeland security

▶ Understand the policing and related activities undertaken by private sector security management

by the Minneapolis bridge collapse, there is much wider recognition that police officers are not merely crime fighters. They are essential civil servants who act quickly and professionally to coordinate efforts in response to disasters. The swift and effective actions of so many different law enforcement agencies in Minneapolis demonstrate the importance of the network of relationships among national, state, and local police forces.

In this chapter, we examine several aspects of the continuing challenges faced by American society in protecting lives and property. We focus on the actual work of the police as they pursue suspects, prevent crimes, and otherwise serve the public. The police must be organized so that their patrol efforts can be coordinated, investigations carried out, arrests made, evidence gathered, and violators prosecuted. Moreover, the responsibilities of police must be carried out effectively in an increasingly diverse society. As shown by the Minneapolis bridge example, law enforcement officials must routinely tackle issues other than traditional crime prevention, such as emergency response. This chapter also examines the emerging challenges stemming from homeland security and antiterrorist efforts. Finally, the chapter discusses the role of private security officials in advancing society's interests in public safety and crime prevention. All of the topics explored in this chapter demonstrate the wide range of issues and problems handled by public police and private security officials in the twenty-first century, as they work toward advancing society's goals of order, safety, and security.

Everyday Actions of Police

We saw in Chapter 4 how the police are organized and which three functions of policing—law enforcement, order maintenance, and service—compose their mandate. We have also recognized that police officers must be guided by policies developed by their superiors as to how policing is to be implemented. Police officers' actions and effectiveness also depend on the resources available to them, as illustrated by the example of computers in patrol cars that will be discussed in greater detail in Chapter 14. In this section, we look at the everyday actions of the police as they deal with citizens in often highly discretionary ways. We then discuss domestic violence, to show how the police respond to serious problems.

Encounters between Police and Citizens

To carry out their mission, the police must have the public's confidence, because they depend on the public to help them identify crime and carry out investigations (see "What Americans Think"). Each year one in five Americans has face-to-face contact with law enforcement officers. A third of these contacts involve people seeking help or offering assistance. Another third involve witnessing or reporting a crime. A little less than a third say that the police initiated the contact.

Although most people are willing to help the police, factors such as fear and self-interest keep some from cooperating. Many people who avoid calling the police do so because they think it is not worth the effort and cost. They do not want to spend time filling out forms at the station, appearing as a witness, or confronting a neighbor or relative in court. In some low-income neighborhoods, citizens are reluctant to assist the police, because their past experience has shown that contact with law enforcement "only brings trouble." Without information about a crime, the police may decide not to pursue an investigation. Clearly citizens have influence over the work of the police through their decisions to call or not to call them.

Officers learn that developing and maintaining effective communication with people is essential to doing their job. As Officer Marcus Laffey of the New York Police Department says, "If you can talk a good game as a cop, you're halfway there." He says that police use of "confrontation and force, of roundhouse punches and high speed chases" makes the movies and the news, but "what you say and how you say it come into play far more than anything you do with your stick or your gun, and can even prevent the need for them" (Laffey, 1998:38).

Citizens expect the police to act both effectively and fairly—in ways consistent with American values. Departmental policy often affects fairness in encounters between citizens and police. When should the patrol officer frisk a suspect? When should a deal be made with the addict-informer? Which disputes should be mediated on the spot, and which left to more formal procedures? Surprisingly, these conflicts between fairness and policy are seldom decided by heads of departments but fall largely to the discretion of the officer on the scene. In many situations, the department has little control over the actions of individual officers.

Police Discretion

Police officers have the power to deprive people of their liberty, to arrest them, to take them into custody, and to use force to control them. In carrying out their professional responsibilities, officers are expected to exercise *discretion*—to make choices in often ambiguous situations as to how and when to apply the law. Discretion can involve ignoring minor violations of the law or holding some violators to rule-book standards. It can mean arresting a disorderly person or taking that person home. In the final analysis, the officer on the scene must define the situation, decide how to handle it, and determine whether and how the law should be applied. Five factors are especially important:

1. *The nature of the crime.* The less serious a crime is to the public, the more freedom officers have to ignore it.

2. *The relationship between the alleged criminal and the victim.* The closer the personal relationship, the more variable the use of discretion. Family squabbles may not be as grave as they appear, and police are wary of making arrests, because a spouse may later decide not to press charges.

3. *The relationship between the police and the criminal or victim.* A polite complainant will be taken more seriously than a hostile one. Similarly, a suspect who shows respect to an officer is less likely to be arrested than one who does not.

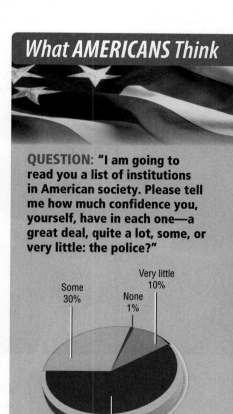

What AMERICANS Think

QUESTION: "I am going to read you a list of institutions in American society. Please tell me how much confidence you, yourself, have in each one—a great deal, quite a lot, some, or very little: the police?"

Some 30%
Very little 10%
None 1%
Great deal/quite a lot 58%

Go to http://www.cengage.com/criminaljustice/cole to compare your opinion on this issue with the opinions of other criminal justice students.

Source: Bureau of Justice Statistics, *Sourcebook of Criminal Justice Statistics, 2008* (Washington, DC: U.S. Government Printing Office, 2009), Table 2.12.2008.

Police officers use their discretion to make many decisions. Who should be stopped and questioned? When should an arrest be made? Who needs an encouraging word and who needs a stern warning? In making decisions, officers can significantly impact the lives of people who come into contact with the criminal justice system. Are there ways that supervisors could better monitor officers' use of discretion?

© Michael Newman/PhotoEdit

4. *Race/ethnicity, age, gender, class.* Although contested by many criminal justice officials, some research shows that officers are more likely to strictly enforce the law against young, minority, poor men while being more lenient to the elderly, to whites, and to affluent women.

5. *Departmental policy.* The policies of the police chief and city officials promote more or less discretion.

■ Domestic Violence

How the police deal with domestic violence can show the links between police–citizen encounters, the exercise of discretion, and actions taken (or not taken) by officers. Domestic violence, also called "battering" and "spouse abuse," is assaultive behavior involving adults who are married or who have a prior or an ongoing intimate relationship.

Violence by an intimate (spouse, ex-spouse, girlfriend, ex-boyfriend, and so forth) accounts for about 20 percent of all violence experienced by female victims, compared with 3 percent for male victims (Rennison, 2002). Historically, however, police departments typically treated domestic violence as a private, family matter rather than as a crime. This viewpoint often reflected male officers' stereotyped opinions about a woman's obligation to obey her husband or boyfriend. Prodded by the women's movement beginning in the 1970s and 1980s, police departments began to rethink this policy of leniency when research in Minneapolis found that abusive spouses who are arrested and jailed briefly are much less likely to commit acts of domestic violence again (Sherman and Berk, 1984:261). Subsequent studies of mandatory arrest policies showed mixed results (Dixon, 2008). Although studies in other cities (Charlotte, Milwaukee, and Omaha) did not produce similar results (Ho, 2000), the research led some departments to order officers to make an arrest in every case in which evidence of an assault existed (Sherman et al., 1991:821). In many states, policies have been changed as a result of lawsuits by injured women who claimed that the police ignored evidence of assaults and in effect allowed the spouse to inflict serious injuries (Robinson, 2000). In addition, there is a growing sense that domestic violence can no longer be left to the discretion of individual patrol officers. Nearly half of the states and the District of Columbia require the arrest without a warrant of suspects in violent incidents, even if the officer did not witness the crime but has probable cause to believe that the suspect committed it (Hoctor, 1997). Most large departments and police academies have programs to educate officers about domestic violence.

Even though we can point to policy changes imposed to deal with domestic violence, the fact remains that the officer in the field is the one who must handle these situations. Each context may differ, both in terms of the officer's perceptions about what occurred and with respect to the victim's desire to see the abuser arrested and punished (Hirschel and Hutchinson, 2003). As with most law enforcement situations, laws, guidelines, and training can help; however, as is often true in police work, in the end the discretion of the officer inevitably determines what actions will be taken. Even if a prosecutor is firmly committed to prosecuting all domestic violence cases, whether or not the victim wants to testify against an intimate partner, no prosecution can occur if the police decline to use their discretionary authority to make an arrest (R. C. Davis et al., 2008).

CHECKPOINT

ANSWERS

① *Why do patrol officers have so much discretion?*

① They deal with citizens, often in private, and are charged with maintaining order and enforcing laws. Many of these laws are ambiguous and deal with situations in which the participants' conduct is in dispute.

② *Why have police in the past failed to make arrests in domestic violence situations?*

② Officers assume family conflicts are private matters, the victim is often uncooperative, and intervention is thought to be dangerous.

Police Response

In a free society, people do not want police to stand on every street corner and ask them what they are doing. Thus, the police are mainly **reactive** (responding to citizen calls for service) rather than **proactive** (initiating actions in the absence of citizen requests). Studies of police work show that 81 percent of actions result from citizen telephone calls, 5 percent are initiated by citizens who approach an officer, and only 14 percent are initiated in the field by an officer. These facts affect the way departments are organized and the way the police respond to incidents.

Because they are mainly reactive, the police usually arrive at the scene only after the crime has been committed and the perpetrator has fled. This means that the police are hampered by the time lapse and sometimes by inaccurate information given by witnesses. For example, a mugging may happen so quickly that victims and witnesses cannot accurately describe what happened. In about a third of cases in which police are called, no one is present when the police arrive on the scene.

Citizens have come to expect that the police will respond quickly to every call, whether it requires immediate attention or can be handled in a more routine manner. This expectation has produced **incident-driven policing**, in which calls for service are the primary instigators of action. Studies have shown, though, that less than 30 percent of calls to the police involve criminal law enforcement—most calls concern order maintenance and service (S. Walker, 1999:80). To a large extent, then, reports by victims and observers define the boundaries of policing.

The police do use proactive strategies such as surveillance and undercover work to combat some crimes. When addressing crimes without victims, for example, they must rely on informers, stakeouts, wiretapping, stings, and raids. Because of the current focus on drug offenses, police resources in many cities have been assigned to proactive efforts to apprehend people who use or sell illegal drugs. As you read "Criminal Justice: Myth and Reality," consider whether the use of proactive strategies will reduce crime.

■ How Bureaucracy Affects Response

The organization of the police bureaucracy influences how the police respond to citizens' calls. Factors that affect the response process include the separation of police into various functional groups (patrol, vice, investigation, and so on), the quasi-military command system, and the techniques used to induce patrol officers to respond in desired ways.

■ **reactive** Occurring in response, such as police activity in response to notification that a crime has been committed.

■ **proactive** Acting in anticipation, such as an active search for potential offenders that is initiated by the police without waiting for a crime to be reported. Arrests for crimes without victims are usually proactive.

■ **incident-driven policing** Policing in which calls for service are the primary instigators of action.

Criminal Justice: MYTH AND REALITY

COMMON BELIEF: If more police officers actively patrolled the streets, instead of having so many at headquarters sitting in offices, crime rates in a city would certainly decline.

Crime rates are shaped by a complex variety of factors that seem unrelated to the number of officers in a city's police department. Some cities with the highest number of officers per capita on the streets also have the highest crime rates. In addition, police patrols do not necessarily reduce crime. Officers cannot be everywhere at once. Moreover, many crimes occur out of public view. Cities that have attempted to flood neighborhoods with officers often simply see the criminals move their activities to a different location. In sum, research raises questions about whether more-numerous or more-active patrols will necessarily impact crime rates.

Police officers are directed to locations needing investigation or assistance through centralized communications with the police department. Police dispatchers play a key role in the effectiveness and responsiveness of officers by prioritizing calls for service; they also provide information so that officers know as much as they can about the problems they will encounter. What kinds of training do police dispatchers need?

© Bonnie Kamin/PhotoEdit

Police departments are being reshaped by new communications technology, which has tended to centralize decision making. The core of the department is the communications center, where commands are given to send officers into action.

Patrol officers are expected to be in constant touch with headquarters and must report each of their actions. Two-way radios, cell phones, and computers are the primary means by which administrators monitor the decisions of officers in the field. In the past, patrol officers might have administered on-the-spot justice to a mischievous juvenile, but now they must file a report, take the youth into custody, and start formal proceedings. Because officers must contact headquarters by radio or computer with reports about each incident, headquarters can more effectively guide officers' discretion and ensure that they comply with departmental policies. Although most large cities and state police agencies have acquired computers for their patrol cars, small towns and rural sheriff's departments often cannot receive immediate funding from their local governments to purchase new technology.

Most residents in urban and suburban areas can call 911 to report a crime or obtain help or information. The 911 system has brought a flood of calls to police departments—many not directly related to police responsibilities. In Baltimore a "311 system" has been implemented to help reduce the number of nonemergency calls, estimated as 40 percent of the total calls. Residents have been urged to call 311 when they need assistance that does not require the immediate dispatch of an officer. Recent studies found that this innovation reduced calls to 911 and resulted in extremely high public support (Mazerolle et al., 2003; *New York Times*, October 10, 1997, p. A12).

■ **differential response** A patrol strategy that assigns priorities to calls for service and chooses the appropriate response.

To improve efficiency, police departments use a **differential response** system that assigns priorities to calls for service. This system assumes that it is not always necessary to rush a patrol car to the scene when a call is received. The appropriate response depends on several factors—such as whether the incident is in progress, has just occurred, or occurred some time ago, as well as whether anyone is or could be hurt. A dispatcher receives the calls and asks for certain facts. The dispatcher may (1) send a sworn officer to the scene right away, (2) give the call a lower rank so that the response by an officer is delayed, (3) send someone other than a sworn officer, or (4) refer the caller to another agency.

Some experts criticize centralized communications and decision making. Many advocates of community policing believe that certain technologies tend to isolate the police from citizens. Community-policing strategies attempt to enhance interaction and cooperation between officers and citizens (Morash and Ford, 2002). Widespread use of motorized patrols has meant that residents get only a glimpse of officers as they cruise through their neighborhoods. Community-oriented policing attempts to overcome some of the negative aspects of centralized response.

■ Productivity

Police response and action in part depend on departmental productivity. A recent innovation in productivity management has brought major changes to police operations. New York's Compstat program emphasizes precinct-level accountability for crime reduction (Rosenfeld, Fornango, and Baumer, 2005). This program has inspired similar approaches in police departments in Baltimore, New Orleans, Indianapolis, and other cities. Through twice-weekly briefings before their peers and senior executives, precinct commanders must explain the results of their efforts to reduce crime. In the Compstat approach, they are held responsible for the success of crime control efforts in their precincts as indicated by crime statistics (Weisburd et al., 2003). Essential to this management strategy is timely, accurate information. Computer systems have been developed to put up-to-date crime data into the hands of managers at all levels (Willis, Mastrofski, and Weisburd, 2004). This allows discussion of department-wide strategies and puts pressure on low producers (Sherman, 1998:430; Silverman, 1999). The Compstat approach has raised questions as to how police work should be measured. It has also raised questions about whether measures of performance based on data tend to move departments away from community policing by emphasizing a centralized hierarchy focused on accountability and control (Walsh and Vito, 2004).

Quantifying police work is difficult in part because of the wide range of duties and day-to-day tasks of officers. In the past, the crime rate and the clearance rate have been used as measures of "good" policing. A lower crime rate might be cited as evidence of an effective department, but critics note that factors other than policing affect this measure. Like other public agencies, the police departments and the citizens in a community have trouble gauging the quantity and quality of police officers' work (see "What Americans Think").

The **clearance rate**—the percentage of crimes known to police that they believe they have solved through an arrest—is a basic measure of police performance. The clearance rate varies by type of offense. In reactive situations this rate can be low. For example, the police may learn about a burglary hours or even days after it has occurred; the clearance rate for such crimes is only about 13 percent. Police have much more success in handling violent crimes, in which victims often know their assailants; the clearance rate for such cases is 46 percent (BJS, 2005e).

In proactive situations, the police are not responding to the call of a crime victim; rather, they seek out crimes. Hence, at least in theory, arrests for prostitution, gambling, and drug selling have a clearance rate of 100 percent, because every crime known to the police is matched with an arrest.

These measures of police productivity are sometimes supplemented by other data, such as the number of traffic citations issued, illegally parked cars ticketed, and suspects stopped for questioning, as well as the value of stolen goods recovered. These additional ways of counting work done reflect the fact that an officer may work hard for many hours but have no arrests to show for his or her efforts. Yet, society may benefit even more when officers spend their time in activities that are hard to measure, such as calming disputes, becoming acquainted with people in the neighborhood, and providing services to those in need. Some research indicates that officers who engage in activities that produce higher levels of measurable productivity, such as issuing citations or making arrests, also receive higher numbers of citizen complaints about alleged misconduct (Lersch, 2002).

One might think that police effectiveness would depend on a city's population, its crime level, and the size of its police force. As seen in Figure 5.1, however these variables are not always related. The size of San Jose's police force is small relative to the population, but its rates of index offenses are low. In contrast, index offenses in Washington, D.C., rank in the middle range of the cities studied, but its force is the largest. The issue grows even more complicated: Police productivity is shaped in part by population density, the number of nonresidents who spend part of their day working or visiting in the area, local politics, and other factors. In sum, like other public agencies, the police have trouble gauging the quantity and quality of their work.

■ **clearance rate**   The percentage of crimes known to the police that they believe they have solved through an arrest; a statistic used to measure a police department's productivity.

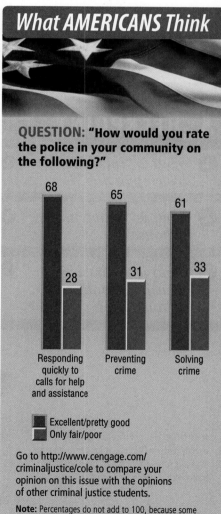

What AMERICANS Think

QUESTION: "How would you rate the police in your community on the following?"

- Responding quickly to calls for help and assistance: 68 (Excellent/pretty good), 28 (Only fair/poor)
- Preventing crime: 65 (Excellent/pretty good), 31 (Only fair/poor)
- Solving crime: 61 (Excellent/pretty good), 33 (Only fair/poor)

■ Excellent/pretty good
■ Only fair/poor

Go to http://www.cengage.com/criminaljustice/cole to compare your opinion on this issue with the opinions of other criminal justice students.

Note: Percentages do not add to 100, because some respondents declined to answer specific questions

Source: Bureau of Justice Statistics, *Sourcebook of Criminal Justice Statistics, 2002* (Washington, DC: U.S. Government Printing Office, 2003), Table 2.23.

FIGURE 5.1
Sworn officers and UCR violent crime index offenses per 1,000 population in 10 U.S. cities (2004)
These major cities have varying numbers of police officers and crimes for every 1,000 residents. As you can see, the amount of crime and numbers of police do not correlate.

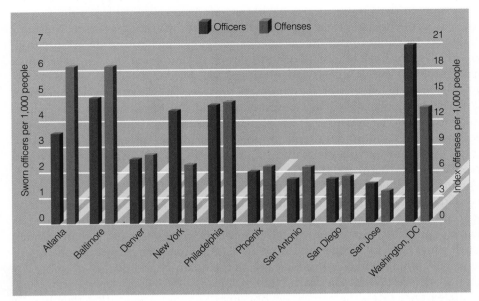

Source: Brian A. Reaves, "Census of State and Local Law Enforcement Agencies, 2004," Bureau of Justice Statistics *Bulletin* (Washington, DC: Bureau of Justice Statistics, 2007), Appendix Table 4; Federal Bureau of Investigation, *Uniform Crime Reports, 2004* (Washington, DC: U.S. Department of Justice, 2005), Section II, Table 8.

CHECKPOINT

ANSWERS

3 What is "incident-driven policing"?

3 Policing in which calls for service are the primary instigators of action.

4 What is "differential response"?

4 Policy that gives priority to calls according to whether an immediate or delayed response is warranted.

5 What is the basic measure of police productivity?

5 Clearance rate—the percentage of crimes known to the police that they believe they have solved through an arrest.

Delivery of Police Services

■ **line functions** Police components that directly perform field operations and carry out the basic functions of patrol, investigation, traffic, vice, juvenile, and so on.

In service bureaucracies like the police, a distinction is often made between line and staff functions. **Line functions** are those that directly involve field operations: patrol, investigation, traffic control, vice and juvenile crimes, and so on. By contrast, *staff functions* supplement or support the line functions. Staff functions are based in the chief's office and the support or services bureau, as well as in the staff inspection bureau. An efficient department maintains an appropriate balance between line and staff duties.

■ Patrol Functions

Patrol is often called the backbone of police operations. The word *patrol* is derived from a French word, *patrouiller*, which once meant "to tramp about in the mud."

This is an apt description of a function that one expert has described as "arduous, tiring, difficult, and performed in conditions other than ideal" (Chapman, 1970:ix). For most Americans, "policing" is the familiar sight of a uniformed and armed patrol officer, on call 24 hours a day.

Every local police department has a patrol unit. Even in large departments, patrol officers account for up to two-thirds of all **sworn officers**—those who have taken an oath and received the powers to make arrests and use necessary force in accordance with their duties. In small communities, police operations are not specialized, and the patrol force is the department. As we have seen, the patrol officer must be prepared for any imaginable situation and must perform many duties.

Television portrays patrol officers as always on the go—rushing from one incident to another and making several arrests in a single shift. A patrol officer may indeed be called to deal with a robbery in progress or to help rescue people from a burning building. However, the patrol officer's life is not always so exciting, often involving routine and even boring tasks such as directing traffic at accident scenes and road construction sites.

Most officers, on most shifts, do not make even one arrest (Bayley, 1994:20). To better understand patrol work, note in Figure 5.2 how the police of Wilmington, Delaware, allocate time to various activities.

The patrol function has three parts: answering calls for help, maintaining a police presence, and probing suspicious circumstances. Patrol officers are well suited to answering calls, because they usually are near the scene and can move quickly to provide help or catch a suspect. At other times, they engage in **preventive patrol**—that is, making the police presence known in an effort to deter crime and to make officers available to respond quickly to calls. Whether walking the streets or cruising in a car, the patrol officer is on the lookout for suspicious people and behavior. With experience, officers come to trust their own ability to spot signs of suspicious activity that merit stopping people on the street for questioning.

When officers earn the trust and respect of the residents of the neighborhoods they patrol, people become much more willing to provide information about crimes and suspicious activities. Effective work by patrol officers can also help reduce citizens' fear of crime and foster a sense of security.

Patrol officers' duties sound fairly straightforward, yet these officers often find themselves in complex situations requiring sound judgments and careful actions. As the first to arrive at a crime scene, the officer must comfort and give aid to victims,

■ **sworn officers** Police employees who have taken an oath and been given powers by the state to make arrests and use necessary force, in accordance with their duties.

■ **preventive patrol** Making the police presence known, to deter crime and to make officers available to respond quickly to calls.

FIGURE 5.2

Time allocated to patrol activities by the police of Wilmington, Delaware

The time spent on each activity was calculated from records for each police car unit. Note the range of activities and the time spent on each.

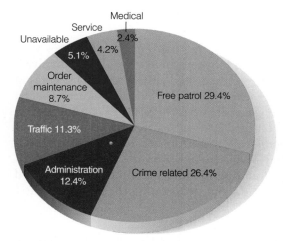

Free patrol: park and walk

Crime related: officer in trouble, suspicious person/vehicle, crime in progress, alarm, investigate crime not in progress, service warrant/subpoena, assist other police

Administration: meal break, report writing, firearms training, police vehicle maintenance, at headquarters, court related

Traffic: accident investigation, parking problems, motor vehicle driving problems, traffic control, fire emergency

Order maintenance: order maintenance in progress, animal complaint, noise complaint

Service: service related

Medical: medical emergency, at local hospital

Source: Jack R. Greene and Carl B. Klockars, "What Police Do," in *Thinking about Police,* 2nd ed., ed. Carl B. Klockars and Stephen D. Mastrofski (New York: McGraw-Hill, 1991), 279.

identify and question witnesses, control crowds, and gather evidence. These roles call for creativity and good communication skills.

Because the patrol officer has the most direct contact with the public, the patrol officer's actions in large part determine the image of the police and their relations with the community. Moreover, successful investigations and prosecutions often depend on patrol officers' actions in questioning witnesses and gathering evidence after a crime. Think of the variety of events that come to the attention of patrol officers. How would you handle them?

Because the patrol officer's job involves the most contact with the public, the best-qualified officers should be chosen to perform it. However, because of the low status of patrol assignments, many officers seek higher-status positions such as that of detective. A key challenge facing policing is to grant to patrol officers a status that reflects their importance to society and the criminal justice system.

■ Investigation

All cities with a population of more than 250,000, and 90 percent of smaller cities, have officers called *detectives*, who are assigned to investigative duties. Detectives make up 15 percent of police personnel. Compared with patrol officers, they enjoy a higher status in the department: Their pay is higher, their hours are more flexible, and they are supervised less closely. Detectives do not wear uniforms, and their work is considered more interesting than that of patrol officers. In addition, they engage solely in law enforcement rather than in order maintenance or service work; hence, their activities conform more closely to the image of the police as crime fighters.

Within federal law enforcement agencies, the work of special agents is similar to that of detectives. In agencies such as the FBI, DEA, and Secret Service, special agents are plainclothes officers who focus on investigations. One key difference between federal special agents and detectives in local departments is that federal agents are more likely to be proactive in initiating investigations to prevent terrorism, drug trafficking, and other crimes. Local detectives are typically reactive, responding to crimes already discovered.

Detectives typically become involved after a crime has been reported and a patrol officer has done a preliminary investigation. The job of detectives is mainly to talk to people—victims, suspects, witnesses—to find out what happened. On the basis of this information, detectives develop theories about who committed the crime; they then set out to gather the evidence that will lead to arrest and prosecution.

In performing an investigation, detectives depend not only on their own experience but also on technical experts. Much of the information they need comes from criminal files, lab technicians, and forensic scientists. Many small departments turn to the state crime laboratory or the FBI for such information. Often depicted as working alone, detectives in fact operate as part of a team.

Although detectives focus on serious crimes, they are not the only ones who investigate such crimes. Patrol, traffic, vice, and juvenile units may also be involved. In small towns and rural areas, patrol officers must conduct investigations, because police departments are too small to have separate detective bureaus. In urban areas, because they are likely to be the first police to arrive at the scene of a crime, patrol officers must do much of the initial investigative work. As we have seen, the patrol unit's investigation can be crucial. Successful prosecution of many kinds of cases, including robbery, larceny, and burglary, is closely linked to the speed with which a suspect is arrested. If patrol officers cannot obtain information from victims and witnesses right away, their odds of arresting and prosecuting the suspect greatly decrease.

Apprehension   The discovery that a crime has been committed sets off a chain of events leading to the capture of a suspect and the gathering of the evidence needed

FIGURE 5.3
The apprehension process
Apprehension of a felony suspect results from a sequence of actions by patrol officers and detectives. Coordination of these efforts is key to solving major crimes.

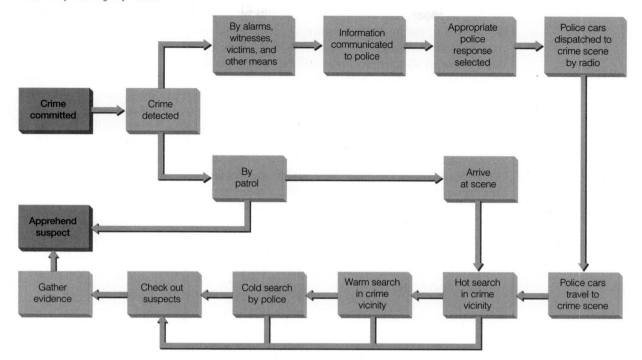

to convict that person. It may also lead to several dead ends, such as a lack of clues pointing to a suspect or a lack of evidence to link the suspect to the crime.

The process of catching a suspect has three stages: detection of a crime, preliminary investigation, and follow-up investigation. Depending on the outcome of the investigation, these three steps may be followed by a fourth: clearance and arrest. As shown in Figure 5.3, these actions are designed to use criminal justice resources to arrest a suspect and assemble enough evidence to support a charge.

Forensic Techniques   American police have long relied on science in gathering, identifying, and analyzing evidence. The public has become increasingly aware of the wide range of scientific testing techniques used for law enforcement purposes, through the television drama *CSI* (crime scene investigation) and its spin-offs (S. Stephens, 2007). Scientific analysis of fingerprints, blood, semen, hair, textiles, soil, weapons, and other materials has helped the police identify criminals. All states and many large cities have forensic labs. However, this does not guarantee that the latest tests can be applied to all pieces of evidence. Not all labs have the same technical machinery and personnel. In addition, some police departments, especially those in small towns and rural areas, have little access to crime labs and other technology (Hickman and Reaves, 2001).

Forensic scientists who work in such labs often have graduate degrees in science. There are three primary areas of forensic science in which these scientists may have received their

A police officer in Santa Ana, California, dusts the door of a stolen car in order to look for fingerprints. Police departments use various forensic techniques to discover evidence. Some techniques are used at crime scenes, while others involve tests in scientific laboratories. Which techniques are likely to be most effective?

training. A background in biological sciences is necessary to examine blood, hair, and DNA samples. Scientists who test bomb residue, textiles, and other materials typically have training in chemistry. Forensic anthropologists examine bone fragments and skeletal remains.

The technological weapons employed to investigate many kinds of crimes include DNA "fingerprinting." This technique identifies people through their distinctive gene patterns (also called genotypic features). DNA, or deoxyribonucleic acid, is the basic component of all chromosomes; all the cells in an individual's body, including those in skin, blood, organs, and semen, contain the same unique type of DNA. The characteristics of certain segments of DNA vary from person to person and thus form a genetic "fingerprint." Analysts can therefore analyze DNA from, say, samples of hair and compare them with those of suspects. Use of the DNA technique has been hampered by the limited number of labs equipped to perform DNA analysis. Many labs have a backlog of cases, especially because of the need to test and record samples from offenders whose DNA must be added to databases (S. Stephens, 2007). Chapter 14 will present more about DNA and other aspects of forensic science in criminal justice.

DNA testing has played a role in thousands of convictions, particularly in sexual contact and abuse cases. It has also been responsible for the release from prison of an increasing number of people after testing has shown that they could not have committed the crimes for which they were imprisoned. As of 2009, more than 220 wrongfully convicted individuals have gained release from prison through DNA testing (Chang, 2009).

Research on Investigation   The results of several studies raise questions about the value of investigations and the role detectives play in apprehension. This research suggests that the police attach too much importance to investigation as a means of solving crimes and shows that most crimes are cleared because of arrests made by the patrol force at or near the scene. Response time is key to apprehension, as is the information given by the victim or witnesses.

A classic study of 153 large police departments found that a crucial factor in solving crimes was identification of the perpetrator by the victim or witnesses. Of those cases that were not solved right away but were cleared later, most were cleared by routine procedures such as fingerprint searches, tips from informants, and mug-shot "show-ups." The report found that actions by the investigative staff mattered in very few cases. In sum, about 30 percent of the crimes were cleared by on-scene arrests and another 50 percent through identification by victims or witnesses when the police arrived. Thus, only about 20 percent could have been solved by detective work. Even among this group, however, the study found that most crimes "were also solved by patrol officers, members of the public who spontaneously provide[d] further information, or routine investigative practices" (Greenwood, Chaiken, and Petersilia, 1977:227).

Does this research show that detectives are not important? No. Some cases are weak, with little evidence; some are strong, with a lot of evidence. Police need not devote a great deal of effort in these polar cases. However, the many cases with moderate evidence do require additional effort by detectives; as one researcher found, this "is extremely important with respect to subsequent making of follow-up arrests" (Bayley, 1998:149). This was confirmed by a study of a Midwestern department's follow-up investigations of burglary and robbery (Brandl and Frank, 1994:163).

■ Special Operations

Patrol and investigation are the two largest and most important units in a police department. In metropolitan areas, however, special units are set up to deal with specific types of problems. The most common of such units concern traffic, vice, juveniles, and SWAT (strategic weapons and tactics) teams. Some cities also have units to deal with organized crime and drugs. Even with special units in place, however, patrol officers and investigators continue to deal with these same issues.

Traffic   Traffic regulation is a major job of the police. On average, 7 percent of officers are assigned to traffic units (Bayley, 1994:94). The police regulate the flow of vehicles, investigate accidents, and enforce traffic laws. This work may not seem to have much to do with crime fighting or order maintenance, but in fact it does. Besides helping to maintain order, enforcement of traffic laws educates the public by promoting safe driving habits and provides a visible service to the community.

Traffic work is mostly proactive and permits officers to use broad discretion about whom to stop and whether to issue a citation. Traffic duty can also help the police catch criminals. In enforcing traffic laws, patrol officers can stop cars and question drivers. Stolen property and suspects linked to other criminal acts are often found this way. Most departments can now automatically check license numbers against lists of wanted vehicles and suspects. See "A Question of Ethics" at the end of this chapter for more on this topic.

Vice   Enforcement of vice laws depends on proactive police work, which often involves the use of undercover agents and informers. Most big-city police departments have a vice unit. Strict enforcement of these laws requires that officers receive wide discretion. They often must engage in degrading activities, such as posing as prostitutes or drug dealers, in order to catch lawbreakers. The special nature of vice work requires members of the unit to be well trained in the legal procedures required for arrests to lead to convictions.

The potential for corruption in this type of police work presents some administrative problems. Undercover officers are in a position to blackmail gamblers and drug dealers and may also be offered bribes. In addition, officers must be transferred when their identities become known.

The growth of undercover work and electronic surveillance, common in vice patrols, troubles critics who favor more-open policing. They fear that the use of these tactics violates civil liberties and increases government intrusion into the private lives of citizens, whether or not those citizens commit crimes.

Drug Law Enforcement   Many large cities have a bureau to enforce drug laws. These agencies may include task forces that deal with organized crime or with gangs involved in drug dealing. Other groups may use sting operations to arrest drug sellers on the street; still others may provide drug education in the community.

Drug enforcement sometimes reflects the goal of *aggressive patrol*, or assigning resources so as to get the largest number of arrests and to stop street dealing. Police executives believe that they must show dealers and the community that drug laws are enforced.

The police have used various strategies to attack drug dealing. One of these involves code or building inspections of houses and buildings used by drug dealers. Those that do not meet city standards can be boarded up in order to rid the neighborhood of dealers. Streets on which drugs are dealt openly can be flooded with officers who engage in proactive stops and questioning. There are risks, however, that drug dealers will simply move their operations to new locations.

Although arrests for drug sale or possession have increased dramatically, some observers believe that this is not the best way to deal with the problem. Many public officials argue that drugs should be viewed as a public health problem rather than as a crime problem. Critics of current policies believe that society would benefit more from drug treatment programs, which can get some people to stop using drugs, than from police actions that fill prisons without doing much to reduce drug use.

CHECKPOINT

ANSWERS

6 *What are the three parts of the patrol function?*

6 Answering calls for assistance, maintaining a police presence, probing suspicious circumstances.

7 *What are the four steps in the apprehension process?*

7 (1) Detection of crime, (2) preliminary investigation, (3) follow-up investigation, (4) clearance and arrest.

8 *What are three kinds of special operations units that police departments often employ?*

8 Traffic, vice, narcotics.

Issues in Patrolling

In the last 30 years, much research has been done on police methods of assigning tasks to patrol officers, deploying them, and communicating with them. Although their conclusions have been mixed, these studies have caused experts to rethink some aspects of patrolling. However, even when researchers agree on which patrol practices are the most effective, those practices often run counter to the desires of departmental personnel. For example, foot patrol may be a key component of community-policing strategies, but many officers would rather remain in squad cars than walk the pavement. Police administrators therefore must deal with many issues in order to develop and implement effective patrol strategies.

■ Assignment of Patrol Personnel

In the past it has been assumed that patrol officers should be assigned where and when they will be most effective in preventing crime, keeping order, and serving the public. For the police administrator, the question has been "Where should the officers be sent, when, and in what numbers?" There are no guidelines to answer this question, and most assignments seem to be based on the notion that patrols should be concentrated in "problem" neighborhoods or in areas where crime rates and calls for service are high. Thus, the assignment of officers is based on factors such as crime statistics, 911 calls, degree of urbanization, pressures from business and community groups, ethnic composition, and socioeconomic conditions. Experimentation with different strategies in various cities has led to numerous choices for police leaders. In addition, research on these strategies sheds light on the strengths and weaknesses of various options. We shall examine several options in greater detail: (1) preventive patrol, (2) hot spots, (3) rapid response time, (4) foot versus motorized patrol, (5) one-person versus two-person patrol units, (6) aggressive patrol, and (7) community policing.

Preventive Patrol   Preventive patrol has long been thought to help deter crime. Many have argued that a patrol officer's moving through an area will keep criminals from carrying out illegal acts. In 1974, this assumption was tested in

Kansas City, Missouri. The surprising results shook the theoretical foundations of American policing (Sherman and Weisburd, 1995).

In the Kansas City Preventive Patrol Experiment, a 15-beat area was divided into three sections, each with similar crime rates, population characteristics, income levels, and numbers of calls to the police. In one area, labeled "reactive," all preventive patrol was withdrawn, and the police entered only in response to citizens' calls for service. In another section, labeled "proactive," preventive patrol was raised to as much as four times the normal level; all other services were provided at the same levels as before. The third section was used as a control, with the usual level of services, including preventive patrol, maintained. After observing events in the three sections for a year, the researchers concluded that the changes in patrol strategies had had no major effects on the amount of crime reported, the amount of crime as measured by citizen surveys, or citizens' fear of crime (Kelling et al., 1974). Neither a decrease nor an increase in patrol activity had any apparent effect on crime.

Despite contradictory findings of other studies using similar research methods, the Kansas City finding "remains the most influential test of the general deterrent effects of patrol on crime" (Sherman and Weisburd, 1995:626). Because of this study, many departments have shifted their focus from law enforcement to maintaining order and serving the public. Some have argued that if the police cannot prevent crime by changing their patrol tactics, they may serve society better by focusing patrol activities on other functions while fighting crime as best they can.

Hot Spots In the past, patrols were organized by "beats." It was assumed that crime can happen anywhere, and the entire beat must be patrolled at all times. Research shows, however, that crime is not spread evenly over all times and places. Instead, direct-contact predatory crimes, such as muggings and robberies, occur when three elements converge: motivated offenders, suitable targets, and the absence of anyone who could prevent the violation. This means that resources should be focused on *hot spots*, places where crimes are likely to occur (L. E. Cohen and Felson, 1979:589).

In a study of crime in Minneapolis, researchers found that a small number of hot spots—3 percent of streets and intersections—produced 50 percent of calls to the police. By analyzing the places from which calls were made, administrators could identify those that produced the most crime (Sherman, Gartin, and Buerger, 1989:27).

With this knowledge, administrators can assign officers to **directed patrol**— a proactive strategy designed to direct resources to known high-crime areas. Research indicates that directed-patrol activities focused on suspicious activities and locations can reduce violent gun crime (McGarrell et al., 2001). However, the extra police pressure may simply cause lawbreakers to move to another neighborhood or lead to other effects, such as increased numbers of arrests that place pressure on jail and court resources (Goldkamp and Vilcica, 2008).

■ **directed patrol** A proactive form of patrolling that directs resources to known high-crime areas.

Rapid Response Time Most departments are organized so that calls for help come to a central section that dispatches the nearest officers by radio to the site of the incident. Because most citizens have access to phones, most cities have 911 systems, and because most officers are in squad cars linked to headquarters by two-way radios, cell phones, and computers, police can respond quickly to calls. But are response times short enough to catch offenders?

Several studies have measured the impact of police response time on the ability of officers to intercept a crime in progress and arrest the criminal. In a classic study, William Spelman and Dale Brown (1984) found that the police succeeded in only 29 of 1,000 cases. It made little difference whether they arrived 2 minutes or 20 minutes after the call. What did matter, however, was how soon the police were called. Figure 5.4 presents these findings.

FIGURE 5.4

Probability of arrest as a function of elapsed time after crime

The probability of arrest declines sharply when the police are not called within seconds. What does this imply for patrol policies?

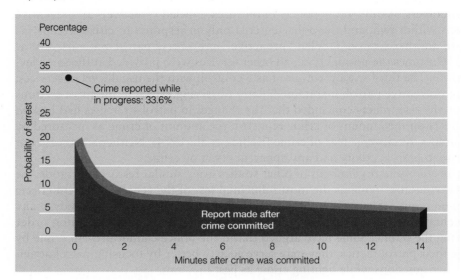

Source: William G. Spelman and Dale K. Brown, *Calling the Police: Citizen Reporting of Serious Crime* (Washington, DC: Police Executive Research Forum, 1984), 65. Reprinted by permission.

Although delayed arrival of the police is often due to slowness in calling, it seems unlikely that arrest rates would be improved merely by educating the public about their key role in stopping crime. As Spelman and Brown (1984) point out, three types of decision-making delays slow the process of calling the police:

1. *Ambiguity delays.* Some people find the situation ambiguous and are not sure whether the police should be called. They might see an event but not know whether it is a robbery or two young men "horsing around."

2. *Coping delays.* Other people are so busy coping—taking care of the victim or directing traffic—that they cannot leave the scene to call the police.

3. *Conflict delays.* Still other people must first resolve conflicts before they call the police. For example, they may call someone else for advice about whether to call the police.

Besides these delays, communication problems can slow response. For example, a telephone may not be available or the dispatcher may not be able to handle the incoming call because she or he is dealing with other problems.

The proliferation of cell phones among the American public has increased people's immediate access to phones when emergencies occur. One-third of 911 calls nationwide come from cell phones. Emergency systems in some counties are being upgraded to enable 911 operators to trace the location of cell phone calls, so that accident or crime victims who do not know their precise location can be found (Purser, 2005). However, with dropped calls and bad connections, cell phones can create their own problems.

Although delay is a major factor in decreasing probability of arrest in certain types of cases, reducing delay would only slightly increase overall arrest rates. In about three-quarters of crime calls, the police are reactive, in that the crimes (burglary, larceny, and the like) are discovered long after have they have occurred. A much smaller portion are "involvement" crimes (robbery, rape, assault) that victims know about right away and for which they can call the police promptly (Spelman and Brown, 1984:4). In addition, the danger created by high-speed response may outweigh any possible increase in effectiveness (Sherman, 1995:334).

Foot versus Motorized Patrol   One of the most frequent citizen requests is for officers to be put back on the beat. This was the main form of police patrol until the 1930s, when motorized patrol came to be viewed as more effective. Of the 195 million Americans served by local police departments, 85 percent are served by a department that uses some amount of foot patrol, bicycle patrol, or both (Hickman and Reaves, 2001; Reaves and Hart, 2000). However, departments typically use these strategies only in selected neighborhoods or districts with a high business or population density. Most patrolling is still conducted in cars, accounting for 94 percent of patrol time in large cities (Reaves, 1992). With advances in communications technologies and onboard computers, patrol officers have direct links to headquarters and to criminal information databases. Now the police can be quickly sent where needed, with crucial information in their possession.

On the other hand, many citizens and some researchers claim that patrol officers in squad cars have become remote from the people they protect and less aware of their needs. By contrast, officers on foot stay close to the daily life of the neighborhood. They detect criminal activity and apprehend lawbreakers more easily than do car patrols. Further, patrol officers who are known to citizens are less likely to be viewed as symbols of oppression by poor or minority residents (Hawdon and Ryan, 2003).

Although studies have shown that foot patrols are costly and do not greatly reduce crime, they do make citizens less fearful, increase satisfaction with the police, and give officers a greater appreciation of neighborhood values (M. Cohen, Miller, and Rossman, 1990; Kelling, 1991). In terms of the cost and benefit, foot patrols are effective in high-density urban neighborhoods and business districts.

One-Person versus Two-Person Patrol Units   The debate over one-person versus two-person patrol units has raged in police circles for years. Officers and their union leaders support the two-person squad car. They claim that police are safer and more effective when two officers work together in dangerous or difficult situations.

However, police administrators contend that the one-person squad car is much more cost-effective and permits them to deploy more cars on each shift. With more cars to deploy, each can be assigned to a smaller area and response time can be decreased. They also contend that an officer working alone is more alert and attentive because he or she cannot be distracted by idle conversation with a colleague.

Aggressive Patrol   **Aggressive patrol** is a proactive strategy designed to maximize police activity in the community. It takes many forms, such as "sting" operations, firearms confiscation, raids on crack houses, programs that encourage citizens to list their valuables, and the tracking of high-risk parolees. Some have argued that the effect of the police on crime depends less on how many officers are deployed in an area than on what they do while they are there.

The zero-tolerance policing of the 1990s in New York City is an example of aggressive patrol linked to the "broken windows" theory. As you will recall, this theory asserts "that if not firmly suppressed, disorderly behavior in public will frighten citizens and attract predatory criminals, thus leading to more serious crime problems" (Greene, 1999:172). Thus,

■ **aggressive patrol** A patrol strategy designed to maximize the number of police interventions and observations in the community.

Many police chiefs credit aggressive take-back-the-streets tactics with reducing urban crime rates in the past two decades. In some cities, however, there are questions about whether such tactics have harmed police–community relations through searches and arrests that neighborhood residents view as unjustified. If you were a police chief, what patrol strategy would you choose and what specific goals would you seek to advance?

© Lou Dematteis/The Image Works

the police should focus on minor, public order crimes such as aggressive panhandling, graffiti, prostitution, and urinating in public. By putting more police on the streets, decentralizing authority to the precinct level, and instituting officer accountability, the zero-tolerance policy was judged to be a factor in reducing New York City's crime rate (Messner et al., 2007; Rosenfeld, Fornango, and Rengifo, 2007).

Aggressive policing has also been applied as part of the war on drugs, with police officers stopping many vehicles and frisking pedestrians on certain streets. In Detroit, aggressive, zero-tolerance police practices reduced gang-related crime in targeted precincts (Bynum and Varano, 2002). Police departments also use aggressive patrol strategies to track high-risk parolees and apprehend them if they commit new offenses.

The most cost-effective of the aggressive patrol strategies seem to be those that encourage officers to carry out more field questioning and traffic stops. To implement such a strategy, the department must recruit certain kinds of officers, train them, and devise requirements and reward systems (traffic ticket quotas, required numbers of field interrogations, chances for promotion) that will encourage them to carry out the intended strategy.

Recent research raises questions about whether the "broken windows" approach actually reduces crime. Several studies present new analyses of data that challenge claims that aggressive policing is what caused crime reduction during the 1990s (Harcourt and Ludwig, 2006). Moreover, the "broken windows" approach might actually lead to citizen hostility. In some urban neighborhoods, there are rumblings that aggressive patrol has gone too far and is straining police relations with young African Americans and Hispanics. This issue centers on balancing the rights of individuals against the community's interest in maintaining order (Kolbert, 1999:50). "Put another way, it's whose son is being hassled" (Reibstein, 1997:66). See "The Policy Debate" for more on the pros and cons of aggressive enforcement.

Community Policing   To a great extent, community policing has been seen as the solution to problems with the crime-fighter stance that prevailed during the professional era (Murphy, 1992). Community policing consists of attempts by the police to involve residents in making their own neighborhoods safer. Based on the belief that citizens are often concerned about local disorder as well as crime in general, this strategy emphasizes cooperation between the police and citizens in identifying community needs and determining the best ways to meet them (M. Moore, 1992).

Community policing has four components (Skolnick and Bayley, 1986):

1. Community-based crime prevention
2. Changing the focus of patrol activities to nonemergency services
3. Making the police more accountable to the public
4. Decentralizing decision making to include residents

As indicated by these four components, community policing requires a major shift in the philosophy of policing. In particular, police officials must view citizens as customers to be served and partners in the pursuit of social goals rather than as a population to be watched, controlled, and served reactively (Morash et al., 2002). Although crime control may remain a priority in community policing, the change in emphasis can strengthen police effectiveness for order maintenance and service (Zhao, He, et al., 2003).

Departments that view themselves as emphasizing community policing do not necessarily have identical patrol strategies and initiatives (Thurman, Zhao, and Giacomazzi, 2001). Some departments emphasize identifying and solving problems related to disorder and crime. Other departments work mainly on strengthening local neighborhoods. A department's emphasis can affect which activities become the focus of officers' working hours.

Organizational factors can also affect the implementation of community policing (E. J. Williams, 2003). For example, community policing could be carried out

THE POLICY DEBATE

Should the Police Aggressively Enforce Public Order Laws?

THE POLICE IN MANY CITIES are now paying greater attention to public order offenses. Officials believe that these "little crimes" can lead to more-serious offenses. They say the police must deal with public order offenses in an aggressive, proactive manner to prevent crime.

Research has shown that high levels of disorder are linked to high levels of crime, and that disorder often leads to community decline, as fearful residents move, property values drop, and businesses close. In some cities a policy of zero tolerance for public order offenses has been instituted. Community crime-fighting initiatives can reduce disorderly behavior, fear, and urban decay, thus improving the lives of citizens.

Newer research raises questions about the "broken windows" theory. This research says the police should encourage the development of collective efficacy in neighborhoods. As described by Robert Sampson and Steve Raudenbush (2001:5–6),

> Informally mobilizing a neighborhood cleanup, for example, would reduce physical disorder while building collective efficacy by creating and strengthening social ties and increasing awareness of residents' commitment to their neighborhood.... By contrast, a police-led crackdown on disorder would probably produce a very different response by residents.

For Aggressively Enforcing Public Order Laws

Supporters of a focus on public order offenses argue that this initiative is necessary to reduce residents' fears and prevent more-serious crimes. Research, they say, has shown that using community policing to deal effectively with public order offenses is the best way to control crime and make urban areas more livable. Through aggressive foot patrol, order can be restored and maintained.

The arguments for aggressively enforcing public order laws are these:

- Enforcing public order laws reduces serious crime, residents' fears, and urban decay.
- When the police deal with low-level offenders, they learn about those who have committed serious offenses.
- Officers walking through a neighborhood become familiar with the residents and gain their cooperation and assistance when serious crime erupts.
- Police action on public order offenses encourages citizens to uphold neighborhood standards for behavior in public spaces.

Against Aggressively Enforcing Public Order Laws

Enforcing the law and improving the quality of urban life may seem to be positive goals for any community. However, some officers say they have

enough to do just dealing with the "bad guys," and they should not divert resources to lesser offenses. Further, recent research challenges the idea that reducing disorder in a neighborhood through police enforcement will produce a decline in serious crime. Recent research suggests that police should encourage community-building projects to empower neighborhood residents rather than swooping in to enforce every small rule. Civil libertarians say the new policies targeting public order offenses are designed to harass the poor, the homeless, and the mentally ill—the people society has pushed into the streets. They emphasize that some officers misuse force in enforcing these policies.

The arguments against aggressive enforcement of public order laws are these:

- Police resources and tactics should be focused on fighting serious crime.
- Recent research has challenged the link among disorder, fear, and crime.
- Aggressive police tactics against people using public spaces are attacks on the poor and other social outcasts.
- The civil liberties of the poor are infringed upon when the police aggressively enforce public order laws.

What Should U.S. Policy Be?

How would the American people react if greater police resources were allocated to deal with public order offenses? Some have argued that by aggressively dealing with disorder, the police reduce residents' fear and prevent more-serious crimes. Others see this new emphasis as targeting primarily the weak—the poor and the outcasts of society. Civil liberties are trampled in the process.

RESEARCHING THE INTERNET

To read research that challenges the assumptions of aggressive policing and the "broken windows" theory, see the corresponding website listed on the Cole/Smith Criminal Justice in America Companion Website: http://www.cengage.com/criminaljustice/cole

FOR CRITICAL ANALYSIS

Does aggressive enforcement of public order laws reduce crime or does it interfere with citizens' personal freedom and generate animosity toward the police?

by patrol officers who are assigned to walk neighborhood beats so that they can get to know residents better. It could entail creating police ministations in the community and police-sponsored programs for youth and the elderly. Police departments could also survey citizens to find out about their problems and needs (Reisig, 2002). The common element in community-policing programs is a high level of interaction between officers and citizens and the involvement of citizens in identifying problems and solving them.

■ **problem-oriented policing** An approach to policing in which officers routinely seek to identify, analyze, and respond to the circumstances underlying the incidents that prompt citizens to call the police.

A central feature of community policing for many departments is **problem-oriented policing**, a strategy that seeks to find out what is causing citizens to call for help (Goldstein, 1990). The police seek to identify, analyze, and respond to the conditions underlying the events that prompt people to call the police (Cordner and Biebel, 2005; DeJong, Mastrofski, and Parks, 2001). Knowing those conditions, officers can enlist community agencies and residents to help resolve them (Braga, 1999). Recent research indicates that problem-solving approaches can impact homicide rates (Chermak and McGarrell, 2004). Police using this approach do not just fight crime (M. D. White et al., 2003); they address a broad array of other problems that affect the quality of life in the community.

Community policing has spread across the country and gained a great deal of support from citizens, legislators, and Congress (Bayley, 1994; Zhao, Schneider, and Thurman, 2003). This support can be seen in the emphasis on community policing in the Violent Crime Control and Law Enforcement Act passed by Congress in 1994. Portions of the act call for increases in the number of officers assigned to community policing and for the development of new community-policing programs.

As with any reform, change might not come easily (Schafer, 2002). Police chiefs and midlevel managers, accustomed to dealing with problems according to established procedures, may feel that their authority decreases when responsibility shifts to precinct commanders and officers on the streets (Alley, Bonello, and Schafer, 2002). Another problem with implementing community policing is that it does not reduce costs; it requires either additional funds or redistribution within existing budgets. Measuring the success of this approach in reducing fear of crime, solving underlying problems, maintaining order, and serving the community is also difficult. In addition, there is the debate about how far the police should extend their role beyond crime fighting to remedying other social problems. Finally, police officers may resist committing themselves to daily activities that emphasize roles other than the crime-fighting role that may have attracted them to a career in law enforcement (Mastrofski, Willis, and Snipes, 2002; E. J. Williams, 2003).

■ The Future of Patrol

Preventive patrol and rapid response to calls for help have been the hallmarks of policing in the United States for the past half century. However, research done in the past 30 years has raised many questions about which patrol strategies police should employ. The rise of community policing has shifted law enforcement toward problems that affect the quality of life of residents. Police forces need to use patrol tactics that fit the needs of the neighborhood. Neighborhoods with crime hot spots may require different strategies than do neighborhoods where residents are concerned mainly with order maintenance. Many researchers believe that traditional patrol efforts have focused too narrowly on crime control, neglecting the order maintenance and service activities for which police departments were originally formed. Critics have urged the police to become more community oriented and return to the first principle of policing: "to remain in close and frequent contact with citizens" (H. Williams and Pate, 1987:53). To see this policy in action, we look to Japan, where most patrolling is done on foot, as described in the Comparative Perspective.

How the national effort to combat terrorism will affect local police-patrol operations remains uncertain. Since the attacks of September 11, state and local police have assumed greater responsibility for investigating bank robberies and other federal crimes as the FBI and other federal agencies devote significant attention to catching people connected with terrorist organizations. In addition, even local police officers must be ready to spot suspicious activities that might relate to terrorist activity. They

COMPARATIVE PERSPECTIVE

Patrol in *JAPAN*

MANY COMMUNITY-POLICING STRATEGIES now being used in the United States have been the tradition in Japan for many years. Patrol officers walking through their assigned neighborhoods and working out of local offices are a hallmark of Japanese policing.

Japanese policemen are addressed by the public as Omawari-san—Mr. Walkabout. This is an accurate reflection of what the public sees the police doing most of the time. Foot patrolling is done out of *kobans* [mini police stations in urban neighborhoods], usually for periods of an hour. Patrols are more common at night, when officers work in pairs.... Patrolmen amble at a ruminative pace that allows thorough observation.... Patrolling by automobile, which is much less common than foot patrolling, can be frustrating too. Due to the narrow congested streets of Japanese cities... patrol cars are forced to move at a snail's pace....

Patrolling is by no means a matter of high adventure. For the most part it consists of watching and occasionally answering questions. Patrolmen rarely discover genuine emergencies; the chance of coincidence between patrolmen and sudden need are simply too great. Patrolling does not reduce reaction time or particularly enhance availability. What patrolling does is to demonstrate the existence of authority, correct minor inconveniences... such as illegally parked cars... and generate trust through the establishment of familiar personal relations with a neighborhood's inhabitants. On patrol, policemen are alert for different kinds of problems in different places. In a residential area they watch for people who appear out of place or furtive. In public parks they give attention to loitering males. Around major railroad stations they look for runaway adolescents, lured by the glamour of a big city, who could be victimized by criminal elements. They also watch for *teyhaishi*...labor contractors...who pick up and sell unskilled laborers to construction companies. In a neighborhood of bars and cabarets, patrolmen stare suspiciously at stylishly dressed women standing unescorted on street corners. They determine whether wheeled carts piled with food or cheap souvenirs are blocking pedestrian thoroughfares. Throughout every city they pay particular attention to illegally parked cars and cars that have been left with their doors unlocked....

When a Japanese policeman is out on patrol he makes a special point of talking to people about themselves, their purposes, and their behavior. These conversations may be innocent or investigatory. The law provides that policemen may stop and question people only if there is reasonable ground for suspecting they have committed or are about to commit a crime or have information about a crime. Nevertheless, standard procedure on patrol is to stop and question anyone whenever the policeman thinks it may be useful. One reason for doing so is to discover wanted persons. And the tactic has proved very effective; 40 percent of criminals wanted by the police have been discovered by patrolmen on the street. Not only do officers learn to question people adroitly on the street, they become adept at getting people to agree to come to the *koban* so that more extended, less public inquiries can be made. People are under no obligation to do so, any more than they are to stop and answer questions. The key to success with these tactics is to be compelling without being coercive. This in turn depends on two factors: the manner of the police officer and a thorough knowledge of minor laws. The first reduces hostility, the second provides pretexts for opening conversations justifiably. People who park illegally, ride bicycles without a light, or fail to wear helmets when riding a motorcycle are inviting officers to stop them and ask probing questions. The importance with which the police view on-street interrogation is indicated by the fact that prefectural and national contests are held each year to give recognition to officers who are best at it.... Senior officers continually impress upon new recruits the importance of learning to ask questions in inoffensive ways so that innocent people are not affronted and unpleasant scenes can be avoided....

The most striking aspect of the variety of situations confronted by policemen is their compelling, unforced naturalness. The police see masses of utterly ordinary people who have been enmeshed in situations that are tediously complex and meaningful only to the persons immediately involved. The outcomes are of no interest to the community at large; the newspapers will not notice if matters are sorted out or not; superior officers have no way of recording the effort patrolmen expend in trying to be helpful; and the people themselves are incapable by and large of permanently escaping their predicaments. Policemen are responsible for tending these individuals, for showing that they appreciate—even when they are tired, hurried, bored, and preoccupied—the minute ways in which each person is unique. It is perhaps, the greatest service they render.

🌐 RESEARCHING THE INTERNET

To learn more about policing in Japan, see the English-language website of Japan's National Police Agency, listed on the Cole/Smith Criminal Justice in America Companion Website: http://www.cengage.com/criminaljustice/cole

Source: David H. Bayley, *Forces of Order: Police Behavior in Japan and the United States* (Berkeley: University of California Press, 1979), 33–34, 37, 41, 51–52. Copyright © 1976 The Regents of the University of California. Reprinted by permission

are the first responders in a bombing or other form of attack. Obviously, federal law enforcement officials must work closely with local police in order to be effective. Yet, many local police chiefs have criticized the FBI for failing to share important information about local suspects (Bowers, 2002). The new concerns will not alter traditional police responsibilities for crime fighting, order maintenance, and service, but they will provide an additional consideration as police administrators plan how to train and deploy their personnel.

CHECKPOINT

ANSWERS

9 What are the advantages of foot patrol? Of motorized patrol?

9 Officers on foot patrol have greater contact with residents of a neighborhood, thus gaining their confidence and assistance. Officers on motorized patrol have a greater range of activity and can respond speedily to calls.

10 What is aggressive patrol?

10 A proactive strategy designed to maximize the number of police interventions and observations in a community.

11 What are the major elements of community policing?

11 Community policing emphasizes order maintenance and service. It attempts to involve members of the community in making their neighborhoods safe. Foot patrol and decentralization of command are usually part of community-policing efforts.

Police and the Community

The work of a police officer in a U.S. city can be very difficult, involving hours of boring, routine work interrupted by short spurts of dangerous crime fighting. Although police work has always been frustrating and dangerous, officers today must deal with situations ranging from helping the homeless to dealing with domestic violence to confronting shoot-outs at drug deals gone sour. Yet, police actions are sometimes mishandled by officers or misinterpreted by the public, making some people critical of the police.

Special Populations

Urban police forces must deal with a complex population. City streets contain growing numbers of people suffering from mental illness, homelessness, alcoholism, drug addiction, or serious medical conditions such as acquired immune deficiency syndrome (AIDS) (Hails and Borum, 2003). In addition, they may find youthful runaways and children victimized by their parents' neglect. Several factors have contributed to increasing numbers of "problem" people on the streets. These factors include overcrowded jails, cutbacks in public assistance, and the closing of many psychiatric institutions, which must then release mental health patients. Most of these "problem" people do not commit crimes, but their presence disturbs many of their fellow citizens and thus they may contribute to fear of crime and disorder.

Patrol officers cooperate with social service agencies in helping individuals and responding to requests for order maintenance. The police must walk a fine line when requiring a person to enter a homeless shelter, obtain medical assistance, or be taken to a mental health unit (McCoy, 1986; Melekian, 1990). Police departments have developed various techniques for dealing with special populations. In some cities, mobile units are equipped with restraining devices, mace, and medical equipment to handle disturbed people.

In multicultural America, police must be sensitive to the perspectives and customs of many different groups. They must enforce the law while treating people equally and upholding civil liberties. These responsibilities can be difficult when people are angry or uncooperative. Have you heard about situations in which police officers' emotions, such as anger or frustration, affected their decisions or behavior?

© Bob Daemmrich/The Image Works

Clearly, dealing with special populations is a major problem for police in most cities. Each community must develop policies so that officers will know when and how they are to intervene when a person may not have broken the law but is upsetting residents. Inevitably, police officers will make mistakes in some situations. For instance, their interactions with troubled people sometimes lead to tragic consequences, such as using lethal force against deaf or mentally ill people whose actions are misperceived as threatening. In 2003, a controversy erupted in Denver after police shot a legally blind, mentally handicapped teenager who was holding a knife (Felch, 2003).

■ Policing in a Multicultural Society

Carrying out the complex tasks of policing efficiently and according to the law is a tough assignment even when the police have the support and cooperation of the public. But policing in a multicultural society such as the United States presents further challenges.

In the last half century, the racial and ethnic composition of the United States has changed. During the mid-twentieth century, many African Americans moved from rural areas of the South to northern cities. In recent years, immigrants from Central and South America have become the fastest-growing minority group in many cities. Latinos are now the largest minority population in the nation. Immigrants from Eastern Europe, Russia, the Middle East, and Asia have entered the country in greater numbers than before. Policing requires trust, understanding, and cooperation between officers and the public. People must be willing to call for help and provide information about wrongdoing. But in a multicultural society, relations between the police and minorities are complicated by stereotypes, cultural variations, and language differences. Most of these immigrants come from countries with cultural traditions and laws that differ from those in the United States. These traditions may be unfamiliar to American police officers. Further, some immigrants cannot communicate easily in English. Lack of familiarity, difficulties in communicating, and excessive suspicion can create risks that officers will violate the American value of equal treatment of all people (C. E. Smith, McCall, and Perez McCluskey, 2005).

Like other Americans who have limited personal experience or familiarity with people from different backgrounds, officers may attribute undesirable traits to members of minority groups. Treating people according to stereotypes, rather than as individuals, creates tensions that harden negative attitudes. Racial profiling, as discussed in Chapter 1, can contribute to mistrust and conflict.

Public opinion surveys have shown that race and ethnicity play a key role in determining people's attitudes toward the police. As seen in "What Americans Think," questions of fair treatment by the police differ among racial groups. Young, low-income, racial-minority men carry the most negative attitudes toward the police (S. Walker, Spohn, and DeLeone, 2007). Inner-city neighborhoods—the areas that need and want effective policing—often significantly distrust the police; citizens may therefore fail to report crimes and refuse to cooperate with the police (P. J. Carr, Napolitano, and Keating, 2007). Encounters between officers and members of these communities are often hostile and sometimes lead to large-scale disorders. In January 2008, hundreds of protestors marched in Lima, Ohio, to express their outrage that police officers, when entering a home to look for a male drug suspect, had shot and killed a young African American woman and wounded her toddler. Twenty-seven percent of Lima's 38,000 residents are African American, yet only two of the city's 77 police officers are African American (Maag, 2008).

Race is not the only factor affecting attitudes toward the police. Attitudes also stem from negative personal experience with the police, a factor associated with race. In some neighborhoods, such experience may contribute to people's unhappiness with the overall quality of life and a lack of cooperation between the public and the police. Clearly, police actions and policies significantly affect the attitudes some citizens have about the fairness of the larger political community.

Why do some urban residents resent the police? John DiIulio argues that this resentment stems from permissive law enforcement and police abuse of power (DiIulio, 1993:3). The police are perceived as failing to give protection and services to minor-

What AMERICANS Think

QUESTION: "Just your impression, are African Americans in your community treated less fairly than whites in the following situations? How about in dealing with the police, such as traffic incidents?"

Yes, African Americans are treated less fairly

- Whites: 33%
- African Americans: 73%

No, not treated less fairly

- Whites: 59%
- African Americans: 24%

Go to http://www.cengage.com/criminaljustice/cole to compare your opinion on this issue with the opinions of other criminal justice students.

Source: Gallup Poll, June 2–24, 2007, http://www.gallup.com.

ity neighborhoods and as abusing residents physically or verbally. Thus, as we have seen, urban ghetto dwellers may think of the police as an army of occupation, and the police may think of themselves as combat soldiers. As noted by Jerome Skolnick and James Fyfe, the military organization of the police and the war on crime can lead to violence against inner-city residents, whom the police see as the enemy (1993:160). All aspects of officers' responsibilities, including service, order maintenance, and crime control, can suffer when police officers and the communities that they serve lack cooperation and trust.

■ Community Crime Prevention

There is a growing awareness that the police cannot control crime and disorder on their own. Social control requires involvement by all members of the community. Community crime prevention can be enhanced if government agencies and neighborhood organizations cooperate. Across the country, community programs to help the police have proliferated (Zhao et al., 2002).

More than six million Americans belong to citizen crime-watch groups, which often have direct ties to police departments. Many communities also use the Crime Stoppers Program to enlist public help in solving crimes. Television and radio stations present the "unsolved crime of the week," sometimes with cash rewards given for information that leads to conviction of the offender. Although these programs help solve some crimes, the number solved remains small compared with the total number of crimes committed.

Research on 40 neighborhoods in six cities shows that while crime-prevention efforts and voluntary community groups have seen some success in relatively affluent neighborhoods, such efforts and groups are less likely to be found in poor neighborhoods with high levels of disorder. In such areas, "residents typically are deeply suspicious of one another, report only a weak sense of community, perceive they have low levels of personal influence on neighborhood events, and feel that it is their neighbors, not 'outsiders,' whom they must watch with care" (Skogan, 1990:130). Scholars say that the citizens of a community must take responsibility for maintaining civil and safe social conditions. Experience has shown that "while police might be able to retake a neighborhood from aggressive drug dealers, police could not hold a neighborhood without significant commitment and actual assistance from private citizens" (Kelling and Coles, 1996:248).

CHECKPOINT

ANSWERS

12 *What "special populations" pose challenges for policing?*

12 Runaways and neglected children; people who suffer from homelessness, drug addiction, mental illness, or alcoholism.

13 *What factors make policing in a multicultural society difficult?*

13 Stereotyping, cultural differences, language differences.

14 *How are citizen watch groups and similar programs helpful to the police?*

14 They assist the police by reporting incidents and providing information.

Homeland Security

The aftermath of 9/11 has brought expansion, redirection, and reorganization among law enforcement agencies, especially those at the federal level. For instance, the emphasis on counterterrorism has led to an increase in intelligence analysts in the FBI, from

1,023 in September 2001 to more than 2,100 in April 2008. In addition, the number of foreign-language specialists in the FBI increased from 784 to more than 1,300 in the same period (Mueller, 2008). The creation of the Department of Homeland Security, the reordering of crime control policies away from street crime and drugs to international and domestic terrorism, and the great increase in federal money to pursue the war against terrorism are greatly affecting law enforcement at all levels of government.

For example, the FBI has an increased budget and a restructuring plan in place to "increase the emphasis in counterterrorism, counterintelligence, cyber crimes, and relations with state and local law enforcement" (Oliver, 2002:1). This new thrust in policy shifts the focus of the FBI from the investigation of local street crimes to cases of international and domestic terrorism. FBI Director Robert Mueller has acknowledged that, following 9/11, many criminal investigations had to be set aside as many agents directed their attention toward Al-Qaida and related threats. Further, the bureau has come to rely on state and local law enforcement to fill the gaps where the FBI could not respond to matters, such as bank robberies, that are crimes under both federal and state laws.

To meet the challenges of terrorist threats as well as the increasingly international nature of criminal organizations, U.S. agencies have dramatically increased the number of officers stationed in foreign countries. The FBI has 70 overseas offices known as Legal Attaches or Legats. These offices focus on coordination with law enforcement personnel in other countries. Their activities are limited by the formal agreements negotiated between the United States and each host country. In many other countries, American agents are authorized only to gather information and facilitate communications between countries. American agencies are especially active in working with other countries on counterterrorism, drug trafficking, and cyber crime (Mueller, 2008).

Another vehicle for international antiterrorist and anticrime efforts is Interpol, the International Criminal Police Organization created in 1946 to foster cooperation among the world's police forces. Based today in Lyon, France, Interpol maintains an intelligence database and serves as a clearinghouse for information gathered by agencies of its 186 member nations, including the United States. In 2008, Interpol's six priority crime areas were (1) drugs and criminal organizations, (2) public safety and terrorism, (3) financial and high-tech crime, (4) trafficking in human beings, (5) fugitive apprehension, and (6) corruption (http://www.interpol.int). Despite the benefits of international cooperation, Interpol's secretary-general has complained that individual countries have not shared enough information with Interpol in a timely manner (Noble, 2006).

■ Preparing for Threats

The events of September 11 altered the priorities of government agencies and pushed law enforcement agencies at the federal, state, and local levels to make plans for the possibility of future significant threats to homeland security. The FBI and DHS make concerted efforts to identify and combat risks in order to reduce the threat of additional attacks. The FBI switched a significant portion of its personnel away from traditional crime control activities in order to gather intelligence on people within the United States who may pose a threat to the nation. At the same time, the creation of DHS reflected a desire to have better coordination between agencies that were previously scattered through the federal government. The DHS also instituted new security procedures at airports and borders as a means of identifying individuals and contraband that pose threats. Many critics believe that the federal government has not done enough to protect ports and critical infrastructure, including nuclear power plants, information systems, subway systems, and other elements essential for the functioning of U.S. society. Attacks with devastating consequences could range from computer hackers disabling key military information systems or computerized controls

The White House and U.S. Capitol were evacuated, and U.S. Air Force planes scrambled in May 2005, when authorities became alarmed about the approach of an unidentified aircraft. The Cessna airplane had inadvertently violated the restricted airspace surrounding Washington, D.C. Incidents such as this are treated with much more urgency since the September 11 terrorist attacks.

© Ken Cedeno/CORBIS

at energy companies to a suicide airline hijacker hitting a nuclear power or chemical plant. If an attack should target and disable any of these entities, it would fall to local police to maintain order and rescue victims.

Security at borders is an important component of homeland security. U.S. Border Patrol agents do not merely look for illegal immigrants and drug traffickers; they must also be aware that terrorists might try to sneak across the border, bringing with them weapons, explosives, and other dangerous materials. As you read "Careers in Criminal Justice," consider whether you would want a challenging career working in the Border Patrol.

Police agencies have traditionally gathered **law enforcement intelligence** about criminal activities and organizations, especially in their efforts to monitor motorcycle gangs, hate groups, drug traffickers, and organized crime. The new emphasis on homeland security broadens the scope of information that agencies need to gather. According to Jonathan White (2004:73), police must be trained to look for and gather information about such things as

- Emergence of radical groups, including religious groups
- Suspicious subjects observing infrastructure facilities
- Growth of phony charities that may steer money to terrorists
- Groups with links to foreign countries
- Unexpected terrorist information found during criminal searches
- Discovery of bomb-making operations

Local police agencies need training about what to look for and whom to contact if any suspicious activities or materials are discovered. One of the disconcerting aspects of the September 11 tragedy was that specific agencies and officers possessed suspicions about unusual students at flight schools and individuals who had entered the country. If the agencies had shared information more effectively, some people believe that at least some of the September 11 hijackers would have been apprehended and questioned. In light of this lesson, law enforcement agencies at all levels are working harder to coordinate their efforts and share information. Local police officials still complain that the FBI and other federal agencies do not share enough information with them about potential threats within their communities.

One effort to share information emerged in the form of *fusion centers*. These are state and local intelligence operations that "use law enforcement analysts and sophisticated computer systems to compile, or fuse, disparate tips and clues and pass along the refined information to other agencies" (O'Harrow, 2008). The federal government has provided nearly $250 million for the development and operation of these centers. In addition, the Department of Homeland Security has assigned its personnel to work at these centers. According to the DHS website, "As of March 2008, there were 58 fusion centers around the country. The Department has deployed 23 officers as of March 2008 and plans to have 25 professionals deployed by the end of [fiscal year] 2008." Nineteen of the centers have security clearances that permit them to access information classified as "secret" from the federal government's National Counterterrorism Center (U.S. Department of Homeland Security, 2008). Authorities hope that the gathering, processing, and sharing of information can help prevent plots from being executed (Sheridan and Hsu, 2006).

■ **law enforcement intelligence** Information, collected and analyzed by law enforcement officials, concerning criminal activities and organizations, such as gangs, drug traffickers, and organized crime.

U.S. Border Patrol agents and other officials who work for U.S. Customs and Border Protection have been trained to give extra attention to the threat of terrorism. They still retain traditional responsibilities for laws related to immigration, drug trafficking, and smuggling, but all of these issues are now recognized as important components of homeland security. Should the United States impose greater restrictions on entry into our country? What would be the economic and political impact of such restrictions?

© Jack Kurtz/The Image Works

CAREERS IN CRIMINAL JUSTICE

Border Patrol Agent

KARL HUETHER, U.S. BORDER PATROL AGENT
U.S. BORDER PATROL, ARIZONA

THE UNITED STATES BORDER PATROL is the mobile, uniformed law enforcement arm of the U.S. Customs and Border Protection (CBP) within the Department of Homeland Security. Since the terrorist attacks of September 11, 2001, the focus of the Border Patrol has shifted to emphasize the detection, apprehension and/or deterrence of terrorists and terrorist weapons. Its overall mission remains unchanged: to detect and prevent the illegal entry of aliens and contraband into the United States. Together with other law enforcement officers, the Border Patrol helps maintain borders that work—facilitating the flow of legal immigration and goods while preventing the illegal trafficking of people and contraband.

The Border Patrol is specifically responsible for patrolling the 6,000 miles of Mexican and Canadian international land borders and 2,000 miles of coastal waters surrounding Florida and Puerto Rico. Agents work around the clock on assignments, in all types of terrain and weather conditions. Agents also work in many isolated communities throughout the United States.

To become a United States Border Patrol Agent, one must meet a few basic qualifications. A candidate must be a U.S. citizen, possess a valid automobile driver's license, and pass the CBP Border Patrol entrance exam. Candidates must also have substantial work experience. A four-year college degree may substitute for the required work experience, or candidates may qualify through a combination of education and work experience.

Karl Huether earned an undergraduate degree in criminal justice, as well as a certificate in homeland security studies. In addition, he gained experience in the field of criminal justice through participation in internships with state police and state probation offices.

As a Border Patrol Agent, I face different challenges every day when I go out into the field. Line watch is one of the most crucial activities that a Border Patrol Agent will conduct. While conducting line watch, agents detect, prevent, and apprehend terrorists, undocumented aliens, and smugglers of aliens at or near the land border. To make line watch successful, agents must keep up with daily intelligence reports, training, and the laws which are enforced by the U.S. Border Patrol.

During the 1960s and 1970s, government agents spied on American citizens for merely expressing their views about civil rights and the Vietnam War. Critics who remember such activities publicly voice suspicion regarding fusion centers and other recent intelligence operations. For example, fusion centers in various states create massive databases that include such information as citizens' credit reports, car rental records, unlisted cell phone numbers, drivers' license photographs, and identity theft reports. Some feel that the government is intruding too broadly into the lives of all Americans, including those who are not suspected of any wrongdoing (German and Stanley, 2007; O'Harrow, 2008). In addition, the accumulation of so much information into connected networks raises concerns about the risk of a security breach, either through the work of an ingenious hacker or through a government employee losing a laptop computer on a business trip. Such a breach would create massive problems, including identity theft. As law enforcement agencies in the United States continue to develop methods to combat terrorism and protect homeland security, many people will reexamine the balance between providing the government with appropriate tools and safeguarding the rights of Americans against government intrusions.

The emphasis on information analysis and coordination among agencies at all levels of U.S. government, as well as coordination with foreign governments, also impacts law enforcement operations concerning other major problems, such as drug trafficking, money laundering, gun smuggling, and border security. For example, homeland security efforts overlap with initiatives to combat transnational street gangs. For instance, the MS-13 gang from Central America has spread from Los Angeles to such places as

Washington, D.C., and Charlotte, North Carolina, bringing with it various criminal activities, including a series of gang-related homicides (Axtman, 2005a).

Within local police departments, the emphasis on homeland security has led to changes in training, equipment, and operations to prepare first responders to deal with the possibility of weapons of mass destruction and terrorist attacks. The police must also develop regional coordination with neighboring communities and state governments, because large-scale emergencies require the resources and assistance of multiple agencies. Communities need plans for conducting evacuations of buildings and neighborhoods. Police officials must work more closely with firefighters, public health officials, and emergency medical services to prepare for anything from a bomb to a bioterrorist attack using anthrax, smallpox, or other harmful agents (Hinton, 2002). Some of these threats require the acquisition of new equipment, such as protective suits for suspected biological or chemical hazards or communications equipment that can be used to contact multiple agencies. Many police departments are giving renewed attention to training specialized teams, such as bomb squads and SWAT teams, that will intervene in emergency situations. In addition, they must give all officers additional training on hazardous materials, coordination with outside agencies, and evacuation procedures for malls, central business districts, and hospitals.

CHECKPOINT

ANSWER

15 *What have law enforcement officials done to enhance the protection of homeland security?*

15 Planning and coordinating with other agencies, intelligence gathering, new equipment, and training.

■ New Laws and Controversies

The hijackers' devastating attacks on September 11, 2001, spurred a variety of government actions intended to protect homeland security and combat terrorism. The Bush administration asserted new presidential powers to arrest and detain indefinitely without trial Americans whom it accused of terrorist activities. In 2004, however, the U.S. Supreme Court ruled that the president does not possess unlimited authority and that American detainees are entitled to challenge their confinement through court procedures (*Hamdi v. Rumsfeld*, 2004). The Supreme Court's decision illustrates one aspect of the challenge facing the United States: how to provide government with sufficient power to fight terrorism while also protecting individuals' constitutional rights.

Other controversies arose concerning new state and federal statutes created after September 11. Both Congress and state legislatures enacted new laws aimed at addressing various aspects of homeland security. More than 30 states added new terrorism-related laws. These laws ranged from narrow to broad—from statutes addressing specific problems to authorizations of new powers for law enforcement officials and the definition of new crimes. At the narrow end of the spectrum, for example, Virginia passed a law to make it more difficult for foreign nationals to obtain a driver's license without possession of specific legal documents. This was in direct response to the discovery that several of the September 11 hijackers had obtained Virginia driver's licenses.

Because new laws provide tools for justice system officials, controversies can arise when those officials apparently stretch their authority beyond the intentions of the relevant statutes. For example, prosecutors in several cases have used new terrorism laws as a means to prosecute people for criminal acts that are not commonly understood to be related to terrorism. In New York, for example, one of the first prosecutions under the state's antiterrorism laws enacted after September 11 arose when the Bronx district attorney charged street gang members for various crimes. There was no allegation that the gang members had connections to any foreign terrorist networks. Instead, the prosecutor used the state's antiterrorism law to charge gang members with shootings committed with the intent to intimidate or coerce a civilian population (Garcia, 2005). In another example, a North Carolina prosecutor charged the operator of a small meth lab under a terrorism statute for manufacturing a nuclear or chemical weapon ("Charging Common Criminals," 2003). These cases generated criticism in newspaper editorials and raised concerns that government officials would exploit terrorism laws for improper purposes. The language of many terrorism laws is sufficiently vague to give prosecutors great flexibility in seeking convictions. The severe penalties for terrorism-related acts can also give prosecutors more leverage to pressure defendants to plead guilty to lesser charges.

The most controversial legislation came from Congress in the form of the Uniting and Strengthening America by Providing Appropriate Tools Required to Intercept and Obstruct Terrorism Act. It is best known by its shorthand name, the **USA Patriot Act**. The Patriot Act moved quickly through Congress after the September 11 attacks and covered a wide range of topics, including the expansion of government authority for searches and surveillance and the expansion of definitions and penalties for crimes related to terrorism. Critics have raised concerns about many provisions because of fears that the government's assertions of excessive power will infringe individuals' rights (Dority, 2005). The Patriot Act makes it easier for law enforcement officials to monitor email and obtain "sneak-and-peek" warrants, in which they secretly conduct searches and do not inform the home or business owner that the premises have been searched until much later (K. M. Sullivan, 2003). The Patriot Act also authorizes warrantless searches of third-party records, such as those at libraries, financial institutions, phone companies, and medical facilities. This provision has sparked an outcry from librarians and booksellers, who argue that government monitoring of the reading habits of citizens without sufficient evidence to obtain a warrant violates their rights of privacy and free expression. This provision, in particular, was cited by many of the 150 communities across the country that passed resolutions protesting the excessive authority granted to government by the Patriot Act (J. Gordon, 2005).

Some of the concerns about the Patriot Act arose because it sailed through Congress in the aftermath of September 11 with little close examination or debate. Because the law is several hundred pages long, members of Congress had not likely studied the entire law before voting on it. Some of the provisions in the Patriot Act, such as those expanding powers for searches and wiretaps, had been sought by some federal law enforcement officials prior to September 11. Critics claim that the terrorist attacks provided the momentum for powers that these officials had sought to use for crime control purposes unrelated to homeland security. Moreover, some people fear that the Patriot Act authorizes law enforcement officials to undertake investigatory activities that cannot be readily supervised or monitored by judges and legislators.

In light of their new powers, will law enforcement officials act too swiftly in investigating and even arresting people without an adequate basis for suspicion? Read the Close Up box on the arrest of an Oregon lawyer and see whether you think these risks are real.

The Patriot Act has received criticism from both liberals and conservatives. Politicians express concern that law enforcement officials could too easily search people's homes, obtain their personal records, and intercept their communications without a firm basis for suspicion of wrongdoing. For example, government reports revealed in 2008 that the FBI had improperly made blanket demands for phone records instead of requesting specific phone records (Lichtblau, 2008a). In addition, the FBI improperly obtained other personal information on Americans that was not consistent with the authority granted under the Patriot Act. In response, the FBI instituted a new tracking system for national security letters and increased training and supervision for its agents (Lichtblau, 2008b).

Further, the Patriot Act defines domestic terrorism as criminal acts dangerous to human life that appear intended to intimidate civilians or influence public policy by intimidation. Conservatives fear the law could be used against antiabortion protestors who block entrances at abortion clinics, whereas liberals fear that it could be used against environmental activists who take direct actions to prevent the destruction of forests and wildlife. Other critics of the Patriot Act point to provisions making it a crime

■ **USA Patriot Act** A federal statute passed in the aftermath of the terrorist attacks of September 11, 2001, that broadens government authority to conduct searches and wiretaps and that expands the definitions of crimes involving terrorism.

CLOSE UP

Swift Action Based on Limited Evidence

POWERFUL BOMBS ROCKED the train station in Madrid, Spain, on March 11, 2004, killing 191 people and injuring 2,000 others. Authorities suspected Muslim radicals who were targeting Spain because it had joined the United States in the invasion of Iraq. FBI experts examined evidence in the bombing, including a partial fingerprint found on a bag of detonators. The FBI officials used their department's automated searching system for the fingerprint database and determined that the print matched Brandon Mayfield's. The fingerprints of Mayfield, a lawyer from Portland, Oregon, who had converted to Islam 20 years earlier, were in the FBI database because he had once been a U.S. Army officer and military fingerprints are included in the FBI computer. Although Spanish authorities cast doubt on the FBI's conclusions, Mayfield was arrested as a material witness and held in jail. The FBI searched his home, examined his telephone records, and analyzed his relationships with other Muslims who they believed had ties to terrorist organizations. After he spent two weeks in jail, Mayfield was released because Spanish authorities matched the fingerprint to

a man from Algeria. The FBI subsequently apologized to Mayfield for the error and paid him $2 million to settle the lawsuit that he filed against the agency.

 RESEARCHING THE INTERNET

Read the article "Fingerprints: Not a Gold Standard" in *Issues in Science and Technology Online*, on the site listed on the Cole/Smith Criminal Justice in America Companion Website: http://www.cengage.com/criminaljustice/ cole. Should the government rely on a single, partial fingerprint for placing someone in jail? Would the FBI have acted so swiftly against Mayfield if he had belonged to a different religion? How much evidence should the government possess before taking someone into custody?

Sources: "Editorial: The F.B.I. Messes Up," *New York Times*, May 26, 2004, p. A22; Susan Jo Keller, "Judge Rules Provision in Patriot Act to Be Illegal," *New York Times*, September 27, 2007, http://www.nytimes.com; MSNBC, "U.S. Lawyer Freed in Madrid Bombing Case," May 20, 2004, http://www.MSNBC.com.

to provide material support for terrorism; they raise concerns that people who donate money to the antiabortion movement or environmental causes could unwittingly find themselves prosecuted for serious terrorist offenses (Lithwick and Turner, 2003).

The debates about new laws enacted as part of homeland security and counterterrorist efforts illustrate the struggle to maintain American values of personal liberty, privacy, and individual rights while simultaneously ensuring that law enforcement personnel have sufficient power to protect the nation from catastrophic harm. There are no easy answers for the questions raised about whether the government has too much power and whether Americans' rights have been violated.

Now that we have considered the government's role in homeland security, we turn our attention to the private sector. Corporations and other entities must safeguard their assets, personnel, and facilities. They, too, have heightened concerns about terrorism and other homeland security issues. For example, nuclear power plants, chemical factories, energy companies, and other private facilities make up part of the nation's critical infrastructure. Because terrorists might target such facilities, private sector officials must address these concerns, just as they have long needed to address other security issues such as employee theft, fires, and trade secrets.

CHECKPOINT

ANSWER

16 *What are the criticisms directed at the USA Patriot Act?*

16 Permits too much government authority for searches and wiretaps; defines domestic terrorism in ways that might include legitimate protest groups.

Security Management and Private Policing

Only a few years ago, the term *private security* called to mind the image of security guards, people with marginal qualifications for other occupations who ended up accepting minimal wages to stand guard outside factories and businesses. This image reflected a long history of private employment of individuals who served limited police-patrol functions. In recent years, by contrast, private sector activities related to policing functions have become more complex and important.

Many threats have spurred an expansion in security management and private policing; these include (1) an increase in crime in the workplace; (2) an increase in fear (real or perceived) of crime; (3) the fiscal crises of the states, which have limited public police protection; and (4) increased public and business awareness and use of more cost-effective private security services (Cunningham, Strauchs, and Van Meter, 1990:236). Today, if one speaks of people employed in private security, it would be more accurate to envision a variety of occupations ranging from traditional security guards to computer security experts to high-ranking corporate vice presidents responsible for planning and overseeing safety and security at a company's industrial plants and office complexes around the world.

Retail and industrial firms spend nearly as much for private protection as all localities spend for police protection. Many government entities hire private companies to provide security at specific office buildings or other facilities. In addition, private groups, such as residents of wealthy suburbs, have hired private police to patrol their neighborhoods. Precise figures are difficult to obtain, but one fairly recent estimate showed that 60,000 private agencies employed more than 1.9 million people in security operations (T. Carlson, 1995:67). Each year businesses, organizations, and individuals together spend about $100 billion on private security. There are now three times as many officers hired by private security companies as there are public police (see Figure 5.5).

Contemporary security managers are well-educated professionals with administrative experience and backgrounds in management and law. Here, Hemanshu Nigam, a former federal prosecutor, poses at the offices of Fox Interactive Media, where he is the chief security officer. Nigam is responsible for online safety and security at MySpace.com, the popular social networking site. Are there any businesses or industries that do not need the services of security personnel in today's fast-changing world?

AP Images/Damian Dovarganes

FIGURE 5.5

Employment in private and public protection, 1970–2010 (projected)

The number of people employed by private security firms has surpassed the number employed by the public police and is growing. Such a large private force presents questions for the criminal justice system.

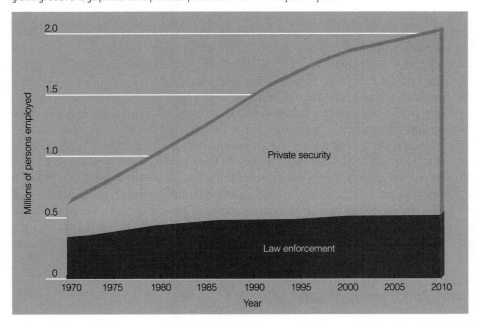

Source: Adapted from William Cunningham, John Strauchs, and Clifford Van Meter, *Private Security: Patterns and Trends* (Washington, DC: National Institute of Justice, U.S. Government Printing Office, 1991), 3. Trend line projection to 2010 by the authors.

Functions of Security Management and Private Policing

Top-level security managers have a range of responsibilities that require them to fulfill multiple roles that separate individuals would handle in the public sector. For their corporations, they simultaneously function as police chiefs, fire chiefs, emergency-management administrators, and computer-security experts. They hire, train, and supervise expert personnel to protect corporate computer systems that may contain credit card numbers, trade secrets, confidential corporate financial information, and other data sought by hackers intent on causing destruction or stealing money. Frequently they combat cyber criminals who are attacking their computer resources from overseas and are therefore beyond the reach of U.S. law enforcement officials. They also plan security systems and fire and other disaster-response plans for buildings. Such plans include provisions for evacuating large buildings and coordinating their efforts with local police and fire departments in a variety of locales. In addition, they develop security systems to prevent employee theft that may involve sophisticated schemes to use company computer systems to transfer financial assets in improper ways. Because so many American companies own manufacturing plants and office buildings overseas, security companies must often implement their services in diverse countries around the globe.

At lower levels, specific occupations in private security compare more closely with those of police officers. Many security personnel are the equivalent of private sector detectives. They must investigate attacks on company computer systems or activities that threaten company assets. Thus, for example, credit card companies have large security departments that use computers to monitor unusual activity on individual customers' credit cards, which may signal that a thief is using the card. Private sector detectives must also investigate employee theft. Because this criminal activity extends beyond simple crimes such as stealing money from a store's cash register, investigations might examine whether people are making false reports on expense accounts, using company computers to run private businesses, or misspending company money.

Other activities compare more directly to those of police patrol officers, especially those of security officers who must guard specific buildings, apartments, or stores. The activities of these private security personnel vary greatly: Some act merely as guards and call the police at the first sign of trouble, others have the power to carry out patrol and investigative duties similar to those of police officers, and still others rely on their own presence and the ability to make a citizen's arrest to deter lawbreakers. In most cases, citizens are authorized by law to make an arrest only when a felony has been committed in their presence. Thus, private security companies risk being held liable for false arrest and violation of civil rights.

Some states have passed laws that give civil immunity to store personnel who reasonably but mistakenly detain people suspected of shoplifting. More ambiguous is the search of a suspect's person or property by a private guard. The suspect may resist the search and file a civil suit against the guard. If such a search yields evidence of a crime, the evidence might not be admitted in court. Yet, the Supreme Court has not applied the *Miranda* ruling to private police. In any case, federal law bars private individuals from engaging in wiretapping, and information so gathered cannot be entered as evidence at trial.

Security managers are often willing to accept responsibility for minor criminal incidents that occur on their employer's premises. They might perform such tasks as responding to burglar alarms, investigating misdemeanors, and carrying out preliminary investigations of other crimes. Some law enforcement administrators have indicated that they might be willing to transfer some of these tasks to private security firms. They cite several police tasks such as providing security in public buildings and enforcing parking regulations that private security might perform more efficiently than the police. In some parts of the country, personnel from private firms already perform some of these tasks.

Private Police and Homeland Security

Private sector corporations control security for vital facilities in the United States, including nuclear power plants, oil refineries, military manufacturing facilities, and other important sites (Nalla, 2002). Fires, tornadoes, or earthquakes at such sites could release toxic materials into the air and water. Thus, emergency planning is essential for public safety. Moreover, because these sites are now recognized as potential targets of terrorist attacks, the role and effectiveness of security managers matter more than ever to society. They must work closely with law enforcement executives and other government officials to institute procedures that reduce known risks and to participate in emergency preparedness planning.

Unfortunately, significant problems have emerged in delegating essential homeland security responsibilities to private companies. The federal government has become increasingly dependent on private contractors for a variety of functions, including safety and security (Shane and Nixon, 2007). Private security firms handle a variety of tasks for government, from guarding military bases, nuclear power plants, and government buildings to providing personal security for diplomats traveling in Iraq and other dangerous locations. For example, private security personnel guard the headquarters of the U.S. Department of Homeland Security. Yet, security guards assigned to the building claim that they do not have proper training or equipment to handle the job. In 2005, guards at the building opened an envelope containing a mysterious white powder. A well-trained security force would have known to put on hazardous materials clothing and carefully seek to dispose of a potentially dangerous chemical or biological hazard. Instead, the private security personnel "carried [the envelope] by the office of [then Homeland Security] Secretary Michael Chertoff, took it outside and then shook it outside Chertoff's window without evacuating people nearby" (Margasak, 2006). If it had been a deadly chemical or biological agent, it might have killed several important officials, including Chertoff. Fortunately, it turned out to be harmless. Other guards at the same building failed tests conducted by the Secret Service, which sent personnel into the building with fake identification cards. Other guards could not tell what to do when a fire alarm sounded; without radios, they could not learn if it was real or a test. And yet another guard said, "I didn't have a clue what to do" when a suspicious bag was reported to be abandoned in the parking lot (Margasak, 2006). Because of these problems, large private security companies have actually lobbied the government for more rules and regulations for their industry (Margasak, 2007).

■ Private Employment of Public Police

The officials responsible for asset protection, safety, and security at the top levels of major corporations are often retired police administrators or former military personnel. For example, New York Police Commissioner Raymond Kelly served as Senior Managing Director of Global Corporate Security for a Wall Street financial firm after he left his position as Director of the U.S. Customs Service and before he was appointed to serve as police commissioner. The reliance on people with public sector experience for important positions in private security management reflects the fact that asset protection and security management have only recently become emphasized as topics in college and university programs. Thus, relatively few professionals have yet gained specific educational credentials in this important area. As a result, the placement of retired law enforcement officials in high-level positions has often created opportunities for strategic communication and coordination between top-level security managers and public sector police administrators. Both entities have reason to seek cooperation throughout the hierarchy of their respective organizations. Unfortunately, however, they cannot always ensure that individual police officers and lower-level security personnel will sufficiently communicate and coordinate with each other when incidents arise.

At operational levels of security management, private security and local police often make frequent contact. Private firms are usually eager to hire public police officers on a part-time basis. About 20 percent of departments forbid their officers from moonlighting for private employers. By contrast, some departments simultaneously facilitate and control the hiring of their officers by creating specific rules and procedures for off-duty employment. For example, the New York City police department coordinates a program called the Paid Detail Unit. Event planners, corporations, and organizations can hire uniformed, off-duty officers for $30 per hour. The police department must approve all events at which the officers will work, and the department imposes an additional

10 percent administrative fee for the hiring of its officers. Thus, the department can safeguard against officers working for organizations and events that will cause legal, public relations, or other problems for the police department. The department can also monitor and control how many hours its officers work so that private, part-time employment does not lead them to be exhausted and ineffective during their regular shifts.

These officers retain their full powers and status as police personnel even when they work for a private firm while off duty. New York and other cities have specific regulations requiring an on-duty officer to be called when a situation arises in which an arrest will be made. While the use of off-duty officers expands the number and visibility of law enforcement officers, it also raises questions, two of which are discussed here.

Conflict of Interest   Police officers must avoid any appearance of conflict of interest when they accept private employment. They are barred from jobs that conflict with their public duties. For example, they may not work as process servers, bill collectors, repossessors, or preemployment investigators for private firms. They also may not work as investigators for criminal defense attorneys or as bail bondsmen. They may not work in places that profit from gambling, and many departments do not allow officers to work in bars or other places where regulated goods, such as alcohol, are sold. No department can know the full range of situations in which private employment of an officer might harm the image of the police or create a conflict with police responsibilities. Thus, departments need to keep tabs on new situations that might require them to refine their regulations for private employment of off-duty officers.

Management Prerogatives   Another issue concerns the impact of private employment on the capabilities of the local police department. Private employment cannot be allowed to tire officers and impair their ability to protect the public when they are on duty. Late-night duties as a private security officer, for example, can reduce an officer's ability to police effectively the next morning.

Departments require that officers request permission for outside work. Such permission can be denied for several reasons. Work that lowers the dignity of the police, is too risky or dangerous, is not in the home jurisdiction, requires more than eight hours of off-duty service, or interferes with department schedules is usually denied.

Several models have been designed to manage off-duty employment of officers. The *department contract model* permits close control of off-duty work, because firms must apply to the department to have officers assigned to them. New York City's system fits this model. Officers chosen for off-duty work are paid by the police department, which is reimbursed by the private firm, along with an overhead fee. Departments usually screen employers to make sure that the proposed use of officers will not conflict with the department's needs. When the private demand for police services exceeds the supply (and that is often the case), the department contract model provides a way of assigning staff so as to ensure that public needs are met.

The *officer contract model* allows each officer to find off-duty employment and to enter into a direct relationship with the private firm. Officers must apply to the department for permission, which is granted if the employment standards listed earlier are met. Problems can arise when an officer acts as an employment agent for other officers. This can lead to charges of favoritism and nepotism, with serious effects on discipline and morale.

In the *union brokerage model*, the police union or association finds off-duty employment for its members. The union sets the standards for the work and bargains with the department over the pay, status, and conditions of the off-duty employment.

Each of these models has its backers. Albert Reiss notes another complication, however: The more closely a department controls off-duty employment, the more liability it assumes for officers' actions when they work for private firms (Reiss, 1988).

■ The Public–Private Interface

The relationship between public and private law enforcement is a concern for police officials. Because private agents work for the people who employ them, their goals might not always serve the public interest. Questions have arisen about the power of private security agents to make arrests, conduct searches, and take part in undercover investigations. A key issue is the boundary between the work of the police and that of private agencies. Lack of coordination and communication between public and private agencies has led to botched investigations, destruction of evidence, and overzealousness.

Growing awareness of this problem has led to efforts to have private security agents work more closely with the police. Current efforts to enhance coordination involve emergency planning, building security, and general crime prevention. In other areas, private security managers still tend to act on their own without consulting the police.

One such area is criminal activity within a company. Many security managers in private firms tend to treat crimes by employees as internal matters that do not concern the police. They report UCR index crimes to the police, but employee theft, insurance fraud, industrial espionage, commercial bribery, and computer crime tend not to be reported to public authorities. In such cases, the chief concern of private firms is to prevent losses and protect assets. Most of these incidents are resolved through internal procedures (private justice). When such crimes are discovered, the offender may be convicted and punished within the firm by forced restitution, loss of the job, and the spreading of information about the incident throughout the industry. Private firms often bypass the criminal justice system so they do not have to deal with prosecution policies, administrative delays, rules that would open the firms' internal affairs to public scrutiny, and bad publicity. Thus, the question arises: To what extent does a parallel system of private justice exist with regard to some offenders and some crimes (M. Davis, Lundman, and Martinez, 1991)?

■ Recruitment and Training

Higher-level security managers are increasingly drawn from college graduates with degrees in criminal justice who have taken additional coursework in such subjects as business management and computer science. These graduates are attracted to the growing private sector employment market for security-related occupations, because the jobs often involve varied, complex tasks in a white-collar work environment. In addition, they often gain corporate benefits such as quick promotion, stock options, and other perks unavailable in public sector policing.

By contrast, the recruitment and training of lower-level private security personnel present a major concern to law enforcement officials and civil libertarians. These personnel carry the important responsibility of guarding factories, stores, apartments, and other buildings. Often on the scene when criminal activity occurs, they are the private security personnel most likely to interact with the public in emergency situations. Moreover, any failure to perform their duties could lead to a significant and damaging event, such as a robbery or a fire. In spite of these important responsibilities, which parallel those of police patrol officers, studies have shown that such personnel often have little education and training. Because the pay is low, the work often attracts people who cannot find other jobs or who seek temporary work. For example, private security firms in San Francisco reported annual staff turnover rates as high as 300 percent because their low pay and benefits led employees continually to seek higher-paying jobs, especially when better-paid public sector security work opened up, such as jobs as airport screeners (Lynem, 2002).

The growth of private policing has brought calls for the screening and licensing of its personnel. Fewer than half of the states require background checks or examine private security applicants' criminal records from states other than the one in which they currently reside. Twenty-two states have no certification or licensing requirements, and only 17 states have regulatory boards to oversee the private security industry. More than half of the states have no training requirements whatsoever for people who will assume important responsibilities in guarding buildings and other private security tasks

Today's security personnel must be aware of numerous potential threats and have the necessary training and equipment to communicate with law enforcement officials. If security guards are minimum-wage employees, are they likely to have the qualifications and commitment to provide adequate security at important private enterprises such as chemical factories and nuclear power plants?

© Jeff Greenberg/PhotoEdit

(PR Newswire, 2002). Several national organizations, such as the National Council on Crime and Delinquency, have offered model licensing statutes that specify periods of training and orientation, uniforms that permit citizens to distinguish between public and private police, and a ban on employment of people with criminal records.

The regulations that do exist tend to focus on contractual, as opposed to proprietary, private policing. Contractual security services are provided for a fee by locksmiths, alarm specialists, polygraph examiners, and firms such as Brink's, Burns, and Wackenhut, which provide guards and detectives. States and cities often require contract personnel to be licensed and bonded. Similar services are sometimes provided by proprietary security personnel, who are employed directly by the organizations they protect—retail stores, industrial plants, hospitals, and so forth. Except for those who carry weapons, proprietary security personnel are not regulated by the state or city. Certainly, the importance of private security and its relation to public policing demands further exploration of these and related issues in the years to come.

CHECKPOINT

ANSWERS

17 What has caused the growth of security management and private policing?

17 Companies' recognition of the need to protect assets and to plan for emergencies, as well as problems with employee theft, computer crime, and other issues that require active prevention and investigation.

18 What are the three models for private employment of police officers?

18 Department contract model, officer contract model, and union brokerage model.

A QUESTION OF ETHICS: WRITING ASSIGNMENT

You are a police officer on road patrol. The previous day there was a report that a man wearing a blue baseball cap and driving a light-colored car attempted to abduct a girl. You are driving behind a silver car, and it appears that the driver is wearing a dark baseball cap. When the car changes lanes, a blinding glare in your eyes from the sun glinting off the silver car makes it difficult to see if the driver used his turn signal. You are curious about whether this driver is connected to the attempted abduction.

WRITING ASSIGNMENT

Would you stop the vehicle? What would be the reason for the stop? Could you make a stop for failure to signal a lane change? Write out what you would say if you were in a private conversation with a new police officer who came to you to seek advice about what to do in such situations.

Summary

Understand the everyday actions of police

▶ To carry out their mission, the police must have the public's cooperation and assistance, because they depend on the public to help them identify crime and carry out investigations.

▶ Five factors affect how police exercise discretion or make choices in often ambiguous situations as to how and when to apply the law.

▶ Police agencies have developed policies to guide officers' decision making in responding to calls about

domestic violence, but officers still must use their discretion in each situation.

Recognize the factors that affect police response

▶ The police are mainly reactive rather than proactive, which often leads to incident-driven policing.

▶ The organization of the police bureaucracy influences how the police respond to citizens' calls.

▶ The productivity of a force can be measured in various ways, including clearance rate; however, measuring proactive approaches is more difficult.

Understand the main functions of police patrol, investigation, and special operations units

- Police services are delivered through the work of the patrol, investigation, and specialized operations units.
- The patrol function has three components: answering calls for assistance, maintaining a police presence, and probing suspicious circumstances.
- The investigative function is the responsibility of detectives, who work in close cooperation with patrol officers.
- The felony apprehension process is a sequence of actions that includes crime detection, preliminary investigation, follow-up investigation, clearance, and arrest.
- Large departments usually have specialized units dealing with traffic, drugs, and vice.

Analyze patrol strategies that departments employ

- Police administrators make choices about possible patrol strategies, which include directed patrol, foot patrol, and aggressive patrol, among others.
- Community policing seeks to involve citizens in identifying problems and working with police officers to prevent disorder and crime.

Recognize the importance of connections between the police and the community

- Police face challenges in dealing with special populations, such as the mentally ill and homeless, who need social services yet often disturb or offend other citizens as they walk the streets.
- Policing in a multicultural society requires an appreciation of the attitudes, customs, and languages of minority group members.

- To be effective, the police must maintain their connection with the community.

Identify issues and problems that emerge from law enforcement agencies' increased attention to homeland security.

- Homeland security has become an important priority for law enforcement agencies at all levels of government since September 11, 2001.
- Agencies need planning and coordination in order to gather intelligence and prepare for possible threats and public emergencies.
- The federal government provides funding for state and local fusion centers and emergency preparedness equipment
- New laws, such as the USA Patriot Act, have caused controversy about the proper balance between government authority and citizens' rights

Understand the policing and related activities undertaken by private sector security management

- The expansion of security management and private policing reflects greater recognition of the need to protect private assets and to plan for emergencies.
- Security management produces new issues and problems, including concerns about the recruitment, training, and activities of lower-level private security personnel.
- Public–private interaction affects security through such means as joint planning for emergencies, hiring private firms to guard government facilities, and hiring police officers for off-duty private security work

Questions for Review

1. What is the purpose of patrol? How is it carried out?
2. What responsibilities are handled in large cities by special operations units?
3. What has research shown about the effectiveness of patrol?
4. What problems do officers face in policing a diverse, multicultural society?
5. What have law enforcement agencies done to enhance homeland security?
6. What problems are associated with private policing?

Key Terms and Cases

aggressive patrol (p. 145)
clearance rate (p. 135)
differential response (p. 134)
directed patrol (p. 143)
incident-driven policing (p. 133)

law enforcement intelligence (p. 154)
line functions (p. 136)
preventive patrol (p. 137)
proactive (p. 133)
problem-oriented policing (p. 148)

reactive (p. 133)
sworn officers (p. 137)
USA Patriot Act (p. 157)

Police and Law

6

AFTER AN ARGUMENT WITH HER HUSBAND, Scott, Janet Randolph called the Americus, Georgia, police department. She complained that Scott had left with their young son. When the police arrived at the house, she told them that her husband used cocaine. Scott Randolph returned to the house minutes later and reported that he had taken the child to a neighbor's house because he feared that his wife would leave and take the boy to Canada as she had done once before. Scott denied that he used cocaine and told the police that his wife's alcohol abuse had harmed the marriage.

After an officer escorted Janet to retrieve the boy, Janet told the police that "items of drug evidence" were inside the house. An officer asked Scott for permission to search the house but Scott said "no" and refused to grant permission for the officers to enter. The officer then asked Janet for permission to search the house. She said "yes." The officers entered the house and seized a section of a drinking straw that appeared to have cocaine residue. When the officers sought to reenter the house, Janet withdrew her consent to search. The officers took the Randolphs to the police station, used the straw as a basis to obtain a warrant to search the house, found further evidence of drugs, and charged Scott Randolph with possession of cocaine. Scott Randolph pursued his case all the way to the Georgia Supreme Court to challenge the validity of the search. He claimed that any evidence against him must be excluded from use in court because it was obtained in violation of the Fourth Amendment.

As you will recall from Chapter 3, the Fourth Amendment provides protection against "unreasonable searches and seizures." The Fourth Amendment is relevant because the officers relied on the consent of one co-homeowner to search a house despite the other co-homeowner's refusal to consent. The state supreme court faced the task of determining whether it was "unreasonable" for the police to conduct the initial search in reliance on Janet's permission when Scott, who had equal authority over the home, clearly said that he would not give consent for the officers to enter the house.

The Georgia Supreme Court agreed with Scott Randolph and said that "the consent to conduct a warrantless search is not valid in the face of the refusal of another occupant who is physically present at the scene to permit a warrantless search." Because Georgia prosecutors disagreed with this decision, they asked the U.S. Supreme Court to review the case.

- Know the extent of police officers' authority to stop people and to conduct searches of people, their vehicles, and other property

- Recognize how police officers seek warrants in order to conduct searches and make arrests

- Identify situations in which police officers can examine property and conduct searches without obtaining a warrant

- Analyze the purpose of the privilege against compelled self-incrimination

- Understand the exclusionary rule and situations in which it applies

- Analyze the problems of police abuse and corruption

- Recognize the mechanisms used to hold police accountable when they violate laws and policies

As you think about the Randolph case, remember that the words of the Fourth Amendment do not provide an answer to the question of whether the search was "unreasonable." Indeed, the eighteenth-century men who wrote the phrase *unreasonable searches and seizures* could not have anticipated the thousands of modern situations in which police officers want to search homes, automobiles, backpacks, computer hard drives, and other possessions and locations for evidence of criminal activity. Thus, today's judges must decide for themselves how each situation falls within the intended purposes of the Fourth Amendment.

In March 2006, the U.S. Supreme Court provided its answer to the question raised in the case of *Georgia v. Randolph*. Five justices agreed with the Georgia Supreme Court. Justice David Souter's majority opinion said that "a physically present inhabitant's express refusal to consent to a police search is dispositive as to him, regardless of the consent of a fellow occupant." Three other justices filed dissenting opinions expressing sharp disagreement with the rule announced by the majority's decision. (The ninth justice, Samuel Alito, had not yet been confirmed by the U.S. Senate when the case was argued.)

As we shall see in this chapter, there are many situations in which police are forbidden to use evidence of criminal activity when the evidence was obtained through improper procedures in conducting a search or questioning a suspect.

For instance, Georgia could not use the cocaine discovered in the house as evidence against Scott Randolph.

Are you surprised by the U.S. Supreme Court's decision? Do you agree with it? Do you believe that Scott Randolph should escape punishment for cocaine possession when the police found clear evidence of his guilt after reasonably relying on Janet's permission to search the house? Would the outcome have been different if Janet had given permission to search and the police had found the cocaine residue before Scott returned from the neighbor's house? As we examine other Supreme Court decisions, think about the challenge of applying brief phrases from the Bill of Rights to actual situations that will determine whether people and places can be searched and suspects questioned and, more importantly, whether certain individuals will spend many years in prison.

In this chapter, we examine individual rights and how those legal protections define the limits of police officers' powers of investigation and arrest. In particular, we look closely at two rights that were introduced in Chapter 3: the Fourth Amendment protection against unreasonable searches and seizures and the Fifth Amendment privilege against compelled self-incrimination. In addition, we look at the challenge of supervising police and holding them accountable in situations when they break the law through rights violations, misuse of force, and corruption.

Legal Limitations on Police Investigations

The provisions of the Bill of Rights embody very important American values regarding individual rights in society. They reflect the belief that we do not want to give government officials absolute power to pursue investigations and prosecutions, because that approach to crime control would impose excessive costs on the values of individual liberty, privacy, and due process. If police could do whatever they wanted to do, then people would lack protections against arbitrary searches and arrests. On the other hand, crime control is an important policy goal. We do not want individuals' expectations about legal protections to block the ability of law enforcement officers to protect citizens from crime and punish wrongdoers. Judges must therefore seek to interpret the Constitution in ways that properly balance crime control and the protection of individual rights.

How does an officer know when his or her actions might violate laws protecting an individual's rights? Individual police officers do not have time to follow the details of the latest court decisions. That responsibility rests with those who train and supervise law enforcement officers. Officers depend on the information provided at the police academy and subsequent updates from city and state attorneys who monitor court decisions. Thus, police officers' compliance with the law depends on their own knowledge and decisions as well as those of their supervisors.

■ Search and Seizure Concepts

The Fourth Amendment prohibits police officers from undertaking "unreasonable searches and seizures." The Supreme Court defines a **search** as an action by law enforcement officials that intrudes on people's **reasonable expectations of privacy**. For example, someone who places a personal diary in a locked drawer within a bedroom of her home has demonstrated a reasonable expectation of privacy. Police officers cannot simply decide to enter her home in order to open the locked drawer and read the diary. Many situations raise questions about people's reasonable expectations. Should people reasonably expect a police officer to reach into their pockets in order to see if they have guns? Should people reasonably expect an officer not to walk up to their houses and attempt to peer through small cracks in the window blinds? Although judges do not always answer these questions in clear, consistent ways, people's reasonable expectations about their privacy play a key role in judges' determinations about legal guidelines for police investigations.

What if a police officer is walking down the public sidewalk and sees a marijuana plant growing quite visibly in the large front window of a home? When police officers examine people's property without violating reasonable expectations of privacy, then no search occurred. In *Coolidge v. New Hampshire* (1971), the Court discussed the **plain view doctrine**, which permits officers to notice and use as evidence items that are visible to them when they are in a location where they are permitted to be, such as a public sidewalk. Similarly, police can see what is in open area, including private property, either by walking through open fields or by flying a helicopter over people's houses and yards. Officers may not break into a home and then claim that the drugs found inside were in plain view on a table. However, if a homeowner invited officers into his home in order to file a report about a burglary, the officers do not need to obtain a warrant in order to seize drugs that they see lying on the kitchen table. Because the drugs were in plain view and the officers had a legal basis for their presence in the house, the owner lost any reasonable expectation of privacy that would otherwise require officers to demonstrate probable cause for a search warrant.

In defining **seizures**, the Supreme Court focuses on the nature and extent of officers' interference with people's liberty and freedom of movement. If an officer who is leaning against the wall of a building says to a passing pedestrian, "Where are you going?" and the person replies, "To the sandwich shop down the street" as she continues to walk without interference by the officer, there is virtually no intrusion on

■ **search** Government officials' examination of and hunt for evidence on a person or in a place in a manner that intrudes on reasonable expectations of privacy.

■ **reasonable expectation of privacy** The objective standard developed by courts for determining whether a government intrusion into an individual's person or property constitutes a search because it interferes with the individual's interests that are normally protected from government examination.

■ **plain view doctrine** Officers may examine and use as evidence, without a warrant, contraband or evidence that is in open view at a location where they are legally permitted to be.

■ **seizures** Situations in which police officers use their authority to deprive people of their liberty or property and which must not be "unreasonable" according to the Fourth Amendment.

her liberty and freedom of movement. Thus, officers are free to speak to people on the street. If people voluntarily stop in order to speak with the officer, they have not been "seized," because they are free to move along their way whenever they choose. However, if people are not free to leave when officers assert their authority to halt someone's movement, then a seizure has occurred and the Fourth Amendment requires that the seizure be reasonable.

One form of seizure is an arrest. This involves taking a suspect into custody. Property can also be subject to seizure, especially if it is evidence in a criminal case.

A **stop** is a brief interference with a person's freedom of movement for a duration that can be measured in minutes, usually under an hour. An interference with freedom of movement that lasts several hours risks being viewed as exceeding the proper duration of a stop and requires greater justification. When police require a driver to pull over in order to receive a traffic citation, that is a stop. Such stops can affect the rights of both drivers and passengers, especially if the stop leads to a search of the individuals or the vehicle (*Brendlin v. California*, 2007; V. Amar, 2008). In order to be permissible under the Fourth Amendment, stops must be justified by **reasonable suspicion**—a situation in which specific articulable facts lead officers to conclude that the person may be engaging in criminal activity. Officers cannot legally make stops based on hunches; they must be able to describe specific aspects of the person's appearance, behavior, and circumstances that led them to conclude that the person should be stopped in order to investigate the occurrence of a crime. As we shall see, however, the courts permit police officers to make many kinds of stops without reasonable suspicion. Such stops can occur, for example, at border crossing points where preventing illegal activities, such as smuggling and drug trafficking, is especially important. Thus, everyone can be stopped in certain situations even if there is no specific basis to suspect them of wrongdoing.

The Concept of Arrest

An arrest is a significant deprivation of liberty, because a person is taken into police custody, transported to the police station or jail, and processed into the criminal justice system. Because arrests involve a more significant intrusion on liberty, they require a higher level of justification. Unlike stops, which require only reasonable suspicion, all arrests must be supported by **probable cause**. Probable cause exists when sufficient evidence is available to support the reasonable conclusion that a person has committed a crime. To obtain an arrest warrant, the police must provide a judicial officer with sufficient evidence to support a finding of probable cause. Alternatively, police officers' on-the-street determinations of probable cause can produce discretionary warrantless arrests. A judge subsequently examines such arrests for probable cause, in a hearing that must occur shortly after the arrest, typically within 48 hours. If the judge determines that the police officer was wrong in concluding that probable cause existed to justify the arrest, the suspect is released from custody.

Warrants and Probable Cause

Imagine that you are a judge. Two police officers come to your chambers to ask you to authorize a search warrant. They swear that they observed frequent foot traffic of suspicious people going in and out of a house. Moreover, they swear that a reliable informant told them that he was inside the house two days earlier and saw crack cocaine being sold. Does this information rise to the level of probable cause, justifying issuance of a search warrant? Can you grant a warrant based purely on the word of police officers, or do you need more-concrete evidence?

■ **stop** Government officials' interference with an individual's freedom of movement for a duration that typically lasts less than one hour and only rarely extends for as long as several hours.

■ **reasonable suspicion** A police officer's belief based on articulable facts that would be recognized by others in a similar situation as indicating that criminal activity is afoot and necessitates further investigation that will intrude on an individual's reasonable expectation of privacy.

■ **probable cause** An amount of reliable information indicating that it is more likely than not that evidence will be found in a specific location or that a specific person is guilty of a crime.

Arrest is the physical taking of a person into custody. What legal requirements must be met to make this a valid arrest? What limits are placed on the officers?

© AP Images/Devin Bruce

These questions are important not only for judges but for prosecutors as well. Police and prosecutors must work closely together. If the police have made errors in seeking warrants or conducting searches, evidence could be excluded from use at trial and, as a result, prosecutors could lose their cases through no fault of their own.

The Fourth Amendment requires that "no Warrants shall issue, but upon probable cause, supported by Oath or affirmation, and particularly describing the place to be searched, and the persons or things to be seized." These particular elements of the Amendment must be fulfilled in order to issue a warrant. If they are not, then a defendant may later challenge the validity of the warrant. The important elements are, first, the existence of probable cause. Second, evidence must be presented to the judicial officer and be supported by "oath or affirmation," which typically means that police officers must say "yes" when the judicial officer asks them if they swear or affirm that all information presented is true to the best of their knowledge. This requirement may be fulfilled by presenting an **affidavit** from the police officers, which is a written statement confirmed by oath or affirmation. Third, the warrant must describe the specific place to be searched. A "general warrant" for searching many locations cannot be issued. Fourth, the warrant must describe the person or items to be seized. Thus, if the warrant authorizes a search for a person suspected of robbery, the officers should not open small dresser drawers or other places a person could not be hiding.

The U.S. Supreme Court has attempted to guide judicial officers in identifying the existence of probable cause. Mere suspicion cannot constitute probable cause, yet the level of evidence to establish probable cause need not fulfill the high level of proof "beyond a reasonable doubt" needed to justify a criminal conviction. In essence, probable cause is a level of evidence sufficient to provide a reasonable conclusion that the proposed objects of a search will be found in a location that law enforcement officers request to search. For an arrest warrant, the essential issue is whether sufficient evidence is presented to lead to the reasonable conclusion that a specific person should be prosecuted for a criminal offense. There is no hard-and-fast definition of *probable cause* that can be applied to every situation. It is a flexible concept that various judicial officers apply differently. In *Illinois v. Gates* (1983), the Supreme Court announced a flexible **totality of circumstances** test for determining the existence

■ **affidavit** Written statement of fact, supported by oath or affirmation, submitted to judicial officers to fulfill the requirements of probable cause for obtaining a warrant.

■ **totality of circumstances** Flexible test established by the Supreme Court for identifying whether probable cause exists to justify a judge's issuance of a warrant.

CHECKPOINT

ANSWERS

1 *What is a search?*

1 A government intrusion into an individual's reasonable expectation of privacy.

2 *What is the "plain view doctrine"?*

2 The "plain view doctrine" permits officers to observe and seize illegal items that are visible to them when they are in a location in which they are legally permitted to be.

3 *What is the difference between an arrest and a stop?*

3 An arrest requires probable cause and involves taking someone into custody for prosecution, whereas a stop is a brief deprivation of freedom of movement based on reasonable suspicion.

4 *What do police officers need to demonstrate in order to obtain a warrant?*

4 The existence of probable cause by the totality of circumstances in the case.

of probable cause. Judges are permitted to make a generalized determination about whether the evidence is both sufficient and reliable enough to justify a warrant.

Warrantless Searches

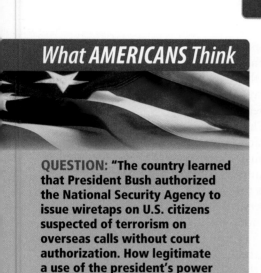

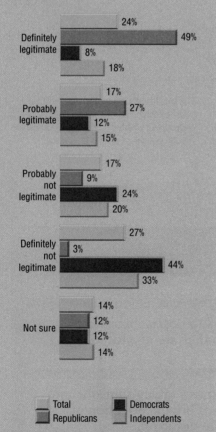

Definitely legitimate
- 24%
- 49%
- 8%
- 18%

Probably legitimate
- 17%
- 27%
- 12%
- 15%

Probably not legitimate
- 17%
- 9%
- 24%
- 20%

Definitely not legitimate
- 27%
- 3%
- 44%
- 33%

Not sure
- 14%
- 12%
- 12%
- 14%

- Total
- Democrats
- Republicans
- Independents

In day-to-day police work, the majority of searches take place without a warrant. It is in this area that the courts have been most active in defining the term *unreasonable*. Six kinds of searches may be legally conducted without a warrant and still uphold the Fourth Amendment: (1) special needs beyond the normal purposes of law enforcement, (2) stop and frisk on the streets, (3) search incident to a lawful arrest, (4) exigent circumstances, (5) consent, and (6) automobile searches. We examine these forms of warrantless searches in this section.

Recent debates raise new issues about whether the threat of terrorism should justify additional opportunities for warrantless searches. For example, the government response to the threat of terrorism after 9/11 included warrantless wiretaps of Americans' telephones and other forms of electronic surveillance. Indeed, the Bush administration asserted that the Fourth Amendment would not apply at all to any antiterrorist actions undertaken by the U.S. military within the United States (Eggen and White, 2008). Do you think such actions should be permissible under the Fourth Amendment? If so, what level of suspicion or evidence should be necessary to justify such intrusions on reasonable expectations of privacy? See "What Americans Think" to compare your own views with those of others in the United States. In addition, think about the impact of heightened concerns about terrorism and homeland security as you read about the career of intelligence analyst in "Careers in Criminal Justice." Consider how these concerns have led to the creation of new kinds of careers in criminal justice.

■ Special Needs beyond the Normal Purposes of Law Enforcement

In certain specific contexts, law enforcement officials have a justified need to conduct warrantless searches of every individual passing through. The use of metal detectors to examine airline passengers, for example, occurs in a specific context in which the need to prevent hijacking justifies a limited search of every passenger. Here, the Supreme Court does not require officers to have any suspicions, reasonable or otherwise, about the illegal activities of any individual.

Similarly, warrantless searches take place at the entry points into the United States—border crossings, ports, and airports. The government's interests in guarding against the entry of people and items (weapons, drugs, toxic chemicals, and so forth) that are harmful to national interests outweigh the individuals' expectations of privacy. Typically, these border stops involve only a few moments as customs officers check any required documents such as passports and visas, ask where the person traveled, and ask what the person is bringing into the United States. The customs officers may have a trained dog sniff around people and their luggage, checking for drugs or large amounts of cash. At the Mexican and Canadian borders and at international airports, people may be chosen at random to have their cars and luggage searched. They may also be chosen for such searches because their behavior or their answers to questions arouse the suspicions of customs officers.

The Supreme Court has expanded the checkpoint concept by approving systematic stops to look for drunken drivers along highways. Michigan's state police implemented a sobriety checkpoint program. They set up a checkpoint at which they stopped every vehicle and briefly questioned each driver (*Michigan Department of State Police v. Sitz*, 1990). A group of citizens filed lawsuits alleging that checkpoints violated drivers' rights. However, the Court

CAREERS IN CRIMINAL JUSTICE

Intelligence Analyst

ERIN GOFF, INTELLIGENCE ANALYST
OHIO DEPARTMENT OF PUBLIC SAFETY,
DIVISION OF HOMELAND SECURITY

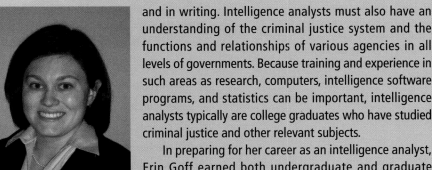

ASSIGNED DUTIES for intelligence analysts vary according to the specific mission of the federal or state agency in which they work. Intelligence analysts collect and analyze information about financial transactions, communication patterns, informants' tips, individuals' and organizations' actions, and other activities that might reveal threats to public safety. By continuously sifting through available information, they produce intelligence products, such as reports, statistical analyses, and suspicious activities notices concerning potential criminal events and threats to homeland security. They also conduct specific research projects, present briefings to law enforcement and other officials, and write reports and other materials that can be used to warn, inform, and train officials.

Qualifications for the position vary according to an agency's specific needs. In general, candidates need experience and skill in research and writing. Critical-thinking skills are especially important, as is the ability to communicate effectively, both orally and in writing. Intelligence analysts must also have an understanding of the criminal justice system and the functions and relationships of various agencies in all levels of governments. Because training and experience in such areas as research, computers, intelligence software programs, and statistics can be important, intelligence analysts typically are college graduates who have studied criminal justice and other relevant subjects.

In preparing for her career as an intelligence analyst, Erin Goff earned both undergraduate and graduate degrees in criminal justice. In addition, she gained experience in the field as a graduate student by working on federally funded projects through which university professors and other experts provided training for police departments concerning homeland security issues.

The biggest challenge I face on a daily basis is the constantly changing picture of terrorism. There are always new threat streams using tactics we've never seen and we are forced to adapt our information analysis. As with other areas of criminal justice, it is essential to stay one step ahead, so I regularly seek additional education to enhance my formal knowledge. In addition, I continuously discuss emerging information and issues with other intelligence analysts.

said that police can systematically stop drivers in order to seek information. The Court more recently approved checkpoints to ask drivers whether they had witnessed an accident (*Illinois v. Lidster*, 2004).

The U.S. Supreme Court has not given blanket approval for every kind of checkpoint or traffic stop that police might wish to use. The Court forbids random stops of vehicles by officers on patrol (*Delaware v. Prouse*, 1979). Officers must have a basis for a vehicle stop, such as an observed violation of traffic laws. The Court also ruled that a city cannot set up a checkpoint in order to check drivers and passengers for possible involvement in drugs or other crimes. The Court declared that a general search for criminal evidence does not justify the use of a checkpoint. Again, such stops must be narrowly focused on a specific objective, such as checking for drunken drivers (*City of Indianapolis v. Edmond*, 2000).

◼ Stop and Frisk on the Streets

Police officers possess the authority to make stops and limited searches of individuals on the streets when specific circumstances justify such actions. In the landmark case of ***Terry v. Ohio* (1968),** the Court upheld the stop-and-frisk procedure when a police officer had good reasons to conclude that a person endangered the public by being involved in criminal activity. In the *Terry* case, a plainclothes detective in downtown Cleveland observed men walking back and forth to look in the window of a store and

◼ *Terry v. Ohio* (1968) Supreme Court decision endorsing police officers' authority to stop and frisk suspects on the streets when there is reasonable suspicion that they are armed and involved in criminal activity.

then conferring with each other. He suspected that they might be preparing to rob the store. He approached the men, identified himself as a police officer, patted down their clothing, and found unlicensed handguns on two individuals. Those individuals challenged the legality of the search.

Although the justices supported the detective's authority to conduct the pat-down search based on his observations of the men's suspicious behavior, they struck a careful balance between police authority and individuals' rights by specifying the circumstances in which such a pat-down search—more commonly known as a **stop-and-frisk search**—can occur. In the *Terry* decision, the Court specifies the following criteria, all of which must be present, to define a legal stop and frisk:

> We merely hold today that
>
> [1] where a police officer observes unusual conduct
>
> [2] which leads him reasonably to conclude in light of his experience
>
> [3] that criminal activity may be afoot and
>
> [4] that the persons with whom he is dealing may be armed and presently dangerous,
>
> [5] where in the course of investigating this behavior
>
> [6] he identifies himself as a policeman and makes reasonable inquiries,
>
> [7] and where nothing in the initial stages of the encounter serves to dispel his reasonable fear for his own or others' safety,
>
> [8] he is entitled for the protection of himself and others in the area to conduct a carefully limited search of the outer clothing of such persons in an attempt to discover weapons which might be used to assault him.

These factors impose an obligation on police officers to make observations, draw reasonable conclusions, identify themselves, and make inquiries before conducting the stop-and-frisk search. In addition, the reasonableness of the search must be justified by a reasonable conclusion that a person is armed, thereby requiring the officer to act in order to protect him- or herself and the public.

As we discuss later with respect to the "exclusionary rule," a suspect who, during a frisk search, is found to be carrying drugs or a weapon can seek to have the evidence excluded from use in court if the stop-and-frisk was not justified by proper observations and reasonable suspicion. Typically, a judge will believe the police officer's version of events rather than accept the claims of a person found to be carrying illegal items. Sometimes, however, the officer's version of events may not be persuasive. When an

■ **stop-and-frisk search** Limited search approved by the Supreme Court in *Terry v. Ohio* that permits police officers to pat down the clothing of people on the streets if there is reasonable suspicion of dangerous criminal activity.

Kansas City, Missouri, police officers conduct a sobriety checkpoint in June 2008. All vehicles were stopped in order to detect whether any drivers had been drinking too much alcohol. Do you think such roadblocks interfere with the rights of drivers who have done nothing to raise suspicions about improper behavior?

© Rich Sugg/MCT/Landov

officer claims to have seen a lump under a suspect's jacket while the officer was standing 20 yards away on a busy street, judges may doubt whether officers can see with such accuracy at that distance. In New York City, for example, concerns arose in 2008 that police officers were regularly searching anyone they saw on the streets, even though the officers did not have the proper justifications established in *Terry v. Ohio* and later cases. In response, federal judges closely examined officers' versions of events. In nearly two dozen cases, the judges concluded that the police officers either were not being truthful or were not carefully following the *Terry* rules (Weiser, 2008).

Court decisions have given officers significant discretion to decide when factors that justify a stop-and-frisk search exist. For example, if officers see someone running at the sight of police in a high-crime neighborhood, their observation can be one consideration in determining whether a stop-and-frisk search is justified (*Illinois v. Wardlow*, 2000). Thus, officers need not actually see evidence of a weapon or interact with the suspect prior to making the stop.

The Supreme Court also expanded police authority by permitting officers to rely on reports from reliable witnesses as the basis for conducting the stop and frisk (*Adams v. Williams*, 1972). However, an unverified anonymous tip does not serve as an adequate reason for a stop-and-frisk search (*Florida v. J. L.*, 2000).

The stopping and frisking of an individual must be carried out according to the law. What does the law require in this situation?

AP Images/Gregory Bull

■ Search Incident to a Lawful Arrest

The authority to undertake a warrantless search incident to a lawful arrest is not limited by the crime for which the arrestee has been taken into custody. Even someone arrested for a traffic offense can be searched. Although there is no reason to suspect the person has a weapon nor to believe that evidence related to the offense will be found in the person's pockets (*United States v. Robinson*, 1973), the arrestee is subject to the same arrest scene search as someone taken into custody for murder.

The justification for searches of arrestees emerged in the Supreme Court's decision in **Chimel v. California (1969)**. The officers must make sure that the arrestee does not have a weapon that could endanger the officers or others in the vicinity. The officers must also look for evidence that might be destroyed or damaged by the arrestee before or during the process of transporting the arrestee to jail. Officers can search the arrestee and the immediate area around the arrestee. Officers can also make a protective sweep through other rooms where the suspect may recently have been. However, the arrest would not justify opening drawers and conducting a thorough search of an entire house. If, after the arrest, officers have probable cause to conduct a more thorough search, they must obtain a warrant that specifies the items that they seek and the places where they will search.

In a traffic stop, because officers possess the authority to make arrests for minor offenses, including acts that would normally only be subject to traffic citations, officers have opportunities to use arrests of drivers as a basis for conducting warrantless searches of automobiles (*Virginia v. Moore*, 2008). However, the search of the passenger compartment must be limited to areas within reach of the arrestee. In 2009, the Supreme Court clarified the limits of police authority by declaring that

■ *Chimel v. California* (1969) Supreme Court decision that endorsed warrantless searches for weapons and evidence in the immediate vicinity of people who are lawfully arrested.

police cannot search the entire passenger compartment of an automobile simply because they have made an arrest (*Arizona v. Gant*, 2009).

■ Exigent Circumstances

Officers can make an arrest without a warrant when there are **exigent circumstances**. This means that officers are in the middle of an urgent situation in which they must act swiftly and do not have time to go to court to seek a warrant. With respect to arrests, for example, when officers are in hot pursuit of a fleeing suspected felon, they need not stop to seek a warrant and thereby risk permitting the suspect to get away (*Warden v. Hayden*, 1967). Similarly, exigent circumstances can justify the warrantless entry into a home or other building and an accompanying search that flows from the officers' response to the urgent situation. For example, the Supreme Court approved police officers' warrantless entry into a home when, on being called to the scene of a loud party, they observed through the home's window a violent altercation between a teenager and an adult (*Brigham City, Utah v. Stuart*, 2006). The unanimous decision by Chief Justice John Roberts said that "law enforcement officers may enter a home without a warrant to render emergency assistance to an injured occupant or to protect an occupant from imminent injury." After the officers make the warrantless entry, the plain view doctrine permits them to examine and seize any criminal evidence that they can see in the course of actions taken to address the exigent circumstances.

In *Cupp v. Murphy* (1973), a man voluntarily complied with police officers' request that he come to the police station to answer questions concerning his wife's murder. At the station, officers noticed a substance on the man's fingernails that they thought might be dried blood. Over his objections, they took a sample of scrapings under his fingernails and ultimately used that tissue as evidence against him when he was convicted of murdering his wife. The Supreme Court said the search was properly undertaken under exigent circumstances. If officers had taken the time to seek a warrant, the suspect could have washed his hands and the evidence would have been lost.

Police officers can use the exigent circumstances justification for warrantless searches for the purpose of seeking evidence. To justify such searches, they do not need to show that there was a potential threat to public safety. As a practical matter, police officers make quick judgments about undertaking certain searches. If incriminating evidence is discovered, courts may be asked after the fact to determine whether the urgency of the situation justified a warrantless search and whether the nature and purpose of the search were reasonable. Judges are usually reluctant to second-guess a police officer's on-the-spot decision that the urgency of a situation required an immediate warrantless search.

■ Consent

If people consent to a search, officers do not need probable cause or even any level of suspicion to justify the search. Consent effectively absolves law enforcement officers of any risk that evidence will be excluded from use at trial or that they will be found liable in a civil lawsuit alleging a violation of Fourth Amendment rights.

Consent searches provide a valuable investigatory tool for officers who wish to conduct warrantless searches. Officers in many police departments are trained to ask people if they will consent to a search. Thus, some officers ask every motorist during a traffic stop, "May I search your car?" Or, if called to the scene of a domestic dispute or a citizen complaint about noise, the officers may say, "Do you mind if I look around the downstairs area of your house?" Criminal evidence is often uncovered in such consent searches—a fact that may indicate that many citizens do not know that they have the option to say "no" when officers ask for permission to search. Moreover, some citizens may fear that they will look more suspicious to the officer if they say "no," so they agree to searches in order to act as if they have nothing to hide. In addition, in *United States v. Drayton* (2002), the Supreme Court said that police officers do not have to inform people of their right to say "no" when asked if they wish to consent to a search.

In deciding if a permissible consent search has occurred, one must address two key issues. First, the consent must voluntary. Police officers may not use coercion or threats to obtain consent. Even subtler tricks, such as dishonestly telling someone that there is a search warrant and thereby implying that the person has no choice but to consent, will result in the search being declared improper (*Bumper v. North Carolina*, 1968). Second, the consent must be given by someone who possesses authority to give consent and thereby waive the right. Someone cannot, for example, consent to have his or her neighbor's house searched. The resident in a dwelling can consent to a search of that dwelling. As we saw in the opening of the chapter, however, the police may not search when one resident of a dwelling is present and objects, even if another resident consents to the search of the house (*Georgia v. Randolph*, 2006).

■ Automobile Searches

The U.S. Supreme Court first addressed automobile searches in *Carroll v. United States* (1925), a case in which federal agents searched a car for illegal alcohol. The *Carroll* case, in which the warrantless search was approved, provided an underlying justification for permitting such searches of automobiles. In essence, because cars are mobile, they differ greatly from houses and other buildings. Automobiles can be driven away and disappear in the time that it would take officers to ask a judicial officer for a search warrant.

Police officers have significant authority to search automobiles and to issue commands to people riding in vehicles. For example, during a traffic stop, officers can order passengers as well as the driver to exit the vehicle, even if there is no basis for suspicion that the passengers engaged in any wrongdoing (*Maryland v. Wilson*, 1997).

Two key questions arise in automobile searches: (1) When can officers stop a car? and (2) How extensively can they search the vehicle? Many automobile searches arise as a result of traffic stops. A stop can occur when an officer observes a traffic violation, including defective safety equipment, or when there is a basis for reasonable suspicion concerning the involvement of the car, its driver, or its passengers in a crime. Police officers are free to make a visible inspection of a car's interior by shining a flashlight inside and looking through the window. They can also look at the vehicle identification number on the dashboard and inside the door of a validly stopped vehicle (*New York v. Class*, 1986).

All sworn officers can make traffic stops, even if they are in unmarked vehicles and serving in special vice or detective bureaus that do not normally handle traffic offenses (*Whren v. United States*, 1996). A traffic violation by itself, however, does not provide an officer with the authority to search an entire vehicle (*Knowles v. Iowa*, 1998). Only specific factors creating reasonable suspicion or probable cause will justify officers' doing anything more than looking inside the vehicle.

For example, the arrest of a driver justifies the search of a passenger's property or other locations in the vehicle if there is reason to believe that those locations could contain criminal evidence or weapons (*Wyoming v. Houghton*, 1999). In addition, the Court has expanded officers' authority to search automobiles even when no formal arrest has yet occurred. In *Michigan v. Long* (1983), the Court approved a search of the car's interior around the driver's seat after officers found the car in a ditch and the apparently intoxicated driver standing outside the car. The Supreme Court justified the search as an expansion of the *Terry* doctrine. In effect, the officers were permitted to "frisk" the car in order to protect themselves and others by making sure no weapon was available to the not-yet-arrested driver. Such a search requires that the officers have reasonable suspicion that the person stopped may be armed and may

Criminal Justice: MYTH AND REALITY

COMMON BELIEF: Under the Fourth Amendment's requirements for searches, only judges make determinations of "probable cause," and they do so in order to decide whether to issue a search warrant.

In *California v. Acevedo* (1991), the Supreme Court said that officers could search anywhere in the car for which they have probable cause to search. This includes a search of closed containers within the car. Further, the officers themselves, rather than a judge, determine whether probable cause exists before conducting the warrantless search of the vehicle. If, however, a judge later disagrees with an officer's conclusion about the existence of probable cause, any evidence found in the search of the automobile might be excluded from use at trial. It may be difficult, however, for a judge to second-guess an officer's decisions, since the judge must make an after-the-fact evaluation based on the officer's description of the facts and circumstances.

If officers are suspicious of a driver who has been stopped for a traffic violation and they are eager to search the vehicle, is there a risk that they will be less careful than a judge in deciding whether probable cause exists to justify a complete search? The Supreme Court's *Acevedo* decision expanded police officers' authority to determine whether to search a vehicle and its contents. At the same time, it imposed on officers a significant responsibility for making careful decisions in order to protect citizens' Fourth Amendment rights.

pose a threat to the officers. As described in "Criminal Justice: Myth and Reality," there are also opportunities for officers to search closed containers within a vehicle.

The Court permits thorough searches of vehicles, without regard to probable cause, when police officers inventory the contents of impounded vehicles (*South Dakota v. Opperman*, 1976). This means that containers found within the course of the inventory search may also be opened and searched when the examination of such containers is consistent with a police department's inventory policies.

Table 6.1 reviews selected Supreme Court cases concerning those circumstances in which the police do not need a warrant to conduct a search or to seize evidence.

TABLE 6.1	Warrantless Searches

The Supreme Court has ruled that there are circumstances when a warrant is not required.

Case	Decision
Special needs	
Michigan Department of State Police v. Sitz (1990)	Stopping motorists systematically at roadblocks designed for specific purposes, such as detecting drunken drivers, is permissible.
City of Indianapolis v. Edmond (2000)	Police traffic checkpoints cannot be justified as a generalized search for criminal evidence, they must be narrowly focused on a specific objective.
Stop and frisk	
Terry v. Ohio (1968)	Officers may stop and frisk suspects on the street when there is reasonable suspicion that they are armed and involved in criminal activity.
Adams v. Williams (1972)	Officers may rely on reports from reliable witnesses as the basis for conducting a stop and frisk.
Illinois v. Wardlow (2000)	When a person runs at the sight of police in a high-crime area, officers are justified in using the person's flight as a basis for forming reasonable suspicion to justify a stop and frisk.
Incident to an arrest	
Chimel v. California (1969)	To preserve evidence and protect the safety of the officer and the public after a lawful arrest, the arrestee and the immediate area around the arrestee may be searched for weapons and criminal evidence.
United States v. Robinson (1973)	A warrantless search incident to an arrest is not limited by the seriousness of the crime for which the arrestee has been taken into custody.
Exigent circumstances	
Warden v. Hayden (1967)	When officers are in hot pursuit of a fleeing suspect, they need not stop to seek a warrant and thereby risk permitting the suspect to get away.
Cupp v. Murphy (1973)	Officers may seize evidence to protect it if taking time to seek a warrant creates a risk of its destruction.
Consent	
Bumper v. North Carolina (1968)	Officers may not tell falsehoods as a means of getting a suspect to consent to a search.
United States v. Drayton (2002)	An officer does not have to inform people of their right to refuse when he or she asks if they wish to consent to a search.
Automobiles	
Carroll v. United States (1925)	Because by their nature automobiles can be easily moved, warrantless searches are permissible when reasonable suspicion of illegal activity exists.
New York v. Class (1986)	An officer may enter a vehicle to see the vehicle identification number when a car has been validly stopped pursuant to a traffic violation or other permissible justification.
California v. Acevedo (1991)	Officers may search throughout a vehicle when they believe they have probable cause to do so.
Maryland v. Wilson (1997)	During traffic stops, officers may order passengers as well as the driver to exit the vehicle, even if there is no basis for suspicion that the passengers engaged in any wrongdoing.
Knowles v. Iowa (1998)	A traffic violation by itself does not provide an officer with the authority to search an entire vehicle. There must be reasonable suspicion or probable cause before officers can extend their search beyond merely looking inside the vehicle's passenger compartment.

CHECKPOINT

ANSWERS

5 *In what situations do law enforcement's special needs justify stopping an automobile without reasonable suspicion?*

5 Warrantless stops of automobiles are permitted at international borders and sobriety checkpoints (unless barred within a specific state by its own supreme court) or when there is reasonable suspicion of a traffic violation or other wrongdoing.

6 *What is an exigent circumstance?*

6 An urgent situation in which evidence might be destroyed, a suspect might escape, or the public would be endangered if police took the time to seek a warrant for a search or an arrest.

7 *What two elements must be present for a valid consent to permit a warrantless search?*

7 Voluntary consent by a person with proper authority to consent.

Questioning Suspects

The Fifth Amendment contains various rights, including the one most relevant to police officers' actions in questioning suspects. The relevant words of the amendment are "No person shall... be compelled in any criminal case to be a witness against himself." The privilege against compelled self-incrimination should not be viewed as simply a legal protection that seeks to assist individuals who may be guilty of crimes. By protecting individuals in this way, the Fifth Amendment discourages police officers from using violent or otherwise coercive means to push suspects to confess.

In addition to discouraging the physical abuse of suspects, the privilege against compelled self-incrimination can also diminish the risk of erroneous convictions. When police officers use coercive pressure to seek confessions, they create a significant risk that innocent people will confess to crimes they did not commit. The worst-case scenario took place in the film *In the Name of the Father* (1993), based on a true story in England, in which police officers gain a confession from a bombing suspect, whom they know to be innocent, by placing a gun in the suspect's mouth and threatening to pull the trigger. This example in England took place at a moment when people there were afraid of terrorist acts by militants who sought to use violence to force Great Britain to remove its soldiers and governing institutions from Northern Ireland. Since 9/11, many Americans feel similar fears about their own country's vulnerability to terrorists. See "What Americans Think" on the next page to assess how the threat of terrorism may have influenced the public's views on coercive questioning of terrorism suspects.

A Santa Ana, California, police officer questions a suspect about a knife that was found by police. In such a confined setting, are you confident that suspects will truly understand the nature of their rights before consenting to be questioned without an attorney present?

© Spencer Grant/PhotoEdit

■ *Miranda* Rules

■ *Miranda v. Arizona* (1966) U.S. Supreme Court decision declaring that suspects in custody must be informed of their rights to remain silent and be represented during questioning.

The decision by the Supreme Court in ***Miranda v. Arizona*** **(1966)** said that as soon as the investigation of a crime begins to focus on a particular suspect and he or she is taken into custody, the so-called *Miranda* warnings must be read aloud before questioning can begin. In the Close Up box, you can read an excerpt from the Court's actual opinion explaining the decision. Suspects must be told four things:

1. They have the right to remain silent.
2. If they decide to make a statement, it can and will be used against them in court.
3. They have the right to have an attorney present during interrogation or to have an opportunity to consult with an attorney.
4. If they cannot afford an attorney, the state will provide one.

Prior to the *Miranda* decision, police officers in some places solved crimes by picking up a poor person or an African American and torturing him or her until a confession was produced. In *Brown v. Mississippi* (1936), the Supreme Court ruled that statements produced after police beat suspects were inadmissible, but it did not insist that counsel be available at the early stages of the criminal process.

Two rulings in 1964 laid the foundation for the *Miranda* decision. In *Escobedo v. Illinois*, the Court made the link between the Fifth Amendment right against self-incrimination and the Sixth Amendment right to counsel. Danny Escobedo was questioned at the police station for 14 hours without counsel, even though he asked to see his attorney. He finally made incriminating statements that the police said were voluntary. The Court's ruling specified that defendants have a right to counsel

> when the investigation is no longer a general inquiry into an unsolved crime, but has begun to focus on a particular suspect, the suspect has been taken into police custody, [and] the police carry out a process of interrogations that lends itself to eliciting incriminating statements.

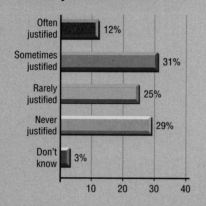

What AMERICANS Think

QUESTION: "Do you think the use of torture against suspected terrorists in order to gain important information can often be justified, sometimes be justified, rarely be justified, or never be justified?"

Often justified	12%
Sometimes justified	31%
Rarely justified	25%
Never justified	29%
Don't know	3%

(scale: 10 20 30 40)

Go to http://www.cengage.com/criminaljustice/cole to compare your opinion on this issue with the opinions of other criminal justice students.

Source: Pew Research Center for the People and the Press, *Trends in Political Values and Core Attitudes: 1987–2007*, p. 106. Reprinted in Bureau of Justice Statistics, *Sourcebook of Criminal Justice Statistics, 2008* (Washington, DC: U.S. Government Printing Office, 2008), Table 2.0007.2007, http://www.albany.edu/sourcebook/.

The Court effectively expanded the right to counsel to apply at an early point in the criminal justice process as a means to guard against law enforcement officers' actions that might violate the Fifth Amendment privilege against compelled self-incrimination. In *Massiah v. United States* (1964), the Supreme Court declared that the questioning of the defendant by a police agent outside of the presence of defense counsel violated the defendant's rights.

The *Miranda* warnings only apply to what are called custodial interrogations. If police officers walk up to someone on the streets and begin asking questions, there is no need to inform the person of his rights. The justices say that people know they can walk away when an officer asks them questions in a public place. When police have taken someone into custody, however, the Supreme Court sees risks of excessive pressure. The loss of liberty and isolation experienced by detained suspects can make them vulnerable to abusive interrogation techniques, especially when interrogations take place out of view of anyone other than police officers. When a suspect is alone in a room with the police, will anyone believe the suspect if he or she claims to have been beaten? If the police say that the suspect confessed, will anyone believe the suspect if he or she denies this? The *Miranda* warnings and presence of counsel during questioning are supposed to prevent such abuses.

The Court has permitted police officers to forgo *Miranda* warnings when a threat to public safety would result from police taking the time to provide the warnings. This exception is similar to the exigent circumstance justification for warrantless searches. The underlying premise is that some urgent, socially significant situation outweighs the necessity of respecting individuals' rights. In the case that created this **"public safety" exception**, police officers chased an armed man into a supermarket after a reported assault. When they found him with an empty shoulder holster, they asked, "Where's the gun?" after he was handcuffed but before he had been informed of his *Miranda*

■ **"public safety" exception** Exception to *Miranda* requirements that permits police to immediately question a suspect in custody without providing any warnings, when public safety would be jeopardized by their taking the time to supply the warnings.

CLOSE UP

Miranda v. Arizona, 384 U.S. 436 (1966)

ERNEST MIRANDA, a loading-dock worker with a prior history of sex offenses, was arrested for rape. Two detectives took him into a private interrogation room for questioning. Eventually, they emerged with his signed confession. Miranda's lawyer challenged the confession, because the questioning took place before the attorney had been appointed to provide representation. Chief Justice Warren delivered the opinion of the Court, as follows.

★★★

Our holding will be spelled out with some specificity in the pages which follow but briefly stated it is this: the prosecution may not use statements... stemming from custodial interrogation of the defendant unless it demonstrates the use of procedural safeguards effective to secure the privilege against self-incrimination. By custodial interrogation, we mean questioning initiated by law enforcement officers after a person has been taken into custody or otherwise deprived of his freedom of action in any significant way. As for the procedural safeguards to be employed, unless other fully effective means are devised to inform accused persons of their right to silence and to assure a continuous opportunity to exercise it, the following measures are required. Prior to any questioning, the person must be warned that he has a right to remain silent, that any statement he does make may be used as evidence against him, and that he has the right to the presence of an attorney, either retained or appointed.

The defendant may waive effectuation of these rights, provided the waiver is made voluntarily, knowingly, and intelligently. If, however, he indicates in any manner and at any stage of the process that he wishes to consult with an attorney before speaking there can be no questioning. Likewise, if the individual is alone and indicates in any manner that he does not wish to be interrogated, the police may not question him. The mere fact that he may have answered some questions or volunteered some statements on his own does not deprive him of the right to refrain from answering any further inquiries until he has consulted with an attorney and thereafter consents to be questioned.

The constitutional issue we decide... is the admissibility of statements obtained from a defendant questioned while in custody or otherwise deprived of his freedom of action in any significant way....

An understanding of the nature and setting of this in-custody interrogation is essential to our decisions today. The difficulty in depicting what transpires at such interrogations stems from the fact that in this country they have largely taken place incommunicado. From extensive factual studies undertaken in the early 1930's, including the famous *Wickersham Report* to Congress by a Presidential Commission, it is clear that police violence and the "third degree" flourished at that time.

In a series of cases decided by this Court long after these studies, the police resorted to physical brutality—beatings, hanging, whipping—and to sustained and protracted questioning incommunicado in order to extort confessions.... The use of physical brutality and violence is not, unfortunately, relegated to the past or to any part of the country. Only recently in Kings County, New York, the police brutally beat, kicked, and placed lighted cigarette butts on the back of a potential witness under interrogation for the purpose of securing a statement incriminating a third party....

The examples given above are undoubtedly the exception now, but they are sufficiently widespread to be the object of concern. Unless a proper limitation upon custodial interrogation is achieved—such as these decisions will advance—there can be no assurance that practices of this nature will be eradicated in the foreseeable future....

★★★

In dealing with statements obtained through interrogation, we do not purport to find all confessions inadmissible. Confessions remain a proper element in law enforcement. Any statement given freely and voluntarily without any compelling influences is, of course, admissible in evidence.... There is no requirement that police stop a person who enters a police station and states that he wishes to confess to a crime, or a person who calls the police to offer a confession or any other statement he desires to make. Volunteered statements of any kind are not barred by the Fifth Amendment and their admissibility is not affected by our holding today....

★★★

In announcing these principles, we are not unmindful of the burdens which law enforcement officials must bear, often under trying circumstances. We also fully recognize the obligation of all citizens to aid in enforcing the criminal laws. This Court, while protecting individual rights, has always given ample latitude to law enforcement agencies in the legitimate exercise of their duties. The limits we have placed on the interrogation process should not constitute an undue interference with a proper system of law enforcement....

RESEARCHING THE INTERNET

An online FBI publication provides a history of the events that led to the *Miranda* decision as well as a description of subsequent Supreme Court decisions that have clarified the obligation to provide warnings in different situations. Visit the site listed on the Cole/Smith Criminal Justice in America Companion Website: http://www.cengage.com/criminaljustice/cole

FOR CRITICAL ANALYSIS

Does Chief Justice Warren's opinion provide a persuasive justification for the required *Miranda* warnings? Does the opinion give clear guidance to police about what they must do? Is the opinion based on a clear requirement from the Constitution, or was the *Miranda* rule created because a majority of the Supreme Court justices thought it would be a good idea?

---

rights (*New York v. Quarles*, 1984). His statement in response to the question could be used against him in court, because the public's safety might have been threatened if the police had taken the time to read him his rights before asking any questions.

Although some legal commentators and police officials have criticized the *Miranda* warnings, the Supreme Court strongly repeated its endorsement of the *Miranda* requirement in 2000 (*Dickerson v. United States*). In declaring that *Miranda* warnings are required by the Constitution, Chief Justice William Rehnquist's majority opinion stated that "*Miranda* has become embedded in routine police practice to the point where the warnings have become part of our national culture." Rehnquist's conclusion was reinforced by a national survey of police chiefs, in which more than three-quarters of respondents supported the Supreme Court's decision to keep the *Miranda* rule in place (Zalman and Smith, 2007).

■ The Consequences of *Miranda*

Miranda rights must be provided before questions are asked during custodial interrogations. However, police officers have adapted their techniques in various ways in order to question suspects without any impediment from the warnings. For example, officers may ask questions while standing on the suspect's doorstep before making an arrest. Even after arrest, the courts do not require that police inform suspects of their rights immediately. Thus, after taking a suspect into custody, some officers may delay providing *Miranda* warnings in case the suspect talks on his or her own. The suspect may be kept in the backseat of a car as officers drive around town, or the suspect may be left alone in a room at the police station. Some suspects will take the initiative to talk to officers because of feelings of guilt. Other suspects may start conversations with officers because they are so eager to convince the officers that they have an alibi or that they want to cooperate. This may lead the suspect to provide contradictory statements that will help build the case.

Officers are also trained in interrogation techniques that are intended to encourage suspects to talk despite *Miranda* warnings (Weisselberg, 2008). The words of the warnings are so familiar from television police shows that many suspects never stop to think about the message being conveyed. In addition, officers may pretend to sympathize with the suspect (Leo, 1996). For example, they may say such things as "We know that you had a good reason to go after that guy with a knife. Tell us how it happened." Police officers are not required to be truthful in speaking to suspects. They are permitted to use deception to induce suspects to talk. It is not uncommon for officers to say, untruthfully, "We have five witnesses that saw you do it. If you tell us everything right now, we may be able to get you a good deal." In reality, there were no witnesses and there will be no deal. Do such statements constitute improper pressure in violation of *Miranda*? Probably not—as long as the officers do not threaten suspects in ways that make them fear for their physical safety or the safety of their loved ones. See "A Question of Ethics" at the end of the chapter for more on this.

Many suspects talk to the police despite being informed of their right to remain silent and their right to have an attorney present during questioning. Some suspects do not fully understand their rights. They may believe that they will look guilty by remaining silent or asking for an attorney. They therefore feel that they must talk to officers in order to have any hope of claiming innocence. More importantly, many suspects believe (often accurately) that they will gain a more favorable charge or plea bargain if they cooperate with officers as fully and as early as possible.

In 2004, the Supreme Court warned police officers not to try to get around *Miranda* warnings by questioning unwarned suspects and obtaining incriminating statements and then giving the warnings and asking the suspects to repeat their statements again. In *Missouri v. Seibert* (2004), Justice Souter's majority opinion concluded,

> Upon hearing warnings only in the aftermath of interrogation and just after making a confession, a suspect would hardly think he had a genuine right to remain silent, let alone persist in so believing once the police began to lead him over the same ground again....Thus, when *Miranda* warnings are inserted in the midst of coordinated and continuing interrogation, they are likely to mislead and "depriv[e] a defendant of knowledge essential to his ability to understand the nature of his rights and the consequences of abandoning them."

Some commentators have argued that officers' efforts to get around the *Miranda* requirement could be prevented by requiring that all police interrogations be videorecorded in order to make sure that suspects' statements are voluntary. Several states have introduced videorecording requirements, but they are often limited to certain categories of cases, such as murders or serious felonies (L. Lewis, 2007). It remains to be seen whether such requirements will become more universal.

CHECKPOINT

8 *What are* Miranda *rights?*

8 Officers must inform suspects before custodial interrogation of the right to remain silent, the prosecution's authority to use any of the suspect's statements, the right to the presence of an attorney during questioning, and the right to have an attorney appointed if the suspect is too poor to hire one.

9 *What is the "public safety" exception?*

9 Officers can ask questions of suspects in custody without first providing *Miranda* warnings, when public safety would be threatened by their taking the time to supply the warnings.

10 *How have police officers adapted their practices in light of* Miranda?

10 Officers ask questions before suspects are in custody, use techniques to pretend to befriend or empathize with suspects being questioned, and misinform suspects about the existence of evidence demonstrating their guilt.

The Exclusionary Rule

■ **exclusionary rule** The principle that illegally obtained evidence must be excluded from trial.

What happens when police commit rights violations? One primary remedy is the exclusion of evidence from court. In 1914, the U.S. Supreme Court declared in *Weeks v. United States* that federal courts must exclude any evidence that was obtained through an improper search by federal law enforcement agents. In *Weeks*, U.S. marshals searched a home without a warrant and found incriminating evidence. According to the Court,

> If letters and private documents can thus be seized and held and used in evidence against a citizen accused of an offense, the protection of the 4th Amendment, declaring his right to be secure against such searches and seizures, is of no value, and, so far as those thus placed are concerned, might as well be stricken from the Constitution.

Thus, the Court required that the improperly obtained evidence be excluded from use in court, even if it meant that a guilty person might go free because of a lack of enough evidence to gain a conviction. As a result of this **exclusionary rule** created by the Court, it was assumed that law enforcement officers would obey the Fourth Amendment in order to avoid the loss of incriminating evidence. The exclusionary rule was later also applied to Fifth Amendment violations caused by improper questioning, such as a failure to inform arrested individuals of their *Miranda* rights.

The exclusionary rule does not necessarily require that cases against defendants be dismissed when constitutional rights have been violated. The prosecution can continue, but it may not use improperly obtained evidence. In some cases, other valid evidence of guilt may exist in the form of witness testimony or confessions. Without such alternative evidence, however, the exclusionary rule can lead to charges being dropped.

■ The Application of the Exclusionary Rule to the States

In *Wolf v. Colorado* (1949), the Supreme Court incorporated the Fourth Amendment. However, the justices declined to apply the exclusionary rule to the states, because they believed states could develop their own

Police officers must take care to follow the rules for conducting proper searches that obey court rulings defining the Fourth Amendment protection against "unreasonable searches and seizures." Evidence will be excluded when the Fourth Amendment is violated, unless the police officers' actions fall within a specific exception to the exclusionary rule.

© Mitch Wojnarowicz/Amsterdam Recorder/The Image Works

remedies to handle improper searches by police. The situation changed during the Supreme Court tenure of Chief Justice Earl Warren (1953–1969), when the Court incorporated most of the criminal justice–related rights in a way that required state law enforcement officials to adhere to the same rules federal law enforcement officials had to follow. Not until *Mapp v. Ohio* (1961) did the Court apply the exclusionary rule to the states.

Why did the Supreme Court see the exclusionary rule as necessary? Several reasons emerge in *Weeks v. United States* (1914) and *Mapp*. First, *Weeks* declared that the exclusionary rule is essential to make the Fourth Amendment meaningful. In essence, the justices believed that constitutional rights are nullified if government officials are permitted to benefit by violating those rights. Second, *Mapp* indicated that the exclusionary rule is required by the Constitution. Third, the majority opinion in *Mapp* concluded that alternatives to the exclusionary rule do not work. The opinion noted that many states had found that nothing short of exclusion of evidence would work to correct constitutional rights violations and limit the number of violations that occur. Fourth, the *Mapp* opinion argued that the use of improperly obtained evidence by officials who are responsible for upholding the law only serves to diminish respect for the law. Fifth, the *Mapp* decision indicates that the absence of an exclusionary rule would diminish the protection of all rights because it would permit all constitutional rights "to be revocable at the whim of any police officer who, in the name of law enforcement itself, chooses to suspend ... [the] enjoyment [of rights]." Sixth, the exclusionary rule is justified in *Mapp* as an effective means of deterring police and prosecutors from violating constitutional rights.

The existence of the exclusionary rule demonstrates the Supreme Court's conclusion that it is sometimes necessary to risk setting a guilty criminal free in order to make sure that constitutional rights are protected.

■ Exceptions to the Exclusionary Rule

The exclusionary rule has many critics who claim that the Court's decision hampers police investigations and allows guilty criminals to go free. However, research has not clearly supported claims about the negative consequences of the exclusionary rule. Studies of the impact of the exclusionary rule have produced two consistent findings. First, only a small minority of defendants file a "motion to suppress," which is used to ask a judge to exclude evidence that has allegedly been obtained in violation of the defendant's rights. Second, only a very small fraction of motions to suppress evidence are granted (Davies 1983; Uchida and Bynum, 1991; S. Walker, 2001:90–91). Despite continuing debates about the rule's impact and effectiveness, the Supreme Court began creating exceptions to the exclusionary rule after Warren Burger became chief justice in 1969.

■ **"good faith" exception** Exception to the exclusionary rule that permits the use of improperly obtained evidence when police officers acted in honest reliance on a defective statute, a warrant improperly issued by a magistrate, or a consent to search by someone who lacked authority to give such permission.

"Good Faith" Exception   The Supreme Court created a **"good faith" exception** to the exclusionary rule when officers use search warrants (*United States v. Leon*, 1984). "Good faith" means that the officers acted with the honest belief that they were following the proper rules, but the judge issued the warrant improperly. In addition, the reliance and honest belief must be reasonable. If officers knew that a judge issued a warrant based on no evidence whatsoever, the officers could not claim that they reasonably and honestly relied on the warrant. But when officers present evidence of probable cause to the judge and the judge issues a warrant based on information that actually falls below the standard of probable cause, the officers may use evidence found in the resulting search, because it was the judge who made the error, not the police. However, evidence can still be excluded if officers undertake a warrantless search based on their own discretionary decision, even if they honestly (but wrongly) believe that such a search is permitted in such circumstances.

Inevitable Discovery Rule Another important exception to the exclusionary rule is the **inevitable discovery rule**. This rule arose from a case involving the tragic abduction and murder of a young girl. The police sought an escapee from a psychiatric hospital who was seen carrying a large bundle. The man being sought contacted an attorney and arranged to surrender to police in a town 160 miles away from the scene of the abduction. The Supreme Court subsequently found that the police improperly questioned the suspect outside of the presence of his attorney while driving him back to the city where the abduction occurred (*Brewer v. Williams*, 1977). The Court declared that the girl's body and the suspect's statements had to be excluded from evidence because they were obtained in violation of his rights. Thus, his murder conviction was overturned and he was given a new trial. At the second trial, he was convicted again. However, at the second trial, the prosecution used the body in evidence against him based on the claim that search parties would have found the body eventually even without his confession. There was a search team within two and one-half miles of the body at the time that it was found. In *Nix v. Williams* **(1984),** the Supreme Court agreed that the improperly obtained evidence can be used when it would later have been inevitably discovered anyway without improper actions by the police. Table 6.2 summarizes selected Supreme Court decisions regarding the exclusionary rule as it applies to the Fourth and Fifth Amendments.

When the Court issued its decisions in *Weeks* and *Mapp*, it appeared that the exclusion of evidence would be guided by a trial judge's answer to the question "Did police violate the suspect's rights?" By contrast, through the development of exceptions to the rule, the Court shifted its focus to the question "Did the police make an error that was so serious that the exclusion of evidence is required?" For example, the "good faith" exception established in *United States v. Leon* (1984) emphasizes the fact that officers did what they thought they were supposed to do. The decision did not rest on the fact that the suspect's Fourth Amendment rights were violated by a search conducted with an improper warrant. Thus, the Supreme Court's creation of exceptions to the exclusionary rule has given police officers the flexibility to make specific kinds of errors without jeopardizing the admissibility of evidence that may help establish a defendant's guilt.

In 2009, some commentators speculated that the Supreme Court was deeply divided on the issue of whether to eliminate the exclusionary rule (Liptak, 2009c). Five justices declined to apply the exclusionary rule to the case of an improper search, when a man was wrongly arrested because of sloppy record keeping in a police database that erroneously informed the officers that there was an arrest warrant (*Herring v. United States*, 2009). Critics of the exclusionary rule hope that this decision moved the Court one step closer to abolishing the rule. In reality, the fate of the rule will be determined

■ **inevitable discovery rule** Supreme Court ruling that improperly obtained evidence can be used when it would later have been inevitably discovered by the police.

■ *Nix v. Williams* **(1984)** Legal decision in which the Supreme Court created the "inevitable discovery" exception to the exclusionary rule.

TABLE 6.2 | **Exclusionary Rule**

The Supreme Court has created the exclusionary rule as a means of ensuring that Fourth and Fifth Amendment rights are protected. It has also provided exceptions to this rule.

Case	Decision
Exclusionary rule	
Mapp v. Ohio (1961)	Because the Fourth Amendment protects people from unreasonable searches and seizures by all law enforcement officials, evidence found through improper searches or seizures must be excluded from use at state and federal trials.
"Good faith" exception	
United States v. Leon (1984)	When officers act in good faith reliance on a warrant, the evidence will not be excluded even if the warrant was issued improperly.
"Inevitable discovery" exception	
Nix v. Williams (1984)	Improperly obtained evidence can be used when it would later have inevitably been discovered without improper actions by the police.

by new justices, who could go either way (C. E. Smith, McCall, and McCall, 2009). In the immediate future, it seems unlikely that President Barack Obama would appoint new justices who would favor the elimination of the exclusionary rule, but presidents cannot always predict accurately how their nominees will decide specific issues.

CHECKPOINT

ANSWERS

11 *Why was the exclusionary rule created and eventually applied to the states?*

11 The exclusionary rule was created to deter officers from violating people's rights, and the Supreme Court considers it an essential component of the Fourth and Fifth Amendments.

12 *What are the criticisms of the exclusionary rule?*

12 The rule is criticized for hampering police investigations and permitting some guilty people to go free.

13 *What are the main exceptions to the exclusionary rule?*

13 A "good faith" exception in warrant situations; cases in which evidence would have been discovered by the police inevitably anyway (inevitable discovery rule).

Police Abuse of Power

The first sections of this chapter discussed legal rules that police are supposed to obey when carrying out their duties. But what happens when police violate the law? What if police make an improper arrest? What if they conduct an improper search but do not find any evidence of wrongdoing? The exclusionary rule provides a limited, after-the-fact remedy, but only in cases for which the police have found evidence of a crime or obtained incriminating statements during improper questioning. How can Americans be protected against illegal actions by the police when the exclusionary rule does not apply?

Think about other circumstances in which police may violate the law. Moreover, think about how such behavior can harm both individuals and society. Individuals' rights can be violated. The image of the police and their relationship to the community can be damaged. Moreover, extreme abuse can result in civil disturbances. For example, the videotaped beating of Rodney King by Los Angeles police officers drew worldwide attention in 1991 and eventually contributed to a major riot that took dozens of lives.

The issue of police misbehavior is not limited to the problem of violating citizens' rights. Police can also break the law and disobey departmental policies through corruption, favoritism, discrimination, and the failure to carry out their duties. Periodically, police corruption and abuse of power become major issues on the public agenda (Skolnick and Fyfe, 1993). Although police scandals have occurred throughout U.S. history, only in the past 40 years has the public been keenly aware of the problems of police misconduct, especially the illegal use of violence by law enforcement officers and the criminal activities associated with police corruption. Although most officers do not engage in misconduct, these problems deserve study because they raise questions about how much the public can control and trust the police. We now turn our attention to the problems of police misbehavior and to approaches for addressing these issues.

Use of Force

Although most people cooperate with the police, officers must at times use force to make arrests, control disturbances, and deal with the drunken or mentally ill (R. A. Thompson, 2001). As noted by Jerome Skolnick and James Fyfe (1993:37),

> As long as some members of society do not comply with the law and [some] resist the police, force will remain an inevitable part of policing. Cops, especially, understand that. Indeed, anybody who fails to understand the centrality of force in police work has no business in a police uniform.

Thus, police may use *legitimate* force to do their job. It is when they use *excessive* force that they violate the law. But what is excessive force? Both officers and experts debate this question.

In cities where racial tensions are high, conflicts between police and residents often result when officers are accused of acting unprofessionally (Kane, 2002). Citizens use the term *police brutality* to describe a wide range of practices, from the use of profane or abusive language to physical force and violence. As shown in "What Americans Think," the percentage of Americans who believe that police brutality exists where they live has increased over the past four decades.

Stories of police brutality are not new. However, unlike the untrained officers of the early 1900s, today's officers are supposed to be professionals who know the rules and understand the need for proper conduct. Thus, reports of unjustified police shootings and beatings are particularly disturbing (Ogletree et al., 1995). Moreover, the public cannot know how often police engage in abusive behavior, even when it comes to light, because most violence remains hidden from public view (Weitzer, 2002). In 2008, a news helicopter filmed a dozen Philadelphia police officers beating and kicking a criminal suspect who had just been pulled from a car (Hurdle, 2008). If not for the videotape, how would the public know that the incident had happened? If criminal suspects claim to be beaten, will the public believe them? How can we prevent such incidents, especially when they occur without witnesses?

The concept "use of force" takes many forms in practice. We can arrange the various types of force on a continuum ranging from most severe (civilians shot and killed) to least severe ("come-alongs," or being grasped by an officer) (Terrill, 2005). Table 6.3 lists many of these forms of force according to their frequency of use. How often must force be used? Most research has shown that in police contacts with suspects, force is used infrequently and the type of force used is usually at the low end of the continuum—toward the less severe. Research in Phoenix found that the single largest predictor of police use of force was use of force by the suspect, to which the police then responded (Garner et al., 1995). For example, resistance by a suspect can contribute to the officers' decision to use force (Garner, Maxwell, and Heraux, 2002). Research in six urban jurisdictions in which 7,512 arrests were examined showed that in 97.9 percent of contacts, the police used no weapon such as a baton, flashlight, handgun, chemical agent, or canine (Garner and Maxwell, 1999:31). Again, it is *excessive* use of force, in violation of departmental policies and state laws, that constitutes abuse of police power.

A report by the National Institute of Justice summarized general conclusions from research about use of force (K. Adams, 1999):

1. Police use force infrequently.

2. Police use of force typically occurs in the lower end of the force spectrum, involving grabbing, pushing, or shoving.

3. Use of force typically occurs when police are trying to make an arrest and the suspect is resisting.

Police grab a protester off his bike after he taunted them at a protest against free trade policies during a meeting of international leaders in Miami, Florida. Does this appear to be an appropriate use of force? Do police officers sometimes use force out of anger rather than out of necessity?

What AMERICANS Think

QUESTION: "In some places in the nation there have been charges of police brutality. Do you think there is any police brutality in your area, or not?"

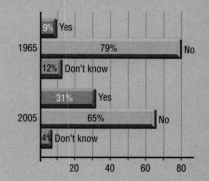

1965
- 9% Yes
- 79% No
- 12% Don't know

2005
- 31% Yes
- 65% No
- 4% Don't know

Go to http://www.cengage.com/criminaljustice/cole to compare your opinion on this issue with the opinions of other criminal justice students.

Source: Source: Gallup Poll, January 3, 2006, reprinted from Bureau of Justice Statistics, *Sourcebook of Criminal Justice Statistics, 2006* (Washington, DC: U.S. Government Printing Office, 2007), Table 2.

TABLE 6.3	Reported Uses of Force by Big-City Police

Police have the legal right to use force to make an arrest, keep the peace, and maintain order. Of the many types of force available to police, the less severe types are used most often.

Type of Force	Rate per Thousand Sworn Officers
Handcuff/leg restraint	490.4
Bodily force (arm, foot, or leg)	272.2
Come-alongs	226.8
Unholstering weapon	129.9
Swarm	126.7
Twist locks/wrist locks	80.9
Firm grip	57.7
Chemical agents (mace or Cap-Stun)	36.2
Batons	36.0
Flashlights	21.7
Dog attacks or bites	6.5
Electrical devices (Taser)	5.4
Civilians shot at but not hit	3.0
Other impact devices	2.4
Neck restraints/unconsciousness-rendering holds	1.4
Vehicle rammings	1.0
Civilians shot and killed	0.9
Civilians shot and wounded but not killed	0.2

Source: Drawn from Bureau of Justice Statistics, *National Data Collection on Police Use of Force* (Washington, DC: U.S. Government Printing Office, 1996) 43.

Although more studies are needed, other research indicates that use of force is not linked to an officer's personal characteristics such as age, gender, and ethnicity. However, a small percentage of officers may be disproportionately involved in use-of-force situations. In addition, use of force occurs more frequently when police are dealing with people affected by drugs, alcohol, or mental illness. At this point, there is a great need for additional research to tell us how frequently wrongful use of force by police occurs and whether specific departmental policies concerning hiring, training, and supervision affect officers' decisions to use force (K. Adams, 1999).

By law, the police have the authority to use force if necessary to make an arrest, keep the peace, or maintain public order. But the questions of just how much force is necessary and under what conditions force may be used are complex and open to debate. In particular, the use of deadly force in apprehending suspects has become a deeply emotional issue with a direct connection to race relations. Research has shown that the most frequent use of deadly force by the police occurs in communities with high levels of economic inequality and large minority populations (Holmes, 2000; Sorensen, Marquart, and Brock, 1993).

When police kill a suspect or bystander while trying to make an arrest, their actions may produce public outrage and hostility. Fears about the possibility of similar public disorders arose in 2005 when a police officer fired ten shots that killed a 13-year-old boy who was driving a stolen car. The officer fired in the aftermath of a chase when the boy skidded across a sidewalk and then struck a police car while backing up (Chavez, 2005). The incident led Los Angeles police officials to revise their policies about firing at moving vehicles.

There are no accurate data on the number of people shot by the police. Researchers estimate that, in the United States, the police shoot about 3,600 people each year, with fatal results for as many as 1,000 of these people (Cullen et al., 1996:449). In Baltimore, the number of police shootings varied in recent years from a low of 11 in 2004 to a high of 31 in 2007 (Fenton, 2009). In the 189 police shootings in the Houston area from 1999 through 2004, the police used firearms against 65 unarmed people (Khanna and Olsen, 2004). An analysis of New York City's detailed records on police shootings in 2008 showed drops in the use of firearms that coincided with the drop in crime rate over the preceding decade. Police opened fire at people only 60 times in 2006, compared with 147 times in 1996 (Baker, 2008). One troubling question that lingers is whether the New York City police are more inclined to use firearms against members of minority groups. Nearly 90 percent of those shot by the New York City police in the late 1990s were African American or Hispanic, but the police department has refused to release more-recent data in this regard. The police department also stopped providing information about injuries to innocent bystanders from police shootings (Baker, 2008). The selective release of information raises questions about whether the public is being kept in the dark about the nature and extent of police use of force. Data from other U.S. cities has also raised questions about use of force against minorities.

Until the 1980s, the police had broad authority to use deadly force in pursuing suspected felons. Police in about half the states were guided by the common-law principle that allowed the use of whatever force was necessary to arrest a fleeing felon. In 1985, the Supreme Court set a new standard in *Tennessee v. Garner*, ruling that the police may not use deadly force in apprehending fleeing felons "unless it is necessary to prevent the escape and the officer has probable cause to believe that the suspect poses a significant threat of death or serious physical injury to the officer or others." As in other cases concerned with use of excessive force, if officers violate standards established by the Supreme Court's decisions, they can be sued for violating individuals' Fourth Amendment right against "unreasonable seizures."

■ *Tennessee v. Garner* (1985) Deadly force may not be used against an unarmed and fleeing suspect unless necessary to prevent the escape and unless the officer has probable cause to believe that the suspect poses a significant threat of death or serious injury to the officers or others.

The standard set by *Tennessee v. Garner* presents problems, because it can be hard to judge how dangerous a suspect may be. Because officers must make quick decisions in stressful situations, the Supreme Court and other courts cannot create clear rules that will guide police in every context that arises. However, to clarify the rules for police, the Supreme Court justices also established the standard of "objective reasonableness," saying that the officer's use of deadly force should be judged in terms of its reasonableness for the specific situation that confronts the officer and requires the officer to make a quick decision about appropriate actions to take (*Graham v. Connor*, 1989). This means that the use of the deadly force should be judged from the point of view of the officer on the scene. The Court's decision recognized that "officers are often forced to make split-second judgments—in circumstances that are tense, uncertain, and rapidly evolving—about the amount of force that is necessary in a particular situation" (Georgiady, 2008).

The risk of lawsuits by victims of improper police shootings looms over police departments and creates a further incentive for administrators to set and enforce standards for the use of force. However, as long as officers carry weapons, some improper shootings will occur. Training, internal review of incidents, and the disciplining or firing of quick-trigger officers may help reduce the use of unnecessary force (Blumberg, 1989:442; Fyfe, 1993:128).

Lawsuits also arise from other uses of force by police officers. Police officers have caused deaths and injuries by using choke holds and striking people in the head with flashlights or batons. Injuries can also result from seemingly routine procedures such as placing a suspect in handcuffs, but making the handcuffs too tight. Additional lawsuits can arise when people are injured by police vehicles, although courts reject some claims if judges conclude that a fleeing suspect's behavior caused the police to take actions—such as bumping the rear fender of the suspect's car—that led to the suspect's injuries (McCall, McCall, and Smith, 2008a; *Scott v. Harris*, 2007).

As a result of lawsuits by people injured at the hands of the police, departments have sought new means of applying force in ways that will not produce injuries. Some of the new methods center on specific holds and pressure points that officers can use to incapacitate people temporarily without causing permanent harm; officers can learn these techniques through training. In addition, police departments seek new weapons that use less-than-lethal force. In Chapter 14, when we discuss the impact of technology on police, we shall examine new weapons that use electric shocks, projectiles, and chemical sprays. Advocates claim that the use of these weapons has saved the lives of citizens and officers by permitting officers to restore order without resorting to the use of guns. However, critics have raised concerns about deaths and injuries produced by less-than-lethal weapons. They have also pointed to the risk that officers will resort too quickly to such weapons when situations could be solved through patience and persuasion (Adang and Mensink, 2004).

■ Corruption

Police corruption has a long history in America. Early in the twentieth century, city officials organized liquor and gambling businesses for their personal gain. In many cities, ties between politicians and police officials assured that favored clients would be protected and competitors harassed. Much of the Progressive movement to reform the police aimed at combating such corrupt arrangements.

Although such political ties have diminished in most cities, corruption still exists. In 2008, for example, a New Haven, Connecticut, police detective was sentenced to 3 years in prison for taking bribes and stealing money seized in drug cases (Orson, 2008). Other New Haven detectives pleaded guilty to related charges stemming from an undercover investigation by the FBI (WFSB, 2007). In April 2005, two police officers in Chicago stood among the 14 reputed organized-crime figures indicted in a major investigation of unsolved mob murders. Both officers were accused of improperly providing information to mob leaders (Lighty, 2005).

Sometimes corruption is defined so broadly that it ranges from accepting a free cup of coffee to robbing businesses or beating suspects. Obviously, corruption is not easily defined, and people disagree about what it includes. As a useful starting point, we can focus on the distinction between corrupt officers who are "grass eaters" and those who are "meat eaters."

"Grass eaters" are officers who accept payoffs that the routines of police work bring their way. "Meat eaters" are officers who actively use their power for personal gain. Although meat eaters are few, their actions make headlines when discovered. By contrast, because grass eaters are numerous, they make corruption seem acceptable and promote a code of secrecy that brands any officer who exposes corruption as a traitor. Grass eaters are the heart of the problem and are often harder to detect than meat eaters.

In the past, researchers have cited low salaries, politics, and poor hiring practices as factors contributing to corruption. However, these arguments fall short of explaining today's corruption. Although some claim that a few "rotten apples" should not taint an entire police force, corruption in some departments has been so rampant that the rotten-apple theory does not fully explain the situation. Some explanations focus on the structure and organization of police work. Much police work involves the enforcement of laws in situations where there is no complainant or it is unclear whether a law has been broken. Moreover, most police work is carried out at the officer's own discretion, without direct supervision. Thus, police officers may have many opportunities to gain benefits by using their discretion to protect people who engage in illegal conduct.

Examples of meat eaters in Cleveland, Ohio, came to light in January 1998 as a result of an FBI sting operation. Forty-one officers were charged with protecting cocaine trafficking. The Cleveland case was one of a series of police-corruption investigations that struck cities across the country around that time. From 1994 to 1997, 508 officers in 47 cities were convicted in federal corruption cases (*New York Times*, January 1, 1998, p. A16).

If police administrators judge success merely by the maintenance of order on the streets and a steady flow of arrests and traffic citations, they may not have any idea what their officers actually do while on patrol. Officers therefore may learn that they

Officers are often placed in situations where they can be tempted to enrich themselves by stealing money, property or drugs, or by accepting favors, gifts, and bribes. If you were a police chief, how would you reduce the risks of police corruption?

© AP Photo/Billings Gazette, James Woodcock

can engage in improper conduct without worrying about investigations by supervisors as long as there is order on the streets and they keep their activities out of the public spotlight.

Enforcement of vice and drug laws creates major problems for police agencies. In many cities, the profits for drug offenders are so high that they can easily afford to make large payments to unethical officers to protect themselves against prosecution. That police operations against victimless crimes are proactive makes the problem worse. Unless drugs are being sold openly, upsetting the residents of a neighborhood, no victims will complain if officers ignore or even profit from the activities of drug dealers.

Over time, illegal activity may become accepted as normal. Ellwyn Stoddard, who studied "blue-coat crime," has said that it can become part of an "identifiable informal 'code'" (Stoddard, 1968:205). He suggests that officers are socialized to the code early in their careers. Those who "snitch" on other officers may be ostracized. Recent research shows that officers risk retaliation from peers if they break the code (Cancino and Enriquez, 2004). When corruption comes to official attention, officers protect the code by distancing themselves from the known offender rather than stopping their own improper conduct (Stoddard, 1968).

Police corruption has three major effects on law enforcement: (1) suspects are left free to engage in further crime, (2) morale is damaged and supervision becomes lax, and (3) the image of the police suffers. The image of the police agency is crucial in light of the need for citizen cooperation. When people see the police as not much different from the "crooks," effective crime control falls even further out of reach. Indeed, recent research has identified connections between violent crime and compromised police legitimacy in disadvantaged communities (Kane, 2005).

What is startling is that many people do not equate police corruption with other forms of crime. Some believe that police corruption is tolerable as long as the streets remain safe. This attitude ignores the fact that corrupt officers serve only themselves, not the public.

CHECKPOINT

ANSWERS

⑭ What kinds of practices could be viewed as police abuse?

⑭ Profanity, abusive language, physical force, violence.

⑮ How did the Supreme Court rule in Tennessee v. Garner?

⑮ Deadly force may not be used in apprehending a fleeing felon unless it is necessary to prevent the escape and unless the officer has probable cause to believe that the suspect poses a significant threat of death or serious physical injury to the officer or to others.

⑯ What is the difference between grass eaters and meat eaters?

⑯ Grass eaters are officers who accept payoffs that police work brings their way. Meat eaters are officers who aggressively misuse their power for personal gain.

Civic Accountability

Relations between citizens and the police depend greatly on citizen confidence that officers will behave in accordance with the law and with departmental guidelines. Rapport with the community is enhanced when citizens feel sure that the police will protect their persons and property and the rights guaranteed by the Constitution.

Making the police responsive to citizen complaints without burdening them with a flood of such complaints is difficult. The main challenge in making the police more accountable is to use citizen input to force police to follow the law and departmental guidelines without placing too many limits on their ability to carry out their primary functions. At present, four less-than-perfect techniques are used in efforts to control the police: (1) internal affairs units, (2) civilian review boards, (3) standards and accreditation, and (4) civil liability lawsuits. We now look at each of these in turn.

■ Internal Affairs Units

Controlling the police is mainly an internal matter that administrators must treat as a top priority. The community must be confident that the department has procedures to ensure that officers will protect the rights of citizens. Yet, department complaint procedures often seem designed to discourage citizen input. People with complaints cannot always be certain that the police department will take any meaningful action.

Depending on the size of the department, a single officer or an entire section can serve as an **internal affairs unit** that receives and investigates complaints against officers. An officer charged with misconduct can face criminal prosecution or disciplinary action leading to resignation, dismissal, or suspension. Officers assigned to the internal affairs unit have duties similar to those of the inspector general's staff in the military. They must investigate complaints against other officers. Hollywood films and television series depict dramatic investigations of drug dealing and murder, but investigations of sexual harassment, alcohol or drug problems, misuse of force, and violations of departmental policies are more common.

The internal affairs unit must receive enough resources to carry out its mission. It must also have direct access to the chief. Internal investigators who assume that a citizen complaint is an attack on the police as a whole will shield officers against such complaints. When this happens, administrators do not get the information they need to correct a problem. The public, in turn, may come to believe that the department condones the practices they complain of and that filing a complaint is pointless. Moreover, even when the top administrator seeks to attack misconduct, he or she may find persuading police to testify against other officers difficult.

Internal affairs investigators find the work stressful, because their status prevents them from maintaining close relationships with other officers. A wall of silence rises around them. Such problems can be especially severe in smaller departments where all the officers know each other well and regularly socialize together.

■ Civilian Review Boards

If a police department cannot show that it effectively combats corruption among officers, the public will likely demand that the department be investigated by a *civilian review board*. Such a board allows complaints to be channeled through a committee of people who are not sworn police officers. The organization and powers of civilian review boards vary, but all oversee and review how police departments handle citizen complaints. The boards may also recommend remedial action. They do not have the power to investigate or discipline individual officers, however (S. Walker and Wright, 1995).

During the 1980s, as minorities gained more political power in large cities, a revival of civilian review boards took place. A survey of the 50 largest cities found that 36 had civilian review boards, as did 13 of the 50 next-largest cities (S. Walker and Wright, 1995).

The main argument made by the police against civilian review boards is that people outside law enforcement do not understand the problems of policing. The police contend that civilian oversight lowers morale and hinders performance and that officers will be less effective if they must worry about possible disciplinary actions. In reality, however, the boards have not been harsh.

Review of police actions occurs some time after the incident has taken place and usually comes down to the officer's word against that of the complainant. Given the

■ **internal affairs unit** A branch of a police department that receives and investigates complaints alleging violation of rules and policies on the part of officers.

low visibility of the incidents that lead to complaints, a great many complaints are not substantiated (Skolnick and Fyfe, 1993:229). The effectiveness of civilian review boards has not been tested, but their presence may improve police–citizen relations.

Standards and Accreditation

One way to increase police accountability is to require that police actions meet nationally recognized standards. The movement to accredit departments that meet these standards has gained momentum during the past decade. It has the support of the Commission on Accreditation for Law Enforcement Agencies (CALEA), a private nonprofit corporation formed by four professional associations: the International Association of Chiefs of Police (IACP), the National Organization of Black Law Enforcement Executives (NOBLE), the National Sheriffs Association (NSA), and the Police Executive Research Forum (PERF).

First published in 1983, the CALEA *Standards* have been periodically updated. The fourth edition, published in 1999, has 439 specific standards. Each standard is a statement, with a brief explanation, that provides clear requirements. For example, under "Limits of Authority," Standard 1.2.2 requires that "a written directive [govern] the use of discretion by sworn officers." The explanation states, "In many agencies, the exercise of discretion is defined by a combination of written enforcement policies, training and supervision. The written directive should define the limits of individual discretion and provide guidelines for exercising discretion within those limits" (CALEA, 1989:1). Because police departments have said almost nothing about their use of discretion, this statement represents a major shift. However, the standard still is not specific enough. For example, it does not cover stop-and-frisk actions, the handling of drunks, and the use of informants.

Police accreditation is voluntary. Departments contact CALEA, which helps them in their efforts to meet the standards. This process involves self-evaluation by departmental executives, the development of policies that meet the standards, and the training of officers. The CALEA representative acts like a military inspector general, visiting the department, examining its policies, and seeing if the standards are met in its daily operations. Departments that meet the standards receive certification. Administrators can use the standards as a management tool, training officers to know the standards and be accountable for their actions. By 1998, over 460 agencies had been accredited (S. Walker, 1999:285).

Obviously, the standards do not guarantee that police officers in an accredited department will not engage in misconduct. However, they serve as a major step toward providing clear guidelines to officers about proper behavior. Accreditation can also show the public a department's commitment to making sure officers carry out their duties in an ethical, professional manner.

Civil Liability Lawsuits

Civil lawsuits against departments for police misconduct can increase police accountability. In 1961, the U.S. Supreme Court ruled that Section 1983 of the Civil Rights Act of 1871 allows citizens to sue public officials for violations of their civil rights. The high court extended this opportunity in 1978 when it ruled that individual officials and local agencies may be sued when a person's civil rights are violated by an agency's "customs and usages." If an individual can show that harm was caused by employees whose wrongful acts were the result of these "customs, practices, and policies, including poor training and supervision," then he or she can sue a local agency (*Monell v. Department of Social Services of the City of New York*, 1978).

Lawsuits charging police officers with brutality, improper use of weapons, dangerous driving, and false arrest are brought in both state and federal courts. Often, these lawsuits provide the basis for punishing officers who violate constitutional rights. Rights that are often subject to lawsuits are the Fourth Amendment right against unreasonable seizures, when police use excessive force or make improper arrests, and the Fourth Amendment right against unreasonable searches, when police wrongly search a house without a warrant.

In several states, people have received damage awards in the millions of dollars, and police departments have settled some suits out of court. For example, the Chicago City Council paid nearly $20 million in 2008 to settle a lawsuit by four former death row inmates who were wrongly convicted of murder after Chicago police used electric shocks and beatings to torture them into falsely confessing (CBS2-TV, 2008). Omaha, Nebraska, paid $8 million between 1993 and 2005 to innocent victims of police chases (N. Hicks, 2005).

Civil liability rulings by the courts tend to be simple and severe: Officials and municipalities are ordered to pay a sum of money, and the courts can enforce that judgment. The threat of significant financial awards often pressures officers, their employing agencies, and their insurance companies to negotiate financial settlements rather than take the risk of being ordered to pay larger sums after a trial. The potential for costly judgments gives police departments a strong incentive to improve the training and supervision of officers (Vaughn, 2001). One study asked a sample of police executives to rank the policy issues most likely to be affected by civil liability decisions. The top-ranked issues were use of force, pursuit driving, and improper arrests (C. E. Smith and Hurst, 1996). Most departments have liability insurance, and many officers have their own insurance policies.

CHECKPOINT

ANSWERS

17 What are the four methods used to increase the civic accountability of the police?

17 Internal affairs units, civilian review boards, standards and accreditation, civil liability suits.

18 What is an internal affairs unit?

18 A unit, within a police department, designated to receive and investigate complaints alleging violation of rules and policies on the part of officers.

19 Why are civilian review boards relatively uncommon?

19 Opposition by the police.

A QUESTION OF ETHICS: WRITING ASSIGNMENT

The desk sergeant approached Detectives Alicia Baird and Eric Houston at 10:00 P.M. "An attorney just called and said that he is representing Linda Franklin. He said that he would come in if you were going to question her, but I told him that you had just finished booking her. Since it's so late, I knew you'd be leaving for home, so I told him that no questioning would start until tomorrow."

"OK," said Detective Baird as the desk sergeant turned and walked down the hall. She turned to Detective Houston. "That's too bad, because I really thought she might start talking about the murder if we asked her some questions right away."

"I agree," said Houston. "So I don't think we can afford to let this opportunity pass by. C'mon."

With a puzzled look on her face, Baird followed him into the interrogation room, where Franklin sat at a table looking tired and frightened.

As Baird stood by the door, Houston read the suspect her *Miranda* rights again—she had already been informed of her rights during the booking process. "Do you understand these rights?" Houston asked.

Franklin nodded her head. "I know. I know." She hesitated before saying, "I guess I don't have any attorney, do I?"

"I don't see one here, do you?" replied Houston. "But you can talk to us if you want to. Just sign this form indicating that you were informed of your rights and that you understand them."

Franklin signed the form and Houston began to ask her questions about the events of the evening that led to the discovery of a murder victim at her apartment.

Baird could not stop thinking about the conversation with the desk sergeant and the fact that the attorney had been told that no questioning would begin until the next day. If the questioning continued, that would mean that the police had deceived the defense attorney and, in effect, been untruthful in stating when questioning would take place.

WRITING ASSIGNMENT

What should Detective Baird do? Should she stop Houston from questioning Franklin? Should she call the attorney to tell him that the questioning of his client has begun? Is she obligated to take any action at all? Write a memo to Detective Baird explaining the legal and ethical implications of the situation. Also, give her advice about what she might do. After you write the memo, go to the Justia website and search for the case *Moran v. Burbine* (1986). The website is listed on the Cole/Smith Criminal Justice in America Companion Website: http://www.cengage.com/criminaljustice/cole. How does your advice compare with the decision of the U.S. Supreme Court?

Summary

Know the extent of police officers' authority to stop people and to conduct searches of people, their vehicles, and other property

▶ The Supreme Court has defined rules for the circumstances and justifications for stops, searches, and arrests in light of the Fourth Amendment's prohibition on unreasonable searches and seizures.

▶ The plain view doctrine permits officers to visually examine and use as evidence, without a warrant, any contraband or criminal evidence that is in open sight when the officers are in a place where they are legally permitted to be.

▶ Most stops must be supported by reasonable suspicion; an arrest or a search warrant must be supported by enough information to constitute probable cause.

Recognize how police officers seek warrants in order to conduct searches and make arrests

▶ In order to obtain a warrant, police officers present an affidavit (sworn statement) verifying the information that they present to the judge that they believe constitutes probable cause to search or make an arrest.

Identify situations in which police officers can examine property and conduct searches without obtaining a warrant

▶ Searches are considered "reasonable" and may be conducted without warrants in specific circumstances that present special needs beyond the normal purposes of law enforcement. For example, borders and airports often require searches without warrants.

▶ Limited searches may be conducted without warrants when officers have reasonable suspicions to justify a stop and frisk for weapons on the streets; when officers make a lawful arrest; under exigent circumstances; when people voluntarily consent to searches of their persons or property; and in certain situations involving automobiles.

Analyze the purpose of the privilege against compelled self-incrimination

▶ The Fifth Amendment privilege against compelled self-incrimination helps protect citizens against violence and coercion by police while helping maintain the legitimacy and integrity of the legal system.

▶ The Supreme Court's decision in *Miranda v. Arizona* required officers to inform suspects of specific rights before custodial questioning, although officers have adapted their practices to accommodate this rule and several exceptions have been created.

Understand the exclusionary rule and the situations in which it applies

▶ By barring the use of illegally obtained evidence in court, the exclusionary rule is designed to deter police from violating citizens' rights during criminal investigations.

▶ The Supreme Court has created several exceptions to the exclusionary rule, including the inevitable discovery rule and the "good faith" exception in defective warrant situations.

Analyze the problems of police abuse and corruption

▶ Police misbehavior, such as violating citizens' rights, misusing force, and engaging in corrupt behavior, erode community support.

▶ Police use of deadly force occurs infrequently and can no longer be applied to unarmed fleeing felons.

▶ Police corruption includes "meat eaters," who actively seek corrupt activities, and "grass eaters," who accept favors and payoffs that come their way.

Recognize the mechanisms used to hold police accountable when they violate laws and policies

▶ Police accountability is improved through internal affairs units, civilian review boards, standards and accreditation, and civil liability lawsuits.

■ Questions for Review

1. What are the requirements for police officers with respect to stops, searches, arrests, and warrants?

2. Under what circumstances are warrantless searches permissible?

3. How have police officers adapted to the requirements of *Miranda v. Arizona*?

4. What are the main exceptions to the exclusionary rule?

5. What are the problems of police misbehavior, and what mechanisms increase police accountability?

■ Key Terms and Cases

affidavit (p. 171)
exclusionary rule (p. 183)
exigent circumstances (p. 176)
"good faith" exception (p. 184)
inevitable discovery rule (p. 185)
internal affairs unit (p. 192)
plain view doctrine (p. 169)
probable cause (p. 170)

"public safety" exception (p. 180)
reasonable expectation of privacy (p. 169)
reasonable suspicion (p. 170)
search (p. 169)
seizures (p. 169)
stop (p. 170)
stop-and-frisk search (p. 174)

totality of circumstances (p. 171)
Chimel v. California (1969) (p. 175)
Miranda v. Arizona (1966) (p. 180)
Nix v. Williams (1984) (p. 185)
Tennessee v. Garner (1985) (p. 189)
Terry v. Ohio (1968) (p. 173)
United States v. Drayton (2002) (p. 176)

Stepping into a New World: Arrested, Booked, Charged, Jailed, and Investigated

Written by Chuck Terry

BY THE MID-1970s I had spent time in jail and was on probation for burglary. My probation officer, thinking I could never stay "clean" (not use heroin), thought I belonged in San Quentin and told me he'd do everything within his power to send me there. He tested my urine for drugs and checked my arms for needle marks with a magnifying glass two or three times a week until I couldn't take it anymore. Eventually I quit reporting and went "on the run." The fact that I had skipped probation and there was now an arrest warrant with my name on it left me feeling like a desperado. Now it was time to get really hooked.

I began selling dope to support my habit. I was living in a Manhattan Beach motel and selling about a thousand dollars' worth of heroin a week. For me this was "doing good," because I wasn't stealing. Not only that, my customers seemed to appreciate my services.

Arrest

One Thursday afternoon, while calling my connection from a phone booth in front of my motel, I noticed several men in suits knocking on the door of my room. I instantly knew they were cops and that I needed to get away from there fast. Trying to be discreet, I opened the booth door and quietly started walking away. Before I took two steps a woman came running out of the nearby motel office, pointing at me and yelling, "There he is! There he is!" Because of the many people she had observed coming and going from my room, she suspected me of dealing and called the Manhattan Beach City Police Department.

I started running but didn't get far. Besides the cops upstairs, other officers were surrounding the motel. Though I hadn't noticed, two of them were within ten feet of where I stood. As soon as I realized that I had been spotted by the police, I bolted from that phone booth as if my life depended on it. Ignoring their commands to "halt," I ran as fast as I could. Before I had gone a hundred yards, they tackled me to the ground and cuffed me. At that moment I felt a sense of fear, helplessness, and anger that is difficult to describe. I was under arrest—again. While one cop held me from behind, the other went into my pockets and pulled out eleven balloons filled with heroin. The plainclothes cops found more heroin, other drugs, and several hundred dollars in my room. Next thing I knew somebody was reading me my *Miranda* rights ("You have the right to remain silent. . . .") and I found myself sitting in the back seat of a cop car, alone, angry, scared, and cuffed, the crackling sounds and voices from the police radio relentlessly assaulting my ears. Welcome to my nightmare—live from Los Angeles County.

During the ride to the Manhattan Beach City Jail, the police lockup, I felt helpless and desperate, like a captured animal. The cops in the front seat seemed excited as they talked about what had just gone down—the chase, the bust. As I listened to their conversation I got a sense of what I must mean to them—a good catch, evidence of a job well done, but little else. They talked about me as if I were invisible. That my whole world had just caved in was apparently insignificant to them. Underneath all these feelings was the unquestionable certainty that I would soon become sick from heroin withdrawal.

Booking

We quickly arrived at the local police lockup—a small facility that functioned as a way station, a place where recently captured "suspects" are held until they can bail out or be transported to the county jail. Once inside I was promptly booked, a process that included being notified of my charges (given paperwork clarifying the specific crimes I was being accused of—possession of heroin with the intent to sell was the most serious) and the amount of my bail (which was high), photographed, fingerprinted, and strip-searched. Because I could not make bail, I was held for a court appearance and confined to a small cell block (the tank), where I was given a blanket, toilet paper, and food twice a day. Because Friday was a holiday I would not be sent to the county jail until Monday. It was here that I began kicking a heroin habit that was so bad I did not sleep for the following three weeks.

For the next four days this cell block was my home. I had never been so physically addicted or experienced such severe withdrawal. I was weak, couldn't eat, ached all over, and had the sweats, chills, and diarrhea.

While I was in the lockup, a few other men came and went. Most had been arrested for crimes that were not as serious as mine—not paying traffic tickets and the like. But they say misery loves company, and having other people around did help. In such facilities there is usually a high level of camaraderie among inmates. Having been stripped of everything we take for granted "on the streets," like personal autonomy, heterosexual relations, jobs, safety, and loved ones, we are left with just about all there is to associate with and find meaning from on the inside—each other.

On the third day, I was called out of the tank and placed inside a room with two men who looked like addicts. One was Chicano and the other white. They had tattoos, tracks on their arms (scars from needle marks), and talked like convicts. By this time I was extremely weak—neither my vision nor my perception was very sharp. To my surprise these guys turned out to be narcotics officers who worked for the local police department. I felt like I was in the Twilight Zone. They wanted me to tell on my connection. "We know you were scoring ounces. We figure if you tell us who your man is we can get to the guy who has the pounds." My head began to spin.

Even though it happens a lot, being a police informant is taboo among prisoners. Informants often spend years in protective custody (special sections of jails or prisons separated from the main population) or are killed for providing information that leads to further arrests. Nevertheless, police relentlessly seek new informants. Payment for cooperation varies. A good example of this is the witness protection programs that keep all sorts of people, including murderers, out of prison in exchange for the information they provide.

I was still consumed by my need for heroin as I sat facing these guys. Sick as I was, I would do just about anything for a shot. Except tell. They said if I cooperated they would give me enough dope to "get well." I told them I could never give up my connection because he was my friend. How could I live with myself if I did that? They told me they'd set it up so nobody would have to know (apparently they didn't understand why I couldn't do it). Their plan was for me to have my connection meet me on a street corner and sell me some dope while they watched from a hidden location. Once the buy was made they would rush in, arrest us, take us both to jail, and then let me go. All my charges would be dropped and they would cut me loose. Luckily, their offer did not tempt me. I knew what time it was. I went to bed in the tank that night sick as a dog, but I still had my dignity. The following Monday I was transported in chains to the county jail.

Courts and Adjudication

LEARNING OBJECTIVES

▶ **Recognize the structure of the American court system**

▶ **Analyze the qualities that the public desires in a judge**

▶ **Identify the ways that American judges are selected**

▶ **Understand the roles of the prosecuting attorney**

▶ **Analyze the process by which criminal charges are filed and what role the prosecutor's discretion plays in that process**

▶ **Identify those with whom the prosecutor interacts in decision making**

▶ **Understand the day-to-day reality of criminal defense work in the United States**

▶ **Know how counsel is provided for defendants who cannot afford a private attorney**

▶ **Understand the courtroom workgroup and how it functions**

7

LAWYERS, SPECTATORS, AND THE DEFENDANT waited in tense silence as the jurors came back into the courtroom on December 21, 2007. Nearly everyone in the room expected a guilty verdict in one of the most gruesome murder cases covered by Michigan news reporters in recent decades. Stephen Grant, a 37-year-old father of two small children, was charged with first-degree murder for strangling his wife, Tara, and then cutting her body into many pieces, some of which were scattered in a park. Other body parts were found in the garage of their family home. The Macomb County prosecutor, Eric Smith, called Grant "evil personified." He believed that he could prove that Grant had a motive for killing his wife because of Grant's sexual relationship with his children's 20-year-old nanny from Germany (L. Williams, 2008; Associated Press, 2007).

The case generated national news media attention when Grant reported his wife missing and then later fled to northern Michigan. He was apprehended after a major manhunt in which dozens of law enforcement officers, using dogs and helicopters, tracked him through a snowy state park. When he was caught, he was suffering from hypothermia and frostbite after losing his shoes and jacket in waist-deep snow as he tried to hide from the approaching police officers. After he was caught, the police recorded his detailed confession to the killing (Hackney, Arboscello, and Swickard, 2007).

Prior to his trial, Grant entered a guilty plea to the charge of a mutilating a corpse (Associated Press, 2007). After a judge ruled that Grant's hospital confession could be used at trial, he and his attorney concluded that there was no way that he could avoid conviction on that charge. By pleading guilty, he may have hoped to get a less-than-maximum sentence on that charge by admitting responsibility rather than forcing the court system to use its time and money on a trial.

In contrast, despite the detailed confession, Grant pleaded not guilty to the first-degree murder charge. First-degree murder requires proof of premeditation—planning and intention in advance. Grant's defense attorneys, Stephen Rabaut and Gail Pamukov, argued during the trial that Grant had killed his wife in the heat of an argument. In Michigan, a conviction for first-degree murder automatically triggers a sentence of life without possibility of parole. A conviction for manslaughter or other lesser homicide, by contrast, could bring a much shorter sentence and the possibility of parole. Thus, the defense attorneys used the trial to challenge the prosecutor's claim that Grant had planned the murder and intended to kill his wife.

In the hushed courtroom, the jury's verdict was announced—guilty—but of second-degree murder, not premeditated first-degree murder. The victim's family was shocked and disappointed that such a gruesome murder could lead to a verdict and sentence from which the killer might eventually gain release on parole. Yet, they recognized that jury trials can be unpredictable, especially because criminal juries in most states must reach unanimous conclusions in order to render a guilty verdict. In the words of Alicia Standerfer, the sister of Tara Grant, "Am I happy with the verdict? No, but those 12 people [on the jury] did the best they could" (Associated Press, 2007).

Although defense attorneys Rabaut and Pamukov argued that he should receive a sentence of 15 to 25 years in prison, Macomb County Circuit Judge Diane Druzinski ultimately gave Grant a sentence of 50 to 80 years for the murder and an additional 6 to 10 years for mutilating the body (L. Williams, 2008). The length of the sentence virtually guaranteed that Grant would not live long enough to become eligible for parole. Thus, the final result satisfied the victim's family and other observers who believed that Grant should have been convicted of first-degree murder.

Because of the high stakes and uncertainty that surround criminal trials, most defendants plead guilty as they get closer to the prospect of being judged by a random group of citizens drawn from the community. Prosecutors also create incentives for guilty pleas by offering reductions in charges and sentences in exchange for admissions of guilt. Defense attorneys advise their clients by predicting the likelihood that a jury might issue a guilty verdict and weighing it against the advantages of taking a plea deal. Even if specific incentives are not offered, defendants may plead guilty in order to demonstrate to the judge that they are taking responsibility for their actions. They may hope that such honesty will lead the judge to soften the sentence. This may have been the motive for Grant's guilty plea for mutilating the corpse.

Stephen Grant's case demonstrates the power and importance of prosecutors and defense attorneys. Prosecutors determine who will be charged with a crime and which charges they will face. Prosecutors also organize and present evidence to prove guilt when defendants decline to plead guilty and instead seek a trial. Defense attorneys must advise their clients and make strategic decisions about whether to plead guilty and what tactics to use during trial. Because the stakes in the case were so high, Grant's defense attorneys fought the murder charge through the entire trial process. In most case defendants plead guilty to reduced charges rather than risk facing a guilty verdict at trial.

The American system places great power and responsibility in the hands of attorneys for each side in a criminal case. The prosecutor and defense attorney are the most influential figures in determining the outcomes of criminal cases. Their discretionary decisions and negotiations determine people's fates. As we shall see in this chapter, the justice system's ability to handle cases and produce fair results depends on the dedication, skill, and enthusiasm of these lawyers. In addition, the lawyers who become judges assume important duties for overseeing court proceedings that decide whether accused defendants will be found guilty and punished. Later in the chapter, when you read "Careers in Criminal Justice" about a career as a prosecutor, imagine the impact of your decisions on people's lives if you pursued such a career.

The Functions and Structure of American Courts
The Functions of Courts
The Structure of Courts

To Be a Judge
Who Becomes a Judge?
Functions of the Judge
How to Become a Judge

The Functions and Structure of American Courts

The United States has a dual court system. Separate federal and state court systems handle matters throughout the nation. Other countries have a single national court system, but American rules and traditions permit states to create their own court systems to handle most legal matters, including most crimes.

In the United States, both state and federal courts use the **adversarial process** to protect the rights of defendants and examine evidence to determine whether a defendant is guilty. In the adversarial process, a professional attorney, trained in the rules of evidence and the strategies of advocacy, represents each side—the prosecution (government) and defense (defendant). These attorneys challenge each other's evidence and arguments while trying to persuade the judge or jury about the defendant's guilt or lack thereof. Even when the attorneys negotiate a guilty plea without going to trial, they are supposed to adopt an adversarial stance that represents the interests of their side. Although they may hold friendly and cooperative discussions, the content of these discussions often reflects probing, bluffing, compromising, and disagreeing. In the adversarial context of American courts, judges often act like referees at a sporting event. They oversee the interactions and enforce the rules without imposing their will on the presentation of evidence by attorneys. The adversarial process came from England and can be found in the United States and other former British colonies. By contrast, other countries typically use an **inquisitorial process**, in which the judge takes an active role in questioning witnesses and asserts herself into the investigation of the case and the examination of evidence.

The federal courts oversee a limited range of criminal cases. For example, they deal with people accused of violating the criminal laws of the national government. Federal crimes include counterfeiting, kidnapping, smuggling, and drug trafficking, among others. But such cases account for only a small portion of the criminal cases that pass through U.S. courts each year. For every felony conviction in federal courts, more than 16 felony convictions take place in state courts, because most crimes are defined by state laws (BJS, 2008e: Tables 5.44.2004, 5.18.2003). This disparity may grow wider as federal law enforcement agencies increasingly emphasize antiterrorist activities rather than traditional crime-control investigations. The gap is even greater for misdemeanors, because state courts bear the primary responsibility for processing the lesser offenses, such as disorderly conduct, that arise on a daily basis.

State supreme courts monitor the decisions of lower courts within their own states by interpreting state constitutions and statutes. The U.S. Supreme Court oversees both court systems by interpreting the U.S. Constitution, which protects the rights of defendants in federal and state criminal cases.

A third court system operates in several states; this adds to the issues of complexity and coordination that the country's decentralized courts face. Native Americans have tribal courts, whose authority is endorsed by congressional statutes and Supreme Court decisions, with **jurisdiction** over their own people on tribal land. The existence of tribal courts permits Native American judges to apply their people's cultural values in resolving civil lawsuits and processing certain criminal offenses (Vicenti, 1995).

■ **adversarial process** Court process, employed in the United States and other former British colonies, in which lawyers for each side represent their clients' best interests in presenting evidence and formulating arguments as a means to discover the truth and protect the rights of defendants.

■ **inquisitorial process** Court process, employed in most countries of the world, in which the judge takes an active role in investigating the case and examining evidence by, for example, questioning witnesses.

■ **jurisdiction** The geographic territory or legal boundaries within which control may be exercised; the range of a court's authority.

■ The Functions of Courts

Courts serve many important functions for society. We often picture courts as the settings for criminal trials, much like those portrayed on television shows such as *Law and Order*. When courts focus on criminal matters, through bail hearings, preliminary hearings, plea bargaining, and trials, they are serving a *norm enforcement* function for society. A *norm* is a value, standard, or expectation concerning people's behavior. In other words, courts play a central role in enforcing society's rules and standards for behavior—a function that contributes to peace and stability in society. In addition, courts handle a wide variety of matters beyond criminal justice, matters that benefit society in ways that extend beyond merely determining the guilt of and punishments for criminal defendants.

Courts also handle *dispute processing* for society. When people disagree about contracts, money, property, and personal injuries in ways that they cannot resolve on their own, they file lawsuits in order to seek government intervention on their behalf. Presumably the availability of courts for dispute processing helps avoid the possibility that people will resort to violence when they become angry about disagreements with business partners, neighbors, and others. In criminal justice, the dispute-processing function plays a significant role when people file lawsuits against police officers or correctional officials for violating constitutional rights. As a result of such lawsuits, judges may order prisons to change their procedures or order police officers or their departments to pay thousands of dollars to compensate a citizen for an erroneous arrest, excessive use of force, or improper search of a home.

Courts also engage in *policy making,* especially the highest courts, such as state supreme courts and the U.S. Supreme Court. When judges interpret the U.S. Constitution or other forms of law and thereby define the rights of individuals, they are simultaneously telling police officers, correctional officers, and other officials what they can and cannot do. Such judicial decisions determine how searches will be conducted, how suspects will be questioned, and how prisons will be managed. This function makes courts in the United States especially important and powerful, because judges in other countries usually do not have the authority to tell officials throughout all levels of government how to carry out their jobs.

■ The Structure of Courts

Both the federal and state court systems have trial and appellate courts. There are three levels of courts: trial courts of limited jurisdiction, trial courts of general jurisdiction, and appellate courts.

Cases begin in a trial court, which handles determinations of guilt and sentencing. **Trial courts of limited jurisdiction** handle only misdemeanors, lawsuits for small amounts of money, and other specific kinds of cases. The full range of felony cases and all other civil lawsuits are heard in **trial courts of general jurisdiction**. Trial courts are the arenas in which evidence is presented, witnesses give testimony and are questioned by attorneys, and lawyers make arguments about the guilt (or lack thereof) of criminal defendants. These are the courts in which jury trials take place and judges impose prison sentences. The federal system has no limited jurisdiction trial courts. All federal cases begin in the general jurisdiction trial courts, the U.S. district courts.

Cases move to intermediate **appellate courts** if defendants claim that errors by police or the trial court contributed to their convictions. Further appeals may be filed with a state supreme court or the U.S. Supreme Court, depending on which court system the case is in and what kind of legal argument is being made. Unlike trial courts, appellate courts do not have juries, nor do lawyers present evidence. Instead, lawyers for each side make arguments about specific alleged errors of law or procedure that the trial judge failed to correct during the proceeding that determined the defendant's

■ **trial courts of limited jurisdiction**
Criminal courts with trial jurisdiction over misdemeanor cases and preliminary matters in felony cases. Sometimes these courts hold felony trials that may result in penalties below a specific limit.

■ **trial courts of general jurisdiction**
Criminal courts with jurisdiction over all offenses, including felonies. In some states, these courts also hear appeals.

■ **appellate courts** Courts that do not try criminal cases but hear appeals of decisions of lower courts.

The Supreme Court of the United
States has the final word on questions
concerning interpretations of the U.S.
Constitution. Should a small group of
appointed judges possess such power in
a democracy?

guilt. Thus, the written and oral arguments presented in an entire appellate case may
focus on a single question, such as "Should the trial judge have excluded the defendant's
confession because the police did not adequately inform her about *Miranda* rights?"
Appellate judges often decide cases by issuing elaborate written opinions to explain
why they answered the question at issue in a certain way.

All states have courts of last resort (usually called state supreme courts), and all
but a few have an intermediate-level appellate court (usually called courts of appeals). In the federal system, the U.S. Supreme Court is the court of last resort, and
the U.S. circuit courts of appeals are the intermediate appellate courts. The U.S. Supreme Court, with its nine justices, controls its own caseload by choosing 75 to 85
cases to hear from among the 7,000 cases submitted annually. It takes the votes of
four justices for the Supreme Court to decide to grant a request to hear a case. After
the justices consider the written and oral arguments in the cases selected for hearing, a majority vote will determine the outcome and the rule of law to be expressed
in the Court's majority opinion. Many decisions are unanimous, but other cases are
decided by a narrow 5-to-4 vote when the justices are deeply divided. For example,
when the Court decided in 2008 that the Second Amendment's "right to bear arms"
gives law-abiding people who live in federal jurisdictions, such as Washington, D.C.,
the constitutional right to own and keep handguns in their homes, the justices split
5-to-4 in reaching the decision (*District of Columbia v. Heller*, 2008; Reynolds and
Denning, 2008). Close decisions can be overturned in later years if the new justices
appointed to replace retiring justices bring viewpoints to the Court that differ from
those of their predecessors.

Although the basic, three-tiered structure is found throughout the United
States, the number of courts, their names, and their specific functions vary
widely. For example, in state systems, 13,000 trial courts of limited jurisdiction typically handle traffic cases, small claims, misdemeanors, and other less
serious matters. These courts handle 90 percent of all criminal matters. Some
limited jurisdiction courts bear responsibility for a specific category of cases,

sometimes including serious offenses. Drug courts, for example, attempt to combine rehabilitation, close supervision, and the threat of punishment in order to push drug offenders to shake free from substance abuse problems (Kassebaum and Okamoto, 2001; Rockwell, 2008). Mental health courts, which are expanding across the country, seek to handle cases of nonviolent offenders with mental disorders and to develop appropriate treatment, supervision, and assistance instead of incarceration (Kimber, 2008; Watson et al., 2001). Some cities have developed domestic violence courts to give focused attention to recurring problems of violence within families and among those with intimate relationships (Gover, MacDonald, and Alpert, 2003).

The federal system begins with the U.S. district courts, its trial courts of general jurisdiction. In the states, these courts have a variety of names (circuit, district, superior, and others) and are reserved for felony cases or substantial lawsuits. These are the courts in which trials take place, judges rule on evidence, and juries issue verdicts. Figure 7.1 shows the basic structure of the dual court system.

American trial courts are highly decentralized. Local political influences and community values affect the courts: Local officials determine their budgets, residents make up the staff, and operations are managed so as to fit community needs. Only a few small states have a court system organized on a statewide basis, with a central administration and state funding. In most of the country, the criminal courts operate under the state penal code but are staffed, managed, and financed by county or city governments. The federal courts, by contrast, have central administration and funding, although judges in each district help shape their own courts' practices and procedures.

Lower courts, especially at the state level, do not always display the dignity and formal procedures of general jurisdiction trial courts and appellate courts. Instead, they may function informally. Decisions and processes in one judge's courtroom may differ from those in another courtroom. In most urban areas, local courts process seemingly endless numbers of people through the crime control model (see Chapter 1), and each defendant's "day in court" usually lasts only a few minutes. People expect their local courts to adhere to the standards that reflect American values of justice. Many are critical when the courts do not meet these ideals.

FIGURE 7.1

The dual court system of the United States and routes of appeal
Whether a case enters through the federal or state court system depends on which law has been broken. The right of appeal to a higher court exists in either system.

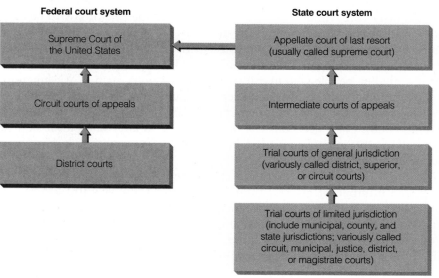

CHECKPOINT

1 What is the dual court system?

1 Separate federal and state court systems handling cases in the United States.

2 What different categories of courts exist within each court system?

2 The federal system is made up of the Supreme Court of the United States, circuit courts of appeals, and district courts. State court systems are made up of an appellate court of last resort, intermediate appellate courts (in most states), trial courts of general jurisdiction, and trial courts of limited jurisdiction.

3 What does it mean for courts to be decentralized?

3 Operated, controlled, and funded by local communities, not a statewide administration. Most state and county courts are decentralized.

To Be a Judge

People tend to see judges as the most powerful actors in the criminal justice process. Their rulings and sentencing decisions influence the actions of police, defense attorneys, and prosecutors. For example, if judges treat certain crimes lightly, police and prosecutors may be less inclined to arrest and prosecute people who commit those offenses. Although judges are thought of primarily in connection with trials, some of their work—signing warrants, setting bail, arraigning defendants, accepting guilty pleas, scheduling cases—takes place outside the formal trial process.

More than any other person in the system, the judge is expected to embody justice, ensuring that the right to due process is upheld and that the defendant receives fair treatment. The prosecutor and the defense attorney each represent a "side" in a criminal case. By contrast, the judge's black robe and gavel symbolize impartiality. Both within and outside the courthouse, the judge is supposed to act according to a well-defined role. Judges are expected to make careful, consistent decisions that uphold the ideal of equal justice for all citizens (McKee, 2007).

Who Becomes a Judge?

In U.S. society, the position of judge, even at the lowest level of the judicial hierarchy, brings high status. Public service, political power, and prestige in the community may matter more than a high-paying job to those who aspire to the judiciary. Many judges take a significant cut in pay to assume a position on the bench. Unlike private practice attorneys, who often work over 50 hours per week preparing cases and counseling clients, judges can typically control their own working hours and schedules better. Although judges carry heavy caseloads, they frequently decide for themselves when to go home at the end of the workday. The ability to control one's own work schedule is therefore an additional attraction for lawyers interested in becoming judges.

Historically, the vast majority of judges have been white men with strong political connections. Women and members of minority groups had few opportunities to enter

Judges bear important responsibilities for ensuring that both prosecutors and defense attorneys follow proper law and procedure. They must ensure that the rights of defendants are protected during court proceedings. Here, Judge Roosevelt Robinson instructs the jury during a trial in Portland, Oregon. What qualifications do you think someone should have in order to become a judge?

AP Images/Greg Wahl-Stephens

the legal profession prior to the 1960s and thus were seldom considered for judge-ships. By the late twentieth century, political factors in many cities dictated that judges be drawn from specific racial, religious, and ethnic groups. One study found, however, that less than 4 percent of state appellate judges were African American men and less than 2 percent were Hispanic men. Women from each of these minority groups comprised less than 1 percent of state appellate judges (Hurwitz and Lanier, 2001). Comparing the racial and ethnic makeup of the judiciary with that of the defendants in urban courts raises important questions (Nava, 2008). If middle-aged white men hold nearly all the power to make judgments about people from other segments of so-ciety, will people believe that decisions about guilt and punishment are being made in an unfair manner? Will people think that punishment is being imposed on behalf of a privileged segment of society rather than on behalf of the entire, diverse U.S. society?

Further, within these questions lurk concerns regarding the essential American val-ues of equality, fairness, and equal opportunity. Indeed, the equal protection clause of the Fourteenth Amendment of the Constitution demonstrates a formal commitment to use law to combat discrimination. However, the political connections necessary to gain judgeships continue to disadvantage women and members of racial minor-ity groups in many communities. Because judges symbolize the law as well as make important decisions about law, the lack of diversity in the judiciary provides a visible contrast with American values related to equal opportunity.

◼ Functions of the Judge

Although people usually think that a judge's job is to preside at trials, in reality the work of most judges extends to all aspects of the judicial process. Defendants see a judge whenever decisions about their future are being made: when bail is set, pre-trial motions are made, guilty pleas are accepted, a trial is conducted, a sentence is pronounced, and appeals are filed (see Figure 7.2). However, judges' duties are not

FIGURE 7.2
Actions of a trial court judge in processing a felony case
Throughout the process, the judge ensures that legal standards are upheld; he or she maintains courtroom decorum, protects the rights of the accused, meets the requirement of a speedy trial, and ensures that case records are maintained properly.

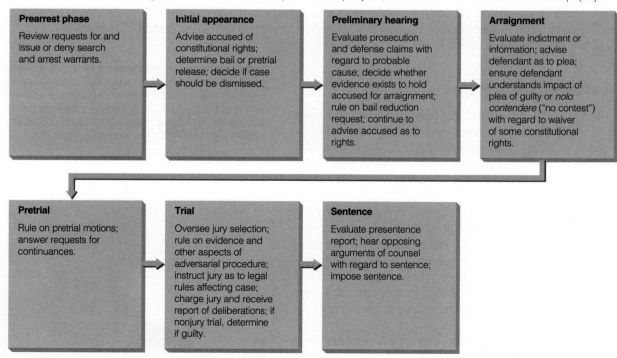

limited to making such decisions about criminal defendants within the courtroom; judges also perform administrative tasks outside of it. Judges have three major roles: adjudicator, negotiator, and administrator.

Adjudicator Judges must assume a neutral stance in overseeing the contest between the prosecution and the defense. They must apply the law in ways that uphold the rights of the accused in decisions about detention, plea, trial, and sentence. Judges receive a certain amount of discretion in performing these tasks—for example, in setting bail—but they must do so according to the law. They must avoid any conduct that could appear biased (Goldschmidt and Shaman, 1996).

Negotiator Many decisions that determine the fates of defendants take place outside of public view, in the judge's private chambers. These decisions come about through negotiations between prosecutors and defense attorneys about plea bargains, sentencing, and bail conditions. Judges spend much of their time in their chambers talking with prosecutors and defense attorneys. They often encourage the parties to work out a guilty plea or agree to proceed in a certain way. The judge may act as a referee, keeping both sides on track in accordance with the law. Sometimes the judge takes a more active part in the negotiations, suggesting terms for an agreement or even pressuring one side to accept an agreement.

Administrator A seldom-recognized function of most judges is managing the courthouse. In urban areas, a professional court administrator may direct the people who keep records, schedule cases, and do the many other jobs that keep a system functioning. But even in cities, judges are in charge of their own courtroom and staff. In rural areas, which do not usually employ professional court administrators, the judges' administrative tasks may expand to include managing labor relations, budgeting, and maintenance of the courthouse building. As administrator, the judge must deal with political actors such as county commissioners, legislators, and members of the state executive bureaucracy. Chief judges in large courts may also use their administrative powers to push other judges to cooperate in advancing the court's goals of processing cases in a timely manner (Jacob, 1973). For judges whose training as lawyers focused on learning law and courtroom advocacy skills, managing a complex organization with a sizable budget and many employees can pose a major challenge (C. E. Smith and Feldman, 2001; Wasby, 2003).

Many observers argue that a fourth role of judges is emerging in some court systems. They see judges acting as "problem solvers" in newly developed courts that seek to address the problems of people arrested for drugs, domestic violence, and other issues for which innovative courts steer people to treatment programs rather than jail. Because judges typically have no training in psychology or social work, critics worry that the development of the problem-solver role will lead judges to make decisions about matters in which they lack expertise.

■ How to Become a Judge

The quality of justice depends to a great extent on the quality of those who make decisions about guilt and punishment. Because judges have the power to deprive a citizen of his or her liberty through a prison sentence, judges should be thoughtful, fair, and impartial. When a judge is rude or hasty or allows the courtroom to become noisy and crowded, the public may lose confidence in the fairness and effectiveness of the criminal justice process (see the Close Up box).

Six methods are used to select state trial court judges: gubernatorial appointment, legislative selection, merit selection, **nonpartisan election, partisan election**, and a

■ **nonpartisan election** An election in which candidates' party affiliations are not listed on the ballot.

■ **partisan election** An election in which candidates openly endorsed by political parties are presented to voters for selection.

CLOSE UP

Improper Judicial Behavior

DURING AN ARRAIGNMENT in New York for a defendant charged with assaulting his wife, the judge reportedly said, "What's wrong with that? You've got to keep them in line once in a while." When authorities acted to remove the judge from office, the judge's lawyer said that the judge makes light-hearted comments from the bench but does not misuse his position.

In another New York case, a judge was "censured" (publicly criticized) by the state's judicial conduct commission for walking toward a defendant in the courtroom and saying, "You want a piece of me?" In another case, the same judge said to a police officer, in reference to a disrespectful defendant, "If you are so upset about it, why don't you just thump the shit out of him outside the courthouse because I am not going to do anything about it." The two members of the commission who wanted to remove the judge from office were outvoted by the six other members who thought removal would be too harsh a punishment.

In California, a judge reportedly indicated to a good-looking defendant that other inmates at the prison would find him attractive. The judge also allegedly called a prosecutor in a drunken-driving case a "hypocrite" who was in all probability guilty of the same offense as the defendant. When a complaint was filed with the state's Commission on Judicial Performance, the judge's attorney claimed that the comments were taken out of context.

In another New York case, a judge charged off the bench, grabbing and screaming at a lawyer during a courtroom proceeding.

 RESEARCHING THE INTERNET

To read about ethics rules for judges, see the Code of Judicial Conduct for judges in Texas at the corresponding website listed on the Cole/Smith Criminal Justice in America Companion Website: http://www.cengage.com/criminaljustice/cole.

FOR CRITICAL ANALYSIS

Do the statements reportedly made by these judges harm the image of the courts? If so, how? If these statements are improper, what should happen to judges who say such things? If the judges apologize, should they receive another opportunity to behave properly? Is there any way to make sure that judges act at all times in accordance with the proper image of their office?

Sources: Drawn from "Court Upholds Removal of Rockland Judge," *New York Times,* March 31, 1999 (Metro News); Richard Marosi, "Hard-line Judge Is Being Judged Herself," *Los Angeles Times,* May 7, 1999, p. B1; Robert H. Tembeckjian, "How Judges Hide from Justice," *New York Times,* May 22, 2005, http://www.nytimes.com; Stephanie Francis Ward, "Confrontation Leads to Censure," *ABA Journal E-Report,* October 13, 2006, http://www.abanet.org/journal/ereport/oc12smack.html.

---

mixture of methods. Table 7.1 shows the method used in each of the states. All the methods bring up persistent concerns about the desired qualities of judges.

Selection by public voting occurs in more than half the states and has long been part of this nation's tradition. This method of judicial selection embodies the underlying American value of democracy because it permits the citizens to control the choice of individuals who will receive the power to make decisions in civil and criminal cases. The fulfillment of this American value also helps ensure that judges will remain connected to the community and demonstrate sensitivity to the community's priorities and concerns. The American value of democracy may, however, have detrimental consequences if it pressures judges to follow a community's prejudices rather than make independent decisions using their best judgment in each case (Saphire and Moke, 2008).

When lawyers are first elected to serve as judges, they obviously have no prior experience in deciding cases and supervising courthouse operations. As a result, judges must learn on the job. This clashes with the belief that judges are trained to "find the law" and apply neutral judgments (M. G. Hall, 1995). In Europe, by contrast, prospective judges are given special training in law school to become professional judges. These trained judges must serve as assistant judges and lower-court judges before they can become judges in general trial and appellate courts (Provine, 1996).

Election campaigns for lower-court judgeships tend to be low-key contests marked by little controversy. Usually, only a small portion of the voters participate, judgeships are not prominent on the ballot, and candidates do not discuss controversial issues because of ethical considerations. Most candidates run on the same two claims that reveal relatively little to the voters about how they will make specific decisions as judges: "I have the best prior experience" and "I'll be tough on crime."

TABLE 7.1   Methods Used by States to Select Judges

States use different methods to select judges. Note that many judges are initially appointed to fill a vacancy, giving them an advantage if they must run for election at a later date.

Partisan Election	Nonpartisan Election	Gubernatorial Appointment	Legislative Selection	Merit Selection
Alabama	Arizona (some trial courts)	California (appellate)	South Carolina	Alaska
Illinois	Arkansas	Maine	Virginia	Arizona (appellate)
Indiana (trial)	California (trial)	Massachusetts (court of last resort)		Colorado
Louisiana	Florida (trial)	New Hampshire		Connecticut
New Mexico	Georgia	New Jersey		Delaware
New York (trial)	Idaho			Florida (appellate)
Pennsylvania (initial)	Kentucky			Hawaii
Tennessee (trial)	Michigan			Indiana (appellate)
Texas	Minnesota			Iowa
West Virginia	Mississippi			Kansas
	Montana			Maryland
	Nevada			Massachusetts (trial, intermediate appellate)
	North Carolina			Missouri
	North Dakota			Nebraska
	Ohio			New York (appellate)
	Oklahoma (trial)			Oklahoma (appellate)
	Oregon			Rhode Island
	Pennsylvania (retention)			South Dakota (appellate)
	South Dakota (trial)			Tennessee (appellate)
	Washington			Utah
	Wisconsin			Vermont
				Wyoming

Source: American Judicature Society, 2008, "Methods of Judicial Selection," http://www.judicialselection.us.

Recent research reveals, however, that even lower-level judicial races are becoming more competitive as candidates raise money and seek connections with interest groups (Abbe and Herrnson, 2002). Political parties typically want local judgeships to be elected posts, because they can use courthouse staff positions to reward party loyalists. When a party member wins a judgeship, courthouse jobs may become available for campaign workers, because the judge often chooses clerks, bailiffs, and secretaries.

In contrast, elections for seats on state supreme courts frequently receive statewide media attention. Because of the importance of state supreme courts as policy-making institutions, political parties and interest groups may devote substantial energy to organizing and funding the election campaigns of their preferred candidates. When organized interests contribute tens of thousands of dollars to judicial campaigns, questions sometimes arise about whether the successful candidates who received those contributions will favor the interests of their donors when they begin to decide court cases (Champagne and Cheek, 1996; T. V. Reid, 1996).

Some states have tried to reduce the influence of political parties in the selection of judges while still allowing voters to select judges. These states hold nonpartisan elections in which only the names of candidates, not their party affiliations, appear on the ballot. However, political parties are often strongly involved in such elections. In Ohio, for example, the Republican and Democratic political parties hold their own primary elections to choose the judicial candidates whose names will go on the nonpartisan ballot for the general election (Felice and Kilwein, 1992). In other states, party organizations raise and spend money on behalf of candidates in nonpartisan elections.

■ **merit selection** A reform plan by which judges are nominated by a commission and appointed by the governor for a given period. When the term expires, the voters approve or disapprove the judge for a succeeding term. If the judge is disapproved, the committee nominates a successor for the governor's appointment.

■ **prosecuting attorney** A legal representative of the state with sole responsibility for bringing criminal charges. In some states, this person is referred to as the district attorney, state's attorney, commonwealth attorney, or county attorney.

■ **United States attorneys** Officials responsible for the prosecution of crimes that violate the laws of the United States. Appointed by the president and assigned to a U.S. district court jurisdiction.

■ **state attorney general** Chief legal officer of a state, responsible for both civil and criminal matters.

Public opinion data show that Americans express concern about the influence of politics on judges, especially with respect to elected judges. If so many Americans are concerned about judges' involvement in political campaigns, why do so many states still rely on elections to select judges?

Merit selection, which combines appointment and election, was first used in Missouri in 1940 and has since spread to other states. When a judgeship becomes vacant, a nominating commission made up of citizens and attorneys evaluates potential appointees and sends the governor the names of three candidates, from which the replacement is chosen. After one year, a referendum is held to decide whether the judge will stay on the bench. The ballot asks, "Shall Judge X remain in office?" The judge who wins a majority vote serves out the term and can then be listed on the ballot at the next election (Cady and Phelps, 2008).

Public opinion polls indicate that Americans are divided in their views about judges' honesty and ethics, and these divisions are based, in part, on race and income. It is unclear whether judges' image would improve if merit selection were more widespread (see "What Americans Think" for specific data).

Merit selection is designed to remove politics from the selection of judges and supposedly allows the voters to unseat judges. However, interest groups sometimes mount publicity campaigns during retention elections in order to turn out judges with whom they disagree on a single issue or to open an important court seat so that a like-minded governor can appoint a sympathetic replacement. It may be difficult for judges to counteract a barrage of one-sided inflammatory television commercials focusing on a single issue such as capital punishment (T. V. Reid, 2000). If merit-selected judges feel intimidated by interest groups that might threaten their jobs at the next retention election, the independence of the judiciary will diminish.

CHECKPOINT

ANSWERS

❹ *What are judges' main functions?*

❹ Adjudicator, negotiator, administrator.

❺ *Why do political parties often prefer that judges be elected?*

❺ To ensure that courthouse positions are allocated to party workers.

❻ *What are the steps in the merit-selection process?*

❻ When a vacancy occurs, a nominating commission is appointed that sends the governor the names of approved candidates. The governor must fill the vacancy from the list. After a year's term, a referendum is held to ask the voters whether the judge should be retained.

The Prosecutorial System

Prosecuting attorneys make discretionary decisions about whether to pursue criminal charges, which charges to make, and what sentence to recommend. They represent the government in pursuing criminal charges against the accused. Except in a few states, no higher authority second-guesses or changes these decisions. Thus, prosecutors are more independent than most other public officials. As with other aspects of

The U.S. Attorney in Illinois, Patrick Fitzgerald, is known for his determination and even-handedness in prosecuting officials from both political parties, including Republican I. Lewis Libby, who was the chief advisor to former Vice President Dick Cheney, and Democrat Rod Blagojevich, the former governor of Illinois. What kinds of political pressures can confront prosecutors?

© Chuck Berman/MCT/Landov

American government, prosecution is mainly a task of state and local governments. Because most crimes violate state laws, county prosecutors bring charges against suspects in court.

Federal cases are prosecuted by **United States attorneys**. One U.S. attorney and a staff of assistant U.S. attorneys prosecute cases in each of the 94 U.S. district courts (Lochner, 2002). Each state has an elected **state attorney general**, who usually has the power to bring prosecutions in certain cases. A state attorney general may, for example, handle a statewide consumer fraud case if a chain of auto repair shops is suspected of overcharging customers. In Alaska, Delaware, and Rhode Island, the state attorney general also directs all local prosecutions. However, the vast majority of state criminal cases are handled in the 2,341 county-level offices of the prosecuting attorney—known in various states as the district attorney, state's attorney, commonwealth attorney, or county attorney—who pursues cases that violate state law. The number of prosecutors who work in these offices increased by more than 35 percent between 1990 and 2001 but then remained stable through 2005 (BJS, 2008e: Tables 1.85, 1.85.2005; DeFrances, 2002). Prosecutors have the power to make independent decisions about which cases to pursue and what charges to file. They can also drop charges and negotiate arrangements for guilty pleas.

In rural areas, the prosecutor's office may consist of merely the prosecuting attorney and a part-time assistant. By contrast, some urban jurisdictions such as Los Angeles have 500 assistant prosecutors and numerous legal assistants and investigators, and the office is organized according to various types of crimes. Many assistant prosecutors seek to use the trial experience gained in the prosecutor's office as a means of moving on to a more highly paid position in a private law firm. Read "Careers in Criminal Justice" to see the responsibilities and career path of an elected prosecutor in a major county.

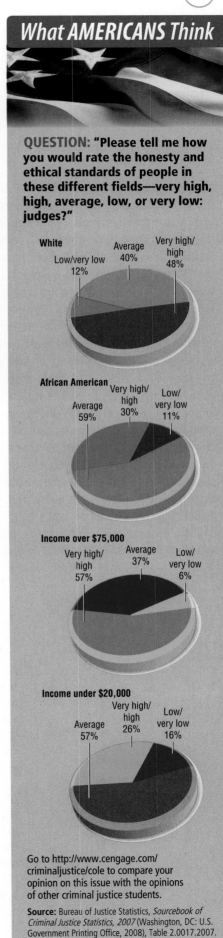

What AMERICANS Think

QUESTION: "Please tell me how you would rate the honesty and ethical standards of people in these different fields—very high, high, average, low, or very low: judges?"

White
Low/very low 12%
Average 40%
Very high/high 48%

African American
Average 59%
Very high/high 30%
Low/very low 11%

Income over $75,000
Very high/high 57%
Average 37%
Low/very low 6%

Income under $20,000
Average 57%
Very high/high 26%
Low/very low 16%

Go to http://www.cengage.com/criminaljustice/cole to compare your opinion on this issue with the opinions of other criminal justice students.

Source: Bureau of Justice Statistics, *Sourcebook of Criminal Justice Statistics, 2007* (Washington, DC: U.S. Government Printing Office, 2008), Table 2.0017.2007.

CAREERS IN CRIMINAL JUSTICE

Prosecuting Attorney

KYM WORTHY, PROSECUTING ATTORNEY
WAYNE COUNTY, MICHIGAN

A COUNTY'S ELECTED PROSECUTOR oversees a staff of assistant prosecutors and support personnel in directing the investigation and prosecution of cases within the county. Wayne County, Michigan, which includes the city of Detroit, is one of the ten largest counties in the United States. The Wayne County prosecutor's office handles tens of thousands of cases each year. The prosecutor's office works with law enforcement agencies to investigate crimes, apply for search and arrest warrants, and gather evidence concerning criminal suspects. The prosecutor and her assistant prosecutors make decisions about which suspects to charge with crimes and what charges to pursue against each suspect. Prosecutors decide whether to offer opportunities for defendants to plead guilty in exchange for dropping charges or recommending specific sentences. They must discuss and negotiate with defense attorneys in defining these plea agreements. Prosecutors also present evidence in trials when defendants decline to plead guilty. They try to present enough evidence to prove a defendant's guilt "beyond a reasonable doubt." Prosecutors in many states may also be involved in appeals if they must fight against defense attorneys' claims that

Regina H. Boone / Detroit Free Press

convictions should be thrown out because of errors by the trial judge. In some states, the state attorney general's office may have primary responsibility for representing the prosecution in appeals.

Kym Worthy completed her undergraduate degree at the University of Michigan and earned her law degree at the University of Notre Dame Law School. She spent ten years as an assistant prosecuting attorney in Wayne County before being elected to a trial court judgeship. After nearly a decade as a trial court judge, she resigned from the bench in order to seek the position of Wayne County Prosecuting Attorney when the previous elected prosecutor resigned. With her significant experience as both an assistant prosecutor and a trial judge, she was elected as prosecutor in 2004 and overwhelmingly reelected in 2008.

When you let the facts and evidence guide you, then you just do the right thing. And the minute I feel that I'm letting any outside pressures dictate what I do, that's the day I no longer should have this position. Any prosecutors that let outside forces dictate how they handle a case or how they dispose of a case other than the facts and the law really shouldn't be doing the job.

Source: Sven Gustafson, "Wayne County Prosecutor Kym Worthy: No One Is above the Law," *Michigan Business Review*, March 4, 2009, http://www.mlive.com/businessreview.

■ Politics and Prosecution

In all states except Alaska, Connecticut, New Jersey, and Rhode Island, prosecutors are elected, usually for a four-year term; local politics thus heavily influence the office. By seeking to please voters, many prosecutors have tried to use their local office as a springboard to a higher office—such as state legislator, governor, or member of Congress. Further, although the power of prosecutors flows directly from their legal duties, prosecutors can often mesh their own ambitions with the needs of a political party. The appointment of assistant prosecutors offers a chance to recruit bright young lawyers for the party.

Prosecutors may choose certain cases for prosecution in order to gain the favor of voters, or investigate charges against political opponents and public officials to get the public's attention. Political factors may also cause prosecutors to apply their powers unevenly within a community. Prosecutors' discretionary power can create the impression that some groups or individuals receive harsh treatment while others receive protection.

Discretion in decision making also creates the risk of discrimination. For example, some scholars see prosecutors' decisions as reflecting biases based on race, social class, and gender (Frohmann, 1997), but other researchers believe that studies have not yet documented the full extent of discrimination by prosecutors (S. Walker, Spohn, and

DeLeone, 2007). Several studies raise questions about discrimination in specific situations, such as prosecutors' decisions to seek the death penalty (Sorensen and Wallace, 1999). For the criminal justice system to fulfill American values concerning equality and fairness, prosecutors must use their decision-making authority carefully to avoid inequality and injustice. Yet, court decisions have made it extraordinarily difficult to use statistical studies to prove and seek remedies for racial discrimination by prosecutors, even when strong social science evidence exists (M. P. Wolf, 2007).

The Prosecutor's Influence

Most decision makers in the criminal justice process are involved in only part of the process. However, prosecutors are concerned with all aspects of the process and can therefore exert great influence. From arrest to final disposition of a case, prosecutors can make decisions that largely determine the defendant's fate. The prosecutor chooses the cases to be prosecuted, selects the charges to be brought, recommends the bail amount, approves agreements with the defendant, and urges the judge to impose a particular sentence (Kingsnorth, MacIntosh, and Sutherland, 2002).

Throughout the justice process, prosecutors' links with the other actors in the system—police, defense attorneys, judges—shape the prosecutors' decisions. Prosecutors may, for example, recommend bail amounts and sentences that match the preferences of particular judges. They may make "tough" recommendations in front of "tough" judges but tone down their arguments before judges who favor leniency or rehabilitation. Similarly, the other actors in the system may adjust their decisions and actions to match the preferences of the prosecutor. For example, police officers' investigation and arrest practices tend to reflect the prosecutor's priorities. Thus, prosecutors influence the decisions of others while also shaping their own actions in ways that reinforce their relationships with police, defense attorneys, and judges.

Prosecutors gain additional power from the fact that their decisions and actions take place away from public view. For example, a prosecutor and a defense attorney may strike a bargain whereby the prosecutor reduces a charge in exchange for a guilty plea or drops a charge if the defendant agrees to seek psychiatric help. In such instances, they reach a decision on a case in a way that is nearly invisible to the public.

The Prosecutor's Roles

As "lawyers for the state," prosecutors face conflicting pressures to press charges vigorously against lawbreakers while also upholding justice and the rights of the accused. These pressures are often called "the prosecutor's dilemma." In the adversarial system, prosecutors must do everything they can to win a conviction, but as members of the legal profession they must see that justice is done even if it means that the accused is not convicted. Even so, they always face the risk of "prosecutor's bias," sometimes called a "prosecution complex." Although they are supposed to represent all the people, including the accused, prosecutors may view themselves as instruments of law enforcement. Thus, as advocates on behalf of the state, their strong desire to close each case with a conviction may keep them from recognizing unfair procedures or evidence of innocence.

Although all prosecutors must uphold the law and pursue charges against lawbreakers, they may perform these tasks in different ways. Their personal values and professional goals, along with the political climate of their city or county, may cause them to define the prosecutor's role differently than do prosecutors in other places. For example, a prosecutor who believes that young offenders can be rehabilitated may define the role differently than one who believes that young offenders should receive the same punishments as adults. One might send juveniles to counseling programs, whereas the other would seek to process them though the adult system of courts and corrections. A prosecutor with no assistants and few resources for conducting full-blown jury trials may be forced to embrace effective plea bargaining, whereas a prosecutor in a wealthier county may have more options when deciding whether to take cases to trial.

When prosecutors are asked about their roles, the following four emerge:

1. *Trial counsel for the police.* Prosecutors who see their main function in this light believe that they should reflect the views of law enforcement in the courtroom and take a crime-fighter stance in public.

2. *House counsel for the police.* These prosecutors believe that their main function is to give legal advice so that arrests will stand up in court.

3. *Representative of the court.* Such prosecutors believe that their main function is to enforce the rules of due process to ensure that the police act according to the law and uphold the rights of defendants.

4. *Elected official.* These prosecutors may be most responsive to public opinion. The political impact of their decisions is one of their main concerns.

Each of these roles involves a different view of the prosecutor's "clients" as well as his or her own responsibilities. In the first two roles, prosecutors appear to believe that the police are the clients of their legal practice. Take a moment to think about who might be the clients of prosecutors who view themselves as representatives of the court or as elected officials.

■ Discretion of the Prosecutor

Because they have such broad discretion, prosecutors can shape their decisions to fit different interests. They might base their decisions on a desire to impress voters through tough "throw-the-book-at-them" charges in a highly publicized case (Maschke, 1995). Decisions may also be driven by changing events in society. For example, an emphasis on pursuing fraudulent business transactions and mortgage loans developed when Americans concluded that the greed of business people had helped to create the economic crisis of 2008 (Segal, 2009). Decisions by prosecutors might also stem from their personal values, such as an emphasis on leniency and rehabilitation for young offenders. They may also shape their decisions to please local judges by, for example, accepting plea agreements that will keep the judges from being burdened by too many time-consuming trials. Prosecutors who have doubts about whether the available evidence actually proves the defendant's guilt may just shrug their shoulders and say, "I'll just let the jury decide" rather than face public criticism for dropping charges. Any or all of these motives may shape prosecutors' decisions, because there is generally no higher authority to tell prosecutors how they must do their jobs. From the time the police turn a case over to the prosecutor, the prosecutor has almost complete control over decisions about charges and plea agreements (M. Stephens, 2008).

Research has also shown that the staffing levels of individual prosecutor's offices may affect decisions to pursue felony charges (P. Walker, 1998). If offices lack sufficient resources to pursue all possible cases, prosecutors may establish priorities and then reduce or dismiss charges in cases deemed less important.

If you were a prosecutor, what would you consider to be the most important factors in deciding whether to pursue a case? Would you have any concerns about the possibility of prosecuting an innocent person? If a prosecutor pursues a case against someone who the prosecutor does not really believe is guilty of a crime, does this pose an ethical problem? As you read "A Question of Ethics" at the end of the chapter, consider what you would do if you were the prosecutor assigned to the case.

After deciding that a case should be prosecuted, the prosecutor has great freedom in deciding what charges to file. Criminal incidents may involve several laws, so the prosecutor can often bring a single charge or more than one. Suppose that Smith, who is armed, breaks into a grocery store, assaults the proprietor, and robs the cash drawer. What charges can the prosecutor file? By virtue of having committed the robbery, the accused can be charged with at least four crimes: breaking and entering, assault, armed robbery, and carrying a dangerous weapon. Other charges or **counts** may be added, depending on the nature of the incident. A forger, for instance, may be charged with one count for each act of forgery committed. By filing as many charges as possible, the prosecutor strengthens his or her position in plea negotiations. In effect, the prosecutor can use discretion in deciding the number of charges and thus increase the prosecution's supply of "bargaining chips."

The discretionary power to set charges does not give the prosecutor complete control over plea bargaining, however. Defense attorneys strengthen their position in the **discovery** process, in which information from the prosecutor's case file must be made available to the defense. For example, the defense has the right to see any statements made by the accused during interrogation by the police, as well as the results of any physical or psychological tests. This information tells the defense attorney about the strengths and weaknesses of the prosecution's case. The defense attorney may use it to decide whether a case is hopeless or whether engaging in tough negotiations is worthwhile.

The prosecutor's discretion does not end with the decision to file a certain charge. After the charge has been made, the prosecutor may reduce it in exchange for a guilty plea or enter a notation of *nolle prosequi* (*nol. pros.*). The latter is a freely made decision to drop the charge, either as a whole or as to one or more counts. When a prosecutor decides to drop charges, no higher authorities can force him or her to reinstate them. When guilty pleas are entered, the prosecutor uses discretion in recommending a sentence.

■ **count** Each separate offense of which a person is accused in an indictment or an information.

■ **discovery** A prosecutor's pretrial disclosure to the defense of facts and evidence to be introduced at trial.

■ *nolle prosequi* An entry, made by a prosecutor on the record of a case and announced in court, indicating that the charges specified will not be prosecuted. In effect, the charges are thereby dismissed.

■ Key Relationships of the Prosecutor

Prosecutors do not base their decisions solely on formal policies and role conceptions (Fridell, 1990). Relationships with other actors in the justice system also influence their choices. Despite their independent authority, prosecutors must consider how police, judges, and others will react. They depend on these other officials in order to prosecute cases successfully. In turn, the success of police, judges, and correctional officials depends on prosecutors' effectiveness in identifying and convicting lawbreakers. Thus, these officials build exchange relationships in which they cooperate with each other.

Police   Prosecutors depend on the police to provide both the suspects and the evidence needed to convict lawbreakers. Because they cannot investigate crimes on their own, prosecutors cannot control the types of cases brought to them. Thus, the police control the initiation of the criminal justice process by investigating crimes and arresting suspects. These actions may be influenced by various factors, such as pressure on police to establish an impressive crime-clearance record. As a result, police actions may create problems for prosecutors if, for example, the police make many arrests without gathering enough evidence to ensure conviction.

Victims and Witnesses   Prosecutors depend on the cooperation of victims and witnesses. Although prosecutors can pursue a case whether or not a victim wishes to press charges, many prosecutors will not do so when the key testimony and other necessary evidence must come from a victim who is unwilling to cooperate (Dawson and Dinovitzer, 2001). In some cases, the decision to prosecute may be influenced by the victim's assertiveness in persuading the prosecutor to file charges (Stickels, Michelsen, and Del Carmen, 2007).

The decision to prosecute is often based on an assessment of the victim's role in his or her own victimization and the victim's credibility as a witness. If a victim has a criminal record, the prosecutor may choose not to pursue the case, in the belief that a jury would not consider the victim a credible witness—despite the fact that the jury will never learn that the victim has a criminal record. If a victim is poorly dressed, uneducated, or somewhat inarticulate, the prosecutor may be inclined to dismiss charges out of fear that a jury would find the victim unpersuasive (Stanko, 1988). Research indicates that victim characteristics, such as moral character, behavior at time of incident, and age, influence decisions to prosecute sexual assault cases more than does the actual strength of the evidence against the suspect (Spears and Spohn, 1997). Studies have shown that prosecutions succeed most when aimed at defendants accused of committing crimes against strangers (Boland et al., 1983). When the victim is an acquaintance, a friend, or even a relative of the defendant, he or she may refuse to act as a witness, and prosecutors and juries may view the offense as less serious.

Judges and Courts   The sentencing history of each judge gives prosecutors an idea of how a case may be treated in the courtroom. Prosecutors may decide to drop a case if they believe that the judge assigned to it will not impose a serious punishment. Because prosecutors' offices have limited resources, they cannot afford to waste time pursuing charges in front of a specific judge if that judge shows a pattern of dismissing those types of charges. Interactions with defense attorneys also affect prosecutors' decisions, as in the case of plea bargains.

The Community   Public opinion and the media can play a crucial role in creating an environment that either supports or scrutinizes the prosecutor. Like police chiefs and school superintendents, county prosecutors will not remain in office long if they fall out of step with community values. They will likely lose at the next election to an opponent who has a better sense of the community's priorities.

Many cities are experimenting with innovations designed to enhance communication and understanding between prosecutors and the community. One innovation called *community prosecution* gives specific assistant prosecutors continuing responsibilities for particular neighborhoods. These prosecutors may become known to people in the neighborhood, attend community meetings and social functions, and learn about residents' specific concerns. In so doing, they can build relationships that will help them gather information and identify witnesses when crimes occur (Boland, 2001; Gray, 2008).

Prosecutors' relationships and interactions with police, victims, defense attorneys, judges, and the community form the core of the exchange relations that shape decision making in criminal cases. Other relationships, such as those with news media, federal and state officials, legislators, and political party officials, also influence prosecutors' decisions. This long list of actors illustrates that prosecutors do not base their decisions solely on whether a law was broken. The occurrence of a crime is only the first step in a decision-making process that may vary from one case to the next. Sometimes charges are dropped or reduced. Sometimes plea bargains are negotiated quickly. Sometimes cases move through the system to a complete jury trial. In every instance, relationships and interactions with a variety of actors both within and outside the justice system shape prosecutors' discretionary decisions.

■ Decision-Making Policies

Despite the many factors that potentially affect prosecutors' decisions, we can draw some general conclusions about how prosecutors approach their office. Prosecutors develop their own policies on how cases will be handled. These policies shape the decisions made by the assistant prosecutors and thus greatly affect the administration of justice. Within the same state, prosecutors may pursue different goals in forming policies on which cases to pursue, which ones to drop, and which ones to plea bargain. For example, prosecutors who wish to maintain a high conviction rate will drop cases with weak evidence. Others, concerned about using limited resources effectively, will focus most of their time and energy on the most serious cases.

Some prosecutors' offices make extensive use of screening and tend not to press charges. Guilty pleas are the main method of processing cases in many offices, whereas pleas of not guilty strain the courts' trial resources in others. Some offices process cases soon after the police bring them to the prosecutor's attention, sometimes diverting or referring them to other agencies; others have disposition occurring as late as the first day of trial. The period from the receipt of the police report to the start of the trial is thus a time of review in which the prosecutor uses discretion to decide what actions should be taken.

The **accusatory process** is the series of activities that take place from the moment a suspect is arrested and booked by the police to the moment the formal charge—in the form of an indictment or information—is filed with the court. In an indictment, evidence is presented to a grand jury made up of citizens who determine whether to issue a formal charge. Grand juries are used in the federal system and in states where legislatures have mandated their use for serious charges. In jurisdictions that do not use grand juries, the prosecutor has full control of the charging decision when the filing of an information initiates prosecution. In other words, when an information is used to present formal charges, no body of citizens can protect a suspect from wrongful prosecution until the case goes to trial and a trial jury hears the case. However, earlier in the process judges may decide at preliminary hearings that there is insufficient evidence to support the pursuit of the charges; in such circumstances, a judge can order that the charges be dismissed.

Clearly, the prosecutor's established policies and decisions play a key role in determining whether charges will be filed against a defendant. Keep in mind, though, that the prosecutor's decision-making power is not limited to decisions about charges. As shown in Figure 7.3, the prosecutor makes important decisions at each stage, both before and after a defendant's guilt is determined. Because the prosecutor's involvement and influence span the justice process, from seeking search warrants during early investigations to arguing against postconviction appeals, the prosecutor is a highly influential actor in criminal cases. No other participant in the system is involved in so many different stages of the criminal process.

■ **accusatory process** The series of events from the arrest of a suspect to the filing of a formal charge (through an indictment or information) with the court.

FIGURE 7.3
Typical actions of a prosecuting attorney in processing a felony case
The prosecutor has certain responsibilities at various points in the process. At each point, the prosecutor is an advocate for the state's case against the accused.

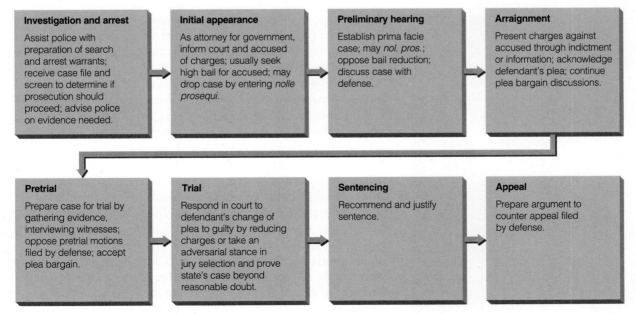

Investigation and arrest
Assist police with preparation of search and arrest warrants; receive case file and screen to determine if prosecution should proceed; advise police on evidence needed.

Initial appearance
As attorney for government, inform court and accused of charges; usually seek high bail for accused; may drop case by entering *nolle prosequi*.

Preliminary hearing
Establish prima facie case; may *nol. pros.*; oppose bail reduction; discuss case with defense.

Arraignment
Present charges against accused through indictment or information; acknowledge defendant's plea; continue plea bargain discussions.

Pretrial
Prepare case for trial by gathering evidence, interviewing witnesses; oppose pretrial motions filed by defense; accept plea bargain.

Trial
Respond in court to defendant's change of plea to guilty by reducing charges or take an adversarial stance in jury selection and prove state's case beyond reasonable doubt.

Sentencing
Recommend and justify sentence.

Appeal
Prepare argument to counter appeal filed by defense.

CHECKPOINT

7 *What are the roles of the prosecutor?*

7 Trial counsel for the police, house counsel for the police, representative of the court, elected official.

8 *How does the prosecutor use discretion to decide how to treat each defendant?*

8 The prosecutor can determine the type and number of charges, reduce the charges in exchange for a guilty plea, or enter a *nolle prosequi* (thereby dropping some or all of the charges).

9 *What are the prosecutor's key exchange relationships?*

9 Police, victims and witnesses, defense attorneys, judges, the community.

The Defense Attorney: Image and Reality

■ **defense attorney** The lawyer who represents accused offenders and convicted offenders in their dealings with criminal justice.

Billy Martin, a prominent defense attorney who has represented such clients as NFL star Michael Vick and U.S. Senator Larry Craig, gives closing arguments in the manslaughter trial of former NBA basketball star Jayson Williams. An effective defense requires respect, openness, and trust between attorney and client. Do defense attorneys need special skills and personal qualities?

AP Photo/Ed Pagliarini, Pool

In an adversarial process, the **defense attorney** is the lawyer who represents accused and convicted persons in their dealings with the criminal justice system. Most Americans have seen defense attorneys in action on television dramas such as *Boston Legal* and *Law and Order*. In these dramas, defense attorneys vigorously battle the prosecution, and the jury often finds their clients innocent. These images gain strength from news stories about prominent defense attorneys, such as Chicago's Ed Genson, who represented Illinois Governor Rod Blagojevich during initial impeachment proceedings and who won an acquittal from child pornography charges for singer R. Kelly in 2008 (St. Clair, 2008). Although these images are drawn from reality, they do not give a true picture of the typical defense attorney, focusing as they do on the few highly publicized cases that result in jury trials. By contrast, most cases find resolution through plea bargaining, discretionary dismissals, and similar decisions by actors in the justice system. In these cases, the defense attorney may seem less like the prosecutor's adversary and more like a partner in the effort to dispose of cases as quickly and efficiently as possible through negotiation.

All the key courtroom actors discussed in this chapter—judges, prosecutors, and defense attorneys—are lawyers who met the same educational requirements. After becoming lawyers, however, they made different decisions about what career to pursue. Some people cannot understand why anyone would want to be a defense attorney and work on behalf of criminals. However, defense attorneys work for people who are *accused* of crimes. Under the American system of criminal justice, defendants are supposedly presumed to be innocent. Indeed, many of them will have charges reduced or dismissed. Others will be found not guilty. Thus, characterizing defense attorneys as representing only criminals is simply not accurate. Moreover, many lawyers who choose to work as defense attorneys see themselves as defending the Bill of Rights by ensuring that prosecutors actually respect the Constitution and provide proof beyond a reasonable doubt before defendants are convicted and punished.

FIGURE 7.4
Typical actions of a defense attorney processing a felony case
Defense attorneys are advocates for the accused. They have an obligation to challenge points made by the prosecution and advise clients about constitutional rights.

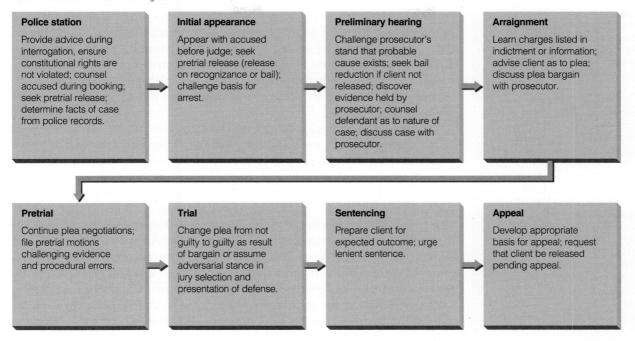

Police station	**Initial appearance**	**Preliminary hearing**	**Arraignment**
Provide advice during interrogation, ensure constitutional rights are not violated; counsel accused during booking; seek pretrial release; determine facts of case from police records.	Appear with accused before judge; seek pretrial release (release on recognizance or bail); challenge basis for arrest.	Challenge prosecutor's stand that probable cause exists; seek bail reduction if client not released; discover evidence held by prosecutor; counsel defendant as to nature of case; discuss case with prosecutor.	Learn charges listed in indictment or information; advise client as to plea; discuss plea bargain with prosecutor.

Pretrial	**Trial**	**Sentencing**	**Appeal**
Continue plea negotiations; file pretrial motions challenging evidence and procedural errors.	Change plea from not guilty to guilty as result of bargain *or* assume adversarial stance in jury selection and presentation of defense.	Prepare client for expected outcome; urge lenient sentence.	Develop appropriate basis for appeal; request that client be released pending appeal.

■ The Role of the Defense Attorney

To be effective, defense attorneys must have knowledge of law and procedure, skill in investigation, experience in advocacy, and, in many cases, relationships with prosecutors and judges that will help a defendant obtain the best possible outcome. In the American legal system, the defense attorney performs the key function of making sure that the prosecution proves its case in court or has substantial evidence of guilt before a guilty plea leads to conviction and punishment.

As shown in Figure 7.4, the defense attorney advises the defendant and protects his or her constitutional rights at each stage of the criminal justice process. The defense attorney advises the defendant during questioning by the police, represents him or her at each arraignment and hearing, and serves as advocate for the defendant during the appeal process. Without knowing the technical details of law and court procedures, defendants have little ability to represent themselves in court effectively. The defense attorney therefore ensures that prosecutors and judges understand and respect the defendant's rights. In light of the important role of defense attorneys, as you read "Criminal Justice: Myth and Reality," consider the qualifications that are necessary for the position.

While filling their roles in the criminal justice system, defense attorneys also psychologically support defendants and their families. Relatives are often bewildered, frightened, and confused. The defense attorney is the only legal actor available to answer the question "What will happen next?" In short, the attorney's relationship with the client matters a great deal. An effective defense requires respect, openness, and trust between attorney and client. If the defendant refuses to follow the attorney's advice, the lawyer may feel obliged to withdraw from the case in order to protect his or her own professional reputation.

■ Realities of the Defense Attorney's Job

How well do defense attorneys represent their clients? Attorneys who are inexperienced, uncaring, or overburdened have trouble representing their clients effectively.

Criminal Justice:
MYTH AND REALITY

COMMON BELIEF: Because defense attorneys are responsible for insuring that constitutional rights are protected and innocent people are not wrongly convicted, such attorneys must have special training and expertise in order to handle criminal cases.

Although detailed knowledge of criminal law, court procedures, and negotiation processes for plea bargaining are essential for effective representation of criminal defendants, the American justice system does not require any special training or qualifications for attorneys who wish to handle criminal cases. After graduation from law school, prospective lawyers take a written licensing exam, called the "bar exam," that covers limited aspects of two dozen legal subjects. Upon passing the exam, all American attorneys are considered qualified to handle any kind of case, even if they have no specific knowledge or experience in that area of law. This approach to education and licensing differs greatly from the approach in the medical field, where medical school graduates must pass exams, gain practical experience through supervised residencies, and undertake additional years of training and experience before they are certified as specialists qualified to work in certain areas of medicine, such as surgery or psychiatry. In countries such as England and Canada, new attorneys must work for a year under the supervision of a judge or lawyer before they can represent their own clients. Among American lawyers who are unable to obtain jobs with law firms, either because of their poor grades in law school or because of limited opportunities in the legal job market, the easiest way to generate income is to handle criminal cases for indigent defendants. Thus, inexperienced lawyers can learn about legal practice through experimentation and errors with the cases of poor clients who, as a result of their attorneys' lack of knowledge, may end up with stiffer sentences than others who commit the same crimes. In the worst-case scenario, the ineffectiveness of an inexperienced defense attorney could even contribute to the conviction of an innocent person. Does the United States take a proper approach to attorney education and licensing? Would criminal defendants be better served if defense attorneys were required to have specific expertise and experience?

The attorney may quickly agree to a plea bargain and then work to persuade the defendant to accept the agreement. The attorney's self-interest in disposing of cases quickly, receiving payment, and moving on to other cases may cause the attorney to, in effect, work with the prosecutor to pressure the defendant to plead guilty. Skilled defense attorneys also consider plea bargaining in the earliest stages of a case; however, unlike their unskilled counterparts, these lawyers would be guided by their role as advocate for the defendant, not by outside pressures. In many cases, a negotiated plea with a predictable sentence serves the defendant better than does a trial spent fending off more-serious charges. An effective defense attorney does not try to take every case all the way to trial.

The defense attorney's job is all the more difficult because neither the public nor defendants fully understand the attorney's duties and goals. The public often views defense attorneys as protectors of criminals. In fact, the attorney's basic duty is not to save criminals from punishment but to protect constitutional rights, keep the prosecution honest in preparing and presenting cases, and prevent innocent people from being convicted. Surveys indicate that lawyers place much greater emphasis on the importance of right to counsel than does the public. Look at the questions presented in "What Americans Think." Do you think that the public may underestimate the necessity of representation by an attorney? Do you agree with the majority of defense attorneys in the survey, or are they too protective of rights for people who might threaten American society?

Three groups of private practice lawyers can be called specialists in criminal defense because they handle criminal cases on a regular basis. The first group is composed of nationally known attorneys who charge large fees in highly publicized cases. The second group, found in each large city, is composed of the lawyers of choice for defendants who can afford to pay high fees. These attorneys make handsome incomes by representing white-collar criminals, drug dealers, and affluent people charged with crimes. The third and largest group of attorneys in full-time criminal practice is composed of courthouse regulars who accept many cases for small fees and who participate daily in the criminal justice system as either retained or assigned counsel. These attorneys handle a large volume of cases quickly. They negotiate guilty pleas and try to convince their clients that these agreements are beneficial. They depend on the cooperation of prosecutors, judges, and other courtroom actors, with whom they form exchange relationships in order to reach plea bargains quickly.

In addition to these defense specialists, many private attorneys sometimes take criminal cases. These attorneys often have little trial experience and lack well-developed relationships with other actors in the criminal justice system. In fact, their clients might be better served by a courthouse regular who has little interest in each case but whose relationships with prosecutors and judges will produce better plea bargains.

Government-salaried attorneys called *public defenders* handle criminal cases for defendants who are too poor to hire their own attorneys. These attorneys focus exclusively on criminal cases and usually develop significant expertise. They cannot always devote as much time as they want to each case, because they often have heavy caseloads.

■ The Environment of Criminal Practice

Defense attorneys have a difficult job. Much of their work involves preparing clients and their relatives for the likelihood of conviction and punishment. Even when they know that their clients are guilty, they may become emotionally involved because they are the only judicial actors who know the defendants as human beings and see them in the context of their family and social environment.

Most defense lawyers constantly interact with lower-class clients whose lives and problems are depressing. They might also visit the local jail at all hours of the day and night. Thus, their work setting is far removed from the fancy offices and expensive restaurants of the world of corporate attorneys. As described by one defense attorney, "The days are long and stressful. I spend a good deal of time in jail, which reeks of stale food and body odor. My clients often think that because I'm court-appointed, I must be incompetent" (Lave, 1998:14).

Defense lawyers must also struggle with the fact that criminal practice does not pay well. Public defenders garner fairly low salaries, and attorneys appointed to represent poor defendants receive small sums. If private attorneys do not demand payment from their clients at the start of the case, they may find that they must persuade the defendants' relatives to pay—because many convicted offenders have no incentive to pay for legal services while sitting in a prison cell. To perform their jobs well and gain satisfaction from their careers, defense attorneys must focus on goals other than money, such as their key role in protecting people's constitutional rights. However, that they are usually on the losing side can make it hard for them to feel like professionals—with high self-esteem and satisfying work. In addition, because they work on behalf of criminal defendants, they also face suspicion from the public.

■ Counsel for Indigents

Since the 1960s, the Supreme Court has interpreted the "right to counsel" in the Sixth Amendment to the Constitution as requiring that the government provide attorneys for indigent defendants who face the possibility of going to prison or jail. *Indigent defendants* are those who are too poor to afford their own lawyers. The Court has also required that attorneys be provided early in the criminal justice process, to protect suspects' rights during questioning and pretrial proceedings. See Table 7.2 for a summary of key rulings on the right to counsel.

Research on felony defendants indicates that 78 percent of those prosecuted in the 75 largest counties and 66 percent of those prosecuted in federal courts received publicly provided legal counsel (Harlow, 2000). The portion

Sean Sullivan, a lawyer who represents indigent clients, carries a heavy caseload under difficult conditions. The quality of representation for poor defendants may vary from courthouse to courthouse, depending on the knowledge and efforts of the attorneys, caseloads, and administrative pressures to resolve cases quickly. How can we improve the quality of defense in criminal cases?

Ruth Fremson/The New York Times/Redux

What AMERICANS Think

QUESTION: The American Bar Association, the largest national association of lawyers, surveyed a small sample of defense attorneys about their views on issues related to the government's response to terrorism.

The terrorism laws passed by Congress have made the U.S. safer.

- No opinion 6%
- Agree 14%
- Disagree 80%

Privacy rights have been unduly compromised as a result of antiterror efforts.

- No opinion 2%
- Disagree 4%
- Agree 94%

Would you be willing to represent Osama Bin Laden in federal court?

- Don't know 18%
- Yes 59%
- No 23%

Go to http://www.cengage.com/criminaljustice/cole to compare your opinion on this issue with the opinions of other criminal justice students.

Source: Mark Hansen and Stephanie Francis Ward, "The 50-Lawyer Poll," *ABA Journal*, September 2007, http://www.abajournal.com.

TABLE 7.2		The Right to Counsel: Major Supreme Court Rulings
Case	**Year**	**Ruling**
Powell v. Alabama	1932	Indigents facing the death penalty who are not capable of representing themselves must be given attorneys.
Johnson v. Zerbst	1938	Indigent defendants must be provided with attorneys when facing serious charges in federal court.
Gideon v. Wainwright	1963	Indigent defendants must be provided with attorneys when facing serious charges in state court.
Douglas v. California	1963	Indigent defendants must be provided with attorneys for their first appeal.
Miranda v. Arizona	1966	Criminal suspects must be informed about their right to counsel before being questioned in custody.
United States v. Wade	1967	Defendants are entitled to counsel at "critical stages" in the process, including postindictment lineups.
Argersinger v. Hamlin	1972	Indigent defendants must be provided with attorneys when facing misdemeanor and petty charges that may result in incarceration.
Ross v. Moffitt	1974	Indigent defendants are not entitled to attorneys for discretionary appeals after their first appeal is unsuccessful.
Strickland v. Washington	1984	To show ineffective assistance of counsel violated the right to counsel, defendants must prove that the attorney committed specific errors that affected the outcome of the case.
Murray v. Giarratano	1989	Death row inmates do not have a right to counsel for habeas corpus proceedings asserting rights violations in their cases.

of defendants who are provided with counsel because they are indigent has increased greatly in the past three decades.

The quality of counsel given to indigent defendants has spurred debate. Ideally, experienced lawyers would be appointed soon after arrest to represent the defendant in each stage of the criminal justice process. Ideal conditions do not always exist, however. As we have seen, inexperienced and uncaring attorneys may be appointed. Some attorneys have little time to prepare the case. Even conscientious attorneys may be unable to provide top-quality counsel if they have heavy caseloads or do not receive enough money to enable them to spend the time required to handle the case well. If they lack the time and desire to interview the client and prepare the case, the appointed counsel may simply persuade defendants to plead guilty right there in the courtroom during their first and only conversation. Of course, not all publicly financed lawyers who represent poor defendants ignore their clients' best interests. Even so, the quality of counsel received by the poor may vary from courthouse to courthouse, depending on the quality of the attorneys, conditions of defense practice, and administrative pressure to reduce the caseload.

Ways of Providing Indigents with Counsel   There are three main ways of providing counsel to indigent defendants: (1) the **assigned counsel** system, in which a court appoints a private attorney to represent the accused; (2) the **contract counsel** system, in which an attorney, a nonprofit organization, or a private law firm contracts with a local government to provide legal services to indigent defendants for a specified dollar amount; and (3) **public defender** programs, which are public or private nonprofit organizations with full-time or part-time salaried staff. Figure 7.5 shows the system in use in the majority of counties in each of the 50 states. Note, however, that 23 percent of counties use both public defenders and assigned counsel to provide representation (S. K. Smith and DeFrances, 1996).

The methods for providing defense attorneys and the quality of defense services may depend on the money available to pay attorneys. Twenty-seven states pay for indigent criminal defense, but in the remaining states each county must fund its own defense service. As a result, resources—and the quality of indigent defense—may vary from county to county within a single state. In 2003, Quitman County, Mississippi, sued the state government because it could not provide sufficient county funds to pay for defense attorneys by itself (Liptak, 2003).

ASSIGNED COUNSEL   In the assigned counsel system, the court appoints a lawyer in private practice to represent an indigent defendant. This system is widely used in small cities and in rural areas, but even some city public defender systems assign counsel in some cases, such as a case with multiple defendants, where a conflict of interest might result if a public lawyer represented all of them.

■ **assigned counsel** An attorney in private practice assigned by a court to represent an indigent. The attorney's fee is paid by the government with jurisdiction over the case.

■ **contract counsel** An attorney in private practice who contracts with the government to represent all indigent defendants in a county during a set period of time and for a specified dollar amount.

■ **public defender** An attorney employed on a full-time, salaried basis by a public or private nonprofit organization to represent indigents.

FIGURE 7.5

Indigent defense system used by the majority of counties in each state

Note that some states use a mixture of methods to provide counsel for indigents; this figure shows only the predominant method per state.

■ Public defender
☐ Contract
■ Assigned counsel

Source: Bureau of Justice Statistics, *Bulletin*, September 1988.

Assigned counsel systems are organized on either an ad hoc or a coordinated basis. In ad hoc assignment systems, private attorneys tell the judge that they are willing to take the cases of indigent defendants. When an indigent requires counsel, the judge either assigns lawyers in rotation from a prepared list or chooses one of the attorneys who are known and present in the courtroom. In coordinated assignment systems, a court administrator oversees the appointment of counsel.

Use of the ad hoc system raises questions about the loyalties of the assigned counsel. Are they trying to vigorously defend their clients or are they trying to please the judges to ensure future appointments? For example, Texas has been criticized for giving judges free rein to assign lawyers to cases without any supervising authority to ensure that the attorneys actually do a good job (Novak, 1999). Additional concerns in Texas and other states where judges run for election center on lawyers' donating to judges' political campaigns. Judges could return the favor by supplying their contributors with criminal defense assignments.

The fees paid to assigned defenders are often low compared with what a lawyer might otherwise charge. As described by one attorney, "The level of compensation impacts the level of representation.... If an attorney takes [an appointed criminal case], it means they lose the opportunity to take other cases at higher rates" ("Economics of CJA Representations," 2008). Whereas a private practice attorney might charge clients at rates that exceed $200 per hour, hourly rates for appointed counsel in Cook County (Chicago), Illinois, are merely $40 per hour for in-court tasks and $30 per hour for out-of-court tasks. These same rates have been in place for more than 30 years. Defense attorneys receive the low rate of $40 per hour for out-of-court work in Oklahoma, Oregon, Alabama, South Carolina, and Tennessee. Many other

TABLE 7.3	Fees Paid to Assigned Counsel in Noncapital Felony Cases		
State	**Out-of-Court Hourly Rate**	**In-Court Hourly Rate**	**Per-Case Maximum**
Alaska	$50	$60	$4,000 trial; $2,000 plea
Georgia	$40	$60	None
Hawaii	$90	$90	$6,000
Maryland	$50	$50	$3,000
New York	$75	$75	$4,400
North Carolina	$65	$65	None
North Dakota	$65	$65	$2,000
Federal	$100	$100	$7,000

Sources: "Economics of CJA Representations Costly to Attorneys," *The Third Branch* 40 (no. 4, April 2008), http://www.uscourts.gov/ttb/2008-04/article05.cfm; Spangenburg Group, "Rates of Compensation Paid to Court-Appointed Counsel in Non-Capital Felony Cases at Trial: A State-by-State Overview," *American Bar Association Information Program*, June 2007.

states pay only $50 to $75 per hour (Spangenberg Group, 2007). The average hourly overhead cost for attorneys—the amount they must make just to pay their secretaries, office rent, and telephone bills—is $64 ("Economics of CJA Representations," 2008). If their hourly fees fall short of their overhead costs, then attorneys actually lose money when spending time on these cases. Look at Table 7.3 to see examples of fees paid to assigned defense counsel.

CONTRACT SYSTEM   A few counties, mainly in Western states that do not have large populations, use the contract system. The government contracts with an attorney, a non-profit association, or a private law firm to handle all indigent cases (Worden, 1994). Some jurisdictions use public defenders for most cases but contract for services in multiple-defendant cases that might present conflicts of interest, in extraordinarily complex cases, or in cases that require more time than the government's salaried lawyers can provide.

This system has its problems. According to Robert Spangenberg and Marea Beeman (1995:49), "There are serious potential dangers with the contract model, such as expecting contract defenders to handle an unlimited caseload or awarding contracts on a low-bid basis only, with no regard to qualifications of contracting attorneys."

PUBLIC DEFENDERS   The position of public defender developed as a response to the legal needs of indigent defendants. The most recent national survey of the 100 most populous counties found that public defender systems handled 82 percent of the 4.2 million indigent criminal cases, whereas appointed counsel handled 15 percent and contract counsel represented only 3 percent of defendants (DeFrances and Litras, 2000). The public defender system, which is growing fast, is used in 43 of the 50 most populous counties and in most large cities. There are about 20 statewide, state-funded systems; in other states, the counties organize and pay for indigent defense, and some counties in 28 states choose to use full-time public defenders. Only two states, North Dakota and Maine, do not have public defenders either statewide or in any individual counties.

Experts and others often view the public defender system as better than the assigned counsel system, because public defenders are specialists in criminal law. Because they are full-time government employees, public defenders, unlike appointed counsel and contract attorneys, do not sacrifice their clients' cases to protect their own financial interests. Public defenders do face certain special problems, however.

They may have trouble gaining the trust and cooperation of their clients. Criminal defendants may assume that attorneys on the state payroll, even with the title public defender, have no reason to protect the defendants' rights and interests. Lack of cooperation from the defendant may make it harder for the attorney to prepare the best possible arguments for use during hearings, plea bargaining, and trials.

Public defenders may also face heavy caseloads. These burdens increase when government budget cuts affect the money devoted to indigent defense. In 2008, for example, a lawsuit in Miami sought to limit public defenders' caseloads after the average number of felony cases handled annually by each attorney grew from 367 to nearly 500. In Missouri, there was no increase in the number of public defenders hired, even though these attorneys were required to handle 12,000 more total cases than in previous years (Eckholm, 2008a). Public defender programs are most effective when they have enough money to keep caseloads manageable. However, these programs do not control their own budgets, and state and local governments usually do not see them as high priorities (Jaksic, 2007). Thus, they find it hard to gain the funds they need to give adequate attention to each defendant's case.

If public defenders do good work on behalf of criminal defendants, they may become the focus of political efforts to reduce their resources or involvement in cases. In 2003, Governor Jeb Bush of Florida proposed cutting state funding for the public defenders who handle death penalty cases. Although he argued that it would be less expensive to hire private attorneys as assigned counsel for capital cases, critics worried that such a move would reduce the quality of representation and increase the risk of errors in such cases (Richey, 2003).

Attorney Effectiveness and Competence   Do defendants who can afford their own counsel get better legal services than those who cannot? Many convicted offenders say, "You get what you pay for," meaning that they would have received better counsel if they had been able to pay for their own attorneys. At one time, researchers thought public defenders entered more guilty pleas than did lawyers who had been either privately retained or assigned to cases. However, studies show little variation in case outcomes by various types of defense (Hanson and Chapper, 1991).

The right to counsel is of little value when the counsel is not competent and effective. Even in death penalty cases, attorneys have shown up for court so drunk that they could not stand up straight (Bright, 1994). In other cases, attorneys with almost no knowledge of criminal law have made blunders that have needlessly sent their clients to death row (C. E. Smith, 1997). For example, lawyers have fallen asleep during their clients' death penalty trials, yet one Texas judge found no problem with such behavior. He wrote that everyone has a constitutional right to have a lawyer, but "the Constitution does not say that the lawyer has to be awake" (Shapiro, 1997:27). An appellate court later disagreed with this conclusion.

The U.S. Supreme Court has examined the question of what requirements must be met if defendants are to receive effective counsel. To prevail in claims that their counsel has been ineffective, defendants must identify specific errors, made by their attorneys, that affected the result of the case and made the case unfair. By focusing on whether errors by an attorney were bad enough to make the trial result unreliable, thereby denying a fair trial, the Court has made it hard for defendants to prove that they were denied effective counsel, even when defense attorneys perform very poorly. As a result, innocent people who were poorly represented have been convicted, even of the most serious crimes (Radelet, Bedeau, and Putnam, 1992).

CHECKPOINT

ANSWERS

10 *What special pressures do defense attorneys face?*

10 Heavy caseloads, poor pay, difficult working conditions, persuading clients to accept pleas, accepting the fact that they will lose most cases.

11 *What are the three main methods of providing attorneys for indigent defendants?*

11 Assigned counsel, contract counsel, public defender.

The Courtroom: How It Functions

Criminal cases throughout the nation follow similar rules and procedures. However, courts differ in the precise ways they apply them. Social scientists are aware that the culture of a community greatly influences how its members behave. *Culture* implies shared beliefs about proper behavior. These beliefs can span entire nations or exist in smaller communities, including organizations such as corporations, churches, or neighborhoods. In any community, large or small, the culture can strongly affect people's decisions and behaviors.

Researchers have identified a **local legal culture** of values and norms shared by members of a particular court community (judges, attorneys, clerks, bailiffs, and others) about how cases should be handled and the way court officials should behave (Church, 1985). The local legal culture influences court operations in three ways:

1. Norms (shared values and expectations) help participants distinguish between "our" court and other courts. Often, a judge or prosecutor will proudly describe how "we" do the job differently and better than officials in a nearby county or city.

2. Norms tell members of a court community how they should treat one another. For example, mounting a strong adversarial defense may be viewed as not in keeping with the norms of one court, but it may be expected in another.

3. Norms describe how cases should be processed. The best example of such a norm is the **going rate**, the local view of the proper sentence, which considers the offense, the defendant's prior record, and other factors. The local legal culture also includes attitudes on such issues as whether a judge should take part in plea negotiations, when **continuances**—lawyers' requests for delays in court proceedings—should be granted, and which defendants qualify for a public defender.

Differences among local legal cultures help explain why court decisions may differ, even though the formal rules of criminal procedure are basically the same. For example, although judges play a key role in sentencing, sentences also stem from understandings of the going rate shared by the prosecutor, defense attorney, and judge. In one court, shared understandings may mean that a court imposes probation on a first-time thief; in other courts, different shared values may send first offenders to jail or prison for the same offense.

Decision making in criminal cases is influenced by the fact that participants are organized in **workgroups**. The judge, prosecutor, and defense attorney, along with the support staff (clerk, reporter, and bailiff), interact in the workplace on a continuing basis, share goals, develop norms regarding how activities should be carried out, and eventually establish a network of roles that differentiates the group from others and that facilitates cooperation. These relationships are necessary if the group is to carry out its task of disposing of cases. The workgroup concept is especially important in analyzing urban courts, which have many courtrooms; large numbers of lawyers, judges, and other court personnel; and a heavy caseload.

Given the factors that define the workgroup, workgroups in various courthouses differ, depending on the strength of these factors in each setting. For example, a rotation system that moves judges among courtrooms in a large courthouse may limit the development of workgroup norms and roles. Although the same prosecutors and defense attorneys may be present every day, the arrival of a new judge every week or month will require them to learn and adapt to new ideas about how cases should be negotiated or tried. When shared norms cannot develop, cases

local legal culture Norms shared by members of a court community as to how cases should be handled and how a participant should behave in the judicial process.

going rate Local court officials' shared view of the appropriate sentence, given the offense, the defendant's prior record, and other case characteristics.

continuance An adjournment of a scheduled case until a later date.

workgroup A collection of individuals who interact in the workplace on a continuing basis, share goals, develop norms regarding how activities should be carried out, and eventually establish a network of roles that differentiates the group from others and that facilitates cooperation.

Criminal cases move through court processes as a result of discussions, interactions, and decisions involving judges, prosecutors, and defense attorneys. Even when the attorneys adopt strongly adversarial positions, courtroom participants interact, cooperate, and negotiate as they fulfill the responsibilities of their positions in the courtroom workgroup. How is the judge a key actor in this process?

will tend to proceed in a more formal manner. The actors in such a courtroom have fewer chances to follow agreed-on routines than would a workgroup with a well-developed pattern of interactions.

By contrast, when there are shared expectations and consistent relationships, the business of the courtroom proceeds in a regular but informal manner, with many shared understandings among members easing much of the work (Worden, 1995). Through cooperation, each member can achieve his or her goals as well as those of the group. The prosecutor wants to gain quick convictions, the defense attorney wants fair and prompt resolution of the defendant's case, and the judge wants cooperative agreements on guilt and sentencing. All of these actors want efficient processing of the steady flow of cases that burden their working lives.

Judges are the leaders of the courtroom team. They ensure that procedures are followed correctly. Even if prosecutors and defense attorneys appear to make the key decisions, the judge must approve them. Judges coordinate the processing of cases. Further, each judge can perform this role somewhat differently. Judges who run a loose administrative ship see themselves as somewhat above the battle. They give other members of the team a great deal of freedom in carrying out their duties and will usually approve group decisions, especially when the members of the group have shared beliefs about the court's goals and the community's values. Judges who exert tighter control over the process play a more active role. They anticipate problems, provide cues for other actors, and threaten, cajole, and move the group toward the efficient achievement of its goals. Such judges command respect and participate fully in the ongoing courtroom drama. Judges' actions can, for example, pressure defense attorneys to encourage their clients to plead guilty instead of insisting on a trial (Lynch, 1999).

CHECKPOINT

ANSWERS

12 *How does the local legal culture affect criminal cases?*

12 The local legal culture consists of norms that distinguish a given court from other jurisdictions, that stipulate how members should treat one another, and that describe how cases should be processed.

13 *What is the courtroom workgroup?*

13 The courtroom workgroup is made up of the judge, prosecutor, defense counsel, and support staff assigned regularly to a specific courtroom. Through the interaction of these members, goals and norms are shared and a set of roles becomes stabilized.

A QUESTION OF ETHICS: WRITING ASSIGNMENT

Assistant County Prosecutor Adam Dow entered the office of his boss, County Prosecutor Susan Graham. "You wanted to see me?" he asked as he closed the door.

"Yes, I do," Graham replied with a flash of anger. "I don't agree with your recommendation to dismiss charges in the Richardson case."

"But the victim was so uncertain in making the identification at the lineup, and the security video from the ATM machine is so grainy that you can't really tell if Richardson committed the robbery."

"Look. We've had six people robbed while withdrawing money at ATM machines in the past month. The community is upset. The banks are upset. The newspapers keep playing up these unsolved crimes. I want to put an end to this public hysteria. Richardson has a prior record for a robbery, and the victim picked him out of the lineup eventually." Graham stared at him coldly. "I'm not going to dismiss the charges."

Dow shifted his feet and stared at the floor. "I'm not comfortable with this case. Richardson may be innocent. The evidence just isn't very strong."

"Don't worry about the strength of the evidence. That's not your problem," said Graham. "We have enough evidence to take the case to trial. The judge said so at the preliminary hearing. So we'll just let the jury decide. Whatever happens, the community will know that we took action against this crime problem."

"But what if he's innocent? The jury could make a mistake in thinking that he's the robber in the grainy videotape. I wouldn't want that on my conscience."

FIGURE 8.1
Typical outcomes of 100 urban felony cases

Prosecutors and judges make crucial decisions during the period before trial or plea. Once cases are bound over for disposition, guilty pleas are many, trials are few, and acquittals are rare.

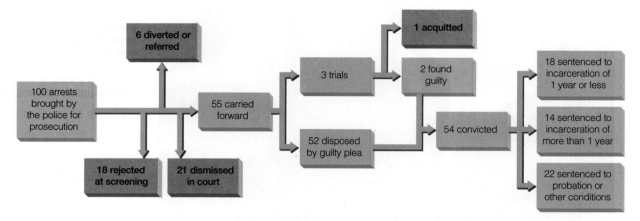

Source: Barbara Boland, Paul Mahanna, and Ronald Stones, *The Prosecution of Felony Arrests, 1988* (Washington, DC: Bureau of Justice Statistics, U.S. Government Printing Office, 1992), 2.

■ **motion** An application to a court requesting that an order be issued to bring about a specific action.

Defense attorneys use pretrial proceedings to challenge the prosecution's evidence. They make **motions** to the court requesting that an order be issued to bring about a specific action. For example, the defense may seek an order for the prosecution to share certain evidence, or for the exclusion of evidence that was allegedly obtained through improper questioning of the suspect or an improper search.

As Figure 8.1 shows, prosecutors use their decision-making power to filter many cases out of the system. The 100 cases illustrated are typical felony cases. The percentage of cases varies from city to city, depending on such factors as the effectiveness of police investigations and prosecutors' policies about which cases to pursue. In the figure, nearly half of those arrested did not ultimately face felony prosecutions. A small number of defendants were steered toward diversion programs. A larger number had their cases dismissed for various reasons, including lack of evidence, the minor nature of the charges, or first-time offender status. Some of the 22 sentenced to probation or other conditions may actually be imprisoned if the offenders commit a crime after release into the community. In these cases, the prosecutor simply chooses to pursue revocation of probation or parole, typically an easier and quicker process than proving guilt for a new crime (Kingsnorth, MacIntosh, and Sutherland, 2002).

During the pretrial process, defendants are exposed to the informal, "assembly-line" atmosphere of the lower criminal courts. Often, decisions are quickly made about bail, arraignment, pleas, and the disposition of cases. Moving cases as quickly

CHECKPOINT

ANSWERS

① *What are the purposes of the initial appearance, arraignment, and motions?*

① The initial appearance determines if there is probable cause to support the arrest. Arraignments involve the formal reading of charges and the entry of a plea. Motions seek information and the vindication of defendants' rights.

② *Why and how are cases filtered out of the system?*

② Cases are filtered out through the discretionary decisions of prosecutors and judges when they believe that there is inadequate evidence to proceed, or when prosecutors believe that their scarce resources are best directed at other cases.

as possible seems to be the main goal of many judges and attorneys during the pretrial process. Courts throughout the nation face pressure to limit the number of cases going to trial. This pressure may affect the decisions of both judges and prosecutors, as well as the defense attorneys who seek to maintain good relationships with them. American courts often have too little money, too few staff members, and too little time to give detailed attention to each case, let alone a full trial.

Bail: Pretrial Release

It is often stated that defendants are presumed innocent until proved guilty or until they enter a guilty plea. However, people who are arrested are taken to jail. They are deprived of their freedom and, in many cases, subjected to miserable living conditions while they await the processing of their cases. The idea that people who are presumed innocent can lose their freedom—sometimes for many months—as their cases work their way toward trial, clashes with the American values of freedom and liberty. It is not clear how committed Americans are to preserving the ideal of freedom for people who have not yet been convicted of crimes. Such concerns may have further diminished in the aftermath of September 11, as the federal government began to hold persons suspected of terrorism, labeled "enemy combatants," without providing any bail hearing, evidence of guilt, or access to defense attorneys. The outcry against such deprivations of liberty has come from civil rights groups and attorneys rather than from the general public (Tashima, 2008).

A conflict is bound to occur between the American value of individual liberty and the need to keep some criminal suspects in jail in order to protect society from violent people or from those who may try to escape prosecution. However, not every person charged with a criminal offense need be detained. Thus, bail and other release methods are used on the condition that the defendants will appear in court as required.

Bail is a sum of money or property, specified by the judge, that defendants present to the court as a condition of pretrial release. They forfeit the bail if they do not appear in court as scheduled. Although people are generally entitled to a bail hearing as part of their right to due process, there is no constitutional right to release on bail, nor even a right to have the court set an amount as the condition of release. The Eighth Amendment to the U.S. Constitution forbids excessive bail, and state bail laws are usually designed to prevent discrimination in setting bail. They do not guarantee, however, that all defendants will have a realistic chance of being released before trial.

Because the accused is presumed to be innocent, bail should not be used as punishment. The amount of bail should therefore be high enough to ensure that the defendant appears in court for trial—but no higher. As we have seen, however, this is not the only purpose of bail. The community must be protected from the crimes that some defendants would likely commit while out on bail (Karnow, 2008). Congress and some of the states have passed laws that permit preventive detention of defendants when the judge concludes that they pose a threat to the community while awaiting trial (Wiseman, 2009).

■ The Reality of the Bail System

The reality of the bail system is far from the ideal. The question of bail may arise at the police station, at the initial court appearance in a misdemeanor case, or at the arraignment in most felony cases. For minor offenses, police officers may have a standard list of bail amounts. For serious offenses, a judge will set bail in court. In both cases, those setting bail may have discretion to set differing bail amounts for various suspects, depending on the circumstances of each case.

In almost all courts, the amount of bail is based mainly on the judge's view of the seriousness of the crime and of the defendant's record. In part, this emphasis results

■ **bail** An amount of money, specified by a judge, to be paid as a condition of pretrial release to ensure that the accused will appear in court as required.

from a lack of information about the accused. Because bail is typically determined 24 to 48 hours after an arrest, there is little time to conduct a more thorough assessment. As a result, judges in many communities have developed standard rates: so many dollars for such-and-such an offense. In some cases, a judge may set a high bail if the police or prosecutor wants a certain person to be kept off the streets.

Critics of the bail system argue that it discriminates against poor people. Imagine that you have been arrested and have no money. Should you be denied a chance for freedom before trial just because you are poor? What if you have a little money, but if you use it to post bail you will not have any left to hire your own attorney? Professional criminals and the affluent have no trouble making bail; many drug dealers, for instance, can readily make bail and go on dealing while awaiting trial. In contrast, a poor person arrested for a minor violation may spend the pretrial period in jail. Should dangerous, wealthy offenders be allowed out on bail while nonviolent, poor suspects are locked up?

According to a study of felony defendants in the nation's most populous counties, 62 percent were released before disposition of their cases, 32 percent were unable to make bail, and 6 percent were detained without bail (T. H. Cohen and Reaves, 2006). Among those who gained release, 25 percent had bail set at less than $5,000. Figure 8.2 shows the amounts of bail set for various types of felony offenses. Those who cannot make bail must remain in jail awaiting trial, unless they can obtain enough money to pay a bail bondsman's fee. Given the length of time between arraignment and trial in most courts and the hardships of pretrial detention, bondsmen are important to defendants in many cities.

◼ Bail Bondsmen

The bail bondsman is a key figure in the bail process. Bail bondsmen (or women) are private businesspeople who are paid fees by defendants who lack the money to make bail. They are licensed by the state and can choose their own clients. In exchange for a fee, which may be 5 to 10 percent of the bail amount, the bondsman will put up the money (or property) to gain the defendant's release. Bondsmen are not obliged to provide bail money for every defendant who seeks to use their services. Instead, they decide which defendants are likely to return for court appearances. If the defendant skips town, the bondsman's money is forfeited and the bondman has a strong incentive to try to locate the missing defendant. Sometimes bondsmen and their employees have used violence or otherwise gone outside the boundaries of the law in their efforts to capture missing defendants.

Bondsmen may build relationships with police officers and jailers to obtain referrals. Many defendants may not know whom to call for help in making bail, and officers can steer them to a particular bondsman. This can lead to corruption if a bondsman pays a jailer or police officer to make such referrals. Moreover, these relationships may lead to improper cooperation, such as a bondsman refusing to help a particular defendant if the police would like to see that defendant remain in jail.

The potential problems of using profit-seeking bondsmen are widely recognized. Only two countries in the world use commercial bail bond systems, the United States and the Philippines. Posting bail for a fee is illegal in many countries. In addition, four states—Illinois, Kentucky, Oregon, and Wisconsin—have abolished private bail bond systems and instead rely on deposits to courts instead of payments to private businesses (Liptak, 2008b).

FIGURE 8.2
Bail amounts for felony defendants by type of offense
The amount of bail varies according to the offense.

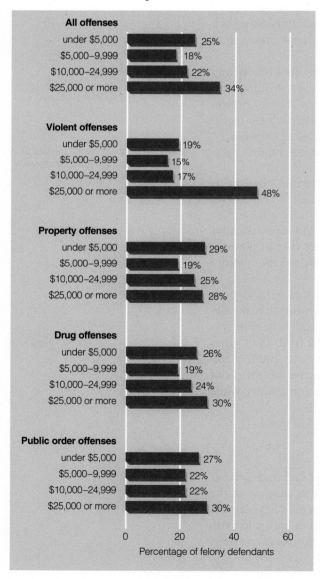

Source: Thomas H. Cohen and Brian A. Reaves, *Felony Defendants in Large Urban Counties, 2002* (Washington, DC: U.S. Government Printing Office, 2006), 18.

Despite the problems posed by the bondsmen's role, and although bondsmen act in their own interest, they can contribute to the smooth processing of cases (Dill, 1975). A major reason that defendants fail to appear for scheduled court appearances is forgetfulness and confusion about when and where they must appear. Courthouses in large cities are huge bureaucracies that do not always clearly communicate to a defendant a change in the time and location of a hearing. Bondsmen can help by reminding defendants about court dates, calling defendants' relatives to make sure that the defendant will arrive on time, and warning defendants about the penalties for failing to appear. Such contributions, however, do not necessarily outweigh the risks and problems caused by bail bondsmen. In 2006, for example, a bail bondsman in Louisiana who was sentenced to prison provided testimony to convict several judges and other employees for accepting his bribes in the form of cash and gifts (M. Gordon, 2006).

Although the justice system benefits from the activities of bondsmen, court and law enforcement officials could handle the same functions as well or better if they had the resources, time, and interest to make sure that released defendants return to court. If all courts had pretrial services offices such as those in the federal courts, defendants could be monitored and reminded to return to court but avoid the risks of discrimination and corruption associated with the use of bail bondsmen (J. G. Carr, 1993; Marsh, 1994; Peoples, 1995).

Further, the problems caused by bondsmen and bounty hunters in using their own means to find and capture fugitives could be avoided if pretrial services offices reduced the role of bail bondsmen (M. Hirsch, 2007). The hunt for fugitives, such as defendants who skip bail, could remain the exclusive responsibility of trained law enforcement personnel. In the federal system, U.S. marshals are the main law enforcement officials in the court system, responsible for court security, prisoner transport, and tracking down fugitives.

■ Setting Bail

When the police set bail at the station house for minor offenses, they usually apply a standard amount for a particular charge. By contrast, when a judge sets bail, the amount of bail and conditions of release result from interactions among the judge, prosecutor, and defense attorney. These actors discuss the defendant's personal qualities and prior record. The prosecutor may stress the seriousness of the crime, the defendant's record, and negative personal characteristics. The defense attorney, if one has been hired or appointed at this point in the process, may stress the defendant's good job, family responsibilities, and place in the community. Like other aspects of bail, these factors may favor affluent defendants over the poor, the unemployed, and people with unstable families. Yet, many of these factors provide no clear information about how dangerous a defendant is or whether he or she will appear in court.

Research highlights the disadvantages of the poor in the bail process. A study of Hispanic arrestees in the Southwest found that those who could afford to hire their own attorneys were seven times more likely to gain pretrial release than were those represented at public expense (Holmes et al., 1996). This result may reflect the fact that affluent defendants are better able to come up with bail money, as well as the possibility that private attorneys fight harder for their clients in the early stages of the criminal process.

Mackenzie Green is a well-known California bondswoman and bounty hunter. Each year, 20 percent of felony defendants out on bail fail to appear for scheduled court hearings. Some forget court dates or misunderstand instructions. Others intentionally skip town. Nearly all of them are eventually found, frequently by bondsmen and their agents. Should such profit-seeking, private businesses be so deeply involved in the criminal justice process?

Thane Plambeck; inset courtesy of Mackenzie Green

The amount of bail may also reflect the defendant's social class or even racial or ethnic discrimination by criminal justice officials. A study by the State Bail Commission of cases in Connecticut showed that at each step in the process African American and Hispanic men with clean records received bail amounts double those given whites. One reason for the difference might be that poor defendants often do not have jobs and a permanent residence, factors that strongly influence setting bail. The study also recognized that the higher bail might result from the fact that African Americans and Hispanics were more likely than whites to be charged with a felony. However, the largest disparities in bail appeared in felony drug cases. In these cases, the average bail for African Americans and Hispanics was four times higher than for whites at the same courthouse (Houston and Ewing, 1991).

■ Reforming the Bail System

Studies of pretrial detention in such cities as Philadelphia and New York have raised questions about the need to hold defendants in jail. Criticisms of the bail system focus on judges' discretion in setting bail amounts, the fact that the poor are deprived of their freedom while the affluent can afford bail, the negative aspects of bail bondsmen, and jail conditions for those detained while awaiting trial.

In response to such criticisms, efforts to reform the bail system have arisen. Such efforts often focus on reducing the number of defendants held in jail. As such, the percentage of defendants released on bail has increased in recent decades, in part because of the use of certain pretrial release methods, which we now discuss.

Citation   A **citation**, or summons, to appear in court—a "ticket"—is often issued to a person accused of committing a traffic offense or some other minor violation. By issuing the citation, the officer avoids taking the accused person to the station house for booking and to court for arraignment and setting of bail. Citations are now being used for more-serious offenses, in part because the police want to reduce the amount of time they spend booking minor offenders and waiting in arraignment court for their cases to come up.

Release on Recognizance   Pioneered in the 1960s by the Vera Institute of Justice in New York City, the **release on recognizance (ROR)** approach is based on the assumption that judges will grant releases if the defendant is reliable and has roots in the community. Soon after the arrest, court personnel talk to defendants about their job, family, prior record, and associations. They then decide whether to recommend release. In the first three years of the New York project, more than ten thousand defendants were interviewed and about 3,500 were released. Only 1.5 percent failed to appear in court at the scheduled time, a rate almost three times better than the rate for those released on bail (Goldfarb, 1965). Programs in other cities have had similar results, although Sheila Royo Maxwell's research (1999) raises questions about whether women and property crime defendants on ROR are less likely than other defendants to appear in court.

Ten Percent Cash Bail   Although ROR is a useful alternative to money bail, judges are unwilling to release some defendants on their own recognizance. Illinois, Kentucky, Nebraska, Oregon, and Pennsylvania have **percentage bail** programs in which the defendants deposit with the court an amount of cash equal to 10 percent of their bail. When they appear in court as required, this amount is returned minus a 1 percent fee for administrative costs. Begun in Illinois in 1964, this plan is designed to release as many defendants as possible without using bail bondsmen.

Bail Guidelines   To deal with the problem of unequal treatment, reformers have written guidelines for setting bail. The guidelines specify the standards judges should use in setting bail and also list appropriate amounts. Judges are expected to follow the

■ **citation** A written order or summons, issued by a law enforcement officer, directing an alleged offender to appear in court at a specific time to answer a criminal charge.

■ **release on recognizance (ROR)** Pretrial release granted, on the defendant's promise to appear in court, because the judge believes that the defendant's ties to the community guarantee that he or she will appear.

■ **percentage bail** Defendants may deposit a percentage (usually 10 percent) of the full bail with the court. The full amount of the bail is required if the defendant fails to appear. The percentage of bail is returned after disposition of the case, although the court often retains 1 percent for administrative costs.

guidelines but may deviate from them in special situations. The guidelines take into account the seriousness of the offense and the defendant's prior record in order to protect the community and ensure that released suspects will likely return for court appearances.

Preventive Detention   Reforms have been suggested not only by those concerned with unfairness in the bail system but also by those concerned with stopping crime. Critics of the bail system point to a link between release on bail and the commission of crimes, arguing that the accused can commit other crimes while awaiting trial. A study of the nation's most populous counties found that 18 percent of felony defendants released on bail were rearrested for another crime (T. H. Cohen and Reaves, 2006). To address this problem, legislatures have passed laws permitting detention of defendants without bail.

For federal criminal cases, Congress enacted the Bail Reform Act of 1984, which authorizes **preventive detention**. Under the act, if prosecutors recommend that defendants be kept in jail, a federal judge holds a hearing to determine (1) if there is a serious risk that the person will flee; (2) if the person will obstruct justice or threaten, injure, or intimidate a prospective witness or juror; or (3) if the offense is one of violence or one punishable by life imprisonment or death. On finding that any of these factors makes setting bail impossible without endangering the community, the judge can order the defendant held in jail until the case is completed (C. E. Smith, 1990).

Critics of preventive detention argue that it violates the Constitution's due process clause because the accused is held in custody until a verdict is rendered (Wiseman, 2009). However, the Supreme Court has ruled that it is constitutional. The preventive detention provisions of the Bail Reform Act of 1984 were upheld in *United States v. Salerno and Cafero* (1987). The justices said that preventive detention was a legitimate use of government power because it was not designed to punish the accused. Instead, it deals with the problem of people who commit crimes while on bail. By upholding the federal law, the Court also upheld state laws dealing with preventive detention (Miller and Guggenheim, 1990).

Supporters of preventive detention claim that it ensures that drug dealers, who often treat bail as a business expense, cannot flee before trial. Research has shown that the nature and seriousness of the charge, a history of prior arrests, and drug use all have a strong bearing on the likelihood that a defendant will commit a crime while on bail.

■ **preventive detention** Holding a defendant for trial, based on a judge's finding that if the defendant were released on bail, he or she would endanger the safety of any other person and the community or would flee.

■ *United States v. Salerno and Cafero* (1987) Preventive detention provisions of the Bail Reform Act of 1984 are upheld as a legitimate use of government power designed to prevent people from committing crimes while on bail.

CHECKPOINT

ANSWERS

3 What factors affect whether bail is set and how much money or property a defendant must provide to gain pretrial release?

3 Bail decisions are based primarily on the judge's evaluation of the seriousness of the offense and the defendant's prior record. The decisions are influenced by the prosecutor's recommendations and the defense attorney's counterarguments about the defendant's personal qualities and ties to the community.

4 What methods are used to facilitate pretrial release for certain defendants?

4 Police citations, release on own recognizance (ROR), and 10 percent cash bail.

Pretrial Detention

People who are not released before trial must remain in jail. Often called the ultimate ghetto, American jails hold almost 750,000 people on any one day. Most are poor, half are in pretrial detention, and the rest are serving sentences (normally of less than one year) or are waiting to be moved to state prison or to another jurisdiction (Clear, Cole, and Reisig, 2009).

Jails holding pretrial detainees may be crowded and lack education and counseling programs. Spending time in detention can be frightening and difficult as people worry about what will happen to them. Why do you think the suicide rate in jails is higher than that in prisons?

AP Images/Matt York

Urban jails also contain troubled people, many with mental health and drug abuse problems, whom police have swept off the streets. Michael Welch calls this process, in which the police remove socially offensive people from certain areas, "social sanitation" (1994:262). Conditions in jails are often much harsher than those in prisons. People awaiting trial are often held in barracks-like cells with sentenced offenders. Thus, a "presumed innocent" pretrial detainee might spend weeks in the same confined space with troubled people or sentenced felons (Beck, Karberg, and Harrison, 2002).

The period just after arrest is the most frightening and difficult time for suspects. Imagine freely walking the streets one minute and being locked in a small space with a large number of troubled and potentially dangerous cell mates the next. Suddenly, you have no privacy and must share an open toilet with hostile strangers. You have been fingerprinted, photographed, searched, and questioned—treated like the "criminal" that the police and the criminal justice system consider you to be (Schlanger, 2008). You are alone with people whose behavior you cannot predict and left to worry about what might happen. If you are female, you may be placed in a cell by yourself (Steury and Frank, 1990). Given the stressful nature of arrest and jailing, it is little wonder that most jail suicides and psychotic episodes occur during the first hours of detention.

Other factors can make the shock of arrest and detention even worse. Many people are arrested for offenses they committed while under the influence of drugs or alcohol. They may be less able than others to cope with their new situation. Young arrestees who face the risk of being victimized by older, stronger cell mates may sink into depression. Detainees also worry about losing their jobs while in jail, because they do not know if or when they will be released.

As you read the Comparative Perspective concerning pretrial detention in the Philippines, ask yourself whether individual U.S. jails could ever have comparable conditions, especially if the county administering the jail has budget problems that hinder the upgrading of facilities and the training of personnel. What factors help keep detainees in American jails from experiencing the hardships endured by those in jails in the Philippines?

Although most Americans arrested for felonies have their cases adjudicated within three months, 31 percent wait for more than six months and 13 percent for more than a year (T. H. Cohen and Reaves, 2006). Imagine the hardships for the 38 percent of arrestees who cannot gain pretrial release if they are among those who must wait six months or a year before the courts complete the processing of their cases. The

COMPARATIVE PERSPECTIVE

Pretrial Detention in the *PHILIPPINES*

Raymund E. Narag

DESPITE LEGAL PRINCIPLES that say an accused suspect has a right to a speedy trial, pretrial detainees in the Philippines can spend years in jail while undergoing trial. Because jails are so overcrowded and unhealthy, time spent in pretrial detention can actually be a death sentence, as many detainees die from tuberculosis and other communicable diseases. In the Quezon City Jail, where I was held for seven years while wrongly accused of a crime, five detainees die every month.

Jail overcrowding combines with a lack of basic services to make life in jail nearly unbearable. The Quezon City Jail was built to hold 700 people, yet it is used to detain 3,500 suspects. I lived with more than 100 men crammed into a room that was actually only large enough to accommodate ten residents. The money spent on food for detainees is the equivalent of 50 cents per day per detainee. Authorities do not provide clothing, sleeping mats, blankets—or even forks and spoons. Detainees must rely on friends and relatives, if they have any nearby, to provide basic provisions. Diseases spread among detainees who are crowded together and must share eating utensils.

Detainees also face dangers from their fellow inmates, including those who are organized into gangs. They may be beaten or killed if they violate the expected inmate code of behavior. The bleak, overcrowded conditions create both physical and psychological harms. Some detainees fight over scarce resources. Others risk their lives trying to escape. Others suffer from psychological problems from the pressure, illness, and boredom.

The average stay of detainees in jail is 3.2 years, but some unlucky defendants may be detained as long as 11 years while undergoing trial. The conditions create pressure on detainees to plead guilty in order to be transferred to the national penitentiary to serve a prison sentence. Ironically, among those who wait in jail for their day in court, only 18 percent will be found "guilty," as the police are frequently ineffective and disorganized in actually discovering and presenting evidence to prove an individual's guilt. Yet, many of the detainees who are found to be "not guilty" will already have had their lives destroyed, as their health has been ruined or their stay in jail has filled them with hate and led them to commit crimes that will bring them back to jail again. The people in jail who must endure these conditions are nearly all poor and uneducated. In light of how few detainees are proved to be guilty of crimes, one must ask whether jails are really holding the powerless people of society rather than the real criminals.

Source: This description of pretrial detention in the Philippines was written specifically for this book by Raymund E. Narag. He was held in jail for seven years for a crime that he did not commit and was eventually declared to be innocent by the Regional Trial Court. While in jail, he organized a literacy program and earned a diploma from the University of the Philippines through correspondence courses. After his release, he advised his country's Supreme Court on criminal justice issues, wrote a book entitled *Freedom and Death inside the City Jail*, and was awarded a Fulbright Fellowship to study in the United States. He is currently a doctoral student in criminal justice at Michigan State University.

psychological and economic hardships faced by pretrial detainees and their families can be significant and prolonged.

Pretrial detention not only imposes stresses and hardships that may reach a crisis level; it can also affect the outcomes of cases (McCoy, 2007). People in jail can give little help to their attorneys. They cannot help find witnesses and perform other useful tasks on their own behalf. In addition, they may feel pressured to plead guilty in order to end their indefinite stay in jail. Even if they believe that they should not be convicted of the crime charged, they may prefer to start serving a prison or jail sentence with a definite end point. Some may even gain quicker release on probation or in a community corrections program by pleading guilty, whereas they might stay in jail for a longer period by insisting on their innocence and awaiting a trial.

CHECKPOINT

ANSWERS

5 *What categories of people are found in jails?*

5 Pretrial detainees for whom bail was not set or those who are too poor to pay the bail amount required, people serving short sentences for misdemeanors, people convicted of felonies awaiting transfer to prison, and people with psychological or substance abuse problems who have been swept off the streets.

6 *What are the sources of stress for people in jail awaiting trial?*

6 Living with difficult and potentially dangerous cell mates; uncertainty about what will happen to their case, family, and job, as well as inability to contribute to preparing a defense.

Plea Bargaining

For the vast majority of cases, plea bargaining—also known as negotiating a settlement, copping a plea, or copping out—is the most important step in the criminal justice process. Very few cases go to trial; instead, a negotiated guilty plea arrived at through the interactions of prosecutors, defense lawyers, and judges determines what will happen to most defendants. The courtroom workgroup, as discussed in Chapter 7, uses plea bargaining to determine the outcomes of cases quickly and efficiently in those courthouses where the same actors work together repeatedly in processing cases. Many people believe that plea bargaining permits offenders to avoid appropriate punishments. As you read "Criminal Justice: Myth and Reality," consider your views on the topic.

Quick resolution of cases through negotiated guilty pleas became common and was upheld by the Supreme Court in the 1971 case of *Santobello v. New York*. In the decision, Chief Justice Warren Burger described plea bargaining in favorable terms in ruling that prosecutors were obliged to fulfill promises made during plea negotiations. According to Burger, "'Plea bargaining' is an essential component of the administration of justice. Properly administered, it is to be encouraged" because it saves time and criminal justice resources while also protecting the community.

In 1976, Justice Potter Stewart revealed the heart and soul of plea bargaining when he wrote in *Blackledge v. Allison* that plea bargaining "can benefit all concerned" in a criminal case. There are advantages for defendants, prosecutors, defense attorneys, and judges. Defendants can have their cases completed more quickly and know what the punishment will be, instead of facing the uncertainty of a judge's sentencing decision. Moreover, the defendant is likely to receive less than the maximum punishment that might have been imposed after a trial. Prosecutors are not being "soft on crime" when they plea bargain. Instead, they gain an easy conviction, even in cases in which enough evidence may not have been gathered to convince a jury to convict the defendant. They also save time and resources by disposing of cases without having to prepare for a trial. Private defense attorneys also save the time needed to prepare for a trial. They earn their fee quickly and can move on to the next case. Similarly, plea bargaining helps public defenders cope with large caseloads. Judges, too, avoid time-consuming trials and the prospect of having to decide what sentence to impose on the defendant. Instead, they often adopt the sentence recommended by the prosecutor in consultation with the defense attorney, provided that it is within the range of sentences that they deem appropriate for a given crime and offender.

Because plea bargaining benefits all involved, it is little wonder that it still exists, even when prosecutors, legislators, or judges claim that they wish to abolish it. In California, for example, voters decided to ban plea bargaining for serious felony cases. Research showed, however, that when plea bargaining was barred in the felony trial courts, it did not disappear. It simply occurred earlier in the justice process, at the suspect's first appearance in the lower-level municipal court (McCoy, 1993). Efforts to abolish plea bargaining may also result in bargaining over the charges instead of over the sentence that will be recommended in exchange for a guilty plea. If a prosecutor forbids his or her staff to plea bargain, judges may become more involved in negotiating and facilitating guilty pleas that result in predictable punishments for offenders. Consider the ban on plea bargaining for several serious violent crimes in Memphis, Tennessee, described in the Close Up box.

■ Exchange Relationships in Plea Bargaining

As we have seen, plea bargaining is a set of exchange relationships in which the prosecutor, the defense attorney, the defendant, and sometimes the judge participate.

Criminal Justice:
MYTH AND REALITY

COMMON BELIEF: Plea bargaining defeats the purposes of the criminal justice system by permitting defense attorneys to arrange for offenders to avoid properly severe punishments for their crimes.

When members of the public believe that a criminal offender has received a "light" sentence or had serious charges reduced, they typically notice that the sentence or charge reduction came as a result of plea bargaining. Thus, they often believe that plea bargaining lets criminals "get off scot-free." In reality, prosecutors maintain significant control over the outcomes of plea bargains. They often file charges despite knowing that they may not have enough evidence to prove a defendant's guilt. However, such charges create pressure on the defendant to plead guilty to something in order to avoid the worst penalties. Recall the discussion in Chapter 7 about the courtroom workgroup's shared understandings concerning the going rate of punishment for particular crimes. These understandings permit the prosecutor, defense attorney, and judge to reach quick agreement on the appropriate charge and sentence without using the court's scarce resources on a trial. The plea bargain in these cases represents the quick arrival at the same case outcome that would otherwise have been produced through the slower, more expensive trial process. In sum, pleading guilty to lesser charges is often merely pleading to the crime for which the prosecution actually would have been able to prove guilt at trial.

■ *Santobello v. New York* (1971) When a guilty plea rests on a promise of a prosecutor, the promise must be fulfilled.

CLOSE UP

Banning Plea Bargaining in Tennessee

IN JANUARY 1997, William Gibbons, the district attorney for Shelby County, Tennessee, which includes the city of Memphis, introduced a policy of refusing to reduce charges of first- and second-degree murder and charges of robbery or rape that involved the use of a deadly weapon. Under the policy, anyone indicted for these crimes must either plead guilty to the charge specified or go to trial. The operation of the policy raises interesting questions about the impact of bans on plea bargaining.

The District Attorney's Office hoped that the "no deal" policy and the resulting tough sentences would deter other potential offenders from committing violent crimes. Thus, the ban on plea bargaining was accompanied by a public relations campaign to spread the word about the new policy. "No Deal" signs, decals, and bumper stickers were distributed to businesses and neighborhood watch groups.

The District Attorney's Office claims that the ban "had a positive impact in reducing violent felonies." But can one truly know whether crime reductions are due to the plea-bargaining policy rather than a general social trend?

The District Attorney's Office says that the effectiveness of the new policy is due to cooperation between the prosecutor and local law enforcement agencies. Under the new policy, representatives of the District Attorney's Office meet with representatives of the Memphis Police Department and the Shelby County Sheriff's Office to screen cases involving the violent crimes covered by the policy. This early review helps ensure that the DA's Office has a good case with strong evidence before someone is charged and a proposed indictment is presented to the grand jury.

By filtering out cases for which the most serious charges are not provable, does this review and screening process perhaps fulfill the function served by plea bargaining in other cities? Elsewhere, the plea negotiation process involves discussions between defense attorneys and prosecutors about the provable facts of a case so that both sides can reach agreement about the going rate of punishment for that particular offender and crime. In effect, then, might the Memphis screening process really just produce the same results in "no deal" cases that would have been produced anyway through plea negotiations in other cities?

In reality, the Memphis ban on plea bargaining is not absolute, even for the specified crimes to which it applies. There can be "exceptions based on legal, factual, or ethical grounds [that] must be approved by a supervisor [in the District Attorney's Office] and documented in writing." Does the possibility of exceptions create incentives for defense attorneys to seek special deals for their clients? Does it create opportunities for prosecutors to use discretion to reduce charges against particular defendants or the clients of particular attorneys?

Consider the following results from the "no deal" policy in 2007. Out of 560 "no deal" cases, 301 defendants entered guilty pleas to the charges and an additional 83 defendants were convicted at trial. The most interesting number represents the 176 defendants who entered "guilty to lesser charges or [had their] cases dismissed" under the "no deal" system. According to the prosecutor's office, the charge reductions were usually the result of the inability of the police to locate crucial witnesses needed for gaining a conviction at trial. Presumably, the dismissals also stemmed from a lack of sufficient evidence. In light of those numbers, does the "no deal" policy really live up to its name? Would the public be surprised to learn that a "no deal" policy permits so many plea bargains resulting in reduced charges? Alternatively, in light of how the criminal justice system operates and its dependence on witnesses and discretionary decisions, would it be unrealistic to have a policy in which there were actually never any charge reductions?

RESEARCHING THE INTERNET

To see a report evaluating Alaska's early effort to abolish plea bargaining, read the report of the Alaska Judicial Council at the corresponding website listed on the Cole/Smith Criminal Justice in America Companion Website: http://www.cengage.com/criminaljustice/cole.

FOR CRITICAL ANALYSIS

Are the "no deal" policy and the accompanying advertising campaign primarily a public relations effort to gain support and credit for the District Attorney's Office? Is it possible that the district attorney honestly believes that the "no deal" policy has positive benefits even if it may have produced little change? What do you think?

Sources: Thomas D. Henderson, "No Deals Policy," Office of the District Attorney General, 30th Judicial District of Tennessee, 1999, http://www.scdag.com/nodeals/htm#top; Michael J. Sniffen, "Crime Down for 7th Straight Year," Associated Press, October 17, 1999; 2007 Annual Report of District Attorney General's Office, Shelby County, Tennessee, 2008, http://www.scdag.com/Portals/0/annualreport/ar2007.pdf1.

All have specific goals, all try to use the situation to their own advantage, and all are likely to see the exchange as a success.

Plea bargaining does not always occur in a single meeting between the prosecutor and defense attorney. One study showed that plea bargaining is a process in which prosecutors and defense attorneys interact again and again as they move further along in the judicial process. As time passes, the discovery of more evidence or new information about the defendant's background may strengthen the prosecutor's hand (Emmelman, 1996). Often, the prosecution rather than the defense is in the best position to obtain new evidence (Cooney, 1994). However, the defense attorney's position may gain strength if the prosecutor does not wish to spend time preparing for a trial.

In 2009, two Pennsylvania judges, Michael Conahan (back left) and Mark Ciavarella (center), pleaded guilty to wire fraud and income tax fraud charges. They had taken more than $2.6 million in kickback payments from private companies that managed juvenile detention facilities, in exchange for sentencing juvenile offenders to serve time in those facilities. Should officials who violate the public's trust be permitted to gain reduced sentences through plea bargains?

■ Tactics of Prosecutor and Defense

Plea bargaining between defense counsel and prosecutor is a serious game in which friendliness and joking can mask efforts to advance each side's cause. Both sides use various strategies and tactics (Brown, 2009). Each side tries to impress the other with its confidence in its own case while pointing out weaknesses in the other side's case. An unspoken rule of openness and candor usually keeps the relationship on good terms. Little effort is made to conceal information that could later be useful to the other side in the courtroom. Studies show that the outcomes of plea bargaining may depend on the relationships between prosecutors and individual attorneys, as well as the defense counsel's willingness to fight for the client (Champion, 1989).

A tactic that many prosecutors bring to plea-bargaining sessions is the multiple-offense indictment. Multiple-offense charges are especially important to prosecutors in handling difficult cases—for instance, those in which the victim is reluctant to provide information, the value of the stolen item is unclear, or the evidence may not be reliable. Prosecutors often file charges of selling a drug when they know they can probably convict only for possession. Because the accused persons know that the penalty for selling is much greater, they are tempted to plead guilty to the lesser charge rather than risk a longer sentence, even if the probability of conviction on the more serious charge is uncertain.

Defense attorneys may threaten to ask for a jury trial if concessions are not made. To strengthen their hand further, they may also file pretrial motions that require a formal response by the prosecutor. Another tactic is to seek to reschedule pretrial activities in the hope that, with delay, witnesses will become unavailable, media attention will die down, and memories of the crime will grow weaker by the time of the trial. Rather than resort to such legal tactics, however, some attorneys prefer to bargain on the basis of friendship. Read about the position of defense attorney in "Careers in Criminal Justice" and consider whether you would want to be involved in plea bargaining and advising defendants.

■ Pleas without Bargaining

Studies have shown that in many courts give-and-take plea bargaining does not occur for certain types of cases, yet they have as many guilty pleas as do other courts (Eisenstein, Flemming, and Nardulli, 1988). The term *bargaining* may be misleading

CAREERS IN CRIMINAL JUSTICE

Criminal Defense Attorney

ABRAHAM V. HUTT, CRIMINAL DEFENSE ATTORNEY
PRIVATE PRACTICE, DENVER, COLORADO

DEFENSE ATTORNEYS must interview their clients and relevant witnesses when hired by a defendant or appointed by a court to handle criminal cases. These interviews may occur under difficult circumstances in jails or on street corners in tough neighborhoods. Defense attorneys must find and evaluate all relevant evidence in light of how they anticipate the prosecution will present its version of the case. They spend a significant amount of time in offices doing legal research, preparing legal documents, and reviewing legal papers. They also must appear in court to represent their clients at hearings where bail is set and judges consider whether there is sufficient evidence for a case to move forward. They discuss possible plea agreements with prosecutors. Occasionally, one of their cases will move through the entire justice process and become the subject of a trial. In the courtroom, defense attorneys present arguments and evidence to show the weaknesses in the prosecution's case. When a guilty verdict is issued, they may continue to represent their clients in the appeals process.

To become a lawyer in the United States, people must earn a four-year college degree in any subject before going to law school for three years of postgraduate study. Gaining admission to law school is a competitive process, so people interested in legal careers must work hard during college, earn good grades, and gain good scores on the Law School Admissions Test (LSAT).

After graduating from law school, prospective lawyers must pass a state's bar exam in order to receive a license to practice law or serve as a judge in that state. Each state has its own bar exam, which typically lasts two days. A separate ethics exam may also be required. In most states, one day is devoted to a six-hour multiple-choice test on six subjects that are common to all states (contract, criminal, tort, evidence, property, and constitutional law). The other day involves six hours of essays on 12 or more subjects focused on state law, including business associations, taxation, and family law.

During college, Abraham Hutt spent two summers as an intern with the Colorado State Public Defender's Office, where he worked as an investigator interviewing witnesses and helping lawyers prepare to represent poor defendants. For one year after college, he worked as an investigator for a former public defender who became a private practice attorney representing criminal defendants who could afford to pay for legal representation. He then went to law school for three years, passed the Colorado bar exam, and worked in a small law firm that specialized in criminal defense. Eventually, he started his own law firm that focused on criminal cases.

One of the many difficult things about counseling clients is advising them to accept plea bargains even when I believe they are innocent. I may advise them to plead guilty and accept a lesser punishment when they face the realistic possibility of horrendous consequences from a mandatory sentence if found guilty by a jury.

---

in that it implies haggling. Many scholars argue that guilty pleas emerge after the prosecutor, the defense attorney, and sometimes the judge have reached an agreement to "settle the facts" (Utz, 1978). In this view, the parties first study the facts of a case. What were the circumstances of the event? Was it really an assault or was it more of a shoving match? Did the victim antagonize the accused? Each side may hope to persuade the other that its view of the defendant's actions is backed up by provable facts. The prosecution wants the defense to believe that strong evidence proves its version of the event. The defense attorney wants to convince the prosecution that the evidence is not solid and that there is a risk of acquittal if the case is heard by a jury.

In some cases, the evidence is strong and the defense attorney has little hope of persuading the prosecutor otherwise. Through their discussions, the prosecutor and defense attorney seek to reach a shared view of the provable facts in the case. Once they agree on the facts, they will both know the appropriate charge, and they can agree on a sentence according to the locally defined going rate. At that point, a guilty plea can be entered without any formal bargaining, because both sides agree on what the case is worth in terms of the seriousness of the charge and the usual punishment.

This process may be thought of as *implicit plea bargaining,* because shared understandings create the expectation that a guilty plea will lead to a less-than-maximum sentence, even without any exchange or bargaining.

As we saw in Chapter 7, the going rates for sentences for particular crimes and offenders depend on local values and sentencing patterns. Often, both the prosecutor and the defense attorney belong to a particular local legal culture and thus share an understanding about how cases should be handled. On the basis of their experiences in interacting with other attorneys and judges, they become keenly aware of local practices in the treatment of cases and offenders (Worden, 1995). Thus, they may both know right away what the sentence will be for a first-time burglar or second-time robber. The sentence may differ in another courthouse, because the local legal culture and going rates vary.

▪ Legal Issues in Plea Bargaining

▪ **Boykin v. Alabama (1969)** Before a judge may accept a plea of guilty, defendants must state that they are making the plea voluntarily.

In *Boykin v. Alabama* (1969), the U.S. Supreme Court ruled that, before a judge may accept a plea of guilty, defendants must state that the plea was made voluntarily. Judges have created standard forms with questions for the defendant to affirm in open court before the plea is accepted. Trial judges also must learn whether the defendant understands the consequences of pleading guilty and ensure that the plea is not obtained through pressure.

▪ **North Carolina v. Alford (1970)** A plea of guilty by a defendant who maintains his or her innocence may be accepted for the purpose of a lesser sentence.

Can a trial court accept a guilty plea if the defendant claims to be innocent? In *North Carolina v. Alford* (1970), the Court allowed a defendant to enter a guilty plea for the purpose of gaining a lesser sentence, even though he maintained that he was innocent. However, the Supreme Court also stated that trial judges should not accept such a plea unless a factual basis exists for believing that the defendant is in fact guilty.

▪ **Ricketts v. Adamson (1987)** Defendants must uphold the plea agreement or suffer the consequences.

▪ **Bordenkircher v. Hayes (1978)** A defendant's rights were not violated by a prosecutor who warned that refusing to enter a guilty plea would result in a harsher sentence.

Another issue is whether the plea agreement will be fulfilled. If the prosecutor has promised to recommend a lenient sentence, the promise must be kept (*Santobello v. New York*, 1971). As ruled in *Ricketts v. Adamson* (1987), defendants must also keep their side of the bargain, such as testifying against a codefendant. However, in *Bordenkircher v. Hayes* (1978), the justices ruled that prosecutors may threaten to seek more-serious charges, as long as such charges are supported by evidence, if defendants refuse to plead guilty. Some scholars criticize this decision as imposing pressures on a defendant that are not permitted elsewhere in the justice process (O'Hear, 2006).

▪ Criticisms of Plea Bargaining

Among the many concerns about plea bargaining, two primary criticisms stand out. The first argues that plea bargaining is unfair because defendants give up some of their constitutional rights, especially the right to trial by jury. The second stresses sentencing policy and points out that plea bargaining reduces society's interest in appropriate punishments for crimes. In urban areas with high caseloads, harried judges and prosecutors are said to make concessions based on administrative needs, resulting in lighter sentences than those required by the penal code.

Plea bargaining also comes under fire because it is hidden from judicial scrutiny. Because the agreement is most often made at an early stage, the judge has little information about the crime or the defendant and thus cannot adequately evaluate the case. The result of "bargain justice" is that the judge, the public, and sometimes even the defendant cannot know for sure who got what from whom in exchange for what.

Other critics believe that overuse of plea bargaining breeds disrespect and even contempt for the law. They say criminals look at the judicial process as a game or a sham, much like other "deals" made in life.

Critics also contend that it is unjust to penalize people who assert their right to a trial, by giving them stiffer sentences than they would have received if they had pleaded guilty. The evidence here is unclear, although it is widely believed that an extra penalty is imposed on defendants who take up the court's time by asserting their right to a trial (Spohn, 1992). Critics note that federal sentencing guidelines also encourage avoidance of trial, because they include a two-point deduction from an offender's base score for a guilty plea—thus lowering the sentence—for "acceptance of responsibility" (McCoy, 1995).

Finally, another concern about plea bargaining is that innocent people will plead guilty to acts that they did not commit. Although it is hard to know how often this happens, some defendants have entered guilty pleas when they have not committed the offense (Bowen, 2008). It may be hard for middle-class people to understand how anyone could possibly plead guilty when innocent. However, people with little education and low social status may lack the confidence to say "no" to an attorney who strongly encourages them to plead guilty.

People may also lack confidence in court processes. What if you feared that a jury might convict you and send you to prison for 20 years based on circumstantial evidence (such as being in the vicinity of the crime and wearing the same color shirt as the robber that day)? Might you plead guilty and take a five-year sentence, even if you knew that you were innocent? How much confidence do you have that juries and judges will always reach the correct result? Poor people in particular may feel helpless in the stressful climate of the courthouse and jail. If they lack faith in the system's ability to protect their rights and find them not guilty, they may accept a lighter punishment rather than risk being convicted for a serious offense.

Examine the scene in "A Question of Ethics" at the end of the chapter. Are all of the courtroom actors behaving in an honest, ethical manner? Does this scene raise questions about how plea bargains operate?

CHECKPOINT

ANSWERS

❼ *Why does plea bargaining occur?*

❼ It serves the self-interest of all relevant actors: defendants gain certain, less-than-maximum sentences; prosecutors gain swift, sure convictions; defense attorneys get prompt resolution of cases; judges preside over fewer time-consuming trials.

❽ *What are the criticisms of plea bargaining?*

❽ Defendants might be pressured to surrender their rights; society's mandated criminal punishments are improperly reduced.

Trial: The Exceptional Case

If cases are not dismissed or terminated through plea bargaining, they move forward for trial. The seriousness of the charge is probably the most important factor influencing the decision to go to trial. Murder, felonious assault, or rape—all charges that bring long prison terms—may require judge and jury, unless the defendant fears a certain conviction and therefore seeks a negotiated plea deal. When the penalty is harsh, however, many defendants seem willing to risk the possibility of conviction at trial. Table 8.1 shows the differences in the percentages of defendants going to trial for offenses of varying severity. Notice that crimes with greater punishments—murder, manslaughter, and rape—produce a higher percentage of trials than do other crimes.

Sitting between his attorneys, defendant Neil Entwistle tearfully watches the presentation of evidence against him in a Massachusetts courtroom in 2008. The jury convicted him of double murder for killing his wife and infant daughter. What other kinds of cases are likely to be processed through jury trials?

■ **bench trials** Trials conducted by a judge who acts as fact finder and determines issues of law. No jury participates.

■ **jury** A panel of citizens selected according to law and sworn to determine matters of fact in a criminal case and to deliver a verdict of guilty or not guilty.

Trials determine the fates of very few defendants. Although the right to trial by jury is ingrained in American ideology—it is mentioned in the Declaration of Independence, the U.S. Constitution and three of its amendments, and myriad opinions of the U.S. Supreme Court—year in and year out fewer than 9 percent of felony cases go to trial. Of these, only about half are jury trials; the rest are **bench trials**, presided over by a judge without a **jury**. In 2004, trials produced only 3 percent of felony convictions in the nation's 75 most populous counties (Kyckelhahn and Cohen, 2008). Defendants may choose a bench trial if they believe a judge will be more capable of making an objective decision, especially if the charges or evidence are likely to arouse emotional reactions in jurors.

The rates of trials also vary from city to city. This difference stems, in part, from the local legal culture. Think about how prosecutors' policies or sentencing practices in different cities may increase or decrease the incentives for a defendant to plead guilty. In addition, defense attorneys and prosecutors in different courthouses may have their own understandings about which cases should produce a plea bargain because of agreements (or disagreements) about the provable facts and the going rate of sentences for an offense.

TABLE 8.1	Percentage of Felony Convictions by Trial and Guilty Pleas, by Offense

Defendants facing severe punishments for the most-serious offenses are mostly likely to go to trial rather than plead guilty.

Offense	Bench Trial	Jury Trial	Guilty Plea
All offenses	3%	2%	95%
Murder/nonnegligent manslaughter	4	27	69
Rape	3	13	83
Robbery	2	6	92
Aggravated assault	4	4	92
Weapons offenses	4	3	93
Drug trafficking	2	2	96
Burglary	3	2	95
Motor vehicle theft	1	2	97
Fraud/forgery	4	1	95

Source: *Sourcebook of Criminal Justice Statistics, 2008* (Washington, DC: Bureau of Justice Statistics, 2008), http://www.albany.edu/sourcebook, Table 5.46.2004.

Trials take considerable time and resources. Attorneys frequently spend weeks or months preparing—gathering evidence, responding to their opponents' motions, planning trial strategy, and setting aside a day to several weeks to present the case in court. From the perspective of judges, prosecutors, and defense attorneys, plea bargaining presents an attractive alternative for purposes of completing cases quickly.

■ Jury Trial

Trials are based on the idea that the prosecution and defense will compete as adversaries before a judge and jury so that the truth will emerge. As such, the rules of criminal law, procedure, and evidence govern the conduct of the trial. Above the battle, the judge ensures that the rules are followed and that the jury impartially evaluates the evidence and reflects the community's interests. In a jury trial, the jury alone evaluates the facts in a case. The adversarial process and inclusion of jurors in decision making often make trial outcomes difficult to predict. The verdict hinges not only on the nature of the evidence but also on the effectiveness of the prosecution and defense and on the jurors' attitudes. Does this adversarial and citizen-based process provide the best mechanism for finding the truth and doing justice in our most serious criminal cases?

However one assesses their effectiveness, juries perform six vital functions in the criminal justice system:

1. Prevent government oppression by safeguarding citizens against arbitrary law enforcement

2. Determine whether the accused is guilty on the basis of the evidence presented

3. Represent diverse community interests so that no one set of values or biases dominates decision making

4. Serve as a buffer between the accused and the accuser

5. Promote knowledge about the criminal justice system by learning about it through the jury duty process

6. Symbolize the rule of law and the community foundation that supports the criminal justice system

As a symbol of law, juries demonstrate to the public, as well as to defendants, that decisions about depriving individuals of their liberty will be made carefully by a group of citizens who represent the community's values. In addition, juries provide the primary element of direct democracy in the judicial branch of government.

Through participation on juries, citizens use their votes to determine the outcomes of cases (C. E. Smith, 1994). This branch of government, which is dominated by judges and lawyers, offers few other opportunities for citizens to shape judicial decisions directly. In addition, as indicated by the responses in "What Americans Think," jury service may help to maintain jurors' confidence in the justice system.

In the United States, a jury in a criminal trial traditionally comprises 12 citizens, but some states now allow as few as 6 citizens to make up a jury. This reform was recommended to modernize court procedures and reduce expenses. It costs less for the court to contact, process, and pay a smaller number of jurors. The use of small juries was upheld by the Supreme Court in ***Williams v. Florida*** **(1970).** Six states use juries with fewer than 12 members in noncapital felony cases, and a larger number of states use small juries for misdemeanors. In *Burch v. Louisiana* (1979), the Supreme Court ruled that 6-member juries must vote unanimously to convict a defendant, but unanimity is not required for larger juries. Some states permit juries to convict defendants by votes of 10–2 or 9–3. The change to 6-person juries has its critics, who charge that the smaller group is less representative of the conflicting views in the community and too quick to bring in a verdict (A. R. Amar, 1997).

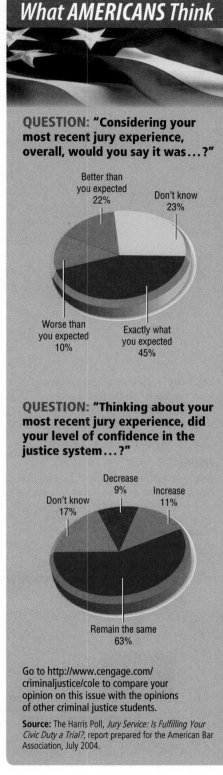

What AMERICANS Think

QUESTION: "Considering your most recent jury experience, overall, would you say it was...?"

- Better than you expected 22%
- Don't know 23%
- Worse than you expected 10%
- Exactly what you expected 45%

QUESTION: "Thinking about your most recent jury experience, did your level of confidence in the justice system...?"

- Decrease 9%
- Increase 11%
- Don't know 17%
- Remain the same 63%

Go to http://www.cengage.com/criminaljustice/cole to compare your opinion on this issue with the opinions of other criminal justice students.

Source: The Harris Poll, *Jury Service: Is Fulfilling Your Civic Duty a Trial?*, report prepared for the American Bar Association, July 2004.

■ ***Williams v. Florida*** **(1970)** Juries of fewer than 12 members are constitutional.

■ The Trial Process

The trial process generally follows eight steps: (1) selection of the jury, (2) opening statements by prosecution and defense, (3) presentation of the prosecution's evidence and witnesses, (4) presentation of the defense's evidence and witnesses, (5) presentation of rebuttal witnesses, (6) closing arguments by each side, (7) instruction of the jury by the judge, and (8) decision by the jury. The details of each step may vary according to each state's rules. Although the proportion of trials may be small, understanding each step in the process and considering the broader impact of this institution are both important.

Jury Selection   The selection of the jury, outlined in Figure 8.3, is a crucial first step in the trial process. Because people always apply their experiences, values, and biases in their decision making, prosecutors and defense attorneys actively seek to identify potential jurors who may be automatically sympathetic or hostile to their side. When they believe they have identified such potential jurors, they try to find ways to exclude those who may sympathize with the other side, while striving to keep those who may favor their side. Lawyers do not necessarily achieve these goals, because the selection of jurors involves the decisions and interactions of prosecutors, defense attorneys, and judges, each of whom has different objectives in the selection process.

Jurors are selected from among the citizens whose names have been placed in the jury pool. The composition of the jury pool tremendously affects the ultimate composition of the trial jury. In most states, the jury pool is drawn from lists of registered voters, but research has shown that nonwhites, the poor, and young people register to vote at much lower rates than does the rest of the population. As a result, members of these groups are underrepresented on juries (Fukurai, 1996).

In many cases, the presence or absence of these groups may make no difference in the ultimate verdict. In some situations, however, members of these groups may interpret evidence differently than do their older, white, middle-class counterparts who dominate the composition of juries (Ugwuegbu, 1999). For example, the poor, nonwhites, and young people may be more likely to have had unpleasant experiences with police officers and therefore be less willing to believe automatically that police officers always tell the truth. Today courts may supplement the lists of registered voters with other lists, such as those for driver's licenses, hunting licenses, and utility bills, in order to diversify the jury pool (Newman, 1996). Several states are also considering increases in jurors' daily pay; Texas, for example, has gone from $6 per day to $40 per day in trials lasting more than one day. It is hoped that such efforts will make jury service more attractive for poor people who might otherwise avoid participating because they cannot afford to lose pay by missing work (Axtman, 2005a).

Only about 15 percent of adult Americans have ever been called for jury duty. Retired people and homemakers with grown children tend to be overrepresented on juries, because they are less inconvenienced by serving and are often less likely to ask to be excused because of job responsibilities or child care problems. To make jury duty less onerous, many states have moved to a system called "one-day-one-trial," in which jurors serve for either one day or for the duration of one trial.

The courtroom process of **voir dire** (which means "to speak the truth") is used to question prospective jurors in order to screen out those who might be biased or otherwise incapable of making a fair decision. Attorneys for each side, as well as the judge, may question jurors about their background, knowledge

■ **voir dire**   A questioning of prospective jurors to screen out people the attorneys think might be biased or otherwise incapable of delivering a fair verdict.

FIGURE 8.3

Jury selection process for a 12-member jury
Potential jurors are drawn at random from a source list. From this pool, a panel is selected and presented for duty. The voir dire examination may remove some, whereas others will be seated. The 14 jurors selected include two alternates.

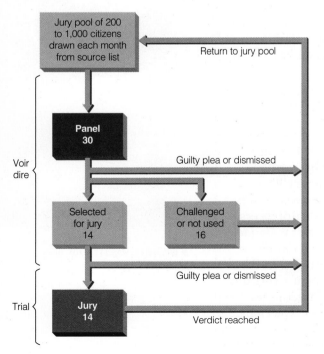

of the case, and acquaintance with any participants in the case. Jurors will also be asked whether they or their immediate family members have been crime victims or otherwise involved in a criminal case in a manner that may prevent them from making open-minded decisions about the evidence and the defendant. If a juror's responses indicate that he or she will not be able to make fair decisions, the juror may be **challenged for cause**. The judge must rule on the challenge, but if the judge agrees with the attorney, then the juror is excused from that specific case (Arterton, 2008). There is usually no limit on the number of jurors that the attorneys may challenge for cause. However, identifying all of a juror's biases through brief questioning is not easy (Dillehay and Sandys, 1996).

Although challenges for cause ultimately fall under the judge's control, the prosecution and defense can exert their own control over the jury's composition through the use of **peremptory challenges**. With these, the prosecution and defense can exclude prospective jurors without giving specific reasons. Attorneys use peremptory challenges to exclude jurors who they think will be unsympathetic to their arguments (Hoffman, 1999). Attorneys usually use hunches about which jurors to challenge; little evidence suggests that they can accurately identify which jurors will sympathize with their side or not (M. S. White, 1995). Normally, the defense is allowed eight to ten peremptory challenges, and the prosecution six to eight.

The use of peremptory challenges has raised concerns that attorneys can use them to exclude, for example, African American jurors when an African American is on trial (Kennedy, 1997) or Latino jurors when there is a Latino defendant (Enriquez and Clark, 2007). In a series of decisions in the late 1980s and early 1990s (such as *Batson v. Kentucky*, 1986), the Supreme Court prohibited using peremptory challenges to systematically exclude potential jurors because of their race or gender. In practice, however, the enforcement of this prohibition is up to the trial judge (C. E. Smith and Ochoa, 1996). If a trial judge is willing to accept flimsy excuses for race-based and gender-based exclusions, then the attorneys can ignore the ban on discrimination (Bray, 1992).

Some lawyers say that trials are won or lost in jury selection. If a lawyer succeeds in seating a favorable jury, he or she may have a receptive audience that will readily support the lawyer's arguments and evidence.

Opening Statements   After the jury has been selected, the trial begins. The clerk reads the complaint (indictment or information) detailing the charges, and the prosecutor and the defense attorney may, if they desire, make opening statements to the jury to summarize the position that each side intends to take. The statements are not evidence. The jury is not supposed to regard the attorneys' statements as proving or disproving anything about the case.

Presentation of the Prosecution's Evidence   One of the basic protections of the American criminal justice system is the assumption that the defendant is innocent until proved guilty. The prosecution carries the burden of proving beyond a reasonable doubt, within the demands of the court procedures and rules of evidence, that the individual named in the indictment committed the crime. This does not mean that absolute certainty is required, only that the evidence sufficiently excludes all reasonable doubt.

In presenting evidence to the jury, the prosecution must establish a case showing that the defendant is guilty. Evidence is classified as real evidence, demonstrative evidence, testimony, direct evidence, and circumstantial evidence. **Real evidence** might include such objects as a weapon, business records, fingerprints, or stolen property. These are real objects involved in the crime. **Demonstrative evidence** is presented for jurors to see and understand without testimony. Real evidence is one form of demonstrative evidence; other forms include maps, X-rays, photographs, models, and diagrams. Most evidence in a criminal trial, however, consists of the **testimony** of witnesses. Witnesses at a trial must be legally competent. Thus, the judge may be required to determine whether the witness whose testimony is challenged has the intelligence

challenge for cause Removal of a prospective juror by showing that he or she has some bias or some other legal disability. The number of such challenges available to attorneys is unlimited.

peremptory challenge Removal of a prospective juror without giving any reason. Attorneys are allowed a limited number of such challenges.

real evidence Physical evidence—such as a weapons, records, fingerprints, and stolen property—involved in the crime.

demonstrative evidence Evidence that is not based on witness testimony but that demonstrates information relevant to the crime, such as maps, X-rays, and photographs; includes real evidence involved in the crime.

testimony Oral evidence provided by a legally competent witness.

■ **direct evidence** Eyewitness accounts.

■ **circumstantial evidence** Evidence provided by a witness from which a jury must infer a fact.

to tell the truth and the ability to recall what was seen. Witnesses with inadequate intelligence or mental problems might not be regarded as qualified to present testimony. **Direct evidence** refers to eyewitness accounts such as "I saw John Smith fire the gun." **Circumstantial evidence** requires that the jury infer a fact from what the witness observed: "I saw John Smith walk behind his house with a gun. A few minutes later I heard a gun go off, and then Mr. Smith walked toward me holding a gun." The witness's observation that Smith had a gun and that the witness then heard a gun go off does not provide direct evidence that Smith fired his gun; however, the jury may link the described facts and infer that Smith fired his gun. After a witness has given testimony, counsel for the other side may cross-examine him or her.

The attorney for each side challenges the other side's presentation of evidence. If evidence violates the rules, reflects untrustworthy hearsay, is a statement of opinion, or is not relevant to the issues in the case, an attorney will object to the presentation of it. In effect, the attorney is asking the judge to rule that the jury cannot consider the opponent's questionable evidence.

After the prosecution has presented all of the state's evidence against the defendant, the court is informed that the people's case rests. It is common for the defense then to ask the court to direct the jury to bring forth a verdict of not guilty. Such a motion is based on the defense argument that the state has not presented enough evidence to prove its case. If the motion is sustained by the judge (it rarely is), the trial ends; if it is overruled, the defense presents its evidence.

Prosecutors and defense attorneys present various forms of evidence during trials, including physical objects ("real evidence") as well as witness testimony. Do you think that the communication skills and persuasiveness of the attorneys could distract the jurors' attention from the actual evidence presented in the case?

AP Images/Lawrence K. Ho, pool

Presentation of the Defense's Evidence The defense is not required to answer the case presented by the prosecution. As it is the state's responsibility to prove the case beyond a reasonable doubt, it is theoretically possible—and in fact sometimes happens—that the defense rests its case immediately, as we have seen. Usually, however, the accused's attorney employs one strategy or a combination of three strategies: (1) contrary evidence is introduced to rebut or cast doubt on the state's case, (2) an alibi is offered, or (3) an affirmative defense is presented. As discussed in Chapter 3, defenses include self-defense, insanity, duress, and necessity.

A key issue for the defense is whether the accused will take the stand. The Fifth Amendment protection against self-incrimination means that the defendant does not have to testify. The Supreme Court has ruled that the prosecutor may not comment on, nor can the jury draw inferences from, the defendant's decision not to appear in his or her own defense. The decision is not made lightly, because if the defendant does testify, the prosecution may cross-examine. *Cross-examination,* which is questioning by the opposing attorney, is broader than direct examination. The prosecutor may question the defendant not only about the crime but also about his or her past, including past criminal convictions. On the other hand, if the defendant does not testify, jurors may make assumptions about the defendant's guilt, even though they have been instructed not to do so.

For example, when Michael Skakel, a cousin of the Kennedy family, was convicted in 2002 of bludgeoning a girl with a golf club 27 years earlier as a teenager, he never took the witness stand in his own defense. The prosecution gained the conviction based on testimony from several witnesses who claimed that Skakel had told them years earlier about killing a girl with a golf club. Skakel's attorneys used an alibi defense by presenting testimony from witnesses who said that he had been at home watching television with friends at the time of the murder. The defense also sought to cast suspicion on another suspect. The jury, however, accepted the version of events presented by the prosecution's witnesses and, upon conviction, Skakel received a sentence of 20 years to life (Goldman, 2002).

Presentation of Rebuttal Witnesses   When the defense's case is complete, the prosecution may present witnesses whose testimony is designed to discredit or counteract testimony presented on behalf of the defendant. If the prosecution brings rebuttal witnesses, the defense has the opportunity to question them and to present new witnesses in rebuttal.

Closing Arguments by Each Side   When each side has completed its presentation of the evidence, the prosecution and defense make closing arguments to the jury. The attorneys review the evidence of the case for the jury, presenting interpretations of the evidence that favor their own side. The prosecutor may use the summation to connect the individual pieces of evidence in a way that forms a basis for concluding that the defendant is guilty. The defense may set forth the applicable law and try to show that the prosecution has not proved its case beyond a reasonable doubt. Each side may remind the jury of its duty to evaluate the evidence impartially and not to be swayed by emotion. Yet, some attorneys may hope that the jurors react emotionally, especially if they think that those emotions will benefit their side.

Judge's Instructions to the Jury   The jury decides the facts of the case, but the judge determines the law. Before the jurors depart for the jury room to decide the defendant's fate, the judge instructs them on how the law should guide their decision. The judge may discuss basic legal principles such as proof beyond a reasonable doubt, the legal requirements necessary to show that all the elements have been proved by the prosecution, or the rights of the defendant. More-specific aspects of the law bearing on the decision—such as complicated court rulings on the nature of the insanity defense or the ways certain types of evidence have been gathered—may be included in the judge's instructions. In complicated trials, the judge may spend an entire day instructing the jury.

The concept of **reasonable doubt** forms the heart of the jury system. As we have seen, the prosecution is not required to prove the guilt of the defendant beyond all doubt. Instead, if a juror is

■ **reasonable doubt**   The standard used by a jury to decide if the prosecution has provided enough evidence for conviction.

> satisfied to a moral certainty that this defendant…is guilty of any one of the crimes charged here, you may safely say that you have been convinced beyond a reasonable doubt. If your mind is wavering, or if you are uncertain…you have not been convinced beyond a reasonable doubt and must render a verdict of not guilty. (Phillips, 1977:214)

Listening to the judge may become an ordeal for the jurors, who must hear and understand perhaps two or three hours of instruction on the law and the evidence (Bradley, 1992). It is assumed that somehow jurors will fully absorb these details on first hearing them, so that they will thoroughly understand how they are supposed to decide the case in the jury room (G. P. Kramer and Koenig, 1990). In fact, the jurors may be confused by the instructions and reach a decision through an inaccurate understanding of the law that applies to the case, such as the legal definitions of intent, premeditation, and other elements of the crime that must be proved in order to justify a conviction (Armour, 2008).

Decision by the Jury   After they have heard the case and received the judge's instructions, the jurors retire to a room where they have complete privacy. They elect a foreperson to run the meeting, and deliberations begin. Until now, the jurors have been passive observers of the trial, unable to question witnesses or to discuss the case among themselves; now they can discuss the facts that have been presented. Throughout their deliberations the jurors may be *sequestered*—kept together day and night, away from the influences of newspapers and conversations with family and friends. If jurors are allowed to spend nights at home, they are ordered not to discuss the case with anyone. The jury may request that the judge reread to them portions of the instructions, ask for additional instructions, or hear portions of the transcript detailing what was said by specific witnesses.

If the jury becomes deadlocked and cannot reach a verdict, the trial ends with a hung jury and the prosecutor must decide whether to try the case all over again in front of a new jury. When a verdict is reached, the judge, prosecution, and defense reassemble in the courtroom to hear it. The prosecution or the defense may request that the jury be polled: Each member individually tells his or her vote in open court. This procedure presumably ensures that no juror has felt pressured to agree with the other jurors.

■ Evaluating the Jury System

Early research found that, consistent with theories of group behavior, participation and influence in the jury process are related to social status. Men were found to be more active participants than women, whites more active than minority members, and the better educated more active than those less educated. Much of the discussion in the jury room did not center on the testimony but rather on trial procedures, opinions about the witnesses, and personal reminiscences (Strodtbeck, James, and Hawkins, 1957). In 30 percent of the cases, a vote taken soon after entering the jury room was the only one necessary to reach a verdict; in the rest of the cases, the majority on the first ballot eventually prevailed in 90 percent of the cases (Broeder, 1959). Because of group pressure, only rarely did a single juror produce a hung jury. Although some individual jurors may view the case differently, they may doubt their own views or go along with the others if everyone else disagrees. More-recent findings have upheld the influence of group pressure on decision making (Hastie, Penrod, and Pennington, 1983).

A recent examination of trials in the 75 largest U.S. counties found that 88 percent of bench trials ended in convictions but only 80 percent of jury trials ended so (T. H. Cohen and Reaves, 2006). These numbers alone do not reveal whether judges and juries decide cases differently. However, research on trials provides clues about differences between these two decision makers.

Juries tend to take a more liberal view of such issues as self-defense than do judges and are likely to minimize the seriousness of an offense if they dislike some characteristic of the victim (S. J. Adler, 1994:200–207). For example, if the victim of an assault is a prostitute, the jury may minimize the assault. Perceived characteristics of the defendant may also influence jurors' assessments of guilt (Abwender and Hough, 2001). Because judges have more experience with the justice process, they are more likely than juries to base their convictions on evidence that researchers characterize as moderately strong (Eisenberg et al., 2005). As explained by the premier jury researchers Neil Vidmar and Valerie Hans (2007:227),

> the jury's distinctive approach of common sense justice, and the judges' greater willingness to convict based on the same evidence, best explain why juries and judges sometimes reach different conclusions. These juror values affect the verdicts primarily in trials in which the evidence is relatively evenly balanced and a verdict for either side could be justified.

CHECKPOINT

ANSWERS

9 What functions do juries serve in the criminal justice system?

9 Safeguard citizens against arbitrary law enforcement, determine the guilt of the accused, represent diverse community interests and values, serve as buffer between accused and accuser, become educated about the justice system, and symbolize the law.

10 What is voir dire?

10 The jury selection process in which lawyers and/or judges ask questions of prospective jurors and make decisions about using peremptory challenges and challenges for cause to shape the jury's composition.

11 What are the stages in the trial process?

11 Jury selection, attorneys' opening statements, presentation of prosecution's evidence, presentation of defense's evidence, presentation of rebuttal witnesses, closing arguments by each side, judge's instructions to the jury, and jury's decision.

Appeals

Imposition of a sentence does not mean that the case is necessarily over; the defendant typically has the right to appeal the verdict to a higher court, and the right to counsel continues through the first appeal (Priehs, 1999). Some states have limited the right to appeal when defendants plead guilty. An **appeal** is based on a claim that one or more errors of law or procedure were made during the investigation, arrest, or trial process (C. E. Smith, 2000b). Such claims usually assert that the trial judge made errors in courtroom rulings or in improperly admitting evidence that the police gathered in violation of some constitutional right. A defendant might base an appeal, for example, on the claim that the judge did not instruct the jury correctly or that a guilty plea was not made voluntarily.

■ **appeal** A request to a higher court that it review actions taken in a trial court.

AP Images/Bob Child

In appellate courts, several judges sit as a group to hear and decide cases. The appeals process provides an opportunity to correct errors that occurred in trial court proceedings. What are the advantages and disadvantages of having a group of appeals court judges decide a case together?

Appeals are based on questions of procedure, not on issues of the defendant's guilt or innocence. The appellate court will not normally second-guess a jury. Instead, it will check to make sure that the trial followed proper procedures. If there were significant errors in the trial, then the conviction is set aside. The defendant may be tried again if the prosecutor decides to pursue the case again. Most criminal defendants must file an appeal shortly after trial to have an appellate court review the case. By contrast, many states provide for an automatic appeal in death penalty cases (Alarcon, 2007). The quality of defense representation is important, because the appeal must usually meet short deadlines and carefully identify appropriate issues (Wasserman, 1990).

A case originating in a state court is first appealed through that state's judicial system. When a state case involves a federal constitutional question, however, a later appeal can go to the U.S. Supreme Court. State courts decide almost four-fifths of all appeals.

Most appeals do not succeed. In almost 80 percent of the cases examined in one study (Chapper and Hanson, 1989), the decision of the trial courts was affirmed. Most of the other decisions produced new trials or resentencing; relatively few decisions (1.9 percent) produced acquittals on appeal.

■ Habeas Corpus

habeas corpus A writ or judicial order requesting the release of a person being detained in a jail, prison, or mental hospital. If a judge finds the person is being held improperly, the writ may be granted and the person released.

After people use their avenues of appeal, they may pursue a writ of habeas corpus if they claim that their federal constitutional rights were violated during the lower-court processes. Known as "the great writ" from its traditional role in English law and its enshrinement in the U.S. Constitution, **habeas corpus** is a judicial order requesting that a judge examine whether an individual is being properly detained in a jail, prison, or mental hospital. If there is no legal basis for the person to be held, then the judge may grant the writ and order the person to be released. In the context of criminal justice, convicted offenders claim that their imprisonment is improper because one of their constitutional rights was violated during the investigation or adjudication of their case. Statutes permit offenders convicted in both state and federal courts to pursue habeas corpus actions in the federal courts. After first seeking favorable decisions by state appellate courts, convicted offenders can start their constitutional claims anew in the federal district courts and subsequently pursue their habeas cases in the federal circuit courts of appeal and the U.S. Supreme Court.

Only about 1 percent of habeas petitions succeed (Flango, 1994). One reason may be that an individual has no right to be represented by counsel when pursuing a habeas corpus petition. Few offenders have sufficient knowledge of law and legal procedures to identify and present constitutional claims effectively in the federal courts (Hanson and Daley, 1995). In the late 1980s and early 1990s, the U.S. Supreme Court issued many decisions that made filing habeas corpus petitions more difficult for convicted offenders (Alexander, 1993; C. E. Smith, 1995a). Specifically, the Court created tougher procedural rules that are more difficult for convicted offenders to follow. The rules also unintentionally created some new problems for state attorneys general and federal trial courts, because they must now examine the procedural rules affecting cases rather than simply addressing the constitutional violations that the offender claims occurred (C. E. Smith, 1995c). In 1996, the Antiterrorism and Effective Death Penalty Act placed additional restrictions on habeas corpus petitions. The statute was quickly approved by the U.S. Supreme Court. These reforms were based, in part, on a belief that prisoners' cases were clogging the federal courts (C. E. Smith, 1995b). Ironically, habeas corpus petitions in the federal courts have increased by 50 percent since the passage of the restrictive legislation (Scalia, 2002). By imposing strict filing deadlines for petitions, the legislation may have inadvertently focused more prisoners' attention on the existence of habeas corpus and thereby encouraged them to move forward with petitions in order to meet the deadlines.

■ Evaluating the Appellate Process

The public seems to believe that many offenders are being "let off" through the appellate process. In addition, frustrated by the problems of crime, some conservatives have argued that opportunities for appeal should be limited. They claim that too many offenders delay imposition of their sentences and that others completely evade punishment by filing appeals endlessly. This practice not only increases the workload of the courts but also jeopardizes the concept of the finality of the justice process. However, given that 90 percent of accused persons plead guilty, the number of cases that might be appealed is relatively small.

The appeals process performs the important function of righting wrongs. It also helps ensure consistency in the application of law by judges in different courts. Beyond that, its presence constantly influences the daily operations of the criminal justice system, as prosecutors and trial judges must consider how a higher court might later evaluate their decisions and actions.

CHECKPOINT

ANSWERS

12 *How does the appellate court's job differ from that of the trial court?*

12 Unlike trial courts, which have juries, hear evidence, and decide if the defendant is guilty or not guilty, appellate courts focus only on claimed errors of law or procedure in trial court proceedings. Victory for a defendant in a trial court means an acquittal and instant freedom. Victory in an appellate court may mean only a chance at a new trial—which often leads to a new conviction.

13 *What is a habeas corpus petition?*

13 The habeas corpus process may be started after all appeals have been filed and lost. Convicted offenders ask a federal court to review whether any constitutional rights were violated during the course of a case investigation and trial. If rights were violated, the person's continued detention in prison or jail may be improper.

▌A QUESTION OF ETHICS: WRITING ASSIGNMENT

Lisa Davidson stood silently in the courtroom of Judge Helen Iverson. Defense attorney Bill Dixon whispered in Davidson's ear as they waited for Judge Iverson to finish reading Davidson's file. "Are we ready to proceed?" asked the judge.

"Yes, your honor," came the simultaneous replies from both Dixon and the prosecutor standing nearby.

Judge Iverson stared at Davidson momentarily with a serious expression. "Ms. Davidson, you are charged with larceny. Because it is your third offense, I can send you to prison. Do you understand that?"

"Yes, your honor," replied Davidson, her voice quivering.

"Are you pleading guilty to this crime because you are guilty?" asked the judge.

"Yes, your honor."

The judge continued. "Are you pleading guilty of your own free will?"

"Yes, your honor."

"Did anyone threaten you to make you plead guilty?"

"No, your honor."

"Did anyone make any promises to you to induce you to plead guilty?"

Davidson nodded her head. "Yes. Mr. Dixon said that if I plead guilty to this charge then the prosecutor promised that my sentence would be only..."

"Excuse me, Judge Iverson!" Dixon interrupted in a loud voice. "Could I please have a moment to speak with my client?" Judge Iverson nodded.

Taking Davidson by the arm, Dixon moved her three feet farther away from the judge's bench. Dixon whispered into Davidson's ear as his hands punched the air with emphatic gestures. A few moments later, they returned to their positions, standing in front of the judge. "We are ready to continue, your honor," said Dixon.

Judge Iverson looked at Davidson once again. "Did anyone promise you anything to induce you to plead guilty?"

Davidson glanced sideways at Dixon before replying, "No, your honor."

"You understand that you are waiving your constitutional right to a trial and you are freely waiving that right?"

"Yes, your honor."

"Then I find you guilty as charged and I will set sentencing for one month from today at 10:00 A.M."

WRITING ASSIGNMENT

Imagine that you are an ethics expert who has been asked to evaluate court processes. Write a memo addressing the following questions. Should Judge Iverson have accepted the guilty plea? What role did the defense attorney play in staging the guilty plea ceremony? Were there any ethical problems? What would you have done if you were the judge?

Summary

Understand the pretrial process in criminal cases

▷ Pretrial processes determine the fates of nearly all defendants through case dismissals, decisions defining charges, and plea bargains, all of which affect more than 90 percent of cases.

▷ Defense attorneys use motions to their advantage to gain information and delay proceedings to benefit their clients.

Recognize how the bail system operates

▷ The bail process provides opportunities for many defendants to gain pretrial release, but poor defendants may be disadvantaged by their inability to come up with the money or property needed to secure release. Some preventive detention statutes permit judges to hold defendants considered dangerous or likely to flee.

▷ Bail bondsmen are private businesspeople who charge a fee to provide money for defendants' pretrial release. Their activities create risks of corruption and discrimination in the bail process, but bondsmen may also help the system by reminding defendants about court dates.

▷ Although judges bear the primary responsibility for setting bail, prosecutors are especially influential in recommending amounts and conditions for pretrial release.

▷ Initiatives to reform the bail process include police-issued citations, release on own recognizance (ROR), percentage bail, bail guidelines, and preventive detention.

Understand the context of pretrial detention

▷ Despite the presumption of innocence, pretrial detainees endure difficult conditions in jails containing mixed populations of convicted offenders, detainees, and troubled people. The shock of being jailed creates risks of suicide and depression.

Analyze how and why plea bargaining occurs

▷ Most convictions are obtained through plea bargaining, a process that exists because it fulfills the self-interest of prosecutors, judges, defense attorneys, and defendants.

▷ Plea bargaining is facilitated by exchange relations between prosecutors and defense attorneys. In many courthouses, there is little actual bargaining, as outcomes are determined through the implicit bargaining process of settling the facts and assessing the going

rate of punishment according to the standards of the local legal culture.

▷ Plea bargaining has been criticized for pressuring defendants to surrender their rights and for reducing the sentences imposed on offenders.

Know why cases go to trial and how juries are chosen

▷ Americans tend to presume that, through the dramatic courtroom battle of prosecutors and defense attorneys, trials are the best way to discover the truth about a criminal case.

▷ Only about 5 percent of cases go to trial, and half of those are typically bench trials in front of a judge, not jury trials.

▷ Typically, cases go to trial because they involve defendants who are wealthy enough to pay attorneys to fight to the very end or because they involve charges that are too serious to create incentives for plea bargaining.

▷ The U.S. Supreme Court has ruled that juries need not be made up of 12 members, and 12-member juries can, if permitted by state law, convict defendants by a less-than-unanimous super-majority vote.

▷ Juries serve vital functions for society by preventing arbitrary action by prosecutors and judges, educating citizens about the justice system, symbolizing the rule of law, and involving citizens from diverse segments of the community in judicial decision making.

▷ The jury selection process, especially in the formation of the jury pool and the exercise of peremptory challenges, often creates juries that do not fully represent all segments of a community.

Identify the stages of a criminal trial

▷ The trial process consists of a series of steps: jury selection, opening statements, presentation of prosecution's evidence, presentation of defense's evidence, presentation of rebuttal witnesses, closing arguments, judge's jury instructions, and jury's decision.

▷ Rules of evidence dictate what kinds of information may be presented in court for consideration by the jury. Types of evidence are real evidence, demonstrative evidence, testimony, direct evidence, and circumstantial evidence.

Understand the basis for an appeal of a conviction

▷ Convicted offenders have the opportunity to appeal, although defendants who plead guilty, unlike those convicted through a trial, often have few grounds for an appeal.

▶ Appeals focus on claimed errors of law or procedure in the investigation by police and prosecutors or the decisions by trial judges. Relatively few offenders win their appeals, and most of those simply gain an opportunity for a new trial, not release from jail or prison.

▶ After convicted offenders have used all of their appeals, they may file a habeas corpus petition to seek federal judicial review of claimed constitutional rights violations in their cases. Very few of such petitions succeed.

Questions for Review

1. What is bail and how has it been reformed to limit its traditionally harsh impact on poor defendants?

2. Why are some defendants held in pretrial detention?

3. Why does plea bargaining exist?

4. Given that there are so few jury trials, what types of cases would you expect to find adjudicated in this manner? Why?

5. What is the purpose of the appeals process?

Key Terms and Cases

appeal (p. 255)
arraignment (p. 233)
bail (p. 235)
bench trials (p. 248)
challenge for cause (p. 251)
circumstantial evidence (p. 252)
citation (p. 238)
demonstrative evidence (p. 251)
direct evidence (p. 252)
habeas corpus (p. 256)

jury (p. 248)
motion (p. 234)
percentage bail (p. 238)
peremptory challenge (p. 251)
preventive detention (p. 239)
real evidence (p. 251)
reasonable doubt (p. 253)
release on recognizance (ROR) (p. 238)
testimony (p. 251)
voir dire (p. 250)

Bordenkircher v. Hayes (1978) (p. 246)
Boykin v. Alabama (1969) (p. 246)
North Carolina v. Alford (1970) (p. 246)
Ricketts v. Adamson (1987) (p. 246)
Santobello v. New York (1971) (p. 242)
United States v. Salerno and Cafero (1987) (p. 239)
Williams v. Florida (1970) (p. 249)

Punishment and Sentencing

IN APRIL 2008, throngs of onlookers, reporters, and photographers waited in anticipation outside the courthouse as Hollywood actor Wesley Snipes, the star of numerous action movies, arrived for his sentencing hearing in Ocala, Florida. The federal government charged Snipes with tax fraud and conspiracy as well as failing to file tax returns for six years. Although he made more than $58 million from his acting career during those years, Snipes refused to pay income taxes and claimed that the federal income tax was illegal. The IRS had adopted the strategy of prosecuting a select number of prominent people for violating tax laws, with the hope that sending a celebrity to prison would scare other Americans from cheating on their taxes. The government was particularly interested in prosecuting people who were part of the "tax deniers" movement; people who claimed that the government had no authority to collect taxes from them. Snipes had become part of that movement after getting financial advice from two men, Eddie Ray Kahn and Douglas Rosile, who were also charged with criminal offenses in conjunction with the prosecution of Snipes (Johnston, 2008).

Snipes originally faced the possibility of 16 years in prison if he had been convicted of all charges. Much to the government's dismay, however, the jury acquitted the actor on the most serious fraud and conspiracy charges as well as charges for failing to pay taxes during three years of the six-year period in question. The jurors apparently accepted the defense attorney's argument that Snipes genuinely believed that he was not obligated to pay taxes and therefore lacked the necessary criminal intent (*mens rea*, discussed in Chapter 3) to be guilty of a crime. With respect to failing to file a tax return, the jury convicted him of three misdemeanor charges—one for each of the three years prior to his learning that he was the focus of an IRS investigation. The jurors apparently regarded his failure to file a return in the subsequent three years as merely his assertion of his Fifth Amendment right to remain silent and not feel forced to engage in self-incrimination. By contrast, the codefendants Kahn and Rosile, who helped to advise people to refuse to pay their taxes, were convicted on felony charges (Johnston, 2008).

At the daylong sentencing hearing, the attorneys for Snipes argued that he should receive leniency because he was merely the naive victim of misguided financial advice from Kahn and Rosile. Snipes arrived at the court with checks totaling $5 million in order to pay the government a portion of the $17 million that he owed in back taxes and interest penalties. In a prepared statement that he read in the courtroom, Snipes said, "I'm very sorry for my mistakes. I acknowledge that I have failed myself and others" ("Wesley Snipes," 2008).

The prosecution argued for the maximum penalty: three years in prison—one year for each of the misdemeanor convictions. They complained that even when Snipes claimed to be "sorry," he never acknowledged his legal duty to pay income taxes, never withdrew his prior assertions that federal taxes are illegal, and never showed genuine remorse for breaking the law ("Wesley Snipes," 2008).

Ultimately, U.S. District Judge William Terrell Hodges demonstrated that he agreed with the prosecution's position. He sentenced Snipes to one year in prison for each misdemeanor conviction and ordered that the sentences be served *consecutively*, one right after the other, for a total of three years in prison plus one year of probation afterward. In addition, Snipes was ordered to pay the remaining portion of the $17 million that he owed to the government. In other cases, offenders convicted of multiple charges are ordered to serve their sentences concurrently, meaning that each year in prison counts as a year toward each sentence. If Snipes had received concurrent sentences, he would have been sent to prison for one year instead of three. Thus, Snipes received the maximum penalty possible for the misdemeanor charges ("Wesley Snipes," 2008).

His codefendants, Kahn and Rosile, received prison sentences of ten years and four and a half years, respectively, because of their felony convictions. Throughout the case, Kahn refused to accept that the court had any authority to make decisions about him. He stayed in his jail cell rather than attend many of the court proceedings, as a way of demonstrating his view that the government lacked any legal authority to

prosecute him for tax law violations (Johnston, 2008; "Wesley Snipes," 2008). In some cases, defendants risk receiving severer sentences if they show disrespect to the judge or fail to show remorse for their crimes. The severity of Kahn's sentence raises the possibility that his attitude and behavior led to harsher punishment.

The outcome of Wesley Snipes's case brings up many questions about the role of sentencing in the criminal justice system. Did Snipes's sentence achieve justice? Did it appropriately advance society's goals? Which goals? For example, did it compensate the "victim"? Make an example of Snipes? Help him become a law-abiding citizen? Further, was he treated fairly when compared with others who commit similar crimes? Should someone who refuses to accept responsibility or fails to cooperate receive a maximum sentence? What sentence do you believe Wesley Snipes deserved? What about his codefendants? As such questions indicate, criminal behavior may produce a wide variety of punishments that depend on the goals being pursued by officials who make laws and determine sentences.

The criminal justice system aims to solve three basic issues: (1) What conduct is criminal? (2) What determines guilt? (3) What should be done with the guilty? Earlier chapters emphasized the first two questions. The answers given by the legal system to the first question compose the basic rules of society: Do not murder, rob, sell drugs, commit treason, and so forth. The law also spells out the process for determining guilt or innocence; however, the administrative and interpersonal considerations of the actors in the criminal justice system greatly affect this process. In this chapter, we begin to examine the third problem: sanction and punishment. First, we consider the four goals of punishment: retribution, deterrence, incapacitation, and rehabilitation. We then explore the forms punishment takes to achieve its goals. These are incarceration, intermediate sanctions, probation, and death. Finally, we look at the sentencing process and how it affects punishment.

The Goals of Punishment

Criminal sanctions in the United States have four main goals: retribution (deserved punishment), deterrence, incapacitation, and rehabilitation. Ultimately, all criminal punishment aims at maintaining the social order, but the justifications for sentencing proceed from the American values of justice and fairness. There is no universal agreement, however, on how to make the severity of punishment just and fair. Further, the justice sought by crime victims often conflicts with fairness to offenders.

Punishments reflect the dominant values of a particular moment in history. By the end of the 1960s, for example, the number of Americans who were sentenced to imprisonment decreased because of a widespread commitment to rehabilitating offenders. By contrast, since the mid-1970s an emphasis on imposing strong punishments for the purposes of retribution, deterrence, and incapacitation has resulted in record numbers of offenders being sentenced to prison. At the beginning of the twenty-first century, voices are calling for the addition of restorative justice as a fifth goal of the criminal sanction.

■ Retribution—Deserved Punishment

Retribution is punishment inflicted on a person who has harmed other people and so deserves to be penalized (Cahill, 2007b). The biblical expression "An eye for an eye, a tooth for a tooth" illustrates the philosophy underlying this kind of punishment. Retribution means that those who commit a particular crime should be punished alike, in proportion to the gravity of the offense or to the suffering it has caused others. Retribution is deserved punishment; offenders must "pay their debts."

Some scholars claim that the desire for retribution is a basic human emotion. They maintain that if the state does not provide retributive sanctions to reflect community revulsion at offensive acts, citizens will take the law into their own hands to punish offenders. Under this view, the failure of government to satisfy the people's desire for retribution could produce social chaos.

This argument may not be valid for all crimes, however. If a rapist is inadequately punished, then the victim's family and other members of the community may be tempted to exact their own retribution. But what about a young adult smoking marijuana? If the government failed to impose retribution for this offense, would the community care? The same apathy may hold true for offenders who commit other nonviolent crimes that modestly impact society. Even in these seemingly trivial situ-

■ **retribution** Punishment inflicted on a person who has harmed others and so deserves to be penalized.

ations, however, retribution may serve as a necessary public reminder of the general rules of law and the important values they protect.

Since the late 1970s, retribution as a justification for the criminal sanction has aroused new interest, largely because of dissatisfaction with the philosophical basis and practical results of rehabilitation. Using the concept of "just deserts or deserved punishment" to define retribution, some theorists argue that one who infringes on the rights of others deserves to be punished. This approach rests on the philosophical view that punishment is a moral response to harm inflicted on society. In effect, these theorists believe that basic morality demands that wrongdoers be punished (von Hirsch, 1976:49). According to this view, punishment should be applied only for the wrong inflicted and not primarily to achieve other goals such as deterrence, incapacitation, or rehabilitation.

■ Deterrence

Many people see criminal punishment as a basis for affecting the future choices and behavior of individuals. Politicians frequently talk about being "tough on crime" in order to send a message to would-be criminals. The roots of this approach, called deterrence, lie in eighteenth-century England among the followers of social philosopher Jeremy Bentham.

Bentham was struck by what seemed to be the pointlessness of retribution. His fellow reformers adopted Bentham's theory of utilitarianism, which holds that human behavior is governed by the individual's calculation of the benefits versus the costs of his or her acts. Before stealing money or property, for example, potential offenders would consider the punishment that others have received for similar acts and would thereby be deterred.

■ **general deterrence** Punishment of criminals that is intended to be an example to the general public and to discourage the commission of offenses.

There are two types of deterrence. **General deterrence** presumes that members of the general public, on observing the punishments of others, will conclude that the costs of crime outweigh the benefits. For general deterrence to be effective, the public must receive constant reminders of the likelihood and severity of punishment for various acts. They must believe that they will be caught, prosecuted, and given a specific punishment if they commit a particular crime. Moreover, the punishment must be severe enough to instill fear of the consequences of committing crimes. For example, public hanging was once considered to be an effective general deterrent.

■ **specific deterrence** Punishment inflicted on criminals to discourage them from committing future crimes.

By contrast, **specific deterrence** targets the decisions and behavior of offenders who have already been convicted. Under this approach, the amount and kind of punishment are calculated to discourage that criminal from repeating the offense. The punishment must be severe enough to cause the criminal to say, "The consequences of my crime were too painful. I will not commit another crime, because I do not want to risk being punished again."

The concept of deterrence presents obvious difficulties (Stafford and Warr, 1993). Deterrence assumes that all people think before they act. As such, deterrence does not account for the many people who commit crimes while under the influence of drugs or alcohol, or those whose harmful behavior stems from psychological problems or mental illness. Deterrence also does not account for people who act impulsively in stealing or damaging property. In other cases, the low probability of being caught defeats both general and specific deterrence. To be generally

Depending on a state's sentencing laws, those who commit the most-serious offenses, such as murder, will typically receive long prison sentences or the death penalty. In 2009, Ohio teenager Daniel Petric received a sentence of 23 years to life in prison for killing his mother and wounding his father after they took away his video games. What goals of punishment are advanced by sending someone to prison? What about the death penalty?

© Marvin Fong/The Plain Dealer /Landov

deterrent, punishment must be perceived as relatively fast, certain, and severe. But punishment does not always occur that way.

Knowledge of the effectiveness of deterrence is limited as well (Nagin, 1998). For example, social science cannot measure the effects of general deterrence, because only those who are not deterred come to the attention of researchers. A study of the deterrent effects of punishment would have to examine the impact of different forms of the criminal sanction on various potential lawbreakers. How can we truly determine how many people—or even if any people—stopped themselves from committing a crime for any reason, let alone because they were deterred by the prospect of prosecution and punishment? Therefore, although legislators often cite deterrence as a rationale for certain sanctions, no one really knows the extent to which sentencing policies based on deterrence achieve their objectives. Because contemporary U.S. society has shown little ability to reduce crime by imposing increasingly severe sanctions, the effectiveness of deterrence for many crimes and criminals should be questioned (Tonry, 2008).

■ Incapacitation

Incapacitation assumes that society can use detention in prison or execution to keep offenders from committing further crimes. Many people express such sentiments, urging officials to "lock 'em up and throw away the key!" In primitive societies, banishment from the community was the usual method of incapacitation. In early America, offenders often agreed to move away or to join the army as an alternative to some other form of punishment. In the United States today, imprisonment serves as the usual method of incapacitation. Offenders can be confined within secure institutions and effectively prevented from committing additional harm against society for the duration of their sentence. Capital punishment is the ultimate method of incapacitation. Any sentence that physically restricts an offender may incapacitate the person, even when the underlying purpose of the sentence is retribution, deterrence, or rehabilitation.

Sentences based on incapacitation are future oriented. Whereas retribution requires focusing on the harmful act of the offender, incapacitation looks at the offender's potential actions. If the offender is likely to commit future crimes, then the judge may impose a severe sentence—even for a relatively minor crime.

For example, under the incapacitation theory, a woman who kills her abusive husband as an emotional reaction to his verbal insults and physical assaults could receive a light sentence. As a one-time impulse killer who felt driven to kill by unique circumstances, she is not likely to commit additional crimes. By contrast, someone who shoplifts merchandise and has been convicted of the offense on ten previous occasions may receive a severe sentence. The criminal record and type of crime indicate that he or she will commit additional crimes if released. Thus, incapacitation focuses on characteristics of the offenders instead of aspects of their offenses.

Does it offend your sense of justice that a person could receive a severer sentence for shoplifting than for manslaughter? This question embodies one of the criticisms of incapacitation. Questions also arise about how to determine the length of sentence. Presumably, offenders will not be released until the state is reasonably sure that they will no longer commit crimes. However, can we accurately predict any person's behavior? Moreover, on what grounds can we punish people for anticipated behavior that we cannot accurately predict?

In recent years, greater attention has been paid to the concept of **selective incapacitation**, whereby offenders who repeat certain kinds of crimes receive long prison terms. Research has suggested that a relatively small number of offenders commit a large number of violent and property crimes (Clear, 1994:103). Burglars, for example, tend to commit many offenses before they are caught. Thus, these "career criminals" should be locked up for long periods (Auerhahn, 1999). Such policies could be costly, however. Not only would correctional facilities have to be expanded,

■ **incapacitation** Depriving an offender of the ability to commit crimes against society, usually by detaining the offender in prison.

■ **selective incapacitation** Making the best use of expensive and limited prison space by targeting for incarceration those individuals whose incapacity will do the most to reduce crime in society.

but the number of expensive, time-consuming trials also might increase if severer sentences caused more repeat offenders to plead not guilty. Another difficulty with this policy is that we cannot accurately predict which offenders will commit more crimes upon release (Vitiello, 2008).

■ Rehabilitation

■ **rehabilitation** The goal of restoring a convicted offender to a constructive place in society through some form of vocational or educational training or therapy.

Rehabilitation refers to the goal of restoring a convicted offender to a constructive place in society through some form of training or therapy. Americans want to believe that offenders can be treated and resocialized in ways that allow them to lead a crime-free, productive life upon release. Over the last hundred years, rehabilitation advocates have argued for techniques that they claim identify and treat the causes of criminal behavior. If the offender's criminal behavior is assumed to result from some social, psychological, or biological imperfection, the treatment of the disorder becomes the primary goal of corrections.

Rehabilitation focuses on the offender. Its objective does not imply any consistent relationship between the severity of the punishment and the gravity of the crime. People who commit lesser offenses can receive long prison sentences if experts believe effective rehabilitation requires it. By contrast, a murderer might win early release by showing signs that the psychological or emotional problems that led to the killing have been corrected.

According to the concept of rehabilitation, offenders are treated, not punished, and they will return to society when they are "cured." Consequently, judges should not set fixed sentences but rather ones with maximum and minimum terms so that parole boards can release inmates when they have been rehabilitated.

From the 1940s until the 1970s, the goal of rehabilitation was so widely accepted that treatment and reform of the offender were generally regarded as the only issues worth serious attention. Crime was assumed to be caused by problems affecting individuals, and modern social sciences had the tools to address those problems. During the past 30 years, however, researchers and others have questioned the assumptions of the rehabilitation model. Studies of the results of rehabilitation programs have challenged the idea that criminal offenders can be cured (Martinson, 1974). Moreover, scholars no longer take for granted that crime is caused by identifiable, curable problems such as poverty, lack of job skills, low self-esteem, and hostility toward authority. Instead, some argue that we cannot identify the cause of criminal behavior for individual offenders.

During the first decade of the twenty-first century, rehabilitation reemerged as a goal of corrections. As we shall see in Chapter 13, it came to be discussed and applied through the concept of "reentry" rather than through a declaration that rehabilitation is a primary goal of the justice system (Butterfield, 2004). States and the federal government endured significant financial costs through the expansion of prison systems and the growth of prison populations, caused by the imposition of severer prison sentences during the preceding two decades. Eventually, they confronted the reality that hundreds of thousands of prisoners were returning to society each year after serving long sentences. In addition, as governments at all levels experienced budget crises, officials sought ways to reduce prison populations. Thus, policies and programs emerged that were intended to prepare offenders for successful integration into society (Eckholm, 2008b). These programs are rehabilitative in nature, by providing education, counseling, skill training, and other services to help change offenders' behavior and prospects for success in society. As you can see in "What Americans Think," public opinion supports efforts to reform offenders through such rehabilitative efforts (Cullen, 2007).

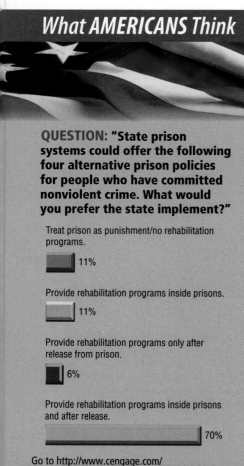

What AMERICANS Think

QUESTION: "State prison systems could offer the following four alternative prison policies for people who have committed nonviolent crime. What would you prefer the state implement?"

Treat prison as punishment/no rehabilitation programs.

11%

Provide rehabilitation programs inside prisons.

11%

Provide rehabilitation programs only after release from prison.

6%

Provide rehabilitation programs inside prisons and after release.

70%

Go to http://www.cengage.com/criminaljustice/cole to compare your opinion on this issue with the opinions of other criminal justice students.

Source: Barry Krisberg and Susan Marchionna, "Attitudes of U.S. Voters toward Prisoners Rehabilitation and Reentry Policies," National Council on Crime and Delinquency *Focus*, April 2006. Based on results of a February 2006 national survey of likely voters.

CLOSE UP

Restorative Justice in Vermont

ONE NIGHT IN MORRISVILLE, VERMONT, Newton Wells went looking for a good time and wound up in an experiment. The 22-year-old college student was charged with assault after nearly driving into two police officers who were breaking up a party. Facing a felony conviction, Wells took a different way out. He pleaded guilty to a lower charge and volunteered to be sentenced by a county "reparative" board. Instead of a judge, a businessman, a counselor, a retired chemistry teacher, and a civil servant issued his punishment.

Restorative justice programs are designed to compensate victims, rehabilitate offenders, and involve the community in a new and direct way in the justice process. Today some Vermont offenders may be sentenced to make public apologies, make restitution, or chop wood for the elderly—to "repair" the community.

Vermont's sentencing boards, typically four to six volunteers, handle misdemeanors and low-grade felonies such as drunken driving and writing bad checks. Although such crimes normally would not merit jail time, removing the cases from the traditional criminal justice system frees up correctional department resources.

Board members meet with offenders in hour-long sessions, hear explanations and apologies, and tailor the penalties. The idea is to make the punishment related to the crime, which often occurs in novel ways:

- In Morrisville, college student Wells was ordered to work 30 hours with troubled youths and to meet with the police he menaced so that they could vent their anger about his driving.

- In Rutland, a man who drove 105 mph down a residential street was sentenced to work with brain-injured adults, some of them survivors of high-speed crashes.

- In Hyde Park, a teenager who vandalized a home got 55 hours on a work crew. His job was repairing plaster on an aging opera house.

Panel members get involved in ways they never could if they were serving as jurors. In Rutland, Jack Aicher tells shoplifters they've committed crimes against the "community." Everyone pays higher prices, he says, to cover the store's loss.

Proponents say board sanctions are typically tougher than conventional probation.

But offenders opt for the citizen panels to get their sentences concluded quickly. In Vermont, probation can last more than a year and can include special sanctions such as drug tests and rehabilitation programs. Reparative board punishments are concluded within 90 days.

The percentage of nonviolent offenders in the state's eight prisons has dropped from about 50 percent to 28 percent. The decline is ascribed, in part, to the effect of the boards. By handling low-level offenders, the community panels have freed state probation officers to deal with more serious cases. Those probation officers can then monitor criminals serving their sentences in work camps or on furlough rather than in jail, as a way of relieving overcrowding.

🌐 RESEARCHING THE INTERNET

Read the article entitled "Restorative Justice Dialogue: Evidence-Based Practice." You'll find it at the corresponding website listed on the Cole/Smith Criminal Justice in America Companion Website: http://www.cengage.com/criminaljustice/cole.

FOR CRITICAL ANALYSIS

Would the restorative justice approach work in your community? What criticisms is such a program likely to face?

Source: *USA Today*, February 12, 1997, http://www.usatoday.com. Copyright © 1997 USA Today. Reprinted by permission.

■ A New Approach to Punishment: Restorative Justice

In keeping with the focus on community justice for police, courts, and corrections, many people are calling for **restorative justice** to be added to the goals of the criminal sanction (Basemore and Umbreit, 1994; Braithwaite, 2007). The restorative justice perspective views crime as more than a violation of penal law. The criminal act practically and symbolically denies community. It breaks trust among citizens and requires community members to determine how "to contradict the moral message of the crime that the offender is above the law and the victim beneath its reach" (Clear and Karp, 1999:85). Crime victims suffer losses involving damage to property and self. The primary aim of criminal justice should be to repair these losses (Waldman, 2007). Crime also challenges the heart of community, to the extent that community life depends on a shared sense of trust, fairness, and interdependence.

■ **restorative justice** Punishment designed to repair the damage done to the victim and community by an offender's criminal act.

Restorative justice seeks to repair the damage done to the victim and community by an offender's criminal act. Here, Susanna Kay Cooper sits next to David Lee Myers as she looks at the photo of his dead wife. Cooper pled guilty to vehicular homicide in the death of Elaine Myers, received a 34-month prison sentence, and agreed to enter into talks with the victim's family

Rose Howerter/The Oregonian

TABLE 9.1 The Goals of Punishment

At sentencing, the judge usually gives reasons for the punishments imposed. Here are statements that Judge William Terrell Hodges might have given Wesley Snipes, each promoting a different goal for the sanction.

Goal	Judge's Possible Statement
Retribution	I am imposing this sentence because you deserve to be punished for the economic harm caused by violating laws concerning tax evasion. Your criminal behavior is the basis of the punishment. Justice requires that I impose a sanction at a level that illustrates the importance that the community places on obedience to tax laws.
Deterrence	I am imposing this sentence so that your punishment for tax evasion will serve as an example and deter others who may contemplate similar actions. In addition, I hope that this sentence will deter you from ever again committing an illegal act.
Incapacitation	I am imposing this sentence so that you will be incapacitated and hence unable to engage in tax evasion in the free community during the length of this term.
Rehabilitation	The trial testimony and information contained in the presentence report make me believe that there are aspects of your personality that led to the tax evasion. I am therefore imposing this sentence so that you can receive treatment that will rectify your behavior so you will not commit another crime.

Shifting the focus to restorative justice requires a three-way approach that involves the offender, the victim, and the community. This approach may include mediation in which the three actors devise ways that all agree are fair and just that the offender can repair the harm done to victim and community.

This new approach to criminal justice means that losses suffered by the crime victim are restored, the threat to local safety is removed, and the offender again becomes a fully participating member of the community. The Vermont Reparative Sentencing Boards, described in the Close Up box, exemplify one way of implementing restorative justice.

As yet, restorative justice represents a small minority of sanctions. To see how the four main punishment goals might be enacted in real life, consider again the sentencing of actor Wesley Snipes for tax crimes. Table 9.1 shows various hypothetical sentencing statements that the judge might have given, depending on prevailing correctional goals.

As we next consider how such goals are expressed though the various forms of punishment, keep in mind the underlying goal—or mix of goals—that justifies each form of sanction.

CHECKPOINT

ANSWERS

1 What are the four primary goals of the criminal sanction?

1 Retribution, deterrence, incapacitation, rehabilitation.

2 What are the difficulties in showing that a punishment acts as a deterrent?

2 It is impossible to show who has been deterred from committing crimes; punishment isn't always certain; people act impulsively rather than rationally; people commit crimes while on drugs.

Forms of the Criminal Sanction

Incarceration, intermediate sanctions, probation, and death are the basic ways that the criminal sanction, or punishment, is applied. The United States does not have a single, uniform set of sentencing laws. The criminal codes of each of the states and of the federal government specify the punishments. Each code differs to some extent in the severity of the punishment for specific crimes and in the amount of discretion given judges to tailor the sanction to the individual offender.

As we examine the various forms of criminal sanction, bear in mind that applying these legally authorized punishments gives rise to complex problems. Judges often receive wide discretion in determining the appropriate sentence within the parameters of the penal code.

■ Incarceration

Imprisonment is the most visible penalty imposed by U.S. courts. Although less than 30 percent of people under correctional supervision are in prisons and jails, incarceration remains the standard for punishing those who commit serious crimes. Imprisonment is thought to contribute significantly to deterring potential offenders. However, incarceration is expensive. It also creates the problem of reintegrating offenders into society upon release.

In penal codes, legislatures stipulate the types of sentences and the amount of prison time that can be imposed for each crime. Three basic sentencing structures are used: (1) indeterminate sentences (36 states), (2) determinate sentences (14 states), and (3) mandatory sentences (all states). Each type of sentence makes certain assumptions about the goals of the criminal sanction, and each provides judges with varying degrees of discretion.

Indeterminate Sentences   When the goal of rehabilitation dominated corrections, legislatures enacted **indeterminate sentences** (often called indefinite sentences) (Fisher, 2007). In keeping with the goal of treatment, indeterminate sentencing gives correctional officials and parole boards significant control over the amount of time a prisoner serves. Penal codes with indeterminate sentences stipulate a minimum and a maximum amount of time to be served in prison (for example, 1–5 years, 10–15 years, or 1 year to life). At the time of sentencing, the judge informs the offender about the range of the sentence. The offender also learns that he or she will probably be eligible for parole at some point after the minimum term has been served. The parole board determines the actual release date. Because it is based on the idea that the time necessary for treatment cannot be set, the indeterminate sentence is closely associated with rehabilitation.

Determinate Sentences   Dissatisfaction with the rehabilitation goal and support for the concept of deserved punishment led many legislatures in the 1970s to shift to **determinate sentences** (Dansky, 2008). With a determinate sentence, a convicted offender is imprisoned for a specific period (for example, 2 years, 5 years, 15 years). At the end of the term, minus credited good time (to be discussed shortly), the prisoner is automatically freed. The time of release depends neither on participation in treatment programs nor on a parole board's judgment concerning the offender's likelihood of returning to criminal activities.

Some determinate-sentencing states have adopted penal codes that stipulate a specific term for each crime category. Others allow the judge to choose a range of time to be served. Some states emphasize a determinate **presumptive sentence**: The legislature, or often a commission, specifies a term based on a time range (for example, 14–20 months) into which most cases should fall. Only in special circumstances should judges deviate from the presumptive sentence. Whichever variation is used, however, the offender theoretically knows at sentencing the amount of time to be served. One result of determinate sentencing is that, by reducing the judge's discretion, legislatures have tended to limit sentencing disparities and to ensure that terms correspond to those the elected body thinks are appropriate (Griset, 1993).

■ **indeterminate sentence**   A period, set by a judge, that specifies a minimum and a maximum time to be served in prison. Sometime after the minimum, the offender may be eligible for parole.

■ **determinate sentence**   A sentence that fixes the term of imprisonment at a specific period.

■ **presumptive sentence**   A sentence for which the legislature or a commission sets a minimum and maximum range of months or years. Judges are to fix the length of the sentence within that range, allowing for special circumstances.

Of all correctional measures, incarceration represents the greatest restriction on freedom. These inmates at Alabama's Staton Correctional Facility are part of America's huge incarcerated population. Since 1980, the number of Americans held in prisons and jails has quadrupled. What are the costs to society from having such a large population of prisoners?

AP Images/Rob Carr

■ **mandatory sentence** A sentence determined by statutes and requiring that a certain penalty be imposed and carried out for convicted offenders who meet certain criteria.

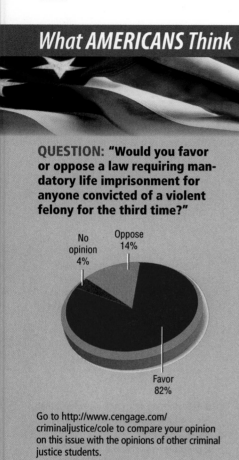

What AMERICANS Think

QUESTION: "Would you favor or oppose a law requiring mandatory life imprisonment for anyone convicted of a violent felony for the third time?"

No opinion 4%

Oppose 14%

Favor 82%

Go to http://www.cengage.com/criminaljustice/cole to compare your opinion on this issue with the opinions of other criminal justice students.

Source: Telephone interviews of a national adult sample by ABC News, February 27–March 3, 2002. Data provided by the Roper Center for Public Opinion Research, University of Connecticut.

■ **good time** A reduction of an inmate's prison sentence, at the discretion of the prison administrator, for good behavior or participation in vocational, educational, or treatment programs.

Mandatory Sentences   As part of the public's fear and anger about crime, politicians and the public periodically complain that offenders are released before serving long enough terms, and legislatures have responded (Zimring, 2007). All states and the federal government now have some form of **mandatory sentences** (often called mandatory minimum sentences), stipulating some minimum period of incarceration that people convicted of selected crimes must serve. The judge may consider neither the circumstances of the offense nor the background of the offender, and he or she may not impose nonincarcerative sentences. Mandatory prison terms are most often specified for violent crimes, drug violations, habitual offenders, or crimes in which a firearm was used (see "What Americans Think"). As you read "Criminal Justice: Myth and Reality," consider the various assumptions and motives of legislators who support mandatory sentences and want to increase the length of sentences for various crimes.

The "three strikes and you're out" laws adopted by 26 states and the federal government provide an example of mandatory sentencing (Schultz, 2000). These laws require that judges sentence offenders with three felony convictions (in some states two or four convictions) to long prison terms, sometimes to life without parole. In some states, these laws have inadvertently clogged the courts, lowered the rates of plea bargaining, and caused desperate offenders to violently resist arrest. Mandatory minimum sentences resulted in a great increase in the number of drug offenders serving very long terms in America's prisons, mostly for nonviolent offenses (Gezari, 2008). Across the country, mandatory prison terms are applied more often to African American drug offenders than to their white counterparts (Crawford, 2000).

A study in California found a reduction in repeat offenders' participation in certain kinds of crimes, but a troubling increase in the violence of third-strike offenses (Iyengar, 2008). This raises the possibility that career criminals who are willing to risk the three-strikes ultimate punishment may commit more-serious crimes, such as robbery, since the penalty will be no greater than that for a lesser felony, such as larceny (Fisman, 2008). The study also raised the possibility that offenders with prior strikes may be inclined to migrate to other states, thus merely moving their criminal activities to a new location (Iyengar, 2008).

The Sentence versus Actual Time Served   Regardless of how much discretion judges have to fine-tune the sentences they give, the prison sentences that are imposed may bear little resemblance to the actual amount of time served. In reality, parole boards in indeterminate-sentencing states have broad discretion in release decisions once the offender has served a minimum portion of the sentence. In addition, offenders can have their prison sentence reduced by earning **good time** for good behavior, at the discretion of the prison administrator.

Most states have good-time policies. Days are subtracted from prisoners' minimum or maximum term for good behavior or for participating in various types of vocational, educational, or treatment programs. Correctional officials consider these policies necessary for maintaining institutional order and for reducing crowding. Good-time credit serves as an incentive for prisoners to follow institutional rules, because recently earned credits can be taken away for misbehavior (King and Sherry, 2008). Prosecutors and defense attorneys also take good time into consideration during plea bargaining. In other words, they think about the actual amount of time a particular offender will likely serve.

The amount of good time one can earn varies among the states, usually from 5 to 10 days a month. In some states, once 90 days of good time are earned, they are vested; that is, the credits cannot be taken away as a punishment for misbehavior. Prisoners who then violate the rules risk losing only days not vested.

Judges in the United States often prescribe long periods of incarceration for serious crimes, but good time and parole reduce the amount of time spent in prison. Figure 9.1 shows the estimated time actually served by offenders in state prisons, versus the average (mean) sentence. Note that the national average for time served is 27 months, or 51 percent of the mean sentence of 53 months.

This type of national data often hides the impact of variations in sentencing and releasing laws in individual states. In many states, because of prison crowding and release policies, offenders serve less than 20 percent of their sentences. In other states, where three-strikes and truth-in-sentencing laws are employed, the average time served will be longer than the national average.

Truth-in-Sentencing   *Truth-in-sentencing* refers to laws that require offenders to serve a substantial proportion (usually 85 percent for violent crimes) of their prison sentence before being released on parole (Mayrack, 2008).

FIGURE 9.1
Estimated time served in state prison compared with mean length of sentence
Most offenders serve a third or less of their mean sentences. Why is there such a difference between the sentence and actual time served?

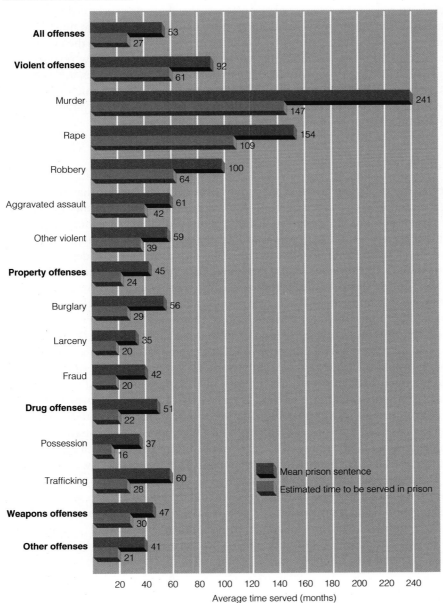

Sources: Matthew R. Durose and Patrick A. Langan, "Felony Sentences in State Courts, 2004," Bureau of Justice Statistics *Bulletin,* July 2007; "State Court Sentencing of Convicted Felons, 2004—Statistical Tables," http://www.ojp.usdoj.gov/bjs/abstract/scscfst.htm, Table 1.5.

Criminal Justice:
MYTH AND REALITY

COMMON BELIEF: Long, mandatory sentences will deter people from committing crimes, because they will stop themselves from causing harm to society out of fear of the severe punishments that await them.

Effective deterrence requires two elements: (1) potential offenders must think rationally and weigh the costs and benefits of crimes before committing criminal acts, and (2) potential offenders must fear that they will be caught. In fact, many offenders do not think rationally. They act impulsively in deciding to rob someone or steal an item from a store. They may also be driven by substance abuse problems that cloud their ability to think rationally and/or create an immediate need for money in order to obtain drugs and alcohol. In addition, many offenders do not believe that they will be caught. They erroneously believe that they are smarter than the police or that they are committing their crime in a manner that will let them escape without being apprehended. When offenders are overconfident about their ability to get away with crimes, then deterrence is unlikely to prevent them from committing illegal acts. Moreover, some offenders do not fear the prospect of prison. They regard stretches in prison as merely an inevitable part of their lives. All of the foregoing factors mean that legislators should not assume that severe sentences will have a deterrent effect, even if they say to themselves, "I would never commit crimes if sentences were long and mandatory."

Truth-in-sentencing became such a politically attractive idea that the federal government allocated almost $10 billion for prison construction to those states adopting truth-in-sentencing (Donziger, 1996:24). Critics maintain, however, that truth-in-sentencing increases prison populations at a tremendous cost.

◾ Intermediate Sanctions

■ **intermediate sanctions** A variety of punishments that are more restrictive than traditional probation but less severe and costly than incarceration.

Prison crowding and the low levels of probation supervision have spurred interest in the development of **intermediate sanctions**, punishments that are less severe and costly than prison but more restrictive than traditional probation (R. Warren, 2007). Intermediate sanctions provide a variety of restrictions on freedom, such as fines, home confinement, intensive probation supervision, restitution to victims, community service, boot camp, and forfeiture of possessions or stolen property (Morris and Tonry, 1990).

In advocating intermediate punishments, Norval Morris and Michael Tonry (1990:37) stipulate that these sanctions should not be used in isolation, but rather in combination, to reflect the severity of the offense, the characteristics of the offender, and the needs of the community. In addition, intermediate punishments must be supported and enforced by mechanisms that take seriously any breach of the conditions of the sentence. Too often, criminal justice agencies have devoted few resources to enforcing sentences that do not involve incarceration. If the law does not fulfill its promises, offenders may feel that they have "beaten" the system, which makes the punishment meaningless. Citizens viewing the ineffectiveness of the system may develop the attitude that nothing but stiffer sentences will work.

◾ Probation

■ **probation** A sentence that the offender is allowed to serve under supervision in the community.

The most frequently applied criminal sanction is **probation**, a sentence that an offender serves in the community under supervision. Nearly 60 percent of adults under correctional supervision are on probation. Ideally, under probation, offenders attempt to straighten out their lives. Probation is a judicial act granted by the grace of the state, not extended as a right. Conditions are imposed specifying how an offender will behave through the length of the sentence. Probationers may have to undergo regular drug tests, abide by curfews, enroll in educational programs or remain employed, stay away from certain people or parts of town, and meet regularly with probation officers. If probationers do not meet the required conditions, the supervising officer recommends to the court that the probation be revoked and that the remainder of the sentence be served in prison. Probation may also be revoked for commission of a new crime.

Although probationers serve their sentences in the community, the sanction is often tied to incarceration. In some jurisdictions, the court is authorized to modify an offender's prison sentence, after a portion is served, by changing it to probation. This is often referred to as **shock probation** (or split probation): An offender is released after a period of incarceration (the "shock") and resentenced to probation. An offender on probation may be required to spend intermittent periods, such as weekends or nights, in jail. Whatever its specific terms, a probationary sentence will emphasize guidance and supervision in the community.

■ **shock probation** A sentence in which the offender is released after a short incarceration and resentenced to probation.

Probation is generally advocated as a way of rehabilitating offenders whose crimes are not serious or whose past records are clean. It is viewed as less expensive yet more effective than imprisonment. For example, imprisonment may embitter youthful or first-time offenders and mix them with hardened criminals so that they learn more-sophisticated criminal techniques.

◾ Death

Although other Western democracies abolished the death penalty years ago, the United States continues to use it. Capital punishment was imposed and carried out regularly prior to the late 1960s. Amid debates about the constitutionality of the death penalty and with public opinion polls showing opposition to it, the U.S. Supreme Court suspended its use from 1968 to 1976. Eventually, the Court decided that capital punishment does not violate the Eighth Amendment's prohibition of cruel and unusual punishments. Executions resumed in 1977 as a majority of states began, once again, to sentence murderers to death.

The numbers of people facing the death penalty has increased dramatically, as Figure 9.2 reveals. As of January 1, 2008, 3,309 people awaited execution in death penalty states. Two-thirds of those on death row are in the South. The greatest number of death row inmates are in California, Texas, Florida, and Pennsylvania (see Figure 9.3). Although about 200 people are sent to death row each year, since 1977 the annual number of executions has never exceeded 98 (which occurred in 1999).

The Death Penalty and the Constitution   Death differs from other punishments in that it is final and irreversible. The Supreme Court has therefore examined the decision-making process in capital cases to ensure that it fulfills the Constitution's requirements regarding due process, equal protection, and cruel and unusual punishments. Because life is in the balance, capital cases must be conducted according to higher standards of fairness and more-careful procedures than are other kinds of cases. Several important Supreme Court cases illustrate this concern.

Prisoners sentenced to death typically must wait several years as their cases move through the appeals process. Michael Rodriguez was among a group of Texas prison escapees who killed a police officer during a robbery in 2000. Here he was interviewed on death row just two weeks prior to his execution by lethal injection in August 2008. Should appeals in death penalty cases be accelerated in order to speed up executions, or would speedy appeals increase the risk of executing an innocent person?

AP Images/Mike Graczyk

FIGURE 9.2

People under sentence of death and people executed, 1953–2008

In recent years, 115 or more new offenders have been added to death row each year, but the number of executions has never exceeded 98. What explains this fact?

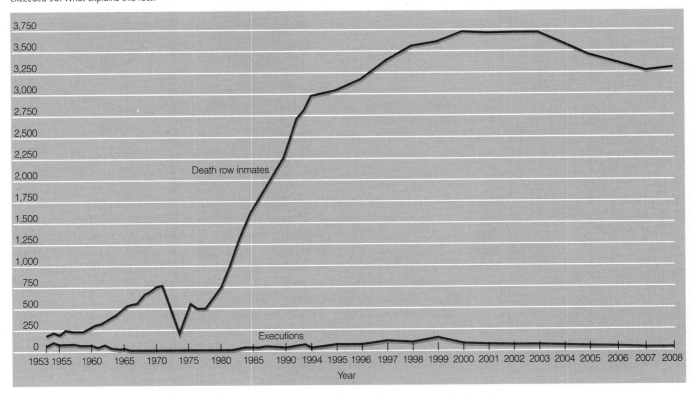

Sources: Death Penalty Information Center: *The Death Penalty in 2008: Year End Report*, December 2008, p. 7; *Facts about the Death Penalty*, June 1, 2008, http://www.deathpenaltyinfo.org/.

FIGURE 9.3
Death row census, 2008

Many of the inmates on death row are concentrated in certain states. African Americans make up about 13 percent of the U.S. population but 42 percent of the death row population. How might you explain this higher percentage of death sentences in proportion to the population?

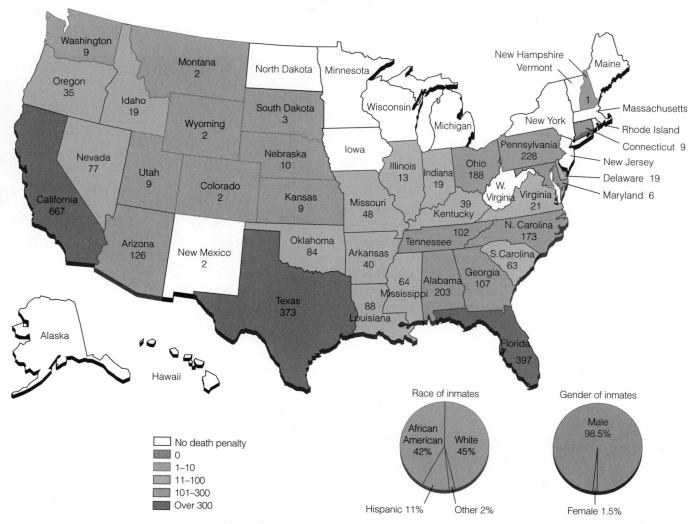

Race of inmates

African American 42%
White 45%
Hispanic 11%
Other 2%

Gender of inmates

Male 98.5%
Female 1.5%

No death penalty
0
1–10
11–100
101–300
Over 300

Note: The two offenders on death row in New Mexico remain under sentence of death although the state abolished the death penalty for crimes in 2009 and thereafter.

Sources: Death Penalty Information Center, *The Death Penalty in 2008: Year End Report,* December 2008, p. 7.

■ *Furman v. Georgia* (1972) The death penalty, as administered, constitutes cruel and unusual punishment.

■ *Gregg v. Georgia* (1976) Death penalty laws are constitutional if they require the judge and jury to consider certain mitigating and aggravating circumstances in deciding which convicted murderers should be sentenced to death. Proceedings must also be divided into a trial phase and a punishment phase, and there must be opportunities for appeal.

In *Furman v. Georgia* (1972), the Supreme Court ruled that the death penalty, as administered, constituted cruel and unusual punishment. The decision invalidated the death penalty laws of 39 states and the District of Columbia. A majority of justices found that the procedures used to impose death sentences were arbitrary and unfair. Over the next several years, more than three dozen states eventually enacted new capital punishment statutes that provided for different procedures and methods of execution, such as lethal injection.

The new laws were tested before the Supreme Court in *Gregg v. Georgia* (1976). The Court upheld those laws that required the sentencing judge or jury to take into account specific aggravating and mitigating factors in deciding which convicted murderers should be sentenced to death. Further, the Court decided that, rather than having a single proceeding determine the defendant's guilt and whether the death sentence would be applied, states should use "bifurcated proceedings." In this two-part process, the defendant has a trial that finds him guilty or not guilty and then a separate hearing that focuses exclusively on the issues of punishment. It seeks to ensure a thorough deliberation before someone receives the ultimate punishment.

Under the *Gregg* decision, the prosecution uses the punishment phase hearing to focus attention on the existence of aggravating factors, such as excessive cruelty or a defendant's prior record of violent crimes. The defense may focus on mitigating factors, such as the offender's youthfulness, mental condition, or lack of a criminal record. Before the judge or jury can decide to impose a death sentence, they must weigh these aggravating and mitigating factors. The Supreme Court has ruled that the defendant may not be brought into court for the sentencing hearing wearing chains and shackles. Such visible restraints might make the individual seem exceptionally dangerous and therefore influence the jury to favor the death penalty (*Deck v. Missouri*, 2005). Because of the Court's emphasis on fair procedures and individualized decisions, state appellate courts review trial court procedures in virtually every capital case.

In *McCleskey v. Kemp* (1987), opponents of the death penalty felt that the U.S. Supreme Court failed to accept strong evidence. In this case, the Court rejected a challenge to Georgia's death penalty law, made on the grounds of racial discrimination. Warren McCleskey, an African American, was sentenced to death for killing a white police officer. Before the U.S. Supreme Court, McCleskey's attorney cited research that showed a disparity in the imposition of the death penalty in Georgia, based on the race of the victim and, to a lesser extent, the race of the defendant (Baldus, Woodworth, and Pulaski, 1994). In particular, when African American men were murdered, there was little likelihood that the death penalty would be pursued. When an African American man was convicted of killing a white person, the likelihood of the death penalty increased dramatically (M. R. Williams, Demuth, and Holcomb, 2007).

By a 5–4 vote, the justices rejected McCleskey's assertion that Georgia's capital-sentencing practices violated the equal protection clause of the Constitution by producing racial discrimination. The slim majority of justices declared that McCleskey would have to prove that the decision makers acted with a discriminatory purpose in deciding his particular case. The Court also concluded that statistical evidence showing discrimination throughout the Georgia courts did not provide adequate proof. McCleskey was executed in 1991. The decision made it very difficult to prove the existence of racial discrimination in capital cases, but it did not alleviate continuing concerns that death penalty cases can be infected with racial bias (R. N. Walker, 2006).

In June 2002, the Supreme Court broke new ground in a way that heartened opponents of the death penalty. First, in *Atkins v. Virginia*, it ruled that execution of the mentally retarded was unconstitutional. Daryl Atkins, who has an IQ of 59, was sentenced to death for killing Eric Nesbitt in a 7-Eleven store parking lot. As the majority opinion noted, the characteristics of mentally retarded offenders, people with IQs of less than 70, "undermine the strength of the procedural protections." This point is in keeping with the argument of mental health experts who say their suggestibility and willingness to please leads developmentally disabled people to confess. At trial, they have problems remembering details, locating witnesses, and testifying credibly in their own behalf.

The Supreme Court further reduced the scope of capital punishment, in *Roper v. Simmons* (2005). A slim majority of justices decided that offenders cannot be sentenced to death for crimes that they committed before they reached the age of 18. Prior to that decision, the United States was among only a half-dozen countries in the entire world with laws that permitted death sentences for juveniles. The same five-member majority also ruled that the death penalty cannot be imposed as a punishment for the crime of child rape (*Kennedy v. Louisiana*, 2008). Because the Court was deeply divided on these issues, some observers wonder if further changes in the Court's composition may lead to a reversal of these decisions.

All states use lethal injection as the means to conduct executions, although a few states permit the condemned prisoners to choose the electric chair or another means that was in existence at the time of their conviction (Liptak, 2008a). Lethal injection

■ *McCleskey v. Kemp* (1987) The Supreme Court rejects a challenge of Georgia's death penalty on grounds of racial discrimination.

■ *Atkins v. Virginia* (2002) Execution of the mentally retarded is unconstitutional.

■ *Roper v. Simmons* (2005) Execution of offenders for crimes committed while under the age of 18 is unconstitutional.

remains controversial as a method of execution because of botched executions. In these cases, prolonged and painful deaths resulted from improperly inserted needles or malfunctioning tubes that carry the chemicals (Radelet, 2004). The constitutionality of lethal injection as a means of execution was examined by the U.S. Supreme Court in *Baze v. Rees* (2008). All of the justices concluded that the attorneys for the death row inmates had not proved that the use of lethal injection violates the Eighth Amendment. The case was notable because of Justice John Paul Stevens's separate opinion. In it, he announced that he had concluded, after more than 30 years on the Supreme Court, that "the death penalty represents 'the pointless and needless extinction of life . . .' [that] is patently excessive and cruel and unusual punishment violative of the Eighth Amendment." It remains to be seen whether future changes in the Supreme Court's composition will increase the number of justices who question the constitutionality of capital punishment.

Continuing Legal Issues   The case law since *Furman* indicates that capital punishment is legal so long as it is imposed fairly. However, opponents continue to raise several issues in litigation and in arguments presented to legislatures and the public (Acker, 2007). Now that the mentally retarded and juvenile offenders have been excluded from eligibility for the death penalty, some people argue that mentally ill offenders should also be excluded. Issues have arisen about the effectiveness of representation provided for capital defendants by defense attorneys. Many critics are concerned about the impact of using death-qualified juries. Other cases continue to raise issues about methods of execution and the lengthy periods that condemned offenders spend on death row because of appeals. Finally, issues have arisen concerning the requirements of international law on the administration of capital punishment in the United States. We look at each of these in turn.

EXECUTION OF THE MENTALLY ILL   As we saw in Chapter 3, insanity is a recognized defense for commission of a crime. Moreover, the Supreme Court has said that people who become insane after entering prison cannot be executed (*Ford v. Wainwright*, 1986). But many people with mental illnesses do not meet the legal tests for insanity. They can be convicted of crimes and punished, and there is no guarantee that they will receive psychiatric treatment in prison. What happens if these people commit capital crimes? Is it appropriate to execute people whose mental illnesses may have affected their behavior? Opponents of the death penalty will undoubtedly seek to persuade the Supreme Court that mentally ill offenders should be excluded from capital punishment, following the rulings regarding the mentally retarded and juveniles.

Critics have also questioned whether it is medically ethical to treat an offender's mental illness so that he or she can be executed. In 2003, the U.S. 8th Circuit Court of Appeals held that Arkansas could force a death row inmate to take antipsychotic drugs to make him sane enough to execute. Similarly, ethical concerns related to the physicians' oath to "do no harm" led California to postpone executions by lethal injection, because doctors refused to participate. Such issues may be raised on behalf of mentally ill offenders in future court cases.

EFFECTIVE COUNSEL   In *Strickland v. Washington* (1984), the Supreme Court ruled that defendants in capital cases had the right to representation that meets an "objective standard of reasonableness." As noted by Justice Sandra Day O'Connor, the appellant must show "that there is a reasonable probability that, but for the counsel's unprofessional errors, the result of the proceeding would be different." Although it is possible to identify errors made by an attorney, it can be difficult to persuade judges that anything less than truly major errors actually affected the outcome of the case.

In the past decade, the public has learned of cases placing the defense attorney's competency in doubt, such as the case of a defense attorney sleeping during a murder trial. In 1999, the *Chicago Tribune* conducted an extensive investigation of capital punishment in Illinois. Reporters found that 33 defendants sentenced to death since 1977 were represented by attorneys who had been, or were later, disbarred or suspended for conduct that was "incompetent, unethical or even criminal." These attorneys included David Landau, who was disbarred one year after representing a Will County defendant sentenced to death, and Robert McDonnell, a convicted felon and the only lawyer in Illinois to be disbarred twice. McDonnell represented four men who landed on death row (K. Armstrong and Mills, 1999).

In March 2000, a federal judge in Texas ordered the release of Calvin Jerold Burdine after 16 years on death row. At his 1984 trial, Burdine's counsel slept through long portions of the proceedings. As the judge said, "Sleeping counsel is equivalent to no counsel at all" (*New York Times*, March 2, 2000, p. A19).

These highly publicized cases may have caught the attention of the Supreme Court. In 2003, the Court issued a decision that seemed designed to remind lawyers and judges about the need for competent defense attorneys in capital cases. In *Wiggins v. Smith* (2003), the Court found that the Sixth Amendment right to counsel was violated when a defense attorney failed to present mitigating evidence concerning the severe physical and sexual abuse suffered by the defendant during childhood. Whether the justices create clearer or stricter standards for defense attorneys remains to be seen.

DEATH-QUALIFIED JURIES Should people who are opposed to the death penalty be excluded from juries in capital cases? In *Witherspoon v. Illinois* (1968), the Supreme Court held that potential jurors who have general objections to the death penalty or whose religious convictions oppose its use cannot be automatically excluded from jury service in capital cases. However, it upheld the practice of removing, during voir dire (preliminary examination), those people whose opposition is so strong as to "prevent or substantially impair the performance of their duties." Such jurors have become known as *"Witherspoon excludables."* The decision was later reaffirmed in *Lockhart v. McCree* (1986).

Because society is divided on capital punishment, opponents argue that death-qualified juries do not represent a cross section of the community. Researchers have also found that "juries are likely to be nudged toward believing the defendant is guilty and toward an imposition of the death sentence by the very process of undergoing death qualification" (Luginbuhl and Burkhead, 1994:107).

Mark Costanzo (1997:24–25) points to research indicating that death qualification has several impacts. First, those who are selected for jury duty are more conviction prone and more receptive to aggravating factors presented during the penalty phase. A second, subtler impact is that jurors answering the questions about their willingness to vote for a death sentence often conclude that both defenders and prosecutors anticipate a conviction and a death sentence.

APPEALS Ongoing controversy surrounds the long appeals process for death penalty cases. The 65 prisoners executed in 2003 had been under sentence of death an average of 10 years and 11 months (Bonczar and Snell, 2004). During this time, sentences were reviewed by the state courts and through the writ of habeas corpus by the federal courts.

The late Chief Justice William Rehnquist, who served as chief justice from 1986 to 2005, actively sought to reduce the opportunities for capital punishment defendants to have their appeals heard by multiple courts. In 1996, President Bill Clinton signed the Anti-Terrorism and Effective Death Penalty Act that requires death row inmates to file habeas appeals within one year and requires federal judges to issue their decisions within strict time limits.

Appellate review is a time-consuming and expensive process, but it also makes an impact. From 1977 through 2003, 7,061 people entered prison under sentence of death. During those 26 years, 885 people were executed, 282 died of natural causes, and 2,542 were removed from death row as a result of appellate court decisions and reviews, commutations, or death while awaiting execution (Bonczar and Snell, 2004).

Michael Radelet and his colleagues have examined the cases of 68 death row inmates later released because of doubts about their guilt (Radelet, Lofquist, and Bedau, 1996:907). This number is equivalent to one-fifth of the inmates executed during

■ ***Witherspoon v. Illinois* (1968)** Potential jurors who object to the death penalty cannot be automatically excluded from service; however, during voir dire, those who feel so strongly about capital punishment that they could not give an impartial verdict may be excluded.

the period 1970–1996. Correction of the miscarriage of justice for about one-third of the defendants took four or less years, but it took nine years or longer for another third of the defendants. Had the expedited appeals process and limitations on habeas corpus been in effect, would these death sentences have been overturned?

INTERNATIONAL LAW   The United States has signed the Vienna Convention on Consular Relations, which requires notification of consular officials when a foreign national is arrested. This aspect of international law benefits Americans who are arrested abroad, by enabling the U.S. embassy to help find a lawyer and monitor the prosecution of Americans who face criminal punishment in foreign countries. However, individual prosecutors and police throughout the United States are apparently unaware of the law, because several dozen foreign nationals have been convicted and sentenced to death in the United States without their consular officials being informed.

Mexico, Germany, and Paraguay filed complaints against the United States for violating the Vienna Convention in death penalty cases. In April 2004, the International Court of Justice in The Hague, Netherlands, ruled that international law had been violated and ordered the United States to review the death sentences of Mexicans held on American death rows. The International Court has no power to force the United States to take action, but President George W. Bush announced in February 2005 that the United States would comply with the Vienna Convention in the future. President Bush did not, however, have any means to ensure that each county prosecutor throughout the United States would follow the Vienna Convention. In light of the president's announcement, the Supreme Court decided not to rule in a pending case brought to it by a Mexican citizen on death row in Texas (*Medellin v. Dretke*, 2005). Instead, the majority of justices decided to see how the Texas courts would handle the issue.

The Texas courts subsequently rejected the notion that the treaty was superior to state law and procedure. They also refused to follow the president's order to follow the Vienna Convention. When the case returned to the U.S. Supreme Court in 2008, a majority of justices concluded that the president lacked the power to order the states to follow the treaty (*Medellin v. Texas*, 2008). It remains to be seen whether additional issues and arguments based on international law will arise concerning the death penalty.

The Death Penalty: A Continuing Controversy

Various developments in the twenty-first century appear to indicate a weakening of support for capital punishment in the United States. On January 13, 2000, Illinois Governor George Ryan, a long-time supporter of the death penalty, called for a moratorium on executions in his state. Ryan said that he was convinced that the death penalty in Illinois was "fraught with errors," noting that since 1976 Illinois had executed 12 people yet freed 13 from death row as innocent. Similar calls followed from the governors of Kansas and Maryland, the Louisiana Bar Association, and the Philadelphia City Council. In May 2000, the New Hampshire legislature became the first in more than two decades to vote to repeal the death penalty; the governor vetoed it, however. In January 2003, Governor Ryan pardoned four death row inmates and commuted the sentences of 167 to life imprisonment without parole.

Both Illinois and Massachusetts appointed commissions to study whether and how the courts could process death penalty cases fairly and with little risk that an innocent person would be erroneously convicted. The recommendations from commissions in both states emphasized providing high-quality representation for defendants; using scientific evidence, such as DNA testing, when appropriate; and careful appeals processes. Mitt Romney, the governor of Massachusetts at the time, sought to use his commission report as the basis for proposing the limited use of capital punishment in a state that currently does not use the death penalty.

Subsequently, the legislatures of New Jersey (Richburg, 2007) and New Mexico (Urbina, 2009), as well as the House of Representatives in New Hampshire

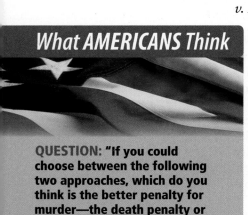

What AMERICANS Think

QUESTION: "If you could choose between the following two approaches, which do you think is the better penalty for murder—the death penalty or life imprisonment with absolutely no possibility of parole?"

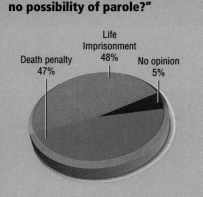

Death penalty 47%

Life Imprisonment 48%

No opinion 5%

Go to http://www.cengage.com/criminaljustice/cole to compare your opinion on this issue with the opinions of other criminal justice students.

Source: Gallup Poll, May 5–7, 2006, http://www.gallup.com.

THE POLICY DEBATE

Should the Death Penalty Be Abolished?

THE EXECUTION MORATORIUM imposed by Illinois Governor George Ryan in January 2000 reinvigorated debate on the death penalty. His announcement was soon followed by a national poll that found support for the penalty to be the lowest in 19 years, the release of a national study of appeals that found two-thirds of death sentences overturned, and research questioning the quality of counsel given to many defendants. Within months, the policy debate shifted to whether it was possible to construct a system that could ensure that innocent people would not be executed.

Opponents of capital punishment continue the fight to abolish it. They argue that poor people and minorities receive a disproportionate number of death sentences. They also point to the numbers of innocent people discovered on death row, to argue that the system is too fallible and flawed ever to produce error-free results.

Even the proponents of capital punishment remain dissatisfied with how it is applied. They point to the fact that although there are more than 3,300 convicted murderers on death row, the number of executions since 1976 has never exceeded 98 in a year. The appeals process is a major factor halting this pace, given that executions are delayed for years as cases are appealed through the courts.

For the Death Penalty

Supporters argue that society should apply swift, severe punishments to killers to address the continuing problems of crime and violence. Execution should occur quite soon after conviction so that the greatest deterrent value will result. They say that justice requires that a person who murders another must be executed. To do less is to denigrate the value of human life.

The arguments for the death penalty include the following:

- The death penalty deters criminals from committing violent acts.

- The death penalty achieves justice by paying killers back for their horrible crimes.

- The death penalty prevents criminals from doing further harm while on parole.

- The death penalty is less expensivle than holding murderers in prison for life.

Against the Death Penalty

Opponents believe that the death penalty lingers as a barbaric practice from a less civilized age. They point out that most other developed democracies in the world have ceased to execute criminals. Opponents challenge the death penalty's claims for effectiveness in reducing crime. They also raise concerns about whether the punishment can be applied without errors and discrimination.

The arguments against the death penalty include the following:

- No hard evidence proves that the death penalty is a deterrent.

- It is wrong for a government to participate in the intentional killing of citizens.

- The death penalty is applied in a discriminatory fashion.

- Innocent people have been sentenced to death.

- Some methods of execution are inhumane, causing painful, lingering deaths.

What Should U.S. Policy Be?

With more and more people now being sentenced to death row but fewer than a hundred individuals executed each year, death penalty policy is at a significant crossroads. Will the United States increase the pace of executions, allow the number of capital offenders in prison to keep growing, or take a middle ground that satisfies neither side completely, such as life imprisonment without parole for convicted murderers?

RESEARCHING THE INTERNET

Compare the perspectives presented at the websites of Pro-Death Penalty and the Death Penalty Information Center. Both are listed on the Cole/Smith Criminal Justice in America Companion Website: http://www.cengage.com/criminaljustice/cole.

FOR CRITICAL ANALYSIS

Evaluate the pros and cons of the death penalty debate. What political factors might influence your state's legislators to abolish, modify, or retain the death penalty?

(Chiaramida, 2009), voted to abolish capital punishment. The governors of New Jersey and New Mexico signed the law, but New Hampshire's Senate and governor blocked enactment (as the governor in 2000 had done). The Maryland legislature declined to follow the governor's request to abolish the death penalty, but instead severely restricted the application of the punishment in that state by requiring DNA evidence and a videotaped confession in any murder case for which the prosecution seeks capital punishment (Wagner, 2009).

Although public opinion polls still reflect significant support for the death penalty (see "What Americans Think"), the number of executions remains low. Recent surveys show that the public is split when asked to choose between life imprisonment (without parole) and death. Does this mean that Americans are ambivalent about carrying out the punishment? What might it say about capital punishment in the next decade? Debate on this important public policy issue has gone on for more than two hundred years, yet there is still no consensus (see "The Policy Debate" for more).

TABLE 9.2 The Punishment of Offenders

The goals of the criminal sanction are carried out in a variety of ways, depending upon the provisions of the law, the characteristics of the offender, and the discretion of the judge. Judges may impose sentences that combine several forms to achieve punishment objectives.

Form of Sanction	Description	Purposes
Incarceration	Imprisonment	
Indeterminate sentence	Specifies a maximum and minimum length of time to be served	Incapacitation, deterrence, rehabilitation
Determinate sentence	Specifies a certain length of time to be served	Retribution, deterrence, incapacitation
Mandatory sentence	Specifies a minimum amount of time that must be served for given crimes	Incapacitation, deterrence
Good time	Subtracts days from an inmate's sentence because of good behavior or participation in prison programs	Rewards behavior, relieves prison crowding, helps maintain prison discipline
Intermediate sanctions	Punishment for those requiring sanctions more restrictive than probation but less restrictive than prison	Retribution, deterrence
Administered by the judiciary		
Fine	Money paid to state by offender	Retribution, deterrence
Restitution	Money paid to victim by offender	Retribution, deterrence
Forfeiture	Seizure by the state of property illegally obtained or acquired with resources illegally obtained	Retribution, deterrence
Administered in the community		
Community service	Requires offender to perform work for the community	Retribution, deterrence
Home confinement	Requires offender to stay in home during certain times	Retribution, deterrence, incapacitation
Intensive probation supervision	Requires strict and frequent reporting to probation officer	Retribution, deterrence, incapacitation
Administered institutionally		
Boot camp/shock incarceration	Short-term institutional sentence emphasizing physical development and discipline, followed by probation	Retribution, deterrence, rehabilitation
Probation	Allows offender to serve a sentence in the community under supervision	Retribution, incapacitation, rehabilitation
Death	Execution	Incapacitation, deterrence, retribution

The criminal sanction takes many forms, with offenders punished in various ways to serve various purposes. Table 9.2 summarizes how these sanctions operate and how they reflect the underlying philosophies of punishment.

CHECKPOINT

ANSWERS

3 What are the three types of sentences used in the United States?

3 Determinate, indeterminate, and mandatory sentences.

4 What are thought to be the advantages of intermediate sanctions?

4 Intermediate sanctions give judges a greater range of sentencing alternatives, reduce prison populations, cost less than prison, and increase community security.

5 What requirements specified in Gregg v. Georgia must exist before a death sentence can be imposed?

5 Judge and jury must be able to consider mitigating and aggravating circumstances, proceedings must be divided into a trial phase and a punishment phase, and there must be opportunities for appeal.

The Sentencing Process

Regardless of how and where guilt has been determined—misdemeanor court or felony court, plea bargain or adversarial context, bench or jury trial—judges hold the responsibility for imposing sentences. Often difficult, sentencing usually involves more than applying clear-cut principles to individual cases. In one case, a judge may decide to sentence a forger to prison as an example to others, even though the offender poses no threat to community safety and probably does not need rehabilitative treatment. In another case, the judge may impose a light sentence on a youthful offender who has committed a serious crime but may be a candidate for rehabilitation if moved quickly back into society.

Legislatures establish the penal codes that set forth the sentences judges can impose. These laws generally give judges discretion in sentencing. Judges may combine various forms of punishment in order to tailor the sanction to the offender. The judge may specify, for example, that the prison terms for two charges are to run either concurrently (at the same time) or consecutively (one after the other), or that all or part of the period of imprisonment may be suspended. In other situations, the offender may receive a combination of a suspended prison term, a fine, and probation. Judges may suspend a sentence as long as the offender stays out of trouble, makes restitution, or seeks medical treatment. They may also delay imposing any sentence but retain the power to set penalties at a later date if the offender misbehaves.

Within the discretion allowed by the code, various elements influence the decisions of judges. Social scientists believe that several factors influence the sentencing process: (1) the administrative context of the courts, (2) the attitudes and values of judges, (3) the presentence report, and (4) sentencing guidelines.

■ The Administrative Context of the Courts

Judges are strongly influenced by the administrative context within which they impose sentences. As a result, differences are found, for example, between the assembly-line style of justice in misdemeanor courts and the more formal proceedings in felony courts.

Misdemeanor Courts: Assembly-Line Justice   Misdemeanor or lower courts have limited jurisdiction because they normally can impose only jail sentences of less than one year. These courts hear about 90 percent of criminal cases. Whereas felony cases are processed in lower courts only for arraignments and preliminary hearings, misdemeanor cases are processed completely in the lower courts. Only a minority of cases adjudicated in lower courts end in jail sentences. Most cases result in fines, probation, community service, restitution, or a combination of these.

Most lower courts are overloaded and allot minimal time to each case. Judicial decisions are mass produced because actors in the system share three assumptions. First, any person appearing before the court is guilty, because the police and prosecution have presumably filtered out doubtful cases. Second, the vast majority of defendants will plead guilty. Third, those charged with minor offenses will be processed in volume, with dozens of cases being decided in rapid succession within a single hour. The citation will be read by the clerk, a guilty plea entered, and the sentence pronounced by the judge for one defendant after another.

In misdemeanor cases, judges' sentencing decisions may be influenced by many factors, including the defendant's remorse, the availability of space for new offenders in the county jail, and the defendant's prior record. Here, Eric Feltner, a former government official in Missouri, is sentenced to probation and community service for public display of explicit sexual materials. Is it important for judges to impose comparable sentences on offenders who are convicted of similar crimes?

AP Images/Kelley McCall

TABLE 9.3   Types of Felony Sentences Imposed by State Courts

Although a felony conviction is often equated with a prison sentence, almost a third of felony offenders receive probation.

Most Serious Conviction Offense	Percentage of Felons Sentenced to		
	Prison	Jail	Probation
All offenses	41	28	31
Violent offenses	52	25	23
Murder	91	4	5
Sexual assault	59	23	18
Rape	67	22	11
Other sexual assault	55	23	22
Robbery	71	15	14
Aggravated assault	42	29	29
Other violent	42	35	23
Property offenses	38	28	34
Burglary	46	26	28
Larceny	36	31	33
Motor vehicle	37	39	24
Fraud	31	28	41
Drug offenses	39	27	34
Possession	34	28	38
Trafficking	42	26	32
Weapons offenses	45	28	27
Other offenses	35	35	30

Note: For persons receiving a combination of sanctions, the sentence designation came from the most severe penalty imposed—prison being the most severe, followed by jail and then probation.

Source: Matthew R. Durose and Patrick A. Langan, "Felony Sentences in State Courts, 2002," Bureau of Justice Statistics *Bulletin*, December 2004, p. 2.

Defendants whose cases are processed through the lower court's assembly line may appear to receive little or no punishment. However, people who get caught in the criminal justice system experience other punishments, whether or not they are ultimately convicted. A person who is arrested but eventually released still incurs various tangible and intangible costs. Time spent in jail awaiting trial, the cost of a bail bond, and days of work lost create an immediate and concrete impact. Poor people may lose their jobs or be evicted from their homes if they fail to work and pay their bills for even a few days. For most people, simply being arrested is a devastating experience. It is impossible to measure the psychological and social price of being stigmatized, separated from family, and deprived of freedom.

Felony Courts   Felony cases are processed and felony offenders are sentenced in courts of general jurisdiction. Because of the seriousness of the crimes, the atmosphere is more formal and generally lacks the chaotic, assembly-line environment of misdemeanor courts. Caseload burdens can affect how much time individual cases receive. Exchange relationships among courtroom actors can facilitate plea bargains and shape the content of prosecutors' sentencing recommendations. Sentencing decisions are ultimately shaped, in part, by the relationships, negotiations, and agreements among the prosecutor, defense attorney, and judge. Table 9.3 shows the types of felony sentences imposed for conviction on different charges.

■ Attitudes and Values of Judges

All lawyers recognize that judges differ from one another in their sentencing decisions. Administrative pressures, the conflicting goals of criminal justice, and the influence of community values partly explain these differences. Sentencing decisions also depend on judges' attitudes concerning the offender's blameworthiness, the protection of the community, and the practical implications of the sentence (Steffensmeier and Demuth, 2001).

Blameworthiness concerns such factors as offense severity (such as violent crime or property crime), the offender's criminal history (such as recidivist or first timer), and role in commission of the crime (such as leader or follower). For example, a judge might impose a harsh sentence on a repeat offender who organized others to commit a serious crime.

Protection of the community hinges on similar factors, such as dangerousness, recidivism, and offense severity. However, it centers mostly on the need to incapacitate the offender or to deter would-be offenders.

Finally, the practical implications of a sentence can affect judges' decisions. For example, judges may take into account the offender's ability to "do time," as in the case of an elderly person. They may also consider the impact on the offender's family; a mother with children may receive a different sentence than a single woman would. Finally, costs to the corrections system may play a role in sentencing, as judges consider probation officers' caseloads or prison crowding (Steffensmeier, Kramer, and Streifel, 1993).

CAREERS IN CRIMINAL JUSTICE

District Associate Judge

OTTUMWA, IOWA
KIRK DAILY, DISTRICT ASSOCIATE JUDGE

UNDER IOWA LAW, district associate judges have the authority to hear Class D felonies as well as serious and aggravated misdemeanors. Substance abuse crimes can form a significant component of the court's docket. Such crimes include operating a motor vehicle while intoxicated and possession of controlled substances. The penalties for crimes handled by this limited-jurisdiction court can range from probation and other community-based sanctions to one year in county jail and up to five years in state prison. Thus, these judges' decisions significantly impact the lives of people charged with such crimes.

Judges in such courts make determinations of probable cause and decide whether to issue search warrants. They also conduct preliminary hearings in criminal cases. District associate judges also have jurisdiction over civil suits when the amount in controversy is $10,000 or less. Finally, these judges handle appeals for both criminal and civil matters that have been decided in the limited-jurisdiction magistrate court

After graduating from college and law school, Kirk Daily entered private law practice as an attorney in his hometown of Ottumwa, Iowa. The career path to a judgeship, whether in a

system of elected judges or appointed judges, typically depends on building a solid reputation for wisdom, intelligence, ethics, and industriousness. Daily gained significant knowledge and experience concerning many areas of law through a broad, general law practice that ranged from representing criminal defendants for serious crimes, including murder, to civil cases such as medical malpractice and divorce. The breadth of his experience as a lawyer provided exceptionally good training for his later role as judge. As a judge, he must use his knowledge of law to make decisions concerning a wide variety of cases, both criminal and civil. Iowa uses a merit-selection process for choosing judges, and Daily's solid experience and impressive performance as an attorney led to his selection for a judgeship.

Substance abuse crimes, such as the use and manufacture of meth-amphetamine and drunk driving, take up a great deal of my time. There are high recidivism rates among substance abusers, and their cases require a high level of follow-up supervision to assist these individuals to deal with their addictions. In sentencing substance abusers, judges must often weigh public safety against treatment. Creating a sentence that aims to treat a person's addiction, rather than simply imposing prison, increases a judge's options.

Judges' decisions have profound impacts on the lives of people drawn into the criminal justice system. Would you want to make sentencing decisions that determine the fates of people convicted of crimes? Consider how you would perform as a judge when you read "Careers in Criminal Justice."

■ Presentence Report

Even though sentencing is the judge's responsibility, the **presentence report** has become an important ingredient in the judicial mix. Usually, a probation officer investigates the convicted person's background, criminal record, job status, and mental condition to suggest a sentence that is in the interests of both the offender and society. Although the presentence report serves primarily to help the judge select the sentence, it also assists in the classification of probationers, prisoners, and parolees for treatment planning and risk assessment. In the report, the probation officer makes judgments about what information to include and what conclusions to draw from that information. In some states, however, probation officers present only factual material to the judge and make no sentencing recommendation. Because the probation officers do not necessarily follow evidentiary rules, they may include hearsay statements as well as firsthand information. The Close Up box gives an example of a presentence report.

■ **presentence report** A report, prepared by a probation officer, that presents a convicted offender's background and is used by the judge in selecting an appropriate sentence.

CLOSE UP

Sample Presentence Report

STATE OF NEW MEXICO
Corrections Department Field Service Division
Santa Fe, New Mexico 87501
Date: March 4, 2006
To: The Honorable Manuel Baca
From: Presentence Unit, Officer Brian Gaines
Re: Richard Knight

EVALUATION

Appearing before Your Honor for sentencing is 20-year-old Richard Knight, who on November 10, 2005, pursuant to a Plea and Disposition Agreement, entered a plea of guilty to Aggravated Assault Upon a Peace Officer (Deadly Weapon) (Firearm Enhancement), as charged in Information Number 95-5736900. The terms of the agreement stipulate that the maximum period of incarceration be limited to one year, that restitution be made on all counts and charges whether dismissed or not, and that all remaining charges in the Indictment and DA Files 39780 be dismissed.

The defendant is an only child, born and raised in Albuquerque. He attended West Mesa High School until the eleventh grade, at which time he dropped out. Richard declared that he felt school was "too difficult" and that he decided that it would be more beneficial for him to obtain steady employment rather than to complete his education. The defendant further stated that he felt it was "too late for vocational training" because of the impending one-year prison sentence he faces, due to the Firearm Enhancement penalty for his offense.

The longest period of time the defendant has held a job has been for six months with Frank's Concrete Company. He has been employed with the Madrid Construction Company since August 2004 (verified). Richard lives with his parents, who provide most of his financial support. Conflicts between his mother and himself, the defendant claimed, precipitated his recent lawless actions by causing him to "not care about anything." He stressed the fact that he is now once again "getting along" with his mother. Although the defendant contended that he doesn't abuse drugs, he later contradicted

himself by declaring that he "gets drunk every weekend." He noted that he was inebriated when he committed the present offense.

In regard to the present offense, the defendant recalled that other individuals at the party attempted to stab his friend and that he and his companion left and returned with a gun in order to settle the score. Richard claimed remorse for his offense and stated that his past family problems led him to spend most of his time on the streets, where he became more prone to violent conduct. The defendant admitted being a member of the 18th Street Gang.

RECOMMENDATION

It is respectfully recommended that the defendant be sentenced to three years incarceration and that the sentence be suspended. It is further recommended that the defendant be incarcerated for one year as to the mandatory Firearm Enhancement and then placed on three years probation under the following special conditions:

1. That restitution be made to Juan Lopez in the amount of $622.40.

2. That the defendant either maintain full-time employment or obtain his GED [general equivalency diploma].

3. That the defendant discontinue fraternizing with the 18th Street Gang members and terminate his own membership in the gang.

RESEARCHING THE INTERNET

You can see the actual forms that probation officers fill out in preparing a presentence report, at the corresponding website listed on the Cole/Smith Criminal Justice in America Companion Website: http://www.cengage.com/criminaljustice/cole.

FOR CRITICAL ANALYSIS

Do you agree with Probation Officer Gaines's recommendation to Judge Baca? Do you see problems carrying out this sentence? For Richard Knight? For the Corrections Department?

In the federal court system, the presentence report is supplemented by an additional report written by a pretrial services officer (PSO). This report focuses on the defendant's behavior and compliance with conditions while out on bail—prior to trial or plea or between the date of conviction and the date of sentencing.

The presentence report is one means by which judges ease the strain of decision making. The report lets judges shift partial responsibility to the probation department. Because a substantial number of sentencing alternatives are open to judges, they often rely on the report for guidance. "A Question of Ethics" at the end of this chapter illustrates some of the difficulties faced by a judge who must impose a sentence with little more than the presentence report to consider.

■ Sentencing Guidelines

sentencing guidelines A mechanism to indicate to judges the expected sanction for certain offenses, in order to reduce disparities in sentencing.

Since the 1980s, **sentencing guidelines** have been established in the federal courts and in more than two dozen states. Such guidelines indicate to judges the expected sanction for particular types of offenses. They are intended to limit the sentencing discretion of judges and to reduce disparity among sentences given for similar offenses. Although statutes provide a variety of sentencing options for particular crimes, guidelines attempt to direct the judge to more-specific actions that should be taken. The range of sentencing options provided for most offenses centers on the seriousness of the crime and on the criminal history of an offender.

Legislatures and, in some states and the federal government, commissions construct sentencing guidelines as a grid of two scores (Tonry, 1993:140). As shown in Table 9.4, the Minnesota Guidelines, one dimension relates to the seriousness of the offense, the other to the likelihood of offender recidivism. The offender score is obtained by totaling the points allocated to such factors as the number of juvenile, adult misdemeanor, and adult felony convictions; the number of times incarcerated; the status of the accused at the time of the last offense, whether on probation or parole or escaped from confinement; and employment status or educational achievement. Judges look at the grid to see what sentence should be imposed on a particular offender who has committed a specific offense. Judges may go outside the guidelines if aggravating or mitigating circumstances exist; however, they must provide a written explanation of their reasons for doing so (J. H. Kramer and Ulmer, 1996).

TABLE 9.4   Minnesota Sentencing Guidelines Grid (presumptive sentence length in months)

The italicized numbers in the grid are the range within which a judge may sentence without the sentence being considered a departure. The criminal-history score is computed by adding one point for each prior felony conviction, one-half point for each prior gross misdemeanor conviction, and one-quarter point for each prior misdemeanor conviction.

Less Serious ← **Criminal-History Score** → More Serious

Severity of Offense (Illustrative Offenses)		0	1	2	3	4	5	6 or more
Murder, second degree (intentional murder, drive-by shootings)	XI	306 *261–367*	326 *278–391*	346 *295–415*	366 *312–439*	386 *329–463*	406 *346–480*	426 *363–480*
Murder, third degree Murder, second degree (unintentional murder)	X	150 *128–180*	165 *141–198*	180 *153–216*	195 *166–234*	210 *179–252*	225 *192–270*	240 *240–288*
Assault, first degree Controlled substance crime, first degree	IX	86 *74–103*	98 *84–117*	110 *94–132*	122 *104–146*	134 *114–160*	146 *125–175*	158 *135–189*
Aggravated robbery, first degree Controlled substance crime, second degree	VIII	48 *41–57*	58 *50–69*	68 *58–81*	78 *67–93*	88 *75–105*	98 *84–117*	108 *92–129*
Felony DWI	VII	36	42	48	54 *46–64*	60 *51–72*	66 *57–79*	72 *62–84*
Controlled substance crime, third degree	VI	21	27	33	39 *34–46*	45 *39–54*	51 *44–61*	57 *49–68*
Residential burglary Simple robbery	V	18	23	28	33 *29–39*	38 *33–45*	43 *37–51*	48 *41–57*
Nonresidential burglary	IV	12	15	18	21	24 *21–28*	27 *23–32*	30 *26–36*
Theft crimes (over $5,000)	III	12	13	15	17	19 *17–22*	21 *18–25*	23 *20–27*
Theft crimes ($5,000 or less) Check forgery ($251–$2,500)	II	12	12	13	15	17	19	21 *18–25*
Sale of simulated controlled substance	I	12	12	12	13	15	17	19 *17–22*

☐ At the discretion of the judge, up to a year in jail and/or other nonjail sanctions can be imposed instead of prison sentences as conditions of probation for most of these offenses. If prison is imposed, the presumptive sentence is the number of months shown.

☐ Presumptive commitment to state prison for all offenses.

Note: First-degree murder has a mandatory life sentence and is excluded from the guidelines by law.
Source: Minnesota Sentencing Guidelines Commission, *Minnesota Sentencing Guidelines and Commentary,* August 1, 2008.

Sentencing guidelines are to be reviewed and modified periodically so that recent decisions will be included. Given that guidelines are constructed on the basis of past sentences, some critics argue that because the guidelines reflect only what has happened, they do not reform sentencing. Others question the choice of characteristics included in the offender scale and charge that some are used to mask racial criteria. Paula Krautt (2002:655) found differences in drug-trafficking sentences among federal district and circuit courts. However, Lisa Stolzenberg and Stewart J. D'Alessio (1994) studied the Minnesota guidelines and found, compared with preguideline decisions, an 18 percent reduction in disparity for the prison/no-prison outcome and a 60 percent reduction in disparity of length of prison sentences.

Although guidelines make sentences more uniform, many judges object to having their discretion limited in this manner (J. B. Weinstein, 1992). However, Peter Rossi and Richard Berk (1997) found a fair amount of agreement between the sentences prescribed in the federal guidelines and those desired by the general public.

The future of sentencing guidelines is uncertain. In 2004, the U.S. Supreme Court decided that aspects of Washington state sentencing guidelines violated the Sixth Amendment right to trial by jury, by giving judges too much authority to enhance sentences based on unproved factual determinations (*Blakely v. Washington*). One year later, the Supreme Court applied the *Blakely* precedent to the federal sentencing guidelines and found a similar violation of the Sixth Amendment when judges enhance sentences based on their own determinations (*United States v. Booker*, 2005). In 2008, however, the Supreme Court ruled that federal judges are not required to give advance notice to defendants prior to imposing a sentence that varies from the guidelines (*Irizarry v. United States*, 2008). Observers anticipate that the U.S. Supreme Court will need to revisit this issue in order to provide guidance about how sentencing guidelines can be properly designed and applied.

■ Who Gets the Harshest Punishment?

Harsh, unjust punishments can occur because of sentencing disparities and wrongful convictions. The prison population in most states contains a higher proportion of African American and Hispanic men than occurs in the general population. Are these disparities caused by racial prejudices and discrimination, or are other factors at work? Wrongful conviction occurs when people who are in fact innocent are nonetheless found guilty by plea or verdict. It also includes those cases in which the conviction of a truly guilty person is overturned on appeal because of due process errors.

Racial Disparities   Studies of racial disparities in sentencing are inconclusive. Because some studies show disparities in specific states or cities, though, there are grave concerns about the possibility of racial discrimination. Studies of sentencing in Pennsylvania, for example, found that there is a "high cost of being black, young (21–29 years), and male." Sentences given these offenders resulted in a higher proportion going to prison and incurring longer terms (Steffensmeier, Ulmer, and Kramer, 1998:789). While supporting the Pennsylvania results, research in Chicago, Kansas City, Missouri, and Miami found variation among the jurisdictions as to sentence length (Spohn and Holleran, 2000).

Do these disparities stem from the prejudicial attitudes of judges, police officers, and prosecutors? Are African Americans and Hispanics viewed as a "racial threat" when they commit crimes of violence and drug selling, which are thought to be spreading from the urban ghetto to the "previously safe places of the suburbs" (Crawford, Chiricos, and Kleck, 1998:484)? Are enforcement resources distributed so that certain groups are subject to closer scrutiny than are other groups?

Scholars have pointed out that the relationship between race and sentencing is complex and that judges consider many defendant and case characteristics. According to this view, judges assess not only the legally relevant factors of blameworthiness, dangerousness, and recidivism risk, but also race, gender, and age characteristics.

The interconnectedness of these variables, not judges' negative attitudes, is what culminates in the disproportionately severe sentences given young black men.

Federal sentencing guidelines were adjusted in 2007 and 2008 to reduce the impact of a highly criticized source of racial disparities in prison sentences for offenders convicted of cocaine-related offenses. The federal sentencing guidelines for crack cocaine offenses—which disproportionately affected African American defendants—were adjusted to be more closely aligned with shorter sentences for possessing and selling similar amounts of powder cocaine, crimes more commonly associated with white offenders. The U.S. Sentencing Commission voted to apply these new guidelines retroactively, meaning that offenders currently serving long sentences for crack cocaine offenses were eligible to be resentenced to shorter terms in prison. In many cases, this adjustment led to the release in 2008 of offenders who had already served for longer periods than those required under the new sentencing guidelines (Gezari, 2008; "National Summits," 2008).

Thomas McGowan (center) celebrates his release from prison in 2008. After he served more than two decades in prison, DNA evidence demonstrated his innocence. One of his lawyers is Barry Scheck (left), a founder of the Innocence Project, which seeks to free wrongly convicted prisoners. How could criminal justice processes be changed to reduce the risk of erroneous conviction?

© Fort Worth Star-Telegram/MCT /Landov

Wrongful Convictions   A serious dilemma for the criminal justice system concerns people who are falsely convicted and sentenced. Whereas the public expresses much concern over those who "beat the system" and go free, they pay comparatively little attention to those who are innocent yet convicted. Many of these people are wrongly convicted because victims and witnesses make mistakes in identifying alleged criminals from photographs and lineups.

The development of DNA technology has increased the number of people exonerated after being convicted. However, many cases do not have DNA evidence available. C. Ronald Huff notes that "because the great majority of cases do not produce biological material to be tested, one can only speculate about the error rate in those cases" (2002:2). Even when there is DNA evidence available, the U.S. Supreme Court has ruled that convicted offenders do not have a constitutional right to have the stored evidence tested. According to a five-member majority on the Court, state legislatures and Congress should develop their own rules concerning opportunities to have old evidence tested (*District Attorney's Office v. Osborne*, 2009). Each year, several cases of the conviction of innocent people come to national attention, yet there is no way to know how many more innocent people may be wrongly confined in prisons today.

Whether from racial discrimination or wrongful convictions, unjust punishments do not serve the ideals of justice. Such punishments raise fundamental questions about the criminal justice system and its links to the society it serves.

CHECKPOINT

ANSWER

6 *What are the four factors thought to influence the sentencing behavior of judges?*

6 The administrative context of the courts, the attitudes and values of judges, the presentence report, and sentencing guidelines.

A QUESTION OF ETHICS: WRITING ASSIGNMENT

Seated in her chambers, Judge Ruth Carroll read the presentence investigation report of the two young men she would sentence when court resumed. She had not heard these cases. As often happened in this very busy courthouse, the cases had been given to her only for sentencing. Judge Harold Krisch had handled the arraignment, plea, and trial.

The codefendants had held up a convenience store in the early morning hours, terrorizing the young manager and taking $47.50 from the till.

As she read the reports, Judge Carroll noticed that they looked pretty similar. Each offender had dropped out of high school, had held a series of low-wage jobs, and had one prior conviction for which probation had been imposed. Each had been convicted of Burglary 1, robbery at night with a gun.

Then she noticed the difference. David Bukowski had pleaded guilty to the charge in exchange for a promise of leniency. Richard Leach had been convicted on the same charge after a one-week trial. Judge Carroll pondered the decisions that she would soon have to make. Should Leach receive a stiffer sentence because he had taken the court's time and resources? Did she have an obligation to impose the light sentence recommended for Bukowski by the prosecutor and the defender?

There was a knock on the door. The bailiff stuck his head in. "Everything's ready, Your Honor."

"Okay, Ben, let's go."

WRITING ASSIGNMENT

Write a memo as if you were the judge, addressing the following questions: How will you decide? What factors will you weigh in your decision? How will you explain your decision?

Summary

Recognize the goals of punishment

▷ In the United States, the four main goals of the criminal sanction are retribution, deterrence, incapacitation, and rehabilitation.

▷ Restoration, a new approach to punishment, has not become mainstream yet.

▷ The goals of the criminal sanction are carried out through incarceration, intermediate sanctions, probation, and death.

Identify the types of sentences judges can impose

▷ Penal codes vary as to whether the permitted sentences are indeterminate, determinate, or mandatory. Each type of sentence makes certain assumptions about the goals of the criminal sanction.

▷ Good time allows correctional administrators to reduce the sentence of prisoners who live according to the rules and participate in various vocational, educational, and treatment programs.

▷ The U.S. Supreme Court allows capital punishment only when the judge and jury are allowed to take into account mitigating and aggravating circumstances.

▷ Judges often have considerable discretion in fashioning sentences to take into account factors such as the seriousness of the crime, the offender's prior record, and mitigating and aggravating circumstances.

Understand what really happens in sentencing

▷ The sentencing process is influenced by the administrative context of the courts, the attitudes and values of the judges, the presentence report, and sentencing guidelines.

Analyze whether the system treats wrongdoers equally

▷ Many states have formulated sentencing guidelines as a way of reducing disparity among the sentences given offenders in similar situations.

▷ Harsh, unjust punishments may result from racial discrimination or wrongful convictions.

Questions for Review

1. What are the major differences among retribution, deterrence, incapacitation, and rehabilitation?

2. What is the main purpose of restoration (restorative justice)?

3. What are the forms of the criminal sanction?

4. What purposes do intermediate sanctions serve?

5. What has been the Supreme Court's position on the constitutionality of the death penalty?

6. Is there a link between sentences and race?

Key Terms and Cases

determinate sentence (p. 269)
general deterrence (p. 264)
good time (p. 270)
incapacitation (p. 265)
indeterminate sentence (p. 269)
intermediate sanctions (p. 272)
mandatory sentence (p. 270)
presentence report (p. 283)

presumptive sentence (p. 269)
probation (p. 272)
rehabilitation (p. 266)
restorative justice (p. 267)
retribution (p. 263)
selective incapacitation (p. 265)
sentencing guidelines (p. 284)
shock probation (p. 272)

specific deterrence (p. 264)
Atkins v. Virginia (2002) (p. 275)
Furman v. Georgia (1972) (p. 274)
Gregg v. Georgia (1976) (p. 274)
McCleskey v. Kemp (1987) (p. 275)
Roper v. Simmons (2005) (p. 275)
Witherspoon v. Illinois (1968) (p. 277)

Written by Chuck Terry

Prosecution, Adjudication, and Sentencing

LOS ANGELES COUNTY has the largest jail system in the country. On any given day it houses roughly 20,000 inmates. As I walked into the main jail I was so sick I could hardly stand. Once the chains were removed I was placed in a holding tank with other "new arrivals." Whereas getting booked at the city jail took less than an hour, here it took two days. Remember, I had yet to be formally charged and had not had contact with an attorney.

As time passed, more and more bodies were packed inside the tank. Before long we were standing shoulder to shoulder, butt to butt, like sardines in a can. My nightmare was at a high point. I felt like I wouldn't be able to do this much longer—like I might collapse or lose consciousness. Right then this guy looked at me and said, "Hey, brother, you're sick as hell aren't you?" When I said yes, he directed those around me to move over just enough so I could sit down. Never have I been so glad to sit.

We were eventually herded into a larger holding tank that had one seatless toilet and a sink for everyone. In this world privacy does not exist. Hours are spent in these concrete enclosures with others who are arrested for everything from public drunkenness to robbery. Most are addicts, skid-row winos, homeless people, or a mixture of all three. Many have mental problems. Within these rooms one hears a constant mixture of echoes from slamming cell doors, people yelling, wailing, vomiting, and laughing. Strange how, over time, I got used to it.

The next step of the journey involved being strip-searched. As our clothes were removed, the stench of body odor permeated the room. It took effort not to gag. After having every orifice of our naked bodies examined by deputies, we were steered to a shower area, given about thirty seconds to wash, and then sprayed with bug repellent. Next came jail clothing, a wool blanket, and a towel.

Before being assigned to a cell we were photographed, fingerprinted, and given receipts for our property. Finally, after nearly two days, I was led to a four-man cell—my next temporary home. There were already six men living there—two sleeping on the floor (these cells had enough space for two bunks, a toilet, a sink, and about thirty inches between the bunks). I, along with two of the others, slept on the concrete floor. Whereas they slept directly underneath each of the bunks, I took the space between them—and was glad to have it. No mattress. No pillow. But the blanket and the space sure were nice.

I welcomed the chance to rest. I still couldn't sleep, but it felt good to just lie there. Around 3:30 A.M. a guard came down the tier (the walkway in front of the rows of cells), waking up people whose names were on the daily court list. I was one of the fortunate few. Within a few minutes the cell door opened and I was guided to a holding tank where I waited with other court-bound men to be taken downstairs for breakfast. Once given food and seated, we had about three minutes to eat.

Our next stop was an area containing dozens of holding tanks—each acting as way stations for different courts. Deputies, reading names and court destinations from printouts, directed us to the appropriate tanks. I soon learned that I'd be going to the Torrance court. Before long we could hear the rattling of chains—a signal that we would soon be departing. As our names were called, we walked forward and placed our wrists in cuffs. After we were chained, we were led out of the jail into a parking lot where a huge fleet of black-and-white buses sat, waiting to take us to courts all over the county.

A jail bus ride can be an eventful occasion. For a short time you are almost in the world. Through steel-meshed windows you see cars, buildings, parks, streetlights, and people who are free—including women. Many of the men yell and joke about whatever crosses their mind. Others stare idly through the steel grillwork—silent and serious looking. Five days after my arrest I was finally going before a judge.

After arriving at the Torrance courthouse, we were taken to a basement holding tank and unchained. Because I didn't have money for a lawyer I was assigned a public defender (PD), whom I met through the bars of a holding cell located next to the courtroom. His name was Robert Harrison. Like every other lawyer I ever had, he was white.

He carried a briefcase packed with papers, had a suit on, and looked like he was in his late twenties. Although clearly hurried, he treated me with respect. After introducing himself he informed me that this would be my initial appearance and that I'd be back in two weeks for a preliminary hearing. Our meeting took about three minutes.

During the initial appearance I was arraigned in municipal court (the lower, or misdemeanor, court), which meant being legally charged, given a set amount of bail, and given a date on which to return. The district attorney (DA) and public defender introduced themselves to the judge as participants in the case. The entire proceeding took less than a minute. Afterward, as bailiffs escorted me from the courtroom, my PD told me, "See you soon."

Two weeks later, still in jail and running on no sleep, I returned for my preliminary hearing—the phase of the process in which the district attorney tries to convince the court that a felony has been committed while the PD shoots for dismissal based on lack of evidence or an unlawful arrest. The woman who called the police testified that she had seen suspicious activity around my room—strangers coming and going. The police testified that I evaded arrest. The heroin, money, and other drugs taken from my pockets and room were used as evidence. My PD tried to get the case dismissed by arguing that the police searched me without probable cause. The DA said the search had been lawful. The court ruled against me, and I was bound over for arraignment in the superior court (felony court). After the hearing, my lawyer told me, "It doesn't look good." I asked him, "How much time do you think I'll have to do?" He said I'd "better plan on doing five" (that meant years and that meant prison).

Arraignment in the superior court came two weeks later. This time, as well as being told what I was charged with, I made a plea. In another brief meeting before the hearing, my lawyer told me, "When they ask you to plead, say 'Not guilty.' The judge will then set a trial date. Before that time arrives I hope to know more about what the DA wants from this case." I did as he suggested and a trial date was set. Within a few weeks my PD came to visit me in the county jail to tell me about a deal being offered by the district attorney. If I pled guilty to possession of a controlled substance (heroin), the rest of the charges would be dropped and I would be sent to the Southern California Regional Guidance Center at Chino—state prison, for a ninety-day evaluation, a process designed to assist the court at sentencing. He said, "Because of the evidence in this case I don't think we'd have a chance to win at trial. If you take the deal there is the possibility that a positive evaluation by the people at Chino might influence the judge to send you to a drug program. The worst-case scenario, though, is two to ten years for possession. On the other hand, if you go to trial and lose, you will most likely get five to fifteen years for possession with the intent to sell."

I knew my situation was bleak. The court already had a presentence investigation (PSI) report from my last case, in which I received jail time and probation. I didn't think I had a chance of being found not guilty for my current charges. Plus I had heard about guys getting breaks after going to Chino. So the deal sounded good and I went for it.

To formally accept the deal I had to plead guilty in court to the charge of possession of heroin. My PD told me I needed to understand that doing so must be a decision I willingly made and that the judge possibly would not accept the deal. Finally, there were no guarantees as to what type of sentence I'd get. He said he'd recommend a drug program, but the chances were good that I'd have to do prison time, regardless of what type of evaluation I received from Chino.

When the court date arrived I appeared in Judge Barrett's courtroom. The district attorney told the judge that in exchange for a guilty plea to possession of a controlled substance, the people would agree to drop the rest of the charges. My PD said that we agreed. Then the judge said, "Mr. Terry, before accepting this plea I must ensure that you are doing so voluntarily. Has anyone coerced you in any way to plead guilty to this charge?" I said, "No." "Has anyone promised that you will receive a specific sentence if you plead guilty?" "No." "Do you understand that you do not have to make this plea and that you have a right to a trial by a jury of your peers?" "Yes." "And understanding all this, do you waive that right at this time?" By now I was wondering if I was making a mistake. It seemed as if the judge was trying to talk me out of it. I looked at my PD for assurance. He nodded his head, indicating it was OK. I said, "Yes." After accepting my plea of guilty the judge sent me to Chino as expected and said that sentencing would take place upon my return to court.

The "evaluation" from the ninety-day observation came from a twenty-minute interview by a counselor who recommended a drug program and a fifteen-minute interview by a psychologist (nicknamed San Quentin Sally) who said I was a threat to society and belonged in prison. Within three months I was back in the county jail awaiting my final court date.

Finally, five days after I returned from Chino, I was again taken before Judge Barrett for sentencing. Inside the courtroom, before the actual hearing took place, my PD showed me a copy of the evaluation from Chino that clearly indicated the likelihood of a prison sentence. San Quentin Sally not only recommended prison but also said I was a chronic liar with a dismal future. Once I read that I lost all hope for a drug program. Right then I also felt alone, isolated, like it was me against the world and I was definitely losing. I had no friends or family in the courtroom, I was surrounded by strangers dressed in suits and fancy dresses, and the only person who seemed to care about my well-being was my PD.

When the hearing began, the DA used my criminal history and the evaluation from Chino as justification for a prison sentence. My PD suggested a drug program because I had an extensive history of addiction and no arrests for violent crimes. He pointed out that this was also the conclusion of the counselor at Chino. Before imposing the sentence, the judge asked me if I had anything to say. I said no. Then he said, "After considering all sides of this matter I feel little choice but to send you to the department of corrections for the term prescribed by law. I understand you have a problem with drugs, but you've had your chances in the past. It is my hope that when you get to prison you do something to better yourself so when you get out you can live a normal, decent life. With this said, I sentence you to do not less than two but no more than ten years in the California Department of Corrections for possession of narcotics."

I felt good that day when they chained me up to take me back to the county jail. It had been a while since I got arrested, and I was finally headed for the last leg of my journey. I figured that with the time I had already spent in custody, plus good time, I would be out within eighteen months to two years.

Corrections

I N 2008, a report released by the Pew Center on the States showed that, for the first time in history, one in 100 American adults were behind bars in prisons (1,596,127) and jails (723,000). Anyone who pays any attention to public issues knows that the United States has a large and expanding prison population, but the "one in 100" report brought home this fact. The report also noted that the United States incarcerates more of its residents than does any other country. China is second, with 1.5 million behind bars (Pew Center on the States, 2008:3). The United States has less than 5 percent of the world's population, but almost a quarter of the world's prisoners. Closer to home, the United States has ten times the population of Canada but about 35 times the prison population. The quadrupling of the prison population over the past four decades has raised the need to build new prisons, resulting in a construction boom and increased employment of correctional officers. Correctional budgets have climbed an average of 10 percent annually, and many states have diverted money from education, welfare, and health programs to meet the soaring needs of corrections.

Corrections refers to the great number of programs, services, facilities, and organizations responsible for the management of people accused or convicted of criminal offenses. In addition to prisons and jails, corrections includes probation, halfway houses, education and work release programs, parole supervision, counseling, and community service. Correctional programs operate in Salvation Army hostels, forest camps, medical clinics, and urban storefronts.

About 7.3 million men and women were under correctional supervision in 2008. An astounding 3.2 percent of U.S. adults (one of every 15 men and one of every 100 women) were incarcerated or on probation or parole (BJS, 2008d). Corrections is authorized by all levels of government, is administered by both public and private organizations, and costs $60 billion a year (BJS, 2006c:4). This chapter will examine (1) the history of corrections, (2) the organization of corrections, (3) the law of corrections, and (4) the policy trends in community corrections and incarceration.

Opposite page: © David Sanders/The New York Times/Redux

■ **corrections** The variety of programs, services, facilities, and organizations responsible for the management of people who have been accused or convicted of criminal offenses.

Development of Corrections

How did corrections get where it is today? Why are offenders now placed on probation or incarcerated instead of being whipped or burned as in colonial times? Over the past two hundred years, ideas about punishment have moved like a pendulum from one far position to another (see Table 10.1). As we review the development of present-day policies, think about how future changes in society may lead to new forms of corrections.

■ Invention of the Penitentiary

The late eighteenth century stands out as a remarkable period. At that time, scholars and social reformers in Europe and America were rethinking the nature of society and the place of the individual in it. During the **Enlightenment**, as this period is known, philosophers and reformers challenged tradition with new ideas about the individual, about limitations on government, and about rationalism. Such thinking was the main intellectual force behind the American Revolution and laid the foundation of American values. The Enlightenment also affected the new nation's views on law and criminal justice. Reformers began to raise questions about the nature of criminal behavior and the methods of punishment.

■ **Enlightenment** A movement during the eighteenth century in England and France in which concepts of liberalism, rationalism, equality, and individualism dominated social and political thinking.

Prior to 1800, Americans copied Europeans in using physical punishment such as flogging, branding, and maiming as the main criminal sanction. Yet, criminals were regularly sentenced to death for picking pockets, burglary, robbery, and horse stealing (Rothman, 1971:49). Jails existed throughout the country, but they served only to hold people awaiting trial or to punish people unable to pay their debts. As in England, the American colonies maintained houses of correction, where offenders were sentenced to terms of "hard labor" as a means of turning them from crime (A. J. Hirsch, 1992).

With the spread of Enlightenment ideas during the late eighteenth century, physical punishments began to wane. Gradually, "modern" penal systems emerged that emphasized fitting the punishment to the individual offender. The new goal was not to inflict pain on the offender's body (corporal punishment) but to change the individual and set him or her on the right path.

Many people promoted the reform of corrections, but John Howard (1726–1790), sheriff of Bedfordshire, England, was especially influential. His book, *The State of*

| TABLE 10.1 | History of Corrections in America |

Note the extent to which correctional policies have shifted from one era to the next and are influenced by societal factors.

	Correctional Era					
Colonial (1600s–1790s)	Penitentiary (1790s–1860s)	Reformatory (1870s–1890s)	Progressive (1890s–1930s)	Medical (1930s–1960s)	Community (1960s–1970s)	Crime Control (1970s–2000s)
Features						
Anglican Code Capital and corporal punishment, fines	Separate confinement Reform of individual Power of isolation and labor Penance Disciplined routine Punishment according to severity of crime	Indeterminate sentences Parole Classification by degree of individual reform Rehabilitative programs Separate treatment for juveniles	Individual case approach Administrative discretion Broader probation and parole Juvenile courts	Rehabilitation as primary focus of incarceration Psychological testing and classification Various types of treatment programs and institutions	Reintegration into community Avoidance of incarceration Vocational and educational programs	Determinate sentences Mandatory sentences Sentencing guidelines Risk management
Philosophical Basis						
Religious law Doctrine of predestination	Enlightenment Declaration of Independence Human perfectibility and powers of reason Religious penitence Power of reformation Focus on the act Healing power of suffering	National Prison Association Declaration of Principles Crime as moral disease Criminals as "victims of social disorder"	The Age of Reform Positivist school Punishment according to needs of offender Focus on the offender Crime as an urban, immigrant ghetto problem	Biomedical science Psychiatry and psychology Social work practice Crime as signal of personal "distress" or "failure"	Civil rights movement Critique of prisons Small is better	Crime control Rising crime rates Political shift to the right New punitive agenda

Prisons in England and Wales, published in 1777, described the horrible conditions he observed in the prisons he visited (Howard, 1777/1929). Public response to the book resulted in Parliament's passing the Penitentiary Act of 1779, which called for the creation of a house of hard labor where offenders would be imprisoned for up to two years. The institution would be based on four principles:

1. A secure and sanitary building
2. Inspection to ensure that offenders followed the rules
3. Abolition of the fees charged offenders for their food
4. A reformatory regime

At night, prisoners were to be confined to individual cells. During the day, they were to work silently in common rooms. Prison life was to be strict and ordered. Influenced by his Quaker friends, Howard believed that the new institution should be a place of industry. More important, it should be a place that offered criminals opportunities for penitence (sorrow and shame for their wrongs) and repentance (willingness to change their ways). In short, the **penitentiary** served to punish and to reform.

■ **penitentiary** An institution intended to punish criminals by isolating them from society and from one another so they can reflect on their past misdeeds, repent, and reform.

Howard's idea of the penitentiary was not implemented in England until 1842, 50 years after his death. Although England was slow to act, the United States applied Howard's ideas much more quickly.

■ Reform in the United States

From 1776 to around 1830, a new revolution occurred in the American idea of criminal punishment. Although based on the work of English reformers, the new

Until the early 1800s, Americans followed the European practice of relying on punishment that was physically painful, such as death, flogging, and branding. Would such punishments be appropriate today?

Photo by Time Life Pictures/Mansell/Time Life Pictures/Getty Images

■ **separate confinement** A penitentiary system, developed in Pennsylvania, in which each inmate was held in isolation from other inmates. All activities, including craft work, took place in the cells.

correctional philosophy reflected many ideas expressed in the Declaration of Independence, including an optimistic view of human nature and of individual perfectibility. Emphasis shifted from the assumption that deviance was part of human nature to a belief that crime resulted from environmental forces. The new nation's humane and optimistic ideas focused on reforming the criminal.

In the first decades of the nineteenth century, the creation of penitentiaries in Pennsylvania and New York attracted the attention of legislators in other states, as well as investigators from Europe. By the mid-1800s, the U.S. penitentiary had become world famous.

The Pennsylvania System   Several groups in the United States dedicated themselves to reforming the institutions and practices of criminal punishment. One of these groups was the Philadelphia Society for Alleviating the Miseries of Public Prisons, formed in 1787. This group, which included many Quakers, was inspired by Howard's ideas. They argued that criminals could best be reformed if they were placed in penitentiaries—isolated from one another and from society to consider their crimes, repent, and reform.

In 1790, the Pennsylvania legislature authorized the construction of two penitentiaries for the solitary confinement of "hardened and atrocious offenders." The first, created out of an existing three-story stone structure in Philadelphia, was the Walnut Street Jail. This 25-by-40-foot building had eight dark cells, each measuring 6 by 8 by 9 feet, on each floor. A yard was attached to the building. Only one inmate occupied each cell, and no communications of any kind were allowed. From a small, grated window high on the outside wall, prisoners "could perceive neither heaven nor earth."

From this limited beginning, the Pennsylvania system of **separate confinement** evolved. It was based on five principles:

1. Prisoners would not be treated vengefully but should be convinced that, through hard and selective forms of suffering, they could change their lives.

2. Solitary confinement would prevent further corruption inside prison.

3. In isolation, offenders would reflect on their transgressions and repent.

4. Solitary confinement would be punishment, because humans are by nature social animals.

5. Solitary confinement would be economical, because prisoners would not need a long time to repent, and so fewer keepers would be needed and the cost of clothing would be lower.

The opening of the Eastern Penitentiary near Philadelphia in 1829 culminated 42 years of reform activity by the Philadelphia Society. On October 25, 1829, the first prisoner, Charles Williams, arrived. He was an 18-year-old African American sentenced to two years for larceny. He was assigned to a 12-by-8-by-10-foot cell with an individual exercise yard 18 feet long. In the cell was a fold-up steel bed, a simple toilet, a wooden stool, a workbench, and eating utensils. Light came from an 8-inch window in the ceiling. Solitary labor, Bible reading, and reflection were the keys to the moral rehabilitation that was supposed to occur within the penitentiary. Although the cell was larger than most in use today, it was the only world the prisoner would see throughout the entire sentence. The only other human voice heard would be that of a clergyman who would visit on Sundays. Nothing was to distract the penitent prisoner from the path toward reform.

Eastern State Penitentiary, located outside Philadelphia, became the model for the Pennsylvania system of separate confinement. The building was designed to ensure that each offender was separated from all human contact so that he could reflect on his misdeeds. If you designed a prison, what details would it contain?

The Library Company of Philadelphia

Within five years of its opening, Eastern endured the first of several outside investigations. The reports detailed the extent to which the goal of separate confinement was not fully observed, physical punishments were used to maintain discipline, and prisoners suffered mental breakdowns from isolation. Separate confinement had declined at Eastern by the 1860s, when crowding required doubling up in each cell, yet it was not abolished in Pennsylvania until 1913 (Teeters and Shearer, 1957:ch. 4).

The New York System   In 1819, New York opened a penitentiary in Auburn that evolved as a rival to Pennsylvania's concept of separate confinement. Under New York's **congregate system**, prisoners were held in isolation at night but worked with other prisoners in shops during the day. Working under a rule of silence, they were forbidden to exchange glances while on the job or at meals.

Auburn's warden, Elam Lynds, was convinced that convicts were incorrigible and that industrial efficiency should be the overriding purpose of the prison. He instituted a reign of discipline and obedience that included the lockstep and the wearing of prison stripes. He also started a **contract labor system**. By the 1840s, Auburn was producing footwear, barrels, carpets, harnesses, furniture, and clothing. American reformers, seeing the New York approach as a great advance, copied it throughout the Northeast. Because the inmates produced goods for sale, advocates said operating costs would be covered.

During this period, advocates of the Pennsylvania and New York plans debated on public platforms and in the nation's periodicals. Advocates of both systems agreed that the prisoner must stay isolated from society and follow a disciplined routine. In their view, criminality resulted from pervasive corruption that the family and the church did not sufficiently counterbalance. Only when offenders were removed from the temptations and influences of society and kept in a silent, disciplined environment could they reflect on their sins and offenses and become useful citizens. The convicts were not inherently depraved; rather, they were victims of a society that had not protected them from vice. While offenders were being punished, they would become penitent and motivated to place themselves on the right path. See Table 10.2 for a comparison of the Pennsylvania and New York systems.

■ **congregate system**   A penitentiary system, developed in Auburn, New York, in which each inmate was held in isolation during the night but worked and ate with other prisoners during the day under a rule of silence.

■ **contract labor system**   A system under which inmates' labor was sold on a contractual basis to private employers who provided the machinery and raw materials with which inmates made salable products in the institution.

TABLE 10.2	Comparison of Pennsylvania and New York (Auburn) Penitentiary Systems			
	Goal	**Implementation**	**Method**	**Activity**
Pennsylvania (separate system)	Redemption of the offender through the well-ordered routine of the prison	Isolation, penance, contemplation, labor, silence	Inmates kept in their cells for eating, sleeping, and working	Bible reading, work on crafts in cell
New York (Auburn) (congregate system)	Redemption of the offender through the well-ordered routine of the prison	Strict discipline, obedience, labor, silence	Inmates sleep in their cells but come together to eat and work	Work together in shops making goods to be sold by the state

■ **lease system** A system under which inmates were leased to contractors who provided prisoners with food and clothing in exchange for their labor.

Prisons in the South and West   Scholars tend to emphasize the nineteenth-century reforms in the populous Northeast, neglecting penal developments in the South and the West. Before 1817, four Southern states—Georgia, Kentucky, Maryland, and Virginia—had built prisons, some following the penitentiary model. Later prisons, such as the ones in Jackson, Mississippi (1842), and Huntsville, Texas (1848), followed the Auburn model. Further expansion ended with the Civil War, however. With the exception of San Quentin (1852), the sparse population of the West did not lend itself to the construction of many prisons until the latter part of the nineteenth century.

After the Civil War, southerners began to rebuild their communities and primarily agricultural economy. They lacked funds to build prisons but faced an increasing population of offenders. Given these challenges, a large African American inmate labor force, and the states' need for revenue, southern states developed the **lease system**. Businesses in need of workers negotiated with the state for the care of prisoners and their labor (logging, agriculture, mining, railroad construction). Because these entrepreneurs had no ownership interest in the prisoners, they exploited the prisoners worse than they had been as slaves (Rotman, 1995:176). The prisoner death rate soared.

Settlement in the West did not take off until the California gold rush of 1849. The prison ideologies of the East did not greatly influence corrections in the West, except in California. Prior to statehood, western prisoners were held in territorial facilities or federal military posts and prisons. Until Congress passed the Anticontract Law of 1887, restricting the employment of federal prisoners, leasing programs existed in California, Montana, Oregon, and Wyoming. In 1852, a lessee chose Point San Quentin and, using convict labor, built two prison buildings. In 1858, after reports of deaths, escapes, and brutal discipline, the state of California took over the facility. The Oregon territory had erected a log prison in the 1850s but soon leased it to a private company. On joining the Union in 1859, however, the state discontinued the lease system. In 1877, Oregon built a state prison on the Auburn plan, but with labor difficulties and an economic depression in the 1890s, the state turned it over to a lessee in 1895 (McKelvey, 1977:228).

■ Reformatory Movement

By the middle of the nineteenth century, reformers had become disillusioned with the penitentiary. Within 40 years of being built, penitentiaries had become overcrowded, understaffed, and minimally financed. Discipline was lax, brutality was common, and administrators were viewed as corrupt.

Cincinnati, 1870   The National Prison Association (the predecessor of today's American Correctional Association), at its 1870 meeting in Cincinnati, embodied a new spirit of reform. In its famous Declaration of Principles, the association advocated a new design for penology: that prisons should operate according to a philosophy of inmate change, with reformation rewarded by release. Sentences of indeterminate length would replace fixed sentences, and proof of reformation—rather than mere lapse of time—would be required for a prisoner's release. Classification of prisoners on the basis of character and improvement would encourage the reformation program.

Elmira Reformatory   The first **reformatory** took shape in 1876 at Elmira, New York, when Zebulon Brockway was appointed superintendent. Brockway believed that diagnosis and treatment were the keys to reform and rehabilitation. An interview with each new inmate resulted in an individualized work and education treatment program. Inmates followed a rigid schedule of work during the day, followed by courses in academic, vocational, and moral subjects during the evening. Inmates who did well achieved early release.

Designed for first-time felons aged 16–30, the approach at Elmira incorporated a **mark system** of classification, indeterminate sentences, and parole. Each offender entered the institution at grade 2, and if he earned nine marks a month for six months by working hard, completing school assignments, and causing no problems, he could be moved up to grade 1—necessary for release. If he failed to cooperate and violated the rules, he would be demoted to grade 3. Only after three months of satisfactory behavior could he reembark on the path toward eventual release. In sum, this system placed "the prisoner's fate, as far as possible, in his own hands" (Pisciotta, 1994:20).

By 1900, the reformatory movement had spread throughout the nation, yet by the outbreak of World War I in 1914, it was already in decline. In most institutions, the architecture, the attitudes of the guards, and the emphasis on discipline differed little from those of the past. Too often, the educational and rehabilitative efforts took a back seat to the traditional emphasis on punishment. Yet, the reformatory movement contributed the indeterminate sentence, rehabilitative programs, and parole. The Cincinnati Principles and the reformatory movement set goals that inspired prison activists well into the twentieth century.

■ **reformatory** An institution for young offenders that emphasizes training, a mark system of classification, indeterminate sentences, and parole.

■ **mark system** A point system in which prisoners can reduce their term of imprisonment and gain release by earning "marks" or points through labor, good behavior, and educational achievement.

■ Improving Prison Conditions for Women

Until the beginning of the nineteenth century, female offenders in Europe and North America were treated no differently than men and were not separated from them when they were incarcerated. Only with John Howard's 1777 exposé of prison conditions in England and the development of the penitentiary in Philadelphia did attention begin to focus on the plight of the female offender. Among the English reformers, Elizabeth Gurney Fry, a middle-class Quaker, was the first person to press for changes. When she and other Quakers visited London's Newgate Prison in 1813, they were shocked by the conditions in which the female prisoners and their children were living (Zedner, 1995:333).

News of Fry's efforts spread to the United States. The Women's Prison Association was formed in New York in 1844 with the goal of improving the treatment of female prisoners and separating them from men. Elizabeth Farnham, head matron of the women's wing at Sing Sing from 1844 to 1848, implemented Fry's ideas until male overseers and legislators thwarted her, forcing her to resign.

The Cincinnati Declaration of Principles did not address the problems of female offenders. It only endorsed the creation of separate treatment-oriented prisons for women. Although the House of Shelter, a reformatory for

In the 1860s, at Wethersfield Prison for Women (Connecticut), the inmates were trained for ironing, laundry work, and cooking; time was also spent learning such "ladylike" games as croquet. Today, should prisons for men and women be identical?

© Archive/Getty Images

women, was created in Detroit following the Civil War, not until 1873 did the first independent female-run prison open in Indiana. Within 50 years, 13 other states had followed this lead.

Three principles guided female prison reform during this period: (1) the separation of female prisoners from men, (2) the provision of care in keeping with the needs of women, and (3) the management of women's prisons by female staff. "Operated by and for women, female reformatories were decidedly 'feminine' institutions"(Rafter, 1983:147).

As time passed, the original ideas of the reformers faltered. In 1927, the first federal prison for women opened in Alderson, West Virginia, with Mary Belle Harris as warden. Yet, by 1935, the women's reformatory movement had "run its course, having largely achieved its objective (establishment of separate prisons run by women)" (Heffernan, 1972; Rafter, 1983:165).

■ Rehabilitation Model

In the first two decades of the twentieth century, reformers known as the Progressives attacked the excesses of big business and urban society and advocated government actions against the problems of slums, vice, and crime. The Progressives urged that knowledge from the social and behavioral sciences should replace religious and traditional moral wisdom as the guiding ideas of criminal rehabilitation. They pursued two main strategies: (1) improving conditions in social environments that seemed to be the breeding grounds of crime and (2) rehabilitating individual offenders. By the 1920s, probation, indeterminate sentences, presentence reports, parole, and treatment programs were being promoted as a more scientific approach to criminality.

■ **rehabilitation model** A model of corrections that emphasizes the need to restore a convicted offender to a constructive place in society through some form of vocational or educational training or therapy.

Although the Progressives were instrumental in advancing the new penal ideas, not until the 1930s did reformers attempt to implement fully what became known as the **rehabilitation model** of corrections. Taking advantage of the new prestige of the social sciences, penologists helped shift the emphasis of corrections. The new approach saw the social, intellectual, or biological deficiencies of criminals as causing their crimes. Because the essential elements of parole, probation, and the indeterminate sentence were already in place in most states, incorporating the rehabilitation model meant adding classification systems to diagnose offenders and treatment programs to rehabilitate them.

■ **medical model** A model of corrections based on the assumption that criminal behavior is caused by biological or psychological conditions that require treatment.

Because penologists likened the new correctional methods to those used by physicians in hospitals, this approach was often referred to as the **medical model**. Correctional institutions were to be staffed with people who could diagnose the causes of an individual's criminal behavior, prescribe a treatment program, and determine when the offender was cured and could be safely released to the community.

Following World War II, rehabilitation won new followers. Group therapy, behavior modification, counseling, and several other approaches became part of the "new penology." Yet even during the 1950s, when the medical model reached its height, only a small proportion of state correctional budgets went to rehabilitation. What frustrated many reformers was that, even though states adopted the rhetoric of the rehabilitation model, the institutions were still run with custody as the overriding goal.

Because the rehabilitation model failed to achieve its goals, it became discredited in the 1970s. According to critics of rehabilitation, its reportedly high recidivism rates prove its ineffectiveness. Robert Martinson undertook probably the most thorough analysis of research data from treatment programs. Using rigorous standards, he surveyed 231 studies of rehabilitation programs. Martinson summarized his findings by saying, "With few and isolated exceptions, the rehabilitative efforts that have been reported so far have had no appreciable effect on recidivism" (Martinson, 1974:25). The report had an immediate impact on legislators and policy makers, who took up the cry, "Nothing works!" As a result of dissatisfaction with the rehabilitation model, new reforms emerged.

Community Model

The social and political values of particular periods have long influenced correctional goals. During the 1960s and early 1970s, U.S. society experienced the civil rights movement, the war on poverty, and resistance to the war in Vietnam. People challenged the conventional ways of government. In 1967, the U.S. President's Commission on Law Enforcement and Administration of Justice (1967:7) argued for a model of **community corrections**, which claimed that the purpose of corrections should be to reintegrate the offender into the community.

Proponents of this model viewed prisons as artificial institutions that hindered offenders from finding a crime-free lifestyle. They argued that corrections should focus on providing psychological treatment and on increasing opportunities for offenders to succeed as citizens. Programs were supposed to help offenders find jobs and remain connected to their families and the community. Imprisonment was to be avoided, if possible, in favor of probation, so that offenders could seek education and vocational training that would help their adjustment. The small proportion of offenders who had to be incarcerated would spend a minimal amount of time in prison before release on parole. To promote reintegration, correctional workers were to serve as advocates for offenders in dealing with government agencies providing employment counseling, medical treatment, and financial assistance.

The community model dominated corrections until the late 1970s, when it gave way to a new punitiveness in criminal justice, in conjunction with the rebirth of the determinate sentence. Advocates of reintegration claimed, as did advocates of previous reforms, that the idea was never adequately tested. Nevertheless, community corrections remains one of the significant ideas and practices in the recent history of corrections.

> ■ **community corrections** A model of corrections based on the goal of reintegrating the offender into the community.

Crime Control Model

As the political climate changed in the 1970s and 1980s, legislators, judges, and officials responded with an emphasis on crime control through incarceration and risk containment. The critique of rehabilitation led to changes in the sentencing structures in more than half of the states and the abolition of parole release in many.

Compared with the community model, this **crime control model of corrections** is more punitive and makes greater use of incarceration (especially for violent offenders and career criminals), longer sentences, mandatory sentences, and strict supervision of probationers and parolees.

> ■ **crime control model of corrections** A model of corrections based on the assumption that criminal behavior can be controlled by more use of incarceration and other forms of strict supervision.

The effect of these get-tough policies shows in the record number of people incarcerated, the long terms being served, the great number of parolees returned to prison, and the huge size of the probation population. In some states, the political fervor to be tough on criminals has resulted in the reinstitution of chain gangs and the removal of television sets, body-building equipment, and college courses from prisons. Some advocates point to the crime control policies as the reason for the fall of the crime rate. Others ask whether the crime control policies have really made a difference, considering the smaller number of men in the crime-prone age group and other changes in U.S. society.

The history of corrections in the United States reflects a series of swings from one model to another. The time may now be ripe for another look at correctional policy. The rhetoric used in criminal justice journals today differs markedly from that found in their pages 40 years ago. For example, the optimism that once suffused corrections has waned. Researchers are now scrutinizing the financial and human costs of the retributive crime control policies of the 1990s. Are the costs of incarceration and surveillance justified? Has crime been reduced? Is society safer today than it was 25 years ago? Many researchers think not. Will corrections, then, find a new direction? If so, what will it be?

CHECKPOINT

1 What was the Enlightenment and how did it influence corrections?

1 A period in the late eighteenth century when philosophers rethought the nature of society and the place of the individual in the world. The Enlightenment affected views on law and criminal justice; reformers began to raise questions about the nature of criminal behavior and the methods of punishment.

2 How did the Pennsylvania and New York systems differ?

2 The Pennsylvania system of separate confinement held inmates in isolation from one another. The New York congregate system kept inmates in their cells at night, but they worked together in shops during the day.

3 What are the underlying assumptions of the rehabilitation, community, and crime control models of corrections?

3 Rehabilitation model: Criminal behavior is the result of a biological, psychological, or social deficiency; clinicians should diagnose the problem and prescribe treatment; when cured, the offender may be released. Community model: The goal of corrections is to reintegrate the offender into the community, so rehabilitation should be carried out in the community rather than in prison if possible; correctional workers should serve as advocates for offenders in their dealings with government agencies. Crime control model: Criminal behavior can be controlled by greater use of incarceration and other forms of strict supervision.

Organization of Corrections in the United States

The organization of corrections in the United States is fragmented, with each level of government holding some responsibility for corrections. The federal government, the 50 states, the District of Columbia, the 3,047 counties, and most cities all have at least one correctional facility and many correctional programs. State and local governments pay about 95 percent of the cost of all correctional activities in the nation (BJS, 2006c:5).

Federal Corrections System

The correctional responsibilities of the federal government are divided between the Department of Justice, which operates prisons through the Federal Bureau of Prisons, and the Administrative Office of the United States Courts, which covers probation and parole supervision.

Federal Bureau of Prisons   The Federal Bureau of Prisons, created by Congress in 1930, now operates a system of prisons located throughout the nation and housing over 195,000 inmates, supervised by a staff of more than 30,000. Facilities and inmates are classified by security level, ranging from Level l (the least secure, camp-type settings such as the Federal Prison Camp in Tyndall, Florida) through Level 5 (the most secure, such as the supermax penitentiary in Florence, Colorado). Between these extremes are Levels 2 through 4 federal correctional institutions—other U.S. penitentiaries, administrative institutions, medical facilities, and specialized institutions for women and juveniles. The Bureau enters into contractual agreements with states, cities, and private agencies to provide community services such as halfway houses, prerelease programs, and electronic monitoring.

Federal Probation and Parole Supervision   Probation and parole supervision for federal offenders are provided by the Federal Probation and Pretrial Services System, a branch of the Administrative Office of the U.S. Courts. The federal judiciary appoints probation officers, who serve the court. The first full-time federal probation officer was appointed in 1927; today, 3,842 are assigned to the judicial districts across the country. They assist with presentence investigations but focus primarily on supervising offenders on probation and those released either on parole or by mandatory release.

■ State Corrections Systems

Although states vary considerably in how they organize corrections, in all states the administration of prisons falls under the executive branch of state government. However, the judiciary often controls probation, parole may be separate from corrections, and in most states the county governments run the jails.

Community Corrections   States vary in how they carry out the community punishments of probation, intermediate sanctions, and parole. In many states, probation and intermediate sanctions are administered by the judiciary, often by county and municipal governments. By contrast, parole is a function of state government. The decision to release an offender from prison is made by the state parole board in those states with discretionary release. Parole boards are a part of either the department of corrections or an independent agency. In states with a mandatory system, the department of corrections makes the release. In all states, a state agency supervises the parolees.

State Prison Systems   A wide range of state correctional institutions, facilities, and programs exists for adult felons; these include prisons, reformatories, prison farms, forestry camps, and halfway houses. Because of the smaller female prisoner population, this variety does not exist for women.

State correctional institutions for men are usually classified by level of security: maximum, medium, and minimum. With changes in the number of prisoners and their characteristics, the distinction between maximum and medium security has disappeared in some systems. Crowding has forced administrators to house maximum-security inmates in medium-security facilities.

Prisoners in Nevada's Warm Springs Correctional Center play cards in their small cell. Offenders in other states' prisons live under similarly crowded conditions. How should society address the issue of prison overcrowding?

AP Images/Cathleen Allison

Forty states have created prisons that exceed maximum security. An estimated 20,000 inmates are currently kept in these "supermax" prisons. These institutions, such as California's Pelican Bay and Connecticut's Northern Correctional Facility, hold the most disruptive, violent, and incorrigible offenders—the "toughest of the tough." In such institutions, inmates spend up to 23 hours a day in their cells. They are shackled whenever they are out of their cells—during recreation, showers, and telephone calls. All of these measures are designed to send a message to other inmates. Not surprisingly, supermax prisons generate controversy (Pizarro, Stenius, and Pratt, 2006).

The maximum-security prison (holding about 21 percent of state inmates) is built like a fortress, usually surrounded by stone walls with guard towers. It is designed to prevent escape. New facilities are surrounded by double rows of chain-link fences with rolls of razor wire in between and along the tops of the fences. Inmates live in cells that include plumbing and sanitary facilities. Some facilities' barred doors operate electronically so that an officer can confine all prisoners to their cells with the flick of a switch. The purposes of the maximum-security facility are custody and discipline. It maintains a military-style approach to order, with prisoners following a strict routine (Pizarro and Narag, 2008). Some of the most famous prisons, such as Attica (New York), Folsom (California), Stateville (Illinois), and Yuma (Arizona), are maximum-security facilities.

The medium-security prison (holding 40 percent of state inmates) externally resembles the maximum-security prison, but it is organized somewhat differently and its atmosphere is less rigid. Prisoners have more privileges and contact with the outside world through visitors, mail, and access to radio and television. The medium-security prison usually places greater emphasis on work and rehabilitative programs. Although the inmates may have committed serious crimes, they are not perceived as hardened criminals.

The minimum-security prison (with 33 percent of state inmates) houses the least-violent offenders, long-term felons with clean disciplinary records, and inmates who have nearly completed their term. The minimum-security prison lacks the guard towers and stone walls associated with correctional institutions. Often, chain-link fencing surrounds the buildings. Prisoners usually live in dormitories or even in small private rooms rather than in barred cells. There is more personal freedom: Inmates may have television sets, choose their own clothes, and move about casually within the buildings. The system relies on rehabilitation programs and offers opportunities for education and work release. It also provides reintegration programs and support to inmates preparing for release.

In addition to the three types of institutions just described, a small percentage of state inmates are held in other settings such as work camps and county jails. Sentenced offenders may remain in local jails while they await transfer to a state prison or when there are agreements between state correctional officials and county sheriffs in response to overcrowding in state prisons.

Correctional officers face different challenges, depending on the security level of the institution in which they work. As you read about the job of a correctional officer in "Careers in Criminal Justice," ask yourself about the rewards, accomplishments, and other sources of job satisfaction that are available to those who work directly with prisoners.

State Institutions for Women   Only 7 percent of incarcerated people are women (BJS, 2008b:1). Although the ratio of arrests is approximately six men to one woman, the ratio in state and federal prisons is 14 men to one woman. A higher proportion of female defendants are sentenced to probation and intermediate punishments, partly as a result of male offenders' tendency to commit most of the violent crimes. However, the growth rate in number of incarcerated women has exceeded that for men since 1981. In fact, from 2000 to 2006, the annual growth of the female inmate population averaged 3.2 percent, higher than the 1.9 percent growth in male inmate population. The increase in the number of women prisoners seems driven by the war on drugs. This increase has significantly affected program delivery, housing conditions, medical care, staffing, and security (BJS, 2007b:1; A. Wolf, Bloom, and Krisberg, 2008).

CAREERS IN CRIMINAL JUSTICE

Resident Unit Supervisor

SCOTT YOKOM, ASSISTANT RESIDENT UNIT SUPERVISOR
MICHIGAN REFORMATORY PRISON, IONIA, MICHIGAN

THE MICHIGAN REFORMATORY is a multilevel facility that houses prisoners at both the Level II security status and the more restrictive Level IV status. In addition, the Michigan Reformatory has a segregation unit that houses temporarily segregated prisoners and those on detention status.

Careers in a state department of corrections typically begin with the position of corrections officer. In Michigan, job candidates are required to have taken college-level courses in corrections. When hired as corrections officers, they spend eight weeks in the state's corrections training academy, where they learn policy and procedures as well as weapons training and physical methods for controlling prisoners who threaten safety and security. They must pass a physical fitness test, written exams, and eventually a weapons qualification test. They subsequently spend eight weeks in on-the-job training while paired with a senior corrections officer. During the remainder of their first year on the job, they are probationary employees who are subject to dismissal for violating policies and procedures. Corrections officers oversee prisoners in common areas such as the yard and dining hall, conduct searches of prisoners and cells, write "tickets" when prisoners engage in misconduct, supervise prisoners' work assignments, and respond to calls for assistance when there are fights, assaults on staff, or medical emergencies. Some corrections officers become resident unit officers who supervise prisoners within housing units, called "cell blocks" in some prisons. They share the same responsibilities as other corrections

officers but have additional duties for controlling the movement of prisoners, conducting counseling sessions, and inspecting cells. The resident unit officers report to the Assistant Resident Unit Supervisor, who has oversight responsibilities for solving problems and ensuring the enforcement of policies and procedures in multiple housing units.

Scott Yokom earned an undergraduate degree in sociology with concentrations in criminal justice and social work and a minor in psychology—all fields that are relevant to his work in corrections. Currently working on a graduate degree in criminal justice, he began his career as a corrections officer. As he gained experience, he demonstrated the knowledge of policies and procedures, leadership abilities, decision-making skill in responding to problems, and communication skills that are necessary for promotion to supervisory positions. As Assistant Resident Unit Supervisor, he must identify and address problems caused by corrections officers' mistakes as well as issues that arise from prisoners' misbehavior or failure to understand institutional rules.

Most prisoners return to society. Our duty is not only to protect society by incapacitating the prisoner, but also to prepare them for their release so that they do not reoffend. We must deal every day with many prisoners who are hostile, manipulative, and violent. Working within corrections will change you, and it is up to you to decide if that change will be positive or negative. Thus, I often share with new employees a quote from an unknown source: "For those who fight evil and monsters must take care, that in the process, they themselves do not become evil and monstrous."

Conditions in correctional facilities for women are more pleasant than those of similar institutions for men. Usually the buildings have no gun towers and barbed wire. Because of the small population, however, most states have only one facility, which is often located in a rural setting far removed from urban centers. Thus, women prisoners may be more isolated than men from their families and communities.

■ Private Prisons

Corrections is a multibillion-dollar government-funded enterprise that purchases supplies and services from the private sector. Many jurisdictions have long contracted with private vendors to furnish food and medical services, educational and vocational training, maintenance, security, and the operation of aftercare facilities (Antonuccio, 2008). All of this has been referred to as the "prison-commercial complex," which we discuss later in the chapter.

One response to prison and jail crowding and rising staff costs has come from private entrepreneurs who argue that they can build and run prisons at least as effectively, safely, and humanely as any level of government can, at a profit and at a lower cost to taxpayers. The management of entire institutions for adult felons under private contract is a relatively new approach in corrections that was launched in the 1980s.

At the end of 2006, 32 states and the federal system reported a total of almost 114,000 inmates held in privately operated prisons. Private facilities held 6.2 percent of all state prisoners and 14.4 percent of all federal prisoners. This equals 5 percent of the total incarcerated population. Among the states, Texas (with 18,627) and Florida (with 6,350) reported the largest numbers in privately run prisons (BJS, 2007b:4).

The $1 billion-a-year private prison business is dominated by the Corrections Corporation of America (CCA) and the GEO Group (formerly Wackenhut Corrections Corporation), which together manage 72,000 beds in 65 facilities in 19 states and the District of Columbia. This makes up half of all beds under contract. Because of budget issues in many states, growth of the private prison business is expected to level off somewhat. However, federal detention of illegal immigrants may increase.

Advocates of privately operated prisons claim that they provide the same level of care as the states but do it more cheaply and flexibly (Antonuccio, 2008). However, many of the "true costs" (fringe benefits, contracting supervision, federal grants) are not taken into consideration. A recent study of 48 juvenile correctional facilities found little difference between private and public institutions in terms of environmental quality (G. S. Armstrong and MacKenzie, 2003). The Bureau of Justice Statistics found that, compared with private prisons, a greater proportion of state facilities provide access to work, educational, and counseling programs. However, they also found that the percentage of private facilities with education programs had substantially increased since 1995 (BJS, 2003b:6).

Before corrections becomes too heavily committed to the private ownership and operation of prisons, researchers must examine many political, fiscal, ethical, and administrative issues. The political issues, including questions concerning the delegation of social-control functions to people other than state employees, may be the most difficult to overcome. Some people believe that the administration of justice is a basic function of government that should not be delegated. They fear that private operations would skew correctional policy, because contractors would use their political influence to continue programs not in the public interest. Joseph Hallinan describes the extent to which executives and shareholders of the Corrections Corporation of America and U.S. Corrections have funded political campaigns in Indiana, Kentucky, Oklahoma, and Tennessee (2001:168–70).

Some experts also fear that the private corporations will press to maintain high occupancy and will be interested only in skimming off the best inmates, leaving the most troublesome ones to the public corrections system. The profit incentive may also lead to corruption. In 2009, for example, two Pennsylvania juvenile court judges pleaded guilty to federal wire fraud and income tax fraud for taking more than $2.6 million in kickbacks to send teenagers to privately run youth detention centers (Urbina and Hamill, 2009).

Although some states have shown evidence of cost savings (J. F. Blumstein, Cohen, and Seth, 2008), the fiscal value of private corrections has not yet been fully demonstrated. However, labor unions have opposed these incursions into the public sector, pointing out that the salaries, benefits, and pensions of workers in spheres such as private security are lower than in their public counterparts. Finally, questions have arisen about quality of services, accountability of service providers to correctional officials, and problems related to contract supervision. Opponents cite the many instances in which privately contracted services in group homes, day-care centers, hospitals, and schools have been terminated because of reports of corruption, brutality, or substandard services. Research shows that staff turnover, escapes, and drug use are problems in private prisons (S. D. Camp and Gales, 2002).

The idea of privately run correctional facilities has stimulated much interest among the general public and within the criminal justice community, but the future of this approach remains quite uncertain. The controversy about privatization has forced corrections to rethink some strongly held beliefs. In this regard, the possibility of competition from the private sector may have a positive impact on corrections. See "A Question of Ethics" at the end of this chapter for more on private prisons.

■ Jails: Detention and Short-Term Incarceration

Most Americans do not distinguish between jails and prisons. A **prison** is a federal or state correctional institution that holds offenders who are sentenced to terms of more than one year. A **jail** is a local facility for the detention of people awaiting trial (about 50 percent of inmates) and sentenced misdemeanants. Jail also serves as a holding facility for social misfits—derelicts, junkies, prostitutes, the mentally ill, and disturbers of public order.

Of the 3,376 jails in the United States, 2,700 operate at the county level, with most administered by an elected sheriff. About 600 fall under municipal jurisdiction. Only in six states—Alaska, Connecticut, Delaware, Hawaii, Rhode Island, and Vermont—does the state administer jails for adults. There are also 13,500 police lockups (or drunk tanks) and similar holding facilities authorized to detain people for up to 48 hours. The Federal Bureau of Prisons operates 11 jails for detained prisoners only, holding a total of 11,000 inmates. Another 47 privately operated jails, under contract to state or local governments, house 2.4 percent of the total jail population (BJS, 2005c:96).

The capacity of jails varies greatly. The 50 largest jail jurisdictions hold 31 percent of the nation's jailed inmates. The two jurisdictions with the most inmates, Los Angeles County and New York City, together hold approximately 32,400 inmates, nearly 5 percent of the national total (BJS, 2005a:9). Most jails, however, are much smaller, with 40 percent holding fewer than 50 people each (BJS, 2008a:2) However, the number of these small facilities is dwindling because of new jail construction and the creation of regional, multicounty facilities.

Increasingly, jails are being used to detain illegal immigrants prior to the processing of charges or prior to deportation by U.S. Immigration and Customs Enforcement (ICE) of the Department of Homeland Security. Of an estimated 300,000 detainees in 2008, 46 percent were housed, under contract, in county jails (*New York Times*, March 28, 2008, p. A15; SignOnSanDiego.com, 2008). In recent years, the federal crackdown on illegal immigrants has escalated sharply. Holding ICE detainees not only adds to the overcrowding problems of some jails but is also costly to local governments, even with partial reimbursement by the federal government.

Who Is in Jail?   With an estimated 11 million jail admissions per year, more people directly experience jails than experience prisons, mental hospitals, and halfway houses

■ **prison** An institution for the incarceration of people convicted of serious crimes, usually felonies.

■ **jail** An institution authorized to hold pretrial detainees and sentenced misdemeanants for periods longer than 48 hours.

AP Images/The Oklahoman, Chris Landsberger

Jails contain both pretrial detainees, who are presumptively innocent until proved guilty, and convicted offenders awaiting transfer to prison or serving short sentences. Should as-yet-unconvicted detainees, some of whom may eventually be found not guilty, experience the same conditions and deprivations as convicted offenders inside jails? Or should pretrial detainees be kept in separate areas and given more-extensive privileges? What if the jail lacks the space and resources to treat the groups differently?

combined. Even if we consider that some of the people represented in this total are admitted more than once, probably at least six to seven million people are detained at some time during the year. Nationally, more than 780,000 people, both the convicted and the unconvicted, sit in jail on any one day (BJS, 2008a:1) However, the number of people held at any one time in jail does not tell the complete story. Many are held for less than 24 hours; others may reside in jail as sentenced inmates for up to one year; a few may await their trial for more than a year. Compared with the American population as a whole, jails are disproportionately inhabited by men, minorities, the poorly educated, and people with low incomes, as seen in Figure 10.1.

Managing Jails   Jail administrators face several problems that good management practices cannot always overcome. These problems include (1) the perceived role of the jail in the local criminal justice system, (2) the characteristics of the inmate population, and (3) fiscal problems.

ROLE OF THE JAIL   As facilities to detain accused people awaiting trial, jails customarily have been run by law enforcement agencies. Most of the 150,000 correctional officers in the jail system work under the direction of the county sheriff. We might reasonably expect that the agency that arrests and transports defendants to court should also administer the facility that holds them. Typically, however, neither sheriffs nor deputies have much interest in corrections. Further, almost half the jail inmates are sentenced offenders under correctional authority. Thus, many experts argue that jails have outgrown police administration.

INMATE CHARACTERISTICS   The mixture of offenders of widely diverse ages and criminal histories in U.S. jails is an often-cited problem. Because criminal justice

FIGURE 10.1
Characteristics of adult jail inmates in U.S. jails
Compared with the American population as a whole, jails are disproportionately inhabited by men, minorities, the poorly educated, and those with low incomes.

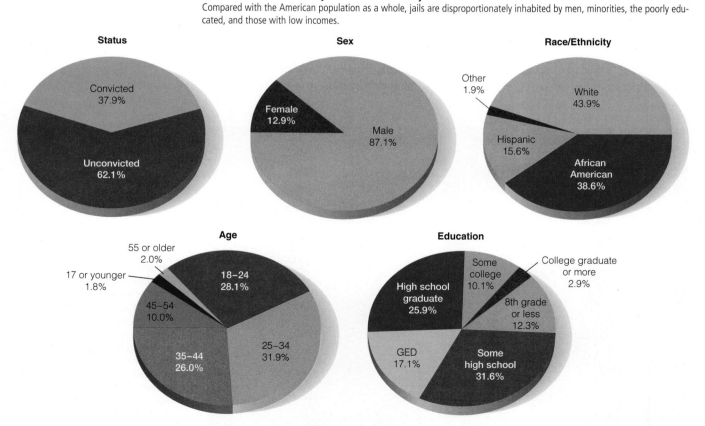

Sources: Bureau of Justice Statistics, *Bulletin*, June 2007, p. 6; Amanda Petteruti and Nastassia Walsh, *Jailing Communities: The Impact of Jail Expansion and Effective Public Safety Strategies* (Washington, DC: Justice Policy Institute, April 2008): 7.

professionals view most inmates as temporary residents, they make little attempt to classify them for either security or treatment purposes. Horror stories of the mistreatment of young offenders by older, stronger, and more violent inmates occasionally come to public attention. The physical condition of most jails aggravates this situation, because most are old, overcrowded, and lacking in basic facilities. Many sentenced felons prefer to move on to state prison, where the conditions tend to be better.

Because inmate turnover is high and because local control provides an incentive to keep costs down, jails usually lack correctional services. They do not usually offer recreational facilities or treatment programs, and medical services are generally minimal. Such conditions add to the idleness and tensions of the inmates. Suicides and high levels of violence are hallmarks of many jails. In any one year, almost half the people who die while in jail have committed suicide.

FISCAL PROBLEMS Jails help control crime but also drain local revenues. The tension between these two public interests often surfaces in debates over expenditures for jail construction and operation. Because revenues often fall short, many jails are overcrowded, lack programs, and do not have enough officers for effective supervision. In some areas, multicounty jails serve an entire region as a means of operating facilities in a cost-efficient way.

As criminal justice policy has become more punitive, jails, like prisons, have become crowded. Surveys have documented increases averaging 6 percent during each of the past five years. Even with new construction and with alternatives such as release on recognizance programs, diversion, intensive probation supervision, and house arrest with electronic monitoring, the jail population continues to rise. The $4.5 billion annual cost of operating jails heavily burdens local governments.

CHECKPOINT

ANSWERS

④ What agencies of the U.S. government are responsible for prisons and probation?

④ The Federal Bureau of Prisons, which handles prisons, and the Administrative Office of the U.S. Courts, which handles probation.

⑤ What agencies of state government are responsible for prisons, probation, intermediate sanctions, and parole?

⑤ Prisons: department of corrections (executive branch). Probation: judiciary or executive department. Intermediate sanctions: judiciary, probation department, department of corrections. Parole: executive agency.

⑥ What are the functions of jails?

⑥ Holding of offenders before trial and incarceration of offenders sentenced to short terms.

The Law of Corrections

Prior to the 1960s, most courts maintained a **hands-off policy** with respect to corrections. Only a few state courts had recognized rights for offenders. Most judges felt that prisoners and probationers did not have protected rights and that courts should not interfere with the operational agencies dealing with probation, prisons, and parole.

■ **hands-off policy** Judges should not interfere with the administration of correctional institutions.

Since the 1960s, however, offenders have gained access to the courts to contest correctional officers' decisions and challenge aspects of their punishment that they believe violate basic rights. Judicial decisions have defined and recognized the constitutional rights of probationers, prisoners, and parolees, as well as the need for policies and procedures that respect those rights. As you read "Criminal Justice: Myth and Reality," consider your own views about the recognition of constitutional rights for convicted criminal offenders.

■ Constitutional Rights of Prisoners

■ *Cooper v. Pate* (1964) Prisoners are entitled to the protection of the Civil Rights Act of 1871 and may challenge in federal courts the conditions of their confinement.

The U.S. Supreme Court decision in *Cooper v. Pate* (1964) signaled the end of the hands-off policy. The court said that through the Civil Rights Act of 1871 (referred to here as Section 1983), state prisoners were *persons* whose rights are protected by the Constitution. The act imposes *civil liability* on any official who violates someone's constitutional rights. It allows suits against state officials to be heard in the federal courts. Because of *Cooper v. Pate*, the federal courts now recognize that prisoners may sue state officials over such things as brutality by guards, inadequate nutrition and medical care, theft of personal property, and the denial of basic rights.

The first successful prisoners' rights cases involved the most excessive of prison abuses: brutality and inhumane physical conditions. Gradually, however, prison litigation has focused more directly on the daily activities of the institution, especially on the administrative rules that regulate inmates' conduct (C. E. Smith, 2007). This focus has resulted in a series of court decisions concerning the First, Fourth, Eighth, and Fourteenth Amendments to the Constitution. (See Chapter 3 for the full text of these amendments.)

First Amendment The First Amendment guarantees freedom of speech, press, assembly, petition, and religion. In the courts, prisoners have successfully challenged many of the restrictions of prison life—access to reading materials, censorship of mail, and rules affecting some religious practices (Burns, 2007). However, the Supreme Court has also approved restrictions on access to written materials, including Pennsylvania's denial of access to newspapers and magazines for prisoners housed in a disciplinary segregation unit (*Beard v. Banks*, 2006).

Since 1970, courts have extended the rights of freedom of speech and expression to prisoners. They have required correctional administrators to show why restrictions on these rights must be imposed. For example, in 1974 the Supreme Court ruled that censorship of mail was permissible only when officials could demonstrate a compelling government interest in maintaining security (*Procunier v. Martinez*). Communication between inmates and the outside world has since increased markedly. However, in *Turner v. Safley* (1987), the Court upheld a Missouri ban on correspondence between inmates in different institutions, as a means of combating gang violence and the communication of escape plans.

The First Amendment prevents Congress from making laws respecting the establishment of religion or prohibiting its free exercise. Cases concerning the free exercise of religion have caused the judiciary some problems, especially when the religious practice may interfere with prison routine and the maintenance of order.

The growth of the Black Muslim religion in prisons set the stage for suits demanding that this group be granted the same privileges as other faiths (special diets, access to clergy and religious publications, opportunities for group worship). Attorneys for the Muslims succeeded in winning several important cases that helped establish for prisoners the First Amendment right to free exercise of religion. These decisions also helped Native Americans, Orthodox

Criminal Justice: MYTH AND REALITY

COMMON BELIEF: People convicted of crimes should forfeit all constitutional rights, because they have violated laws and harmed people. They have broken their "social contract" with our country, through which they receive the benefits of rights and the opportunity for economic success in exchange for their commitment to follow the country's rules.

The U.S. Constitution does make the possession of rights contingent on specific behavior. In fact, many provisions of the Bill of Rights are clearly written as specific limitations on what the government can do to people, including people who commit crimes. The Eighth Amendment's prohibition on "cruel and unusual punishments" implies that there are limits on what the government may do to criminal offenders. If offenders literally had no rights, they could be tortured, starved, and killed without any legal intervention to save them. Is the American value of justice upheld if an 18-year-old who is sentenced to two years in prison for stealing cars can be beaten, starved, deprived of medical care, and even killed because he has no rights whatsoever? In other words, should a short prison sentence actually be a potential death sentence, even for nonviolent offenders?

As you shall see, prisoners have very limited rights that are defined in light of the institution's needs to maintain safety and security. These rights establish a basis for humane treatment from institutions that carry out the punishments announced by the court. Offenders thus lose their liberty for a period of time under stark conditions, rather than facing a potentially deadly environment in which they have no entitlement to food, shelter, protection from violence, and treatment for serious illnesses. Is there widespread agreement about exactly which rights prisoners should possess? No. However, American history itself demonstrates that an absence of rights creates risks of abuses that are contrary to our country's conceptions of justice.

Jews, and other prisoners practice their religions. Court decisions have upheld prisoners' rights to be served meals consistent with religious dietary laws, to correspond with religious leaders, to possess religious literature, to wear a beard if their belief requires it, and to assemble for services. In sum, members of religious minorities have broken new legal ground on First Amendment issues.

Fourth Amendment   The Fourth Amendment prohibits *unreasonable* searches and seizures, but courts have not extended these protections much to prisoners. Thus, regulations viewed as reasonable to maintain security and order in an institution may be justified. For example, *Hudson v. Palmer* (1984) upheld the authority of officials to search cells and confiscate any materials found.

The Supreme Court's opinions with regard to the Fourth Amendment reveal the balance between institutional need and the right to privacy. Body searches have been harder for administrators to justify than cell searches, for example. But body searches have been upheld when they advance policies clearly related to identifiable and legitimate institutional needs and when they are not intended to humiliate or degrade (*Bell v. Wolfish*, 1979).

Prisoners enjoy relatively few protected rights while incarcerated. Among the most important rights for prisoners is the First Amendment right to free exercise of religion, an element that many observers believe can increase some prisoners' odds of becoming rehabilitated. Here, a volunteer minister leads a class for prisoners in Louisiana. Prisoners also need to access law books in order to work on their own appeals and other legal actions. What would the consequences be if these two rights were eliminated?

AP Images/The News-Star, Brandi Jade Thomas

■ *Hudson v. Palmer* (1984)   Prison officials have the authority to search cells and confiscate any materials found.

Eighth Amendment   The Constitution's prohibition of cruel and unusual punishments has been tied to prisoners' needs for decent treatment and minimum health standards. The courts have traditionally applied three principal tests under the Eighth Amendment to determine whether conditions are unconstitutional: (1) whether the punishment shocks the conscience of a civilized society, (2) whether the punishment is unnecessarily cruel, and (3) whether the punishment goes beyond legitimate penal aims. In the past two decades, however, courts have coupled their concerns about these issues with a focus on the intentions of correctional administrators, especially the question of whether officials intentionally ignored problems within their institutions.

Federal courts have ruled that, although some aspects of prison life may be acceptable, the combination of various factors—the *totality of conditions*—may be such that life in the institution constitutes cruel and unusual punishment. When courts have found brutality, unsanitary facilities, overcrowding, and inadequate food, judges have used the Eighth Amendment to order sweeping changes and even, in some cases, to take over administration of entire prisons or corrections systems. In these cases, judges have ordered wardens to follow specific internal procedures and to spend money on certain improvements. The U.S. Supreme Court has instructed lower court judges to focus findings of Eighth Amendment violations on those situations in which correctional officials showed "deliberate indifference" to substandard living conditions (*Wilson v. Seiter*, 1991).

In a February 2009, a judicial panel of the Ninth Circuit of the Federal Court of Appeals ordered California to release 55,000 inmates over the next three years, so that the state could provide a constitutional level of medical and mental health care to the rest of its prisoners. The judges said that without the population reduction, conditions would deteriorate and inmates might regularly die of suicide or lack of proper care (S. Moore, 2009a).

Fourteenth Amendment   One word and two clauses of the Fourteenth Amendment are key to the question of prisoners' rights. The relevant word is *state*, which is found in several clauses of the Fourteen Amendment. It was not until the 1960s that the Supreme Court ruled that, through the Fourteenth Amendment, the Bill of Rights restricts state government actions affecting criminal justice.

The first important clause concerns procedural due process, which requires that government officials treat all people fairly and justly and that official decisions be made according to procedures prescribed by law. The second important clause is the equal protection clause. Assertions that prisoners have been denied equal protection of the law are based on claims of racial, gender, or religious discrimination.

■ *Wolff v. McDonnell* (1974) Basic elements of procedural due process must be present when decisions are made about the disciplining of an inmate.

DUE PROCESS IN PRISON DISCIPLINE   In *Wolff v. McDonnell* (1974), the Supreme Court ruled that basic procedural rights must be present when decisions are made about the disciplining of inmates for serious infractions of prison rules. Specifically, prisoners have the right to receive notice of the complaint, to have a fair hearing, to confront witnesses, to get help in preparing for the hearing, and to be given a written statement of the decision. However, the Court also recognized special conditions of incarceration in that prisoners do not have the right to cross-examine witnesses and that the evidence presented by the offender shall not be unduly hazardous to institutional safety or correctional goals.

As a result of these Supreme Court decisions, prison officials have established rules that provide elements of due process in disciplinary and other proceedings. In many institutions, a disciplinary committee receives the charges, conducts hearings, and decides guilt and punishment. Even with these protections, prisoners remain powerless and may risk further punishment if they challenge the warden's decisions too vigorously.

EQUAL PROTECTION   In 1968, the Supreme Court firmly established that racial discrimination may not be official policy within prison walls (*Lee v. Washington*). Segregation can only be justified in rare instances by compelling circumstances, such as a temporary expedient during periods when violence between races is demonstrably imminent (*Johnson v. California*, 2005). In recent decades, some cases have concerned equal protection issues affecting female offenders. Judges in state courts and lower federal courts have addressed these issues. For example, in a series of decisions spanning nearly two decades, female inmates in Michigan successfully argued that their equal protection rights were violated because programs and services were not as good as those provided to male inmates (*Glover v. Johnson*, 1991). Critics who believe that prisons neglect the needs of women prisoners argue that judges have generally permitted too many differences in facilities and programs for women without providing sufficient attention to issues of equality (Carroll-Ferrary, 2006).

Impact of the Prisoners' Rights Movement   The Supreme Court in recent years has reduced its support of the expansion of prisoners' rights. Nonetheless, the prisoners' rights movement has spurred some positive changes in American corrections since the late 1970s. The most obvious are improvements in institutional living conditions and administrative practices. Law libraries and legal assistance are now generally available, communication with the outside is easier, religious practices are protected, inmate complaint procedures have been developed, and due process requirements are emphasized. Prisoners in solitary confinement undoubtedly suffer less neglect than they did before. Although overcrowding remains a major problem, many conditions have greatly improved and the most brutalizing elements of prison life have diminished. These changes did not entirely result from court orders, however. They also coincide with the growing influence of college-educated correctional professionals who have sought on their own to improve prisons (C. E. Smith, 2000a).

Law and Community Corrections

Although most correctional law concerns prisons and jails, two-thirds of adults under supervision live in the community on probation and parole. However, as with prisoners, offenders in the community have certain rights, and courts have addressed issues concerning due process and searches and seizures.

Probationers and parolees must live according to conditions specified at the time of their sentencing or parole release. These conditions may interfere with their constitutional rights. The conditions typically limit the right of free association by restricting offenders from contact with their crime partners or victims. However, courts have struck down conditions preventing parolees from exercising their First Amendment rights by giving public speeches and receiving publications.

The case of *Griffin v. Wisconsin* (1987) presents a good example of the clash between the Fourth Amendment and community corrections. Learning that Griffin might have a gun, probation officers searched his apartment without a warrant. Noting the practical problems of obtaining a search warrant while a probationer was under supervision, the Supreme Court said that the probation agency must be able to act before the offender damages himself or society. In Griffin's case, the Court felt that the agency had satisfied the Fourth Amendment's reasonableness requirement. Similarly, in *Samson v. California* (2006), the Supreme Court approved a California statute that requires every parolee to agree to be subject to warrantless searches, even in the absence of any suspicion of wrongdoing.

When parole is revoked, prisoners are returned to prison to complete their sentences. Before that happens, a revocation hearing takes place. In a 1998 case, *Pennsylvania Board of Pardons and Parole v. Scott*, a closely divided Court ruled that evidence that would be barred from use in a criminal trial can be used in parole revocation hearings. Operating without a search warrant, officers found guns in the home of a paroled murderer who was barred from owning weapons. Although the Pennsylvania courts decided that an improper search had been conducted, the U.S. Supreme Court concluded that the weapons could be used as evidence at a parole revocation hearing, despite any Fourth Amendment violations that may have occurred. The exclusionary rule does not apply to parole revocation proceedings.

The Supreme Court has also addressed the question of due process when revocation is being considered. In **Mempa v. Rhay (1967)**, the justices determined that a probationer had the right to counsel in revocation and sentencing hearings before a deferred prison sentence could be imposed. Similarly, in **Morrissey v. Brewer (1972)**, the court ruled that parolees facing revocation must be given a two-stage hearing process. In the first stage, a hearing officer determines whether there is probable cause that a violation has occurred. Parolees have the right to be notified of the charges against them, to know the evidence against them, to be allowed to speak on their own behalf, to present witnesses, and to confront the witnesses against them. In the second stage, the revocation hearing, the parolee must receive a notice of charges, the evidence of a violation is disclosed, and he or she may cross-examine witnesses. The hearing body determines if the violation is sufficiently severe to warrant revocation. It must give the parolee a written statement outlining the evidence, with reasons for the decision.

In the following year, the Supreme Court applied the *Morrissey* procedures to probation revocation proceedings in **Gagnon v. Scarpelli (1973)**. In *Gagnon*, however, the Court also looked at the question of the right to counsel. It ruled that there was no absolute requirement but that in some cases probationers and parolees might request counsel, to be allowed on a case-by-case basis depending on the complexity of the issues, mitigating circumstances, and the competence of the offender.

■ **Mempa v. Rhay (1967)** Probationers have the right to counsel at a combined revocation-sentencing hearing.

■ **Morrissey v. Brewer (1972)** Due process rights require a prompt, informal, two-stage inquiry before an impartial hearing officer before parole may be revoked. The parolee may present relevant information and confront witnesses.

■ **Gagnon v. Scarpelli (1973)** Before probation can be revoked, a two-stage hearing must be held and the offender provided with specific elements of due process. Requested counsel will be allowed on a case-by-case basis.

Law and Correctional Personnel

Just as law governs relationships among inmates, probationers, and parolees, laws and regulations also define the relationships between correctional administrators and their staff. With the exception of those working for private, nonprofit organizations, correctional personnel are public employees. Here we consider two important aspects of correctional work. First, as public employees, all correctional employees are governed by civil service rules and regulations. Second, correctional clients may sue state employees using Section 1983 of the United States Code.

Civil Service Laws   Civil service laws set the procedures for hiring, promoting, assigning, disciplining, and firing public employees. These laws protect public employees from arbitrary actions by their supervisors. Workplace rules also come to be developed through collective-bargaining agreements between correctional-employee unions and the government. These agreements have the force of law and contain rules concerning assignments, working conditions, and grievance procedures.

Like their counterparts in the private sector, government employees are protected from discrimination. With the Civil Rights Act of 1964, Congress prohibited employment discrimination based on race, gender, national origin, and religion. Subsequent federal legislation prohibits some forms of age discrimination (Age Discrimination in Employment Act) and discrimination against people with disabilities (Americans with Disabilities Act). States have their own antidiscrimination laws. All these laws have increased the number of minorities and women who work in corrections.

Unlike many public employees, those who work in corrections operate from a difficult position. They must assert authority over persons who have shown that they lack self-control or have little regard for society's rules. Whether in prison, in a probationer's home, or on the street, this responsibility creates pressures and difficult—sometimes dangerous—situations.

Liability of Correctional Personnel   In *Cooper v. Pate* (1964), the Supreme Court said that Section 1983 provides a means for prisoners, but also probationers and parolees, to bring lawsuits against correctional officials. *Monell v. Department of Social Services of the City of New York* (1978) clarified the meaning of Section 1983. Individual public employees and their agency may be sued when a person's civil rights are violated by the agency's "customs and usages." Specifically, if an individual can show that harm was caused by employees whose wrongful acts were the result of these "customs, practices, and policies, including poor training and supervision," then the employees may be sued.

Although huge financial settlements make headlines, and the number of Section 1983 filings is large, few cases come to trial and very few correctional employees must personally pay financial awards to plaintiffs. However, no correctional employee wants to be involved in such legal situations.

CHECKPOINT

ANSWERS

7 *Why is the case of Cooper v. Pate important to the expansion of prisoners' rights?*

7 It allowed state prisoners to challenge, in the federal courts, the conditions of their confinement.

8 *Which two clauses of the Fourteenth Amendment have been interpreted by the Supreme Court to apply to prisoners' rights?*

8 The due process and equal protection clauses.

to provide the offender with food, clothing, and housing, as it must do in prisons. Home confinement programs have grown and proliferated.

The development of electronic monitoring equipment has made home confinement an enforceable sentencing option. The number of offenders currently being monitored is difficult to estimate, because the equipment manufacturers consider this confidential information. However, the best estimates say about 17 different companies provide electronic monitoring of nearly 100,000 offenders (Conway, 2001).

Two basic types of electronic monitoring devices exist. Passive monitors respond only to inquiries; most commonly, the offender receives an automated telephone call from the probation office and is told to place the device on a receiver attached to the phone. Active monitors send continuous signals that a receiver picks up; a computer notes any break in the signal.

Despite favorable publicity, home confinement with electronic monitoring poses certain legal, technical, and correctional issues that must be addressed before it can become a standard punishment. First, some criminal justice scholars question its constitutionality. Monitoring may violate the Fourth Amendment's protection against unreasonable searches and seizures. At issue is a clash between the constitutionally protected reasonable expectation of privacy and the invasion of one's home by surveillance devices. Second, the monitoring devices still have extensive technical problems, such as frequently giving erroneous reports that the offender is home. Third, offender failure rates may prove to be high. Being one's own warden is difficult, and visits by former criminal associates and other enticements may become problematic for many offenders. Anecdotal evidence suggests that four months of full-time monitoring is about the limit before a violation will occur. Furthermore, some crimes—such as child abuse, drug sales, and assaults—can be committed while the offender is at home. Home confinement seems best suited to low-risk offenders who have relatively stable residences.

Community Service   A **community service** sentence requires the offender to perform a certain amount of unpaid labor in the community. Community service can take a variety of forms, including assisting in social service agencies, cleaning parks and roadsides, or helping the poor. The sentence specifies the number of hours to be worked and usually requires supervision by a probation officer. Judges can tailor community service to the skills and abilities of offenders. For example, less educated offenders might pick up litter along the highway, whereas those with schooling might teach reading in evening literacy classes. Many judges order community service when an offender cannot pay a fine. The offender's effort to make reparation to the community harmed by the crime also serves a symbolic function.

Although community service has many supporters, some labor unions and workers criticize it for possibly taking jobs away from law-abiding citizens. In addition, some experts believe that if community service is the only sanction, it may be too mild a punishment, especially for upper-class and white-collar criminals. Examine your own views about community service as a punishment when you read "Criminal Justice: Myth and Reality."

Day Reporting Centers   Another intermediate sanction is the **day reporting center**—a community correctional center to which the offender must report each day to carry out elements of the sentence. Designed to ensure that probationers follow the employment and treatment stipulations attached to their sentence, day reporting centers also increase the likelihood that offenders and the general public will consider probation supervision to be credible.

■ **community service** A sentence requiring the offender to perform a certain amount of unpaid labor in the community.

■ **day reporting center** A community correctional center where an offender reports each day to comply with elements of a sentence.

In 2006, 1980s pop singer Boy George (center) swept the streets of New York City as part of his community service sanction after pleading guilty to drug possession. Such sanctions can provide benefits to the community. There may also be a "shaming" effect if offenders are embarrassed to be seen in public fulfilling a criminal punishment. Can you think of creative and effective ways to expand the use of community service sanctions?

© Dennis Van Tine/Landov

Criminal Justice:
MYTH AND REALITY

COMMON BELIEF: Community service does not punish those who receive the sanction.

There are elements of punishment in the community service sanction. Individuals suffer a partial loss of liberty as they must report to specific locations, surrender their time and freedom of movement, and obey authorities' orders to complete tasks that they would otherwise not do. They also risk feeling the shame and embarrassment of being seen doing tasks, such as collecting trash along a highway, that indicates to other people that they have gotten into trouble with the law. Does this mean that community service is sufficiently severe to serve as a punishment for all kinds of nonviolent offenses? No. Society may legitimately conclude that greater restrictions on liberty and behavior, such as those associated with home confinement, may be appropriate for some offenses and repeat offenders. However, we should recognize that community service carries sanctioning elements while simultaneously avoiding the high costs of more expensive sanctions and permitting minor offenders to stay connected to their families and communities by retaining their jobs or continuing in school.

■ **intensive supervision probation (ISP)**
Probation granted under conditions of strict reporting to a probation officer with a limited caseload.

Most day reporting centers incorporate multiple correctional methods. For example, in some centers offenders must remain in the facility for eight hours or report for drug-related urine checks before going to work. Centers with a rehabilitation component carry out drug and alcohol treatment, literacy programs, and job searches. Others provide staff–offender contact levels equal to or greater than those in intensive supervision programs. However, one study found that offenders sentenced to day reporting plus intensive supervision probation were no more or less likely to return to crime than were those on intensive supervision alone (Marciniak, 2000:34).

The overall success or failure of these programs remains unclear. One study of New York City's program found that its stiff eligibility requirements resulted in few cases entering the center. A study of six day reporting centers in Massachusetts found that about 80 percent of offenders successfully completed the program (McDivitt and Miliano, 1992:160). Such success, however, depends at least in part on who is being treated. If such centers are used only for selected offenders with a low risk of returning to crime, knowing whether the centers themselves are effective will be difficult.

Intensive Supervision Probation (ISP)   Intensive supervision probation (ISP) is a means of dealing with offenders who need greater restrictions than traditional community-based programs can provide. Jurisdictions in every state have programs to intensively supervise such offenders. ISP uses probation as an intermediate form of punishment by imposing conditions of strict reporting to a probation officer who has a limited caseload.

There are two general types of ISP programs. *Probation diversion* puts under intensive surveillance those offenders thought to be too risky for routine supervision. *Institutional diversion* selects low-risk offenders sentenced to prison and provides supervision for them in the community. Daily contact between the probationer and the probation officer may cut rearrest rates. Such contact also gives the probationer greater access to the resources the officer can provide, such as treatment services in the community. Offenders have incentives to obey rules, knowing that they must meet with their probation officers daily and in some cases must speak with them even more frequently. Offenders often face additional restrictions as well, such as electronic monitoring, alcohol and drug testing, community service, and restitution.

ISP programs have been called "old-style" probation because each officer has only 20 clients and requires frequent face-to-face contact. Nonetheless, some people question how much of a difference constant surveillance can make to probationers with numerous problems. Such offenders frequently need help to get a job, counseling to deal with emotional and family situations, and a variety of supports to avoid drug or alcohol problems that may have contributed to their criminality. Yet, ISP may be a way of getting the large number of drug-addicted felons into treatment.

Because it presents a "tough" image of community supervision and addresses the problem of prison crowding, ISP has become popular among probation administrators, judges, and prosecutors. Most ISP programs require a specific number of monthly contacts with officers, performance of community service, curfews, drug and alcohol testing, and referral to appropriate job-training, education, or treatment programs.

Some observers warn that ISP is not a "cure" for the rising costs and other problems facing corrections systems. Ironically, ISP can increase the number of probationers sent to prison. All evaluations of ISP find that, probably because of the closer contact with clients, probation officers uncover more violations of rules than they do in regular probation. Therefore, ISP programs often have higher failure rates than do regular probation, even though their clients produce fewer arrests (Tonry and Lynch, 1996:116).

Another surprising finding is that, when given the option of serving prison terms or participating in ISP, many offenders choose prison. In New Jersey, 15 percent of offenders withdrew their applications for ISP once they learned the conditions and requirements. Similarly, when offenders in Marion County, Oregon, were asked if they would participate in ISP, one-third chose prison instead (Petersilia, 1990). Apparently, some offenders would rather spend a short time in prison, where tough conditions may differ little from their accustomed life, than a longer period under demanding conditions in the community. To these offenders, ISP does not represent freedom, because it is so intrusive and the risk of revocation seems high.

Despite problems and continuing questions about its effectiveness, ISP has rejuvenated probation. These programs have carried out some of the most effective offender supervision. As with regular probation, the size of a probation officer's caseload, within reasonable limits, often matters less in preventing recidivism than does the quality of supervision and assistance provided to probationers. If properly implemented, ISP may improve the quality of supervision and services that foster success for more kinds of offenders.

■ Intermediate Sanctions Administered in Institutions and the Community

Among the most publicized intermediate sanctions are **boot camps**. Often referred to as "shock incarceration," these programs vary; however, all stem from the belief that young offenders (usually 14- to 21-year-olds) can be "shocked" out of their criminal ways. Boot camps put offenders through a 30-to-90-day physical regimen designed to develop discipline and respect for authority. Like the Marine Corps, most programs emphasize a spit-and-polish environment and keep the offenders in a disciplined and demanding routine that seeks ultimately to build self-esteem. Most camps also include education, job-training programs, and other rehabilitation services. On successful completion of the program, offenders are released to the community. At this point, probation officers take over, and the conditions of the sentence are imposed.

Boot camps proliferated in the 1980s. By 1995, some states and the Federal Bureau of Prisons operated 93 camps for adults and 30 for juveniles. At their peak, boot camps held more than 7,000 offenders. By 2000, however, about one-third of the camps had closed, and the decline in boot camp operations have continued. In January 2005, the Federal Bureau of Prisons announced that it would phase out its remaining boot camps over six months. Further, the public uproar following the death of teenager Martin Anderson caused Florida to scrap its system of juvenile boot camps. Anderson died after being pummeled by a group of guards at a Panama City boot camp. He had been sent to the camp for joyriding in his grandmother's automobile (Caputo and Miller, 2006).

Evaluations of boot camp programs have reduced the initial optimism about such approaches. Critics suggest that the emphasis on physical training ignores young offenders' real problems. Some point out that, like the military, boot camp builds esprit de corps and solidarity, characteristics that can improve the leadership qualities of the young offender and therefore enhance a criminal career. In fact, follow-up studies of boot camp graduates show they do no better after release from the program than do other offenders. Research has also found that, like intensive supervision probation, boot camps do not automatically reduce prison crowding. A National Institute of Justice summary of the boot camp experiment notes that they fail to reduce recidivism or prison populations (NIJ, 2003).

Defenders of boot camps argue that the camps are accomplishing their goals; the failure lies in the lack of educational and employment opportunities in the

■ **boot camp** A short-term institutional sentence, usually followed by probation, that puts the offender through a physical regimen designed to develop discipline and respect for authority. Also referred to as *shock incarceration*.

Military-type drills and physical workouts are part of the regimen at most boot camps, such as this one in Massachusetts. Evaluations of boot camps have reduced the initial optimism about this approach. Boot camps have been closed in many states. What are the potential shortcomings of using boot camps as punishment?

© Joel Stettenheim/Corbis

CLOSE UP

After Boot Camp, a Harder Discipline

NELSON COLON misses waking up to the blast of reveille. He sometimes yearns for those 16-hour days filled with military drills and 9-mile runs. He even thinks fondly of the surly drill instructors who shouted in his face.

During his four months at New Jersey's boot camp, Mr. Colon adapted to the rigors of military life with little difficulty. He says it was a lot easier than what he faces now. He is back in his old neighborhood, trying to stay away from old friends and old ways.

So far, Colon, at age 18, has managed to stay out of trouble since he graduated with the camp's first class of 20 cadets in June. Yet each day, he said, he fears he will be pulled back onto the corner, only two blocks away, where he was first arrested for selling drugs at age 15.

A 10:00 P.M. curfew helps keep Colon off the streets. His parole officer checks in with him almost daily, sometimes stopping by at 11:00 to make sure he is inside. He is enrolling in night classes to help him earn his high school equivalency certificate, and he plans on attending Narcotics Anonymous meetings.

His biggest problems are the same ones that tens of thousands of Camden residents confront daily. Camden's unemployment rate exceeds 20 percent. There are few jobs in this troubled city, particularly for young men who have dropped out of high school. Colon has found work as a stock clerk in a sneaker store, but it is miles away at a shopping center on a busy highway, and he has no transportation there.

Selling drugs paid a lot more than stacking shoe boxes, and it did not require commuting. Mr. Colon says he pushes those thoughts of easy money out of his head and tries to remember what the boot camp's drill instructors told him over and over again.

"They used to tell us, 'It's up to you.' You have to have self-accountability. You have to be reliable for your own actions, not because some person wanted you to do it. They taught us not to follow, to lead. That was one of the most important things."

Mr. Colon said his immediate goal was to find a job that he could get to more easily, and then save enough to get as far away from Camden as possible. "I want to get out of here," he said.

"The people's mentality here is real petty. Life isn't nothing to them. The other night, they killed one of the guys I grew up with. They shot him a couple of times. My old friends came around and knocked on my door at one o'clock in the morning to tell me." He said it was his eighth childhood friend to die.

RESEARCHING THE INTERNET

For more on boot camps, access the Washington State Report that summarizes research on the effectiveness of boot camp, at the website listed on the Cole/Smith Criminal Justice in America Companion Website: http://www.cengage.com/criminaljustice/cole.

FOR CRITICAL ANALYSIS

Do youthful offenders need special programs and services after they leave boot camp and return to their communities? If so, what do they need?

Source: Adapted from *New York Times*, September 3, 1995, p. B1.

participants' inner-city communities (see the Close Up box). A national study found that few boot camp graduates received any aftercare assistance on returning to their communities (Bourque, Han, and Hill, 1996). Because boot camps have been popular with the public, which imagines that strict discipline and harsh conditions will instill positive attitudes in young offenders, such camps will probably continue operating whether or not they are more effective than probation or prison.

■ Implementing Intermediate Sanctions

Although the use of intermediate sanctions has spread rapidly, three major questions have emerged about their implementation: (1) Which agencies should implement the sanctions? (2) Which offenders should be admitted to these programs? (3) Will the "community corrections net" widen as a result of these policies so that more people will come under correctional supervision?

As in any public service organization, administrative politics play an ongoing role in corrections. In many states, agencies compete for the additional funding needed to run the programs. The traditional agencies of community corrections, such as probation offices, could receive the funding, or the new programs could be contracted out to nonprofit organizations. Probation organizations argue that they know the field, have the experienced staff, and—given the additional resources—could do an excellent job. They correctly point out that a great many offenders sentenced to intermediate sanctions are also on probation. Critics of giving this role to probation services argue that the established agencies are not receptive to innovation. They say that probation agencies place a high priority on the traditional supervision function and would not actively help clients solve their problems.

The different types of offenders who receive intermediate sanctions prompt a second issue in the implementation debate. One school of thought focuses on the seriousness of the offense; the other centers on the problems of the offender.

If categorized by the seriousness of their offense, offenders may receive such close supervision that they will not be able to abide by the sentence. Sanctions for serious offenders may accumulate to include, for example, probation, drug testing, addiction treatment, and home confinement. As the number of sentencing conditions increases, even the most willing probationers find fulfilling every one of them difficult.

Some agencies want to accept into their intermediate sanctions program only those offenders who *will* succeed. These agencies are concerned about their success ratio, especially because of threats to future funding if the program does not reduce recidivism. Critics point out that this strategy leads to "creaming," taking the most-promising offenders and leaving those with worse problems to traditional sanctions.

The third issue concerns **net widening**, a process in which the new sanction increases the control over offenders' lives, rather than reducing it. This can occur when a judge imposes a more intrusive sentence than usual. For example, rather than merely giving an offender probation, the judge might also require that the offender perform community service. Critics of intermediate sanctions in this regard argue that they have created the following:

- *Wider nets.* Reforms increase the proportion of individuals in society whose behavior is regulated or controlled by the state.

- *Stronger nets.* By intensifying the state's intervention powers, reforms augment the state's capacity to control individuals.

- *Different nets.* Reforms transfer jurisdictional authority from one agency or control system to another.

Some have advocated intermediate sanctions as a less costly alternative to incarceration and a more effective alternative to probation. But how have they been working? Michael Tonry and Mary Lynch have discouraging news: "Few such programs have diverted large numbers of offenders from prison, saved public monies or prison beds, or reduced recidivism rates" (1996:99). With incarceration rates still at record highs and probation caseloads increasing, intermediate sanctions will probably play a major role in corrections through the first decade of this century. However, correctional reform has always had its limitations, and intermediate sanctions may not achieve the goals of their advocates.

■ **net widening** Process in which new sentencing options increase rather than reduce control over offenders' lives.

CHECKPOINT

ANSWERS

4 *What is the main argument for intermediate sanctions?*

4 Judges need a range of sentencing options that are less restrictive than prison and more restrictive than simple probation.

5 *How does intensive supervision probation differ from traditional probation?*

5 In ISP, the offender is required to make stricter and more frequent reporting to an officer with a much smaller caseload.

6 *What are three problems in the implementation of intermediate sanctions?*

6 Deciding which agencies should implement the sanctions, deciding which offenders should be admitted to these programs, and the possible widening of the "community corrections net."

The Future of Community Corrections

In 1995, 3.7 million Americans were under community supervision; by 2007, this figure had grown to 7.3 million (BJS, 2008b:1). Despite this tremendous growth, community corrections still lacks public support. Community corrections suffers from the image of being "soft on crime." As a result, some localities provide adequate resources for prisons and jails but not for community corrections.

Community corrections also faces the challenge that offenders today require closer supervision. The crimes, criminal records, and drug problems of these offenders are often worse than those of lawbreakers of earlier eras. Nationally, 30 percent of convicted felons are sentenced to probation with no jail or prison time, and about one-fourth of these have been found guilty of violent crimes (BJS, 2007a:1). Those people are supervised by probation officers whose caseloads number in the hundreds. Such officers, and their counterparts in parole, cannot provide effective supervision and services to all their clients.

Community corrections is burdened by even greater caseload pressures than in the past. With responsibility for about three-fourths of all offenders under correctional supervision, community corrections needs an infusion of resources. For community corrections to succeed, the public must support it. However, such support will come only if citizens believe that offenders are receiving appropriate punishments.

Citizens must realize that policies designed to punish offenders in the community yield not mere "slaps on the wrists" but meaningful sanctions, even while these policies allow offenders to retain and reforge their ties to their families and society. Joan Petersilia argues that too many crime-control policies focus solely on the short term. She believes that long-term investments in community corrections will pay off for the offender and the community (Petersilia, 1996). Again, before new policies can be put in place, public opinion must shift toward support of community corrections.

A QUESTION OF ETHICS: WRITING ASSIGNMENT

As you look over the Recommendation for Revocation Report sent to you by Officer Sawyer, you are struck by the low-level technical violations used to justify sending James Ferguson, a minor drug offender, to prison. Sawyer cites Ferguson's failure to attend all the drug treatment sessions, to complete his community service, to pay a $500 fine. You call Sawyer in to discuss the report.

"Bill, I've looked over your report on Ferguson and I'm wondering what's going on here. Why isn't he fulfilling the conditions of his probation?"

"I'm really not sure, but it seems he just doesn't want to meet the conditions. I think he's got a bad attitude, and I don't like the guys he hangs around with. He's always mouthing off about the 'system' and says I'm on his case for no reason."

"Well, let's look at your report. You say that he works for Capital Services cleaning offices downtown from midnight till 8:00 A.M. yet has to go to the drug programs three mornings a week and put in ten hours a week at the Salvation Army Thrift Store. Is it that he isn't trying or does he have an impossible situation?"

"I think he could do it if he tried, but also, I think he's selling cocaine again. Perhaps he needs to get a taste of prison."

"That may be true, but do you really want to revoke his probation?"

WRITING ASSIGNMENT

What's going on here? Is Sawyer recommending revocation because of Ferguson's attitude and the suspicion that he is selling drugs again? Do the technical violations warrant prison? Analyze the information as presented and then make a choice: Write Officer Sawyer's report describing the reasons why Ferguson's probation should be revoked or write a memo as a judge who decides that probation revocation is not appropriate in this case.

Summary

Describe the philosophical assumptions that underlie community corrections

- Community corrections is based on four assumptions: (1) Many offenders' crimes do not warrant incarceration. (2) Community supervision is cheaper than incarceration. (3) Recidivism is no greater for those under community supervision than those who go to prison. (4) Ex-inmates require both support and supervision when they return to the community.

- Community supervision through probation, intermediate sanctions, and parole is a growing part of the criminal justice system.

Explain how probation evolved and how probation sentences are implemented today

▶ Probation evolved as a humanitarian effort to allow first-time and minor offenders a second chance.

▶ Probation is imposed on more than half of offenders. People with this sentence live in the community according to conditions set by the judge and under the supervision of a probation officer.

List the types of intermediate sanctions and how they are administered

▶ Intermediate sanctions are designed as punishments that are more restrictive than probation and less restrictive than prison.

▶ The range of intermediate sanctions allows judges to design sentences that incorporate one or more of these punishments.

▶ Some intermediate sanctions are implemented by courts (fines, restitution, forfeiture), others in the community (home confinement, community service, day reporting centers, intensive supervision probation), and others in institutions and the community (boot camps).

Discuss the key issues faced by community corrections at the beginning of the twenty-first century

▶ Despite tremendous growth, community sanctions lack public support.

▶ Many offenders today require closer supervision with attendant higher costs.

▶ The use of community corrections is expected to grow in the twenty-first century, in spite of the problems of implementing them.

■ Questions for Review

1. What is the aim of community corrections?

2. What is the nature of probation, and how is it organized?

3. What is the purpose of intermediate sanctions?

4. What are the primary forms of intermediate sanctions?

5. Why is net widening a concern?

■ Key Terms and Cases

boot camp (p. 337)
community service (p. 335)
day reporting center (p. 335)
fine (p. 333)

forfeiture (p. 334)
home confinement (p. 334)
intensive supervision probation (ISP) (p. 336)

net widening (p. 339)
recidivism (p. 326)
restitution (p. 333)
technical violation (p. 330)

professional treatment specialists carry a higher status than do other employees. Since the rethinking of the rehabilitation goal in the 1970s, treatment programs still exist in most institutions, but few prisons conform to this model today.

3. The **reintegration model** is linked to the structures and goals of community corrections. Recognizing that prisoners will be returning to society, this model emphasizes maintaining the offenders' ties to family and community as a method of reform. Prisons following this model gradually give inmates greater freedom and responsibility during their confinement, moving them to halfway houses or work release programs before giving them community supervision.

■ **reintegration model** A model of a correctional institution that emphasizes maintaining the offender's ties to family and community as a method of reform, recognizing that the offender will be returning to society.

Although one can find correctional institutions that conform to each of these models, most prisons are mainly custodial. Nevertheless, treatment programs do exist, and because almost all inmates return to society at some point, even the most custodial institutions must prepare them for their reintegration. See "What Americans Think" on page 348 for a look at how the public views the goals of incarceration.

Much is asked of prisons. As Charles Logan notes, "We ask them to correct the incorrigible, rehabilitate the wretched, deter the determined, restrain the dangerous, and punish the wicked" (Logan, 1993:19). Because prisons are expected to pursue many different and often incompatible goals, they are almost doomed to fail as institutions. Logan believes that the mission of prisons is confinement. He argues that imprisonment serves primarily to punish offenders fairly and justly through lengths of confinement proportionate to the seriousness of their crimes. He summarizes the mission of prison as follows: "to keep prisoners—to keep them in, keep them safe, keep them in line, keep them healthy, and keep them busy—and to do it with fairness, without undue suffering, and as efficiently as possible" (Logan, 1993:21). If the purpose of prisons is punishment through confinement under fair and just conditions, what are the implications of this purpose for correctional managers?

CHECKPOINT

ANSWER

2 *What three models of prison have predominated since the 1940s?*

2 The custodial, rehabilitation, and reintegration models.

Prison Organization

The prison's physical features and function set it apart from almost every other institution and organization in modern society. It is a place where a group of employees manage a group of captives. Prisoners must live according to the rules of their keepers, and their movements remain sharply restricted. Unlike managers of other government agencies, prison managers

- Cannot select their clients
- Have little or no control over the release of their clients
- Must deal with clients who are there against their will
- Must rely on clients to do most of the work in the daily operation of the institution—work they are forced to do and for which they are not paid
- Must depend on the maintenance of satisfactory relationships between clients and staff

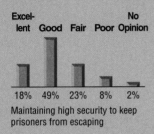
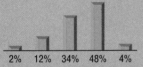
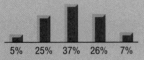
Given these unique characteristics, how should a prison be run? What rules should guide administrators? As the description just given indicates, wardens and other key personnel are asked to perform a difficult job, one that requires skilled and dedicated managers.

Most prisons are expected to fulfill goals related to keeping (custody), using (working), and serving (treating) inmates. Because individual staff members are not equipped to perform all functions, separate lines of command organize the groups of employees that carry out these different tasks. One group is charged with maintaining custody over the prisoners, another group supervises them in their work activities, and a third group attempts to treat them.

The custodial employees are the most numerous. They are normally organized along military lines, from warden to captain to officer, with accompanying pay differentials down the chain of command. The professional personnel associated with the using and serving functions, such as industry supervisors, clinicians, and teachers, are not part of the custodial structure and have little in common with its staff. All employees are responsible to the warden, but the treatment personnel and the civilian supervisors of the workshops have their own salary scales and titles. Figure 12.1 presents the formal organization of staff responsibilities in a typical prison.

The multiple goals and separate lines of command often cause ambiguity and conflict in the administration of prisons. For example, the goals imposed on prisons are often contradictory and unclear. Conflict between different groups of staff (custodial versus treatment, for instance), as well as between staff and inmates, presents significant challenges for administrators.

How, then, do prisons function? How do prisoners and staff try to meet their own goals? Although the U.S. prison may not conform to the ideal goals of corrections and the formal organization may bear little resemblance to the ongoing reality of the informal relations, order *is* kept and a routine *is* followed.

FIGURE 12.1
Formal organization of a prison for adult felons
Prison staff are divided into various sections consistent with the goals of the organization. Custodial employees are the most numerous.

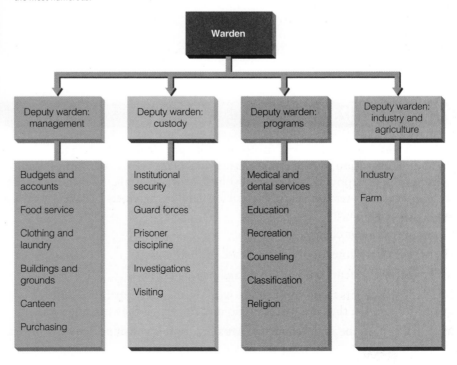

CHECKPOINT

3 How do prisons differ from other organizations in society?

3 It is a place where a group of workers manages a group of captives.

Governing a Society of Captives

Much of the public believes that prisons are operated in an authoritarian manner. In such a society, correctional officers give orders and inmates follow orders. Strictly enforced rules specify what the captives may and may not do. Staff members have the right to grant rewards and to inflict punishment. In theory, any inmate who does not follow the rules could be placed in solitary confinement. Because the officers have a monopoly on the legal means of enforcing rules and can call in the state police and the National Guard if necessary, many people believe that no question should arise as to how the prison is run. Read "Criminal Justice: Myth and Reality" to test your perceptions about the power of correctional officials.

What quality of life should be maintained in prison? According to John DiIulio, a good prison is one that "provides as much order, amenity, and service as possible given the human and financial resources" (1987:12). *Order* is here defined as the absence of individual or group misconduct that threatens the safety of others—for example, assault, rapes, and other forms of violence or threat. *Amenities* include anything that enhances the comfort of the inmates, such as good food, clean cells, and recreational opportunities. *Service* includes programs designed to improve the lives of inmates: vocational training, remedial education, and work opportunities. Here, too, we expect inmates to be engaged in activities during incarceration that will make them better people and enhance their ability to lead crime-free lives upon release.

If we accept the premise that inmates, staff, and society need well-run prisons, what problems must correctional administrators address? The correctional literature points to four factors that make governing prisons different from administering other public institutions: (1) the defects of total power, (2) the limitation on the rewards and punishments officials can use, (3) the co-optation of correctional officers by inmates through exchange relationships, and (4) the strength of inmate leadership. After reviewing each of these research findings, we examine what kind of administrative systems and leadership styles ensure that prisons are safe and humane and serve inmates' needs.

■ The Defects of Total Power

Imagine a prison society in which officers use force to rule hostile and uncooperative inmates. Prisoners could legally be isolated from one another, physically abused until they cooperate, and put under continuous surveillance. Although all of these things are possible, such practices would probably not be countenanced for long, because the public expects correctional institutions to be run humanely.

In reality, the power of officers is limited, because many prisoners have little to lose by misbehaving, and unarmed officers have only limited ability to force compliance with rules. Perhaps more important is the fact that forcing people to follow commands is an inefficient way to make them carry out complex tasks; efficiency further diminishes because of the ratio of inmates to officers (typically 40 to 1) and the potential danger.

Criminal Justice: MYTH AND REALITY

COMMON BELIEF: Because correctional officers have access to guns, clubs, tear gas, and other weapons, they can readily control the behavior of prisoners through the threat of force or, if necessary, the use of force, including lethal force.

Although prison officials typically have firearms locked in an accessible area for emergencies, and the correctional officers in towers or walking outside the prison's perimeter carry guns, most correctional officers cannot carry weapons. These officers must supervise, question, and frisk prisoners close at hand and in a context in which they are heavily outnumbered by the prisoners. If they carried weapons, they might easily be overpowered and have their weapons taken by the prisoners. Thus, effective officers cannot rely on the threat of force to accomplish their daily tasks smoothly. Instead, they must encourage the cooperation and obedience of the prisoners by communicating effectively, establishing their own reputations for toughness and fairness, and showing some understanding and flexibility in the enforcement of minor rules. If a violent event or uprising occurs, prison staff members will use force to restore order. However, the use of force throughout the day is not an efficient way to keep the institution running smoothly. Moreover, there are now legal rules that limit when and how force may be used, and prisoners may file lawsuits for rights violations and personal injuries suffered through the improper use of force.

Officers face significant challenges in maintaining order and safety while outnumbered by prisoners, especially when many prisons are understaffed. What qualities and skills do correctional officers need in order to be effective?

AP Images/The Herald-Mail, Ric Dugan

Rewards and Punishments

Correctional officers often rely on rewards and punishments to gain cooperation. To maintain security and order among a large population in a confined space, they impose extensive rules of conduct. Instead of using force to ensure obedience, however, they reward compliance by granting privileges and punish rule violators by denying these same privileges.

To promote control, officers may follow any of several policies. One is to offer cooperative prisoners rewards such as choice job assignments, residence in the honor unit, and favorable parole reports. Inmates who do not break rules receive good time. Informers may also be rewarded, and administrators may ignore conflict among inmates on the assumption that it keeps prisoners from uniting against authorities.

The system of rewards and punishments has some deficiencies. One is that the punishments for rule breaking do not represent a great departure from the prisoners' usual circumstances. Because inmates already lack many freedoms and valued goods—heterosexual relations, money, choice of clothing, and so on—not being allowed to attend, say, a recreational period does not carry much weight. Further, inmates receive authorized privileges at the start of the sentence and lose them if rules are broken, but officials authorize few rewards for progress or exceptional behavior. However, as an inmate approaches release, opportunities for furloughs, work release, or transfer to a halfway house can serve as incentives to obey rules.

Gaining Cooperation: Exchange Relationships

One way that correctional officers obtain inmate cooperation is by tolerating minor rule infractions in exchange for compliance with major aspects of the custodial regime. The correctional officer plays the key role in these exchange relationships. Officers and prisoners remain in close proximity both day and night—in the cell block, workshop, dining hall, recreation area, and so on. Although the formal rules require a social distance between officers and inmates, the physical closeness makes them aware that each relies on the other. The officers need the cooperation of the prisoners so that they will look good to their superiors, and the inmates count on the officers to relax the rules or occasionally look the other way. For example, officers in a Midwestern prison told researcher Stan Stojkovic that flexibility in rule enforcement especially mattered as it related to the ability of prisoners to cope with their environment. As one officer said, "Phone calls are really important to guys in this place. You cut off their calls and they get pissed. So what I do is give them a little extra and they are good to me." Yet the officers also told Stojkovic that prison personnel would be crazy to intervene to stop illicit sex or drug use (Stojkovic, 1990:214).

Correctional officers must take care not to pay too high a price for the cooperation of their charges. Under pressure to work effectively with prisoners, officers may be blackmailed into doing illegitimate favors in return for cooperation. Officers who establish *sub-rosa*, or secret, relationships can be manipulated by prisoners into smuggling contraband or committing other illegal acts. At the end of the chapter, "A Question of Ethics" presents a dilemma that correctional officers frequently face.

Inmate Leadership

In the traditional prison of the big-house era, administrators enlisted the inmate leaders to help maintain order. Inmate leaders had been "tested" over time so that they were neither pushed around by other inmates nor distrusted as stool pigeons. Because the staff could rely on them, they served as the essential communications link between staff and inmates. Their ability to acquire inside information and gain access to higher officials brought inmate leaders the respect of other prisoners and special privileges from officials. In turn, they distributed these benefits to other prisoners, thus bolstering their own influence within the prison society.

Prisons seem to function more effectively now than they did in the recent past. Although prisons are more crowded, riots and reports of violence have declined. In many prisons, the inmate social system may have reorganized, so that correctional officers again can work through prisoners respected by fellow inmates. Yet, some observers contend that when wardens maintain order in this way, they enhance the positions of some prisoners at the expense of others. The leaders profit by receiving illicit privileges and favors, and they influence other prisoners by distributing benefits.

Further, descriptions of the contemporary maximum-security prison raise questions about administrators' ability to run institutions in this way. In most of today's institutions, prisoners are divided by race, ethnicity, age, and gang affiliation, so that no single leadership structure exists.

The Challenge of Governing Prisons

The factors of total power, rewards and punishments, exchange relationships, and inmate leadership exist in every prison and must be managed. How they are managed greatly influences the quality of prison life. John DiIulio's research (1987) challenges the common assumption of many correctional administrators that "the cons run the joint." Instead, successful wardens have made their prisons function well by applying management principles within the context of their own style of leadership. Prisons can be governed, violence minimized, and services provided to the inmates if correctional executives and wardens exhibit leadership. Although governing prisons poses an extraordinary challenge, it can be and has been effectively accomplished.

CHECKPOINT

4 *What four factors make governing prisons different from administering other public institutions?*

ANSWER

4 The defects of total power, a limited system of rewards and punishments, exchange relations between correctional officers and inmates, and the strength of inmate leadership.

Correctional Officers: The Linchpin of Management

A prison is simultaneously supposed to keep, use, and serve its inmates. The achievement of these goals depends heavily on the performance of its correctional officers. Their job is not easy. Not only do they work long and difficult hours with a hostile client population, but their superiors also expect them to do so with few resources or punishments at their disposal. Most of what they are expected to do must be accomplished by gaining and keeping the cooperation of the prisoners.

Much of the work of correctional officers involves searches and counting. Officers have a saying: "We're all doing time together, except guards are doing it in eight-hour shifts." What are the professional rewards—if any—of working as a correctional officer?

AP Images/Rich Pedroncelli

■ The Officer's Role

Over the past 30 years, the correctional officer's role has changed greatly. No longer responsible merely for "guarding," the correctional officer now stands as a crucial professional who has the closest contact with the prisoners and performs a variety of tasks. Officers are expected to counsel, supervise, protect, and process the inmates under their care. But the officer also works as a member of a complex bureaucratic organization and is expected to deal with clients impersonally and to follow formal procedures. Fulfilling these contradictory role expectations is difficult in itself, and the physical closeness of the officer and inmate over long periods exacerbates this difficulty.

■ Recruitment of Officers

Employment as a correctional officer is neither glamorous nor popular. The work is thought to be boring, the pay is low, and career advancement is minimal. Studies have shown that one of the primary incentives for becoming involved in correctional work is the security that civil service status provides. In addition, because most correctional facilities are located in rural areas, prison work often is better than other available employment. Because correctional officers are recruited locally, most of them are rural and white, in contrast to the majority of prisoners, who come from urban areas and are often either African American or Hispanic (see Figure 12.2). Yet, some correctional officers see their work as a way of helping people, often the people most in need in U.S. society.

Today, because they need more well-qualified correctional officers, most states recruit quality personnel. Salaries have been raised so that the average entry-level pay runs from $16,000 a year in some southern and rural states to over $30,000 in states such as Massachusetts, New Jersey, Nevada, and Rhode Island (Editor, 2003). In addition to their salaries, most officers can earn overtime pay, supplementing base pay by up to 30 percent. However, low salaries, the massive increase in the prison population, and a tougher, more violent class of prisoners have all probably contributed to a shortage of correctional officers in some states.

Correctional administrators have made special efforts to recruit women and minorities. Today, approximately 30 percent of correctional officers belong to minority groups, and 23 percent are women. Female officers are no longer restricted to working with female offenders. For example, in South Carolina, approximately 41 percent of correctional officers are women. In Arkansas, 51 percent of officers

FIGURE 12.2
Racial/ethnic composition of correctional officers and inmates, adult systems
Although the racial/ethnic composition of correctional officers does not equal that of the inmate population, the past quarter century has seen great strides toward equality.

Source: Camille Camp and George Camp, *Corrections Yearbook 2002* (Middletown, CT: Criminal Justice Institute, 2003), 158. Includes both federal and state prisoners.

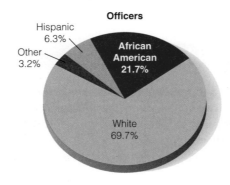

Officers
Hispanic 6.3%
Other 3.2%
African American 21.7%
White 69.7%

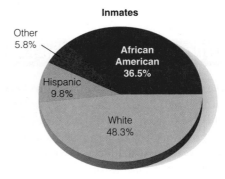

Inmates
Other 5.8%
African American 36.5%
Hispanic 9.8%
White 48.3%

are women. However, in the Federal Bureau of Prisons, only 13.5 percent of the correctional officers are women (C. G. Camp, 2003:158).

Most states require cadets, or new recruits, to complete a preservice training program. The length of preservice training varies from state to state. For example, cadets in California and Michigan receive 640 hours of training. In contrast, new recruits in Kentucky receive only 40 hours. During the typical six-week program, recruits receive at least a rudimentary knowledge of the job and correctional rules. Classroom work includes learning about report writing, communicable diseases, inmate classification, self-defense, and use of force. The classroom work, however, often bears little resemblance to problems confronted on the cell block or in the yard. On completing the course, the new officer is placed under the supervision of an experienced officer. On the job, the new officer experiences real-life situations and learns the necessary techniques and procedures. Through encounters with inmates and officers, the recruit becomes socialized to life behind the walls and gradually becomes part of that subculture.

For most correctional workers, being a custodial officer is a dead-end job. Although officers who perform well may be promoted to higher ranks such as correctional counselor, few ever move into administrative positions. However, in some states and in the Federal Bureau of Prisons, people with college degrees can move up the career ladder to management positions without having to rise through the ranks of the custodial force.

■ Use of Force

The use of force by correctional officers, as that by the police, generates much controversy. Although corporal punishment and the excessive use of force are not permitted, correctional officers use force in many situations. They often confront inmates who challenge their authority or are attacking other inmates. Though unarmed and outnumbered, officers must maintain order and uphold institutional rules. Under these conditions they feel justified in using force.

All correctional agencies now have policies regarding the legitimate use of force. Officers violating these policies may face an inmate lawsuit and dismissal. There are five situations in which the use of force is legally acceptable:

1. *Self-defense.* If officers are threatened with physical attack, they may use a level of force that is reasonable to protect themselves from harm.

2. *Defense of third persons.* As in self-defense, an officer may use force to protect an inmate or another officer. Again, only reasonably necessary force may be used.

3. *Upholding prison rules.* If prisoners refuse to obey prison rules, officers may need to use force to maintain safety and security. For example, if an inmate refuses to return to his or her cell, using handcuffs and forcefully transferring the prisoner may be necessary.

4. *Prevention of a crime.* Force may be used to stop a crime, such as theft or destruction of property, from being committed.

5. *Prevention of escapes.* Officers may use force to prevent escapes, because they threaten the well-being of society and order within correctional institutions. Some agencies limit the use of deadly force to prisoners thought to be dangerous, whereas others require warning shots.

Correctional officers face challenges to self-control and professional decision making. Inmates often "push" officers in subtle ways such as moving slowly, or they use verbal abuse to provoke officers. Correctional officers are expected to run a "tight ship" and maintain order, often in situations where they are outnumbered and dealing with troubled people. In confrontational situations, they must defuse hostility yet uphold the rules—a difficult task at best.

CHECKPOINT

5 *Name three of the five legally acceptable reasons for the use of force.*

ANSWER

5 Self-defense, defense of third persons, upholding prison rules, prevention of crime, prevention of escapes.

Who Is in Prison?

The age, education, and criminal history of the inmate population influence how correctional institutions function. What are the characteristics of inmates in our nation's prisons? Do most offenders have long records of serious offenses, or are many of them first-time offenders who have committed minor crimes? Do some inmates have special needs that dictate their place in prison? These questions are crucial to understanding the work of wardens and correctional officers.

Data on the characteristics of prisoners are limited. The Bureau of Justice Statistics reports that a majority of prisoners are men, aged 25 to 44, and members of minority groups. Approximately 40 percent of state prisoners have not completed high school (see Figure 12.3).

FIGURE 12.3

Sociodemographic and offense characteristics of state prison inmates

These data reflect the types of people found in state prisons. What do they indicate about the belief that many offenders do not "need" to be incarcerated?

Sources: Bureau of Justice Statistics: *Bulletin,* December 2007, p. 25; *Education and Correctional Populations* (Washington, DC: U.S. Government Printing Office, January 2003), 2.

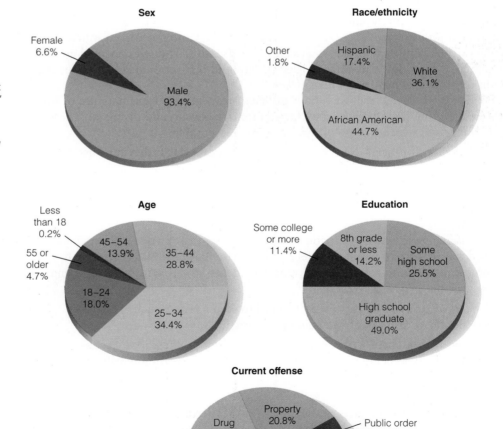

Recidivists and those convicted of violent crimes make up an overwhelming portion of the prison population. Research shows that 44 percent of prisoners are rearrested within the first year after release. Within three years, approximately 25 percent of all released inmates will return to prison (BJS, 2002:3). Most of today's prisoners have a history of persistent criminality. Four additional factors affect correctional operations: the increased number of elderly prisoners, the many prisoners with HIV/AIDS, the thousands of prisoners who are mentally ill, and the increase in long-term prisoners.

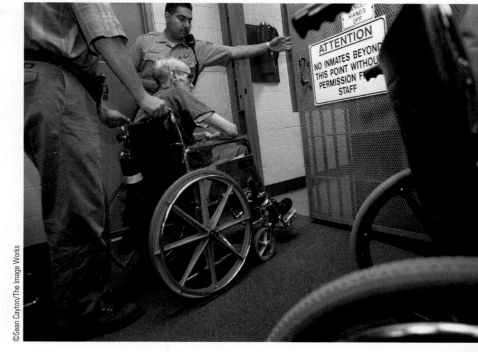

The imposition of long mandatory sentences increased the population of elderly prisoners and also prolonged the confinement of many prisoners who need medical care. These prisoners create extra financial burdens on correctional budgets. Are there less expensive ways to punish elderly and chronically ill prisoners?

Elderly Prisoners

Correctional officials have only recently become aware of the increasing number of inmates over age 55. In 2007, U.S. prisons held more than 73,000 offenders over 55 years old, an increase of 33 percent since 2000 (BJS, 2008b: Appendix 11). In Florida, which defines *elderly* as over age 50, there are now 14,000 elderly prisoners, 71 of whom are over age 80. A number of states have created "geriatric prisons" designed to hold older inmates classified according to need: geriatric, wheelchair users, and long-term (nursing home) care.

To some extent, the prison population is growing older because it reflects the aging of the overall citizenry, but more so because sentencing practices have changed. Consecutive lengthy sentences for heinous crimes, long mandatory minimum sentences, and life sentences without parole mean that more people who enter prison will spend most or all of the rest of their lives behind bars.

Elderly prisoners have medical and security needs that differ from those of the average inmate. For example, they can't climb into top bunks. In many states, special sections of the institution have been designated for this older population so they will not have to mix with the younger, tougher inmates. Elderly prisoners are more likely to develop chronic illnesses such as heart disease, stroke, and cancer. The costs for maintaining an elderly inmate averages about $69,000 per year, triple the average cost for a younger inmate. Ironically, while in prison, the offender will benefit from much better medical care and live a longer life than if he or she were discharged.

Prisoners with HIV/Aids

In the coming years, AIDS is expected to be a leading cause of death among men aged 35 and younger. With 52 percent of the adult inmate population under age 35, correctional officials must cope with the problem of HIV as well as AIDS and related health issues. By the end of 2006, there were more than 21,000 HIV-positive inmates (1.9 percent of the prison population) and 6,000 offenders (0.5 percent) with AIDS. The number of HIV-positive inmates is undoubtedly low, because only 21 states conduct mandatory testing of inmates. Further, the rate of confirmed AIDS cases in state and federal prisons is two and a half times higher than in the total U.S. population. In 2006, 167 inmates died of AIDS, the third largest single cause of inmate death, behind "natural death" and "suicide" (Maruschak, 2008:2). Because many inmates who are HIV infected remain undiagnosed, these numbers underestimate the scope of the problem.

To deal with offenders who have AIDS symptoms or who test positive for the virus, prison officials can develop policies on methods to prevent transmission of the disease, housing of those infected, and medical care for inmates with the full range of symptoms. However, administrators face a host of competing pressures as they decide what actions the institution should take.

■ Mentally Ill Prisoners

Mass closings of public hospitals for the mentally ill began in the 1960s. At the time, new antipsychotic drugs made treating patients in the community seem a more humane and less expensive alternative to long-term hospitalization. It soon became apparent, however, that community treatment works only if the drugs are taken and that clinics and halfway houses do not exist to assist the mentally ill. Mentally ill inmates tend to follow a revolving door from homelessness to incarceration and then back to the streets, with little treatment.

Currently, far more mentally ill live in the nation's jails and prisons (191,000) than in state hospitals (62,000) (BJS, 2001b:3; *Ill-Equipped*, 2003:1). The incarceration rate of the mentally ill is four times that of the general population. The prison has become the largest psychiatric facility in some states. For example, New York City's Rikers Island houses three thousand mentally ill inmates (Winerip, 1999:42). In Los Angeles, 50 percent of those entering the county jail are identified as mentally ill (Butterfield, 1998b).

Correctional workers are usually unprepared to deal with the mentally ill. Cell-block officers, for instance, often do not know how to respond to disturbed inmates. Although most corrections systems have mental health units that segregate the ill, many inmates with psychiatric disorders live among other prisoners in the general population, where they are teased and otherwise exploited. Mentally ill prisoners often suffer as the stress of confinement deepens their depression, intensifies delusions, or leads to mental breakdown. Some commit suicide.

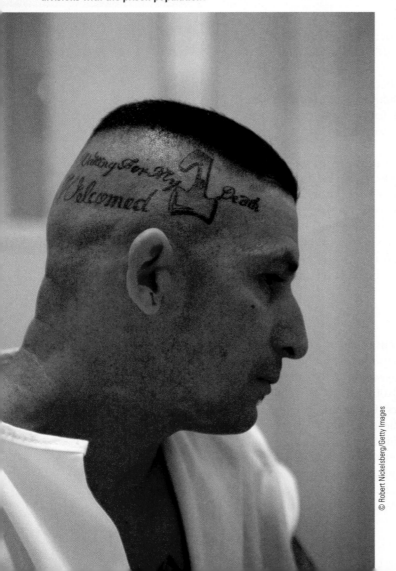

Contemporary prison society is divided along social, ethnic, and gang subgroups. There is no longer a single inmate code to which all prisoners subscribe. As a correctional officer, how would you deal with white supremacists and other gangs based on racial and ethnic divisions with the prison population?

© Robert Nickelsberg/Getty Images

■ Long-Term Prisoners

More prisoners in the United States serve longer sentences than do prisoners in other Western nations. A recent survey shows that nearly 310,000 prisoners are currently serving at least 20-year sentences. Of all inmates, about 10 percent are serving "natural life," which means there is no possibility that they will be paroled, a tripling since 1992. These long-term prisoners are often the same people who will become elderly offenders, with all their attendant problems. Each life sentence costs the taxpayers over $1 million.

Severe depression, feelings of hopelessness, and other health problems are common among long-termers. Such emotional stress tends to take place earlier in the sentence as these inmates lose contact with their families. Addressing the mental health needs of this special population is critical to preventing suicide attempts.

Long-term prisoners are generally not seen as control problems. They receive disciplinary infractions about half as often as do short-term inmates. Rather, administrators must find ways to make long terms bearable. Experts suggest that administrators follow three main principles: (1) maximize opportunities for the inmate to exercise choice in his or her living circumstances, (2) create opportunities for meaningful living, and (3) help the inmate maintain contact with the outside world (Flanagan, 1995:256). Many long-term inmates will eventually be released after spending their prime years incarcerated. Will offenders be able to support themselves when they return to the community at age 50, 60, or 70?

The contemporary inmate population presents several challenges to correctional workers. Resources may not be available to provide rehabilitative programs for most inmates. Even if the resources exist, the goal of maintaining a safe and healthy environment may tax the staff's abilities. These difficulties are multiplied still further by AIDS and the increasing numbers of elderly and long-term prisoners. The contemporary corrections system must also deal with a different type of inmate, one who is more prone to violence, and with a prison society where racial tensions can soar. How well it meets this correctional challenge will greatly affect U.S. society.

CHECKPOINT

ANSWER

6 *What are the major characteristics of today's prisoners?*

6 Today's prisoners are largely men in their late twenties to early thirties with less than a high school education. They are disproportionately members of minority groups.

The Convict World

Inmates of a maximum-security prison do not serve their time in isolation. Rather, prisoners form a society with its own traditions, norms, and leadership structure. Some choose to associate with only a few close friends; others form cliques along racial or "professional" lines. Still others serve as the politicians of the convict society; they attempt to represent convict interests and distribute valued goods in return for support. Just as the free world has a social culture, the "inside" has a prisoner subculture. Membership in a group provides mutual protection from theft and physical assault, the basis of wheeling and dealing, and a source of cultural identity.

As in any society, the convict world has certain norms and values. Often described as the **inmate code**, these norms and values develop within the prison social system and help define the inmate's image of the model prisoner. As Robert Johnson notes, "The public culture of the prison has norms that dictate behavior 'on the yard' and in other public areas of the prison such as mess halls, gyms, and the larger program and work sites" (2002:100). Prison is an ultramasculine world. The culture breathes masculine toughness and insensitivity, impugning softness, and emphasizes the use of hostility and manipulation in one's relations with fellow inmates and staff. It makes caring and friendly behavior, especially with respect to the staff, look servile and silly (Sabo, Kupers, and London, 2001:7).

The code also emphasizes the solidarity of all inmates against the staff. For example, inmates should never inform on one another, pry into one another's affairs, "run off at the mouth," or put another inmate on the spot. They must be tough and trust neither the officers nor the principles for which the guards stand. Further, guards are "hacks" or "screws"; the officials are wrong and the prisoners are right.

Some sociologists believe that the code emerges within the institution as a way to lessen the pain of imprisonment (Sykes, 1958); others believe that it is part of the criminal subculture that prisoners bring with them (Irwin and Cressey, 1962). The inmate who follows the code enjoys a certain amount of admiration from other

■ **inmate code** The values and norms of the prison social system that define the inmates' idea of the model prisoner.

CLOSE UP

Survival Tips for Beginners

TJ GRANACK

OKAY, so you just lost your case. Maybe you took a plea bargain. Whatever. The point is you've been sentenced. You've turned yourself over to the authorities and you're in the county jail waiting to catch the next chain to the R Unit (receiving) where you'll be stripped and shaved and photographed and processed and sent to one of the various prisons in your state.

So what's a felon to do? Here are some survival tips that may make your stay less hellish:

1. *Commit an Honorable Crime.* Commit a crime that's considered, among convicts, to be worthy of respect. I was lucky. I went down for first-degree attempted murder, so my crime fell in the "honorable" category. Oh, goodie. So I just had to endure the everyday sort of danger and abuse that comes with prison life.

2. *Don't Gamble.* Not cards, not chess, not the Super Bowl, and if you do, don't bet too much. If you lose too much and pay up (don't even think of doing otherwise), then you'll be known as a rich guy who'll be very popular with the vultures.

3. *Never Loan Anyone Anything.* Because if you do, you'll be expected to collect one way or another. If you don't collect you will be known as a mark, as someone without enough heart to take back his own. . . .

6. *Make No Eye Contact.* Don't look anyone in the eye. Ever. Locking eyes with another man, be he a convict or a guard, is considered a challenge, a threat, and should therefore be avoided.

7. *Pick Your Friends Carefully.* When you choose a friend, you've got to be prepared to deal with anything that person may have done. Their reputation is yours, and the consequences can be enormous.

8. *Fight and Fight Dirty.* You have to fight, and not according to the Marquis of Queensbury Rules, either. If you do it right, you'll only have to do it once or twice. If you don't, expect regular whooping and loss of possessions. . . .

10. *Mind Your Own Business.* Never get in the middle of anyone else's discussion/argument/confrontation/fight. Never offer unsolicited knowledge or advice.

11. *Keep a Good Porn Collection.* If you don't have one, the boys will think you're funny. . . .

14. *Don't Talk to Staff, Especially Guards.* Any prolonged discussion or associations with staff make you susceptible to rumor and suspicion of being a snitch.

15. *Never Snitch.* Or even appear to snitch. And above all, avoid the real thing. And if you do, you'd better not get caught.

RESEARCHING THE INTERNET

Compare this set of rules with the official information provided to North Carolina prisoners, given to them to convey the rules and regulations of prison; go to the website listed on the Cole/Smith Criminal Justice in America Companion Website: http://www.cengage.com/criminaljustice/cole.

FOR CRITICAL ANALYSIS

If you were sent to prison, how would you seek to learn the code that prisoners enforce among themselves?

Source: Drawn from TJ Granack, "Welcome to the Steel Hotel: Survival Tips for Beginners," in *The Funhouse Mirror*, ed. Robert Gordon Ellis (Pullman: Washington State University Press, 2000), 6–10.

---

inmates as a "right guy" or a "real man." Those who break the code are labeled "rat" or "punk" and will probably spend their prison life at the bottom of the convict social structure, alienated from the rest of the population and targeted for abuse (Sykes, 1958:84).

A single, overriding inmate code probably does not exist in today's prisons. Instead, convict society has divided itself along racial lines (Carroll, 1974; Irwin, 1980). The level of adherence to the inmate code also differs among institutions, with greater modifications to local situations found in maximum-security prisons. Still, the core code described by Sykes over 50 years ago remains.

In a changing society that has no single code of behavior accepted by the entire population, the tasks of administrators become much more difficult. They must be aware of the different groups, recognize the norms and rules that members hold in each, and deal with the leaders of many cliques rather than with a few inmates who have risen to top positions in the inmate society. In the Close Up box, TJ Granack provides "Survival Tips for Beginners."

■ Adaptive Roles

On entering prison, a newcomer ("fish") is confronted by the question "How am I going to do my time?" Some decide to withdraw and isolate. Others decide to become full participants in the convict social system. The choice, influenced by prisoners' values and experiences, helps determine strategies for survival and success.

Most male inmates use one of four basic role orientations to adapt to prison: "doing time," "gleaning," "jailing," and functioning as a "disorganized criminal" (Irwin, 1970:67).

Doing Time   Men "doing time" view their prison term as a brief, inevitable break in their criminal careers, a cost of doing business. They try to serve their terms with the least amount of suffering and the greatest amount of comfort. They avoid trouble by living by the inmate code, finding activities to fill their days, forming friendships with a few other convicts, and generally doing what they think is necessary to survive and to get out as soon as possible.

Gleaning   Inmates who are "gleaning" try to take advantage of prison programs to better themselves and improve their prospects for success after release. They use the resources at hand: libraries, correspondence courses, vocational training, schools. Some make a radical conversion away from a life of crime.

Jailing   "Jailing" is the choice of those who cut themselves off from the outside and try to construct a life within the prison. These are often "state-raised" youths who have spent much of their lives in institutional settings and who identify little with the values of free society. These are the inmates who seek power and influence in the prison society, often becoming key figures in the politics and economy of prison life.

Disorganized Criminal   A fourth role orientation—the "disorganized criminal"—describes inmates who cannot develop any of the other three orientations. They may be of low intelligence or afflicted with psychological or physical disabilities, and they find functioning in prison society difficult. They are "human putty" to be manipulated by others. These are also the inmates who cannot adjust to prison life and who develop emotional disorders, attempt suicide, and violate prison rules (K. Adams, 1992).

As these roles suggest, prisoners are not members of an undifferentiated mass. Individual convicts choose to play specific roles in prison society. The roles they choose reflect the physical and social environment they have experienced and also influence their relationships and interactions in prison. How do most prisoners serve their time? Although the media generally portray prisons as violent, chaotic places, research shows that most inmates want to get through their sentence without trouble. As journalist Pete Earley found in his study of Leavenworth, roughly 80 percent of inmates try to avoid trouble and do their time as easily as possible (1992:44).

■ The Prison Economy

In prison, as outside, individuals want goods and services. Although the state feeds, clothes, and houses all prisoners, amenities remain sparse. Prisoners lack everything but bare necessities. Their diet and routine are monotonous and their recreational opportunities scarce. They experience a loss of identity (due to uniformity of treatment) and a lack of responsibility. In short, the prison is relatively unique in having been deliberately designed as "an island of poverty in the midst of a society of relative abundance" (V. Williams and Fish, 1974:40).

The number of items that a prisoner can purchase or receive through legitimate channels differs from state to state and from facility to facility. For example, prisoners in some state institutions may have televisions, civilian clothing, and hot plates. Not all prisoners enjoy these luxuries, nor do these amenities satisfy the lingering desire for a variety of other goods. Some state legislatures have decreed that amenities will be prohibited and that prisoners should return to spartan living conditions.

Recognizing that prisoners do have some basic needs that are not met, prisons have a commissary or "store" from which inmates may, on a scheduled basis, purchase a limited number of items—toilet articles, tobacco, snacks, and other food products—in exchange for credits drawn on their "bank accounts." The size of a bank account depends on the amount of money deposited at the inmate's entrance, gifts sent by relatives, and amounts earned in the low-paying prison industries.

However, the peanut butter, soap, and cigarettes of the typical prison store in no way satisfy the consumer needs and desires of most prisoners. Consequently, an informal, underground economy acts as a major element in prison society. Many items taken for granted on the outside are inordinately valued on the inside. For example, talcum powder and deodorant become more important because of the limited bathing facilities. Goods and services that a prisoner would not have consumed at all outside prison can take on an exaggerated importance inside prison. For example, unable to get alcohol, offenders may seek a similar effect by sniffing glue. Or, to distinguish themselves from others, offenders may pay laundry workers to iron a shirt in a particular way, a modest version of conspicuous consumption.

Many studies point to the pervasiveness of this economy. The research shows that a market economy provides the goods (contraband) and services not available or not allowed by prison authorities. In many prisons, inmates run private "stores." Food stolen from the kitchen for late-night snacks, homemade wine, and drugs such as marijuana are available in these stores.

As a principal feature of prison culture, this informal economy reinforces the norms and roles of the social system and influences the nature of interpersonal relationships. The extent of the underground economy and its ability to produce desired goods and services—food, drugs, alcohol, sex, preferred living conditions—vary according to the scope of official surveillance, the demands of the consumers, and the opportunities for entrepreneurship. Inmates' success as "hustlers" determines the luxuries and power they can enjoy.

Because real money is prohibited and a barter system is somewhat restrictive, the standard currency of the prison economy is cigarettes. They are not contraband, are easily transferable, have a stable and well-known standard of value, and come in "denominations" of singles, packs, and cartons. Furthermore, they are in demand by smokers. Even those who do not smoke keep cigarettes for prison currency. As more prisons become "nonsmoking," cans of tuna fish, postage stamps, and soap have emerged as a new form of currency (M. Santos, 2004:120).

Certain positions in the prison society enhance opportunities for entrepreneurs. For example, inmates assigned to work in the kitchen, warehouse, and administrative office steal food, clothing, building materials, and even information to sell or trade to other prisoners. The goods may then become part of other market transactions. Thus, the exchange of a dozen eggs for two packs of cigarettes may result in the reselling of the eggs in the form of egg sandwiches made on a hot plate for five cigarettes each. Meanwhile, the kitchen worker who stole the eggs may use the income to get a laundry worker to starch his shirts, to get drugs from a hospital orderly, or to pay a "punk" for sex.

Economic transactions can lead to violence when goods are stolen, debts are not paid, or agreements are violated. Disruptions of the economy can occur when officials

CHECKPOINT

ANSWERS

7 *Why is it unlikely that a single, overriding inmate code exists in today's prisons?*

7 The prison society is fragmented by racial and ethnic divisions.

8 *What are the four role orientations found in adult male prisons?*

8 Doing time, gleaning, jailing, and functioning as a disorganized criminal.

9 *Why does an underground economy exist in prison?*

9 To provide goods and services not available through regular channels.

conduct periodic "lockdowns" and inspections. Confiscation of contraband can result in temporary shortages and price readjustments, but gradually business returns. The prison economy, like that of the outside world, allocates goods and services, rewards and sanctions, and it is closely linked to the society it serves.

Women in Prison

Most studies of prisons have focused on institutions for men. How do prisons for women differ, and what special problems do female inmates face?

Women constitute only 7.1 percent (about 115,000) of the entire U.S. prison population (BJS, 2008b:6). However, the growth rate in the number of incarcerated women has exceeded that of men since 1981. In fact, from 1995 to 2005, the male population increased by 34 percent, whereas that of women increased by 57 percent (BJS, 2006a:4–6). This growth is particularly acute in the federal system, which has absorbed an additional six thousand female inmates during the past 20 years, because of the war on drugs (BJS, 2004a:5). The increased number of women in prison has significantly affected the delivery of programs, housing conditions, medical care, staffing, and security.

Female offenders are incarcerated in 98 confinement facilities for women and 93 facilities that house men and women separately. Life in these facilities both differ from and resemble life in institutions for men alone. Women's prisons are smaller, with looser security and less structured relationships; the underground economy is not as well developed; and female prisoners seem less committed to the inmate code. Women also serve shorter sentences than do men, so their prison society is more fluid as new members join and others leave.

Many women's prisons have the outward appearance of a college campus, often seen as a group of "cottages" around a central administration/dining/program building. Generally these facilities lack the high walls, guard towers, and cyclone fences found at most prisons for men. In recent years, however, the trend has been to upgrade security for women's prisons by adding barbed wire, higher fences, and other devices to prevent escapes.

The characteristics of correctional facilities for women also include geographic remoteness and inmate heterogeneity. Few states operate more than one institution for women, so inmates generally live far from children, families, friends, and attorneys. In many institutions, the small numbers of inmates limit the extent to which the needs of individual offenders can be recognized and treated. Housing classifications are often so broad that dangerous or mentally ill inmates are mixed with women who have committed minor offenses and have no psychological problems. Similarly, available rehabilitative programs are often not used to their full extent, because correctional departments fail to recognize women's problems and needs.

In most respects, we can see incarcerated women, like male prisoners, as disadvantaged losers in this complex and competitive society. However, the two groups differ with regard to types of offenses and length of sentences, patterns of drug use, and criminal history. Thirty-two percent of female prisoners are sentenced for violent

Women's experiences in prison can differ markedly from those of men. Although there is less violence between prisoners in women's institutions, women often have fewer options for educational and vocational programs. In addition, many prisons have discovered problems with male correctional officers sexually abusing women prisoners. How would you organize the selection of staff, staff training, and the development of programs to properly run a prison for women?

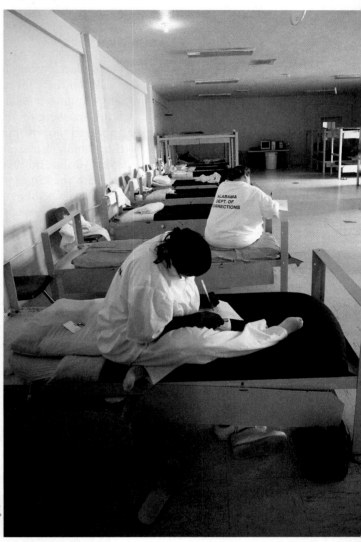

AP Images/Jamie Martin

offenses, compared with 49 percent of male prisoners, and 30 percent for drug-related offenses, versus 20 percent of the men (BJS, 2003a:10). Overall, women receive shorter maximum sentences than do men. Half of the women have a maximum sentence of 5 years or less, whereas half of the men have a sentence of 10 years or less (BJS, 2000a). Figure 12.4 summarizes some characteristics of female prisoners.

■ The Subculture of Women's Prisons

Studies of the subculture of women's prisons have been less extensive than those of male convict society. Further, just as few ethnographic studies of men's prisons have taken place during the past two decades, very few of women's prisons exist.

Much early investigation of women's prisons focused on types of social relationships among female offenders. As in all types of penal institutions, same-sex relationships were found, but unlike in male prisons, such relationships among women appeared more voluntary than coerced. Perhaps more importantly, scholars reported that female inmates tended to form pseudofamilies in which they adopted various roles—father, mother, daughter, sister—and interacted as a unit, rather than identifying with the larger prisoner subculture (Girshick, 1999; Propper, 1982). Esther Hefferman views these "play" families as a "direct, conscious substitution for the family relationships broken by imprisonment, or . . . the development of roles that perhaps were not fulfilled in the actual home environment" (1972:41–42). She also notes the

FIGURE 12.4
Characteristics of female inmates in state prisons
Like their male counterparts, female prisoners are young, have little education, are members of minority groups, and are incarcerated for a serious offense.

Sources: Bureau of Justice Statistics: *Bulletin,* July 2003, p. 10; *Special Report,* December 1999.

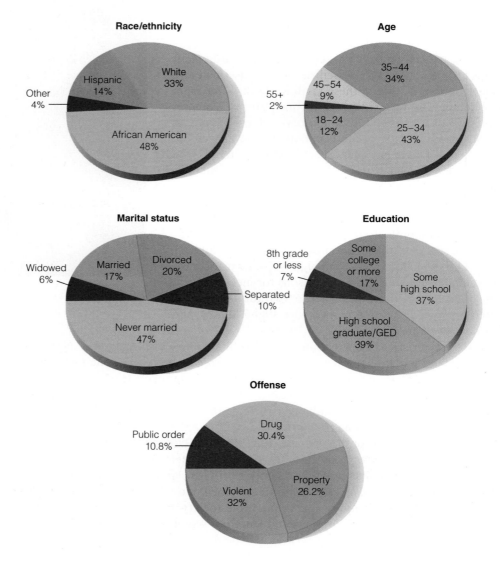

economic aspect of the play families and the extent to which they are formed to provide for their members. Such cooperative relationships help relieve the tensions of prison life, assist the socialization of new inmates, and permit individuals to act according to clearly defined roles and rules.

In discussing the available research on women in prison, we need to consider the most recent shifts in prison life. Just as the subculture of male prisons has changed since the pioneering research of the 1950s, the climate of female prisons has undoubtedly changed. Kimberly Greer (2000) found support for the idea that, compared with male prisons, prisons for women are less violent, involve less gang activity, and lack racial tension; however, the respondents indicated that their interpersonal relationships may be less stable and less familial than in the past. They reported higher levels of mistrust among women and greater economic manipulation.

In one of the few recent studies of prison culture, Barbara Owen (1998) found that the inmates at the Central California Women's Facility developed various styles of doing time. She observed that the vast majority wanted to avoid "the mix"—"behavior that can bring trouble and conflict with staff and other prisoners." A primary feature of "the mix" is anything for which one can lose "good time" or can result in being sent to administrative segregation. Being in "the mix" was related to "'homo-secting,' involvement in drugs, fights, and 'being messy,' that is being involved in conflict and trouble." Owen found that most women want to do their time and go home, but some "are more at home in prison and do not seem to care if they 'lost time'" (Owen, 1998:179).

Male versus Female Subcultures

Comparisons of male and female prisons are complicated by the nature of the research: Most studies have been conducted in single-sex institutions, and most follow theories and concepts first developed in male prisons. However, the following facts may explain the differences in subculture:

- Nearly half of male inmates but only a third of female inmates are serving time for violent offenses.
- There is less violence in prisons for women than in prisons for men.
- Women show greater responsiveness to prison programs.
- Men's prison populations are divided by security level, but most women serve time in facilities where the entire population is mixed.
- Men tend to segregate themselves by race; this is less true of women.
- Men rarely become intimate with their keepers, but many women share their lives with officers.

A major difference between the two types of prisons relates to interpersonal relationships. Male prisoners act for themselves and are evaluated by others according to how they adhere to subcultural norms. As James Fox (1982) notes in his early comparative study of one women's prison and four men's prisons, men believe they must demonstrate physical strength and consciously avoid any mannerisms that might imply homosexuality. To gain recognition and status within the convict community, the male prisoner must strictly adhere to these values. Men form cliques, but not the family networks found in prisons for women. Male norms stress autonomy, self-sufficiency, and the ability to cope with one's own problems, and men are expected to "do their own time." Fox found little sharing in the men's prisons.

Women, on the other hand, place less emphasis on achieving status or recognition within the prisoner community. Fox writes that women are also less likely "to impose severe restrictions on the sexual (or emotional) conduct of other members" (1982:100). As noted previously, in prisons for women, close ties seem to exist among small groups akin to extended families. These family groups provide emotional support and share resources.

The differences between male and female prisoner subcultures have been ascribed to the nurturing, maternal qualities of women. Some critics charge that such an analysis stereotypes female behavior and imputes a biological basis to personality where none exists. Of importance as well is the issue of inmate–inmate violence in male and female institutions. The few data that exist indicate that women are less likely to engage in violent acts against other inmates than are men (Kruttschnitt and Krmpotich, 1990:371). In any case, it will be interesting to see whether such gender-specific differences continue to be found among prisoners as the feminist perspective gains influence among researchers and as society moves toward viewing women and men as equals.

■ Issues in the Incarceration of Women

As noted, the number of incarcerated women has greatly increased over the past 20 years. Under pressures for equal opportunity, states seem to believe that they should run women's prisons as they do prisons for men, with the same policies and procedures. Joycelyn Pollock (1998) believes that when prisons emphasize parity, then use a male standard, women lose. She says that with the increased numbers of women in prison and more equality in programming, more security measures and more formalist approaches to supervision have also arisen.

Although correctional departments have been playing "catch up" to meet the challenges of the influx of women offenders, sexual misconduct by officers persists, along with women prisoners' demands for education and training, medical services, and methods for dealing with the problems of mothers and their children. We next examine each of these issues and the policy implications they pose for the future.

Sexual Misconduct As the number of female prisoners has increased, cases of sexual misconduct by male correctional officers have escalated. After an investigation of sexual misconduct of officers in the women's prisons of five states—California, Georgia, Illinois, Michigan, and New York—Human Rights Watch reported that male officers had raped, sexually assaulted, and abused female inmates. Guards had also "used their near total authority to provide or deny goods and privileges to female prisoners to compel them to have sex or, in other cases, to reward them for having done so" (*New York Times*, December 27, 1996, p. A18).

To deal with the problem of sexual abuse in prison, all but eight states have enacted statutes prohibiting sexual misconduct with correctional clients. Whereas some of these laws focus on correctional officers, several states are revising their statutes to include anyone who supervises offenders (*Criminal Justice Research Reports*, 2001). Beyond the new laws, corrections faces a great need for the implementation of effective sexual harassment policies, the training of officers, and tougher screening of recruits.

Educational and Vocational Training Programs A major criticism of women's prisons is that they lack the variety of vocational and educational programs available in male institutions. Critics also charge that existing programs tend to conform to sexual stereotypes of "female" occupations—cosmetology, food service, housekeeping, sewing. Such training does not correspond to the wider

Companies are finding that prison labor can be more efficient than outsourcing to low-wage countries elsewhere in the world. Prisoners at Wabash Valley Correctional Facility assemble yo-yos as part of a joint venture between the Indiana Department of Corrections' prison industry program and the Flambeau Products Corporation. Are these prisoners doing jobs that would otherwise provide wages for law-abiding citizens?

AP Images/Tribune-Star, Jim Avelis

employment opportunities available to women in today's world. Both men's and women's facilities usually offer educational programs so inmates can become literate and earn general equivalency diplomas (GEDs). Such programs matter a great deal, considering that upon release most women must support themselves, and many must support their children as well.

Merry Morash and her colleagues found that gender stereotypes shape vocational programs (Morash, Haarr, and Rucker, 1994). However, the American Correctional Association reports that the few work assignments available for incarcerated women do teach marketable job skills.

Medical Services   Women's prisons lack proper medical services. Yet, because of their socioeconomic status and limited access to preventive medical care, women usually have more serious health problems than do men. Compared with men, they have a higher incidence of asthma, drug abuse, diabetes, and heart disorders, and many women also have gynecological problems (Bershard, 1985; Yang, 1990). Although a higher percentage of women than men report receiving medical services in prison, women's institutions are less likely than men's to have a full-time medical staff or hospital facilities.

Saying that corrections must "defuse the time bomb," Leslie Acoca argues that failure to provide female inmates with basic preventive and medical treatments such as immunizations, breast cancer screenings, and management of chronic diseases "is resulting in the development of more serious health problems that are exponentially more expensive to treat" (1998:67). She says that poor medical care for the incarcerated merely shifts costs to overburdened community health care systems after release.

Mothers and Their Children   Of greatest concern to incarcerated women is the fate of their children. Over 65 percent of women inmates are mothers with, on average, two dependent children. Thus, on any given day, 115,500 American children—two-thirds of whom are under ten years old—have mothers who are in jail or prison. Roughly half of these children do not see their mothers the entire time they are in prison (BJS, 2000e:1).

Because about 65 percent of incarcerated mothers were single caretakers of minor children before they entered prison, they do not have partners to take care of their children. Other relatives care for nearly 78 percent of these children, whereas 10 percent are in state-funded foster care (Acoca, 1997).

Imprisoned mothers have difficulty maintaining contact with their children. Because most states have only one or two prisons for women, mothers may be incarcerated 150 miles or more away. This makes transportation difficult, visits short and infrequent, and phone calls uncertain and irregular. When the children do visit the prison, they face strange and intimidating surroundings. In some institutions, children must conform to the rules governing adult visitations: strict time limits and no physical contact.

Other correctional facilities, however, seek ways to help mothers maintain links to their children. For example, the Dwight Correctional Center in Illinois schedules weekend retreats, similar to camping trips, for women and their children. In some states, children can meet with their mothers at almost any time, for extended periods, and in playrooms or nurseries where contact is possible. Some states transport children to visit their mothers; some institutions even let children stay overnight with their mothers. A few prisons have family visitation programs that let the inmate, her legal husband, and her children be together, often in a mobile home or apartment, for up to 72 hours.

The future of women's correctional institutions is hard to predict. More women are being sent to prison now, and more have committed the violent crimes and drug offenses that used to be more typical of male offenders. Will these changes affect the adaptive roles and social relationships that differentiate women's prisons from men's? Will women's prisons need to become more security conscious and to enforce rules through more-formal relationships between inmates and staff? These important issues need further study.

CHECKPOINT

ANSWERS

10 What accounts for the neglect of facilities and programs in women's prisons?

10 The small number of female inmates compared with the number of male inmates.

11 How do the social relationships among female prisoners differ from those among their male counterparts?

11 Men are more individualistic and their norms stress autonomy, self-sufficiency, and the ability to cope with one's own problems. Women are more sharing with one another.

12 What problems do female prisoners face in maintaining contact with their children?

12 The distance of prisons from homes, intermittent telephone privileges, and unnatural visiting environment.

Prison Programs

Modern correctional institutions differ from those of the past in the number and variety of programs provided for inmates. Early penitentiaries included prison industries; educational, vocational, and treatment programs were added when rehabilitation goals became prevalent. During the last 35 years, as the public called for harsher punishment of criminals, legislators have gutted prison educational and treatment programs as "frills" that only "coddled" inmates. In addition, the great increase in the number of prisoners has limited access to those programs that are still available. Yet, a majority of respondents to one survey said that prisons do a poor or very poor job of rehabilitating prisoners (see "What Americans Think").

Administrators argue that programs help them deal with the problem of time on the prisoners' hands. They know that the more programs prisons offer, the less likely that inmate idleness will turn into hostility; the less cell time, the fewer tensions. Evidence suggests that inmate education and jobs may positively affect the running of prisons, as well as reducing recidivism.

■ Classification of Prisoners

Determining the appropriate program for an individual prisoner usually involves a process called **classification**. A committee—often comprising the heads of the security, treatment, education, and industry departments—evaluates the inmate's security level, treatment and educational needs, work assignment, and eventually readiness for release.

Classification decisions are often based on the institution's needs rather than on those of the inmates. For example, inmates from the city may be assigned to farm work because that is where they are needed. Further, certain programs may remain limited, even though the demand for them is great. Thus, inmates may find that the few places in, for example, a computer course are filled and that there is a long waiting list. Prisoners often become angered and frustrated by the classification process

■ **classification** The process of assigning an inmate to a category specifying his or her needs for security, treatment, education, work assignment, and readiness for release.

and the limited availability of programs. Although release on parole can depend on a good record of participation in these programs, entrance for some inmates is blocked.

Educational Programs

Offenders constitute one of the most undereducated groups in the U.S. population. In many systems, all inmates who have not completed eighth grade are assigned full-time to prison school. Many programs provide remedial help in reading, English, and math. They also permit prisoners to earn their GED. Some institutions offer courses in cooperation with a college or university, although funding for such programs has come under attack. The Comprehensive Crime Control Act of 1994 bans federal funding (Pell Grants) to prisoners for postsecondary education (Buruma, 2005). Studies have shown that prisoners assigned to education programs tend to avoid committing crimes after release (Andrews and Bonta, 1994). However, it remains unclear whether education helps rehabilitate these offenders or whether the types of prisoners ("gleaners") assigned to education programs tend to be those motivated to avoid further crimes.

Vocational Education

Vocational education programs attempt to teach offenders a marketable job skill. Unfortunately, too many programs train inmates for trades that already have an adequate labor supply or in which new methods have made the skills taught obsolete.

Offenders often lack the attitudes necessary to obtain and keep a job—punctuality, accountability, deference to supervisors, cordiality to coworkers. Therefore, most prisoners need to learn not only a skill but also how to act in the work world.

Yet another problem is perhaps the toughest of all. In one state or another, the law bars ex-felons from practicing certain occupations, including nurse, beautician, barber, real estate salesperson, chauffeur, worker where alcoholic beverages are sold, cashier, and insurance salesperson. Unfortunately, some prison vocational programs actually train inmates for jobs they can never hold.

Prison Industries

Prison industries, which trace their roots to the early workshops of New York's Auburn Penitentiary, are intended to teach work habits and skills that will assist prisoners' reentry into the outside workforce. In practice, institutions rely on prison labor to provide basic food, maintenance, clerical, and other services. In addition, many prisons contain manufacturing facilities that produce goods, such as office furniture and clothing, used in correctional and other state institutions.

The prison industries system carries a checkered career. During the nineteenth century, factories were established in many prisons, and inmates manufactured items that were sold on the open market. With the rise of the labor movement, however, state legislatures and Congress passed laws restricting the sale of prison-made goods so that they would not compete with those made by free workers. In 1979, Congress lifted restrictions on the interstate sale of prison-made products and urged correctional administrators to explore with the private sector possible improvements for prison industry programs. Industrial programs would relieve idleness, allow inmates to earn wages that they could save until release, and reduce the costs of incarceration. The Federal Bureau of Prisons and some states have developed industries, but generally their products are not sold on the free market and the percentage of prisoners employed varies greatly. For example, in North Carolina and Utah, more than 20 percent of prisoners work in prison industries, whereas in most states 5 percent

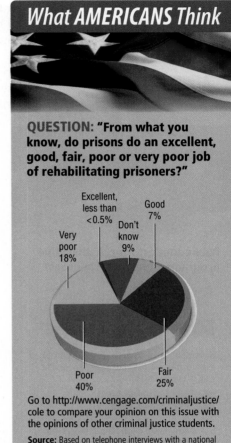

What AMERICANS Think

QUESTION: "From what you know, do prisons do an excellent, good, fair, poor or very poor job of rehabilitating prisoners?"

Excellent, less than <0.5%
Good 7%
Don't know 9%
Very poor 18%
Poor 40%
Fair 25%

Go to http://www.cengage.com/criminaljustice/cole to compare your opinion on this issue with the opinions of other criminal justice students.

Source: Based on telephone interviews with a national adult sample conducted by the public opinion polling firm of Belden, Russonello, and Stewart, January 5–22, 2001. Data provided by the Roper Center for Public Opinion Research, University of Connecticut.

or less do (C. G. Camp and Camp, 1999:96). Nonetheless, in 2002, about 3.5 percent of the prisoners in the United States produced goods and services worth $1.5 billion (Swarz, 2004).

Although the idea of employing inmates sounds attractive, the inefficiencies of prison work may offset its economic value. Turnover is great, because many inmates are transferred among several institutions or released over a two-year period. Many prisoners have little education and lack steady work habits, making it difficult for them to perform many of the tasks of modern production. An additional cost to efficiency is the need to stop production periodically to count heads and to check that tools and materials have not been stolen.

Rehabilitative Programs

Rehabilitative programs seek to treat the personal defects thought to have brought about the inmate's criminality. Most people agree that rehabilitating offenders is a desirable goal, but they disagree a great deal on the amount of emphasis that these programs should receive.

Reports in the 1970s cast doubt on the ability of treatment programs to stem recidivism. They also questioned the ethics of requiring inmates to participate in rehabilitative programs in exchange for the promise of parole (Martinson, 1974). Supporters of treatment programs argue that certain programs, if properly run, work for certain offenders (Andrews et al., 1990; Palmer, 1992). A national survey found support for rehabilitative programs (see "What Americans Think").

Most corrections systems still offer a range of psychological, behavioral, and social services programs. How much they are used seems to vary according to the goals of the institution and the attitudes of the administrators. Nationally, little money is spent on treatment services, and these programs reach only 5 percent of the inmate population. Although rehabilitative programs remain a part of correctional institutions, then, their emphasis has diminished. Incarceration's current goal of humane custody implies no effort to change inmates.

Can you imagine yourself working closely with criminal offenders to help them improve themselves? Consider the challenges of such jobs as you read "Careers in Criminal Justice."

Medical Services

Most prisons offer medical services through a full-time staff of nurses, augmented by part-time physicians under contract to the corrections system. Nurses take care of routine health care and dispense medicines from a secure in-prison pharmacy; regularly scheduled visits to the prison by doctors can enable prisoners to obtain checkups and diagnoses. For cases needing a specialist, surgery, or emergency medical assistance, prisoners must be transported to local hospitals, under close supervision by correctional staff. The aim is for the prison system to provide a range of medical assistance to meet the various needs of the population as a whole. Most states spend about $2,500 per inmate for health care, but some spend up to $5,000 and many under $2,000 (Pennsylvania Prison Society, 2004).

Medical services in some states have not kept up with the increase in the incarcerated population. In 1976, the U.S. Supreme Court ruled that prisoners have a constitutional right to health care. In 2009, as we have seen, a judicial panel of the federal appeals court of the Ninth Circuit ordered California to reduce its incarcerated population by 55,000 over three years as a means of reducing overcrowding so as to create a healthier prison environment. Earlier federal judges had ruled that the state's failure to provide medical and mental health care was killing at least one inmate every month and was subjecting prisoners to cruel and unusual punishment, which is prohibited by the Constitution. The ruling ordered the state to build

What AMERICANS Think

Public support for rehabilitative programs (selective responses)

1. It is a good idea to provide treatment for offenders who are in prison.

Agree   92%

5. Rehabilitative programs should be available even for offenders who have been involved in a lot of crime in their lives.

Agree   69%

6. The best way to rehabilitate offenders is to give them an education.

Agree   71%

7. The best way to rehabilitate offenders is to teach them a skill that they can use to get a job when they are released from prison.

Agree   89%

9. It is important to try to rehabilitate adults who have committed crime and are now in the correctional system.

Agree   88%

Go to http://www.cengage.com/criminaljustice/cole to compare your opinion on this issue with the opinions of other criminal justice students.

Source: Francis T. Cullen, Jennifer A. Pealer, Bonnie S. Fisher, Brandon K. Applegate, and Shannon A. Santana, "Public Support for Correctional Rehabilitation in America: Change and Consistency?" in *Changing Attitudes to Punishment,* ed. Julian V. Roberts and Mike Hough (Cullompton, Devon, UK: Willan, 2002), 137.

CAREERS IN CRIMINAL JUSTICE

Clinical Director

LISA ZIMMER, ASSISTANT CLINICAL DIRECTOR
TALBERT HOUSE, CINCINNATI, OHIO

THE ASSISTANT CLINICAL DIRECTOR assists in training clinical supervisors and other staff members who work with offenders. The position also involves developing and implementing treatment strategies and program improvements. In addition, the position's administrative responsibilities include ensuring that the agency complies with relevant laws and policies regarding best treatment practices, clients' rights, and proper expenditure of funds. Such careers require knowledge of substance abuse and other problems affecting offenders, as well as approaches to treatment. The position requires excellent communication skills, the ability to listen carefully to staff and clients, and the capacity to solve problems.

Lisa Zimmer studied journalism and sociology in earning her undergraduate degree. After beginning a career as a professional writer creating annual reports and other publications for hospitals,

she decided to shift careers so she could work at providing direct benefits to troubled people. While working full-time, she went back to school in the evenings to earn a master's degree in social work with an emphasis on counseling. After gaining the necessary certifications and licenses, she worked as a counselor in various correctional settings. Over time, she was promoted to supervisory and administrative positions for these programs. She now works for Talbert House, a nonprofit agency that provides substance abuse counseling, mental health treatment, and other services in jails, community corrections programs, reentry programs, and other correctional settings in Cincinnati, Ohio.

The work is challenging and rewarding at the same time. Generally, pay is not commensurate with other jobs requiring similar education, experience, and responsibility, so people who choose chemical dependency counseling or to work within the mental health or criminal justice systems aren't in it for the money. They are in it to make a difference, and they do. They help to give people back their lives.

new medical facilities and upgrade existing ones at its 33 state prisons at a cost of $8 billion (S. Moore, 2008; 2009a).

Although inmates' medical needs often echo those of the general population, prisoners pose two special needs, one due to poverty and the other to aging. Because prisoners as a group are very poor, they often bring to the prison years of neglect of their general health. Other consequences of being poor, such as an inadequate diet and poor hygiene, also affect the general health of the prison population.

CHECKPOINT

ANSWERS

13 Why are prison programs important from the standpoint of prison administrators?

13 Programs keep prisoners busy and reduce security problems.

14 Why have legislators and the general public been so critical of educational and rehabilitative programs in prisons?

14 Such programs are thought to "coddle" prisoners and give them resources not available to free citizens.

Violence in Prison

Prisons provide a perfect recipe for violence. They confine in cramped quarters a thousand men, some with histories of violent behavior. While incarcerated, these men are not allowed contact with women and live under highly restrictive conditions. Sometimes these conditions spark collective violence, as in the riots at Attica, New York (1971), Santa Fe, New Mexico (1980), Atlanta, Georgia (1987), Lucasville, Ohio (1993), and Florence, Colorado (2008).

Although prison riots are widely reported in the news, few people have witnessed the level of everyday interpersonal violence in U.S. prisons. For example, each year about 34,000 inmates are physically attacked by other inmates. In 2002, 48 assault victims died. An additional 168 prisoners committed suicide (BJS, 2005d:1). Great numbers of prisoners live in a state of constant uneasiness, always on the lookout for people who might demand sex, steal their few possessions, or otherwise hurt them. Some researchers suggest that the level of violence varies by offender age, institutional security designation, and administrative effectiveness (Maitland and Sluder, 1998:55).

■ Assaultive Behavior and Inmate Characteristics

For the person entering prison for the first time, the anxiety level and fear of violence run especially high. Gary, an inmate at Leavenworth, told Pete Earley, "Every convict has three choices, but only three. He can fight (kill someone), he can hit the fence (escape), or he can fuck (submit)" (1992:55). Even if a prisoner is not assaulted, the potential for violence permeates the environments of many prisons, adding to the stress and pains of incarceration.

Violence in correctional institutions raises serious questions for administrators, criminal justice specialists, and the general public. What causes prison violence? What can be done about it? We consider these questions by examining three main categories of prison violence: prisoner–prisoner, prisoner–officer, and officer–prisoner. First, we discuss three characteristics of prisoners that underlie these behavioral factors: age, attitudes, and race.

Age   Studies have shown that young men aged 16–24, both inside and outside prison, are more prone to violence than are older men. Not surprisingly, 96 percent of adult prisoners are men, with an average age of 27 at time of admission. Studies also show that younger prisoners face a greater risk of being victimized than do older inmates (Wooldredge, 1998:489).

Besides having greater physical strength than their elders, young men lack the commitments to career and family that can restrict antisocial behavior. In addition, many have difficulty defining their position in society. Thus, they interpret many things as challenges to their status.

Machismo, the concept of male honor and the sacredness of one's reputation as a man, requires physical retaliation against those who insult one's honor. Some inmates adopt a preventive strategy of trying to impress others with their bravado, which may result in counterchallenges and violence. The potential for violence among such prisoners is clear.

When officers must remove an uncooperative or violent prisoner from a cell, trained cell extraction teams must overwhelm the prisoner through the use of force while also limiting the risk of injury to themselves. Such events are often filmed to prevent false claims by prisoners that officers used excessive force. Are there additional precautions that these officers should take in order to avoid injuries to themselves and to the prisoner?

Attitudes Some sociologists suggests that a subculture of violence exists among certain socioeconomic, racial, and ethnic groups. In this subculture, found in the lower class and in its value system, violence is "tolerable, expected, or required" (Wolfgang and Ferracuti, 1967:263). Arguments are settled and decisions are made by the fist rather than by verbal persuasion. Many inmates bring these attitudes into prison with them.

Race Race has become a major divisive factor in today's prisons. Racist attitudes, common in the larger society, have become part of the convict code. Forced association—having to live with people one would not likely associate with on the outside—exaggerates and amplifies racial conflict. Violence against members of another race may be how some inmates deal with the frustrations of their lives. The presence of gangs organized along racial lines contributes to violence in prison.

■ Prisoner–Prisoner Violence

Although prison folklore may attribute violence to sadistic guards, most prison violence occurs between inmates. As Hans Toch has observed, the climate of violence in prisons has no free-world counterpart: "Inmates are terrorized by other inmates, and spend years in fear of harm. Some inmates request protective custody segregation, others lock themselves in, and some are hermits by choice" (1976:47–48). The Bureau of Justice Statistics reports that the rate of prisoner–prisoner assaults between inmates is 28 attacks per 1,000 inmates (BJS, 2003c:10). But official statistics likely do not reflect the true amount of prisoner–prisoner violence, because many inmates who are assaulted do not make their victimization known to prison officials.

Prison Gangs Racial or ethnic gangs (also referred to as "security threat groups") are now linked to acts of violence in most prison systems. Gangs make it difficult for wardens to maintain control. By continuing their street wars inside prison, gangs make some prisons more dangerous than any American neighborhoods. Gangs are organized primarily to control an institution's drug, gambling, loan-sharking, prostitution, extortion, and debt-collection rackets. In addition, gangs protect their members from other gangs and instill a sense of macho camaraderie.

Prison gangs exist in the institutions of most states and the federal system. In Illinois, as much as 60 percent of the population belongs to gangs (Hallinan, 2001:95). The Florida Department of Corrections has identified 240 street gangs operating in their prisons (Davitz, 1998). A study by the American Correctional Association found more than 46,000 gang members in the federal system and in the prisons of at least 35 states (1994:21).

Many facilities segregate rival gangs by housing them in separate units of the prison or moving members to other facilities (Knox, 2000). Administrators have also set up intelligence units to gather information on gangs, particularly about illegal acts both in and outside of prison. In some prisons, however, these policies create a power vacuum within the convict society that newer groups with new codes of behavior soon fill.

Prison Rape Much of the mythology of prison life revolves around sexual assaults. Perpetrators are typically strong, experienced cons, either African American or white, who are serving sentences for violent offenses. Victims are portrayed as young, white, physically weak, mentally challenged, effeminate first-time nonviolent offenders.

Prison rape is a crime hidden by a curtain of silence. Inmate–inmate and inmate–staff sexual contact is prohibited in all prisons, yet it exists, and much of it remains hidden from authorities. Sexual violence ranges from unwanted touching to nonconsensual sex. When incidents are reported, correctional officers say that it is difficult to distinguish between rapes and consensual sex. Most officers do not catch the inmates in the act; when they do observe sexual activity, only a few officers report that they ignored the inmates' violations of prison rules (Eigenberg, 2000).

The 2004 Prison Rape Elimination Act establishes a zero-tolerance standard for the incidence of rape in prison. This law requires the Bureau of Justice Statistics to conduct annual surveys in the nation's prisons and jails to measure the incidence of rape. The law also requires the Attorney General to provide a list of the incidence of prison rape in each institution.

In 2006, the Bureau of Justice Statistics released data on prison sexual assault that were based on reports to prison administrators. The survey found 1,865 allegations of inmate–inmate sexual assaults among state prisoners, a rate of 1.5 attacks per 1,000 inmates. Perpetrators of substantial incidents tended to be male (85.7 percent) and African American (42 percent) or white (42 percent). Victims were most likely to be male (84.8 percent), under age 30 (57 percent), and white (78 percent) (BJS, 2006d:4) A second study, published in 2007, was based on sexual victimization reported by inmates in 146 prisons. Researchers found that 60,500 inmates (4.5 percent of all federal and state prisoners) experienced one or more incidents of sexual victimization. The inmates reported 56 incidents of inmate–inmate nonconsensual acts per 1,000 prisoners. They also reported 85 incidents of unwilling sexual contacts with staff members per 1,000 inmates and 82 incidents of "willing" sexual contacts with staff members (BJS, 2007e:1, 3).

Victims of prisoner–prisoner sexual victimization have few options. According to the inmate code, prisoners should "stand and fight" their own battles. For many, this is not feasible. Alternatively, some may seek the protection of a gang or a stronger inmate to whom the victim is then indebted. Others may try to fade into the shadows. Still others may seek protective custody. Each option has its pluses and minuses, but none provides victims with the ability to serve their time without constantly looking over their shoulder.

Protective Custody   For many victims of prison violence, protective custody offers the only way to escape further abuse. About 5,000 state prisoners are in protective custody (C. G. Camp and Camp, 2001:26). Life is not pleasant for these inmates. Often, they are let out of their cells only briefly to exercise and shower (McGee, Warner, and Harlow, 1998). Inmates who ask to "lock up" have little chance of returning to the general prison population without being viewed as a weakling—a snitch or a punk—to be preyed on. Even when they are transferred to another institution, their reputations follow them through the grapevine.

■ Prisoner–Officer Violence

The mass media have focused on riots in which guards are taken hostage, injured, and killed. However, violence against officers typically occurs in specific situations and against certain individuals. Yearly, inmates assault more than 18,000 staff members (BJS, 2003c:10). Correctional officers do not carry weapons within the institution, because a prisoner might seize them. However, prisoners do manage to obtain lethal weapons and can use the element of surprise to injure an officer. In the course of a workday, an officer may encounter situations that require the use of physical force against an inmate—for instance, breaking up a fight or moving a prisoner to segregation. Because such situations are especially dangerous, officers may enlist others to help them minimize the risk of violence. The officer's greatest fear is unexpected attacks, such as a missile thrown from an upper tier or an officer's "accidental" fall down a flight of stairs. The need to watch constantly against personal attacks adds stress and keeps many officers at a distance from the inmates.

■ Officer–Prisoner Violence

A fact of life in many institutions is unauthorized physical violence by officers against inmates. Stories abound of guards giving individual prisoners "the treatment" when supervisors are not looking. Many guards view physical force as an everyday, legitimate procedure. In some institutions, authorized "goon squads" composed of physically powerful officers use their muscle to maintain order.

Correctional officers are expected to follow departmental rules in their dealings with prisoners, yet supervisors generally cannot observe staff–prisoner confrontations directly. Further, prisoner complaints about officer brutality are often not believed until the officer involved gains a reputation for harshness. Even in this case, wardens may feel they must support their officers in order to retain their support.

Decreasing Prison Violence

Five factors contribute to prison violence: (1) inadequate supervision by staff members, (2) architectural design that promotes rather than inhibits victimization, (3) the easy availability of deadly weapons, (4) the housing of violence-prone prisoners near relatively defenseless people, and (5) a general high level of tension produced by close quarters (Bowker, 1982:64). The physical size and condition of the prison and the relations between inmates and staff also affect violence.

The Effect of Architecture and Size   The fortresslike prison certainly does not create an atmosphere for normal interpersonal relationships, and the size of the larger institutions can create management problems. The massive scale of the megaprison, which may hold up to 3,000 inmates, provides opportunities for aggressive inmates to hide weapons, dispense private "justice," and engage more or less freely in other illicit activities. The size of the population in a large prison may also result in some inmates' "falling through the cracks"—being misclassified and forced to live among more-violent offenders.

Much of the emphasis on "new generation prisons"—small housing units, clear sight lines, security corridors linking housing units—is designed to limit such opportunities and thus prevent violence. However, a study of rape in Texas prisons found that cell blocks with solid doors may contribute to sexual assault (Austin et al., 2006).

The Role of Management   The degree to which inmate leaders are allowed to take matters into their own hands can affect the level of violence among inmates. When administrators run a tight ship, security measures prevent sexual attacks in dark corners, the making of "shivs" and "shanks" (knives) in the metal shop, and open conflict among inmate groups. A prison must afford each inmate defensible space, and administrators should ensure that every inmate remains secure from physical attack.

Effective management can decrease the level of assaultive behavior by limiting opportunities for attacks. Wardens and correctional officers must therefore recognize the types of people with whom they are dealing, the role of prison gangs, and the structure of institutions. John DiIulio argues that no group of inmates is "unmanageable [and] no combination of political, social, budgetary, architectural, or other factors makes good management impossible" (1991:12). He points to such varied institutions as the California Men's Colony, New York City's Tombs and Rikers Island, the Federal Bureau of Prisons, and the Texas Department of Corrections under the leadership of George Beto. At these institutions, good management practices have resulted in prisons and jails where inmates can "do time" without fearing for their personal safety. Wardens who exert leadership can manage their prisons effectively, so that problems do not fester and erupt into violent confrontations.

In sum, prisons must be made safe. Because the state puts offenders there, it has a responsibility to prevent violence and maintain order. To exclude violence from prisons, officials may have to limit movement within institutions, contacts with the outside, and the right of inmates to choose their associates. Yet, these measures may run counter to the goal of producing men and women who will be accountable when they return to society.

CHECKPOINT

15 *What five factors are thought to contribute to prison violence?*	**A N S W E R** **15** Inadequate supervision, architectural design, availability of weapons, housing of violence-prone inmates with the defenseless, and the high level of tension of people living in close quarters.

A QUESTION OF ETHICS: WRITING ASSIGNMENT

After three years of daily contact, correctional officer Bill MacLeod and Jack Douglas, who was serving a 3–5 year sentence, knew each other very well. They were both devoted to the Red Sox and the Celtics. Throughout the year, they would chat about the fortunes of their teams and the outlook ahead. MacLeod got to know and like Douglas. They were about the same age and had come from similar backgrounds. Why they were now on opposite sides of the cell bars was something that MacLeod could not figure out.

One day, Douglas called to MacLeod and said that he needed money because he had lost a bet gambling on the Red Sox. Douglas said that his wife would send him the money but that it couldn't come through the prison mail to him in cash. And a check or money order would show on his commissary account.

"The guy wants cash. If he doesn't get it, I'm dead." Douglas took a breath and then rushed on with his request. "Could you bring it in for me?

She'll mail the money to you at home. You could just drop the envelope on my bed."

"You know the rules. No gambling and no money," said MacLeod.

"But I'm scared shitless. It will be no big deal for you and it will make all the difference for me. Come on, we've gotten along well all these years. I think of you as being different from those other officers."

WRITING ASSIGNMENT

What should MacLeod do? Is this kind of request likely to be a one-time occurrence with Douglas? What if MacLeod's sergeant finds out? What if other inmates learn about it? In a short essay, describe the conflict that MacLeod must face. How should he resolve it?

Summary

Describe how contemporary institutions differ from the old-style "big-house" prisons

▷ The typical "big-house" was a walled prison with large tiered cell blocks, a yard, and workshops.

▷ Prisoners came from both rural and urban areas, were poor, and outside of the South were mainly white.

▷ The prison society in the past was isolated, with restrictions on visitors, mail, and other communications. The inmates' days were highly structured with rules enforced by the guards.

Understand the three models of incarceration that have predominated since the 1940s

▷ The custodial model emphasizes the maintenance of security.

▷ The rehabilitation model views security and housekeeping activities as mainly a framework for treatment efforts.

▷ The reintegration model recognizes that prisoners must be prepared for their return to society.

Explain how a prison is organized

▷ Most prisons are expected to fulfill goals related to keeping (custody), using (working), and serving (treating) inmates. They are organized to fulfill these goals.

Know how a prison is governed

▷ The public's belief that the warden and officers have total power over the inmates is outdated.

▷ Good management through effective leadership can maintain the quality of prison life as measured by levels of order, amenities, and services.

▷ Four factors make managing prisons different from administering other public institutions: defects of total power, limited use of rewards and punishments, exchange relationships, and strength of inmate leadership.

Understand the role of correctional officers in a prison

▷ Because they remain in close contact with the prisoners, correctional officers are the linchpins of the prison system. The effectiveness of the institution rests on their shoulders.

Explain the characteristics of the incarcerated population

▶ Most prisoners are male, young, members of minority groups, with low educational levels.

▶ Prison administrators must deal with the special needs of some groups, including elderly prisoners, prisoners with HIV/AIDS, mentally ill prisoners, and long-term prisoners.

Discuss what prison is like for men and for women

▶ Inmates do not serve their time in isolation but are members of a subculture with its own traditions, norms, and leadership structure. Such norms are often described as the inmate code.

▶ Today's prisons, unlike those of the past, do not have a uniform inmate code but several, in part because of the influence of gangs.

▶ Inmates deal with the pain of incarceration by assuming an adaptive role and lifestyle.

▶ Male inmates are individualistic, and their norms stress autonomy, self-sufficiency, and the ability to cope with one's own problems. Female inmates share with one another and place less emphasis on achieving status or recognition within the prisoner community. There is less violence in female prisons than in male ones.

List some of the programs and services available to prisoners

▶ Educational, vocational, industrial, and rehabilitative programs are available in prisons. Administrators believe that these programs are important for maintaining order.

▶ Medical services are provided to all inmates.

Describe the nature of prison violence

▶ Violence occurs between prisoners and between prisoners and guards.

▶ Violence in prison depends on such things as administrative effectiveness, the architecture and size of prisons, and inmate characteristics such as age, attitudes, and race. Prison gangs play an increasing role in causing prison violence.

■ Questions for Review

1. How do modern prisons differ from those in the past?

2. What characteristics of prisons distinguish them from other institutions?

3. What must a prison administrator do to ensure successful management?

4. What is meant by an adaptive role? Which roles are found in male prison society? In female prison society?

5. How does the convict society in institutions for women differ from that in institutions for men?

6. What are the main forms of prison programs, and what purposes do they serve?

7. What are forms and causes of prison violence?

■ Key Terms and Cases

classification (p. 366)
custodial model (p. 346)

inmate code (p. 357)
rehabilitation model (p. 346)

reintegration model (p. 347)

Reentry into the Community

Opposite page: © Michael Stravato/The New York Times/Redux

THIS YEAR, nearly 700,000 people will be released from state and federal prisons. They will join the worst economy in decades. Many of them have limited education and little or no legitimate employment experience, and a criminal record will make it that much harder to find a job.

Yet, newly released prisoners need to work, not just to support themselves and their families, but also because having a job means staying out of trouble. One study, in December 2006, found that 89 percent of people who violate the terms of their parole or probation were unemployed.

In the past few years, several programs have been introduced to teach prisoners, who may have problems finding traditional employment after their release, how to work for themselves. "We try to help these guys realize that the skills they already possess from illegal ventures have real value in the business world," explains Catherine Rohr, founder and chief executive of the Prison Entrepreneurship Program, based in Houston. "Major drug dealers are already proven entrepreneurs."

Prisoners accepted into the five-month P.E.P. program attend class for 35 hours a week. Curtis Hogue, a former security analyst, teaches an intensive M.B.A.-style curriculum, with lessons in finance, accounting, marketing, and sales. Several dozen executives and business students volunteer as guest lecturers or as judges at a competition for the best business plan.

A few days each week, Rohr teaches a course on character development. She stresses what she calls "consequence trails" and encourages students to recognize the suffering and pain unleashed in the wake of bad decisions. Rohr says she believes the focus on character is essential. Without it, the program might, as she puts it, "take an old dope dealer, equip him with a skill set and help him to become a better dope dealer when he gets out."

P.E.P. also sponsors comprehensive postrelease programs for its graduates in Houston and Dallas. Services include housing, free or low-cost dental and medical care, and an evening entrepreneurship school taught by volunteers who also serve as professional mentors.

Since the program's inception, 441 men, roughly a quarter of whom had been incarcerated for violent crimes, have graduated. Only about 8 percent have returned to prison, while the national recidivism rate exceeds 25 percent (Berlin, 2009).

With the great expansion of incarceration during the past three decades, the number of offenders now returning to the community has increased dramatically.

LEARNING OBJECTIVES

▶ **Understand what is meant by the "reentry problem"**

▶ **Explain the origins of parole and how it operates today**

▶ **Identify the mechanisms for the release of felons to the community**

▶ **Describe how ex-offenders are supervised in the community**

▶ **Understand the problems that parolees face during their reentry**

Ex-prisoners are mostly male and unskilled, and 47 percent belong to minority groups. Many have alcohol and drug problems, and about one-third of state inmates have a physical or mental impairment. Some are "churners" who have already served terms for prior offenses and are being let out again. About two-thirds will return to a few metropolitan areas in their states where they will live in poor, inner-city neighborhoods. Some researchers believe that this leads to further instability in areas that already have high levels of crime, drug abuse, and other social problems (Clear et al., 2003). In this chapter, we examine the mechanisms by which prisoners are released from incarceration; we also look at their supervision in the community. Finally, we discuss the many problems facing parolees as they reenter society.

Prisoner Reentry

Reentry has been described as a "transient state between liberty and recommitment" (A. Blumstein and Beck, 2005:50). It is a limited period of supervision whereby an inmate either moves to full liberty in the community or returns to prison for committing a new crime or for violating the terms of parole. Prisoner reentry has become an important public issue. The sudden flood of offenders leaving prison, as well as the eventual return of so many to prison, raises serious questions as to how the criminal justice system deals with the reentry of ex-felons. What is the crux of this problem?

Jeremy Travis and Joan Petersilia (2001) point to several factors contributing to the reentry problem. They argue that, beginning in the 1970s, the power of parole boards to make release decisions was abolished in mandatory release states and severely restricted in discretionary release states. This means that more inmates are automatically leaving prison, ready or not, when they meet the requirements of their sentence. It also means that there has been little or no prerelease planning to ensure that the new parolee has a job, housing, and a supportive family when he or she hits the streets.

A second factor they believe contributes to the reentry problem is the curtailment of prison education, job training, and other rehabilitation programs designed to prepare inmates for their return to the community. There are very few programs like the Texas P.E.P. described in the chapter opening.

Finally, Travis and Petersilia note that the profile of returning prisoners has changed in ways that pose new challenges to successful reentry. In particular, the conviction offense and time served differ from what they were 20 years ago. Now, more than a third of prisoners released to parole are incarcerated for a drug offense—up from 12 percent in 1985. The average time served has also increased by almost a half year since 1990. Further, some drug and violent offenders are exiting prison after very long terms, perhaps 20 or more years. The longer time in prison means a longer period the prisoner has lived apart from family and friends.

CAREERS IN CRIMINAL JUSTICE

Reentry Specialist

RICHARD ROSALES, REENTRY SPECIALIST
INDIANA DEPARTMENT OF CORRECTION,
PLAINFIELD RE-ENTRY EDUCATIONAL FACILITY

THE POSITION OF REENTRY SPECIALIST is unique in the field of corrections, because it exists only at the Plainfield Re-Entry Educational Facility (PREF), which is in turn the only "application facility" in the United States. Offenders must apply from another facility in Indiana; if they meet the criteria for admittance, they are then transferred to PREF. At PREF, offenders are called "residents" to facilitate a different atmosphere. Residents dress in civilian clothes, live in dormitory-style housing, and manage their own daily schedule. PREF has numerous programs designed to assist successful reentry; these include educational, vocational, substance abuse, and spiritual programs.

A reentry specialist is responsible for fulfilling three different roles: case manager, counselor, and custody officer. Specialists manage a caseload of residents, including every aspect of their reentry preparation. Their reentry accountability plan, for instance, details everything—the programs and plans for self-improvement and preparation—that will facilitate a successful reentry back into society. Residents who need counseling for personal problems and other matters rely on their specialist for assistance. Specialists also handle the custody functions that are necessary for safety and security in any correctional institution. Among other duties, they conduct counts and shakedowns and monitor residents' compliance with rules.

A reentry specialist must have thorough knowledge of the criminal justice system in order to understand the documents and procedures. They must understand the processes that lead an offender to incarceration and also the challenges that confront parolees in the community. Superior communication skills are essential to working with both offenders and staff. Anyone in corrections can expect to be manipulated and tested and therefore must maintain constant vigilance regarding their surroundings and interactions. A reentry specialist is also expected to prepare numerous reports, both in-house and for outside criminal justice agencies such as the courts and those dealing with probation and parole.

Richard Rosales prepared for this position by obtaining undergraduate and graduate degrees in criminal justice. During college and graduate school, he completed internships with a state police agency. He first worked with the Indiana Department of Correction through the AmeriCorps*VISTA program, a public service program funded by the federal government. At the conclusion of his year of service, he applied and was accepted for his current position.

The best part of my position in the field of corrections is that every day I have the chance to make a difference in the lives of my residents. The work I do today can prevent someone from returning to prison tomorrow and in turn make the community safer for the citizens of Indiana. We are seeing the direction of corrections shift to reentry, and PREF is at the forefront of this exciting movement.

Many have expressed concern regarding how the corrections system prepares prisoners to live as law-abiding citizens. Successful prisoner reentry requires that parole and services focus on linking offenders with community institutions—churches, families, self-help groups, and nonprofit programs. As emphasized by Joan Petersilia, "We must share the responsibility for transitioning offenders with the community." Ultimately, family and neighborhood stability and public safety depend on successful reentry (Petersilia, 2003:3). As you read "Careers in Criminal Justice," about the job of a reentry specialist in the Indiana corrections system, think about what kinds of programs and services prisons should provide to offenders before they are released into the community.

CHECKPOINT

ANSWER

❶ *What three factors have likely contributed to the reentry problem?*

❶ Changes in the powers of parole boards, reduction in programs designed to assist ex-prisoners, and the changing profile of those being released from prison.

Release and Supervision

Except for the less than 7 percent of inmates who die in prison, all will eventually be released to live in the community. Currently about 77 percent of felons will be released on parole and will remain under correctional supervision for a specific period. About 19 percent will be released at the expiration of their sentence, having "maxed out" and earned the freedom to live in the community without supervision.

■ **parole** The conditional release of an inmate from incarceration, under supervision, after part of the prison sentence has been served.

Parole is the *conditional* release of an offender from incarceration but not from the legal custody of the state. Thus, offenders who comply with parole conditions and do not further conflict with the law receive an absolute discharge from supervision at the end of their sentences. If a parolee breaks a rule, parole can be revoked and the person returned to a correctional facility. Parole rests on three concepts:

1. *Grace.* The prisoner could be kept incarcerated, but the government extends the privilege of release.
2. *Contract.* The government enters into an agreement with the prisoner whereby the prisoner promises to abide by certain conditions in exchange for being released.
3. *Custody.* Even though the offender is released from prison, he or she remains a responsibility of the government. Parole is an extension of correctional programs into the community.

Only felons are released on parole; adult misdemeanants are usually released immediately after they have finished serving their sentences. Today, about 825,000 people are under parole supervision, a threefold increase since 1980 (Glaze and Bonczar, 2008).

■ The Origins of Parole

Parole in the United States evolved during the nineteenth century from the English, Australian, and Irish practices of conditional pardon, apprenticeship by indenture, transportation of criminals from one country to another, and issuance of "tickets of leave." These were all methods of moving criminals out of prison as a response to overcrowding, unemployment, and the cost of incarceration.

A key figure in developing the concept of parole in the nineteenth century was Captain Alexander Maconochie, an administrator of British penal colonies in Tasmania and elsewhere in the South Pacific. A critic of definite prison terms, Maconochie devised a system of rewards for good conduct, labor, and study. Under his classification procedure, prisoners could pass through stages of increasing responsibility and freedom: (1) strict imprisonment, (2) labor on government chain gangs, (3) freedom within a limited area, (4) a ticket of leave or parole resulting in a conditional pardon, and (5) full restoration of liberty. Like modern correctional practices, this procedure assumed that prisoners should be prepared gradually for release. The roots of the American system of parole lie in the transition from imprisonment to conditional release to full freedom.

Maconochie's idea of requiring prisoners to earn their early release caught on first in Ireland. There, Sir Walter Crofton built on Maconochie's idea to link an offender's progress in prison to a ticket of leave. Prisoners who graduated through Crofton's three successive levels of treatment were released on parole under a series of conditions. Most significant was the requirement that parolees submit monthly reports to the police. In Dublin, a special civilian inspector helped releasees find jobs, visited them periodically, and supervised their activities.

■ The Development of Parole in the United States

In the United States, parole developed during the prison reform movement of the latter half of the nineteenth century. Relying on the ideas of Maconochie and Crofton, American reformers such as Zebulon Brockway of the Elmira State

Reformatory in New York began to experiment with the concept of parole. After New York adopted indeterminate sentences in 1876, Brockway started to release prisoners on parole. Under the new sentencing law, prisoners could be released when their conduct showed they were ready to return to society. This idea spread, so that 20 states had parole systems by 1900, and 44 states and the federal government had them by 1932 (Friedman, 1993:304). Today, every state has some procedure for the release of offenders before the end of their sentences.

Although it has been used in the United States for more than a century, parole remains controversial. To many people, parole allows convicted offenders to avoid serving the full sentence they deserve. Public pressure to be tougher on criminals has led half the states and the federal government to restructure their sentencing laws and release mechanisms (Petersilia, 1999:479). The public hue and cry following commission of a particularly heinous act by a parolee pressures authorities to limit release.

CHECKPOINT

ANSWER

2 *In what countries did the concept of parole first develop?*

2 England, Australia, Ireland.

Release Mechanisms

From 1920 to 1973, there was a nationwide sentencing and release policy. During this period, all states and the federal government used indeterminate sentencing, authorized discretionary release by parole boards, and supervised prisoners after release, and they did this all in the interest of the rehabilitation of offenders.

With the 1970s came critiques of rehabilitation, the move to determinate sentencing, and the public's view that the system was "soft" on criminals. By 2002, 16 states and the federal government had abolished discretionary release by parole boards. Another five states had abolished discretionary parole for certain offenses (Petersilia, 2003:65). Further, in some of the states that kept discretionary release, parole boards have been reluctant to grant it.

There are now four basic mechanisms for people to be released from prison: (1) discretionary release, (2) mandatory release, (3) other conditional release, and (4) expiration release. Figure 13.1 shows the percentage of felons released by the various mechanisms.

■ Discretionary Release

States retaining indeterminate sentences allow **discretionary release** by the parole board within the boundaries set by the sentence and the penal law. This is a conditional release to parole supervision. This approach (illustrated in the Close Up box) lets the board members assess the prisoner's readiness for release within the minimum and maximum terms of the sentence. In reviewing the prisoner's file and asking questions, the parole board focuses on the nature of the offense, the inmate's behavior, and his or her participation in rehabilitative programs. This process places great faith in the ability of parole board members to predict the future behavior of offenders. See "A Question of Ethics" at the end of the chapter for more on parole boards.

■ **discretionary release** The release of an inmate from prison to conditional supervision at the discretion of the parole board within the boundaries set by the sentence and the penal law.

Parole hearings are often brief proceedings in which board members ask questions of the prisoner who is eligible for parole. In many places, the crime victim or the victim's family are permitted to communicate with the board, in writing or in person, to express their views about the prospect of the offender's early release from prison. How much influence should crime victims have over parole decisions?

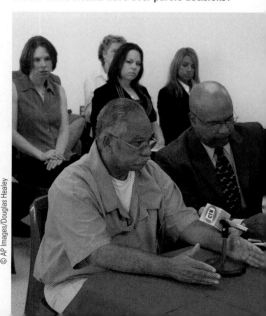

© AP Images/Douglas Healey

FIGURE 13.1

Methods of release from state prison
Felons are released from prison to the community, usually under parole supervision, through various means depending on the law.

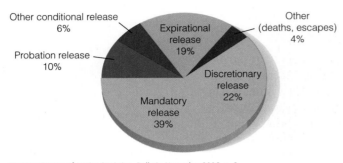

Other conditional release
6%

Probation release
10%

Expirational release
19%

Other (deaths, escapes)
4%

Discretionary release
22%

Mandatory release
39%

Source: Bureau of Justice Statistics, *Bulletin*, November 2006, p. 8.

■ **mandatory release** The required release of an inmate from incarceration to community supervision upon the expiration of a certain period, as specified by a determinate-sentencing law or parole guidelines.

■ **other conditional release** A term used in some states to avoid the rigidity of mandatory release, by placing convicts in various community settings, under supervision.

■ **expiration release** The release of an inmate from incarceration, without further correctional supervision; the inmate cannot be returned to prison for any remaining portion of the sentence for the current offense.

■ Mandatory Release

Mandatory release occurs after an inmate has served time equal to the total sentence minus good time, if any, or to a certain percentage of the total sentence as specified by law. Mandatory release is found in federal jurisdictions and states with determinate sentences and good-time provisions (see Chapter 9). Without a parole board to make discretionary decisions, mandatory release is a matter of bookkeeping to check the correct amount of good time and other credits and make sure the sentence has been accurately interpreted. The prisoner is conditionally released to parole supervision for the rest of the sentence.

■ Other Conditional Release

Because of the growth of prison populations, many states have devised ways to get around the rigidity of mandatory release, by placing inmates in the community through furloughs, home supervision, halfway houses, emergency release, and other programs (BJS, 2000b; Griset, 1995:307). These types of **other conditional release** also avoid the appearance of the politically sensitive label "discretionary parole."

■ Expiration Release

An increasing percentage of prisoners receive an **expiration release**. As noted earlier, such offenders have served the maximum court sentence, minus good time—they have "maxed out." These inmates are released from any further correctional supervision and cannot be returned to prison for their current offense.

■ Impact of Release Mechanisms

Parole release mechanisms do more than simply determine the date at which a particular prisoner will be sent back into the community. Parole release also greatly affects other parts of the system, including sentencing, plea bargaining, and the size of prison populations.

An increasing number of offenders are leaving prison at the expiration of their sentences. They have "maxed out" and leave without the requirements of parole supervision. What is their future?

© AP Images/Joseph Kaczmarek

One important effect of discretionary release is that an administrative body—the parole board—can shorten a sentence imposed by a judge. Even in states that have mandatory release, various potential reductions built into the sentence mean that the full sentence is rarely served. Good time, for example, can reduce punishment even if there is no eligibility for parole.

To understand the impact of release mechanisms on criminal punishment, we must compare the amount of time actually served in prison with the sentence specified by the judge. In most states, good time and jail time are the main factors that reduce the time actually served. On a national basis, felony inmates serve an average of two and a half years before release. Figure 13.2 shows the average time served for selected offenses.

Supporters of discretion for the paroling authority argue that parole benefits the overall system. Discretionary release mitigates the harshness of the penal code. If the legislature must establish exceptionally

CLOSE UP

A Roomful of Strangers

AFTER FIVE YEARS, three months, and four days in Stanhope Correctional Facility, Ben Brooks was ready to go before the Board of Parole. He woke with butterflies in his stomach, realizing that at nine o'clock he was to walk into the hearing room to confront a roomful of strangers. As he lay on his bunk, he rehearsed the answers to the questions he thought the board members might ask: "How do you feel about the person you assaulted? What have you done with your time while incarcerated? Do you think you have learned anything here that will convince the board that you will follow a crime-free life in the community? What are your plans for employment and housing?" According to prison scuttlebutt, these were the types of questions asked, and you had to be prepared to answer that you were sorry for your past mistakes, had taken advantage of the prison programs, had a job waiting for you, and planned to live with your family. You had to "ring bells" with the board.

At breakfast, friends dropped by Ben's table to reassure him that he had it made. As one said, "Ben, you've done everything they've said to do. What else can they expect?" That was the problem—*What did they expect?*

At eight-thirty, Officer Kearney came by the cell. "Time to go, Ben." They walked out of the housing unit and down the long prison corridors to a group of chairs outside the hearing room. Other prisoners were already seated there. "Sit here, Ben. They'll call when they're ready. Good luck."

At ten minutes past nine, the door opened and an officer called, "First case, Brooks." Ben got up, walked into the room. "Please take a seat, Mr. Brooks," said the African American seated in the center at the table. Ben knew he was Reverend Perry, a man known as being tough but fair. To his left was a white man, Mr. MacDonald, and to his right a Hispanic woman, Ms. Lopez. The white man led the questioning.

"Mr. Brooks. You were convicted of armed robbery and sentenced to a term of six to ten years. Please tell the board what you have learned during your incarceration."

Ben paused and then answered hesitantly, "Well, I learned that to commit such a stupid act was a mistake. I was under a lot of pressure when I pulled the robbery and now am sorry for what I did."

"You severely injured the woman you held up. What might you tell her if she were sitting in this room today?"

"I would just have to say, I'm sorry. It will never happen again."

"But this is not the first time you have been convicted. What makes you think it will never happen again?"

"Well this is the first time I was sent to prison. You see things a lot differently from here."

Ms. Lopez spoke up. "You have a good prison record—member of the Toastmaster's Club, gotten your high school equivalency diploma, kept your nose clean. Tell the board about your future plans should you be released."

"My brother says I can live with him until I get on my feet, and there is a letter in my file telling you that I have a job waiting at a meat-processing plant. I will be living in my hometown but I don't intend to see my old buddies again. You can be sure that I am now on the straight and narrow."

"But you committed a heinous crime. That woman suffered a lot. Why should the board believe that you won't do it again?"

"All I can say is that I'm different now."

"Thank you, Mr. Brooks," said Reverend Perry. "You will hear from us by this evening." Ben got up and walked out of the room. It had only taken eight minutes, yet it seemed like hours. Eight minutes during which his future was being decided. Would it be back to the cell or out on the street? It would be about ten hours before he would receive word from the board as to his fate.

RESEARCHING THE INTERNET

For more on this subject, see the corresponding website listed on the Cole/Smith Criminal Justice in America Companion Website: http://www.cengage.com/criminaljustice/cole.

FOR CRITICAL ANALYSIS

What is going on here? Analyze discretionary release from the standpoint of the inmate and the board members. What is each trying to accomplish?

---

strict punishments as a means of conveying a "tough on crime" image to frustrated and angry voters, parole can effectively permit sentence adjustments that make the punishment fit the crime. Not everyone convicted of larceny has done equivalent harm, yet some legislatively mandated sentencing schemes impose equally strict sentences. Early release on parole can be granted to an offender who is less deserving of strict punishment, such as someone who voluntarily makes restitution, cooperates with the police, or shows genuine regret.

A major criticism of discretionary release is that it shifts responsibility for many primary criminal justice decisions from a judge, who holds legal procedures uppermost, to an administrative board, where discretion rules. Judges know a great deal about constitutional rights and basic legal protections, but parole board members may not have such knowledge. In most states with discretionary release, parole hearings are secret, with only board members, the inmate, and correctional officers present. Often, no published criteria guide decisions, and prisoners receive no reason for denial or granting of parole. However, an increasing number of states permit oral or written testimony by victims and by members of the offender's family.

FIGURE 13.2
Estimated time to be served (in months) by state prisoners for selected crimes
The data indicate that the average felony offender going to prison for the first time spends about two years incarcerated. How would you expect the public to react to that fact?

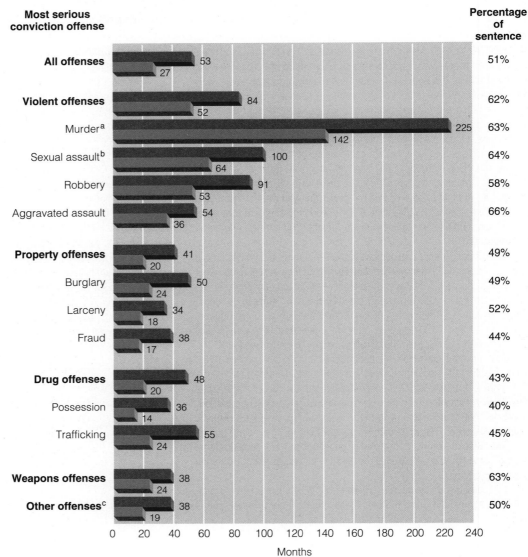

Most serious conviction offense	Months	Percentage of sentence
All offenses	53 / 27	51%
Violent offenses	84 / 52	62%
Murder[a]	225 / 142	63%
Sexual assault[b]	100 / 64	64%
Robbery	91 / 53	58%
Aggravated assault	54 / 36	66%
Property offenses	41 / 20	49%
Burglary	50 / 24	49%
Larceny	34 / 18	52%
Fraud	38 / 17	44%
Drug offenses	48 / 20	43%
Possession	36 / 14	40%
Trafficking	55 / 24	45%
Weapons offenses	38 / 24	63%
Other offenses[c]	38 / 19	50%

[a] Includes nonnegligent manslaughter
[b] Includes rape
[c] Composed of nonviolent offenses such as receiving stolen property and vandalism

■ Mean prison sentence
■ Average time served

Source: Bureau of Justice Statistics, *Bulletin*, November 2004, p. 5.

CHECKPOINT

A N S W E R

❸ *What are the four release mechanisms for prisoners?*

❸ Discretionary release, mandatory release, other conditional release, and expiration release.

Parole Supervision in the Community

Parolees are released from prison on condition that they abide by laws and follow rules, known as **conditions of release**, designed to aid their readjustment to society and control their movement. As in probation, the parolee may be required to abstain from alcohol, keep away from undesirable associates, maintain good work habits, and not leave the state without permission. If they violate these conditions, they could be returned to prison to serve out the rest of their sentence. Nearly 80 percent of released prisoners are subject to some form of community supervision (Petersilia, 1999:489). Only those who have served their full sentence minus good time ("maxed out") are free from supervision.

The restrictions are justified on the ground that people who have been incarcerated must readjust to the community so that they will not fall back into preconviction habits and associations. The strict enforcement of these rules may create problems for parolees who cannot fulfill all the demands placed on them. For example, a parolee may find it impossible to be tested for drugs, attend an Alcoholics Anonymous meeting, and work full-time while also meeting family obligations.

The day they come out of prison, parolees face a staggering array of problems. In most states, they receive only clothes, a token amount of money, a list of rules governing their conditional release, and the name and address of the parole officer to whom they must report within 24 hours. Although a promised job is often required for release, an actual job may be another matter. Most former convicts are unskilled or semiskilled, and the conditions of release may prevent them from moving to areas where they could find work. If the parolee is African American, male, and under 30, he joins the largest demographic group of unemployed people in the country. Figure 13.3 shows the personal characteristics of parolees.

Parolees bear the added handicap of former convict status. In most states, laws prevent former prisoners from working in certain types of establishments—where alcohol is sold, for example—thus ruling out many jobs. In some states, those who have served time are assumed to have "a lack of good moral character and trustworthiness," a condition required to acquire a license to be a barber, for example. Finally, ex-convicts face a significant dilemma. If they are truthful about their backgrounds, many employers will not hire them. If they are not truthful, they can be fired for lying if the employer ever learns about their conviction. Some problems that parolees encounter when they reenter the community are illustrated in the Close Up box on page 387. As you read about Jerome Washington's experience, ask yourself what problems you might encounter after a long term in "max."

Other reentry problems plague parolees. For many, the transition from the highly structured life in prison to open society is too difficult to manage. Many just do not have the social, psychological, and material resources to cope with the temptations and complications of modern life. For these parolees, freedom may be short-lived as they fall back into forbidden activities such as drinking, using drugs, and stealing.

■ **conditions of release** Conduct restrictions that parolees must follow as a legally binding requirement of being released.

Grace Bernstein, an administrative law judge at the Harlem Parole Reentry Court in New York City, conducts a hearing to discuss and resolve issues related to parolees under supervision in the community. Should parolees be given second chances if they violate conditions of release, such as rules about curfews or consumption of alcohol?

■ Community Programs Following Release

There are various programs to assist parolees. Some help prepare offenders for release while they are still in prison; others provide employment and housing assistance after release.

FIGURE 13.3
Personal characteristics of parolees
Prison releases tend to be men in their thirties who have inadequate education and were incarcerated for a nonviolent offense.

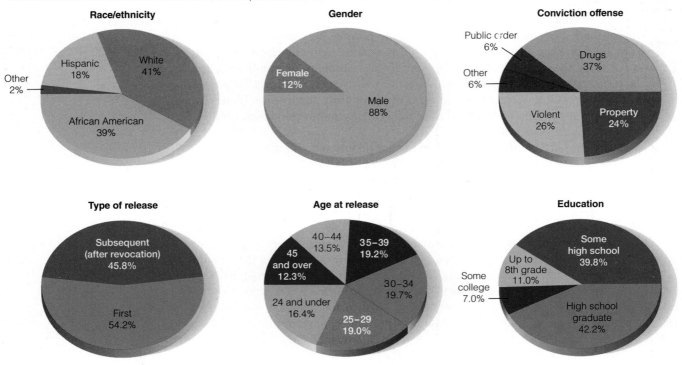

Source: Bureau of Justice Statistics: *Bulletin*, November 2007, p. 4; *Special Report*, October 2001, p. 1.

Together, the programs are intended to help the offender progress steadily toward reintegration into the community. Almost all penologists agree that there should be pre- and postrelease programs to assist reentry, yet more than 90 percent of prisoners do not now participate in such programs (Petersilia, 2003:98). Although all states offer reentry programs, relatively few prisoners have access to them.

Among the many programs developed to help offenders return to the community, three are especially important: work and educational release, furloughs, and halfway houses. Although similar in many ways, each offers a specific approach to helping formerly incarcerated individuals reenter the community.

Work and Educational Release   Programs of **work and educational release**, in which inmates are released from correctional institutions during the day to work or attend school, were first established in Vermont in 1906. However, the Huber Act, passed by the Wisconsin legislature in 1913, is usually cited as the model on which such programs are based. By 1972, most states and the federal government had instituted these programs. Nonetheless, by 2002, only about one-third of prisons operated them for fewer than 3 percent of U.S. inmates (Petersilia, 2003:99).

Although most work and educational release programs are justifiable in terms of rehabilitation, many correctional administrators and legislators also like them because they cost relatively little. In some states, a portion of the inmate's earnings from work outside may be deducted for room and board. One problem with these programs is that they allegedly take jobs from free citizens, a complaint often given by organized labor.

Furloughs   Isolation from loved ones is one of the pains of imprisonment. Although correctional programs in many countries include conjugal visits, only a few U.S. corrections systems have used them. Many penologists view the **furlough**—the temporary release of an inmate from a correctional institution for a visit home—as a meaningful approach to inmate reintegration.

■ **work and educational release** The daytime release of inmates from correctional institutions so they can work or attend school.

■ **furlough** The temporary release of an inmate from a correctional institution for a brief period, usually one to three days, for a visit home. Such programs help maintain family ties and prepare inmates for release on parole.

CLOSE UP

Returning to America

JEROME WASHINGTON

RETURNING TO AMERICA after living in France, China, Swaziland, or the high Himalayas is one thing, but returning to America after serving sixteen years and three months in maximum security, mostly in Attica, is something altogether different.

In 1972 when I went to prison, Richard M. Nixon was president and politicians were still thought to be ethical; . . . the Supreme Court was reasonably balanced; the Vietnam War was winding down, but the weekly body count was still news. The HIV virus was unknown and free sex had more fans than the Super Bowl. Although everybody was not living the American Dream, and some people felt that life was hopeless, most were optimistic about their future and many had a strong commitment to social activism. People cared, and even the most disadvantaged could still dream without fear of having nightmares.

Soon after I got out I was with my brother Freddy. We were standing at Columbus Circle, a major hub, a New York City crossroads. Freddy was my guide. He asked where I'd like to go; what I'd like to do; what I'd like to see. Did I want to meet new people, or just hang out, drift from place to place? Suddenly, life was a smorgasbord, a cornucopia of enticements and alluring temptations. I didn't know where to start, what to do first. Prison was my immediate reference point and, there, decisions related to physical movement were made by the guards, not by me. "We can't stand here all day," my brother said, over and over.

"Go slow," I told myself as I recalled a number of prisoners who shortly after release returned to prison with new convictions, and new sentences. They tried to make everything happen at once, all at the same time. Like children, they wanted instant gratification. Played all their cards at the same time, swung before the ball got to the plate, struck out and found themselves back in a cell where their only landscape was the sun setting against the prison wall.

I decided to do life the same way I did prison. Nothing fancy. One step at a time, one day at a time, and most of all, don't forget to breathe.

Freddy was supportive and sensitive. He understood that I needed to re-learn the rhythm of the streets, tune in on the city, explore my new freedom and tune out on prison. I had no preference which direction we'd walk, or which street we'd take. Freddy didn't seem to have any preference either. He just started off, leaving me to stay where I was or to catch up. I learned

a quick but important lesson. It was this kind of small, ordinary decision—often taken for granted and overlooked—that I missed most in prison. Now, by just walking off and letting me decide what to do, Freddy was tuning me in again to this level of free choice.

The morning after my release found me in Harlem. I was staying with Bert, a long-time family friend. I awoke at dawn. There was no excitement. No stage fright or butterflies to signal the first day of the rest of my life. Looking up from sleep I could have dreamed my release from prison the day before. The sky was as gray as a prison sky—the same sky I had seen for the past sixteen years and three months.

Not long after I went to prison, I woke in the middle of the night and sat up on the side of the bed. The cell was so quiet I could hear cockroaches foraging in my garbage.

"When I get out of prison," I said to myself, "sex can wait." Thinking of what I would most like to do, I said, "I'm going to eat strawberries! Big! Fresh! Red strawberries!" And that became my mantra for the rest of the time I was in prison.

On the day I was released, Kathrin, a friend, a sister, my confidante, came to pick me up. She was there with her camera, taking photos of me as I walked through the last gate to freedom. She drove me to the house where she lived with her husband and son, and fed me steamed shrimp, French champagne, and *strawberries!*

RESEARCHING THE INTERNET

To learn about reentry services offered to parolees, go to the corresponding website listed on the Cole/Smith Criminal Justice in America Companion Website: http://www.cengage.com/criminaljustice/cole.

FOR CRITICAL ANALYSIS

Having overcome the initial shock of reentry, what are some of the problems that parolees such as Jerome Washington must face?

Note: Jerome Washington, a writer, is now discharged from parole supervision and is living in California.

Source: Jerome Washington, *Iron House: Stories from the Yard* (New York: Vintage, 1994), 155–63.

Furloughs are thought to offer an excellent means of testing an inmate's ability to cope with the larger society. Through home visits, the inmate can renew family ties and relieve the tensions of confinement. Most administrators also feel that furloughs increase prisoners' morale. The general public, however, does not always support the concept. Public outrage is inevitable if an offender on furlough commits another crime or fails to return. Correctional authorities are often nervous about using furloughs, because they fear being blamed for such incidents.

Halfway Houses   As its name implies, the **halfway house** is a transitional facility for soon-to-be-released inmates that connects them to community services, resources, and support. Usually, felons work in the community but reside in the halfway house during nonworking hours. Halfway houses range from secure institutions in the community, with programs designed to assist inmates who are preparing for release on parole, to group homes where parolees, probationers, or others diverted from the system live with minimal supervision and direction. Some halfway houses deliver special treatment services, such as programs designed to deal with alcohol, drug, or mental problems.

■ **halfway house** A correctional facility housing convicted felons who spend a portion of their day at work in the community but reside in the halfway house during nonworking hours.

The transition from prison to the community can be difficult for offenders. Work release programs and halfway houses are intended to facilitate the return to society, but often there are only limited opportunities to participate in such programs. Many offenders go straight from prison to parole. Should the United States invest more money in reentry programs so that all parolees have help transitioning back into society?

AP Images/Kitsap Sun, Carolyn J. Yaschur

Residential programs have problems. Few neighborhoods want to host halfway houses or treatment centers for convicts. Community resistance has significantly impeded the development of community-based correctional facilities and has even forced some successful facilities to close. Many communities, often wealthier ones, have blocked the placement of halfway houses or treatment centers within their boundaries. One result of the NIMBY ("not in my backyard") attitude is that many centers are established in deteriorating neighborhoods inhabited by poor people, who lack the political power and resources to block unpopular programs.

In the 1970s, during the community corrections era, one could find halfway houses across the nation. However, a survey by the American Correctional Association (2000) recently found only 55 halfway houses being operated by ten state agencies. This means that such residential programs served fewer than 20,000 inmates. At a time when the need to assist offenders returning to their communities is great, lawmakers have deleted funding for residential support services from most state budgets.

◼ Parole Officer: Cop or Social Worker?

After release, a parolee's principal contact with the criminal justice system is the parole officer, who must provide both surveillance and assistance. Thus, parole officers are asked to play two different, some might say incompatible, roles: cop and social worker. Whereas parole was originally designed to help offenders make the transition from prison to the community, supervision has shifted ever more toward surveillance, drug testing, monitoring curfews, and collecting restitution. Safety and security have become major issues in parole services.

The Parole Officer as Cop   In their role as cop, parole officers have the power to restrict many aspects of the parolee's life, to enforce the conditions of release, and to initiate revocation proceedings if parole conditions are violated. Like other officials in the criminal justice system, the parole officer has extensive discretion in low-visibility situations. In many states, parole officers have the authority to search the parolee's house without warning; to arrest him or her, without the possibility of bail, for suspected violations; and suspend parole pending a hearing before the board. This authoritarian component of the parole officer's role can give the ex-offender a sense of insecurity and hamper the development of mutual trust.

The parole officer is responsible for seeing that the parolee follows the conditions imposed by the parole board or department of corrections. Typically, the conditions require the parolee to follow the parole officer's instructions; to permit the officer to visit the home and place of employment; to maintain employment; not to leave the state without permission; not to marry without permission; not to own a firearm; not to possess, use, or traffic in narcotics; not to consume alcohol to excess; and to comply with all laws and be a good citizen.

Parole officers are granted law enforcement powers in order to protect the community from offenders coming out of prison. However, because these powers diminish the possibility for the officer to develop a close relationship with the client, they can weaken the officer's ability to help the parolee adjust to the community.

The Parole Officer as Social Worker   Parole officers must act as social workers by helping the parolee find a job and restore family ties. Officers channel parolees to social agencies, such as psychiatric, drug, and alcohol clinics, where they can obtain help. As caseworkers, officers try to develop a relationship that allows parolees to confide their frustrations and concerns.

Because parolees are not likely to do this if they are constantly aware of the parole officer's ability to send them back to prison, some researchers have suggested that parole officers' conflicting responsibilities of cop and social worker should be separated. Parole officers could maintain the supervisory aspects of the position, and other personnel—perhaps a separate parole counselor—could perform the casework functions. Another option would be for parole officers to be charged solely with social work duties, while local police check for violations.

■ The Parole Bureaucracy

Although parole officers have smaller caseloads than do probation officers, parolees require more-extensive services. One reason is that parolees, by the very fact of their incarceration, have generally committed much more serious crimes. Another reason is that parolees must make a difficult transition from the highly structured prison environment to a society in which they have previously failed to live as law-abiding citizens. It is exceptionally difficult for a parole officer to monitor, control, and assist clients who may have little knowledge of or experience with living successfully within society's rules.

The parole officer works within a bureaucratic environment. Like most other human services organizations, parole agencies are short on resources and expertise. Because the difficulties faced by many parolees are so complex, the officer's job is almost impossible. As a result, parole officers frequently must classify parolees and give priority to those most in need. For example, most parole officers spend extra time with the newly released. As the officers gain greater confidence in the parolees, they can adjust their level of supervision to "active" or "reduced" surveillance. Depending on how the parolees have functioned in the community, they may eventually be allowed to check in with their officers periodically instead of submitting to regular home visits, searches, and other intrusive monitoring.

■ Adjustment to Life Outside Prison

With little preparation, the ex-offender moves from the highly structured, authoritarian life of the institution into a world filled with temptations and complicated problems. Suddenly, ex-convicts who are unaccustomed to undertaking even simple tasks such as going to the store for groceries are expected to assume pressing, complex responsibilities. Finding a job and a place to live are not the only problems the newly released person faces. The parolee must also make significant social and psychological role adjustments. A male ex-convict, for example, must suddenly become not only a parolee but also an employee, a neighbor, a father, a husband, and a son. The expectations, norms, and social relations in the free world differ greatly from those learned in prison. The relatively predictable inmate code gives way to society's often unclear rules of behavior—rules that the offender had failed to cope with during his previous life in free society.

In terms of living a crime-free life, today's parolees face even greater obstacles than did those released prior to 1990. Since that time, Congress and many state legislatures have imposed new restrictions on ex-felons. These include denial of many things, including welfare benefits such as food stamps, for those convicted of even minor drug crimes; access to public housing; receipt of student loans; and in some states voting rights. Studies have found that returning inmates often face so many restrictions after long periods of incarceration that the conditions amount to years of "invisible punishment" (Mauer and Chesney-Lind, 2002:1). The effects of these policies impact not only the individual parolee, but also their families and communities (Travis, 2002).

What AMERICANS Think

QUESTION: "Some people think that if a person convicted of a crime serves his or her sentence and then does not violate the law for a period such as five years, government agencies SHOULD NOT make that criminal record available to employers or licensing agencies. Other people believe employers and licensing agencies SHOULD have access to such records and be able to consider the fact of a conviction in the hiring or licensing process. What do you think?"

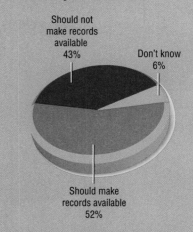

Should not make records available 43%

Don't know 6%

Should make records available 52%

Go to http://www.cengage.com/criminaljustice/cole to compare your opinion on this issue with the opinions of other criminal justice students.

Source: Bureau of Justice Statistics, *Sourcebook of Criminal Justice Statistics, 2001* (Washington, DC: U.S. Government Printing Office, 2002), Table 2.55.

Criminal Justice:
MYTH AND REALITY

COMMON BELIEF: Offenders who never qualify for parole will still inevitably be returned to society upon completion of their sentences.

The foregoing statement is generally true for those offenders who are not serving life sentences. However, some states, such as Kansas and Washington, enacted laws to prolong the detention of offenders whom officials regard as especially dangerous: predatory sex offenders. Under these laws, offenders who are diagnosed with mental conditions that make them highly likely to commit further sex crimes are transported to secure mental facilities upon the completion of their prison sentences. In other words, even after serving their full prison sentences, they remain locked up in state facilities. The U.S. Supreme Court ruled that such indefinite detention statutes are permissible as long as the purpose of the laws is treatment rather than punishment (*Kansas v. Hendricks, 1997*). In theory, these individuals will be released when psychiatrists conclude that they can safely reenter society. In practice, they may never receive such approval. One of those most significant risks of such laws is that they will be applied to people who actually do not pose a significant risk of reoffending. This is especially true because the psychiatric conditions that justify postsentence detentions are vaguely defined and difficult to diagnose accurately.

Sex offender registration laws have made adjustment to the community difficult for many parolees. Residents of some neighborhoods, such as these in Placentia, California, have protested the renting or sale of property to paroled sex offenders. To what extent have these laws resulted in all parolees being labeled as "dangerous"?

AP Images/Francis Specker

News accounts of brutal crimes committed by ex-offenders on parole fuel a public perception that parolees pose a threat to the community. The murder of 12-year-old Polly Klaas by a parolee and the rape and murder of 7-year-old Megan Kanka by a paroled sex offender spurred legislators across the nation to enact "sexual offender notification" laws. These laws require that the public be notified of the whereabouts of "potentially dangerous" sex offenders. In some states, paroled sex offenders must register with the police, whereas in others, the immediate neighbors must be informed. Many states now have publicly accessible sex offender websites listing the names and addresses of those registered. The state of Washington recently created a statewide online database that not only lets you see which sex predators are in your midst, but also can alert you by email if an offender moves close by (J. Sullivan, 2009). "What Americans Think" on the previous page presents public attitudes on the availability of criminal records of ex-offenders.

These laws have generated several unintended consequences. For example, parolees have been "hounded" from communities, the media have televised the parolees' homecomings, homes have been burned, parolees have been killed, and neighbors have assaulted parolees they erroneously thought were sex offenders. In some states, legislators wrote laws so broadly that consensual sex between teenagers and third-degree assault that might constitute inappropriate touching or sexual contact are included in the notification mandate. In 2006, two Maine parolees were shot by a man intent on killing registered sex offenders. One of those killed was on the list because, at age 19, he had been convicted of having consensual sex with his underage girlfriend. His murder heightened national debate as to whether the online registries put those who are listed at risk (G. Adams, 2006).

The fact of repeat violence fuels a public perception that parolees represent a continuing threat to the community. Although the new laws primarily focus on people who have committed sex offenses against children, some fear that the community will eventually target all parolees. This preoccupation with potential parolee criminality makes successful reentry even more difficult for ex-offenders. Read "Criminal Justice: Myth and Reality" and consider your views on the policies adopted by some states to control the offenders whom they fear most.

■ Revocation of Parole

The potential revocation of parole, for committing a new crime or violating the conditions of release, hangs constantly over the ex-inmate's head. The public tends to view the high number of revocations as a failure of parole. Correctional officials point to the great number of parolees who are required to be drug-free, be employed, and pay restitution—conditions that many find difficult to fulfill. Yet, as shown in "What Americans Think," there is strong support for sending back to prison those parolees who fail a drug test.

As discussed in Chapter 10, the Supreme Court ruled in *Morrissey v. Brewer* (1972) that if the parole officer alleges a technical violation, a two-step revocation proceeding is required. In the first stage, a hearing determines whether there is probable cause to believe the conditions have been violated. The parolee has the right to be notified of the charges, to be informed of the evidence, to present witnesses, and to confront the witnesses. In the second stage, the parole authority decides if the violation is severe enough to warrant return to prison.

Despite the increase in the number of parolees supervised, the percentage of those who are returned to prison because of a

TABLE 13.1	Reasons for Revocation among Parole Violators in State Prison

An increasing number of parolees are being returned to prison because of new arrests or technical violations. What factors might be causing this increase?

Reason for Revocation	Percentage of Parolees Returned
Arrest/conviction for new offense	**69.9%**
Drug-related violations	**16.1%**
Positive test for drug use	7.9
Possession of drugs	6.6
Failure to report for drug testing	2.3
Failure to report for drug treatment	1.7
Absconders	**22.3%**
Failure to report/absconded	18.6
Left jurisdiction without permission	5.6
Other reasons	**17.8%**
Possession of gun(s)	3.5
Failure to report for counseling	2.4
Failure to meet financial obligations	2.3
Failure to maintain employment	1.2
Maintained contact with known offenders	1.2

Source: Bureau of Justice Statistics, *Special Report*, October 2001, p. 14.

What AMERICANS Think

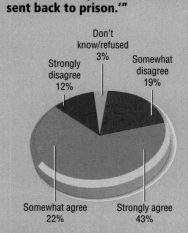

QUESTION: **"Please tell me if you agree or disagree with the following statement: 'People who are out of prison on parole and who fail a drug test should be sent back to prison.'"**

- Don't know/refused 3%
- Strongly disagree 12%
- Somewhat disagree 19%
- Somewhat agree 22%
- Strongly agree 43%

Go to http://www.cengage.com/criminaljustice/cole to compare your opinion on this issue with the opinions of other criminal justice students.

Source: Telephone interviews with a national adult sample by the public opinion polling firm of Beldon, Russonello, and Stewart, January 5–22, 2001. Data provided by the Roper Center for Public Opinion Research, University of Connecticut.

technical violation or conviction for a new offense has remained at about 39 percent (BJS 2007b:7). However, the percentage of violators returned to prison varies by state, accounting for more than half of prison admissions in California (67 percent), Utah (55 percent), and Louisiana (53 percent) but less than 10 percent in Alabama and Florida. The percentage of parolees returned for technical violations also varies. For example, 17 percent of California's prison population consists of inmates who were returned for a technical violation, whereas in the state of Washington, only 1 percent were (Austin, 2001:319). As shown in Table 13.1,

CHECKPOINT

ANSWERS

4 *What are three programs designed to ease the reentry of offenders into the community?*

4 Work and educational release programs, furlough programs, and halfway houses.

5 *What are the main tasks of parole officers?*

5 Surveillance and assistance.

6 *What two conditions can result in the revocation of parole?*

6 Arrest for a new crime, or a technical violation of one or more of the conditions of parole.

of those returned to prison, 70 percent had been arrested or convicted of a new offense.

The Future of Prisoner Reentry

The rising number of offenders returning to the community has only recently come to the attention of policy makers. One underrecognized impact of the incarceration policies of the 1980s is that "more prisoners in prison means that, eventually, more prisoners will be let out" (Butterfield, 2000). Corrections today faces a sudden flood of offenders leaving prison—about 700,000 per year—with about a third of these returning to prison, often within a year of their release. The recidivism rate demonstrates a failure of the criminal justice system to deal with the reentry problems of ex-felons. What lies at the heart of this problem?

As you read earlier, Travis and Petersilia (2001) point to several factors that seem to have contributed to the reentry problem. First, the decline of parole boards, from mandatory release and other measures, means that more inmates must leave when their time is up—regardless of whether they have been prepared for the outside world of work, family, and other responsibilities. The percentage of releasees who have "maxed out" has also increased. Second, with the curtailment of rehabilitation and prerelease programs, parolees now have fewer prison programs preparing them for reentry into society and thus may be more vulnerable to returning to prison. Finally, the changing profile of returning prisoners has also affected reentry. Over a third of parolees were in prison for drug offenses, almost three times the percentage of 30 years ago. These prisoners may be at risk of slipping back into substance abuse. Prison terms also tend to be longer, so that parolees have a harder time adjusting to life on the "outside" because they have been away for so long.

As prison populations rise, demands that felons be allowed to serve part of their time in the community will undoubtedly mount. These demands will not come from the public, which typically believes that all offenders should serve their full sentences. Instead, they will come from legislators and correctional officials who recognize that government lacks the money and facilities to incarcerate all offenders for the complete terms of their sentences. Although many offenders are not successfully integrated into the community, most will end up back in free society whether or not they serve their full sentences. Parole and community programs represent an effort to address the inevitability of their return. Even if such programs do not prevent all offenders from returning to crime, they do help some to turn their lives around.

A QUESTION OF ETHICS: WRITING ASSIGNMENT

The five members of the parole board questioned Jim Allen, an offender with a long history of sex offenses involving teenage boys. Now approaching age 45 and having met the eligibility requirement for a hearing, Allen respectfully answered the board members.

Toward the end of the hearing, Richard Edwards, a dentist who had recently been appointed to the board, spoke up: "Your institutional record is good, you have a parole plan, a job has been promised, and your sister says she will help you. All of that looks good, but I just can't vote for your parole. You haven't attended the behavior modification program for sex offenders. I think you're going to repeat your crime. I have a 13-year-old son, and I don't want him or other boys to run the risk of meeting your kind."

Allen looked shocked. The other members had seemed ready to grant his release.

"But I'm ready for parole. I won't do that stuff again. I didn't go to that program because electroshock to my private area is not going to help me.

I've been here five years of the seven-year max and have stayed out of trouble. The judge didn't say I was to be further punished in prison by therapy." After Jim Allen left the room, the board discussed his case. "You know, Rich, he has a point. He has been a model prisoner and has served a good portion of his sentence," said Brian Lynch, a long-term board member. "Besides we don't know if Dr. Hankin's program works."

"I know, but can we really let someone like that out on the streets?"

WRITING ASSIGNMENT

Are the results of the behavior-modification program for sex offenders relevant to the parole board's decision? Is the purpose of the sentence to punish Allen for what he *did* or for what he *might* do in the future? Would you vote for his release on parole? Prepare a statement for the parole board describing your response to these questions.

Summary

Understand what is meant by the "reentry problem"

▶ Prisoner reentry to the community has become an important public issue because of the large number of offenders who gain parole eligibility or complete their sentences each year.

▶ Preventing recidivism by assisting parolees to become law-abiding citizens requires government resources and the development of helpful programs to prepare offenders for release.

Explain the origins of parole and how it operates today

▶ Parole is the conditional release from prison and is the primary method by which inmates return to society. While on parole, they remain under correctional supervision.

▶ Parole in the United States evolved during the nineteenth century from the English, Australian, and Irish practices of conditional pardon, apprenticeship by indenture, transportation to distant colonies, and issuance of "tickets of leave."

▶ Today, most felons leave prison and are supervised by parole officers for a period of time. They may be returned to prison if they commit another crime or violate the conditions (rules) of their release.

Identify the mechanisms for the release of felons to the community

▶ There are four types of release: discretionary release, mandatory release, other conditional release, and expiration release.

▶ Discretionary release is based on a decision by the parole board within the boundaries set by the sentence and the penal law.

▶ Mandatory release is the required release of an inmate to the community upon the expiration of a certain period, as specified by a determinate-sentencing law or parole guidelines.

▶ Other conditional release is the placement of convicts in various community settings while under supervision; some states use this to avoid the rigidity of mandatory release.

▶ Expiration release occurs when inmates have completed their full sentence. They have "maxed out" and leave the prison without community supervision.

Describe how ex-offenders are supervised in the community

▶ Parole officers are assigned to supervise and assist ex-inmates making the transition to society and to ensure that they follow the conditions of their release.

▶ Parole officers' functions include roles as cops and as social workers.

▶ Parole may be revoked for commission of a crime or for violating the rules governing behavior while on parole (failing to appear for meetings with parole officers, using drugs or alcohol, and so forth).

Understand the problems that parolees face during their reentry

▶ Upon release, offenders face many problems. For instance, they must find housing and employment and reestablish relationships with family and friends.

▶ Adjustment to life outside the prison is often difficult, in that those released must move from the highly structured environment of an institution into a world with temptations and complicated problems.

Questions for Review

1. What are the basic assumptions of parole?

2. How do mandatory release, discretionary release, and unconditional release differ?

3. What roles does the parole officer play?

4. What problems confront parolees upon their release?

Key Terms and Cases

conditions of release (p. 385)
discretionary release (p. 381)
expiration release (p. 382)

furlough (p. 386)
halfway house (p. 387)
mandatory release (p. 382)

other conditional release (p. 382)
parole (p. 380)
work and educational release (p. 386)

INSIDE THE CRIMINAL JUSTICE SYSTEM AND BEYOND: ONE MAN'S JOURNEY

Written by Chuck Terry

Prison

THE TRIP FROM THE COUNTY JAIL to prison, a bus ride known among prisoners as "the chain," can be an unsettling experience. On this particular trip I was accompanied by about thirty other inmates. The scenery we saw outside the grilled windows changed as we headed southeast out of Los Angeles. Freeways, business districts, and suburban neighborhoods were left behind and replaced by small towns, farms, and livestock. During the ride I thought about all I would be missing out there, all the things I wouldn't be able to do wherever I was going, and wondered what my future would bring. For first-termers "the chain" can be as scary as hell. For others it may be routine. Most probably wonder if they'll get out alive. I always did.

Once again, my destination was the Regional Guidance Center at Chino. Only this time, rather than coming for a ninety-day evaluation, I would be classified as a "new commitment." Instead of being "evaluated," I would be processed and sent to another facility somewhere within the state. As we approached the institution I saw the familiar-looking guard towers, chain-link fences covered with barbed razor wire, and the outside windows of the cell blocks. Once we arrived, the bus passed through an electronically operated gate. Our entrance was monitored by armed guards. It was here that I experienced that fleeting sense of impending doom, the feeling that I might never get out of prison again. After the bus stopped we sat for several minutes, chained together and relatively quiet, until the guards came and escorted us inside.

After entering the guidance center I was again booked—fingerprinted, photographed, searched—and told where to live. Given that I had just come from here, being new wasn't that big a deal. Besides, I was getting used to these places. Yet the time I spent inside in the years to come unquestionably affected my sense of identity and ideas about life. After two months of processing, including psychological and physical examinations, I was sent to the California Correctional Center at Lassen, a facility more commonly known as "Susanville," the town in which it is located.

In prison I learned to hate and to do whatever I could to use drugs without compromising my integrity. All myths aside, drugs are hard to get in prison. I learned what it's like to be a minority. Mostly, I learned to see myself and the world from the perspective of a convict.

Life inside is extremely monotonous, although life-threatening situations can arise in a heartbeat. Prison is a world in which you can never show weakness, where you adapt to survive, and where race and "fitting in" are very important. In prison it's not so much what crime you did (except for heinous crimes such as sex offenses or crimes against children—those offenders get no respect), but who you are within that world that determines how you are seen and treated both by fellow inmates and prison workers. And who you are is gauged by the people you run with, how you carry yourself, and your character. And it all takes place within a structure of nearly total control and oppression.

People often ask me what it is really like in prison. The answer depends on historical context, where you are doing time, and who you are. It is different now than it was twenty years ago. It will vary and depend on political ideology, level of custody (maximum or minimum), what color you are (and how that matches with the racial composition of the prison), how old you are, how much experience you have within the system, and, of course, the perspectives you bring with you into the institution. But the degrading,

dehumanizing effects of prison are usually similar because they stem from the same structural roots.

Prisoners are, by definition, a threat to society and in need of control. Therefore, we (I include myself here because I am writing from the perspective of a convict) must be confined, observed, and kept in our place. To achieve these goals our keepers tell us where and when to eat, sleep, go to the bathroom, exercise, and work. What we see, hear, smell, touch, and do on a daily basis depends on them. We are deprived of privacy, heterosexual relationships, education, employment (except at the most menial levels), and the ability to attain material things. Adding to these effects is the contempt with which we are often treated by prison officials.

Sadly, most of the hate and anger generated from the structure of prisons are directed toward other inmates. We seldom focus our attention on changing the conditions and people who bind us. For the most part, we accept our situation as being "the way it is." Perhaps we do this because we believe we deserve it. After all, we are in prison and the guards are just doing their jobs. But sometimes the veils we hide behind are ripped apart as the harsh realities of life become impossible to deny, often as a result of institutionalized violence.

One day, during my months at Susanville, a friend told me that everyone was getting together to have a work strike. Once in the yard I saw something that I never saw before or since: all the races (brown, white, black) were participating in a single act of defiance against the conditions of the prison. Leaders from each race acted as representatives, spoke openly about our needs, and emphasized that this was to be a nonviolent strike. We would simply not go to work until our demands were met.

Within fifteen minutes of this gathering, we heard "Yard recall, yard recall, all men return to your dorms" over the loudspeakers. To establish more control than was possible from the gun towers, extra guards armed with rifles appeared at strategic locations on the roofs of our housing units. We were herded inside our dorms, placed on lockdown status, and fed sack lunches (two baloney sandwiches and an apple) twice a day.

On the afternoon of the fourth day we heard bullets ricocheting against the bricks that made up the lower part of the dorm walls. Above the bricks were windows, out of which we could see the yard, the gun towers, and the guards on the roofs. The bullets made a loud pinging sound like you hear in movies. A friend of mine, five feet away, turned toward me and said, "They're poppin' caps out there [shooting bullets]!" Someone else said, "Those ain't real bullets," as if it weren't possible for such a thing to happen. Next thing I know, my friend fell to the ground and said, "I'm hit." Thinking he was joking, I told him, "Quit bullshitting, get up." But I quickly saw blood coming from his groin area. He really had been shot.

With reality becoming obvious and the bullets still pinging, we all dropped to the floor. I grabbed my friend (who was moaning in agony), dragged him under my bunk for safety, put a tourniquet on his wound, and tried to calm him until the guards came and took him out of there. That evening, after things had settled down, we saw the "goon squad," a row of twelve guards, three in each row, dressed in full battle gear with helmets and clubs, coming across the yard toward our end of the prison. For a few minutes we lost sight of the "gooners," but before long we saw all the men from an upstairs dorm running across the yard, the goon squad right behind them.

Over the course of that long night every man in the prison was "guided" to what is called a "classification hearing," a legal procedure that must take place before a body can be transferred to another institution. Until the early hours of the following day, many inmates were openly beaten during their journeys to the hearing. It was like watching a live version of the Rodney

King beating, right in front of our eyes. At classification we were asked, "Are you ready to work?" Those who said no were shipped to another prison.

Of the more than one thousand inmates housed in that prison, over 120 were transferred that night. Three were shot and many more seriously hurt. Interestingly, television newscasters reported that "inmates were violently rioting" (a lie) in the local prison but were now "back under control."

After the strike was "resolved," I went back to my clerk job in "Receiving and Release" (the place where inmates enter and leave the prison). After seeing my friend shot and all the beatings that had taken place, I had to ask my boss (a sergeant) why the guards had to hurt so many people that night. He answered, "They just want you guys to know who is running this joint."

Over the next several months the story about what happened got out. People from the state capital came to investigate. About 200 inmates took lie detector tests to validate their stories. Not one guard would agree to do the same. And nobody forced the issue. To my knowledge, nothing was ever done to rectify the damage that had been done that day. It is as if it never happened.

Similarly, the harsh reality of living in prison is seldom acknowledged. Does anyone deserve to live in such an environment? Does it matter if one is convicted for murder or possession of drugs? Apparently not. Why you are sentenced to prison makes little difference once you're on the inside.

After being in prison for twelve months I appeared before a parole board that consisted of two men who talked to me as if I were some kind of dog. Their comments were based on my "history," which they had in front of them in a file: rap sheet, prior presentence investigations, police reports, and the results from the ninety-day evaluation. For the most part they harassed and belittled me with questions about my past. The only thing I said was yes when they asked me if I understood them. After they'd had their say, I was asked to step outside the room while they made a decision. They told me they decided to give me a total of twenty-six months (from the time of arrest until release), which was about what I'd expected. They also told me that

if I didn't start acting right, the next time they saw me would be at Folsom Prison and they would bury me so deep I'd never see daylight again. As I left the room I felt great. Many people I knew didn't get a "date" at all and had to wait another year just to appear.

In my final years in prison, the perception I had about myself and the world took a dramatic shift, largely as the result of attending two years of college classes. Learning was exciting. It opened my eyes to things I never knew and helped me see that there were other, more important things to do besides using heroin. In 1992 I was discharged from parole.

Coming Home

Getting released from prison is like coming home from a war. The more time you do the greater the shock. From a world where great meaning comes from the color of your skin, whom you hang out with, which bench you sit on in the yard, and where you eat in the chow hall, you find yourself out here. Choices. Kids. Shopping. Women. Asshole car drivers. Pets. Around people who define themselves based on their jobs, how many "things" they have, or their political affiliation. Life inside was structured. You clearly knew your place—count time, chow line, yard line, sick line. Out here it's really different.

I was assigned to a parole officer known as "Lock-'em-up Tom." Like my old probation officer, Tom told me he didn't think I had a chance of making it. He said I would have to regularly test for drugs and attend Twelve-Step meetings at least three times a week. When I informed him that I no longer had a drug problem, he smiled and said, "Well, Chuck, that might be true. But you also don't know how to live out here. It's kinda like the first time you went to jail—it was something new. You had to learn about it and adapt in order to survive. As I see it, that's what you need to do now—only in reverse. By getting involved with other clean addicts you might just learn how." Tom never did lock me up. He spied on me, tested me, and always talked down to me. Yet his ideas about what I'd have to do to make it were definitely grounded in reality. In many ways I am still learning how to live out here.

Technology and Criminal Justice

O**N A QUIET MORNING IN MAY 2009,** Susan Gerdhart pulled her wallet from her purse to pay for her lunch at the café inside the bookstore for Wesleyan University in downtown Middletown, Connecticut. When she heard four loud pops, she quickly turned around. In the next moment, she witnessed the horrifying sight of a gunman firing three additional shots at close range into a young waitress. As the gunman ran away, Johanna Justin-Jinich, a popular 21-year-old student at Wesleyan, lay dying on the floor (Kovaleski and Cowan, 2009).

The gunman wore a wig to disguise himself, and the police found both the wig and the gun in the bookstore when they rushed to the scene of the crime (Associated Press, 2009a; Standora, 2009). Dramatic crimes, such as the shooting at the bookstore, can occur in a matter of seconds. When there are few witnesses and the perpetrator wears a disguise, it can be extremely difficult to identify the criminal. In fact, the Middletown police unknowingly interviewed the shooter as a potential witness when he lingered outside the bookstore, as part of a growing crowd of concerned passersby who had observed the sudden arrival of the police (Kovaleski and Cowan, 2009). Without any awareness that they had spoken to the actual killer, the police had no reason to detain him, and he walked away. The next day, the suspect surrendered, reportedly after seeing his photo in the newspaper, thus communicating to him that the police knew or would soon know his identity (Associated Press, 2009b; Burke et al., 2009).

Throughout much of history, identifying or apprehending criminals was nearly impossible unless there were eyewitnesses to the crime, the criminal was caught at the crime scene, or the criminal was found later to be in possession of stolen items or other incriminating evidence. In the case of a disguised assailant whose motive is murder rather than robbery, it can be exceptionally difficult to solve the case unless someone is caught with the murder weapon. Technological developments, however, have enhanced the ability of law enforcement officers to identify and apprehend lawbreakers. In the murder of the Wesleyan student, the bookstore's video security system provided instant evidence about the killer's identity. The police immediately released a photo of the killer that was published in newspapers nationally, broadcast on television, and prominently displayed on the Internet. Even if the police had not found the murder weapon and the killer's laptop and journals, the picture from the surveillance camera alone would have provided

LEARNING OBJECTIVES

▶ **Understand how adaptation and belief in science can affect the use of technology**

▶ **Recognize the many aspects of cyber crime and counterfeiting**

▶ **Analyze the role of communications, computers, and databases in policing**

▶ **Describe developments and problems in DNA testing and new weapons technologies**

▶ **Understand the use of technology in courts and corrections**

▶ **Recognize the continuing questions about the effects of technology on civil liberties**

a basis for identifying the suspect. In this case, it was Stephen P. Morgan, a troubled drifter from an affluent family who had been acquainted with his targeted victim after previously meeting her in a summer class at New York University (Kovaleski and Cowan, 2009).

Contemporary Americans take for granted the availability and usefulness of technology. American television viewers are fascinated by *CSI: Crime Scene Investigation* and other programs that show the impressive ability of scientists to identify criminal suspects by examining microscopic bits of evidence. Because the United States is a relatively wealthy and technologically sophisticated country, it can fund and benefit from the development of new technologies that provide crucial assistance in various operations of the criminal justice system. However, the invention of a new device or the development of new software, no matter how potentially useful, does not automatically benefit actors in the criminal justice system. Agencies must have enough money to acquire new technology, and their personnel must have expertise and resources for training in order to make effective use of it.

Further, Americans readily recognize that many countries in the world are too poor and their infrastructure resources, such as electricity, are too unreliable to use technologies that benefit the criminal justice system.

Less recognized, but equally important, is that the benefits of technology are not distributed equally through the United States, because of fragmentation and limited resources. For example, some cities' police departments can afford to put computers into all police patrol cars, but others cannot. As we learn about the role of technology in criminal justice, we must remember that existing technological resources are not universally available, even in the United States.

In this chapter, we examine the role of technology in criminal justice. Each year brings new inventions—as well as improvements to existing technologies—that affect crime and justice. As we shall see, technological change affects the nature of crime as well as the capacity of law enforcement officials to prevent criminal acts and apprehend criminal offenders. Technology also affects the processing of criminal cases in courts and the monitoring and control of convicted offenders in correctional settings. The use of technology increases the capability of criminal justice officials to perform their vital functions effectively. Simultaneously, however, technology creates its own issues and problems, including concerns about the ways in which it may collide with citizens' expectations about their privacy and other constitutional rights.

Technological Development and Criminal Justice

Throughout history, humans have sought to invent tools to advance their goals. The invention of early tools and wheels, for example, promoted agriculture and transport. Over time, simple farming tools have given way to gigantic tractors and other farm machinery. The wheel has similarly been updated through advancing transportation mechanisms—from horse-drawn wagons through steam trains to jet planes. The appreciation for the advantages of technology naturally leads to inventive developments affecting all areas of human experience, including criminal justice.

However, the use of technology in criminal justice differs from its use in many other areas of human activity. Technology in this case is not merely an effort to overcome the natural environment by increasing productivity, ease of daily life, and the range of travel. In criminal justice, as in military affairs, technology becomes an element in the interaction, competition, and conflict among human beings who have opposing objectives. In this case, the clash is between those who would seek to profit or cause harm by breaking society's laws (as in theft or murder) and those who seek to stop, identify, apprehend, process, and punish criminals. This observation highlights two important points about technological development in criminal justice. First, new developments that benefit one side in this competition, whether lawbreaker or law enforcer, will lead to adjustments and adaptations by the other. Second, the pressure to find new and better devices to combat crime can lead to excessive faith in the effectiveness of technology; this can lead to problems when people do not stop to examine the consequences of new technology. After we briefly examine each of these points, keep them in mind to see how they relate to the topics discussed in the rest of this chapter.

■ Competition and Adaptation

Throughout history, the development of both weapons and protective devices affected the preservation of persons and property, which is one of the fundamental goals of criminal justice. As weaponry advanced from daggers and swords to firearms and then later to multishot pistols that could be concealed inside pockets, the threats posed by robbers increased. Thus, when American policing expanded in the nineteenth century, law enforcement officers in the western frontier, and later throughout the country, armed themselves in a way that would help them deal with pistol-toting criminals. These developments continue. News reports have made contemporary Americans well aware that many police departments now struggle to match the firepower of the automatic weapons possessed by some criminal offenders and organized-crime groups (A. Klein, 2008).

Similarly, the development of fortified walls, door locks, and safes led to criminals' adaptive strategies for overcoming these barriers. For example, the creation of locks spawned devices and techniques for picking locks. So, too, the creation of safes led to the birth of professional safecrackers. Later, the introduction of police radar to detect speeders led to a profitable industry selling radar detectors to motorists who wanted to drive at excessive speeds without paying fines. Today, criminals' efforts to overcome residential burglar alarms, as well as cyber criminals' creativity in overcoming security software, illustrate the interactions among technological development, criminals' adaptive behavior, and society's efforts to counteract new forms of criminality.

Fundamentally, these examples should remind us that technological developments do not always help criminal justice officials. New technologies can be developed and used by those who seek to violate criminal laws. Moreover, new devices designed specifically to protect property or to assist police officers will generate adaptive behavior by would-be lawbreakers who adjust their behavior, invent their own devices, or otherwise develop strategies to overcome new barriers to the attainment of their goals. James Byrne (2008:10–11) summarizes the overall impact of technology:

> Advances…in technology have resulted in new *opportunities* for crime (through the Internet), new *forms* of criminality (e.g., Internet scams…), new *techniques* for committing crimes (e.g., computer software programs,…the use of tasers as weapons in robberies), and new *categories* of offenders and victims (such as online predators and identity theft victims).

■ Science and the Presumption of Progress

From the mid-nineteenth century through today, Americans have benefited from industrialization, the development of electricity, the rise of the scientific method, and advances in various scientific fields, such as medicine and engineering. In light of the extraordinary advancements in human knowledge and the new inventions that have dramatically altered the nature of American society, it is not surprising that many people equate technological advancements with "progress." However, contemporary Americans are regularly reminded that new developments can produce consequences, such as side effects from new medicines, that are unexpected and undesirable. Thus, in the field of criminal justice, as in other fields, we need to guard against the assumption that new technologies will always be better than older techniques and devices. Similarly, even when the benefits of new technologies are clear, we need to consider the possibility of undesirable risks and consequences that have not yet been discovered.

Many people presumed that the electric chair provided a quicker, more humane way to execute criminals because the use of electricity was developed through experimentation and other methods of science. In fact, many such executions seemed to be far more painful and prolonged than the traditional use of hanging. Are there any new technologies in criminal justice that are likely to have unexpected and undesirable consequences?

© Lake County Museum/CORBIS

In the late nineteenth century, the development of electricity brought with it efforts to apply this "miracle" resource to various societal needs. One idea applied to criminal justice was the invention of the electric chair as a modern method to produce an instantaneous and presumably humane execution for criminals sentenced to death. At that time, most executions were carried out through hanging. This "old-fashioned" execution method had been used for centuries, with little change in its use of rope and a means to drop the condemned person's body so that the neck would break or the person would be strangled.

The first man condemned to execution by electric chair was William Kemmler, a convicted murderer in New York. Kemmler challenged his sentence through the court system, eventually presenting to the U.S. Supreme Court a claim that execution by electricity constituted "cruel and unusual punishment" in violation of Kemmler's constitutional rights. After all, what could be more "unusual" than to be the first person executed through the use of a newfangled invention?

In rejecting Kemmler's claim in 1890, the U.S. Supreme Court noted that the New York statute permitting execution by electric chair "was passed in the effort to devise a more humane method of reaching the result [of extinguishing life and] that courts were bound to presume that the legislature was possessed of the facts upon which it took action" (*In re Kemmler*, 1890). Thus, there was acceptance of the idea that this new scientific method would be more effective and humane than hanging. When Kemmler was actually executed, however, the first jolt of 1,000 volts did not kill him, and witnesses saw that he was still breathing despite the attending physician's initial declaration that he was dead (Moran, 2002). The wires were reattached to his head, and the chair was revved up to 2,000 volts for an extended period.

> Froth oozed out of Kemmler's strapped mouth. The small blood vessels under his skin began to rupture. Blood trickled down his face and arms…. The awful smell of burning flesh filled the death chamber. Kemmler's body first smoldered and then caught fire…. From the moment he first sat down on the chair until the electricity was shut off the second time, eight minutes had elapsed. (Moran, 2002:15–19)

Did the electric chair fulfill its presumed function of using science to provide instantaneous, humane executions? Although it was used in two thousand executions in the century after Kemmler's death, highly publicized instances of other gruesome death-chamber scenes eventually led to a complete reconsideration of its use. In 2001, Georgia's Supreme Court declared that this method of execution imposed unconstitutional "cruel and unusual punishment" on condemned offenders (H. Weinstein, 2001). By the time that the Nebraska Supreme Court made an identical ruling in 2008, states had moved toward the use of lethal injection as the method of execution. Clearly, the original presumptions about the electric chair had been rejected nationwide (Mears, 2008).

The story of the electric chair provides a graphic example of slow reconsideration of the effects of one particular technological invention. Today we see similar examples concerning the actual risks and consequences of certain technologies. For example, in 2009, the National Academy of Sciences (2009) produced a report that questioned the validity and accuracy of many forensic science methods used by police and prosecutors. In one section, the report said that forensic science "analyses are often handled by poorly trained technicians who then exaggerate the accuracy of their methods in court" (S. Moore, 2009c). Obviously, the effectiveness of technology is limited by the errors made by the human beings who use that technology, despite the seeming infallibility of forensic techniques in *CSI* and other popular shows. Indeed, even the use of a simple photo from a surveillance camera can cause problems when people make mistakes. This point was experienced by Cornell sociology professor Stephen Morgan, when he saw that his old driver's license photo was being mistakenly circulated on the Internet—instead of a photo of the actual Stephen Morgan being sought for the Wesleyan bookstore shooting—as officials sought the public's help in finding the shooter (M. Spencer, 2009). In addition, the technology itself, even when properly used, may also produce unanticipated risks and consequences. An accurate understanding of the role of technology in criminal justice requires recognition of the potential for undesirable results. Think about your own perceptions of the scientific testing of criminal evidence as you read "Criminal Justice: Myth and Reality."

Criminal Justice: MYTH AND REALITY

COMMON BELIEF: As long as forensic scientists do not mishandle evidence, modern scientific methods ensure that reliable conclusions can be drawn after the laboratory testing of various forms of evidence, including fingerprints, hair, soil, handwriting, and bite marks.

In reality, the National Academy of Sciences concluded that "many forensic disciplines—including analysis of fingerprints, bite marks, and the striations and indentations left by a pry bar or a gun's firing mechanism—were not grounded in the kind of rigorous, peer-reviewed research that is the hallmark of classic science" (Fountain, 2009). Major scandals have emerged when experts purported to state definitive conclusions about bite marks, handwriting analysis, and other forms of evidence after scientific testing, only to discover later that these conclusions were incorrect and had led to the conviction of innocent people (F. Santos, 2007). DNA analysis is the only form of scientific evidence that has been subjected to rigorous testing through the methods of science. Although courts admit into evidence other forms of scientific testing, as well as conclusions drawn about such evidence by scientists, many of these other tests have not been validated through rigorous research. Thus, judges and attorneys should display caution in examining and accepting such evidence.

CHECKPOINT

ANSWER

1. What are two reasons to be cautious about assuming that new technological developments automatically provide benefits for the criminal justice system?

1. Lawbreakers can develop and use technology for the purpose of committing crimes; new technologies produce the risks of unanticipated, undesirable risks and consequences.

Crime and Technology

As new technologies emerge, so do people who take advantage of them for their own gain. One has only to think of how the invention of the automobile enhanced criminals' mobility to realize the extent to which computers and other new technologies will enhance existing criminal enterprises. For example, the acquisition of automatic weapons can make drug traffickers more dangerous in battling their rivals and threatening witnesses. Instantaneous transfers of funds between banks via computer networks can make it easier for criminals to move money in order to purchase weapons, drugs, and other contraband, as well as to hide assets from government agencies responsible for law enforcement and tax collection. Computers and other technologies also create opportunities to commit new kinds of crimes, such as cyber crime and counterfeiting. We should note as well that individual citizens can respond by using technology themselves to thwart crime through improved lighting and alarm systems in their homes, security software on their computers, and pepper spray canisters and other weapons for personal protection.

■ Cyber Crime

As we saw in Chapter 2, cyber crimes involve the use of computers and the Internet to commit acts against people, property, public order, or morality. Cyber criminals use computers to steal information, resources, or funds. These thefts can be aimed at simply stealing money or they can involve the theft of companies' trade secrets, chemical formulas, and other valuable information. Others use computers for malicious, destructive acts, such as releasing Internet viruses and "worms" to harm computer systems. They may also use innocent victims' computers, via remote commands, to assist in crimes such as the dissemination of child pornography.

In addition, the illegal downloading of software, music, videos, and other copyrighted materials is widespread (Hinduja, 2007). Doing so is a federal crime. However, although millions of Americans perform illegal downloads every day, they are seldom prosecuted unless the government identifies individuals or organizations with substantial involvement in such activities. Further, new issues continually arise that produce suggestions about criminalizing new forms of cyber behavior, such cyber bullying among teens that may lead to psychological harms and behavioral problems (Hinduja and Patchin, 2007; Patchin and Hinduja, 2006).

Identity theft has become a huge problem affecting many middle-class and affluent Americans who would otherwise seldom find themselves victimized by criminals (J. Collins, 2005). Perpetrators of identity theft use other people's credit card numbers and social security numbers to secure fraudulent loans and steal money and merchandise. Other offenders use the Internet to disseminate child pornography, to advertise sexual services, or to stalk the unsuspecting. Police departments have given special emphasis to stopping computer predators who establish online relationships with juveniles in order to manipulate those children into sexual victimization. Thus, officers often pose as juveniles in "chat rooms" in order to see if sexual predators will attempt to cultivate a relationship and set up a personal meeting (Eichenwald, 2006).

The various forms of cyber crime present a serious concern to Americans. See "What Americans Think" and compare your own concerns and awareness with those of the rest of the country.

In attacking these problems, the FBI's National Computer Crime Squad lists its responsibilities as covering the following:

● Intrusions of the Public Switched Network (the telephone company)
● Major computer network intrusions
● Network integrity violations
● Privacy violations
● Industrial espionage
● Pirated computer software
● Other crimes where the computer is a major factor in committing the criminal offense

■ **identify theft** The theft of social security numbers, credit card numbers, and other information in order to secure loans, withdraw bank funds, and purchase merchandise while posing as someone else: the unsuspecting victim who will eventually lose money in these transactions.

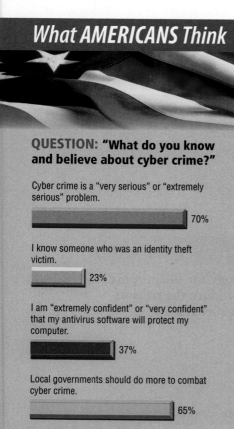

What AMERICANS Think

QUESTION: "What do you know and believe about cyber crime?"

Cyber crime is a "very serious" or "extremely serious" problem.

70%

I know someone who was an identity theft victim.

23%

I am "extremely confident" or "very confident" that my antivirus software will protect my computer.

37%

Local governments should do more to combat cyber crime.

65%

Go to http://www.cengage.com/criminaljustice/cole to compare your opinion on this issue with the opinions of other criminal justice students.

Source: Kelly Jackson Higgins, "Poll: 65% of Consumers Want Local Government to Do More about Cybercrime," April 23, 2009, national poll by Competitive Edge Research and Communication, http://cerc.net.

The global nature of the Internet presents new challenges to the criminal justice system. For example, in 2008, a Colombian man was sentenced to nine years in prison by a U.S. district court for installing keystroke logging software on computers in hotel business centers and other public-access computer locations. He collected personal information, such as bank account numbers and passwords, from 600 people who used those computers. Subsequently, the personal and financial information enabled him to steal $1.4 million. The FBI arrested him during one of his trips to the United States (U.S. Department of Justice, 2008). In another example, stolen credit card numbers are sold on the Internet, primarily by dealers based in states that were formerly part of the Soviet Union. Computer hackers steal large numbers of credit card numbers from the computer systems of legitimate businesses and sell the numbers in bulk to dealers who sell them throughout the world via members-only websites. Credit card fraud costs online merchants more than $1 billion each year (Richtel, 2002).

Law enforcement officers need up-to-date knowledge and equipment to have any hope of pursuing cyber criminals on the Internet. Local police officers often successfully pretend to be teenagers in chat rooms, drawing out people who would sexually abuse children. Local officials cannot usually maintain the expertise to counteract international cyber crime operations, so the FBI takes the lead in those efforts. Should computer courses become a required component of every college criminal justice program?

It is extremely difficult to know how many cyber crimes occur and how much money is lost through identity theft, auction fraud, investment fraud, and other forms of financial computer crime. As indicated by Table 14.1, many destructive attacks and thefts carried out by computer are done by people inside a company. Moreover, many of these events are not reported to the police. The federal government's Internet Crime Complaint Center (IC3) publishes an annual report that provides perspective on the question by compiling information on complaints filed each year. In 2007, the IC3 received nearly 207,000 complaints about cyber crime financial losses totalling more than $239 million (Internet Crime Complaint Center, 2008). These cyber crimes primarily were committed by perpetrators in the United States (63%), but other people in other countries also victimized Americans regularly. The other leading country of origin for cybercriminal enterprises were Great Britain (15%), Nigeria (6%), Canada (6%), and Romania (2%) (Internet Crime Complaint Center, 2008).

Efforts to create and enforce effective laws that will address such activities have been hampered by the international nature of cyber crime. Agencies in various countries are seeking to improve their ability to cooperate and share information. However, not all law enforcement officials throughout the world are equally committed to nor capable of catching cyber thieves and hackers. Criminals in some countries may have better computer equipment and expertise than do the officials trying to catch them. However, the FBI and other law enforcement agencies have made a concerted effort to improve their equipment, hire computer experts, and train their officers to investigate cyber crime. The FBI uses Cyber Action Teams or CATs to act quickly in addressing large-scale or very damaging cyber crimes. The FBI describes CATs as "small, highly trained teams of FBI agents, analysts, and computer forensics and malicious code experts who travel around the world on a moment's notice to respond to cyber intrusions" (FBI, 2006b). For example, in 2006 an FBI CAT team traveled to Morocco and Turkey to help those governments apprehend cyber criminals who were unleashing malicious codes on the Internet and stealing credit card numbers (FBI, 2006b).

TABLE 14.1	Prevalence of Computer Security Incidents, Types of Offenders, and Reporting to Law Enforcement, 2005			
	Percentage of Businesses by Type of Incident			
Characteristic	**All Incidents**	**Cyber Attack**	**Cyber Theft**	**Other**
All businesses responding	67%	58%	11%	24%
Number of employees				
2–24	50%	44%	8%	15%
25–99	59	51	7	17
100–999	70	60	9	24
1,000 or more	82	72	20	36
Industries with the highest prevalence of cyber crime				
Telecommunications	82%	74%	17%	32%
Computer system design	79	72	15	25
Manufacturing, durable goods	75	68	15	32
Suspected offender was an—[a]				
Insider	40%	27%	74%	30%
Outsider	71	74	32	72
Incidents were reported—[b]				
Within the business	80%	81%	46%	69%
To another organization	15	14	9	7
To law enforcement authorities	15	6	56	12

Note: A total of 7,818 businesses responded to the National Computer Security Survey. Detail may sum to more than 100% because businesses could detect multiple types of incidents.

[a] Percentages are based on businesses that detected an incident and provided information on suspected offenders.
[b] Percentages are based on businesses that detected an incident and provided information on reporting incidents to authorities.

Source: Ramona R. Rantala, "Cybercrime against Businesses, 2005," Bureau of Justice Statistics *Special Report*, September 2008, p. 1.

Differences in legal principles and social values also impact the effectiveness of pursuing cyber crime. For instance, in the United States, some laws intended to punish people involved in online pornography have been struck down for violating First Amendment rights to free expression.

Since the events of September 11, many countries' law enforcement agencies have increased their communication and cooperation in order to thwart terrorist activities. As these countries cooperate in investigating and monitoring the financial transactions of groups that employ terror tactics, it seems likely that they will also improve their capacity to discover and pursue cyber criminals. For example, the FBI has also joined forces with the national police agencies of Australia, Canada, New Zealand, and the United Kingdom to form the Strategic Alliance Cyber Crime Working Group, an international organization for sharing information and cooperating in cyber crime investigations (FBI, 2008b).

Law enforcement agencies cannot prevent cyber crimes from occurring. Normally, they react to such harmful activities in order to limit theft and damage. People cannot rely on law enforcement efforts to protect them from such harms. The first defense against some forms of cyber crime is citizen awareness and caution. Do you think most people know enough about cyber crime to protect themselves from becoming victims?

■ Counterfeiting

Traditional counterfeiting involves the creation of fake currency that can be used for illegal profit. Counterfeiting not only constitutes theft by permitting criminals to exchange fake bills for actual products and services; it also harms the economy by placing into circulation bills that have no monetary value. Additional victims may receive the worthless paper as change in a purchase transaction or in payment for products and services. Historically, currency counterfeiters in the United States had difficulty matching the paper, ink, and intricate designs of real currency. While they could produce counterfeit bills that might fool individual clerks in stores, restaurants, and banks, criminals rarely avoided the eventual discovery that the bills were fakes. As image reproduction technology developed, especially photocopiers and scanners, criminals found new ways of counterfeiting. Among the reasons that it is a crime to make any reproduction of U.S. currency is that counterfeiters initially found ways to photocopy currency images and feed those images into change machines. In went the fake paper currency and out came an equal amount of coins with real monetary value that the counterfeiters could then take to a bank and exchange for real paper money.

Continued improvements in computer and printing technology permitted counterfeiters to produce fake currency of increasing quality. Thus, in 1996, the United States began to redesign American currency and employ new technological techniques in order to make imitation more difficult:

> Almost everything about the new design was aimed at frustrating potential counterfeiters, including a security thread embedded in the paper, a watermark featuring a shadow portrait of the figure on the bill and new "microprinting," tiny lettering that is hard to imitate. The most significant addition was the use of optically variable ink, better known as O.V.I. Look at the bills in circulation today: all 10's, 20's, 50's and 100's now feature this counterfeiting deterrent in the denomination number on the lower-right-hand corner. Turn the bill one way, and it looks bronze-green; turn it the other way, and it looks black. O.V.I is very expensive, costing many times more than conventional bank-note ink. (Mihm, 2006)

Despite the effort to prevent counterfeiting, in 2004 and 2005, FBI and Secret Service agents began to intercept large shipments of "supernotes" that featured the same color-shifting ink and paper as real American currency. Apparently, the government of North Korea had purchased the same currency-printing technology that a Swiss company had sold to the U.S. Department of Treasury. North Korean defectors claimed that the country's dictator, Kim Jong Il, had ordered his scientists to counterfeit U.S. money as a means to generate income for the isolated, impoverished country and with the specific intention to "fight America, and screw up the American economic system" (Mihm, 2006). Although U.S. officials believe that too few fake bills have made it into the United States in order to affect the U.S. economy, they have serious concerns about how the bills are used elsewhere in the world to purchase weapons for terrorist activities.

Clearly, the advancement and availability of copying and printing technologies will continue to pose new risks as they fall into the hands of hostile governments as well as terrorist organizations and traditional organized crime groups. As such, U.S. officials constantly seek to improve America's ability to identify fake currency and discourage counterfeiting. As we have seen, these efforts include the federal government's recent redesign of paper currency. Other measures range from the special felt markers used by supermarket cashiers to the use of scientific laboratories to detect fake bills. At Secret Service headquarters, all suspect bills are "examined under a microscope, scrutinized in ultraviolet light and otherwise dissected to reveal their flaws and shortcomings, as well as the printing techniques used in their manufacture... [and] then cross-checked with a database of all known counterfeits" (Mihm, 2006).

Currency is not the only product susceptible to counterfeiting through the use of available reproduction technologies. For example, legitimate businesses lose billions of dollars in potential sales each year when consumers purchase illegally copied, or "pirated," Hollywood DVDs, as well as counterfeit luxury products that purport to be from name brands such as Gucci, Chanel, Louis Vuitton, and Prada. The pirated American movies, music, and computer software produced in China alone cost legitimate businesses more than $2 billion in sales each year (LaFraniere, 2009). Although American law enforcement agencies can attempt—with limited success—to prevent the importation of counterfeit and pirated products, they can do little to prevent the manufacture of such products without the cooperation of authorities in the countries where the counterfeiters are located.

Counterfeiting poses serious problems for the American economy through the production of phony currency and bogus consumer products. What should the United States government do to stop the importation of counterfeit currency, such as high-quality fake bills produced by North Korea to harm the American economy?

AP Images/Damian Dovarganes

Although counterfeit consumer products impose significant costs on American businesses, far worse human costs result from the counterfeiting of another product: prescription drugs. Technological advancements produced a sharp increase in counterfeit medications during the first decade of the twenty-first century. The discovery of counterfeit versions of specific medications increased from five different prescription and over-the-counter drugs per year in the late 1990s to more than 20 new counterfeit drugs per year beginning in 2000 (Grady, 2003). The dangers of counterfeit drugs are obvious: They can cause the deaths of patients who believe that they are taking genuine drugs or prevent patients from recovering appropriately from nonfatal illnesses. In 2008, a counterfeit version of the blood-thinning drug Heparin came to the United States from China and led to the deaths of 19 Americans as well as to hundreds of serious allergic reactions (Bogdanich, 2008). The serious risks from counterfeit drugs include the following:

> Counterfeit drugs are worthless fakes passed off as genuine. They may contain inactive substances like tap water or chalk, wrong ingredients, incorrect dosages or contaminants. Expensive drugs for severe cases of cancer and AIDS have been among the targets. In one case, aspirin tablets were substituted for the schizophrenia drug, Zyprexa. (Grady, 2003)

Imagine needing immediate medications in order to fight a dangerous illness, but unknowingly receiving counterfeit drugs that will have no effect on the illness. This kind of illegal activity can easily kill vulnerable people.

Because counterfeiting prescription drugs can be quite profitable, it has attracted organized crime groups. In one case, criminals in Florida copied the packaging and labels of the anemia drug Procrit, which is used to treat people with cancer and AIDS. They diluted the dosages in some bottles and filled other bottles with water. Because Procrit sells for $500 per dosage bottle, the criminals gained an estimated $46 million in profit before the scheme was discovered (Grady, 2003).

The U.S. Food and Drug Administration (FDA) and other government agencies face significant challenges in finding and seizing counterfeit drugs. New efforts to inspect and supervise pharmaceutical production facilities in the United States and abroad and to track individual medications as they move from factory to pharmacy have sought to reduce the risks for the American public. Unfortunately, profit-seeking criminals are working just as hard to defeat any new monitoring systems that are developed to intercept counterfeits. The proliferation of Internet pharmacies, which sell prescription medications online, has presented new challenges. Such enterprises may be located outside the borders of the United States. FDA officials have worked to warn Americans against purchasing medications from online sources other than the websites of established pharmacy retail chains. However, because many Americans do not have medical insurance or have incomplete prescription drug coverage, some people will purchase medications inexpensively over the Internet, without being aware that they may be purchasing counterfeit drugs. Other people use online sources to seek medications, such as painkillers, for which they do not have legal prescriptions. These people face the potentially grave risks of ingesting fake medications.

CHECKPOINT

ANSWERS

② *What actions have been taken to combat counterfeit currency in the United States?*

② **Redesign of U.S. currency; efforts to detect counterfeit currency from the level of individual cashiers at stores to international investigations leading to the seizure of large quantities of fake currency.**

③ *What harms are caused by counterfeit products in the United States?*

③ **Billions of dollars in losses for American businesses because of counterfeit and pirated products; deaths and other harmful health consequences from counterfeit medications.**

Policing and New Technology

Policing has long made use of technological developments. Twentieth-century police departments adopted the use of automobiles and radios in order to increase the effectiveness of their patrols, including better response time to criminal events and emergencies. Over time, technological advances also helped to provide better protection for police officers, including stronger, lighter bulletproof vests and protective features of patrol cars. Technology has affected the investigation of crime as well. As early as 1911, fingerprint evidence was used to convict an offender. Police officers have collected fingerprints, blood, fibers, and other crime-scene materials to be analyzed through scientific methods in order to identify and convict criminal offenders.

Police officers also use polygraphs, the technical name for lie detectors, that measure people's heart rates and other physical responses as they answer questions. Although polygraph results are typically not admissible as evidence, police officers have often used these examinations on willing suspects and witnesses as a basis for excluding some suspects or for pressuring others to confess.

In recent years, scientific advances have enabled police and prosecutors to place greater reliance on **DNA analysis**. This technique identifies people through their distinctive gene patterns (also called genotypic features). DNA, or deoxyribonucleic acid, is the basic component of all chromosomes; all the cells in an individual's body, including those in skin, blood, organs, and semen, contain the same unique DNA. The characteristics of certain segments of DNA vary from person to person and thus form a genetic fingerprint. Forensic labs can analyze DNA from, for example, samples of

■ **DNA analysis** A scientific technique that identifies people through their distinctive gene patterns (also called genotypic features). DNA, or deoxyribonucleic acid, is the basic component of all chromosomes; all the cells in an individual's body, including those in skin, blood, organs, and semen, contain the same unique DNA.

hair and compare them with those of suspects. As described by several law enforcement officials, the increasing effectiveness of DNA testing as an investigative tool has stemmed from "improved technology, better sharing of DNA databases among states and a drop in crime...that allowed detectives more time to work on unsolved cases" (Yardley, 2006). Although fingerprint evidence is still used, advances in DNA technology have greatly reduced any reliance on the less-precise testing of blood and hair evidence as the sole means of identifying suspects.

Several issues arise as police adopt new technologies. First, questions about the accuracy and effectiveness of technological developments persist, even though the developments were originally embraced with great confidence. For example, despite the long and confident use of fingerprint evidence by police and prosecutors, its accuracy has been questioned. In 2002, a federal judge ruled that expert witnesses could compare crime scene fingerprints with those of a defendant, but they could not testify that the prints definitely matched. The judge pointed out that, unlike DNA evidence, fingerprint evidence processes have not been scientifically verified, the error rate for such identifications has never been measured, and there are no scientific standards for determining when fingerprint samples match (Loviglio, 2002). Prosecutors later persuaded the judge to reverse his original decision and admit the expert testimony about a fingerprint match, but the judge's first decision raises the possibility that other judges will scrutinize fingerprint evidence more closely.

Second, some worry that new technologies will create new collisions with citizens' constitutional rights. As police gain greater opportunities for sophisticated electronic surveillance, for example, new questions arise about what constitutes a search that violates citizens' reasonable expectations of privacy. For example, new technology that allows law enforcement agencies to intercept email messages raises questions about privacy that were not foreseeable in prior decades. Similarly, in several cities, police officers with DNA evidence from a rape have asked all of the men in a particular community to submit a DNA sample from inside the cheek in order to find a match with DNA of the perpetrator. Many critics believe that innocent citizens who have done nothing suspicious should not be pressured to provide the government with a sample of their DNA.

■ Communications and Computer Technology

Communications and the exchange of information serve as central elements in effective law enforcement. Dispatchers receive calls for service and bear responsibility for communicating citizens' immediate needs to patrol officers. In addition, police officers have traditionally relied on communication with dispatchers in order to obtain essential information, such as queries about whether a particular car was stolen or whether a particular individual is being sought under an arrest warrant. New computer technology has altered both citizens' communications with dispatchers and police officers' reliance on their central headquarters. In addition, the use of computers and databases has enhanced the ability of law enforcement officers to investigate many kinds of crimes.

Communications   In many places, the number of calls to 911 emergency operators increased significantly as the spread of cell phones made it easier for people to call as incidents arose. In 1997, the Federal Communications Commission (FCC) set aside "311" as an option for cities to use as a nonemergency number. First Baltimore, then Detroit and New York, implemented the 311 call system, but many cities have not done so. The FCC later set aside "211" for social services information and "511" for traffic information, but relatively few cities have implemented call centers to use these numbers (McMahon, 2002). Although 911 systems can automatically trace the location of calls made from landlines, many cities are struggling to upgrade their 911 systems so that they can trace wireless calls to the vicinity of nearest cell phone tower (Dewan, 2007). Such efforts to upgrade equipment, procedures, and training become more visible in the aftermath of tragedies. One such example is the murder of a University of Wisconsin student in 2008 who dialed 911 from her cell phone, apparently when confronted by an intruder in her apartment; the operator did not know her precise location or the nature of the emergency (Arnold, 2008). The 911 system remains the primary means for callers to reach their local government, but there are always concerns that those lines may become too tied up with emergency calls and thereby disrupt the ability of police and other emergency responders to receive quick reports about urgent situations.

Computers The use of computers inside patrol cars has improved police efficiency and reduced officers' demands on central office dispatchers. Computers enable instant electronic communication that permits the radio airwaves to be reserved for emergency calls rather than being used for requests to check license numbers and other routine matters. Computer programs permit officers to type information about traffic violations, crime suspects, and investigations directly into central computers without filling out numerous, separate forms by hand. For example, new computers in the patrol cars of the Lansing, Michigan, police department permit officers to swipe the bar code on Michigan drivers' licenses to call up a driver's record instantly (Miller, 2009).

Officers can also gain quick access to information about automobile license plates and pending warrants (Fields and Peveto, 2008). For example, new computer technology tested by officers in the Texas Department of Public Safety reduced the time required for an officer to process a drunken-driving arrest from four hours to less than one hour. A study of the Washington State Police found that officers with laptop computers in their cars were able to ticket twice as many speeders and three times as many drunken drivers as were officers who filled out paperwork by hand. The computer-connected officers also made more felony and misdemeanor arrests, presumably because paperwork absorbed less of their time.

The increase in efficiency gained through the use of computers may give police administrators greater flexibility in deciding how to deploy officers on patrol. However, the new technology has its costs and consequences. Patrol car computers can require increased time and money for training officers. They also raise safety issues in that the computers become dangerous projectiles within the vehicles during high-speed pursuits or collisions. In addition, because local police departments are under the control of local governments that do not possess equal resources, some departments cannot afford to purchase computers for patrol cars.

Among departments with more than 100 sworn officers, the percentage of state agencies using in-vehicle computers increased from 14 percent to 59 percent between 1990 and 2000. The use of such computers and unmounted laptops in vehicles over the same time period increased from 19 percent to 68 percent for local police agencies (Reaves and Hickman, 2004). By 2003, nearly 90 percent of departments in cities with 25,000 or more inhabitants used in-vehicle computers. In contrast, police had access to computers in their vehicles in only 58 percent of towns with populations from 2,500 to 10,000 and in only 36 percent of towns with populations below 2,500 (Hickman and Reaves, 2006). From these figures, we can see that the availability of communications and information technology varies, depending on departmental resources. Table 14.2 shows how differences in resources affect police officers' computer access.

As mentioned, patrol car computers enhance police officers' investigative capabilities through quick access to databases and other sources of information that help identify suspects. Depending on the software used and the organization of databases, many officers can make quick checks of individuals' criminal histories, driving records, and outstanding warrants (A. Davis, 2001). With more-advanced computers and software, some officers can even receive mug shots and fingerprint records on their computer screens. Advances in technology provide a variety of possibilities for improving officers' ability to evaluate evidence at the scene of an event. With mobile scanners, officers can potentially run a quick check of an individual's fingerprints against the millions of fingerprint records stored in the FBI's database (Pochna, 2002). The Seal Beach, California, Police Department has worked with high-tech companies to develop streaming video capabilities that can permit officers to view live video from crime scene cameras as they approach the location of an incident. For example, officers using their computers to access surveillance cameras in banks and convenience stores can see the details of a robbery in progress as they approach the scene

TABLE 14.2	Analytic Functions of Computers in Local Police Departments, by Size of Population Served, 2003				
	Percentage of Agencies Using Computers for—				
Population Served	**Traffic Stop Data Collection**	**Crime Analysis**	**Intelligence Gathering**	**Crime Mapping**	**Hotspot Identification**
All sizes	46%	32%	28%	19%	11%
1,000,000 or more	56%	69%	50%	69%	56%
500,000–999,999	57	78	67	67	54
250,000–499,999	51	85	61	81	63
100,000–249,999	49	82	61	74	54
50,000–99,999	50	74	49	61	40
25,000–49,999	64	62	50	41	29
10,000–24,999	58	48	37	30	17
2,500–9,999	52	31	28	14	8
Under 2,500	35	16	19	9	3

Source: Matthew J. Hickman and Brian A. Reaves, *Local Police Departments* (Washington, DC: Bureau of Justice Statistics, May 2006), 30.

("Law Enforcement Solution," 2002). Thus, technology can improve the safety and effectiveness of police officers, especially in their crime-fighting role.

One snapshot of the speed with which the use of patrol vehicle technology is expanding is represented in Figure 14.1. Note how rapidly video cameras came into use in more and more patrol cars when this study was conducted a few years ago. Just imagine how much more technology has been put into use today.

Computers have become very important for investigating specific types of crimes, especially cyber crimes (Hinduja, 2004). Many police departments have begun to train and use personnel to investigate people who use computers to meet children online in order to lure them into exploitative relationships. As we have seen, computer investigations also involve pursuing people who commit identity theft, steal credit card numbers, and engage in fraudulent financial transactions using computers (J. Collins, 2005). At the national level, federal officials must use computers to detect and prevent sophisticated efforts to hack into government and corporate computer systems in order to steal secrets or harm critical infrastructures, such as regional electrical systems and emergency warning systems (Kilgannon and Cohen, 2009; Markoff, 2009).

Computers are also essential for crime analysis and crime mapping, methods used with increasing frequency by local police departments. Through the use of **Geographic Information System (GIS)** technology and software, police departments can analyze

■ **Geographic Information System (GIS)**
Computer technology and software that permits law enforcement officials to map problem locations in order to understand calls for service and the nature and frequency of crimes and other issues within specific neighborhoods.

FIGURE 14.1
Local police departments using video cameras in patrol cars, 2000 and 2003

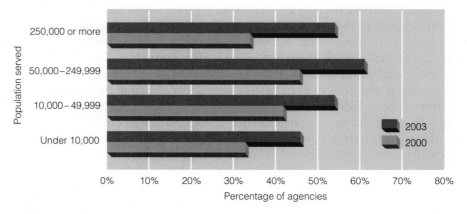

Source: Matthew J. Hickman and Brian A. Reaves, *Local Police Departments* (Washington, DC: Bureau of Justice Statistics, May 2006), 29.

hot spots, crime trends, and other crime patterns with a level of sophistication and precision that was previously unavailable. By analyzing the locations and frequencies of specific crimes, such as burglary, or the nature of calls for service in various neighborhoods, police are better able to deploy their personnel effectively and plan targeted crime-prevention programs (Stroshine, 2005).

One example of promising innovation is the Los Angeles Police Department's development of a "smart car" that incorporates various cutting-edge computer and video technologies. The car contains a camera that scans license plates at high speed, after which the car's computer tells the officers if the car was stolen or if the owner of the vehicle is wanted. The camera-computer system can process 8,000 license plates during a 10-hour shift. By contrast, an officer could manually process only about 100 license plates during the same time period. When the system detects a stolen car, another camera photographs the car and records the GPS location. In addition to the commonly used dashboard video camera, the car also has a rear-facing video camera to monitor any prisoners being transported. The car's computer system can also receive streaming video from surveillance cameras located in housing projects and commercial areas in order to permit officers to spot suspicions persons or crimes in progress. Finally, the car also contains a launcher in the front grill that shoots a small GPS-tracking device; this attaches itself to the car the officers are following. Even if the officers lose the vehicle in a chase, the car's location can be tracked. The LAPD has high hopes for adding a fleet of cars with these technologies to the few "smart cars" that already exist, but adding expensive technological devices to hundreds of police vehicles raises issues of cost (Bennett, 2009; Cheung, 2007; Valencia-Martinez, 2006).

Another promising computerized tool for police is a system for detecting gunshots, quickly analyzing their location, and instantly communicating the information to police without reliance on human witnesses to dial the phone and guess where a shooting took place. These systems were originally developed for the military in order to identify the location of snipers. They operate through the use of sensors, installed in a neighborhood, that can distinguish gunshots from other sounds and detect the location of the gunshots through interaction with other sensors. The expensive systems have been used in specific neighborhoods within such cities as East Orange, New Jersey; Newport News, Virginia; and Roosevelt, New York (Domash, 2008; Holl, 2005).

Databases   Computer technology permits law enforcement officials to gather, store, and analyze data. In minutes, or even seconds, computers can sort through data with the effectiveness that spares a user from spending hours combing through papers stored in a filing cabinet. For example, New York City detectives solved an armed robbery case in 2005 by taking a witness's description of the robber's tattoo and running it through the police department's computerized tattoo database. Very quickly, the detectives identified a suspect, showed his mug shot to the robbery victim, and tracked him down to make the arrest. The New York Police Department's database contains records on criminal complaints, warrants, 911 calls, individuals' criminal and parole records, and other kinds of property and public records (T. Hays, 2006).

In the discussion that follows, keep in mind that the accuracy and usefulness of any database, including that of New York, depends on the accurate input of correct information and methods to permit the information to be accessed efficiently by police officers. Human errors in database development and management can not only limit the usefulness of this technology but also wreak havoc on the lives of people whose information is misclassified. For example, since 9/11, many innocent people, including small children, have faced problems trying to board airplanes because their names were among the thousands on

The development of databases and improvements in nationwide computer access to them help investigators identify suspects through DNA samples, fingerprints, tattoos, and other markers. Here, the FBI's lead ballistics examiner, Walter Dandridge, studies the grooves of a .223 slug through a developing database of ballistics signatures from guns used in crimes. Is there any information about Americans that should *not* be recorded in a centralized database?

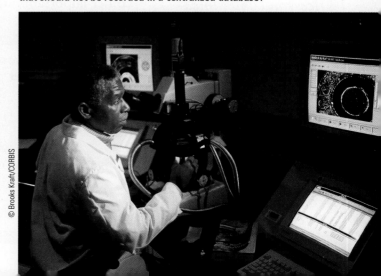

© Brooks Kraft/CORBIS

the Transportation Safety Agency's overly broad terrorist watch list. Even the late Senator Edward Kennedy of Massachusetts found himself denied plane tickets when the name "Edward Kennedy" appeared on the list (Sharkey, 2008; Swarns, 2004).

One of the largest and historically most important criminal justice databases is the fingerprint database. Police departments throughout the country can submit fingerprints from a crime scene in the hope of finding the criminal's identity from among the more than 47 million sets of fingerprints stored in the FBI computers. Local and federal law enforcement officials routinely submit the fingerprints of everyone arrested for a serious charge so that the prints can be added to the database. If a suspect is found not guilty, the prints are supposed to be removed from the system. These databases may also be used for background checks on people who work in regulated industries such as casinos and banks (Engber, 2005).

A few years ago, matching fingerprints was time consuming because fingerprints had to be sent to the FBI on cards. Since 1999, however, the Integrated Automated Fingerprint Identification System (IAFIS) has enabled police to send fingerprints electronically and then have those prints matched against the millions of prints in the database. The FBI can also provide electronic images of individuals' fingerprints to local law enforcement agencies upon request. Finally, the FBI provides training for state and local police on taking fingerprints and transmitting those prints to the IAFIS for evaluation.

The Department of Homeland Security has developed its own fingerprint database from two primary sources. New post-9/11 rules require the collection of fingerprints from every noncitizen entering the United States. This has created a database of more than 64 million fingerprints, which can be linked to the FBI database containing an additional 40 million sets. Military and intelligence officials are also collecting unidentified **latent fingerprints** from cups, glasses, firearms, ammunition, doorknobs, and any other objects that they find overseas in abandoned Al-Qaida training camps, safe houses, and battle sites. These prints are the patterned residue of natural skin secretions or contaminating materials such as ink, blood, or dirt that were present on the fingertips at the time of their contact with the objects. The hope is that terrorists will be identified if their fingerprints match those of visitors to the United States (Richey, 2006). As we shall see later in this chapter, DNA databases present similar hopes for identifying perpetrators, especially in domestic criminal cases.

New debates have emerged about whether there should be a national database of ballistic evidence. Advocates argue that every gun sold should undergo a firing test so that its ballistic fingerprint can be stored in the database, just in case the weapon is later used in a crime. Opponents claim that this is an undesirable step toward national gun registration and that such a database would be useless because the ballistic

■ **latent fingerprints** Impressions of the unique pattern of ridges on the fingertip that are left behind on objects; these impressions are the residue of natural skin secretions or contaminating materials such as ink, blood, or dirt that were present on the fingertips at the time of their contact with the objects.

CHECKPOINT

ANSWERS

4 *How do computers in patrol cars aid officers in communication issues?*

4 Officers do not need to tie up the radio airwaves and the attention of dispatchers in order to check on stolen cars, drivers' records, and other important information that can be accessed via computer.

5 *How can the use of Geographic Information Systems (GIS) assist criminal justice officials?*

5 They can create sophisticated maps for the analyses of crime patterns and other problems in neighborhoods.

6 *What kinds of information can be collected in law enforcement databases?*

6 Fingerprints, tattoos, DNA samples, gun/ballistics records.

characteristics of a gun's fired bullets change as the gun is used over time (Chaddock, 2002). The usefulness of these databases depends on the accuracy of technology to match evidence with stored information and the accessibility of database information to police departments and individual officers. In addition, as indicated by the debate about ballistic evidence, the nature and use of evidence databases rely in part on public policy debates about what information can be gathered and how it will be used.

■ DNA Analysis

Forensic science laboratories perform many kinds of scientific tests. As indicated in Table 14.3, many of these labs examine narcotics, firearms, and fingerprints as well as DNA. Although many publicly funded labs are not equipped to do DNA testing, DNA analysis has become especially important in criminal justice. It is revolutionizing the use of science for the investigation of crimes. Because scientists are increasing their capacity to extract testable DNA samples from tiny samples of biological material, law enforcement officials are increasingly able to tie specific individuals to a location or piece of evidence. When the local government lab is not able to conduct DNA tests, agencies hire private labs to do the analysis.

DNA Databases In spite of questions about which offenders should be required to submit DNA samples, many states and the federal government are building a national database of DNA records that is maintained by the FBI. Known as CODIS, which stands for Combined DNA Index System, the project began in 1990 as a pilot project serving a few state and local laboratories. CODIS has now grown to include 137 laboratories in 47 states and the District of Columbia.

The federal Justice for All Act, enacted in October 2004, greatly expanded the number of offenders in the federal justice system who must submit DNA samples. Previously, samples were taken only from those who had committed specific violent crimes. Later, collection expanded to federal offenders convicted of any felony, violent act, or conspiracy. In 2009, collection of DNA samples expanded further to all people arrested for federal crimes and all noncitizens who are detained (Weiss, 2008). The Federal Bureau of Prisons obtains DNA through blood samples from *all* incoming offenders. In addition, federal probation offices must now obtain samples under the newer law. Federal probation offices are scrambling to find qualified phlebotomists (people trained to draw blood samples), as well as to acquire enough test kits for

TABLE 14.3	Forensic Functions Performed by Crime Laboratories in 2005, by Type of Jurisdiction			
Forensic Function	Total[a]	State	County	Municipal
Controlled substances	89%	88%	94%	85%
Firearms/toolmarks	59	60	59	56
Biology screening	57	58	61	51
Latent prints	55	50	51	76
Trace evidence	55	57	59	44
DNA analysis	53	55	61	42
Toxicology	53	57	49	47
Impressions	52	50	53	56
Crime scene	40	36	46	56
Questioned documents	20	18	22	24
Computer crimes	12	9	16	15
Number of labs reporting	351	207	79	55

Note: Detail sums to more than 100% because some laboratories reported performing more than one function.
[a] Includes federal labs, not shown separately

Source: Matthew R. Durose, "Census of Publicly Funded Forensic Crime Laboratories, 2005" Bureau of Justice Statistics *Bulletin,* July 2008, p. 3.

thousands of additional offenders. Moreover, Congress mandated that the samples be collected but did not provide any funds for the probation offices within federal courts to collect these samples (Administrative Office of the U.S. Courts, 2005). Thus, the new requirement is causing budget problems in the justice system.

States have their own laws governing DNA and which people are required to submit a sample. Efforts are underway to expand the collection of samples. In 2007, for example, New York officials proposed expanding the required sample collection, which included convicted felons, to include convicted misdemeanants as well (McGeehan, 2007). In 2008, Maryland joined a dozen other states in collecting samples from people arrested, but not yet convicted, for murder, rape, and assault (Arena and Bohn, 2008). California began taking samples from everyone arrested on felony charges in 2009, whether or not they are ultimately convicted of a crime (Felch and Dolan, 2008). Georgia instituted a new law in 2008 to permit investigators to compare DNA evidence with samples collected from suspects when a search warrant is obtained to require a subject to provide a sample. Previously, DNA evidence in Georgia could only be compared with samples taken from convicted felons ("Perdue OK's Bill," 2008). One southern California prosecutor regards DNA databases as such a useful resource for solving serious crimes that he began to dismiss some misdemeanor and drug charges against defendants if they would agree to provide a DNA sample. Skeptics questioned whether the so-called "spit and acquit" program was appropriate, since it permitted drug offenders to go free without any treatment (Weiss, 2009). By 2009, every state except Idaho, Nebraska, and New Hampshire collected DNA samples from all convicted felons. An additional 15 states collected samples from people arrested, even if they have not been convicted of any crime, and 19 additional states had pending proposals in their legislatures to do the same (Protess, 2009).

Another proposal to expand the use of DNA testing and evidence concerns searches that look for relatives rather than the exact person whose DNA was left at the crime scene. Although only exact matches of crime scene evidence and an individual's DNA are supposed to be used in court, it is possible to identify other suspects through wider comparisons. For example, DNA comparisons may indicate that a convicted felon whose sample is in the database is not the perpetrator of a rape, but that he is a relative of the rapist. Thus, police would have reason to undertake further investigations of the convicted felon's close male relatives. So-called "kinship-based DNA searching" is already used in Great Britain but is not used as widely in the United States (Wade, 2006).

By taking samples from people convicted of specific crimes in the state and federal systems, officials hope that CODIS will enable them to close unsolved crimes that involve DNA evidence. Unfortunately, problems and delays in collecting and processing the samples persist. Nonetheless, the use of DNA testing and databases has led to arrests in a growing number of unsolved cases.

Recent examples illustrate the use of DNA identification to close cold cases. In April 2005, DNA tests linked a man in Georgia with 25 unsolved rapes in three states, including a rape committed in New York in 1973. The man had fled New York nearly 20 years earlier when facing different rape charges. He was eventually located when Georgia conducted a routine background check when the man attempted to purchase a gun. At the time, officials did not know he was linked to the other unsolved rapes, but the matches emerged when his sample was run through the national database (Preston, 2005). The successful use of the DNA database to close an old case raised officials' optimism about solving other cold cases by testing evidence that had been saved from many years ago. Such was the case, for example, of an imprisoned man in Georgia whose DNA analysis in 2006 indicated that he was responsible for four unsolved murders in Connecticut in the late 1980s and early 1990s (Yardley, 2006) and a serial murderer-rapist in Buffalo, New York, whose unsolved crimes spanned two decades (Staba, 2007).

Issues and Problems with DNA Analysis   Such examples illustrate the benefit of using DNA testing and databases, but other cases demonstrate problems that need to be addressed. In Truro, Massachusetts, a writer was raped and murdered in her home in 2002. Her bloody body was found on the floor with her two-year-old daughter, who was clinging to it when a friend came to check on her whereabouts. The police sought DNA samples from all men in the small community. Their efforts to obtain these samples led to protests by civil liberties advocates who believed the rights of innocent men were threatened, especially when police said that they would look closely at men who refused to provide a sample. In April 2005, police arrested a man after his sample matched DNA from the crime scene. The suspect was the trash collector who went to the victim's house each week. Unfortunately, although the suspect had volunteered to provide a sample in April 2002, the police did not collect the sample until March 2004. Further, because of a backlog of DNA samples to be tested at the state crime lab, the sample was not evaluated until April 2005 (Belluck, 2005). This means that suspect could have committed additional crimes during the long delay.

In another example, it took police only five days to learn that a man's DNA sample in Vermont identified him as a murder suspect. Unfortunately, however, five years had already passed from the time when the man provided the DNA sample to the time when Vermont crime lab officials could put the sample in the state's database (Ring, 2005). Thus, the long delay prevented quick identification and arrest. The lack of resources for prompt tests always raises the possibility that crimes could have been prevented if a suspect had been identified and arrested earlier in the process.

The problem of too few laboratories and inadequate staff and equipment plagues many states and the federal government. A report from the Bureau of Justice Statistics estimates that we would need 1,900 additional laboratory staff members at a cost of more than $70 million to reduce backlogs in DNA labs throughout the nation (Peterson and Hickman, 2005). These backlogs are compounded when government officials expand the categories of individuals from whom samples are taken. The move from collecting samples of convicted felons to also testing arrestees in many states, as well as detained illegal immigrants, greatly expanded the number of samples to be processed and tested. Technological advances may eventually reduce this problem. For example, the FBI laboratory now has robotic systems for processing DNA samples. The FBI's new system is expected to process 90,000 samples per month by 2010, a stark contrast to the 5,000 sample per year processed by the lab in 2002 (S. Moore, 2009b).

Another potential problem with DNA testing, along with other aspects of forensic science, concerns the ethics and competence of scientists and technicians. Such problems have emerged in the FBI crime labs as well as in various states. For example, crime laboratories in Houston and Fort Worth, Texas, were investigated and shut down after improper handling and analyzing of DNA evidence led to the convictions of people who were actually innocent. Scandals involving improper lab procedures and erroneous testimony by forensic scientists have led states such as Oklahoma and Texas to enact laws requiring crime labs to meet national accreditation standards (Kimberly, 2003). The federal government now requires crime labs to meet these standards in order to receive federal funds, but many labs have not yet gone through the credential process. Moreover, critics contend that accreditation will not prevent mistakes and erroneous testimony by scientists and technicians with questionable ethics, skills, or knowledge. This is especially true in the worst cases, such as that of a West Virginia forensic scientist who falsified test results and provided false testimony in order to help prosecutors gain convictions (Roane and Morrison, 2005). Scientists have an obligation to present truthful and impartial analyses, so they must avoid seeing themselves as part of the law enforcement team that seeks to convict people of crimes.

The expansion of DNA databases is raising a new issue that ultimately may be viewed as related to ethics. Sometimes, genetic material from an unsolved case deteriorates over the years. By the time it is tested against a database, forensic scientists may not be able to identify all 13 markers that are usually used to match individuals. However, using fewer markers creates risks that the person matched to the sample really is not guilty. In one case in Britain, a man's DNA sample matched six markers from criminal evidence, but when officials identified and tested four more markers, his DNA no longer matched (Felch and Dolan, 2008). This issue creates risks that the growing public belief in the infallibility of DNA testing may lead to erroneous convictions if a DNA sample is not complete.

For example, when evidence from an unsolved 1972 rape-murder in California was tested in 2004, the degraded sample provided only 5.5 markers to use in seeking to identify the perpetrator. The scientists used evidence from additional makers that were too faint to be considered conclusive in order to produce the seven markers necessary for the computer search. These markers matched a man who had been convicted of rape in the late 1970s and were the basis for his prosecution and conviction for the 1972 case. The prosecution told the jury the remote odds that the match was a coincidence, but the defense was barred from telling the jury that there was also a one in three risk that the match was in error because of the small number of genetic markers and the hundreds of thousands of people in the database whose samples were compared. A juror later said that the verdict would likely have been different if the jury had been given complete information about how this DNA match differed from those that match a complete set of 13 markers (Felch and Dolan, 2008).

DNA is an investigative tool for law enforcement, but it can also be used to correct grave errors by exonerating wrongly convicted people. By 2009, more than 200 people had been released from prison after being exonerated by DNA testing of preserved or newly discovered evidence. However, it can only serve this aspect of justice when evidence is properly preserved and available for later testing as DNA technology steadily improves. In the 1990s, states belatedly began to create laws concerning the preservation of evidence and opportunities for convicted offenders to obtain tests on old and on newly discovered evidence. However, errors by court clerks and lab technicians have led to the disposal of relevant evidence, even in states with laws that require preservation. In addition, many such laws impose strict time limits and other restrictions on opportunities for convicted offenders to have evidence tested. Most troubling to many critics is the tendency of prosecutors to fight against having tests conducted, even when those tests might prove that an innocent person has wrongly spent many years in prison (Dewan, 2009). A more uniform and structured system of evidence preservation is necessary in order for DNA to benefit the justice system fully.

The increasing importance of DNA and other forensic evidence is reflected in the issues arising in the Supreme Court. In 2009, the Supreme Court decided two important cases about forensic evidence. In narrow 5-to-4 decisions, the justices decided that convicted offenders have no constitutional right to have available DNA evidence tested (*District Attorney's Office v. Osborne*, 2009) and that laboratory technicians who test evidence must be available for cross-examination by defense attorneys during trials (*Melendez-Diaz v. Massachusetts*, 2009). The Supreme Court will undoubtedly consider additional issues as technological advancements affect the nature of evidence presented in criminal cases.

Consider whether you would like to become a laboratory scientist who conducts DNA testing when you read "Careers in Criminal Justice."

CHECKPOINT

ANSWERS

7 From whom is DNA collected for submission to the national database?

7 The federal system and some states collect samples from all arrestees. Others collect samples from convicted felons. Very few states do not have laws mandating collection of DNA samples from offenders.

8 What problems exist in the effective use of DNA analysis?

8 Inadequate resources to test the backlog of DNA samples; careless testing or unethical testimony from some labs; prosecutors' opposition to permitting convicted offenders to have DNA tests performed on old or new evidence.

CAREERS IN CRIMINAL JUSTICE

Forensic DNA Analyst

LINDSEY MURRAY, FORENSIC DNA ANALYST
BODE TECHNOLOGY

A FORENSIC DNA ANALYST, also called a forensic biologist or criminalist, is responsible for analyzing evidentiary items for biological material. This can include blood, saliva, semen, bone, or "touch DNA": samples of skin cells left behind when someone touches objects at a crime scene. The job of a DNA analyst requires meticulous laboratory skills, a desire to solve crime, and the ability to remain unbiased. The forensic DNA analyst determines whether biological material is, in fact, present on the evidence and, if so, who contributed that biological material. Although some state and local laboratories require that a DNA analyst attend the crime scene to collect the evidence, most labs, including private labs, do not have this option. Rather, the evidence is collected by a crime scene technician and sent to the agency for analysis. DNA obtained from the evidence item is then compared with a known sample, and a conclusion is made in a formal report. In addition to laboratory work, a forensic DNA analyst may be required to testify in court about his or her findings.

In order to become a forensic DNA analyst, an individual must have a B.S. in biology, chemistry, or a related field and complete four core courses: biochemistry, genetics, molecular biology, and population genetics (or statistics). Many labs recommend that an analyst obtain a master's degree in forensic science, biology, chemistry, or a related field, as this is required for higher positions such as laboratory technical leader.

In preparing for a career as forensic DNA scientist, Lindsey Murray earned an undergraduate degree in biological sciences and a graduate degree in forensic science, with a concentration in forensic biology. In addition, she gained experience in the field by taking on a thesis research project in biology and anthropology involving DNA analysis of skeletal remains. She now works for Bode Technology, a private laboratory that does scientific testing for law enforcement agencies.

One of the widespread challenges that DNA analysts face today is what's known as the "CSI Effect." This is the result of popular television shows portraying a forensic DNA analyst as the primary investigator on the case. Often, these shows suggest DNA results can be obtained in just seconds from any source. This misconception may influence jurors, heighten the expectations of law enforcement agencies, and, worst of all, may show potential criminals how to cover up a crime.

■ Surveillance and Identification

Police have begun using surveillance cameras in many ways. American cities increasingly use surveillance cameras at intersections to monitor and ticket people who run red lights or exceed speed limits, although quality problems affecting the video and photographs can limit the effectiveness of these efforts (Hensley and Wynn, 2009). In Scotland, England, and Australia, law enforcement officials have adopted the use of surveillance cameras that permit police to monitor activities that occur in downtown commercial areas or other selected locations. Officials in a control room can watch everyone who passes within the cameras' fields. Advances in camera technology can enable these officials to see clearly the license plate numbers of cars and other specific information. American cities, such as New York and Washington, have made moves toward experimenting with this approach to combating crime in specific areas.

Chicago has moved forward with plans for the widespread use of surveillance cameras in public places. Using a $5 million grant from the U.S. Department of Homeland Security, Chicago's 2,000 cameras will rotate 360 degrees, possess night-vision capability, and use software designed to detect suspicious activity such as someone leaving a suitcase or other potential bomb container in a busy, public place (Howlett, 2004). City officials hope that surveillance will help them fight crime as well as improve their ability to identify and prevent potential acts of terrorism. Thus, the increased use of surveillance cameras in cities may become one element

What AMERICANS Think

QUESTION: "Do you favor or oppose the following forms of monitoring and surveillance?"

Expanded camera surveillance on streets and in public places

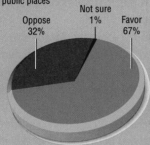

Oppose 32%   Not sure 1%   Favor 67%

Closer monitoring of banking and credit card transactions, to trace funding sources

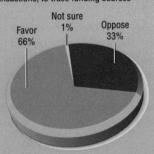

Favor 66%   Not sure 1%   Oppose 33%

Law enforcement monitoring of Internet discussions in chat rooms and other forums

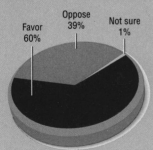

Favor 60%   Oppose 39%   Not sure 1%

Expanded government monitoring of cell phones and email, to intercept communications

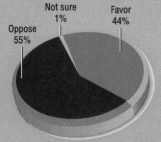

Oppose 55%   Not sure 1%   Favor 44%

Go to http://www.cengage.com/criminaljustice/cole to compare your opinion on this issue with the opinions of other criminal justice students.

Source: Harris Poll, February 2006, http://harrisinteractive.com.

of local police departments' increased emphasis on homeland security. It seems clear that surveillance cameras have helped police solve crimes, as illustrated in the earlier discussion of the shooting at the Wesleyan University bookstore, but it is less certain whether cameras are consistently effective in deterring crime (J. Lee, 2009).

Critics complain that constant surveillance by the government intrudes on the privacy of innocent, unsuspecting citizens and that there is insufficient evidence that this surveillance leads to reduced crime rates (Taifa, 2002). Judges and lawyers, including civil liberties advocates, see no problem with public surveillance; these cameras do not infringe on any rights, because people do not have a reasonable expectation of privacy when they are in public places (Howlett, 2004). In "What Americans Think," see how Americans view various forms of government monitoring and surveillance, and ask yourself why there are different levels of support for the various forms of surveillance.

There may be other problems with surveillance. For example, there are allegations in some British cities that bored officers in the control booth spend their time engaged in close-up monitoring of attractive women and ignore or hide evidence of police misconduct that is caught on camera. Training, supervision, and the establishment of clear procedures will be necessary to avoid such problems. Despite these allegations, the 500,000 surveillance cameras in London proved especially valuable in the aftermath of the July 2005 subway and bus terrorist bombings, when officials used recorded images to identify the bombing suspects (Stecklow, Singer, and Patrick, 2005).

Cameras can also help protect rights and hold police accountable when used in different surveillance contexts. For example, some states now mandate the videotaping of police interrogations for murder cases and other serious crimes. When police know that their actions are being recorded, they are less likely to engage in questionable behavior that may violate suspects' rights. Similarly, video cameras in police cars and surveillance cameras on buildings have caught officers engaged in crimes or using excessive force. For example, a surveillance camera showed two police officers entering and exiting an apartment building multiples times—and trying to avoid the camera in the process—on a night that led a woman to file a rape complaint against an officer who had escorted her back to her building when she was drunk (J. Lee, 2009). In California, a camera in 2009 recorded an officer kicking a suspect in the head after a chase (Vives and Blankstein, 2009).

American law enforcement officials have experimented with other surveillance and detection technologies. The National Institute of Justice provides funding to help scientists develop devices that will assist the police. For example, scanners are being developed that will permit officers to detect whether individuals are carrying weapons, bombs, or drugs. Some of these devices detect foreign masses hidden on the human body, while others detect trace particles and vapors that are differentiated from those associated with human bodies and clothing (Business Wire, 2001b; PR Newswire, 2001). The first versions of such scanners are undergoing testing as security measures at airports, prisons, schools, and stadiums. However, officers on the streets could eventually use smaller, more mobile versions, especially if they could point a handheld device at an individual passerby to detect whether the person is carrying weapons or contraband. Read the Close Up box and consider whether advancements in scanner technology may reveal too much information to law enforcement officials.

In another example, acting under a search warrant, the FBI installed a keystroke-logging device on the computer of a suspected organized crime figure named Nicodemo Scarfo, Jr. The device detects the exact keystrokes typed, and the agents hoped to use it to discover the suspect's passwords. If police can monitor the exact keystrokes on a computer, they can learn the content of documents, outgoing Internet messages, and passwords to enable

CLOSE UP

Backscatter X-Ray

THE DEVELOPMENT OF NEW TECHNOLOGIES can enhance our capacity to detect and prevent crimes as well as gather evidence of criminal guilt. Traditional crime-fighting technologies such as fingerprints and crime scene photographs have been supplemented by a range of inventions that detect microscopic bits of evidence.

New technologies can also create new dilemmas and problems. For example, they can increase government officials' ability to examine previously private aspects of lives—and bodies. As we consider whether and how to use new devices, we must also consider whether we are sacrificing other important values. Fundamentally, we must ask ourselves whether we are so committed to preventing crime and capturing criminals that we are willing to surrender elements of our privacy and liberty.

An excellent example emerged in 2003 when news reports described the federal Transportation Security Administration (TSA)'s experiments with backscatter X-ray devices to detect whether airline passengers are carrying weapons, bombs, or other contraband. Fully clothed people who are examined with such machines will appear naked in the television-type monitor while also revealing any objects that they are carrying under their clothes. According to the director of the TSA's security laboratory, "It does basically make you look fat and naked—but you see all this stuff [that is hidden under clothes]." The thought that a government monitor can see the image of someone's unclothed body is likely to make many people uncomfortable. Indeed, when the TSA began experimenting with the machines at selected airports in 2005, one security expert objected that the devices are too intrusive and described the job of airport screeners as being "paid to go to a peep show." Moreover, he argued that because the low-level X-ray does not penetrate the skin, very overweight people could still hide explosives beneath the folds of their skin.

By 2009, these scanners were in use at 19 airports. Privacy advocates began planning a national campaign to persuade the Department of Homeland Security that these scanner are too intrusive and that citizens do not realize the extent to which the scanners reveal their bodies under their clothing. They raised concerns about whether TSA screeners, in violation of departmental policies, might use a cell phone camera to record the image of someone's body that appears on the monitor, especially if it is the body of some celebrity whose unclothed picture might be worth a lot of money to a tabloid magazine. In response, TSA officials claimed that the faces of people are blurred by the machine and that people have the option of a full-body pat down instead of going past the scanner.

RESEARCHING THE INTERNET

For an online description of backscatter X-ray devices, go to the corresponding site listed on the Cole/Smith Criminal Justice in America Companion Website: http://www.cengage.com/criminaljustice/cole.

FOR CRITICAL ANALYSIS

If you were boarding an airplane, would you want the security monitor to, in effect, see you naked in order to prevent anyone from carrying weapons on planes? What if such devices could be carried by police officers on the street to detect whether pedestrians were carrying concealed weapons? Should limits be placed on the use of such technologies?

Sources: Austin Considine, "Will New Airport X-Rays Invade Privacy?" *New York Times*, October 9, 2005, http://www.nytimes.com; Leslie Miller, "Airport Screeners May Get X-Ray Eyes" [Associated Press Wire Service], *Lansing State Journal*, June 26, 2003, p. 4A; Office of National Drug Control Policy, "2001 Counterdrug Research and Development Blueprint Update," 2001, Appendix D, http://www.ncjrs.org/ondcppubs/publications; Jessica Ravitz, "Scanners Take 'Naked' Pics, Group Says," CNN, May 18, 2009, http://www.cnn.com; Joe Sharkey, "Airport Screeners Could Get X-Rated X-Ray Views," *New York Times*, May 24, 2005, http://www.nytimes.com.

them to overcome encryption software. With such monitoring devices in place, little remains private on an individual's computer. The use of such technology is likely to expand as part of the government's efforts to identify suspected terrorists. The USA Patriot Act enhances federal law enforcement officials' authority to monitor electronic communications, including the use of "roving" surveillance aimed at particular individuals without identifying or limiting specific facilities and devices to be monitored (Chidi, 2002).

Not all technological innovations have proved to be effective. At the Super Bowl in 2001, police officers used a surveillance system with facial-recognition technology in an attempt to identify people being sought on outstanding warrants. Casinos in Atlantic City also use facial-recognition technology with surveillance cameras to identify people whom they know to be skilled at cheating. Conceivably, the system could also be used to identify suspected terrorists attempting to enter the country at airports (Meyer and Gorman, 2001). This technology poses enough problems, however, that some cities have abandoned their initial experiments. It cannot identify faces and match them with database pictures quickly enough to prevent suspects from disappearing into a crowd and thus requiring officers to search for them. In addition, questions persist about the accuracy of the facial-recognition technology. According to one researcher who has tested some systems, "One out of every 50 people looks like Carlos the Jackal, [the infamous terrorist], and the real Carlos the Jackal has only a 50 percent chance of looking like himself" (Meyer and Gorman, 2001:1). Whether facial-recognition technology will become an effective tool for police remains to be seen.

Researchers claim that iris-recognition technology, which examines the interior of the eye and matches its unique characteristics with information in a database, is much more accurate than facial-recognition technology or technologies that attempt to match voices, fingerprints, or the palm of the hand (Business Wire, 2001a). Such iris-recognition technology appeared throughout the fictional futuristic world in the Stephen Spielberg film *Minority Report*. It is not clear, however, that such technology could be developed for use in police surveillance work. Moreover, such a technology would require the development of an entirely new type of database containing records of people's eyes. As with other developing technologies, significant questions arise about the costs of developing and producing new scientific devices for wide distribution. Even if the scientific community develops technologies that might benefit policing, the expense of implementing these devices may be far more than individual cities and counties can afford.

Scientists are working to develop technology to detect deceptions that suspects may use when questioned by police. Polygraph tests are considered insufficiently reliable, because some liars are very calm when they lie, and thereby avoid detection, while some truthful people are quite nervous when asked questions. Thus, truthful people may look like liars on a polygraph test if their palms sweat and their heart rates increase as they answer. One approach under investigation is the use of a thermal-imaging camera that can detect faint blushing in the faces of people who answer questions in an untruthful manner. Critics warn, however, that this technology may simply reproduce the problems with polygraphs by looking only at physical responses that vary by individual (R. Callahan, 2002).

An alternative technology detects people's brain-wave responses to words and images. The subject wears an electronic headband while being shown words or images flashed on a screen. If the person shows a brain-wave response to words or pictures that would be familiar only to the witness or perpetrator of a crime, then law enforcement officials might be able to move forward with an investigation that ultimately solves the crime (Paulson, 2004). Other scientists have taken this approach a step further by asking volunteers questions during an examination of the brain through magnetic resonance imaging (MRI). The research indicates that specific areas of the brain show activity when someone is telling a lie (American Society of Neuroradiology, 2003). These approaches have not been fully tested, nor have the courts accepted them yet. Moreover, they raise concerns that a court would regard this technique as violating the Fifth Amendment privilege against compelled self-incrimination.

The U.S. Supreme Court has already given a sign that it will look critically at some new police technologies. In *Kyllo v. United States* (2001), law enforcement officials pointed a thermal-imaging device at a house to detect unusual heat sources that might indicate marijuana being cultivated under grow lights. Their efforts led to a search of the home and the discovery of 100 marijuana plants. In the majority opinion, Justice An-

■ *Kyllo v. United States* (2001) Law enforcement officials cannot examine a home with a thermal-imaging device unless they obtain a warrant.

CHECKPOINT

ANSWER

❾ *What kinds of experimental technologies are being tested to assist police in the discovery of crimes and the identification of criminal suspects?*

❾ Facial-recognition technology, iris-recognition technology, thermal-imaging cameras, brain-wave technology.

tonin Scalia declared the use of the device in this manner to be an illegal search. According to Scalia, "Obtaining by sense-enhancing technology any information regarding the interior of the home that could not otherwise have been obtained without physical intrusion into a constitutionally protected area constitutes a search" and is therefore covered by the limitations of the Fourth Amendment, especially the warrant requirement (*Kyllo v. United States*, 2001:2043). Thus, it is not clear how judges may evaluate the constitutionally permissible uses of new technologies.

■ Weapons Technology

Police officers have been sued in many cases when they injured or killed people without proper justification. Some of these lawsuits have resulted in cities and counties paying millions of dollars to people who were injured when police used guns or nightsticks improperly or in an inappropriate situation. To avoid future lawsuits, departments have given greater attention to the training of officers. They have also sought nonlethal weapons that could be used to incapacitate or control people without causing serious injuries or deaths. Traditional **less-lethal weapons**, such as nightsticks and pepper spray, can be used only when officers are in close contact with suspects, and they are not suitable for all situations that officers face.

Police officers need to have the ability to incapacitate agitated people who are threatening to harm themselves or others. This need arises when they confront someone suspected of committing a serious crime as well as when they are attempting to control a crowd causing civil disorder. They also seek to enhance their ability to stop criminal suspects from fleeing. A variety of less-lethal weapons have been developed to accomplish these goals. Police use some of them widely, while others are still undergoing testing and refinement.

Projectile weapons shoot objects at people whom the police wish to subdue. Some projectiles, such as rubber bullets, can travel a long distance. Others are employed only when suspects are within a few yards of the officers. Rubber bullets have been used for many years. Although they are generally nonlethal, they can cause serious injuries or death if they hit someone in the eye or elsewhere in the head. Many departments have turned to the use of beanbags, small canvas bags containing tiny lead beads, fired from a shotgun (C. Spencer, 2000). They are intended to stun people on impact without causing lasting injury. Several police departments in the Los Angeles area, however, have abandoned the use of beanbags because of concerns about injuries and a few deaths caused by these projectiles as well as dissatisfaction with their accuracy when fired at a target (Leonard, 2002).

Other departments have begun to use air guns that shoot PepperBalls, small plastic pellets filled with a peppery powder that causes coughing and sneezing on release after the suspect is stunned by the impact of the pellet. This weapon drew increased scrutiny after an Emerson College student died when she was hit in the eye by such a pellet as police officers attempted to disperse a crowd of revelers who were celebrating a Boston Red Sox victory (CNN, 2004a). Officers can also fill the pellets with green dye in order to mark and later arrest individuals in an out-of-control crowd (Randolph, 2001). Other weapons under development include one that shoots nets that wrap around individual suspects and another that sprays a fountain of foam that envelops the suspect in layers of paralyzing ooze. Law enforcement agencies may also eventually have versions of new weapons being developed for the military, such as devices that send out incapacitating blasts of heat or blinding flash explosions

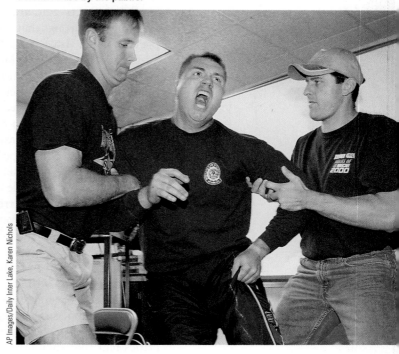

Kalispell, Montana, Police Officer Mike Whitcher reacts as he receives a jolt from a Taser. The Taser fires two wire filaments that send an incapacitating jolt into the body. Whitcher had to endure the jolt for a second or two in order to become certified in the use of the weapon. Should such incapacitating weapons also be available for ownership and defensive use by the public?

AP Images/Daily Inter Lake, Karen Nichols

■ **less-lethal weapons** Weapons such as pepper spray and air-fired beanbags or nets that are meant to incapacitate a suspect without inflicting serious injuries.

(Hambling, 2005). For example, a new military weapon called "Silent Guardian" shoots a focused beam of radiation that is tuned precisely to stimulate human pain nerves. It inflicts unbearable, incapacitating pain but, according to the inventors, does not cause injuries (Hanlon, 2007). A law enforcement version, if it worked as intended, could be an alternative to using lethal firearms in some situations.

For suspects who are close at hand, many police departments use the Taser, a weapon with prongs that sends an incapacitating electric jolt of 50,000 volts into people on contact (Ith, 2001). More than 12,000 law enforcement agencies in the United States use these devices. However, the human rights organization Amnesty International has documented more than 300 cases since 2001 in which people died after police used a Taser on them. The manufacturer of Tasers as well as some researchers dispute whether the device actually caused the deaths. Issues have also arisen about whether officers are too quick to use Tasers when they could use persuasion or other means to calm agitated or uncooperative people. The controversy reached a high point when Miami police officers used a Taser on a six-year-old child who was threatening to harm himself (CNN, 2004b). A study by Amnesty International found that more than 330 people died in the United States between 2001 and 2008 after being shocked by Tasers (Ferretti and Feighan, 2009). Nearly all of them were unarmed. Some of those who received shocks for failing to obey police commands reportedly suffered from mental or physical disabilities that impeded their ability to cooperate. Thus, debates about Tasers and other electroshock devices will likely persist in the future, as when two unarmed teenagers in Michigan died after being tasered in separate incidents within a one-month period in 2009 (Ferretti and Feighan, 2009). A related controversy expanded in 2008 when lawsuits by Taser International, the device's manufacturer, succeeded in persuading a judge to throw out a county medical examiner's conclusion that the device had caused the death of a jail inmate. Some critics fear that such lawsuits may have a chilling effect on doctors and deter them from reporting findings about any links between the Taser and injuries or deaths experienced by those who receive electrical shocks from the device (Anglen, 2008).

The development of less-lethal weapons has undoubtedly saved officers from firing bullets in many situations in which they previously would have felt required to shoot threatening suspects. However, as with all technologies, these weapons do not magically solve the problem of incapacitating suspects safely. Mechanical problems or misuse by the officer may make the new weapons ineffectual. In addition, officers may act too quickly in firing a less-lethal weapon during inappropriate situations. In such circumstances, needless minor injuries may be inflicted, or the targeted person may become more enraged and thus more threatening to the officers who later must transport the person to jail. Moreover, an officer can carry only so many weapons in his or her arms. The existence of less-lethal weapons will not ensure that such weapons are actually handy when officers must make difficult, on-the-spot decisions about how to handle a threatening situation.

Technology in Courts and Corrections

Much of the investment in new technology has been directed toward surveillance equipment and investigation techniques, including DNA analysis, that will assist law enforcement officers in identifying and convicting criminal offenders. Although fewer

CHECKPOINT

ANSWER

⑩ *What kinds of new weaponry have police employed?*

⑩ Less-lethal weapons including beanbag projectiles, Tasers, and PepperBall projectiles.

resources have been directed toward technology in other segments of the criminal justice system, courts and corrections both face new issues and opportunities stemming from the use of technology.

■ Courts

Many local courthouses struggle to keep up with the processing of cases and the attendant consequences of case backlogs. One of the central issues for many busy courthouses is simply the matter of having case files up-to-date and readily available for judges, prosecutors, and defense attorneys. The volume of files in many courthouses can create storage and accessibility problems. There are only so many rooms and filing cabinets available for storing files in any building. Thus, older files may be moved to remote locations where they are not easily accessible and must be retrieved if a case is reexamined on appeal or through later motions concerning the discovery of new evidence and other matters.

Technology provides a mechanism for reducing the problems of "too much paper" in courthouse files. Many courts have moved toward **electronic file management** systems in which records are digitized and made available as computer files. Such systems typically also use electronic filing systems in which attorneys file motions and other documents via email rather than as traditional paper documents.

One example of a court moving toward a reduction in paper used for case processing is the state circuit court in Eaton County, Michigan. The prosecutors carry into the courtroom laptops that can wirelessly access police reports, 911 calls, court orders, and crime scene photos. As noted by the county prosecutor, "We go to court with much more information than a prosecutor carrying a stack of files" (Grasha, 2009a). Gradually, other courts throughout the country are purchasing equipment and software to enable efficient access to information and to reduce the costs of producing and storing paper documents.

Computers can also help increase efficiency in judges' calculation of possible sentencing options. The development of sentencing guidelines has reduced judges' discretion for determining appropriate sentences. Instead, judges add up points, based on the offense and the prior record, to determine the sentence range mandated by the legislature. Private computer companies have developed software that will do sentencing calculations quickly for judges and for the probation officers who write presentence reports. Thus, with the push of a few keys, the computer produces the offender's sentence (P. Egan, 1999).

Advocates of sentencing software believe it will help speed up court processes. In addition, it may be useful during plea negotiations for exploring various sentencing options by quickly producing calculations based on different combinations of charges that the prosecution and defense are considering as part of a guilty plea (P. Egan, 1999).

Does relying on computer calculations pose any risks? Most basically, if incorrect numbers are included in the calculations, an improper sentence will be produced. For defendants with complex records, such as numerous arrests and probation violations, the person inputting the data could easily miscount arrests and reported probation violations in the score, even though the sentence is supposed to be based on the number of actual criminal convictions. More importantly, does the software program diminish the image of justice, giving the impression that sentencing occurs by machine? State judges are supposed to represent the community, delivering messages about justice on the community's behalf as they make rulings.

The presentation of evidence in court is changing through the introduction of new technology. Previously, lawyers presenting documents and objects as evidence often needed to carry them in front of jurors or have jurors pass them through the jury box. This meant that jurors often got only a fleeting glimpse of specific pieces of evidence. Now, many courthouses are developing electronic courtrooms, using presentation technologies that have long been used in business meetings. These mechanisms include projection screens or multiple monitors that permit jurors to

■ **electronic file management**
Computerization of court records, done to reduce reliance on paper documents and make documents easily accessible to the judge and attorneys via computer.

Computers, projection screens, and other technologies permit attorneys to present evidence more effectively in the courtroom. Do these high-tech presentations necessarily advance the search for truth?

Don Hogan Charles/The New York Times/Redux

study documents and photographs simultaneously. Websites of U.S. district courts often list the equipment available in each courtroom and instruct attorneys on how to use the equipment. For example, a partial list of equipment presented on one district court's website includes the following:

- *Evidence presentation cart,* containing
  Evidence camera
  Annotation monitor
  Microphone
  VCR
  Auxiliary connections
- *Counsel table,* containing
  PC connection
  Internet access
  Realtime court reporting connection
- *Jury box/plasma screen.* A 50-inch retractable plasma screen over the jury box can be lowered when needed.
- *Gallery.* Two monitors are located on the sides of the gallery to allow spectators to see evidence being presented during a court proceeding.
- *Side camera.* A side camera is located near the ceiling above the jury box. It is used to display demonstrative exhibits which may be placed on an tripod easel in front of the jury box or by the witness stand. Use of the side camera allows the judge, the witness, the jury, all counsel and those seated in the gallery to view the exhibit with ease.
- *Hearing assistance system.* Wireless headphones are available for use by the hearing impaired, or for language interpretation.
- *Color video printer.* The printer is available should counsel wish to print a displayed image for admission into evidence.

Such technologies are obviously useful in communicating more effectively to everyone in the courtroom. There are risks, however, that some uses of technology may distort rather than clarify an accurate understanding of the evidence. For example, the use of computer simulations raises issues about the accurate presentation of evidence.

Attorneys have traditionally attempted to use their words to "paint a picture" for the jurors. In a criminal case, the prosecutor and defense each tries to present its own version of a chain of events or the circumstances under which a crime allegedly occurred. It is entirely possible that, after hearing the same presentations, individual jurors will leave the courtroom with very different perceptions about what happened at the crime scene (McCormick, 2000). Contemporary attorneys have attempted to use computer technology to advance an image of their version of events. Much like realistic video games, similar realism has now been developed in computer-generated re-creations of crime scenes (McCormick, 2000). The jury may see, for example, a computer-generated film of a person being struck from behind or falling in a manner consistent with the victim's injuries. Yet, this film will be prepared in accordance with a particular version of events, the prosecutor's or the defendant's. There are risks that the realism of the re-created events on the screen will stick in the minds of jurors, even if the presentation is not an objective interpretation of the facts in the case.

Observers have serious concerns about the use of such computer programs in trials. Such re-creations are available only to those who can afford them. Thus, poor defendants have little hope of using this technology to present their side of the story (McCormick, 2000). In addition, computer scenes could be developed or manipulated in ways that are not consistent with the available evidence. Jurors may believe the realistic scenes that they watch on the screen despite contrary evidence that they hear from witness testimony (McCormick, 2000). Judges and attorneys must be wary about the use of such technologies if they may distort perceptions rather than contribute to accurate fact-finding.

Problems also arise through jurors' use of technology. Typically, a judge will tell jurors that they cannot investigate the facts of a case on their own. They are sometimes instructed not to read any articles in a newspaper about a case being presented before them. The widespread use of the Internet, however, makes seeking information about a case not only easy, but also quite tempting for some jurors. While a judge may hear if a juror attempted to visit a crime scene and thereby exclude the juror from the trial for misconduct, it is much more difficult to know whether jurors have sought information about a case through an Internet search. The use of such devices as iPhones and BlackBerrys has even enabled disobedient jurors to do their own research on a case during a lunch break in the middle of the attorneys' arguments. In one case in Florida, 8 out of 12 jurors eventually admitted that they had done their own Internet research on the case, including finding information that was excluded from presentation at trial through the rules of evidence. Thus, the judge had to declare a mistrial, and eight weeks of work by prosecutors and defense attorneys went to waste and the long, complex trial had to begin again after the selection of a new jury (Schwartz, 2009). See "A Question of Ethics" to consider the dilemmas that can be created when jurors violate court rules.

Problems have also arisen as jurors use blogs and Twitter to post announcements about the progress of a case or about jury deliberations. There is evidence that some jurors even send out messages by cell phone during breaks in the trial (Schwartz, 2009). Thus, judges have become more keenly aware of the need to bar jurors from bringing cell phones to court as well as the need to give thorough and stern warnings about

Many prosecutors and judges worry that the "CSI effect" may help guilty defendants go free if there is no DNA or other scientific evidence to use against them. Critics claim that the "CSI effect" is a myth that is perpetuated by prosecutors and the media. What evidence would you want to see in order to conclude whether or not the "CSI effect" exists?

Michael Desmond/© Warner Bros. Television / courtesy Everett Collection

the rule against jurors conducting their own investigations. Under the adversary system, evidence is presented by the opposing attorneys who have been trained to respect the rules of evidence. Independent examinations of evidence by jurors acting as amateur detectives can enhance risks of inaccurate conclusions about facts.

■ **"CSI effect"** A widely discussed but unproved belief that television dramas revolving around forensic science raise jurors' expectations about the use of scientific evidence in criminal cases and thereby reduce the likelihood of "guilty" verdicts in trials that rely solely on witness testimony and other forms of nonscientific evidence.

Another potential impact of technology on jury trials is the so-called **"CSI effect"** that makes jurors unwilling to render "guilty" verdicts unless there is scientific evidence to link the defendant to the crime. Americans are fascinated by dramatized television programs that show the use of science for solving crimes and medical mysteries. According to a 2009 Harris Poll, the television show *CSI: Crime Scene Investigations* set in Las Vegas is Americans' all-time, favorite television series (Harris Poll, 2009). The show was so popular that the CBS network created two *CSI* spin-off shows, set in Miami and New York, respectively. The fourth most popular show is *NCIS*, a parallel drama about the U.S. Navy's Criminal Investigative Service, which also portrays the use of forensic science. The third most popular program, *House*, shows the use of science to solve medical mysteries (Harris Poll, 2009). Because these popular programs portray specialists using science to make definitive conclusions, many judges and prosecutors believe jurors now erroneously think that there should be DNA evidence, soil sample testing, and other scientific evidence in every criminal case (Toobin, 2007). In fact, the evidence in many cases consists of witness testimony, circumstantial evidence, and objects with no fingerprints or DNA on them. Moreover, the television programs show fictional situations in which experts instantly make accurate and definitive conclusions about a "match" between hair samples, fiber samples, handwriting samples, or other materials for which real forensic scientists have grave doubts about anyone's ability to make definitive identifications of suspects.

Students of criminal justice should regard claims about the "CSI effect" with caution. The claims emerge from individual prosecutors' and judges' feelings of surprise or disappointment with the decisions and questions of juries in particular cases. Moreover, because news stories have presented the "CSI effect" as if it were a real phenomenon, prosecutors and judges may merely assume that it has impact when, in fact, it does not even exist.

In reality, the existence of any actual "CSI effect" remains the subject of debate (S. Stephens, 2007). Actual research on the "CSI effect" calls its existence into question (Podlas, 2006). Whether or not such an effect actually makes jurors less likely to convict defendants, the debate about the "CSI effect" illustrates the possibility that decision making within the criminal justice system can be affected by popular perceptions and assumptions about the role of technology and science in the investigation of criminal cases.

CHECKPOINT

ANSWERS

11 How is technology employed in courthouses?

11 Electronic file management for records and presentation technology in courtrooms for displaying evidence.

12 How can technology disrupt jury trials?

12 Jurors using the Internet to investigate cases or use blogs and Twitter to reveal information about jury deliberations; risks of the so-called "CSI effect."

■ Corrections

Many of the technologies previously discussed for policing and courts also have applications in corrections. Computerized record-keeping and statewide databases can reduce the burden of maintaining, storing, and transporting paper files on each prisoner. Instead, officials throughout the state can access records instantly via computer. In fact, many states have set up online records-retrieval systems that are accessible to the public. Often called OTIS (Offender Tracking Information Systems), these accessible databases permit crime victims to keep track of when specific offenders gain release on parole. They can also help employers to do background checks on job applicants. Separate public-access information systems often provide specific information on the residences of convicted sex offenders. Typically, members of the public can use the state correctional departments' website to discover the identities and home addresses of sex offenders within a specific zip code. These databases are intended to warn people about the presence of a specific category of ex-convicts in their neighborhoods.

Public access to information about ex-offenders can cause serious problems. In Maine, Washington, and New Hampshire, individuals looked up the names and address of released sex offenders on a state database, then hunted them down and shot them. As we saw in Chapter 13, one of the murder victims in Maine was on the sex offender registry for the "sex crime" of misdemeanor sexual abuse because, as a 19-year-old youth, he had consensual sex with his girlfriend who was two weeks shy of making their sexual contact legal by reaching her sixteenth birthday (Ellement and Smalley, 2006). These crimes led to debates about which offenders should actually be listed in databases and whether such databases should be open to any member of the public.

In correctional institutions, technology enhances safety and security through the use of such developments as electronically controlled cell doors and locks, motion sensors, surveillance cameras, and small radios attached to the shirts of correctional officers. Note that surveillance cameras are not always popular with correctional officers, because cameras also reveal whether officers are doing their jobs conscientiously and properly.

Because security is the top priority for correctional institutions, most technology resources are devoted to this goal rather on prisoners' vocational training and rehabilitation. In a fast-changing world, prisoners who face the challenges of reentry are often like Rip Van Winkle, the character in the Washington Irving short story who awakens after sleeping for 20 years and discovers many changes in the world. For a contemporary prisoner emerging from prison after serving a long sentence, basic facts of modern life, such as email and cell phones, may be completely unknown or baffling. Released prisoners may also lack basic skills for modern employment, such as the use of computers, word processing, and spreadsheet programs. Although new technologies change modern life, limited resources cause correctional officials to focus on improvements in security rather than on a fuller range of goals serving prisoners.

As in policing, technological developments increase the variety of less-lethal weapons that are available for correctional officers to use in subduing and controlling offenders who pose a threat to institutional safety or who attempt to escape. For example, the transportation of prisoners presents a daily challenge for officials at courts, jails, and prisons. People in custody must be moved from jails and prisons to courts for hearings. They must be transferred from jails to prisons and moved between different prisons when they begin to serve their sentences. New technologies have been developed to prevent prisoners from attempting to escape or otherwise misbehaving while being transported. The most controversial device is the remote-controlled stun belt that prisoners may be required to wear while being transported. The deputy or bailiff in control of the belt can deliver an excruciating 8-second, 50,000-volt jolt of electricity to prisoners. Americans became aware of the belts when a California prisoner who was zapped in a courtroom at the order of a judge filed a $50 million lawsuit. The prisoner had not attempted to escape or threaten anyone; he had merely talked too much when the judge had told him to be silent (Canto, 1998). The international human rights organization Amnesty International mounted a campaign to have the devices banned as torture (Amnesty International, 1999). Although the New York Corrections Department canceled an order for the devices, 25 state correctional departments and 100 county jails reportedly still use them.

Such devices may reduce the number of officers required to escort a prisoner, and they deter prisoners from misbehaving. However, such a jolt of electricity may kill some people if their heart rhythm is susceptible to disruption or if they hit their heads when they fall during the electric shock. There are also issues about whether officers will limit their use to appropriate circumstances.

As discussed in Chapter 11, one particularly important and expanding use of technology is the electronic monitoring of offenders within the community. Offenders in home confinement or "on tether" in the community wear various electronic devices that help monitor whether they obey curfews, remain at home, or otherwise fulfill restrictions about where they are permitted to be. Increasingly, local jails save money by charging fees to nonviolent offenders who choose to pay for electronic monitoring and home confinement rather than imposing expenses on the county for food and supervision by serving their misdemeanor sentences in jail (Grasha, 2009b). There is also expanded use of monitors with GPS capability to track the movements of criminal stalkers and perpetrators of domestic violence. Thus, law enforcement officials can be warned if individuals under restraining orders attempt to approach the homes of their victims (Green, 2009).

CHECKPOINT

ANSWER

⓭ *What technology is used in community corrections?*

⓭ Electronic monitoring for home confinement and community release; GPS monitors for stalkers and perpetrators of domestic violence.

Current Questions and Challenges for the Future

As we have just seen, technological changes have affected nearly every agency and process within the criminal justice system. Most of this chapter's discussion has focused on new technological devices designed to assist officials with specific tasks. James Byrne (2008) classifies these devices as "hard technology" and contrasts them with the development of "soft technology," such as computer software for crime mapping and sentencing calculations. Both categories of technology are important for criminal justice. In some respects, the soft technology may present especially significant possibilities for affecting the performance of criminal justice officials, as computer experts invent new ways to gather and evaluate information that can be used for training, classification of offenders, assessing risk, and other important purposes. Table 14.4 shows examples of various hard and soft technological innovations that have affected each institutional segment of the criminal justice system.

There is no doubt that the desire for efficiency and effectiveness will lead to continued efforts to create new technologies and refine existing technologies to assist the police in their tasks. One can easily envision increased access to information through computers, better surveillance cameras and body scanners, and expanded use of GPS devices. In addition, there will be continued development and experimentation with less-lethal weapons, some of which are likely to borrow from those being developed by the U.S. military, including devices that rely on heat or light or sound to incapacitate threatening individuals.

In light of financial problems affecting state and local correctional budgets, there will inevitably be efforts to refine and expand the use of surveillance and monitoring technology to reduce the costs associated with confining lesser offenders. For example, the future will likely see the expanded use of ignition interlock systems for convicted drunken drivers. In this system, they blow into a tube set up in their car, and the engine starts only if they have not consumed alcohol. This can help prevent drunken driving without relying so heavily on incarceration for first offenders. New and expanded use of surveillance and control mechanisms may also improve officials' ability to monitor probationers, parolees, and other offenders under correctional supervision in the community.

TABLE 14.4	The Application of Hard and Soft Technology to Crime Prevention and Control

	Hard Technology	Soft Technology
Crime prevention	• CCTV • Street lighting • Citizen protection devices (e.g., Mace, Tasers) • Metal detectors • Ignition interlock systems (drunk drivers)	• Threat assessment instruments • Risk assessment instruments • Bullying ID protocol • Sex offender registration • Risk assessment prior to involuntary civil commitment • Profiling
Police	• Improved police protection devices (helmets, vests, cars, buildings) • Improved/new weapons • Less-than-lethal force (mobile/riot control) • Computers in squad cars • Hands-free patrol car control (Project 54) • Offender and citizen IDs via biometrics/fingerprints • Gunshot location devices	• Crime mapping (hot spots) • Crime analysis (e.g., COMPSTAT) • Criminal history data systems enhancement • Info sharing within CJS and private sector • New technologies to monitor communications (phone, mail, Internet) to/from targeted individuals • Amber alerts
Court	• The high-tech courtroom (computers, video, cameras, design features of buildings) • Weapon detection devices • Video conferencing • Electronic court documents • Drug testing at pretrial stage	• Case flow management systems • Radio frequency identification technology • Data warehousing • Automation of court records • Problem-oriented courts
Institutional corrections	• Contraband detection devices • Duress alarm systems • Language translation devices • Remote monitoring • Perimeter screening • Less-than-lethal force in prison • Prison design (supermax) • Expanded use of segregation units	• Use of simulations as training tools (mock prison riots) • Facial recognition software • New inmate classification systems (external/internal) • Within-prison crime analysis (hot spots; high-rate offenders) • Information sharing with police, community, victims, and community-based corrections (reentry)
Community corrections	• GPS for offender monitoring and location restriction enforcement • New devices (breathalyzers, instant drug tests, language translators, plethysmographs) • Polygraph tests (improved) • Laptops/GPS for line staff • Reporting kiosks	• New classification devices for sex, drugs, and MI offenders • New workload software • New computer monitoring programs for sex offenders • Information sharing with community police, treatment providers (for active offender supervision and for absconder location)

Source: James M. Byrne, "The Best Laid Plans: An Assessment of the Varied Consequences of New Technologies for Crime and Social Control," *Federal Probation* 72 (no. 3, 2008): 11.

As noted, technological developments produce risks, questions, and consequences beyond increased efficiency in carrying out tasks. Technological devices are operated by human beings who can make errors that affect the lives of others. What happens when a forensic scientist makes an error in conducting a test? What happens when incorrect information about an individual is entered into a database? With a perception that new weapons will not cause serious injury or death, are police officers more inclined to use

Tasers, PepperBalls, and other less-lethal weapons in situations that might otherwise have been resolved through determined use of verbal warnings and other communications? These are important questions that arise with increasing frequency as we analyze events in which technology produced unintended and undesirable results.

Equally important are concerns about the impact of technology on the civil rights and liberties of individual Americans. In the post-9/11 era, there are already indications that some government officials will react to perceived threats by making use of available technology without necessarily planning for the protection of civil liberties or adherence to existing law. The administration of President George W. Bush, for example, secretly intercepted Americans' phone calls and emails without the court authorizations required under federal law (Sanger and Lichtblau, 2006). When Congress later granted limited authority to undertake such electronic surveillance of communications, the National Security Agency violated the law by intercepting calls that did not fall within the scope of the law (Lichtblau and Risen, 2009). As with other technologies, the means available could be misused in ways that violate Fourth Amendment restrictions on unreasonable searches and other rights under the Constitution.

Another large question looms. Have new technologies been effective in preventing crime and catching criminals? We know that certain technologies, such as DNA testing, have been highly effective in identifying individuals whose biological matter, such as blood or tissue, is found at a crime scene or on a weapon. It is less clear, however, that all of the surveillance, communications, and search technologies have produced entirely desirable benefits. For example, in pointing to declining clearance rates for homicide crimes, James Byrne concludes, "I would be hard pressed to offer an assessment of the positive effect of new technological innovations during this period given these data on police performance" (2008:14). The underlying point is that we know many new technologies expand the scope of social control by government through collecting information, watching and searching the citizenry, and providing new tools for police to use in coercing compliant behavior (as in Tasers). Are the costs of this social control justified? Can we use the benefits of technology without reducing the extent of Americans' freedom and privacy? These are questions that future criminal justice officials and policy makers must continually reexamine. They can do this through the systematic study of the performance of police, courts, and corrections as well as by evaluating the consequences for Americans' civil liberties.

A QUESTION OF ETHICS: WRITING ASSIGNMENT

Alicia Jones, a criminal defense attorney, walked down a back hallway of the courthouse while returning from a lunch break. She was about to deliver her closing arguments in the two-week trial of an alleged murderer. She felt very good about her representation of the client, because she had been able to cast doubt on the truthfulness of the prosecution's key witness, her client's cell mate in jail, as well as challenge the clarity of a security camera photo that had a grainy image of someone running from the scene of the crime. As she rounded a corner, she approached from behind a man who was standing next to a drinking fountain. She recognized him as a member of the jury and she assumed that he was about to return to the jury room after using the restroom or getting a drink. When she passed him, she caught a few words of a whispered conversation as he spoke into his hands-free phone earpiece.

"This is going to be a quick verdict. You'll probably see me on TV. I think the prosecutor is going to be really surprised."

She pretended not to listen as she walked briskly past the juror and through the doors into the courthouse. As she realized what had just happened, she felt flushed with anger. The juror was violating a clear rule by talking to someone about the case during the trial. She felt on the verge of winning a big case, but if she told the judge what she just heard, there was a risk that a mistrial would be declared and the trial would have to be held all over again—but with a different jury *and* with the prosecutor now better positioned to counteract her strategic arguments.

WRITING ASSIGNMENT

Ms. Jones is professionally obligated to fight for her client, but she is also an officer of the court who must protect court procedures. If the juror is giving a little bit of information to some unknown person at the end of the trial, rather than gathering outside information, does that really hurt anything? Yet, if she reports what she heard, it will likely hurt her client by forcing a long delay prior to a new trial in front of a better-prepared prosecutor. Write a short essay advising Ms. Jones about what to do. Is there any way to handle the situation without telling the judge?

Summary

Understand how adaptation and belief in science can affect the use of technology

▷ New technology can be employed by criminals as well as by criminal justice officials.

▷ Criminal justice officials and the public must be wary of automatically assuming that new scientific developments will achieve their intended goals or will produce only desirable consequences.

Recognize the many aspects of cyber crime and counterfeiting

▷ Cyber crime includes identity theft, Internet child pornography, hackers' theft of trade secrets, and destruction of computer networks.

▷ Counterfeiting extends beyond currency and consumer goods to include dangerous and worthless fake prescription drugs.

Analyze the role of communications, computers, and databases in policing

▷ Calls for service to police have expanded from 911 numbers to 311 and 211 for nonemergency purposes.

▷ Computers in patrol cars have expanded police officers' access to information.

▷ Police also use computers in crime mapping, gunshot detection systems, and investigation of cyber crimes.

▷ Databases permit the collection and matching of information concerning fingerprints, DNA, tattoos, criminal records, and other useful data.

Describe developments and problems in DNA testing and new weapons technologies

▷ DNA testing permits scientists to identify the source of biological material with a high degree of certainty.

▷ Some crime labs have been careless and unethical in testifying about DNA results, and some prosecutors have opposed DNA testing that might benefit criminal defendants.

▷ New less-lethal weapons such as Tasers, PepperBalls, and other projectiles are increasingly used by police.

▷ Less-lethal weapons have been involved in incidents that led to the deaths of individuals against whom the police used these weapons.

Understand the use of technology in courts and corrections

▷ Courts use technology in computerized record-keeping and presentation of evidence.

▷ Jurors' perceptions about forensic science and use of technology during trials may cause problems.

▷ Correctional officials use technology for security purposes and for monitoring offenders in the community.

Recognize the continuing questions about the effects of technology on civil liberties

▷ The expanded use of technology by government raises questions about the protection of Americans' rights.

▷ There are questions about the extent to which many new technologies advance criminal justice goals and do not merely expand mechanisms for societal surveillance and control.

Questions for Review

1. How have criminals adapted to changes in technology?
2. How are computers used to investigate crimes?
3. What questions and problems arise from the development of new weapons for police?
4. What undesirable effects can science and technology have on jury trials?
5. How can GPS devices assist correctional officials?
6. How can the use of technology clash with Americans' expectations about rights, liberty, and privacy?

Key Terms and Cases

"CSI effect" (p. 426)
DNA analysis (p. 407)
electronic file management (p. 423)
Geographic Information System (GIS) (p. 410)
identity theft (p. 402)

latent fingerprints (p. 412)
less-lethal weapons (p. 421)
Kyllo v. United States (2001) (p. 420)

Juvenile Justice

LEARNING OBJECTIVES

▶ **Recognize the extent of youth crime in the United States**

▶ **Understand how the juvenile justice system developed and the assumptions on which it was based**

▶ **Identify what determines the jurisdiction of the juvenile justice system**

▶ **Understand how the juvenile justice system operates**

▶ **Analyze some of the issues facing the American system of juvenile justice**

LONELY, depressed, and afraid, Shaquanda Cotton found herself locked up in the Ron Jackson State Juvenile Correctional Complex in Brownwood, Texas. Confined in close quarters with teenagers who were violent, repeat offenders, she faced the prospect of being incarcerated for seven years. The sentence that she faced was more than twice as long as the average prison sentence served by adult felons who are convicted of aggravated assault. Indeed, her sentence was just a few months shorter than the average served by adults convicted of rape (Durose and Langan, 2004). Yet, her crime consisted of merely shoving a hall monitor at her high school. The despair that she felt eventually led to an unsuccessful suicide attempt.

As a high school freshman in Paris, Texas, 14-year-old Shaquanda arrived at her school 20 minutes early on the morning of September 30, 2005. After being told by a school aide that it was too early to enter the school, she pushed the aide aside, and the aide pushed Shaquanda back. During the altercation, both Shaquanda and the school aide received minor injuries (Richards, 2006).

Shaquanda was charged with felony assault on a public servant. She was offered a lesser sentence by the prosecution in exchange for a plea of guilty, but she maintained that she was innocent of any crime. After a trial in which the jury took a mere ten minutes to deliberate and reach a verdict, Shaquanda was found guilty of felony assault. At the urging of the prosecutor, Lamar County Judge Chuck Superville sentenced her to an indeterminate term of incarceration of no more than seven years, at which time she would be 21 years old and therefore no longer under the jurisdiction of the Texas Youth Commission.

When the *Chicago Tribune* ran a story about her long sentence, it aroused a nationwide storm of controversy about the harshness of her punishment. One source of controversy was the perception that racial discrimination may have affected Shaquanda's case. She was an African American teenager sentenced to seven years of incarceration for pushing a school aide. Yet, the same judge who imposed that sentence had just weeks earlier sentenced a 14-year-old white girl to probation for the more serious felony of arson when she burned down her family's house. As more newspapers and websites focused on the story, the supervisor of the Texas youth prison system ordered Shaquanda's release after only one year of imprisonment (Witt, 2007).

If Shaquanda had not received widespread media attention, she would likely still be locked up. Indeed, very few juvenile justice cases receive attention from the news media and the public, so there are likely other "Shaquandas" out there facing years of confinement for acts that would not be treated so seriously if committed by adults. At the same time, there are many other juveniles like the girl sentenced to probation for arson who would have received much harsher sentences if they had been adults. What do these inconsistent outcomes indicate about the nature of the juvenile justice system? In this chapter, we examine this important question.

Although the juvenile justice system is separate from the adult criminal justice system, the key values of freedom, fairness, and justice undergird both. The formal processes of each differ mainly in emphasis, not in values. Although different, the systems are interrelated. One cannot separate the activities and concerns of policing, courts, and corrections from the problems of youth. With juveniles committing a significant portion of criminal offenses, officials in the adult system must pay serious attention to the juvenile system as well.

Youth Crime in the United States

In Denver, a child visiting the zoo was hit by a bullet fired by one teenager at another. Sixteen-year-old Jeff Weise shot ten people in Red Lake, Minnesota. A British tourist was killed while at a rest stop; a 13-year-old boy was one of the suspects. In 2009, an 11-year-old boy in Pennsylvania was accused of shooting his father's pregnant fiancée in the head (E. Hays, 2009). Such dramatic criminal acts make headlines. Are these only isolated incidents, or is the United States facing a major increase in youth crime?

The juvenile crime incidents just described are rare. In a nation with 74 million people under age 18, about 1.6 million arrests of juveniles occur each year, 73,000 of which are for violent crimes. After rising from 1988 through 1994, the juvenile violent crime rate has dropped by half since 1994 to the lowest levels since 1985 (FBI, 2008c: Table 41). Yet, when American high school seniors are asked to identify the two or three most serious problems they worry about, they cite crime and drugs, as shown in "What Americans Think."

Youth crimes range from UCR Index Crimes (for example murder, rape, robbery, assault) to "youthful crimes" such as curfew violations, loitering, and being a runaway (see Figure 15.1). About 1 in 50 people in the under-18 cohort is taken into police custody each year, and about 1.5 million are processed by juvenile courts (FBI, 2006a). Most juvenile crimes are committed by young men; only 29 percent of arrestees under 18 years of age are female (FBI, 2008c). Some researchers estimate that one boy in three will be arrested by the police at some point before his 18th birthday.

Criminologists have tried to explain the rise of the "epidemic" of violent youth crime that erupted in the mid-1980s, reaching its peak in 1993. Among the explanations, two seem the most promising. One explanation uses a "cohort" approach, arguing that during the 1980s the increase in violence was due to an increase in the prevalence of exceptionally violent individuals—so-called "super predators." Critics of this approach, however, say that the birth cohort that peaked during the early 1990s was not at all exceptional with respect to involvement in violence in their younger years (Cook and Laub, 2002: 2).

FIGURE 15.1
Percentage of arrests of people under 18 years old (rounded)
Juveniles are arrested for a wide range of offenses. For some offenses—such as arson, vandalism, motor vehicle theft, and burglary—juveniles account for a larger proportion of arrests than the percentage of juveniles in the general population would suggest.

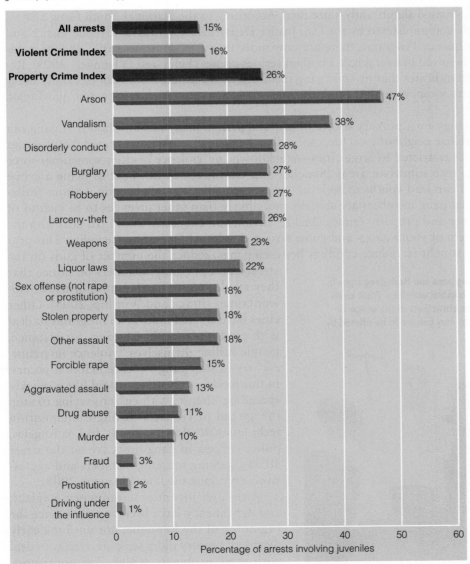

Source: FBI, *Uniform Crime Reports* (Washington, DC: U.S. Government Printing Office, 2008), Table 41.

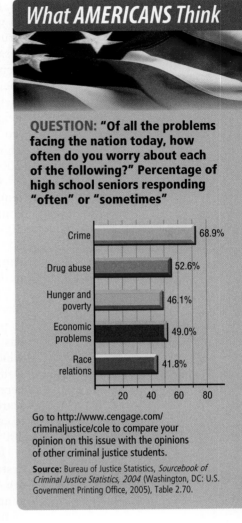

What AMERICANS Think

QUESTION: "Of all the problems facing the nation today, how often do you worry about each of the following?" Percentage of high school seniors responding "often" or "sometimes"

Crime 68.9%
Drug abuse 52.6%
Hunger and poverty 46.1%
Economic problems 49.0%
Race relations 41.8%

Go to http://www.cengage.com/criminaljustice/cole to compare your opinion on this issue with the opinions of other criminal justice students.

Source: Bureau of Justice Statistics, *Sourcebook of Criminal Justice Statistics, 2004* (Washington, DC: U.S. Government Printing Office, 2005), Table 2.70.

A second explanation focuses on environmental factors that influenced the rise in violent youth crime. Scholars holding this position point to the impact of the drug trade, especially crack cocaine and the related increase in gun use and possession by youths. Alfred Blumstein (1996) suggests that as more juveniles, particularly inner-city minority men, were recruited into the drug trade, they armed themselves with guns and used those firearms in battles over market turf. Other factors may have also played a role—violent crime by youth was most prevalent in neighborhoods with deteriorating social and economic conditions. These changes led to increases in family instability and reductions in shared social expectations about behavior, particularly in minority neighborhoods (Strom and MacDonald, 2007).

Certainly, drug use by juveniles has significantly affected the juvenile justice system. From 1985 to 2004, the number of drug offense cases processed by juvenile courts increased from about 75,000 cases to almost 200,000 cases per year (Stahl, 2008a). In addition, drug use cases have skyrocketed for white juveniles, increasing 341 percent from 1984 to 2004 (compared with a 32 percent increase for African American juveniles). This has resulted in higher caseloads handled by juvenile courts in the past 20 years.

Youth gangs are another factor explaining violent youth crime. Gangs such as the Black P Stone Nation, CRIPS (Common Revolution in Progress), and Bloods first came to police attention in the 1970s. Gang membership declined from 1996 to 2001 but has increased significantly since then. According to the National Youth Gang Survey, which is administered by the U.S. Justice Department's Office of Juvenile Justice and Delinquency Programs, there are now more than 27,000 gangs with 788,000 members involved in over a half a million serious crimes (Egley and O'Donnell, 2009). Research indicates that juvenile gang members who commit crimes are especially likely to carry weapons with them during their daily activities (Melde, Esbensen, and Taylor, 2009).

Gangs are a primary source of fear and peril in many neighborhoods. A gang can destabilize neighborhood life, especially when gang members are armed. Youth gangs are not restricted to large cities—crackdowns on violence in cities sometimes force gangs into suburban areas (Sanchez and Giordano, 2008). Fear of being a crime victim can lead youths to seek protection through gang membership without realizing that gang members are actually more likely than other juveniles to be victims of violence and property crimes (Melde, Taylor, and Esbensen, 2009). To deal with the problem of youth gangs and guns, Boston developed Operation Ceasefire. This program sought to reduce conflicts between gangs, reduce the number of guns on the streets, and put gang members on notice that they would receive harsh punishments for violent crimes (Braga and Winship, 2005). Other cities have created innovative programs to deal with gang violence. In Chicago, for instance, people calling themselves "violence interrupters" try to stop gang violence before it occurs. In this model, violence is treated like a quickly spreading disease, with citizens trying to stop the spread of violence through intervention techniques (Kotlowitz, 2008). In Los Angeles, police officers in gang units are on the street all day, looking for gang members and aggressively enforcing the law (Mozingo, 2008).

Although juvenile delinquency, neglect, and dependency have been concerns since the beginning of the Republic, not until the early twentieth century did a separate system to deal with these problems evolve. The contemporary juvenile justice system has gone through a

Youthful members of the Pico Norte 19th Street gang pose and flash gang signs in El Paso, Texas. Gangs can draw youths into serious criminal activities. What kinds of programs might lure young people away from the attractions of the image of toughness, solidarity, respect, and power that youths may believe to be offered by gang membership?

Hector Mata/AFP/Getty Images

CHECKPOINT

ANSWER
1 *What might explain the epidemic of violent crime committed by juveniles in the 1990s?*	**1** Large youth cohorts, gun use related to drug sales, and gangs.

major shift of emphasis as well. The rest of the chapter explores the history of juvenile justice, the process it follows today, and some of the problems associated with it.

The Development of Juvenile Justice

The system and philosophy of juvenile justice that began in the United States during the social reform period of the late nineteenth century was based on the idea that the state should act as a parent would in the interest of the child. This view remained unchallenged until the 1960s, when the Supreme Court ushered in the juvenile rights period. With the rise in juvenile crime in the 1980s, the juvenile justice system shifted again to one focusing on the problem of controlling youth crime. Today, people are again reexamining the philosophy and processes of the juvenile justice system.

The idea that children should be treated differently from adults originated in the common law and in the chancery courts of England. The common law had long prescribed that children under seven years of age were incapable of felonious intent and were therefore not criminally responsible. Children aged 7 to 14 could be held accountable only if it could be shown that they understood the consequences of their actions.

The English chancery courts, established during the Middle Ages, heard only civil cases, mainly concerning property. However, under the doctrine of *parens patriae*, which held the king to be the father of the realm, the chancery courts exercised protective jurisdiction over all children, particularly those involved in questions of dependency, neglect, and property. At this time, the criminal courts, not a separate juvenile court, dealt with juvenile offenders. In legitimizing the actions of the state on behalf of the child, however, the concept of *parens patriae* laid the groundwork for the development of juvenile justice.

■ *parens patriae* The state as parent; the state as guardian and protector of all citizens (such as juveniles) who cannot protect themselves.

Table 15.1 outlines the shifts in how the United States has dealt with the problems of youth. These shifts fall into six periods of American juvenile justice history. Each was characterized by changes in juvenile justice that reflected the social, intellectual, and political currents of the time. During the past two hundred years, population shifts from rural to urban areas, immigration, developments in the social sciences, political reform movements, and the continuing problem of youth crime have all influenced how Americans have treated juveniles

■ The Puritan Period (1646–1824)

The English procedures were maintained in the American colonies and continued into the nineteenth century. The earliest attempt by a colony to deal with problem children was passage of the Massachusetts Stubborn Child Law in 1646. With this law, the Puritans of the Massachusetts Bay Colony imposed the view that the child was evil, and they emphasized the need of the family to discipline and raise youths. Those who would not obey their parents were dealt with by the law.

TABLE 15.1	Juvenile Justice Developments in the United States		
Period	**Major Developments**	**Causes and Influences**	**Juvenile Justice System**
Puritan (1646–1824)	Massachusetts Stubborn Child Law (1646).	A Puritan view of child as evil B Economically marginal agrarian society	Law provides A Symbolic standard of maturity B Support for family as economic unit
Refuge (1824–1899)	Institutionalization of deviants; House of Refuge in New York established (1825) for delinquent and dependent children.	A Enlightenment B Immigration and industrialization	Child seen as helpless, in need of state intervention.
Juvenile Court (1899–1960)	Establishment of separate legal system for juveniles; Illinois Juvenile Court Act (1899).	A Reformism and rehabilitative ideology B Increased immigration, urbanization, large-scale industrialization	Juvenile court institutionalized legal irresponsibility of child.
Juvenile Rights (1960–1980)	Increased "legalization" of juvenile law; *Gault* decision (1967); Juvenile Justice and Delinquency Prevention Act (1974) calls for deinstitutionalization of status offenders.	A Criticism of juvenile justice system on humane grounds B Civil rights movement by disadvantaged groups	Movement to define and protect rights as well as to provide services to children.
Crime Control (1980–2005)	Concern for victims, punishment for serious offenders, transfer to adult court of serious offenders, protection of children from physical and sexual abuse.	A More-conservative public attitudes and policies B Focus on serious crimes by repeat offenders	System more formal, restrictive, punitive; increased percentage of police referrals to court; incarcerated youths stay longer periods.
"Kids Are Different" (2005–present)	Elimination of death penalty for juveniles, focus on rehabilitation, states increasing age of transfer to adult court.	A *Roper v. Simmons* (2005) B Scientific evidence on youth's biological, emotional, and psychological development	Recognition that juveniles are less culpable than adults.

Sources: Adapted from Barry Krisberg, Ira M. Schwartz, Paul Litsky, and James Austin, "The Watershed of Juvenile Justice Reform," *Crime and Delinquency* 32 (January 1986): 5–38; U.S. Department of Justice, *A Preliminary National Assessment of the Status Offender and the Juvenile Justice System* (Washington, DC: U.S. Government Printing Office, 1980), 29.

■ The Refuge Period (1824–1899)

As the population of American cities began to grow during the early 1800s, the problem of youth crime and neglect became a concern for reformers. Just as the Quakers of Philadelphia had been instrumental during the same period in reforming correctional practices, other groups supported changes concerning the education and protection of youths. These reformers focused their efforts primarily on the urban immigrant poor, seeking to have parents declared "unfit" if their children roamed the streets and were apparently "out of control." Not all such children were engaged in criminal acts, but the reformers believed that children whose parents did not discipline and train them to abide by the rules of society would end up in prison. The state would use its power to prevent delinquency. The solution was to create institutions where these children could learn good work and study habits, live in a disciplined and healthy environment, and develop "character."

The first of these institutions was the House of Refuge of New York, which opened in 1825. This half-prison, half-school housed destitute and orphaned children as well as those convicted of crime (Friedman, 1993:164). Similar facilities followed in Boston, Philadelphia, and Baltimore. Children were placed in these homes by court order usually because of neglect or vagrancy. They often stayed until they were old enough to be legally regarded as adults. The houses were run according to a strict program of work, study, and discipline.

Some states created "reform schools" to provide the discipline and education needed by wayward youth in a "homelike" atmosphere, usually in rural areas. The first, the Lyman School for Boys, opened in Westboro, Massachusetts, in 1848. A similar Massachusetts reform school for girls opened in 1855 for "the instruction . . . and reformation, of exposed, helpless, evil disposed and vicious girls" (Friedman, 1993:164). Institutional programs began in New York in 1849, Ohio in 1850, and Maine, Rhode Island, and Michigan in 1906.

Despite these reforms, children could still be arrested, detained, tried, and imprisoned. Even in states that had institutions for juveniles, the criminal justice process for children was the same as that for adults.

The Juvenile Court Period (1899–1960)

With most states providing services to neglected youth by the end of the nineteenth century, the problem of juvenile criminality became the focus of attention. Progressive reformers pushed for the state to provide individualized care and treatment to deviants of all kinds—adult criminals, the mentally ill, juvenile delinquents. They urged adoption of probation, treatment, indeterminate sentences, and parole for adult offenders and succeeded in establishing similar programs for juveniles.

Referred to as the "child savers," these upper-middle-class reformers sought to use the power of the state to save children from a life of crime (Platt, 1977). They shared a concern about the role of environmental factors on behavior and a belief that benevolent state action could solve social problems. They also believed the claim of the new social sciences that they could treat the problems underlying deviance.

Reformers wanted a separate juvenile court system that could address the problems of individual youths by using flexible procedures that, as one reformer said, "banish entirely all thought of crime and punishment" (Rothman, 1980:213). They put their idea into action with the creation of the juvenile court.

Passage of the Juvenile Court Act by Illinois in 1899 established the first comprehensive system of juvenile justice. The act placed under one jurisdiction cases of dependency, neglect, and delinquency ("incorrigibles and children threatened by immoral associations as well as criminal lawbreakers") for children under 16. The act had four major elements:

1. A separate court for delinquent, dependent, and neglected children
2. Special legal procedures that were less adversarial than those in the adult system
3. Separation of children from adults in all portions of the justice system
4. Programs of probation to assist the courts in deciding what the best interest of the state and the child entails

Activists such as Jane Addams, Lucy Flower, and Julia Lathrop, of the settlement house movement; Henry Thurston, a social work educator; and the National Congress of Mothers successfully promoted the juvenile court concept. By 1904, ten states had implemented procedures similar to those of Illinois. By 1917, all but three states provided for a juvenile court.

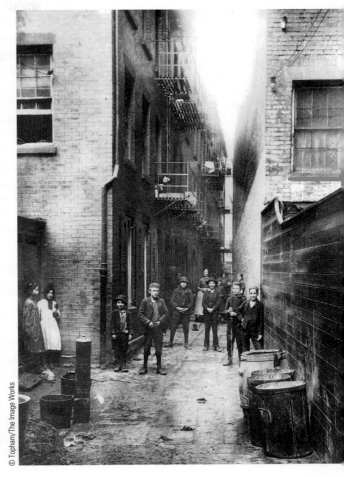

During the nineteenth century, reformers were alarmed by the living conditions of inner-city youths. Reformers in Chicago ushered in the juvenile justice system. Why should juveniles be treated differently than adults when they commit the same criminal acts?

© Topham/The Image Works

The philosophy of the juvenile court derived from the idea that the state should deal with a child who broke the law much as a wise parent would deal with a wayward child. The doctrine of *parens patriae* again helped legitimize the system. Procedures would be informal and private, records would be confidential, children would be detained apart from adults, and probation and social workers would be appointed. Even the vocabulary and physical setting of the juvenile system were changed to emphasize diagnosis and treatment instead of findings of guilt. The term *criminal behavior* was replaced by *delinquent behavior* when referring to the acts of children. The terminology reflected the underlying belief that these children could be "cured" and returned to society as law-abiding citizens.

Because procedures were not to be adversarial, lawyers were unnecessary. The main professionals attached to the system were psychologists and social workers, who could determine the juvenile's underlying behavioral problem. These reforms, however, took place in a system in which children lacked the due process rights held by adults.

While the creation of the juvenile court was a positive development for juveniles in general, some contemporary researchers criticize the tendency for these reformers to hold different standards for girls and boys. For example, girls found guilty of the status offense of "promiscuity" were frequently incarcerated until adulthood (age 18) for their own protection. Boys were rarely charged with this type of offense.

■ The Juvenile Rights Period (1960–1980)

Until the early 1960s, few questioned the sweeping powers of juvenile justice officials. When the U.S. Supreme Court expanded the rights of adult defendants, however, lawyers and scholars began to criticize the extensive discretion given to juvenile justice officials. In a series of decisions (see Figure 15.2), the U.S. Supreme Court expanded the rights of juveniles.

In the first of these cases, *Kent v. United States* (1966), the Supreme Court ruled that juveniles had the right to counsel at a hearing at which a juvenile judge may waive jurisdiction and pass the case to the adult court.

In re Gault (1967) extended due process rights to juveniles. Fifteen-year-old Gerald Gault had been sentenced to six years in a state training school for making a prank phone call. Had he been an adult, the maximum punishment for making such a call would have been a fine of $5 to $50 or imprisonment for two months at most. Gault was convicted and sentenced in an informal proceeding without being represented by counsel. The justices held that a child in a delinquency hearing must be given certain procedural rights, including notice of the charges, right to counsel, right to confront and cross-examine witnesses, and protection against self-incrimination. Writing for the majority, Justice Abe Fortas emphasized that due process rights and procedures have a place in juvenile justice: "Under our Constitution the condition of being a boy does not justify a kangaroo court."

The precedent-setting *Gault* decision was followed by a series of cases further defining the rights of juveniles. In the case of *In re Winship* (1970), the Court held that proof must be established "beyond a reasonable doubt" and not on "a preponderance of the evidence" before a juvenile may be classified as a delinquent for committing an act that would be a crime if it were committed by an adult. The Court was not willing to give juveniles every due process right, however: It held in *McKeiver v. Pennsylvania* (1971) that "trial by jury in the juvenile court's adjudicative stage is not a constitutional requirement." But in *Breed v. Jones* (1975), the Court extended the protection against double jeopardy to juveniles by requiring that, before a case is adjudicated in juvenile court, a hearing must be held to determine if it should be transferred to the adult court.

Another area of change concerned **status offenses**—acts that are not illegal if committed by an adult; these include skipping school, running away from home, and living a "wayward, idle or dissolute life" (Feld, 1993:203). In 1974, Congress passed the Juvenile Justice and Delinquency Prevention Act, which included provisions for taking status offenders out of correctional institutions. Since then, people have

■ *In re Gault* (1967) Juveniles have the right to counsel, to confront and examine accusers, and to have adequate notice of charges when confinement is a possible punishment.

■ *In re Winship* (1970) The standard of proof beyond a reasonable doubt applies to juvenile delinquency proceedings.

■ *McKeiver v. Pennsylvania* (1971) Juveniles do not have a constitutional right to a trial by jury.

■ *Breed v. Jones* (1975) Juveniles cannot be found delinquent in juvenile court and then transferred to adult court without a hearing on the transfer; to do so violates the protection against double jeopardy.

■ **status offense** Any act committed by a juvenile that is considered unacceptable for a child, such as truancy or running away from home, but that would not be a crime if it were committed by an adult.

FIGURE 15.2

Major decisions by the U.S. Supreme Court regarding the rights of juveniles

Since the mid-1960s, the Supreme Court has gradually expanded the rights of juveniles but has continued to recognize that the logic of the separate system for juvenile offenders justifies differences from some adult rights.

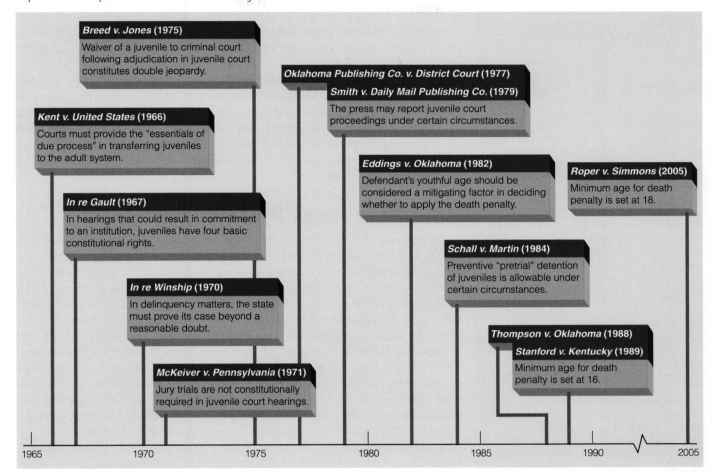

Note: For discussion of death penalty cases, see Chapter 9.

Sources: Office of Juvenile Justice and Delinquency Prevention, *1999 National Report* (Washington, DC: U.S. Government Printing Office, 1999), 90–91; *Roper v. Simmons*, 543 U.S. 551 (2005).

worked on diverting such children out of the system, reducing the possibility of incarceration, and rewriting status offense laws.

Although the courts expanded the definition of rights for juveniles, consider the state of teenagers' rights today as you read "Criminal Justice: Myth and Reality."

As juvenile crime rates continued to rise during the 1970s, the public began calling for tougher approaches in dealing with delinquents. In the 1980s, at the same time that stricter sanctions were imposed on adult offenders, juvenile justice policies shifted to crime control.

■ The Crime Control Period (1980–2005)

The public demands to "crack down on crime" began in 1980. Legislators responded in part by changing the juvenile system. Greater attention began to be focused on repeat offenders, with policy makers calling for harsher punishment for juveniles who commit crimes.

In *Schall v. Martin* (1984), the Supreme Court significantly departed from the trend toward increased juvenile rights. The Court confirmed that the general notion of *parens*

■ *Schall v. Martin* (1984) Juveniles can be held in preventive detention if there is concern that they may commit additional crimes while awaiting court action.

Criminal Justice:
MYTH AND REALITY

COMMON BELIEF: With the exception of convicted criminal offenders, who have limited constitutional rights, all other Americans receive identical protections from the rights contained in the Constitution.

The recognition and expansion of rights for youths in the justice system did not lead to equal application of rights for juveniles and adults. Some of the most obvious differences concern protections against unreasonable searches and seizures, especially in the context of public schools. The U.S. Supreme Court has approved school policies that mandate random drug testing for student athletes (*Vernonia School District v. Acton*, 1995) and for all other students participating in extracurricular activities (*Board of Education v. Earls*, 2002). Schools can mandate such testing, which are a form of searches under the Fourth Amendment, even if there is no reason to suspect wrongdoing by a student. By contrast, the Supreme Court forbade the state of Georgia from requiring drug testing of adult candidates for political office (*Chandler v. Miller*, 1997).

In 2009, the Supreme Court heard oral arguments in a case to determine whether any constitutional rights were violated when school officials strip-searched a teenage girl based on the false claim by another student that the student was carrying prescription-strength painkillers. During oral arguments, only two of the nine justices seemed to see any problem with granting school officials the authority to make such intrusive invasions of schoolchildren's reasonable expectations of privacy (Liptak, 2009a). In the end, the justices surprised observers by ruling against the school, but invasive searches of adults would never even be considered on such a flimsy basis except if the adults were convicted offenders under sentences of imprisonment, parole, or probation (*Safford Unified School District #1 v. Redding*, 2009).

■ **waiver** Procedure by which the juvenile court waives its jurisdiction and transfers a juvenile case to the adult criminal court.

patriae was a primary basis for the juvenile court, equal in importance to the Court's desire to protect the community from crime. Thus, juveniles may be held in preventive detention before trial if they are deemed a "risk" to the community.

The *Schall* decision reflects the ambivalence permeating the juvenile justice system. On one side are the liberal reformers, who call for increased procedural and substantive legal protections for juveniles accused of crime. On the other side are conservatives devoted to crime control policies and alarmed by the rise in juvenile crime.

Crime control policies brought many more juveniles to be tried in adult courts. As noted by Alex Kotlowitz, "the crackdown on children has gone well beyond those accused of violent crimes" (1994:40). Data from the National Juvenile Court Data Archive show that delinquency cases waived to the adult criminal courts increased 83 percent from 1987 to 1994 (Snyder and Sickmund, 2006:186). In addition, some claim that increased penalties on juvenile offenders affect minority youth more than white youth (Feld, 1999, 2003).

■ The "Kids Are Different" Period (2005–Present)

Some observers believe that a new period in juvenile justice may be developing. In *Roper v. Simmons* (2005), discussed in Chapter 9, the United States Supreme Court ruled that executions were unconstitutional for crimes committed by those younger than 18 years of age. This important ruling shepherded in a new era of juvenile justice. In *Roper*, the Court focused on the issue of culpability. The justices ruled that juveniles were less culpable than adults because of factors related to physical and emotional development in turn related to the growth and maturation process of the human brain (MacArthur Foundation, 2007c). Additional research indicates that intellectual maturity occurs at age 16, but other factors (such as control over impulsiveness) are not fully developed until age 24–26. This growing recognition of teenage development provides a basis for new programs and proposed laws designed to treat juveniles differently than adults for purposes of treatment and punishment.

Current program trends aim at helping juvenile offenders through rehabilitation and the prevention of delinquency. Such programs are not yet widespread or fully developed. For example, there are few free substance abuse programs for juveniles outside of correctional institutions. This means that a juvenile must be incarcerated to receive such assistance. Reducing drug use before it increases delinquency seems key to keeping juveniles crime-free, so there is increasing interest in developing more programs that are accessible to youths in the community. Research is also focusing on the relationship between parents and children, and how parenting programs may help to keep kids out of juvenile court (MacArthur Foundation, 2007b).

Once popular, the use of judicial **waiver**, the process to waive juvenile court jurisdiction in order to move juveniles into adult court for prosecution and punishment, declined dramatically in the first years of the twenty-first century, reaching the lowest number of waived cases since 1985 (Snyder and Sickmund, 2006:186). This decrease in waivers mirrors the decrease in juvenile crime during that period (Snyder and Sickmund, 2006:64). Several states are now considering the abolition of juvenile waiver by increasing their minimum age for adult trial to 18. The state of Colorado has recently abolished the use of "life without parole" as a sentence for juvenile offenders, setting a maximum sentence of 40 years for the most serious juvenile offenders. The U.S. Supreme Court has agreed to decide during its 2009–2010 term whether "life without parole" sentences constitute impermissible "cruel and unusual punishment" when applied to juveniles (Liptak, 2009b).

The current movement for more-lenient treatment of juveniles is still in its infancy. It is unknown how states will ultimately react to changes begun by *Roper v. Simmons*, and there is still considerable support for the get-tough stance toward older juveniles. In California, for example, legislators are attempting to count juvenile convictions as "strikes" under their "three strikes and you're out" law mandating long sentences (*People v. Nguyen*, 2008). Opponents point out this violates the spirit of the *parens patriae* philosophy (Juvenile Law Center, 2008). In many places, the juvenile court employs a system of rules and procedures similar to that in adult courts, even though the juvenile system has traditionally functioned through discretion and the desire to rehabilitate. Deserved punishment is still a prominent correctional goal, so juveniles who are repeat offenders continue to receive severe sentences.

In spite of the increasingly tough policies directed at juvenile offenders in the late twentieth century, changes that occurred during the juvenile rights period continue to affect the system profoundly. Lawyers are now routinely present at court hearings and other stages of the process, adding a note of formality that was not present 30 years ago. Status offenders seldom end up in secure, punitive environments such as training schools. The juvenile justice system looks more like the adult justice system than it did, but it remains less formal. Its stated intention is also less harsh: to keep juveniles in the community whenever possible. The ruling in *Roper v. Simmons* may indicate further changes away from tough policies.

Other countries have criticized the United States for our harsh treatment of juveniles. However, treatment of juvenile crime varies by country, each system having its own strengths and weaknesses. As an example, read the Comparative Perspective on the next page to examine how Norway deals with youth crime.

During the final decades of the twentieth century, the police and courts followed crime control policies in reacting to juvenile crime. Many legislators continue to argue for severe sentences for juveniles who commit serious crimes. Can the threat of long prison sentence deter juveniles from committing crimes?

AP Images/Lincoln Journal Star, William Lauer

CHECKPOINT

ANSWERS

2 *What were the major elements of the Illinois Juvenile Court Act of 1899?*

2 A separate court for delinquent, dependent, and neglected children; special legal procedures that were less adversarial than in the adult system; separation of children from adults throughout the system; programs of probation to assist judges in deciding what is in the best interests of the child.

3 *What was the main point of the* In re Gault *decision?*

3 Procedural rights for juveniles, including notice of charges, right to counsel, right to confront and cross-examine witnesses, and protection against self-incrimination.

The Juvenile Justice System

Juvenile justice operates through a variety of procedures in different states; even different counties within the same states vary. Because the offenses committed by juveniles are mostly violations of state laws, there is little federal involvement in

COMPARATIVE PERSPECTIVE

The Hidden Juvenile Justice System in *NORWAY*

THERE IS NO PUNISHMENT for crimes in Norway for a child who is under fifteen. Thus, there are no special courts to try criminal cases against juvenile offenders. Older teenagers may be tried in ordinary courts and sentenced to prison. However, most sentences consist of only a suspended sentence or probation or several months in an open prison.

In practice, the prosecutor transfers the juvenile case directly to a division of the "social office," the *barnevern*—literally, child protection. After a trial the judge may also refer the child to this office. Police evidence is turned over to the social workers, not for prosecution, but for "treatment."

The usual first step in treatment is that the *barnevern* takes emergency custody of the child and places the child in a youth home. If the parents or guardians do not give consent, the child welfare committee will consider arguments against placement. Here the question is the appropriate treatment for the child.

The *barnevern* is most often associated in the public mind with handling of cases of child abuse and neglect. In such a case, the board will turn over custody of the child to the social workers for placement in a foster home or youth home. Once the custody is removed from the parents, the burden of proof is on the parents to retain custody. Social workers are well aware of numerous such cases of recovering alcoholics who, even after recovery, have been unable to retain custody of their children.

In contrast to the U.S. juvenile court, the Norwegian model is wholly dominated by the social worker. The function of the judge is to preside over the hearing and to maintain proper legal protocol, but the child welfare office presents the evidence and directs the case. The five laypeople who constitute the [social welfare committee] are advised by the child welfare office well before the hearing of the "facts" of the case. Before the hearing, the youth will have been placed in a youth home or mental institution "on an emergency basis"; the parents' rights to custody will have already been terminated.

The hearing is thus a mere formality after the fact. There is overwhelming unanimity among members of the board and between the board and social worker administrators. The arguments of the clients and of their lawyers seem to "fall on deaf ears."

Proof of guilt brought before the committee will generally consist of a copy of the police report of the offenses admitted by the accused and a school report written by the principal after he or she has been informed of the lawbreaking. Reports by the *barnevern*-appointed psychologist and social worker are also included. The *barnevern*, in its statement, has summarized the reports from the point of view of its arguments (usually for placement). Otherwise, the reports are ignored.

The hearing itself is a far cry from standard courtroom procedure. The youth and his or her parents may address the board briefly. The attorney sums up the case for a return to the home. Expert witnesses may be called and questioned by the board concerning, for instance, their treatment recommendations.

Following the departure of the parties, the *barnevern* office presents what amounts to the case for the prosecution. There is no opportunity to rebut the testimony and no opportunity for cross-examination.

Placement in an institution is typically for an indefinite period. No notice of the disposition of the matter is given to the press. This absence of public accountability may serve more to protect the social office than the child.

Children receive far harsher treatments than do adults for similar offenses. For instance, for a young adult first offender the typical penalty for thievery is a suspended sentence. A child, however, may languish in an institution for years for the same offense.

A *barnevern's* first work ought to be to create the best possible childhood. However, the *barnevern* also has a control function in relation to both the parents and the child, and the controller often feels a stronger duty to the community than to the parents and child. The institutionalization of children with behavioral problems clearly reflects this social control function. Approximately half of the children under care of the child welfare committee were placed outside the home and the other half placed under protective watch.

The system of justice for children accused of crimes is therefore often very harsh. This is in sharp contrast to the criminal justice system for adults, which is strikingly lenient. Where punishment is called *treatment,* however, the right of the state can almost become absolute. The fact that the state is represented by social work administrators creates a sharp ethical conflict for those whose first duty is to the client.

What we see in Norway is a process of juvenile justice that has not changed substantially since the 1950s. Due to flaws within the system, including the lack of external controls, the best intentions of social workers "have gone awry." Where care and protection were intended, power and secrecy have prevailed. Juvenile justice in Norway today is the justice of America yesterday.

Source: Condensed from Katherine Van Wormer, "The Hidden Juvenile Justice System in Norway: A Journey Back in Time," *Federal Probation*, March 1990, pp. 57–61.

---

the juvenile justice system. Despite internal differences, the juvenile justice system is characterized by two key factors: (1) the age of clients and (2) the categories of cases under juvenile instead of adult court jurisdiction.

■ Age of Clients

Age normally determines whether a person is processed through the juvenile or adult justice system. The upper age limit for original juvenile court jurisdiction varies from 16 to 18. In 39 states and the District of Columbia, it is the 18th birthday; in 10 states, the 17th; and in the remaining 2 states, the 16th. In 45 states, judges have the

FIGURE 15.3

The youngest age at which juveniles may be transferred to adult criminal court by waiver of juvenile jurisdiction

The waiver provisions of states vary greatly, and no clear regional or other factor explains the differences.

Source: National Center for Juvenile Justice, "State Juvenile Justice Profiles 2006," http://www.ncjj.org.

discretion to transfer juveniles to adult courts through a waiver hearing. Figure 15.3 shows the age at which juveniles can be transferred to adult court.

◼ Categories of Cases under Juvenile Court Jurisdiction

Four types of cases fall under the jurisdiction of the juvenile justice system: delinquency, status offenses, neglect, and dependency. Mixing together young criminals and children who suffer from their parents' inadequacies dates from the earliest years of juvenile justice.

Delinquent children have committed acts that if committed by an adult would be criminal—for example, auto theft, robbery, or assault. Juvenile courts handle about 1.6 million delinquency cases each year, 74 percent involving male delinquents, and 29 percent involving African Americans. Among the criminal charges brought before the juvenile court, 24 percent are for crimes against the person, 36 percent for property offenses, 12 percent for drug law violations, and 28 percent for public order offenses (Stahl, Finnegan, and Kang, 2007).

Recall that status offenses are acts that are illegal only if they are committed by juveniles. Status offenders have not violated a penal code; instead, they are charged with being ungovernable or incorrigible: as runaways, truants, or **PINS** (persons in need of supervision). Status offenders make up about 10 percent of the juvenile court caseload. Although female offenders account for only 26 percent of delinquency cases, they make up 44 percent of the status offense cases (Stahl, 2008b).

Some states do not distinguish between delinquent offenders and status offenders; they label both as juvenile delinquents. Those judged to be ungovernable and those judged to be robbers may be sent to the same correctional institution.

Beginning in the early 1960s, many state legislatures attempted to distinguish status offenders and to exempt them from a criminal record. In states that have

◼ **delinquent** A child who has committed an act that if committed by an adult would be a criminal act.

◼ **PINS** Acronym for "person(s) in need of supervision," a term that designates juveniles who are either status offenders or thought to be on the verge of trouble.

decriminalized status offenses, juveniles who participate in these activities may now be classified as dependent children and placed in the care of child-protective agencies.

Juvenile justice also deals with problems of neglect and dependency. Some children are hurt through no fault of their own because their parents have failed to provide a proper environment for them. People see the state's proper role as acting as a parent to a child whose own parents are unable or unwilling to provide proper care. Illinois, for example, defines a **neglected child** as one who is receiving inadequate care because of some action or inaction of his or her parents. This may include not being sent to school, not receiving medical care, being abandoned, living in an injurious environment, or not receiving some other care necessary for the child's well-being. A **dependent child** either has no parent or guardian or is receiving inadequate care because of the physical or mental disability of the parent. The law governing neglected and dependent children is broad and includes situations in which the child is viewed as a victim of adult behavior.

Nationally, about 75 percent of the cases referred to the juvenile courts are delinquency cases, 20 percent of which are status offenses. Twenty percent are dependency and neglect cases, and about 5 percent involve special proceedings, such as adoption. The system, then, deals with both criminal and noncriminal cases. Often, juveniles who have done nothing wrong are categorized, either officially or in the public mind, as delinquents. In some states, little effort is made in pre-judicial detention facilities or in social service agencies to separate the classes of juveniles.

■ **neglected child** A child who is receiving inadequate care because of some action or inaction of his or her parents.

■ **dependent child** A child who has no parent or guardian or whose parents cannot give proper care.

CHECKPOINT

4 *What are the jurisdictional criteria for the juvenile court?*

ANSWER

4 The age of the youth, usually under 16 or 18, and the type of case—delinquency, status offense, neglect, or dependency.

The Juvenile Justice Process

Underlying the juvenile justice system is the philosophy that police, judges, and correctional officials should focus primarily on the interests of the child. Prevention of delinquency is the system's justification for intervening in the lives of juveniles who are involved in either status or criminal offenses.

In theory at least, juvenile proceedings are to be conducted in a nonadversarial environment. The juvenile court is to be a place where the judge, social workers, clinicians, and probation officers work together to diagnose the child's problem and select a treatment program to attack that problem.

Juvenile justice is a bureaucracy based on an ideology of social work. It is staffed primarily by people who think of themselves as members of the helping professions. Not even the recent emphasis on crime control and punishment has removed the treatment philosophy from most juvenile justice arenas. However, political pressures and limits on resources may stymie the implementation of this philosophy by focusing on the punishment of offenders rather than the prevention of delinquency, even though the public is willing to pay more for prevention programs and rehabilitation than continued use of incarceration (Nagin et al., 2006).

Like the adult system, juvenile justice functions within a context of exchange relationships between officials of various government and private agencies that influence decisions. The juvenile court must deal not only with children and their parents, but also with patrol officers, probation officers, welfare officials, social workers, psychologists, and the heads of treatment institutions, all of whom have their own goals, perceptions of delinquency, and concepts of treatment.

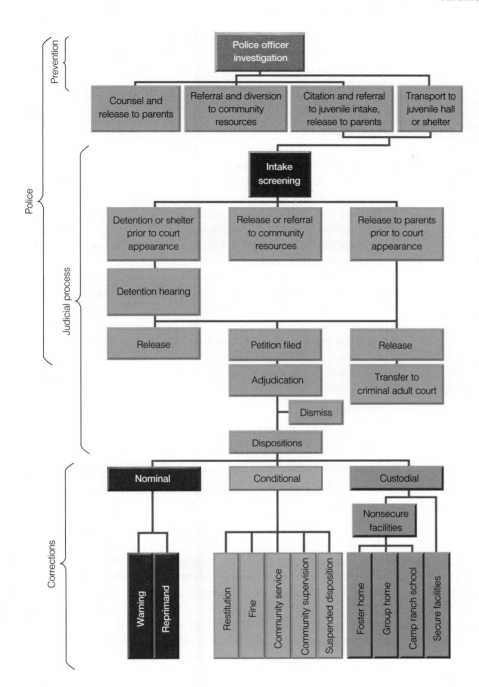

FIGURE 15.4
The juvenile justice system
Decision makers have more options for the disposition of juvenile offenders, compared with options in the criminal justice system for adults.

Source: National Advisory Commission on Criminal Justice Standards and Goals, *Report of the Task Force on Juvenile Justice and Delinquency Prevention* (Washington, DC: Law Enforcement Assistance Administration, 1976).

Figure 15.4 outlines the sequence of steps that are taken from police investigation to correctional disposition. As you examine this figure, compare the procedures with those of the criminal justice system for adults. Note the various options available to decision makers and the extensive discretion that they can exercise.

▓ Police Interface

Many police departments, especially in cities, have special juvenile units. The juvenile officer is often selected and trained to relate to youths, knows much about relevant legal issues, and is sensitive to the special needs of young offenders. This officer also serves as an important link between the police and other community institutions, such as schools and other organizations serving young people. Some communities hire *school resource officers*, who provide counseling and a security presence in school buildings.

Most complaints against juveniles are brought by the police, although an injured party, school officials, and even the parents can initiate them as well. The police must

FIGURE 15.5

Disposition of juveniles taken into police custody

The police have discretion in the disposition of juvenile arrest cases. What factors can influence how a case is disposed?

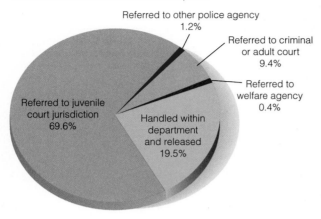

Referred to other police agency 1.2%

Referred to criminal or adult court 9.4%

Referred to welfare agency 0.4%

Referred to juvenile court jurisdiction 69.6%

Handled within department and released 19.5%

Source: Federal Bureau of Investigation, *Uniform Crime Reports 2007* (Washington, DC: U.S. Government Printing Office, 2008), Table 68.

make three major decisions with regard to the processing of juveniles:

1. Whether to take the child into custody
2. Whether to request that the child be detained following apprehension
3. Whether to refer the child to court

The police exercise enormous discretion in these decisions. They do extensive screening and make informal adjustments in the street and at the station house. In communities and neighborhoods where the police have developed close relationships with the residents or where policy dictates, the police may deal with violations by giving warnings to the juveniles and notifying their parents. Figure 15.5 shows the disposition of juveniles taken into police custody.

Initial decisions about what to do with a suspected offender are influenced by such factors as the predominant attitude of the community; the officer's attitude toward the juvenile, the juvenile's family, the offense, and the court; and the officer's conception of his or her own role. The disposition of juvenile cases at the arrest stage also relies on the seriousness of the offense, the child's prior record, and his or her demeanor. To summarize, several key factors influence how the police dispose of a case of juvenile delinquency:

1. The seriousness of the offense
2. The willingness of the parents to cooperate and to discipline the child
3. The child's behavioral history as reflected in school and police records
4. The extent to which the child and the parents insist on a formal court hearing
5. The local political and social norms concerning dispositions in such cases
6. The officer's beliefs and attitudes

Although young people commit many serious crimes, the juvenile function of police work is concerned largely with order maintenance. In most incidents of this sort, the law is ambiguous, and blame cannot easily be assigned. Many offenses committed by juveniles that involve physical or monetary damage are minor infractions: breaking windows, hanging around the business district, disturbing the peace, public sexual behavior, and shoplifting. Here, the function of the investigating officer is not so much to solve crimes as to handle the often legally uncertain complaints involving juveniles. The officer seeks both to satisfy the complainant and to keep the youth from future trouble. Given this emphasis on settling cases within the community instead of strictly enforcing the law, the threat of arrest can be used as a weapon to deter juveniles from criminal activity and to encourage them to conform to the law.

■ Intake Screening at the Court

The juvenile court processing of delinquency cases begins with a referral in the form of a petition, not an arrest warrant as in the adult system. When a petition is filed, an intake hearing is held, over which a hearing officer presides. During this stage, the officer determines whether the alleged facts are sufficient for the juvenile court to take jurisdiction or whether some other action would be in the child's best interest.

Nationally, 43 percent of all referrals are disposed of at this stage, without formal processing by a judge. **Diversion** is the process of screening children out of the system without a decision by the court (Stahl, Finnegan, and Kang, 2007). In 47 percent of these cases, the charges are dismissed; another one-third or so are diverted to an informal probation, 6 percent are placed in a mental health facility or other treatment

■ **diversion** The process of screening children out of the juvenile justice system without a decision by the court.

facility, and 21 percent are dealt with through some agreed-on alternative sanction (Sickmund, 2003).

Would you want to undertake the important and difficult responsibility of determining what should be done with juveniles taken into custody by the police? Consider this question as you read "Careers in Criminal Justice."

■ Pretrial Procedures

When a decision is made to refer the case to the court, the court holds an initial hearing. Here, the juveniles are informed of their rights and told that if a plea is given it must be voluntary.

If the juvenile is to be detained pending trial, most states require a **detention hearing**, which determines if the youth is to be released to a parent or guardian or to be held in a detention facility until adjudication. Some children are detained to keep them from committing other crimes while awaiting trial. Others are held to protect them from the possibility of harm from gang members or parents. Still others are held because, if released, they will likely not appear in court as required. Nationally, about 20 percent of all delinquency cases involve detention between referral to the juvenile court and disposition of the case (Stahl, Finnegan, and Kang, 2007).

The concept of restorative justice has been extended to juveniles. At the Red Hook Youth Court in New York, a 15-year-old arrested for spraying graffiti sits before a jury of his peers with a 16-year-old acting as the judge. The court deals with minor offenses, often where formal charges have not yet been brought. Officials say that 85 percent of the offenders complete restitution, ranging from community service to letters of apology. Is this an effective way to deal with youthful offenders?

© Joe Tabacca

The conditions in many detention facilities are poor; abuse is often reported. In some rural areas, juveniles continue to be detained in adult jails even though the federal government has pressed states to hold youths in separate facilities. In 2003, the city of Baltimore unveiled a new juvenile detention facility, meant to expedite juvenile cases and centralize services to delinquent youth. The new facility was recently termed a "monstrosity," with poor lines of sight (officers cannot easily observe and supervise the juvenile detainees), overcrowding, and increasing rates of violence within its walls (Bykowicz, 2008).

Believing that detaining youths accelerates their delinquent behaviors, some jurisdictions have attempted to stem the tide of rising numbers of juveniles in detention. Indianapolis has implemented a program to increase the use of diversion and send more youths home to live with their families while awaiting trial. This attempt has reduced both the number of incarcerated youths and delinquency rates (Murray, 2008).

■ **detention hearing** A hearing by the juvenile court to determine if a juvenile is to be detained or released prior to adjudication.

■ Transfer (Waiver) to Adult Court

One of the first decisions to be made after a juvenile is referred is whether a case should be transferred to the criminal (adult) justice system. In 45 states, juvenile court judges may waive their jurisdiction. This means that, after considering the seriousness of the charge, the age of the juvenile, and the prospects of rehabilitation, the judge can transfer the case to adult court. In 29 states, certain violent crimes such as murder, rape, and armed robbery are excluded by law from the jurisdiction of the juvenile courts (NIJ, 1997). In 1970, only three states allowed prosecutors the authority to decide whether to file in adult or juvenile court. Today, 15 states give prosecutors the authority to do so (Snyder and Sickmund, 2006). Critics question whether prosecutors will "make

CAREERS IN CRIMINAL JUSTICE

Intake Referee

KIA LOGGINS, INTAKE REFEREE
CIRCUIT COURT—FAMILY DIVISION, LANSING,
MICHIGAN

AN INTAKE REFEREE conducts preliminary inquiries and preliminary hearings regarding juvenile delinquency petitions, traffic violations (such as "minor in possession of alcohol" or "no operator's license"), and abuse and neglect matters. An intake referee takes testimony, investigates family situations, determines probable cause, and decides appropriate legal action. In a hearing, a referee might have to determine the custody of minors, prepare preliminary orders, or assign the case to a juvenile court officer for further investigative work or supervision. When a case is resolved informally, the intake referee must recommend appropriate community-based services such as counseling, community service, behavioral groups, or other diversion programs.

Kia Loggins studied criminal justice as an undergraduate and counseling as a graduate student. In college, she sought out a wide

range of volunteer and internship opportunities to gain experience in juvenile justice. For example, she served as a juvenile court tutor and as an intern in a residential program for troubled boys. After college, she worked in a juvenile detention facility before becoming a juvenile probation officer. She subsequently spent several years working for a nonprofit organization that provides training and consulting services for staff members at juvenile detention facilities throughout the country. By the time she had the opportunity to become an intake referee, Loggins had gained professional experience in many aspects of the juvenile justice system.

The most challenging aspect of my job is working with parents or teens who are not willing to improve themselves but are quick to blame the system. In that situation, I must make the best decision possible while hoping that some positive seeds of change will be planted in the process.

better informed and more appropriate 'criminal adulthood' decisions than would judges in an adversarial waiver hearing" (Feld, 2004:599). See "What Americans Think" for a look at public attitudes about transferring juveniles to the adult court.

After a "tougher" approach to juvenile crime took hold in the 1970s, the number of cases transferred increased dramatically. Several states expanded their ability to transfer juveniles by excluding certain crimes from juvenile court jurisdiction, or lowering their minimum age for transfer to adult court. The likelihood of waiver varies by seriousness of offense, offender age, and offender race. African American youths are more likely to be waived than are white youths (Stahl, Finnegan, and Kang, 2007). This disparity can be affected by offending patterns (that is, which offenses are more frequently committed by which youths) as well as by the risk of biased decision making.

One result of the increased use of the waiver was that more juveniles were being sent to adult state prisons. Between 1985 and 1997, the number doubled from 3,400 to 7,400 (BJS, 2000c). As the use of waiver declined, so, too, did the number of juveniles sent to prison. From 1997 to 2002, there was a 45 percent decline in the number of new admissions of offenders under age 18 into state prisons (Snyder and Sickmund, 2006:237). Critics of the policies claim that waiver subverts the intent of the juvenile justice system and exposes juvenile offenders to harsh conditions in adult prisons—where they are susceptible to physical and sexual victimization (DeJong and Merrill, 2000). In addition, those juveniles tried in adult courts are more likely to reoffend after release (MacArthur Foundation, 2007a). There is also evidence that increased use of waiver has had no effect on juvenile crime rates (Steiner, Hemmens, and Bell, 2006; Steiner and Wright, 2006). Transferring juveniles to be tried in the adult courts remains controversial, as outlined in "The Policy Debate" (page 453).

Adjudication

Juvenile courts deal with almost 1.6 million delinquency cases a year (Stahl, Finnegan, and Kang, 2007). *Adjudication* is the trial stage of the juvenile justice process. If the child has not admitted to the charges and the case has not been transferred to the adult court, an adjudication hearing is held to determine the facts in the case and, if appropriate, label the juvenile "delinquent."

The Supreme Court's decision in *Gault* and other due process rulings mandated changes that have altered the philosophy and actions of the juvenile court. Contemporary juvenile proceedings are more formal than those of the past, although still more informal than adult courts. The parents and child must receive copies of petitions with specific charges; counsel may be present, and free counsel can be appointed if the juvenile cannot pay; witnesses can be cross-examined; and a transcript of the proceedings must be kept.

As with other Supreme Court decisions, local practice may differ sharply from the procedures spelled out in the high court's rulings. Juveniles and their parents often waive their rights in response to suggestions from the judge or probation officer. The lower social status of the offender's parents, the intimidating atmosphere of the court, and judicial hints that the outcome will be more favorable if a lawyer is not present are reasons the procedures outlined in *Gault* might not be followed. The litany of "getting treatment," "doing what's right for the child," and "working out a just solution" may sound enticing, especially to people who are unfamiliar with the intricacies of formal legal procedures. In practice, then, juveniles still lack many of the protections given to adult offenders. Some of the differences between the juvenile and adult criminal justice systems are listed in Table 15.2.

The increased concern about crime has given prosecuting attorneys a more prominent part in the system. In keeping with the traditional child-saver philosophy, prosecuting attorneys rarely appeared in juvenile court prior to the *Gault* decision. Now that a defense attorney is present, the state often uses legal counsel as well. In many jurisdictions, prosecutors are assigned to deal specifically with juvenile cases. Their functions are to advise the intake officer, administer diversion programs, negotiate pleas, and act as an advocate during judicial proceedings.

Juvenile proceedings and court records have traditionally remained closed to the public to protect the child's privacy and potential for rehabilitation. As such, judges in the adult courts usually do not have access to juvenile records. This means that people who have already served time on juvenile probation or in institutions are erroneously perceived to be first offenders when they are processed for crimes as adults. Some people argue that adult courts should have access to juvenile records and that young criminals should be treated more severely than adults to deter them from future illegal activity.

What AMERICANS Think

QUESTION: "Currently, most juvenile offenders are handled in the juvenile justice system. How much would you approve of eliminating this system and handling all juvenile offenders in the same system used for adults?"

Strongly approve 5.7%
Approve 13.9%
Disapprove 40.9%
Strongly disapprove 39.6%

Go to http://www.cengage.com/criminaljustice/cole to compare your opinion on this issue with the opinions of other criminal justice students.

Source: Dan Mears, Carter Hay, Marc Gertz, and Christina Mancini, "Public Opinion and the Foundation of the Juvenile Court," *Criminology* 45 (2007): 223–57.

Disposition

If the court makes a finding of delinquency, the judge will schedule a dispositional hearing to decide what action should be taken. Typically, before passing sentence, the judge receives a *predispositional report* prepared by a probation officer. Similar to a presentence report, it serves to assist the judge in deciding on a disposition that is in the best interests of the child and is consistent with the treatment plan developed by the probation officer.

The juvenile waiver process permits juveniles to be sent to adult court and receive the same punishment as adults for serious crimes. Here Gerardo Gomez, age 15, is led from the courthouse after being charged with a triple homicide in New Jersey. What is the appropriate sentence for a juvenile who commits crimes such as murder or rape?

AP Images/Mike Derer

	Adult System	**Juvenile System**
Philosophical Assumptions	Decisions made as result of adversarial system in context of due process rights	Decisions made as result of inquiry into needs of juvenile within context of some due process elements
Jurisdiction	Violations of criminal law	Violations of criminal law, status offenses, neglect, dependency
Primary Sanctioning Goals	Retribution, deterrence, rehabilitation	Retribution, rehabilitation
Official Discretion	Widespread	Widespread
Entrance	Official action of arrest, summons, or citation	Official action, plus referral by school, parents, other sources
Role of Prosecuting and Defense Attorneys	Required and formalized	Sometimes required; less structured; poor role definition
Adjudication	Procedural rules of evidence in public jury trial required	Less formal structure to rules of evidence and conduct of trial; no right to public trial or jury in most states
Treatment Programs	Run primarily by public agencies	Broad use of private and public agencies

TABLE 15.2　The Adult and Juvenile Criminal Justice Systems Compared

Compare the basic elements of the adult and juvenile systems. To what extent does a juvenile have the same rights as an adult? Are the different decision-making processes necessary because a juvenile is involved?

Application of Bill of Rights Amendments

		Adult System	**Juvenile System**
Fourth:	Unreasonable searches and seizures	Applicable	Applicable
Fifth:	Double jeopardy	Applicable	Applicable (re: waiver to adult court)
	Self-incrimination	Applicable (*Miranda* warnings)	Applicable
Sixth:	Right to counsel	Applicable	Applicable
	Public trial	Applicable	Applicable in less than half of states
	Trial by jury	Applicable	Applicable in less than half of states
Fourteenth:	Right to treatment	Not applicable	Applicable

The court finds most juveniles to be delinquent at trial, because the intake and pretrial processes normally filter out cases in which a law violation cannot be proved. Besides dismissal, four other choices are available: (1) probation, (2) alternative dispositions, (3) custodial care, and (4) community treatment. Alternative dispositions might include assignment to a specific treatment program or suspending the judgment while monitoring the youth's behavior and performance in school with the possibility of later dismissing the charge.

Juvenile court advocates have traditionally believed that rehabilitation is the only goal of the sanction imposed on young people. For most of the twentieth century, judges sentenced juveniles to indeterminate sentences so that correctional administrators could decide when release was appropriate. As in the adult criminal justice system, indeterminate sentences and unbridled discretion in juvenile justice have faced attack during the last three decades. Several states have tightened the sentencing discretion of judges, especially with regard to serious offenses.

■ Corrections

Many aspects of juvenile corrections resemble those of adult corrections. Both systems, for example, mix rehabilitative and retributive sanctions. However, juvenile corrections differs in many respects from the adult system. Some of the differences flow from the *parens patriae* concept and the youthful, seemingly innocent people

THE POLICY DEBATE

Should Juvenile Offenders Be Tried as Adults?

ARRESTS OF JUVENILES for violent crimes more than doubled between 1988 and 1994. Since their peak in 1994, juvenile violent crime arrests have declined, yet cases still come up that are so serious that the public demands severe punishment. Youths are also the primary victims of violent crime. Experts cite the availability of guns, the prevalence of urban youth gangs, and the problem of drugs as the causes of violent youth crimes.

In the face of crimes such as school-yard shootings, the public has loudly called for "getting tough with these young hoods." Politicians and criminal justice planners have urged that steps be taken to ensure that juveniles accused of serious crimes be dealt with in the adult courts.

For Trying Juveniles as Adults

Those who want to make trying juveniles as adults easier point not only to the high levels of violence but also to the heinous nature of some crimes committed by youths. They see the juvenile courts as "coddling" these young predators. Often, only when a youth is transferred to the adult system is his or her long record of felonies revealed—felonies for which the juvenile court ordered little punishment. They say that current level of violence by juveniles requires that offenders be dealt with swiftly and quickly so as to deter the upcoming generation from following in the footsteps of their older siblings.

The arguments for trying serious juvenile offenders in the adult criminal justice system include these:

- Violence by juveniles is a serious problem and must be dealt with in a swift and certain manner.
- Juvenile courts have not been effective in stemming the tide of violence by young people.
- Procedures for waiving juvenile jurisdiction are cumbersome in many states.
- Justice demands that heinous crimes, regardless of the age of the accused, be dealt with to the full extent the law provides.

Against Trying Juveniles as Adults

Although they recognize that serious youth crime is a problem, many experts believe that trying juveniles as adults only makes things worse. They point out that treating adolescents as adults ignores the fact that they are at a different stage of social and emotional development. They argue that children should not be held to the same standards as adults. In an increasingly violent world, children need help to navigate the temptations and threats of adolescence.

The arguments against trying serious juvenile offenders in the adult criminal justice system include these:

- The juvenile justice system is better able to deal with the social and emotional problems of young offenders.
- The basic foundations of criminal law recognize that children carry diminished responsibility for their acts.
- Punishing juveniles in adult institutions robs them of their childhood and threatens their future.
- The problem of violent crime by juveniles must be dealt with by changing the environment within which they live.

What Should U.S. Policy Be?

Under pressure to "do something" about violent juvenile crime, legislators have proposed that the age of adulthood be lowered and that the cases of serious offenders be tried in the adult criminal justice system. Is this the best way to protect community safety—to punish youthful offenders in the adult criminal justice system? Is the juvenile corrections system equipped to treat and guide juvenile offenders in a way that will return them to their communities as productive people?

RESEARCHING THE INTERNET

You can find the article "Delinquents or Criminals: Policy Options for Young Offenders" at the corresponding website listed on the Cole/Smith Criminal Justice in America Companion Website: http://www.cengage.com/criminaljustice/cole.

FOR CRITICAL ANALYSIS

What are the likely consequences of trying juveniles as adults? What are the likely consequences of trying these offenders in the juvenile courts?

---

with whom the system deals. At times, the differences show up in formal operational policies, such as contracting for residential treatment. At other times, the differences appear only in the style and culture of an operation, as they do in juvenile probation.

One predominant aim of juvenile corrections is to avoid unnecessary incarceration. When children are removed from their homes, they are inevitably damaged emotionally, even when the home life is harsh and abusive, for they are forced to abandon the only environment they know. Further, placing children in institutions has labeling effects; the children may perceive themselves as bad because they have received punitive treatment, and children who see themselves as "bad" may actually behave that way. Finally, treatment is believed to be more effective when the child is living in a normal, supportive home environment. For these reasons, noninstitutional forms of corrections are seen as highly desirable in juvenile justice and have proliferated in recent years.

Probation   In 63 percent of cases, the juvenile delinquent is placed on probation and released to the custody of a parent or guardian (Stahl, Finnegan, and Kang, 2007). Often, the judge orders that the delinquent undergo some form of education or counseling. The delinquent can also be required to pay a fine or make restitution while on probation.

Juvenile probation operates in much the same way that adult probation does, and sometimes the same agency carries it out. In two respects, however, juvenile probation can differ markedly from adult probation. First, juvenile probation officers have smaller caseloads. Second, the juvenile probation officer is often infused with the sense that the offender is worthwhile and can change and that the job is valuable and enjoyable. Such attitudes make for greater creativity than adult probation officers usually express. For example, a young offender can be paired with a "big brother" or "big sister" from the community.

Intermediate Sanctions   Although probation and commitment to an institution are the system's two main dispositional options, intermediate sanctions served in the community now account for 15 percent of adjudicated juvenile cases (Stahl, Finnegan, and Kang, 2007). Judges have wide discretion to warn, to fine, to arrange for restitution, to order community service, to refer a juvenile for treatment at either a public or a private community agency, or to withhold judgment.

Judges sometimes suspend judgment—that is, they continue a case without a finding when they wish to put a youth under supervision but are reluctant to apply the label "delinquent." The judge holds off on a definitive judgment but can give one should a youth misbehave while under the informal supervision of a probation officer or parents.

Custodial Care   Of those juveniles declared delinquent, 22 percent are placed in public or private facilities. The placement rate of juveniles over time has decreased from about one in three adjudicated juveniles in 1989 to about one in five juveniles in 2004 (Stahl, Finnegan, and Kang, 2007). The national incarceration rate per 100,000 juveniles aged 10 through 18 is 307—this includes both juveniles held prior to trial and those serving a sentence of incarceration. Like the adult incarceration rate, these rates vary widely among the states, with the highest rate in the District of Columbia (625) and the lowest in Vermont (72) (Snyder and Sickmund, 2006:201). Nationally, 69 percent of incarcerated juveniles are held in public facilities, with the remainder in private facilities (Snyder and Sickmund, 2006:218). See "What Americans Think" for a picture of attitudes toward prisons for juveniles.

Policy makers are concerned about the overrepresentation of incarcerated African American juveniles. Research has found that the disproportionate confinement of minority juveniles often stems from disparity at the early stages of case processing. Thus, if more African Americans are detained than others, more of them will likely be adjudicated in juvenile court, and more placed in residential facilities. Some research suggests that juvenile court actors have biased perceptions of minority juveniles, and thus these youths receive severer treatment at all levels of the juvenile justice system (Leiber and Mack, 2003). Other

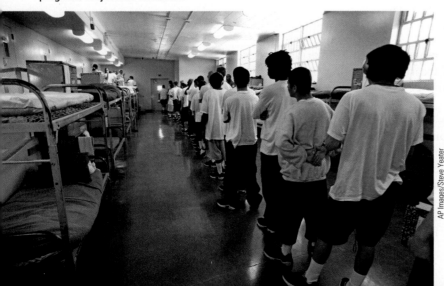

Youths in a sex offender treatment program walk in a single-file line to the exercise yard at California's Close Youth Correctional Facility. Do such overcrowded, stark surroundings provide the best environment for implementing effective treatment programs for juvenile offenders?

AP Images/Steve Yeater

studies indicate the importance of examining both race and gender when analyzing court outcomes, as girls are generally treated more leniently than boys in the justice system (Guevara, Herz, and Spohn, 2006).

Institutions for juvenile offenders are classified as either nonsecure or secure. *Nonsecure* placements (foster homes, group homes, camps, ranches, or schools) include a significant number of nonoffender youths referred for abuse, neglect, or emotional disturbance. *Secure* facilities, such as reform schools and training schools, deal with juveniles who have committed crimes and have serious personal problems. Most secure juvenile facilities are small, designed to hold 40 or fewer residents. However, many states have at least one facility holding two hundred or more hard-core delinquents who are allowed limited freedom. Because the residents are younger and somewhat more volatile than adults, behavioral control is often an everyday issue, and fights and aggression are common. Poor management practices, such as those described in "A Question of Ethics" at the end of this chapter, can lead to difficult situations.

Boot camps for juvenile offenders saw a growth spurt in the early 1990s. By 1997, more than 27,000 teenagers were passing through 54 camps in 34 states annually. However, as with boot camps for adults, the results have not been promising. A national study shows that recidivism among boot camp attendees ranges from 64 percent to 75 percent, slightly higher than for youths sentenced to adult prisons (*New York Times*, January 2, 2000, p. WK3). States are rethinking their policies, with many closing their programs.

A national survey of custodial juvenile institutions showed that 34 percent of juveniles were incarcerated for violent offenses. In addition, 85 percent of the residents were male, only 19 percent had grown up in a household with both parents, and the percentages of African Americans (38 percent) and Hispanics (19 percent) were greater than the percentages of those groups in the general population (Snyder and Sickmund, 2006). The Close Up box on page 456 tells the story of Fernando, whose background matches this profile. Figure 15.6 shows the types of offenses of juveniles in public correctional facilities.

With the elimination of the death penalty as a punishment for juvenile offenders through the Supreme Court's decision in *Roper v. Simmons* (2005), some juvenile offenders receive "life without possibility of parole" (LWOP) for homicide offenses. Referring to this sentence as "a slower form of [the] death [penalty]," some argue that the juvenile justice system must always take age and juveniles' incomplete mental development into account, even for homicide offenses, to avoid giving youths the same sentences imposed on the most serious adult offenders (Feld, 2008).

Institutional Programs   Because of the emphasis on rehabilitation that has dominated juvenile justice for much of the past 50 years, a wide variety of treatment programs has been used. Counseling, education, vocational training, and an assortment of psychotherapeutic methods have been incorporated into the juvenile correctional programs of most states. Unfortunately, research has raised many questions about the effectiveness of rehabilitation programs in juvenile corrections. For example, incarceration in a juvenile training institution primarily seems to prepare many offenders for entry into adult corrections. John Irwin's (1970) concept of the state-raised youth is a useful way of looking at children who come in contact with institutional life at an early age, lack family relationships and structure, become accustomed to living in a correctional facility, and cannot function in other environments. Current recommendations focus on the importance of prevention and keeping juvenile offenders from incarceration at the first signs of problem behavior (Hoge, Guerra, and Boxer, 2008).

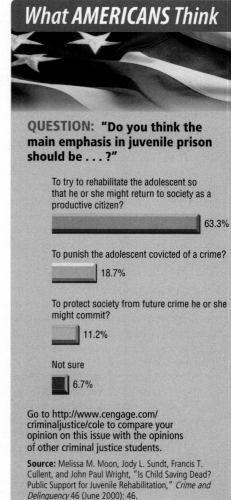

What AMERICANS Think

QUESTION: "Do you think the main emphasis in juvenile prison should be . . . ?"

To try to rehabilitate the adolescent so that he or she might return to society as a productive citizen? 63.3%

To punish the adolescent covicted of a crime? 18.7%

To protect society from future crime he or she might commit? 11.2%

Not sure 6.7%

Go to http://www.cengage.com/criminaljustice/cole to compare your opinion on this issue with the opinions of other criminal justice students.

Source: Melissa M. Moon, Jody L. Sundt, Francis T. Cullent, and John Paul Wright, "Is Child Saving Dead? Public Support for Juvenile Rehabilitation," *Crime and Delinquency* 46 (June 2000): 46.

FIGURE 15.6
Juveniles in public facilities: Types of offenses and nondelinquent reasons for placement

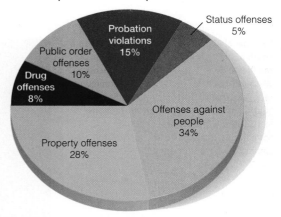

Probation violations 15%
Status offenses 5%
Public order offenses 10%
Drug offenses 8%
Offenses against people 34%
Property offenses 28%

Source: H. N. Snyder and M. Sickmund, *Juvenile Offenders and Victims: 2006 National Report* (Washington, DC: U.S. Office of Juvenile Justice and Delinquency Prevention, 2006), 198.

CLOSE UP

Fernando, 16, Finds a Sanctuary in Crime

FERNANDO MORALES was glad to discuss his life as a 16-year-old drug dealer. He had recently escaped from Long Lane School, a [Connecticut] correctional institution that became his home after he was caught with $1,100 worth of heroin known as P.

"The Five-O caught me right here with the bundles of P," he said, referring to a police officer, as he stood in front of a boarded-up house on Bridgeport's East Side. "They sentenced me to eighteen months, but I jetted after four. Three of us got out a bathroom window. We ran through the woods and stole a car. Then we got back here and the Five-O's came to my apartment, and I had to jump out the side window on the second floor."

What Future?

Since his escape, Fernando has been on the run for weeks. He still went to the weekly meetings of his gang, but he was afraid to go back to his apartment, afraid even to go to a friend's place to pick up the three guns he had stashed away. "I would love to get my baby Uzi, but it's too hot now."

"Could you bring a photographer here?" he asked. "I want my picture in the newspaper. I'd love to have me holding a bundle right there on the front page so the cops can see it. They're going to bug out."

The other dealers on the corner looked on with a certain admiration. They realized that a publicity campaign might not be the smartest long-term career move for a fugitive drug dealer. "Man, you be the one bugging out," another dealer told him but they also recognized the logic in Fernando's attitude. He was living his life according to a common assumption on these streets: There is no future.

When you ask the Hispanic teenagers selling drugs here what they expect to be doing in five years, you tend to get a lot of bored shrugs. Occasionally they'll talk about being back in school or being a retired drug dealer in a Porsche. But the most common answer is the one that Fernando gave without hesitation or emotion: "Dead or in jail."

The story of how Fernando got that way is a particularly sad one, but the basic elements are fairly typical in the lives of drug dealers and gang members in any urban ghetto. He has grown up amid tenements, housing projects, torched buildings, and abandoned factories. His role models have

been adults who use the city and the state primarily as terms for the different types of welfare checks. His neighborhood is a place where 13-year-olds know by heart the visiting hours at local prisons.

The Family: A Mother Leaves, a Father Drinks

Fernando Morales was born in Bridgeport, Connecticut, and a few months after his birth his mother moved out. Since then he has occasionally run into her on the street. Neither he nor his relatives can say exactly why she left or why she didn't take Fernando and her other son with her but the general assumption is that she was tired of being hit by their father.

The father, Bernabe Morales, who was 24 years old and had emigrated from Puerto Rico as a teenager, moved the two boys in with his mother at the P. T. Barnum public housing project. Fernando lived there until the age of 8, when his grandmother died. . . .

After that Fernando and his brother Bernard lived sometimes with their father and his current girlfriend, sometimes with relatives in Bridgeport or Puerto Rico. They eventually settled with their father's cousin, Monserrate Bruno, who already had ten children living in her two-bedroom apartment. . . .

His father, by all accounts, was a charming, generous man when sober but something else altogether when drinking or doing drugs. He was arrested more than two dozen times, usually for fighting or drugs, and spent five years in jail while Fernando was growing up. He lived on welfare, odd jobs, and money from selling drugs, a trade that was taken up by both his sons.

The "Industry": Moving Up in the Drug Trade

Fernando's school days ended two years ago, when he dropped out of ninth grade. School was corny, he explained. "I was smart, I learned quick, but I got bored. I was just learning things when I could be out making money."

Fernando might have found other opportunities—he had relatives working in fast-food restaurants and repair shops, and one cousin tried to interest him in a job distributing bread that might pay $700 a week but nothing with such quick rewards as the drug business flourishing on the East Side.

Staff member Vincent Vaielua (left) talks to a youth at an evening reporting center run by the Pierce County Juvenile Court in Tacoma, Washington. Many courts develop community programs in an effort to avoid confining youthful offenders in juvenile corrections institutions. What are the potential advantages and benefits of emphasizing community-based programs?

AP Images/ Elaine Thompson

He had friends and relatives in the business, and he started as one of the runners on the street corner making sales or directing buyers to another runner holding the marijuana, cocaine, crack, or heroin. The runners on each block buy their drugs paying, for instance, $200 for fifty bags of crack that sell for $250 from the block's lieutenant, who supervises them and takes the money to the absentee dealer called the owner of the block.

By this winter Fernando had moved up slightly on the corporate ladder. "I'm not the block lieutenant yet, but I have some runners selling for me," he explained as he sat in a bar near the block. Another teenager came in with money for him, which he proudly added to a thick wad in his pocket. "You see? I make money while they work for me."

Fernando still worked the block himself, too, standing on the corner watching for cars slowing down, shouting "You want P?" or responding to veteran customers for crack who asked, "Got any slab, man?" Fernando said he usually made between $100 and $300 a day, and that the money usually went as quickly as it came.

He had recently bought a car for $500 and wrecked it making a fast turn into a telephone pole. He spent money on gold chains with crucifixes, rings, Nike sneakers, Timberland boots, an assortment of Russell hooded sweatshirts called hoodies, gang dues, trips to New York City, and his 23-year-old girlfriend.

His dream was to get out of Bridgeport. "I'd be living fat somewhere. I'd go to somewhere hot, Florida or Puerto Rico or somewhere, buy me a house, get six blazing girls with dope bodies." In the meantime, he tried not to think about what his product was doing to his customers.

"Sometimes it bothers me. But see, I'm a hustler. I got to look out for myself. I got to be making money. Forget them. If you put that in your head, you're going to be caught out. You going to be a sucker. You going to be like them." He said he had used marijuana, cocaine, and angel dust himself, but made a point of never using crack or heroin, the drugs that plagued the last years of his father's life. . . .

The Gangs: "Like a Family" of Drug Dealers

"I cried a little, that's it," was all that Fernando would say about his father's death. But he did allow that it had something to do with his subsequent decision to join a Hispanic gang named Neta. He went with friends to a meeting, answered questions during an initiation ceremony, and began wearing its colors, a necklace of red, white, and blue beads.

"It's like a family, and you need that if you've lost your own family," he said. "At the meetings we talk about having heart, trust, and all that. We don't disrespect nobody. If we need money, we get it. If I need anything they're right there to help me."

Neta is allied with Bridgeport's most notorious gang, the Latin Kings, and both claim to be peaceful Hispanic cultural organizations opposed to drug use. But they are financed at least indirectly by the drug trade, because many members like Fernando work independently in drug operations, and the drug dealers' disputes can turn into gang wars . . . .

"I like guns, I like stealing cars, I like selling drugs, and I like money," he said. "I got to go to the block. That's where I get my spirit at. When I die, my spirit's going to be at the block, still making money. Booming." . . .

"I'll be selling till I get my act together. I'm just a little kid. Nothing runs through my head. All I think about is doing crazy things. But when I be big, I know I need education. If I get caught and do a couple of years, I'll come out and go back to school. But I don't have that in my head yet. I'll have my little fun while I'm out."

RESEARCHING THE INTERNET

Read about the problem of youth gangs at the website of the National Youth Violence Prevention Resource Center, listed on the Cole/Smith Criminal Justice in America Companion Website: http://www.cengage.com/criminaljustice/cole.

FOR CRITICAL ANALYSIS

What are the roots of gang affiliations such as Fernando's? What policies might be developed to deal with the gang problem?

Sources: John Tierney, *New York Times*, April 13, 1993, pp. Al, B6. Copyright © 1993 by The New York Times Company. Reprinted by permission.

Aftercare   The juvenile equivalent of parole is known as **aftercare**. Upon release, the offender is placed under the supervision of a juvenile parole officer who assists with educational, counseling, and treatment services. Quality aftercare is associated with lower rates of recidivism after release from incarceration, and many have blamed the failure of boot camps on poor aftercare (Kurlychek and Kempinen, 2006). As with the adult system, juveniles may be returned to custodial care should they violate the conditions of their parole.

■ **aftercare** Juvenile justice equivalent of parole, in which a delinquent is released from a custodial sentence and supervised in the community.

Community Treatment   In the past decade, treatment in community-based facilities has become much more common. Today many private, nonprofit agencies contract with states to provide services for troubled youths. Community-based options include foster homes, in which juvenile offenders live with families, usually for a short period, and group homes, often privately run facilities for groups of 12–20 juvenile offenders. Each group home has several staff personnel who work as counselors or houseparents during 8- or 24-hour shifts. Group-home placements provide individual and group counseling, allow juveniles to attend local schools, and offer a more structured life than most of the residents have received in their own homes. However, critics suggest that group homes often are mismanaged and may do little more than "warehouse" youths.

CHECKPOINT

	ANSWERS
5 *What three discretionary decisions do the police make with regard to processing juveniles?*	**5** Whether to take the child into custody, whether to request that the child be detained, whether to refer the child to court.
6 *What is the purpose of diversion?*	**6** To avoid formal proceedings when the child's best interest can be served by treatment in the community.
7 *What sentencing dispositions are available to the judge?*	**7** Probation, alternative dispositions, custodial care, community treatment.

Problems and Perspectives

Much of the criticism of juvenile justice has emphasized the disparity between the treatment ideal and the institutionalized practices of an ongoing bureaucratic system. Commentators have focused on how the language of social reformers has disguised the day-to-day operations that lack the elements of due process and in which custodial incarceration is all too frequent. Other criticisms claim that the juvenile justice system does not control juvenile crime.

The juvenile court, in both theory and practice, is a remarkably complex institution that must perform a wide variety of functions. The juvenile justice system must play such a range of roles that goals and values will inevitably collide.

In many states, the same judges, probation officers, and social workers are asked to deal with both neglected children and young criminals. Although departments of social services usually deal primarily with cases of neglect, the distinction between the criminal and the neglected child is often not maintained.

In addition to recognizing that the juvenile system has organizational problems, society must acknowledge that little is known about the causes of delinquency and its prevention or treatment. Over the years, people have advanced various social and behavioral theories to explain delinquency. One generation looked to slum conditions as the cause of juvenile crime, and another pointed to the affluence of the suburbs. Psychologists sometimes point to masculine insecurity in a matriarchal family structure, and some sociologists note the peer group pressures of the gang. This array of theories has led to an array of proposed and often contradictory treatments. In such confusion, those interested in the problems of youth may despair. What is clear is that we need additional research on the causes of delinquency and the treatment of juvenile offenders.

Youth gangs pose unique problems to those making decisions in the juvenile justice system. Gangs are responsible for a significant amount of delinquency in communities, and these gangs also thrive in correctional institutions (particularly, adult institutions). How does the presence and behavior of youth gangs affect juvenile justice policy? Recent research has indicated that gang members are more likely than nongang members to carry guns, thereby also increasing the likelihood of severe or lethal violence among these groups. Gang members are also more likely to receive longer sentences, given that gang membership and weapon ownership can increase the severity of punishment for juveniles (Melde, Esbensen, and Taylor, 2009).

In recent years, juveniles have been engaging in delinquent behavior online. The phenomenon of "cyber bullying" involves the use of computers, cell phones, and other electronic devices by youths to mistreat and harm their peers. Approximately one-third of adolescents have been bullied online, while approximately 20 percent of youth admit to cyber bullying others (Hinduja and Patchin, 2009; Patchin and Hinduja, 2006). While additional inquiry is necessary, cyber bullying has been correlated with traditional bullying and various forms of school violence (Hinduja and Patchin, 2007).

What trends foretell the future of juvenile justice? The conservative crime control policies that hit the adult criminal justice system with their emphasis on deterrence, retribution, and getting tough have also influenced juvenile justice in the past 20 years. One can point to growing levels of overcrowding in juvenile institutions, increased litigation challenging the abuse of children in training schools and detention centers, and higher rates of minority youth incarceration. All of these problems have emerged during a period of declining youth populations and fewer arrests of juveniles. With a renewed focus on juvenile crime under the philosophy that "kids are different," the juvenile justice system may be embarking on a less severe path to dealing with juvenile offenders.

On the other hand, future developments and events might ultimately lead to a continuation of the crime control orientation in many states. We must wait to see if we are truly moving into a new era that focuses on juveniles' developmental differences from adults. A future increase in youth crime or highly publicized gang violence could lead policy makers to turn back toward crime control priorities or otherwise slow the current trend toward reemphasizing treatment and rehabilitation for youthful offenders. In recent decades, the United States has not shown a consistent, firm commitment to the original rehabilitative goals of the juvenile justice system. Thus, it remains to be seen which priorities will shape the system's approach to punishing youthful offenders in the future.

A QUESTION OF ETHICS: WRITING ASSIGNMENT

Residents of the Lovelock Home had been committed by the juvenile court because they were either delinquent or neglected. All 25 boys, aged 12 to 16, were streetwise, tough, and interested only in getting out. The institution had a staff of social services professionals who tried to deal with the educational and psychological needs of the residents. Because state funding was short, these services looked better in the annual report than to an observer visiting Lovelock. Most of the time the residents watched television, played basketball in the backyard, or just hung out in one another's rooms.

Joe Klegg, the night supervisor, was tired from the eight-hour shift that he had just completed on his "second job" as a convenience store manager. The boys were watching television when he arrived at seven. Everything seemed calm. It should have been, because Joe had placed a tough 16-year-

old, Randy Marshall, in charge. Joe had told Randy to keep the younger boys in line. Randy used his muscle and physical presence to intimidate the other residents. He knew that if the home was quiet and there was no trouble, he would be rewarded with special privileges such as a "pass" to go see his girlfriend. Joe wanted no hassles and a quiet house so that he could doze off when the boys went to sleep.

WRITING ASSIGNMENT

Does the situation at Lovelock Home raise ethical questions, or does it merely raise questions of poor management practices? What are the potential consequences for the residents? For Joe Klegg? What is the state's responsibility? Write a short essay addressing these questions.

Summary

Recognize the extent of youth crime in the United States

▶ Crimes committed by juveniles remain a serious concern even though crimes of violence in general have decreased.

Understand how the juvenile justice system developed and the assumptions on which it was based

▶ The history of juvenile justice comprises six periods: Puritan, Refuge, juvenile court, juvenile rights, crime control, and "kids are different."

▶ Creation of the juvenile court in 1899 established a separate juvenile justice system.

▶ The *In re Gault* decision by the U.S. Supreme Court in 1967 brought due process to the juvenile justice system.

Identify what determines the jurisdiction of the juvenile justice system

▶ The juvenile system handles cases based on the ages of youths.

▶ Juvenile cases fall into one of three categories: delinquency, dependency, or neglect.

Understand how the juvenile justice system operates

▶ Decisions by police officers and juvenile intake officers dispose of a large portion of the many cases that are never referred to the court.

▶ In juvenile court, most cases are settled through a plea agreement.

▶ After conviction or plea, a disposition hearing is held. Before passing sentence, the judge reviews the offense and the juvenile's social history.

▶ Possible dispositions of a juvenile case include probation, community treatment, or institutional care.

▶ Juvenile court jurisdiction may be waived so that youths can be tried in the adult criminal justice system, but such waivers have decreased since the mid-1990s.

▶ Options for juvenile corrections include probation, alternative dispositions, custodial care, institutional programs, aftercare, and community treatment.

Analyze some of the issues facing the American system of juvenile justice

▶ Juvenile justice faces issues of racial disparities in punishment, criminal activity by gangs, and new behavioral problems, such as cyber bullying, that involve computers.

▶ It remains to be seen whether the current move toward increased rehabilitation will continue or whether crime control policies will remain a priority.

Questions for Review

1. What are the major historical periods of juvenile justice in the United States?

2. What is the jurisdiction of the juvenile court system?

3. What are the major processes in the juvenile justice system?

4. What are the sentencing and institutional alternatives for juveniles who are judged delinquent?

5. What due process rights do juveniles have?

Key Terms and Cases

aftercare (p. 457)
delinquent (p. 445)
dependent child (p. 446)
detention hearing (p. 449)
diversion (p. 448)
neglected child (p. 446)

parens patriae (p. 437)
PINS (p. 445)
status offense (p. 440)
waiver (p. 442)
Breed v. Jones (1975) (p. 440)
In re Gault (1967) (p. 440)

In re Winship (1970) (p. 440)
McKeiver v. Pennsylvania (1971) (p. 440)
Schall v. Martin (1984) (p. 441)

INSIDE THE CRIMINAL JUSTICE SYSTEM AND BEYOND: ONE MAN'S JOURNEY

Written by Chuck Terry

Reflections

THE OTHER DAY, while stopped at a red light, I suddenly thought about all the years I spent in "those places." Cells, segregated chow halls, racial tension, monotony, overcrowded conditions. All the years spent being ordered around by judges, guards, and parole officers. And then I thought about all the people who are there right now. Not only are there many more people doing it than before, but they are doing it for extensively longer periods of time. The thought chilled me to the bone. It hasn't always been like this.

People used to consider rehabilitation as a valid justification for imprisonment. Those who broke the law were seen as less fortunate and in need of help. This was when societal goals included using the law to even up the socioeconomic playing field for women and minorities, when social programs designed to fight poverty were being implemented rather than cut, and when popular enemies included communists and crooked politicians. Now many dwell on the harm created by "single-parent families," "illegal immigrants," "welfare dependency," and the evils of affirmative action. And now we have the perfect scapegoat, someone everyone can hate—the criminal.

Today "criminals" are depicted as inherently "bad" people. They are blamed for, among other things, our economic problems, fear of going out at night, dilapidated schools, rundown neighborhoods, and our children's unhappiness. Prisons and all the things that go along with "protecting" the public (alarm systems, more prisons, gated communities, increased budgets for policing, new laws) are "sold" and "bought" as essential mechanisms of control. By keeping "these people" in their place "we" can live "normal," safe lives.

Our aim now is to punish instead of rehabilitate. Increasing levels of formal social control are the means by which crime is "fought." We seldom address crime-generating factors like our market mentality, which revolves around the need to have, to get, and to have yet more; the increasing economic gap between the "haves" and "have-nots"; capital flight; racism; child abuse; homophobia; chronic unemployment; rampant inequality; economic insecurity; and the desperation that leads to drug addiction and other social ills. Instead, our attention is diverted toward individuals. We seem to blindly accept the sanity of draconian sentencing policies such as mandatory minimum laws that require prison time for selling crack cocaine, even for first-time offenders. Or the "Three Strikes and You're Out Law" in California that, though designed to imprison violent offenders, has been twisted and reshaped so that today roughly 70 percent of those going to prison under this law do so for a nonviolent crime. After spending so many years in "those places," I find what I see today difficult to accept.

Today I find myself around academics and "experts" in the field of criminal justice. I hope that we can learn from each other. I am given the opportunity to write papers like this and speak in front of hundreds of students in undergraduate classes. I feel fortunate to be doing all this, and more than grateful to be free from the grips of addiction and the criminal justice system.

Yet the story is far from over. The nightmare continues. "Those places" are being jammed with bodies faster than they can be built. Prisons and jails become home to the unemployable, addicts, the underprivileged, and outcasts of society. And rather than help, or even punish, doing time on such a massive scale will likely have disastrous effects on individuals, families, and communities that will last lifetimes and beyond. Can it be that we are crippling or incapacitating "those people"? After being oppressed, controlled, and degraded (especially for long periods of time), inmates turn into angry, fearful human beings who are unable to cope with things that people out here deal with all the time. The difficulty of participating in interpersonal relationships, finding and retaining employment, controlling anger, and "fitting in," to name a few, can become insurmountable obstacles. Yet most of our efforts to do anything about the situation only worsens it.

Efforts to improve sophisticated techniques of identifying, labeling, and monitoring parolees, "gang" members, and other "miscreants" are continually being developed. The school I attended inside no longer offers college classes—funding was pulled. Lifting weights—a positive, healthy way to release energy—is no longer allowed in many prisons: can't let "them" get too strong.

Today I have a friend in the county jail facing sixty years to life under California's three-strikes law for possession of less than a gram of cocaine. He is an addict, 48 years old, and if convicted will probably never get out. His first two strikes were for burglaries in the 1970s. Over the last few years he has battled with his addiction and, at one time, made it nearly two years without using. If the laws would have been the way they are today before I got clean, I would have been "striked out" myself. Is there anything wrong with all this?

My hope is that we are entering a new era, one in which we work on replacing blame and increasing levels of social control with understanding and compassion. An era in which we acknowledge the reality of contemporary life, its horrors, and its injustices as well as its joys. And I hope we can begin to alter the way we view those we perceive as being different from ourselves. All of us have fears. All of us need to belong and fit in somewhere. Oppression, hatred, and blame do not build better lives for anyone. We all need hope.

Reducing violence and crime requires lessening the harm we do to one another—including criminals. I know that, for me, the way I lived for so many years in "those places" affected my self-image, outlook, and actions in such a way that I had become almost completely alienated from everything in the outside world. Luckily, education and my motivation to learn gave me a new perspective and some hope. It helped me see more clearly. I was lucky to make it. Maybe it's time that people out here begin to imagine what it's like to be locked up. What it's like to be pushed into a life of crime, addiction, desperation, and hopelessness. Maybe by taking a closer look at the real factors associated with crime, and by changing the way we "see" those who get caught up in the criminal justice system, we can begin to end the nightmare.

accusatory process The series of events from the arrest of a suspect to the filing of a formal charge (through an indictment or information) with the court.

adjudication The process of determining whether the defendant is guilty.

adversarial process Court process, employed in the United States and other former British colonies, in which lawyers for each side represent their clients' best interests in presenting evidence and formulating arguments as a means to discover the truth and protect the rights of defendants.

affidavit Written statement of fact, supported by oath or affirmation, submitted to judicial officers to fulfill the requirements of probable cause for obtaining a warrant.

aftercare Juvenile justice equivalent of parole, in which a delinquent is released from a custodial sentence and supervised in the community.

aggressive patrol A patrol strategy designed to maximize the number of police interventions and observations in the community.

anomie A breakdown or disappearance of the rules of social behavior.

appeal A request to a higher court that it review actions taken in a trial court.

appellate courts Courts that do not try criminal cases but hear appeals of decisions of lower courts.

arraignment The court appearance of an accused person in which the charges are read and the accused, advised by a lawyer, pleads guilty or not guilty.

arrest The physical taking of a person into custody on the grounds that there is reason to believe that he or she has committed a criminal offense. Police may use only reasonable physical force in making an arrest. The purpose of the arrest is to hold the accused for a court proceeding.

assigned counsel An attorney in private practice assigned by a court to represent an indigent. The attorney's fee is paid by the government with jurisdiction over the case.

Atkins v. Virginia (2002) Execution of the mentally retarded is unconstitutional.

bail An amount of money, specified by a judge, to be paid as a condition of pretrial release to ensure that the accused will appear in court as required.

Barron v. Baltimore (1833) The protections of the Bill of Rights apply only to actions of the federal government.

bench trials Trials conducted by a judge who acts as fact finder and determines issues of law. No jury participates.

Bill of Rights The first ten amendments added to the U.S. Constitution to provide specific rights for individuals, including criminal justice rights concerning searches, trials, and punishments.

biological explanations Explanations of crime that emphasize physiological and neurological factors that may predispose a person to commit crimes.

boot camp A short-term institutional sentence, usually followed by probation, that puts the offender through a physical regimen designed to develop discipline and respect for authority. Also referred to as *shock incarceration*.

Bordenkircher v. Hayes (1978) A defendant's rights were not violated by a prosecutor who warned that refusing to enter a guilty plea would result in a harsher sentence.

Boykin v. Alabama (1969) Before a judge may accept a plea of guilty, defendants must state that they are making the plea voluntarily.

Breed v. Jones (1975) Juveniles cannot be found delinquent in juvenile court and then transferred to adult court without a hearing on the transfer; to do so violates the protection against double jeopardy.

challenge for cause Removal of a prospective juror by showing that he or she has some bias or some other legal disability. The number of such challenges available to attorneys is unlimited.

Chimel v. California (1969) Supreme Court decision that endorsed warrantless searches for weapons and evidence in the immediate vicinity of people who are lawfully arrested.

circumstantial evidence Evidence provided by a witness from which a jury must infer a fact.

citation A written order or summons, issued by a law enforcement officer, directing an alleged offender to appear in court at a specific time to answer a criminal charge.

civil law Law regulating the relationships between or among individuals, usually involving property, contracts, or business disputes.

classical criminology A school of criminology that views behavior as stemming from free will, demands responsibility and accountability of all perpetrators, and stresses the need for punishments severe enough to deter others.

classification The process of assigning an inmate to a category specifying his or her needs for security, treatment, education, work assignment, and readiness for release.

clearance rate The percentage of crimes known to the police that they believe they have solved through an arrest; a statistic used to measure a police department's productivity.

community corrections A model of corrections based on the goal of reintegrating the offender into the community.

community service A sentence requiring the offender to perform a certain amount of unpaid labor in the community.

conditions of release Conduct restrictions that parolees must follow as a legally binding requirement of being released.

congregate system A penitentiary system, developed in Auburn, New York, in which each inmate was held in isolation during the night but worked and ate with other prisoners during the day under a rule of silence.

continuance An adjournment of a scheduled case until a later date.

contract counsel An attorney in private practice who contracts with the government to represent all indigent defendants in a county during a set period of time and for a specified dollar amount.

contract labor system A system under which inmates' labor was sold on a contractual basis to private employers who provided the machinery and raw materials with which inmates made salable products in the institution.

control theories Theories holding that criminal behavior occurs when the bonds that tie an individual to society are broken or weakened.

Cooper v. Pate (1964) Prisoners are entitled to the protection of the Civil Rights Act of 1871 and may challenge in federal courts the conditions of their confinement.

corrections The variety of programs, services, facilities, and organizations responsible for the management of people who have been accused or convicted of criminal offenses.

count Each separate offense of which a person is accused in an indictment or an information.

crime control model A model of the criminal justice system that assumes freedom is so important that every effort must be made to repress crime; it emphasizes efficiency, speed, finality, and the capacity to apprehend, try, convict, and dispose of a high proportion of offenders.

crime control model of corrections A model of corrections based on the assumption that criminal behavior can be controlled by more use of incarceration and other forms of strict supervision.

crimes without victims Offenses involving a willing and private exchange of illegal goods or services that are in strong demand. Participants do not feel they are being harmed, but these crimes are prosecuted on the ground that society as a whole is being injured.

criminogenic Having factors thought to bring about criminal behavior in an individual.

critical criminology Theories that assume criminal law and the criminal justice system are primarily a means of controlling the lower classes, women, and minorities.

"CSI effect" A widely discussed but unproved belief that television dramas revolving around forensic science raise jurors' expectations about the use of scientific evidence in criminal cases and thereby reduce the likelihood of "guilty" verdicts in trials that rely solely on witness testimony and other forms of nonscientific evidence.

custodial model A model of incarceration that emphasizes security, discipline, and order.

cyber crimes Offenses that involve the use of one or more computers.

dark figure of crime A metaphor that emphasizes the dangerous dimension of crimes that are never reported to the police.

day reporting center A community correctional center where an offender reports each day to comply with elements of a sentence.

defense attorney The lawyer who represents accused offenders and convicted offenders in their dealings with criminal justice.

delinquent A child who has committed an act that if committed by an adult would be a criminal act.

demonstrative evidence Evidence that is not based on witness testimony but that

demonstrates information relevant to the crime, such as maps, X-rays, and photographs; includes real evidence involved in the crime.

dependent child A child who has no parent or guardian or whose parents cannot give proper care.

detention hearing A hearing by the juvenile court to determine if a juvenile is to be detained or released prior to adjudication.

determinate sentence A sentence that fixes the term of imprisonment at a specific period.

differential response A patrol strategy that assigns priorities to calls for service and chooses the appropriate response.

direct evidence Eyewitness accounts.

directed patrol A proactive form of patrolling that directs resources to known high-crime areas.

discovery A prosecutor's pretrial disclosure to the defense of facts and evidence to be introduced at trial.

discretion The authority to make decisions without reference to specific rules or facts, using instead one's own judgment; allows for individualization and informality in the administration of justice.

discretionary release The release of an inmate from prison to conditional supervision at the discretion of the parole board within the boundaries set by the sentence and the penal law.

discrimination Differential treatment of individuals or groups based on race, ethnicity, gender, sexual orientation, or economic status, instead of on their behavior or qualifications.

disparity A difference between groups that may either be explained by legitimate factors or indicate discrimination.

diversion The process of screening children out of the juvenile justice system without a decision by the court.

DNA analysis A scientific technique that identifies people through their distinctive gene patterns (also called genotypic features). DNA, or deoxyribonucleic acid, is the basic component of all chromosomes; all the cells in an individual's body, including those in skin, blood, organs, and semen, contain the same unique DNA.

double jeopardy The subjecting of a person to prosecution more than once in the same jurisdiction for the same offense; prohibited by the Fifth Amendment.

dual court system A system consisting of a separate judicial structure for each state in addition to a national structure. Each case is tried in a court of the same

jurisdiction as that of the law or laws broken.

due process model A model of the criminal justice system that assumes freedom is so important that every effort must be made to ensure that criminal justice decisions are based on reliable information; it emphasizes the adversarial process, the rights of defendants, and formal decision-making procedures.

electronic file management Computerization of court records, done to reduce reliance on paper documents and make documents easily accessible to the judge and attorneys via computer.

Enlightenment A movement during the eighteenth century in England and France in which concepts of liberalism, rationalism, equality, and individualism dominated social and political thinking.

entrapment The defense that the individual was induced by the police to commit the criminal act.

exchange A mutual transfer of resources: a balance of benefits and deficits that flow from behavior based on decisions about the values and costs of alternatives.

exclusionary rule The principle that illegally obtained evidence must be excluded from trial.

exigent circumstances When there is an immediate threat to public safety or the risk that evidence will be destroyed, officers may search, arrest, or question suspects without obtaining a warrant or following other usual rules of criminal procedure.

expiration release The release of an inmate from incarceration, without further correctional supervision; the inmate cannot be returned to prison for any remaining portion of the sentence for the current offense.

federalism A system of government in which power is divided between a central (national) government and regional (state) governments.

felonies Serious crimes usually carrying a penalty of death or of incarceration for more than one year.

feminist theories Theories that criticize existing theories for ignoring or undervaluing women's experiences as offenders, victims, and people subjected to decision making by criminal justice officials. These theories seek to incorporate an understanding of differences between the experiences and treatment of men and women while also integrating consideration of other factors, such as race and social class.

filtering process A screening operation; a process by which criminal justice officials screen out some cases while advancing others to the next level of decision making.

fine A sum of money to be paid to the state by a convicted person as punishment for an offense.

forfeiture Government seizure of property and other assets derived from or used in criminal activity.

frankpledge A system in old English law in which members of a tithing (a group of ten families) pledged to be responsible for keeping order and bringing violators of the law to court.

fundamental fairness A legal doctrine supporting the idea that so long as a state's conduct maintains basic standards of fairness, the Constitution has not been violated.

furlough The temporary release of an inmate from a correctional institution for a brief period, usually one to three days, for a visit home. Such programs help maintain family ties and prepare inmates for release on parole.

***Furman v. Georgia* (1972)** The death penalty, as administered, constitutes cruel and unusual punishment.

***Gagnon v. Scarpelli* (1973)** Before probation can be revoked, a two-stage hearing must be held and the offender provided with specific elements of due process. Requested counsel will be allowed on a case-by-case basis.

general deterrence Punishment of criminals that is intended to be an example to the general public and to discourage the commission of offenses.

Geographic Information System (GIS) Computer technology and software that permit law enforcement officials to map problem locations in order to understand calls for service and the nature and frequency of crimes and other issues within specific neighborhoods.

***Gideon v. Wainwright* (1963)** Indigent defendants have a right to counsel when charged with serious crimes for which they could face 6 or more months of incarceration.

going rate Local court officials' shared view of the appropriate sentence, given the offense, the defendant's prior record, and other case characteristics.

"good faith" exception Exception to the exclusionary rule that permits the use of improperly obtained evidence when police officers acted in honest reliance on a defective statute, a warrant improperly issued by a magistrate,

or a consent to search by someone who lacked authority to give such permission.

good time A reduction of an inmate's prison sentence, at the discretion of the prison administrator, for good behavior or participation in vocational, educational, or treatment programs.

grand jury Body of citizens drawn from the community to hear evidence presented by the prosecutor in order to decide whether enough evidence exists to file charges against a defendant.

***Gregg v. Georgia* (1976)** Death penalty laws are constitutional if they require the judge and jury to consider certain mitigating and aggravating circumstances in deciding which convicted murderers should be sentenced to death. Proceedings must also be divided into a trial phase and a punishment phase, and there must be opportunities for appeal.

habeas corpus A writ or judicial order requesting the release of a person being detained in a jail, prison, or mental hospital. If a judge finds the person is being held improperly, the writ may be granted and the person released.

halfway house A correctional facility housing convicted felons who spend a portion of their day at work in the community but reside in the halfway house during nonworking hours.

hands-off policy Judges should not interfere with the administration of correctional institutions.

home confinement A sentence requiring the offender to remain inside his or her home during specified periods.

***Hudson v. Palmer* (1984)** Prison officials have a right to search cells and confiscate any materials found.

identify theft The theft of social security numbers, credit card numbers, and other information in order to secure loans, withdraw bank funds, and purchase merchandise while posing as someone else: the unsuspecting victim who will eventually lose money in these transactions.

***In re Gault* (1967)** Juveniles have the right to counsel, to confront and examine accusers, and to have adequate notice of charges when confinement is a possible punishment.

***In re Winship* (1970)** The standard of proof beyond a reasonable doubt applies to juvenile delinquency proceedings.

incapacitation Depriving an offender of the ability to commit crimes against society, usually by detaining the offender in prison.

inchoate offense Conduct that is criminal even though the harm that the law seeks to prevent has not been done but merely planned or attempted.

incident-driven policing Policing in which calls for service are the primary instigators of action.

incorporation The extension of the due process clause of the Fourteenth Amendment to make binding on state governments the rights guaranteed in the first ten amendments to the U.S. Constitution (the Bill of Rights).

indeterminate sentence A period, set by a judge, that specifies a minimum and a maximum time to be served in prison. Sometime after the minimum, the offender may be eligible for parole.

indictment A document returned by a grand jury as a "true bill" charging an individual with a specific crime on the basis of a determination of probable cause as presented by a prosecuting attorney.

inevitable discovery rule Supreme Court ruling that improperly obtained evidence can be used when it would later have been inevitably discovered by the police.

information A document charging an individual with a specific crime. It is prepared by a prosecuting attorney and presented to a court at a preliminary hearing.

inmate code The values and norms of the prison social system that define the inmates' idea of the model prisoner.

inquisitorial process Court process, employed in most countries of the world, in which the judge takes an active role in investigating the case and examining evidence by, for example, questioning witnesses.

integrated theories Theories that combine differing theoretical perspectives into a larger model.

intensive supervision probation (ISP) Probation granted under conditions of strict reporting to a probation officer with a limited caseload.

intermediate sanctions A variety of punishments that are more restrictive than traditional probation but less severe and costly than incarceration.

internal affairs unit A branch of a police department that receives and investigates complaints alleging violation of rules and policies on the part of officers.

jail An institution authorized to hold pretrial detainees and sentenced misdemeanants for periods longer than 48 hours.

jurisdiction The geographic territory or legal boundaries within which control may be exercised; the range of a court's authority.

jury A panel of citizens selected according to law and sworn to determine matters of fact in a criminal case and to deliver a verdict of guilty or not guilty.

Kyllo v. United States (2001) Law enforcement officials cannot examine a home with a thermal-imaging device unless they obtain a warrant.

labeling theories Theories emphasizing that the causes of criminal behavior are not found in the individual but in the social process that labels certain acts as deviant or criminal.

latent fingerprints Impressions of the unique pattern of ridges on the fingertip that are left behind on objects; these impressions are the residue of natural skin secretions or contaminating materials such as ink, blood, or dirt that were present on the fingertips at the time of their contact with the objects.

law enforcement The police function of controlling crime by intervening in situations in which the law has clearly been violated and the police need to identify and apprehend the guilty person.

law enforcement intelligence Information, collected and analyzed by law enforcement officials, concerning criminal activities and organizations, such as gangs, drug traffickers, and organized crime.

learning theories Theories that see criminal behavior as learned, just as legal behavior is learned.

lease system A system under which inmates were leased to contractors who provided prisoners with food and clothing in exchange for their labor.

legal responsibility The accountability of an individual for a crime because of the perpetrator's characteristics and the circumstances of the illegal act.

less-lethal weapons Weapons such as pepper spray and air-fired beanbags or nets that are meant to incapacitate a suspect without inflicting serious injuries.

life course theories Theories that identify factors affecting the start, duration, nature, and end of criminal behavior over the life of an offender.

line functions Police components that directly perform field operations and carry out the basic functions of patrol, investigation, traffic, vice, juvenile, and so on.

local legal culture Norms shared by members of a court community as to how cases should be handled and how a participant should behave in the judicial process.

mala in se Offenses that are wrong by their very nature.

mala prohibita Offenses prohibited by law but not wrong in themselves.

mandatory release The required release of an inmate from incarceration to community supervision upon the expiration of a certain period, as specified by a determinate-sentencing law or parole guidelines.

mandatory sentence A sentence determined by statutes and requiring that a certain penalty be imposed and carried out for convicted offenders who meet certain criteria.

mark system A point system in which prisoners can reduce their term of imprisonment and gain release by earning "marks" or points through labor, good behavior, and educational achievement.

McCleskey v. Kemp (1987) The Supreme Court rejects a challenge of Georgia's death penalty on grounds of racial discrimination.

McKeiver v. Pennsylvania (1971) Juveniles do not have a constitutional right to a trial by jury.

medical model A model of corrections based on the assumption that criminal behavior is caused by biological or psychological conditions that require treatment.

Mempa v. Rhay (1967) Probationers have the right to counsel at a combined revocation-sentencing hearing.

mens rea "Guilty mind" or blameworthy state of mind, necessary for legal responsibility for a criminal offense; criminal intent, as distinguished from innocent intent.

merit selection A reform plan by which judges are nominated by a commission and appointed by the governor for a given period. When the term expires, the voters approve or disapprove the judge for a succeeding term. If the judge is disapproved, the committee nominates a successor for the governor's appointment.

Miranda v. Arizona (1966) U.S. Supreme Court decision declaring that suspects in custody must be informed of their rights to remain silent and be represented during questioning.

misdemeanors Offenses less serious than felonies and usually punishable by incarceration of no more than a year, probation, or intermediate sanction.

money laundering Moving the proceeds of criminal activities through a maze of businesses, banks, and brokerage accounts so as to disguise their origin.

Morrissey v. Brewer (1972) Due process rights require a prompt, informal, two-stage inquiry before an impartial hearing officer before parole may be revoked. The parolee may present relevant information and confront witnesses.

motion An application to a court requesting that an order be issued to bring about a specific action.

National Crime Victimization Surveys (NCVS) Interviews of samples of the U.S. population conducted by the Bureau of Justice Statistics to determine the number and types of criminal victimizations and thus the extent of unreported as well as reported crime.

National Incident-Based Reporting System (NIBRS) A reporting system in which the police describe each offense in a crime incident, together with data describing the offender, victim, and property.

neglected child A child who is receiving inadequate care because of some action or inaction of his or her parents.

net widening Process in which new sentencing options increase rather than reduce control over offenders' lives.

Nix v. Williams (1984) Legal decision in which the Supreme Court created the "inevitable discovery" exception to the exclusionary rule.

nolle prosequi An entry, made by a prosecutor on the record of a case and announced in court, indicating that the charges specified will not be prosecuted. In effect, the charges are thereby dismissed.

nonpartisan election An election in which candidates' party affiliations are not listed on the ballot.

North Carolina v. Alford (1970) A plea of guilty by a defendant who maintains his or her innocence may be accepted for the purpose of a lesser sentence.

occupational crimes Criminal offenses committed through opportunities created in a legal business or occupation.

order maintenance The police function of preventing behavior that disturbs or threatens to disturb the public peace or that involves face-to-face conflict between two or more people. In such situations, the police exercise discretion in deciding whether a law has been broken.

organized crime A framework for the perpetuation of criminal acts—usually in fields such as gambling, drugs, and prostitution—providing illegal services that are in great demand.

other conditional release A term used in some states to avoid the rigidity of mandatory release, by placing convicts in various community settings, under supervision.

parens patriae The state as parent; the state as guardian and protector of all citizens (such as juveniles) who cannot protect themselves.

parole The conditional release of an inmate from incarceration, under supervision, after part of the prison sentence has been served.

partisan election An election in which candidates openly endorsed by political parties are presented to voters for selection.

penitentiary An institution intended to punish criminals by isolating them from society and from one another so they can reflect on their past misdeeds, repent, and reform.

percentage bail Defendants may deposit a percentage (usually 10 percent) of the full bail with the court. The full amount of the bail is required if the defendant fails to appear. The percentage of bail is returned after disposition of the case, although the court often retains 1 percent for administrative costs.

peremptory challenge Removal of a prospective juror without giving any reason. Attorneys are allowed a limited number of such challenges.

PINS Acronym for "person(s) in need of supervision," a term that designates juveniles who are either status offenders or thought to be on the verge of trouble.

plain view doctrine Officers may examine and use as evidence, without a warrant, contraband or evidence that is in open view at a location where they are legally permitted to be.

plea bargain A defendant's plea of guilty to a criminal charge with the reasonable expectation of receiving some consideration from the state for doing so, usually a reduction of the charge. The defendant's ultimate goal is a penalty lighter than the one formally warranted by the charged offense.

political crime An act, usually done for ideological purposes, that constitutes a threat against the state (such as treason, sedition, or espionage); also describes a criminal act by the state.

positivist criminology A school of criminology that views behavior as stemming from social, biological, and psychological factors. It argues that punishment should be tailored to the individual needs of the offender.

Powell v. Alabama (1932) An attorney must be provided to a poor defendant facing the death penalty.

presentence report A report, prepared by a probation officer, that presents a convicted offender's background and is used by the judge in selecting an appropriate sentence.

presumptive sentence A sentence for which the legislature or a commission sets a minimum and maximum range of months or years. Judges are to fix the length of the sentence within that range, allowing for special circumstances.

preventive detention Holding a defendant for trial, based on a judge's finding that if the defendant were released on bail, he or she would endanger the safety of any other person and the community or would flee.

preventive patrol Making the police presence known, to deter crime and to make officers available to respond quickly to calls.

prison An institution for the incarceration of people convicted of serious crimes, usually felonies.

proactive Acting in anticipation, such as an active search for potential offenders that is initiated by the police without waiting for a crime to be reported. Arrests for crimes without victims are usually proactive.

probable cause An amount of reliable information indicating that it is more likely than not that evidence will be found in a specific location or that a specific person is guilty of a crime.

probation A sentence that the offender is allowed to serve under supervision in the community.

problem-oriented policing An approach to policing in which officers routinely seek to identify, analyze, and respond to the circumstances underlying the incidents that prompt citizens to call the police.

procedural criminal law Law defining the procedures that criminal justice officials must follow in enforcement, adjudication, and corrections.

prosecuting attorney A legal representative of the state with sole responsibility for bringing criminal charges. In some states, this person is referred to as the district attorney, state's attorney, commonwealth attorney, or county attorney.

psychological explanations Explanations of crime that emphasize mental processes and behavior.

public defender An attorney employed on a full-time, salaried basis by a public or private nonprofit organization to represent indigents.

"public safety" exception Exception to *Miranda* requirements that permits police to immediately question a suspect in custody without providing any warnings, when public safety would be jeopardized by their taking the time to supply the warnings.

reactive Occurring in response, such as police activity in response to notification that a crime has been committed.

real evidence Physical evidence—such as a weapons, records, fingerprints, and stolen property—involved in the crime.

reasonable doubt The standard used by a jury to decide if the prosecution has provided enough evidence for conviction.

reasonable expectation of privacy The objective standard developed by courts for determining whether a government intrusion into an individual's person or property constitutes a search because it interferes with the individual's interests that are normally protected from government examination.

reasonable suspicion A police officer's belief based on articulable facts that would be recognized by others in a similar situation as indicating that criminal activity is afoot and necessitates further investigation that will intrude on an individual's reasonable expectation of privacy.

recidivism A return to criminal behavior.

reformatory An institution for young offenders that emphasizes training, a mark system of classification, indeterminate sentences, and parole.

rehabilitation The goal of restoring a convicted offender to a constructive place in society through some form of vocational or educational training or therapy.

rehabilitation model (1) A model of corrections that emphasizes the need to restore a convicted offender to a constructive place in society through some form of vocational or educational training or therapy. (See Chapter 10.) (2) A model of incarceration that emphasizes treatment programs to help prisoners address the personal problems and issues that led them to commit crimes. (See Chapter 12.)

reintegration model A model of a correctional institution that emphasizes maintaining the offender's ties to family and community as a method of reform, recognizing that the offender will be returning to society.

release on recognizance (ROR) Pretrial release granted, on the defendant's promise to appear in court, because the judge believes that the defendant's ties to the community guarantee that he or she will appear.

restitution Repayment—in the form of money or service—by an offender to a victim who has suffered some loss from the offense.

restorative justice Punishment designed to repair the damage done to the victim and community by an offender's criminal act.

retribution Punishment inflicted on a person who has harmed others and so deserves to be penalized.

Ricketts v. Adamson (1987) Defendants must uphold the plea agreement or suffer the consequences.

Roper v. Simmons (2005) Execution of offenders for crimes committed while under the age of 18 is unconstitutional.

Santobello v. New York (1971) When a guilty plea rests on a promise of a prosecutor, the promise must be fulfilled.

Schall v. Martin (1984) Juveniles can be held in preventive detention if there is concern that they may commit additional crimes while awaiting court action.

search Government officials' examination of and hunt for evidence on a person or in a place in a manner that intrudes on reasonable expectations of privacy.

seizures Situations in which police officers use their authority to deprive people of their liberty or property and which must not be "unreasonable" according to the Fourth Amendment.

selective incapacitation Making the best use of expensive and limited prison space by targeting for incarceration those individuals whose incapacity will do the most to reduce crime in society.

self-incrimination The act of exposing oneself to prosecution by being forced to respond to questions whose answers may reveal that one has committed a crime. The Fifth Amendment protects defendants against self-incrimination.

sentencing guidelines A mechanism to indicate to judges the expected sanction for certain offenses, in order to reduce disparities in sentencing.

separate confinement A penitentiary system, developed in Pennsylvania, in which each inmate was held in isolation from other inmates. All activities, including craft work, took place in the cells.

service The police function of providing assistance to the public, usually in matters unrelated to crime.

shock probation A sentence in which the offender is released after a short incarceration and resentenced to probation.

social conflict theories Theories that view crime as the result of conflict in society, such as conflict between economic classes caused by elites using law as a means to maintain power.

social process theories Theories that see criminality as normal behavior. Everyone has the potential to become a criminal, depending on (1) the influences that impel one toward or away from crime and (2) how one is regarded by others.

social structure theories Theories that blame crime on the existence of a powerless lower class that lives with poverty and deprivation and often turns to crime in response.

socialization The process by which the rules, symbols, and values of a group or subculture are learned by its members.

sociological explanations Explanations of crime that emphasize as causes of criminal behavior the social conditions that bear on the individual.

specific deterrence Punishment inflicted on criminals to discourage them from committing future crimes.

state attorney general Chief legal officer of a state, responsible for both civil and criminal matters.

status offense Any act committed by a juvenile that is considered unacceptable for a child, such as truancy or running away from home, but that would not be a crime if it were committed by an adult.

stop Government officials' interference with an individual's freedom of movement for a duration that typically lasts less than one hour and only rarely extends for as long as several hours.

stop-and-frisk search Limited search approved by the Supreme Court in *Terry v. Ohio* that permits police officers to pat down the clothing of people on the streets if there is reasonable suspicion of dangerous criminal activity.

subculture The symbols, beliefs, values, and attitudes shared by members of a subgroup of the larger society.

substantive criminal law Law that defines acts that are subject to punishment and specifies the punishments for such offenses.

sworn officers Police employees who have taken an oath and been given powers by the state to make arrests and use necessary force, in accordance with their duties.

system A complex whole consisting of interdependent parts whose actions are directed toward goals and are influenced by the environment within which they function.

technical violation The probationer's failure to abide by the rules and conditions of probation (specified by the judge), resulting in revocation of probation.

Tennessee v. Garner (1985) Deadly force may not be used against an unarmed and fleeing suspect unless necessary to prevent the escape and unless the officer has probable cause to believe that the suspect poses a significant threat of death or serious injury to the officers or others.

Terry v. Ohio (1968) Supreme Court decision endorsing police officers' authority to stop and frisk suspects on the streets when there is reasonable suspicion that they are armed and involved in criminal activity.

testimony Oral evidence provided by a legally competent witness.

theory of differential association The theory that people become criminals because they encounter more influences that view criminal behavior as normal and acceptable than influences that are hostile to criminal behavior.

totality of circumstances Flexible test established by the Supreme Court for identifying whether probable cause exists to justify a judge's issuance of a warrant.

trial courts of general jurisdiction Criminal courts with jurisdiction over all offenses, including felonies. In some states, these courts also hear appeals.

trial courts of limited jurisdiction Criminal courts with trial jurisdiction over misdemeanor cases and preliminary matters in felony cases. Sometimes these courts hold felony trials that may result in penalties below a specific limit.

Uniform Crime Reports (UCR) An annually published statistical summary of crimes reported to the police, based on voluntary reports to the FBI by local, state, and federal law enforcement agencies.

United States attorneys Officials responsible for the prosecution of crimes that violate the laws of the United States. Appointed by the president and assigned to a U.S. district court jurisdiction.

United States v. Drayton (2002) Legal decision declaring that police officers are not required to inform people of their right to decline to be searched when police ask for consent to search.

United States v. Salerno and Cafero (1987) Preventive detention provisions of the Bail Reform Act of 1984 are upheld as a legitimate use of government power designed to prevent people from committing crimes while on bail.

USA Patriot Act A federal statute passed in the aftermath of the terrorist attacks of September 11, 2001, that broadens government authority to conduct searches and wiretaps and that expands the definitions of crimes involving terrorism.

victimology A field of criminology that examines the role the victim plays in precipitating a criminal incident and also examines the impact of crimes on victims.

visible crime An offense against persons or property, committed primarily by members of the lower class. Often referred to as "street crime" or "ordinary crime," this type of offense is the one most upsetting to the public.

voir dire A questioning of prospective jurors to screen out people the attorneys think might be biased or otherwise incapable of delivering a fair verdict.

waiver Procedure by which the juvenile court waives its jurisdiction and transfers a juvenile case to the adult criminal court.

warrant A court order authorizing police officers to take certain actions, for example, to arrest suspects or to search premises.

Williams v. Florida (1970) Juries of fewer than 12 members are constitutional.

Witherspoon v. Illinois (1968) Potential jurors who object to the death penalty cannot be automatically excluded from service; however, during voir dire, those who feel so strongly about capital punishment that they could not give an impartial verdict may be excluded.

Wolff v. McDonnell (1974) Basic elements of procedural due process must be present when decisions are made about the disciplining of an inmate.

work and educational release The daytime release of inmates from correctional institutions so they can work or attend school.

workgroup A collection of individuals who interact in the workplace on a continuing basis, share goals, develop norms regarding how activities should be carried out, and eventually establish a network of roles that differentiates the group from others and that facilitates cooperation.

working personality A set of emotional and behavioral characteristics developed by members of an occupational group in response to the work situation and environmental influences.

Abbe, O. G., and P. S. Herrnson. 2002. "How Judicial Election Campaigns Have Changed." *Judicature* 85:286–95.

Abwender, D. A., and K. Hough. 2001. "Interactive Effects of Characteristics of Defendant and Mock Juror on U.S. Participants' Judgment and Sentencing Recommendations." *Journal of Social Psychology* 141:603–16.

Acker, J. R. 2007. "Impose an Immediate Moratorium on Executions." *Criminology and Public Policy* 6:641–50.

Acoca, L. 1997. "Hearts on the Ground: Violent Victimization and Other Themes in the Lives of Women Prisoners." *Corrections Management Quarterly* 1 (Spring): 44–55.

———. 1998. "Defusing the Time Bomb: Understanding and Meeting the Growing Health Care Needs of Incarcerated Women in America." *Crime and Delinquency* 44 (January): 49–69.

Adams, G. 2006. "Sex Offenders' Killer Studied States' Lists." http://www.boston.com.

Adams, K. 1992. "Adjusting to Prison Life." In *Crime and Justice: A Review of Research*, vol. 16, ed. M. Tonry. Chicago: University of Chicago Press, 275–359.

———. 1999. "What We Know about Police Use of Force." In *Use of Force by Police: Overview of National and Local Data*. Washington, DC: U.S. Government Printing Office.

Adang, O. M. J., and J. Mensink. 2004. "Pepper Spray: An Unreasonable Response to Suspect Verbal Resistance." *Policing: International Journal of Police Strategies and Management* 27:206–19.

Adler, F. 1975. *Sisters in Crime: The Rise of the New Female Criminal*. New York: McGraw-Hill.

Adler, S. J. 1994. *The Jury: Disorder in the Court*. New York: Doubleday.

Administrative Office of the U.S. Courts. 2005. "Need for DNA Testing Taxes Courts." *The Third Branch* 37 (February): 3.

Alarcon, A. L. 2007. "Remedies for California's Death Row Gridlock." *Southern California Law Review* 80: 697–752.

Alexander, R., Jr. 1993. "The Demise of State Prisoners' Access to Federal Habeas Corpus." *Criminal Justice Policy Review* 6:55–70.

Alley, M. E., E. M. Bonello, and J. A. Schafer. 2002. "Dual Responsibilities: A Model for Immersing Midlevel Managers in Community Policing." In *The Move to Community Policing: Making Change Happen*, ed. M. Morash and J. Ford. Thousand Oaks, CA: Sage, 112–25.

Amar, A. R. 1997. *The Constitution and Criminal Procedure: First Principles*. New Haven, CT: Yale University Press.

Amar, V. 2008. "An Enigmatic Court? Examining the Roberts Court as It Begins Year Three: Criminal Justice." *Pepperdine Law Review* 35:523–31.

American Correctional Association. 1994. *Gangs in Correctional Facilities: A National Assessment*. Laurel, MD: American Correctional Association.

———. 2000. *Vital Statistics in Corrections*. Lanham, MD: American Correctional Association.

American Society of Neuroradiology. 2003. "MRI Technology Shows Promise in Detecting Human Truth and Deception." Press release, May 5. http://www.asnr.org.

Amnesty International. 1999. "Annual General Meeting Highlights USA Campaign." *Amnesty Action*, Summer, p. 10.

Anderson, G., R. Litzenberger, and D. Plecas. 2002. "Physical Evidence of Police Officer Stress." *Policing* 25:399–420.

Andrews, D. A., and J. Bonta. 1994. *The Psychology of Criminal Behavior*. Cincinnati, OH: Anderson.

Andrews, D. A., I. Zinger, R. D. Hoge, J. Bonta, P. Gendreau, and F. T. Cullen. 1990. "Does Correctional Treatment Work? A Clinically Relevant and Psychologically Informed Meta-Analysis." *Criminology* 28:369–404.

Anglen, R. 2008. "Judge Rules for Taser in Cause-of-Death Decisions." *Arizona Republic,* May 2. http://www.azcentral.com.

Anti-Defamation League. 2008. "Anti-Defamation League State Hate Crime Statutory Provisions." Washington, DC: Anti-Defamation League. http://www.adl.org.

Antonuccio, R. 2008. "Prisons for Profit: Do the Social and Political Problems Have a Legal Solution?" *Journal of Corporation Law* 33:577–92.

Arena, K., and K. Bohn. 2008. "Rape Victim Pushes for Expanded DNA Database." May 12. http://www.cnn.com.

Armour, M. 2008. "Dazed and Confused: The Need for a Legislative Solution to the Constitutional Problem of Juror Comprehension." *Temple Political and Civil Rights Law Review* 17:641–73.

Armstrong, G. S., and D. L. MacKenzie. 2003. "Private versus Public Juvenile Facilities: Do Differences in Environmental Quality Exist?" *Crime and Delinquency* 49 (October): 542–63.

Armstrong, K., and S. Mills. 1999. "Death Row Justice Derailed." *Chicago Tribune,* November 14 and 15, p. 1.

Arnold, N. 2008. "Madison Murder Prompts Look at 911 Procedures." May 5. http://www.wbay.com.

Arterton, J. B. 2008. "Unconscious Bias and the Impartial Jury." *Connecticut Law Review* 40:1023–33.

Associated Press. 2007. "Grant Convicted of 2nd-Degree Murder." December 21. http://www.clickondetroit.com.

———. 2009a. "Student Shot to Death in Café at Wesleyan." *New York Times*, May 7. http://www.nytimes.com.

———. 2009b. "Wesleyan Shooting Suspect Surrenders." May 8. http://www.foxnews.com.

Association of Certified Fraud Examiners. 2008. *2008 Report to the Nation on Occupational Fraud and Abuse*. Austin, TX: Author.

Auerhahn, K. 1999. "Selective Incapacitation and the Problem of Prediction." *Criminology* 37:703–34.

Austin, J. 2001. "Prisoner Reentry: Current Trends, Practices, and Issues." *Crime and Delinquency* 47 (July): 314–33.

Austin, J., T. Fabelo, A. Gunter, and K. McGinnis. 2006. *Sexual Violence in the Texas Prison System*. Final report submitted to the National Institute of Justice, September.

Axtman, K. 2005a. "A New Motion to Make Jury Service More Attractive." *Christian Science Monitor*, May 23, pp. 2–3.

Baker, A. 2008. "11 Years of Police Gunfire, in Painstaking Detail." *New York Times*, May 8. http://www.nytimes.com.

Baldus, D. C., G. Woodworth, and C. A. Pulaski. 1994. *Equal Justice and the Death Penalty: A Legal and Empirical Analysis*. Boston: Northeastern University Press.

Bandy, D. 1991. "$1.2 Million to Be Paid in Stray-Bullet Death." *Akron Beacon Journal,* December 3, p. B6.

Basemore, G., and M. S. Umbreit. 1994. Foreword to *Balanced and Restorative Justice: Program Summary*. Washington, DC: Office of Juvenile Justice and Delinquency Prevention, U.S. Government Printing Office.

Bayley, D. H. 1994. *Police for the Future*. New York: Oxford University Press.

———. 1998. *What Works in Policing?* New York: Oxford University Press.

Beck, A. 1997. "Growth, Change, and Stability in the U.S. Prison Population, 1980–1995." *Corrections Management Quarterly* 8 (January): 1–14.

Beck, A. J., J. C. Karberg, and P. M. Harrison. 2002. "Prison and Jail Inmates at Mid-Year 2001." Bureau of Justice Statistics *Bulletin*, April.

Becker, H. S. 1963. *Outsiders: Studies in the Sociology of Deviance*. New York: Free Press.

Beckett, K., K. Nyrop, and L. Pfingst. 2006. "Race, Drugs, and Policing: Understanding Disparities in Drug Delivery Arrests." *Criminology* 44:105–37.

Bell, D. 1967. *The End of Ideology*. 2nd rev. ed. New York: Collier.

Belluck, P. 2005. "DNA Test Leads, at Last, to Arrest in Cape Cod Case." *New York Times*, April 16. http://www.nytimes.com.

Bennett, M. 2009. "Police Car Maker Considers Connersville." *Indianapolis Star*, March 5. http://www.indystar.com.

Berlin, L. 2009. "Running a Business after Doing Time." *New York Times*, February 22, p. YBU3.

Bershard, L. 1985. "Discriminatory Treatment of the Female Offender in the Criminal Justice System." *Boston College Law Review* 26:389–438.

BJS (Bureau of Justice Statistics). 1999. *Special Report*, July.

———. 2000a. *Bulletin*, August.

———. 2000b. *Correctional Populations in the United States, 1997*. Washington, DC: U.S. Government Printing Office.

———. 2000c. Press release, February 27.

———. 2000d. *Sourcebook of Criminal Justice Statistics, 1999*. Washington, DC: U.S. Government Printing Office.

———. 2000e. *Special Report*, August.

———. 2001a. *Bulletin*, August.

———. 2001b. *Special Report*, July.

———. 2002. *Special Report*, June.

———. 2003a. *Bulletin*, July.

———. 2003b. *Bulletin*, December.

———. 2003c. *Census of State and Federal Correctional Facilities, 2000*. Washington, DC: U.S. Government Printing Office.

———. 2004a. *Bulletin*, July.

———. 2004b. *Bulletin*, December.

———. 2004c. "UCR and NIBRS Participation." http://www.ojp.usdoj.gov/bjs/nibrsstatus.htm.

———. 2005a. *Bulletin*, April.

———. 2005b. *Bulletin*, October.

———. 2005c. *Sourcebook of Criminal Justice Statistics, 2004*. Washington, DC: U.S. Government Printing Office.

———. 2005d. *Special Report*, August.

———. 2006a. *Bulletin*, November.

———. 2006b. *Criminal Victimization in the United States, 2004*. Washington, DC: U.S. Government Printing Office.

———. 2006c. *Criminal Victimization in the United States, 2005—Statistical Tables*. Washington, DC: U.S. Government Printing Office.

———. 2006d. *Special Report*, July.

———. 2007a. *Bulletin*, July.

———. 2007b. *Bulletin*, December.

———. 2007c. *Crime in the United States, 2007*. Washington, DC: U.S. Department of Justice.

———. 2007d. *FBI Supplemental Homicide Reports, 1976–2005*. Washington, DC: U.S. Department of Justice.

———. 2007e. *Special Report*, December.

———. 2008a. *Bulletin*, June.

———. 2008b. *Bulletin*, December.

———. 2008c. *Criminal Victimization in the United States, 2006—Statistical Tables*. http://www.ojp.usdoj.gov/bjs/abstract/cvusst.htm.

———. 2008d. Press release, December 11.

———. 2008e. Sourcebook of Criminal Justice Statistics Online. http://www.albany.edu/sourcebook/.

Black, A. D. 2007. "'The War on People': Reframing 'The War on Drugs' by Addressing Racism within American Drug Policy through Restorative Justice and Community Collaboration." *University of Louisville Law Review* 46:177–97.

Bloch, P., and D. Anderson. 1974. *Policewomen on Patrol: First Report*. Washington, DC: Police Foundation.

Blumberg, M. 1989. "Controlling Police Use of Deadly Force: Assessing Two Decades of Progress." In *Critical Issues in Policing*, ed. G. Dunham and G. Alpert. Prospect Heights, IL: Waveland Press.

Blumenson, E., and E. Nilsen. 1998. "The Drug War's Hidden Economic Agenda." *The Nation*, March 9, p. 11.

Blumstein, A. 1996. "Youth Violence, Guns, and Illicit Drug Markets." In *NIJ Research Preview*. Washington, DC: National Institute of Justice, U.S. Government Printing Office.

Blumstein, A., and A. Beck. 2005. "Reentry as a Transient State between Liberty and Commitment." In *Prisoner Reentry and Crime in America*, ed. J. Allen, J. Travis, and C. Visher. New York: Cambridge University Press, 50–79.

Blumstein, J. F., M. A. Cohen, and S. Seth. 2008. "Do Government Agencies Respond to Market Pressures? Evidence from Private Prisons." *Virginia Journal of Social Policy and Law* 15:446–69.

Bogdanich, W. 2008. "Heparin Find May Point to Chinese Counterfeiting." *New York Times*, March 20. http://www.nytimes.com.

Boland, B. 2001. *Community Prosecution in Washington, D.C.: The U.S. Attorney's Fifth District Pilot Project*. Washington, DC: National Institute of Justice, U.S. Government Printing Office.

Boland, B., E. Brady, H. Tyson, and J. Bassler. 1983. *The Prosecution of Felony Arrests*. Washington, DC: Bureau of Justice Statistics, U.S. Government Printing Office.

Bonczar, T. P., and T. L. Snell. 2004. "Capital Punishment, 2003." Bureau of Justice Statistics *Bulletin*, November.

Bonne, J. 2001. "Meth's Deadly Buzz." *MSNBC News Special Report*. February. http://www.msnbc.msn.com.

Bontrager, S., W. Bales, and T. Chiricos. 2005. "Race, Ethnicity, Threat and the Labeling of Convicted Felons." *Criminology* 43:589–622.

Bourque, B. B., M. Han, and S. M. Hill. 1996. "A National Survey of Aftercare Provisions for Boot Camp Graduates." National Institute of Justice *Research in Brief*, May.

Bowen, J. 2008. "Punishing the Innocent." *University of Pennsylvania Law Review* 156:1117–79.

Bowers, F. 2002. "The Intelligence Divide: Can It Be Bridged?" *Christian Science Monitor*, October 8, p. 2.

Bowker, L. H. 1982. "Victimizers and Victims in American Correctional Institutions." In *Pains of Imprisonment*, ed. R. Johnson and H. Toch. Beverly Hills, CA: Sage.

Bradley, C. 1992. "Reforming the Criminal Trial." *Indiana Law Journal* 68:659–64.

Braga, A., and C. Winship. 2005. "Creating an Effective Foundation to Prevent Youth Violence: Lessons Learned from Boston in the 1990s." *Rappaport Institute Policy Brief #PB-2005-5*. Cambridge, MA: Kennedy School of Government at Harvard University, September 26.

Braga, A. A. 1999. "Problem-oriented Policing in Violent Crime Places: A Randomized Controlled Experiment." *Criminology* 37:541–80.

Braithwaite, J. 2007. "Encourage Restorative Justice." *Criminology and Public Policy* 6:689–96.

Brandl, S., and Frank, J. 1994. "The Relationship between Evidence, Detective Effort, and the Disposition of Burglary and Robbery Investigations." *American Journal of Police*, 13:149–68.

Bray, K. 1992. "Reaching the Final Chapter in the Story of Peremptory Challenges." *U.C.L.A. Law Review* 40:517–55.

Brennan, P. A., S. A. Mednick, and J. Volavka. 1995. "Biomedical Factors in Crime." In *Crime*, ed. J. Q. Wilson and J. Petersilia. San Francisco: ICS Press.

Bright, S. B. 1994. "Counsel for the Poor: The Death Sentence Not for the Worst Crime but for the Worst Lawyer." *Yale Law Journal* 103:1850.

Britt, C. 2000. "Social Context and Racial Disparities in Punishment Decisions." *Justice Quarterly* 17:707–32.

Broeder, D. W. 1959. "The University of Chicago Jury Project." *Nebraska Law Review* 38:774–803.

Brown, D. M. 2009. "Calling Your Bluff: How Prosecutors and Defense Attorneys Adapt Plea Bargaining Strategies to Increased Formalization." *Justice Quarterly* 26:2–29.

Bruce, M. 2003. "Contextual Complexity and Violent Delinquency among Black and White Males." *Journal of Black Studies* 35:65–98.

Brunson, R. K. 2007. "'Police Don't Like Black People': African-American Young Men's Accumulated Police Experiences." *Crime and Public Policy* 6:71–102.

Burke, K., J. Crosson, A. Gendar, and R. Shapiro. 2009. "Wesleyan Shooting Suspect Stephen Morgan Turns Self in to Police." *New York Daily News*, May 7. http://www.nydailynews.com.

Burns, A. C. 2007. "*Beard v. Banks*: Restricted Reading, Rehabilitation, and Prisoners' First Amendment Rights." *Journal of Law and Policy* 15:1225–70.

Buruma, I. 2005. "What Teaching a College-Level Class at a Maximum Security Correctional Facility Did for the Inmates—and for Me." *The New York Times Magazine*, February 20, pp. 36–41.

Bushway, S. D., and A. M. Piehl. 2001. "Judging Judicial Discretion: Legal Factors and Racial Discrimination in Sentencing." *Law and Society Review* 35:733–64.

Business Wire. 2001a. "Study Shows Iris Recognition Technology Is Superior among Biometrics; Britain's National Physical Laboratory Publishes Performance Evaluation of Seven Biometric Systems." May 17. Lexis-Nexis.

———. 2001b. "WorldNet Technologies, Creators of a State of the Art Weapons Detection System, Signs Consulting Deal with NuQuest." November 27. Lexis-Nexis.

Butterfield, F. 1998a. "Decline in Violent Crimes Is Linked to Crack Market." *New York Times*, December 18, p. A16.

———. 1998b. "Prisons Replace Hospitals for the Nation's Mentally Ill." *New York Times*, March 5, p. A26.

———. 2000. "Often, Parole Is One Stop on the Way Back to Prison." *New York Times*, November 29, p. A1.

———. 2004. "Repaving the Long Road out of Prison." *New York Times*, May 4. http://www.nytimes.com.

Bykowicz, J. 2008. "Juvenile Center Home to Despair." *Baltimore Sun*, May 25. http://baltimoresun.com.

Bynum, T., and S. Varano. 2002. "The Anti-Gang Initiative in Detroit: An Aggressive Enforcement Approach to Gangs." In *Policing Gangs and Youth Violence*, ed. S. H. Decker. Belmont, CA: Wadsworth, 214–38.

Byrne, J. M. 2008. "The Best Laid Plans: An Assessment of the Varied Consequences of New Technologies for Crime and Social Control." *Federal Probation* 72 (3): 10–21.

Cady, M. S., and J. R. Phelps. 2008. "Preserving the Delicate Balance between Judicial Accountability and Independence: Merit Selection in the Post-White World." *Cornell Journal of Law and Public Policy* 17:343–81.

Cahill, M. T. 2007a. "Attempt, Reckless Homicide, and the Design of Criminal Law." *University of Colorado Law Review* 78:879–956.

———. 2007b. "Retributive Justice in the Real World." *Washington University Law Quarterly* 85:815–70.

Calhoun, F. 1990. *The Lawmen*. Washington, DC: Smithsonian Institution.

Callahan, L. A., M. A. McGreevy, C. Cirincione, and H. J. Steadman. 1992. "Measuring the Effects of the Guilty But Mentally Ill (GBMI) Verdict." *Law and Human Behavior* 16:447–62.

Callahan, R. 2002. "Scientists: Liars Are Betrayed by Their Faces." Associated Press Wire Service, January 2.

Camp, C. G. 2003. *Corrections Yearbook, 2002*. Middletown, CT: Criminal Justice Institute.

Camp, C. G., and G. M. Camp. 1999. *Corrections Yearbook, 1999*. Middletown, CT: Criminal Justice Institute.

———. 2001. *Corrections Yearbook, 2000*. Middletown, CT: Criminal Justice Institute.

Camp, S. D., and G. G. Gales. 2002. "Growth and Quality of U.S. Private Prisons: Evidence from a National Survey." *Criminology and Public Policy* 1:427–50.

Cancino, J. M., and R. Enriquez. 2004. "A Qualitative Analysis of Officer Peer Retaliation: Preserving the Police Culture." *Policing: International Journal of Police Strategies and Management* 27:320–40.

Canto, M. 1998. "Federal Government Investigates Use of Stun Belt." *Lansing* (MI) *State Journal*, August 7, p. 4A.

Caputo, M., and C. M. Miller. 2006. "In Wake of Death, Juvenile Boot Camp System Is Scrapped." *Miami Herald*, April 27. http://www.miami.com/miamiherald/14438114.htm.

Carlon, A. 2007. "Entrapment, Punishment, and the Sadistic State." *Virginia Law Review* 93:1081–1134.

Carlson, T. 1995. "Safety, Inc." *Policy Review*, Summer, pp. 67–73.

Carr, J. G. 1993. "Bail Bondsmen and the Federal Courts." *Federal Probation* 57 (March): 9–14.

Carr, P. J., L. Napolitano, and J. Keating. 2007. "We Never Call the Cops and Here's Why: A Qualitative Examination of Legal Cynicism in Three Philadelphia Neighborhoods." *Criminology* 45:445–80.

Carroll, L. 1974. *Hacks, Blacks, and Cons: Race Relations in a Maximum Security Prison*. Lexington, MA: Lexington Books.

Carroll-Ferrary, N. L. 2006. "Incarcerated Men and Women, the Equal Protection Clause, and the Requirement of 'Similarly Situated.'" *New York Law School Law Review* 51:594–617.

Cauffman, E. L., L. Steinberg, and A. R. Piquero. 2005. "Psychological, Neuropsychological, and Physiological Correlates of Serious Antisocial Behavior in Adolescence: The Role of Self-Control." *Criminology* 43:133–76.

CBS2-TV. 2008. "City Council Approves 19.8M Burge Settlement." January 9. http://www.cbs2chicago.com.

Chaddock, G. R. 2002. "Sniper Revives Prospects for Gun-Tracking Moves." *Christian Science Monitor*, October 17, p. 1.

Champagne, A., and K. Cheek. 1996. "PACs and Judicial Politics in Texas." *Judicature* 80:26–29.

Champion, D. J. 1989. "Private Counsels and Public Defenders: A Look at Weak Cases, Prior Records, and Leniency in Plea Bargaining." *Journal of Criminal Justice* 17:253–63.

Chang, S. S. 2009. "Protecting the Innocent: Post-Conviction DNA Exoneration." *Hastings Constitutional Law Quarterly* 36:285–306.

Chapman, S. G. 1970. *Police Patrol Readings*. 2nd ed. Springfield, IL: Thomas.

Chapper, J. A., and R. A. Hanson. 1989. *Understanding Reversible Error in Criminal Appeals*. Williamsburg, VA: National Center for State Courts.

"Charging Common Criminals under Terrorism Laws Doesn't Fit in America's Justice Values." 2003. *Asheville Citizen-Times*, July 23. http://www.citizentimes.com.

Chavez, P. 2005. "Shooting Raises Racial Tension in L.A." *Sacramento Union*, February 21. http://www.sacunion.com.

Chermak, S., and E. McGarrell. 2004. "Problem-solving Approaches to Homicide: An Evaluation of Indianapolis Violence Reduction Partnership." *Criminal Justice Policy Review* 15:161–92.

Chesney-Lind, M. 2006. "Patriarchy, Crime, and Justice." *Feminist Criminology* 1:6–26.

Cheung, H. 2007. "LAPD's Dart-Firing, License Plate Reading, Video Streaming Car." *TG Daily*, August 22. http://www.tgdaily.com.

Chiaramida, A. 2009. "New Hampshire House Approves Death Penalty Appeal." *Newburyport Daily News*, March 26. http://www.newburyportnews.com.

Chidi, G. A. 2002. "FBI's Use of Keystroke Capture Tool Was Permitted for Investigation, Court Says." *PC World*, January 4. http://www.pcworld.com/.

Chiricos, T., K. Barrick, W. Bales, and S. Bontrager. 2007. "The Labeling of Convicted Felons and Its Consequences for Recidivism." *Criminology* 45:547–81.

Chiricos, T., K. Padgett, and M. Gertz. 2000. "Fear, TV News, and the Reality of Crime." *Criminology* 38:755–85.

Christopher, R. L. 1994. "Mistake of Fact in the Objective Theory of Justification." *Journal of Criminal Law and Criminology* 85:295–332.

Church, T. W. 1985. "Examining Local Legal Culture." *American Bar Foundation Research Journal* 1985 (Summer): 449.

Clear, T. R. 1994. *Harm in American Penology*. Albany: State University of New York Press.

Clear, T. R., G. F. Cole, and M. D. Reisig. 2009. *American Corrections*. 8th ed. Belmont, CA: Cengage/Wadsworth.

Clear, T. R., and D. R. Karp. 1999. *Community Justice: Preventing Crime and Achieving Justice*. New York: Westview Press.

Clear, T. R., D. R. Rose, E. Waring, and K. Scully. 2003. "Coercive Mobility and Crime: A Preliminary Examination of Concentrated Incarceration and Social Disorganization." *Justice Quarterly* 20 (March): 33–63.

CNN. 2004a. "Boston Police Accept 'Full Responsibility' in Death of Red Sox Fan." October 22. http://www.cnn.com.

———. 2004b. "Police Review Policy after Tasers Used on Kids." November 14. http://www.cnn.com.

———. 2007. "Astronaut Granted Bond on Attempted Murder Charge." February 6. http://www.cnn.com.

Cohen, L. E., and M. Felson. 1979. "Social Change and Crime Rates: A Routine Activity Approach." *American Sociological Review* 44:588–608.

Cohen, M., T. R. Miller, and S. B. Rossman. 1990. "The Costs and Consequences of Violent Behavior in the United States." Paper prepared for the Panel on the Understanding and Control of Violent Behavior, National Research Council, National Academy of Sciences, Washington, DC.

Cohen, T. H., and B. A. Reaves. 2006. *Felony Defendants in Large Urban Counties, 2002.* Washington, DC: U.S. Government Printing Office.

Cole, D. 1999. *No Equal Justice: Race and Class in the American Criminal Justice System.* New York: The New Press.

Collins, J. 2005. *Preventing Identity Theft in Your Business: How to Protect Your Business, Customers, and Employees.* New York: Wiley.

Collins, T., and L. Leff. 2009. "Cops' Slayings Stun Oakland Residents." Associated Press. March 23. http://www.news.aol.com/article/oakland-police-shooting/392279.

Commission on Accreditation for Law Enforcement Agencies. 1989. *Standards for Law Enforcement Accreditation.* Fairfax, VA: Author.

Conway, P. 2001. "The 2001 Electronic Monitoring Survey." *Journal of Electronic Monitoring* 14 (Winter–Spring): 7–9.

Cook, P. J., and J. H. Laub. 2002. "After the Epidemic: Recent Trends in Youth Violence in the United States." In *Crime and Justice: A Review of Research*, vol. 29, ed. Michael Tonry. Chicago: University of Chicago Press.

Cooney, M. 1994. "Evidence as Partisanship." *Law and Society Review* 28:833–58.

Cordner, G., and E. P. Biebel. 2005. "Problem-Oriented Policing in Practice." *Criminology and Public Policy* 4:155–80.

Costanzo, M. 1997. *Just Revenge.* New York: St. Martin's Press.

Coyle, M. 2009. "New Report Shows Sharp Rise in Prison Time for Federal Offenders." http://law.com/jsp/law/LawArticleFriendly.

Crawford, C. 2000. "Gender, Race, and Habitual Offender Sentencing in Florida." *Criminology* 38:263–80.

Crawford, C., T. Chiricos, and G. Kleck. 1998. "Race, Racial Threat, and Sentencing of Habitual Offenders." *Criminology* 36 (August): 481–512.

Criminal Justice Research Reports. 2001. July–August, p. 87.

Cullen, F. T. 2007. "Make Rehabilitation Corrections' Guiding Paradigm." *Criminology and Public Policy* 6:717–28.

Cullen, F. T., L. Cao, J. Frank, R. H. Langworthy, S. L. Browning, R. Kopache, and T. J. Stevenson. 1996. "'Stop or I'll Shoot': Racial Differences in Support for Police Use of Deadly Force on Fleeing Felons." *American Behavioral Scientist* 39 (February): 449–60.

Cullen, F. T., T. Leming, B. Link, and J. Wozniak. 1985. "The Impact of Social Supports in Police Stress." *Criminology* 23:503–22.

Cunningham, W. C., J. J. Strauchs, and C. W. Van Meter. 1990. *Private Security Trends, 1970 to the Year 2000.* Boston: Butterworth-Heinemann.

Dansky, K. 2008. "Understanding California Sentencing." *University of San Francisco Law Review* 43:45–86.

Davey, J. D. 1998. *The Politics of Prison Expansion: Winning Elections by Waging War on Crime.* Westport, CT: Praeger.

Davies, T. Y. 1983. "A Hard Look at What We Know (and Still Need to Learn) about the 'Costs' of the Exclusionary Rule: The NIJ Study and Other Studies of 'Lost' Arrests." *American Bar Foundation Research Journal* 1983:611–90.

Davis, A. 2001. "Laptop Computers in Police Cars Keep Officers Informed, on Streets." *Arkansas Democrat-Gazette*, February 24, p. B3.

Davis, M., R. Lundman, and R. Martinez, Jr. 1991. "Private Corporate Justice: Store Police, Shoplifters, and Civil Recovery." *Social Problems* 38:395–408.

Davis, R. C., C. S. O'Sullivan, D. J. Farole, and M. Rempel. 2008. "A Comparison of Two Prosecution Policies in Cases of Intimate Partner Violence: Mandatory Case Filing versus Following the Victim's Lead." *Criminology and Public Policy* 7:633–62.

Davitz, T. 1998. "The Gangs Behind Bars." *Insight on the News*, September 28.

Dawson, M., and R. Dinovitzer. 2001. "Victim Cooperation and the Prosecution of Domestic Violence in a Specialized Court." *Justice Quarterly* 18:593–622.

Decker, S. H., and R. Wright. 1993. "A Woman's Place Is in the House: Females and Residential Burglary." *Justice Quarterly* 10:143–62.

DeFrances, C. J. 2002. "Prosecutors in State Courts, 2001." Bureau of Justice Statistics *Bulletin*, May.

DeFrances, C. J., and J. Litras. 2000. "Indigent Defense Services in Large Counties, 1999." Bureau of Justice Statistics *Bulletin*, November.

DeJong, C., S. Mastrofski, and R. Parks. 2001. "Patrol Officers and Problem Solving: An Application of Expectancy Theory." *Justice Quarterly* 18:31–61.

DeJong, C., and E. S. Merrill. 2000. "Getting 'Tough on Crime': Juvenile Waiver and the Criminal Court." *Ohio Northern University Law Review* 27:175–96.

Dewan, S. 2007. "An SOS for 911 Systems in Age of High-Tech." *New York Times*, April 6. http://www.nytimes.com.

———. 2009. "Prosecutors Block Access to DNA Testing for Inmates." *New York Times*, May 18. http://www.nytimes.com.

Dickerson, B. E. 2008. "Hard Lemonade, Hard Price." *Detroit Free Press*, April 28. http://www.freep.com.

DiIulio, J. J., Jr. 1987. *Governing Prisons.* New York: Free Press.

———. 1991. *No Escape: The Future of American Corrections.* New York: Basic Books.

———. 1993. "Rethinking the Criminal Justice System: Toward a New Paradigm." In *Performance Measures for the Criminal Justice System.* Washington, DC: Bureau of Justice Statistics, U.S. Government Printing Office.

Dill, F. 1975. "Discretion, Exchange, and Social Control: Bail Bondsmen in Criminal Courts." *Law and Society Review* 9:644–74.

Dillehay, R. C., and M. R. Sandys. 1996. "Life under *Wainwright v. Witt*: Juror Dispositions and Death Qualification." *Law and Human Behavior* 20:147–65.

Dixon, J. 2008. "Mandatory Domestic Violence Arrest and Prosecution Policies: Recidivism and Social Governance." *Criminology and Public Policy* 7:663–70.

Dodge, J., and M. Pogrebin. 2001. "African-American Policewomen: An Exploration of Professional Relationships." *Policing* 24:550–52.

Domash, S. F. 2008. "Nassau System Will Pinpoint Gunfire Sites." *New York Times*, July 27. http://www.nytimes.com.

Donziger, S. R., ed. 1996. *The Real War on Crime: The Report of the National Criminal Justice Commission.* New York: HarperCollins.

Dority, B. 2005. "The USA Patriot Act Has Decimated Many Civil Liberties." In *Homeland Security: Current Controversies*, ed. A. Nakaya. Detroit: Thomson/Gale, 130–36.

Durose, M. R., and P. A. Langan. 2004. "Felony Sentences in State Courts, 2002." Bureau of Justice Statistics *Bulletin*, December.

Durose, M. R., E. L. Schmitt, and P. Langan. 2005. *Contacts between Police and Public: Findings from the 2002 National Survey.* Washington, DC: Bureau of Justice Statistics, U.S. Government Printing Office, April.

Earley, P. 1992. *The Hot House: Life inside Leavenworth Prison.* New York: Bantam Books.

Eckholm, E. 2008a. "Citing Workload, Public Lawyers Reject New Cases." *New York Times*, November 9. http://www.nytimes.com.

———. 2008b. "U.S. Shifting Prison Focus to Re-entry into Society." *New York Times*, April 8. http://www.nytimes.com.

"Economics of CJA Representations Costly to Attorneys." 2008. *The Third Branch* 40 (no. 4, April). http://www.uscourts.gov/ttb/2008-04/article05.cfm.

Editor. 2003. "Wages and Benefits Paid to Correctional Employees." *Correctional Compendium*, January 28, pp. 8–26.

Egan, P. 1999. "Software Could Assist in Sentencing." *Lansing* (MI) *State Journal*, May 7, pp. 1A–2A.

Egan, T. 1999. "A Drug Ran Its Course, Then Hid with Its Users." *New York Times*, September 19, p. A1.

Eggen, D., and J. White. 2008. "Administration Asserted a Terror Exception on Search and Seizure." *Washington Post*, April 4, p. A4.

Egley, A., and C. E. O'Donnell. 2009. "Highlights of the 2007 National Youth Gang Survey." *OJJDP Fact Sheet*, April. http://www.ojp.usdoj.gov.

Eichenwald, K. 2006. "On the Web, Pedophiles Extend Their Reach." *New York Times*, August 21. http://www.nytimes.com.

Eigenberg, H. 2000. "Correctional Officers and Their Perceptions of Homosexuality, Rape, and Prostitution in Male Prisons." *Prison Journal* 80 (December): 415–33.

Eisenberg, T., P. Hannaford-Agor, V. P. Hans, N. L. Mott, G. T. Munsterman, S. J. Schwab, and M. T. Wells. 2005. "Judge-Jury Agreement in Criminal Cases: A Partial Replication of Kalven and Zeisel's *The American Jury.*" *Journal of Empirical Legal Studies* 2:171–206.

Eisenstein, J., R. B. Flemming, and P. F. Nardulli. 1988. *The Contours of Justice: Communities and Their Courts.* Boston: Little, Brown.

Ellement, J. R., and S. Smalley. 2006. "Six Crime Disclosure Questioned." *Boston Globe,* April 18. http://www.boston.com.

Elliott, D. S., S. S. Ageton, and R. J. Cantor. 1979. "An Integrated Theoretical Perspective on Delinquent Behavior." *Journal of Research in Crime and Delinquency* 16:3–27.

Elliott, J., and B. Murphy. 2005. "Parole, Probation Violators Add to Crowding." *Houston Chronicle,* January 20. http://www.chron.com/ca/CDA/printstory.mpl/metropolitan/3000503.

Emmelman, D. S. 1996. "Trial by Plea Bargain: Case Settlement as a Product of Recursive Decisionmaking." *Law and Society Review* 30:335–60.

Engber, D. 2005. "Does the FBI Have Your Fingerprints?" *Slate,* April 22. http://www.slate.msn.com/id/2117226.

Engel, R. S., and J. M. Calnon. 2004. "Examining the Influence of Drivers' Characteristics during Traffic Stops with Police: Results from a National Survey." *Justice Quarterly* 21:49–90.

Engel, R. S., J. M. Calnon, and T. J. Bernard. 2002. "Theory and Racial Profiling: Shortcomings and Future Directions in Research." *Justice Quarterly* 19:249–73.

Enriquez, R., and J. W. Clark. 2007. "The Social Psychology of Peremptory Challenges: An Examination of Latino Jurors." *Texas Hispanic Journal of Law and Policy* 13:25–38.

ESPN.com. 2008. "Leyritz Charged Following Accident That Killed 30-Year-Old Woman." January 31. http://sports.espn.go.com.

FBI (Federal Bureau of Investigation). 2006a. *Crime in the United States, 2005.* Washington, DC: U.S. Government Printing Office. http://www.fbi.gov.

———. 2006b. "FBI Cyber Action Teams: Traveling the World to Catch Cyber Criminals." March 6. http://www.fbi.gov.

———. 2007. *Hate Crime Statistics, 2006.* Washington, DC: U.S. Government Printing Office. http://www.fbi.gov.

———. 2008a. *Crime in the United States, 2007.* Washington, DC: U.S. Government Printing Office. http://www.fbi.gov.

———. 2008b. "Cyber Solidarity: Five Nations, One Mission," March 18. http://www.fbi.gov.

———. 2008c. *Uniform Crime Reports.* Washington, DC: U.S. Government Printing Office.

———. 2009a. About Us—Quick Facts. http://www.fbi.gov/quickfacts.htm.

———. 2009b. *Preliminary Semiannual Uniform Crime Report, January–June 2008.* Washington, DC: U.S. Government Printing Office. http://www.fbi.gov.

Felch, J. 2003. "How a 'Calm but Aggravated' Teenager Died on East Thrill Place." *Denver Post,* July 11. http://www.denverpost.com.

Felch, J., and M. Dolan. 2008. "DNA Matches Aren't Always a Lock." *Los Angeles Times,* May 4. http://www.latimes.com.

Feld, B. C. 1993. "Criminalizing the American Juvenile Court." In *Crime and Justice: A Review of Research,* vol. 17, ed. M. Tonry. Chicago: University of Chicago Press, 197–280.

———. 1999. *Bad Kids: Race and the Transformation of the Juvenile Court.* New York: Oxford University Press.

———. 2003. "The Politics of Race and Juvenile Justice: The 'Due Process Revolution' and the Conservative Reaction." *Justice Quarterly* 20:765–800.

———. 2004. "Editorial Introduction: Juvenile Transfers." *Criminology and Public Policy* 3 (November): 599–603.

———. 2008. "A Slower Form of Death: Implications of *Roper v. Simmons* for Juveniles Sentenced to Life without Parole." *Notre Dame Journal of Law, Ethics and Public Policy* 22:101–58.

Felice, J. D., and J. C. Kilwein. 1992. "Strike One, Strike Two . . . : The History and Prospect for Judicial Reform in Ohio." *Judicature* 75:193–200.

Fenton, J. 2009. "Baltimore Police Commissioner Defends Withholding Names." *Baltimore Sun,* January 28. http://www.baltimoresun.com.

Ferretti, C., and M. Feighan. 2009. "Teen Dies after Warren Police Use Taser." *Detroit News,* April 11. http://www.detnews.com.

Feuer, A. 2006. "For Ex-F.B.I. Agent Accused in Murders, a Case of What Might Have Been." *New York Times,* April 15. http://www.nytimes.com.

Fields, J., and K. Peveto. 2008. "Local Cop Cars Going Hi-Tech." *Abilene* (TX) *Reporter News,* December 4. http://www.reporternews.com.

Fishbein, D. H. 1990. "Biological Perspectives in Criminology." *Criminology* 28:27–72.

Fisher, D. M. 2007. "Striking a Balance: The Need to Temper Judicial Discretion against a Background of Legislative Interest in Federal Sentencing." *Duquesne Law Review* 46:65–97.

Fisman, R. 2008. "Going Down Swingin': What If Three-Strikes Laws Make Criminals Less Likely to Repeat Offend—But More Violent When They Do? March 20. http://www.slate.com.

Flanagan, T. J., ed. 1995. *Long-Term Imprisonment.* Thousand Oaks, CA: Sage.

Flango, V. E. 1994. *Habeas Corpus in State and Federal Courts.* Williamsburg, VA: National Center for State Courts.

Fountain, H. 2009. "Plugging Holes in the Science of Forensics." *New York Times,* May 12. http://www.nytimes.com.

Fox, J. A., and M. W. Zawitz. 2007. "Homicide Trends in the United States." July 11. Bureau of Justice Statistics, http://www.ojp.usdoj.gov/bjs/homicide/homtrnd.htm.

Fox, J. G. 1982. *Organizational and Racial Conflict in Maximum Security Prisons.* Lexington, MA: Lexington Books.

Frank, J., S. G. Brandl, F. T. Cullen, and A. Stichman. 1996. "Reassessing the Impact of Race on Citizens' Attitudes toward the Police: A Research Note." *Justice Quarterly* 13 (June): 320–34.

Fridell, L. 1990. "Decision Making of the District Attorney: Diverting or Prosecuting Intrafamilial Child Sexual Abuse Offenders." *Criminal Justice Policy Review* 4:249–67.

Friedman, L. M. 1993. *Crime and Punishment in American History.* New York: Basic Books.

Frohmann, L. 1997. "Convictability and Discordant Locales: Reproducing Race, Class, and Gender Ideologies in Prosecutorial Decisionmaking." *Law and Society Review* 31:531–56.

Fukurai, H. 1996. "Race, Social Class, and Jury Participation: New Dimensions for Evaluating Discrimination in Jury Service and Jury Selection." *Journal of Criminal Justice* 24:71–88.

Fyfe, J. 1993. "Police Use of Deadly Force: Research and Reform." In *Criminal Justice: Law and Politics,* 6th ed., ed. G. F. Cole. Belmont, CA: Wadsworth.

Garcia, M. 2005. "N.Y. Using Terrorism Law to Prosecute Street Gang." *Washington Post,* February 1, p. A3.

Garner J., T. Schade, J. Hepburn, and J. Buchanan. 1995. "Measuring the Continuum of Forced Used by and against the Police." *Criminal Justice Review* 20 (Autumn): 146–68.

Garner, J. H., and C. D. Maxwell. 1999. "Measuring the Amount of Force by and against the Police in Six Jurisdictions." In *Use of Force by the Police.* Washington, DC: National Institute of Justice, U.S. Government Printing Office.

Garner, J. H., C. D. Maxwell, and C. G. Heraux. 2002. "Characteristics Associated with the Prevalence and Severity of Force Used by the Police." *Justice Quarterly* 19:705–46.

Georgiady, B. N. 2008. "An Exceedingly Painful Encounter: The Reasonableness of Pain and De Minimis Injuries for Fourth Amendment Excessive Force Claims." *Syracuse Law Review* 59:123–64.

German, M., and J. Stanley. 2007. *What's Wrong with Fusion Centers?* New York: American Civil Liberties Union.

Gest, T. 2001. *Crime and Politics: Big Government's Erratic Campaign for Law and Order.* New York: Oxford University Press.

Gezari, V. M. 2008. "Cracking Open." *Washington Post,* June 1. http://www.washingtonpost.com.

Giordano, P. C., M. A. Longmore, R. D. Schroeder, and P. Seffrin. 2008. "A Life Course Perspective on Spirituality and Desistance from Crime." *Criminology* 46:99–131.

Girshick, L. B. 1999. *No Safe Haven: Stories of Women in Prison.* Boston: Northeastern University Press.

Glaze, L. E., and T. P. Bonczar. 2008. *Probation and Parole in the United States, 2007—Statistical Tables.* December. Bureau of Justice Statistics, http://ojp.usdoj.gov/bjs/abstract/ppus07st.htm.

Glueck, S., and E. Glueck. 1950. *Unraveling Juvenile Delinquency.* New York: Commonwealth Fund.

Goldfarb, R. L. 1965. *Ransom: A Critique of the American Bail System.* New York: Harper & Row.

Goldkamp, J. S., and E. R. Vilcica. 2008. "Targeted Enforcement and Adverse System Side Effects: The Generation of Fugitives in Philadelphia." *Criminology* 46:371–409.

Goldman, J. 2002. "Skakel Is Found Guilty of 1975 Moxley Murder." *Los Angeles Times,* June 8. http://www.latimes.com.

Goldschmidt, J., and J. M. Shaman. 1996. "Judicial Disqualifications: What Do Judges Think?" *Judicature* 80:68–72.

Goldstein, H. 1979. "Improving Policing: A Problem-oriented Approach." *Crime and Delinquency* 25:236–57.

———. 1990. *Problem-oriented Policing.* New York: McGraw-Hill.

Goodman, J. 1994. *Stories of Scottsboro.* New York: Random House.

Goolkasian, G. A., R. W. Geddes, and W. DeJong. 1989. "Coping with Police Stress." In *Critical Issues in Policing,* ed. R. G. Dunham and G. P. Alpert. Prospect Heights, IL: Waveland Press, 489–507.

Gordon, J. 2005. "In Patriots' Cradle, the Patriot Act Faces Scrutiny." *New York Times,* April 24. http://www.nytimes.com.

Gordon, M. 2006. "Disgraced Bondsman Candid on Eve of Jail." *New Orleans Times-Picayune,* October 27. http://www.nola.com.

Gottfredson, M., and T. Hirschi. 1990. *A General Theory of Crime.* Stanford, CA: Stanford University Press.

Gover, A. R., J. M. MacDonald, and G. P. Alpert. 2003. "Combating Domestic Violence: Findings from an Evaluation of a Local Domestic Violence Court." *Criminology and Public Policy* 3:109–31.

Governor's Office on Drug Control Policy. 2006. *Iowa's Drug Control Strategy, 2006.* http://www.state.ia.us/odcp/docs/Strategy_06.pdf.

Grady, D. 2003. "F.D.A. Outlines Plans to Counter Growing Trade in Counterfeit Pharmaceuticals." *New York Times,* October 3. http://www.nytimes.com.

Grasha, K. 2009a. "Going Paperless." *Lansing (MI) State Journal,* February 9, pp. 1A, 4A.

———. 2009b. "Ingham Co. Jail Inmates May Opt for House Arrest." *Lansing (MI) State Journal,* March 11, pp. 1A–2A.

Gray, K. B. 2008. "Community Prosecution: After Two Decades, Still New Frontiers." *Journal of the Legal Profession* 32:199–214.

Green, A. 2009. "More States Use GPS to Track Abusers." *New York Times,* May 9. http://www.nytimes.com.

Greene, J. A. 1999. "Zero Tolerance: A Case Study of Police Policies and Practices in New York City." *Crime and Delinquency* 45 (April): 171–87.

Greenwood, P., J. M. Chaiken, and J. Petersilia. 1977. *Criminal Investigation Process.* Lexington, MA: Lexington Books.

Greer, K. R. 2000. "The Changing Nature of Interpersonal Relationships in a Women's Prison." *Prison Journal* 80 (December): 442–68.

Grennan, S. A. 1987. "Findings on the Role of Officer Gender in Violent Encounters with Citizens." *Journal of Police Science and Administration* 15:78–85.

Griset, P. L. 1993. "Determinate Sentencing and the High Cost of Overblown Rhetoric: The New York Experience." *Crime and Delinquency* 39:552.

———. 1995. "The Politics and Economics of Increased Correctional Discretion over Time Served: A New York Case Study." *Justice Quarterly* 12:307–23.

Guevara, L., D. Herz, and C. Spohn. 2006. "Gender and Juvenile Justice Decision Making: What Role Does Race Play?" *Feminist Criminology* 1:258–82.

Haarr, R. N., and M. Morash. 1999. "Gender, Race and Strategies of Coping with Occupational Stress in Policing." *Justice Quarterly* 16:303–36.

Hackett, D. P., and J. M. Violanti, eds. 2003. *Police Suicide: Tactics for Prevention.* Springfield, IL: Thomas.

Hackney, S., C. Arboscello, and J. Swickard. 2007. "Fatigue, Frostbite Catch Up to Him." *Detroit Free Press,* March 5, p. 1A.

Hagan, F. E. 1997. *Political Crime: Ideology and Criminality.* Needham Heights, MA: Allyn and Bacon.

Hagan, J., and R. D. Peterson. 1995. "Criminal Inequality in America: Patterns and Consequences." In *Crime and Inequality,* ed. J. Hagan and R. D. Peterson. Stanford, CA: Stanford University Press, 14–36.

Hails, J., and R. Borum. 2003. "Police Training and Specialized Approaches to Respond to People with Mental Illness." *Crime and Delinquency* 49:52–61.

Hall, J. 1947. *General Principles of Criminal Law.* 2nd ed. Indianapolis: Bobbs-Merrill.

Hall, M. G. 1995. "Justices as Representatives: Elections and Judicial Politics in the United States." *American Politics Quarterly* 23:485–503.

Hallinan, J. T. 2001. *Going Up the River: Travels in a Prison Nation.* New York: Random House.

Hambling, D. 2005. "Police Toy with 'Less Lethal' Weapons." April 30. http://www.newscientist.com.

Hanlon, M. 2007. "Run Away the Ray-Gun Is Coming: We Test U.S. Army's New Secret Weapon." *Daily Mail,* September 18. http://www.dailymail.co.uk.

Hans, V., and N. Vidmar. 1986. *Judging the Jury.* New York: Plenum Press.

Hanson, R. A., and J. Chapper. 1991. *Indigent Defense Systems.* Williamsburg, VA: National Center for State Courts.

Hanson, R. A., and H. W. K. Daley. 1995. *Challenging the Conditions of Prisons and Jails: A Report on Section 1983 Litigation.* Washington, DC: Bureau of Justice Statistics, U.S. Government Printing Office.

Harcourt, B. E., and J. Ludwig. 2006. "Broken Windows: New Evidence from New York City and a Five-City Social Experiment." *University of Chicago Law Review* 73:271–320.

Harkin, T. 2005. "Confronting the Meth Crisis." Press release, February 7. http://www.harkin.senate.gov.

Harlow, C. 2000. "Defense Counsel in Criminal Cases." Bureau of Justice Statistics *Bulletin,* November.

Harris Poll. 2009. "Who Are You? *CSI* Answers that Question Each Week and Is America's Favorite TV Show." April 21. http://www.harrisinteractive.com.

Hartley, R., S. Madden, and C. Spohn. 2007. "Prosecutorial Discretion: An Examination of Substantial Assistance Departures in Federal Crack-Cocaine and Powder-Cocaine Cases." *Justice Quarterly* 24:382–407.

Hastie, R., S. Penrod, and N. Pennington. 1983. *Inside the Jury.* Cambridge, MA: Harvard University Press.

Hathaway, W. 2002. "A Clue to Antisocial Behavior: Study Finds Gene Marker for Which Abused Children May Become Troubled Adults." *Hartford Courant,* August 2, p. A17.

Hawdon, J., and J. Ryan. 2003. "Police-Resident Interactions and Satisfaction with Police: An Empirical Test of Community Policing Assertions." *Criminal Justice Policy Review* 14:55–74.

Hays, E. 2009. "Boy, 11, Charged with Killing Father's Fiancee, Who Was 8 Months Pregnant." *New York Daily News,* February 21. http://www.nydailynews.com.

Hays, T. 2006. "NYC Real Time Crime Center Tracks Suspects." *Washington Post,* May 10. http://www.washingtonpost.com.

Heffernan, E. 1972. *Making It in Prison.* New York: Wiley.

Heinzmann, D., and S. St. Clair. 2008. "NIU Noted Gunman's Scholarship." *Chicago Tribune,* February 15. http://www.chicagotribune.com.

Henning, P. J. 1993. "Precedents in a Vacuum: The Supreme Court Continues to Tinker with Double Jeopardy." *American Criminal Law Review* 31:1–72.

———. 2009. "Madoff's Future: Where the Case Is Likely to Go." *New York Times,* March 11. http://www.nytimes.com.

Henriques, D. B. 2009. "Madoff Is Sentenced to 150 Years for Ponzi Scheme." *New York Times,* June 29. http://www.nytimes.com.

Henriques, D. B., and J. Healy. 2009. "Madoff Is Jailed after Pleading Guilty." *New York Times*, March 13. http://www.nytimes.com.

Henry, S., and M. M. Lanier. 2006. *The Essential Criminology Reader*. Boulder, CO: Westview.

Hensley, J. J., and M. Wynn. 2009. "Close to Two-Thirds of Photos Taken by Speed Cameras Tossed." *Arizona Republic*, May 15. http://www.azcentral.com.

Herbert, S. 1996. "Morality in Law Enforcement: Chasing 'Bad Guys' with the Los Angeles Police Department." *Law and Society Review* 30:799–818.

Hickey, T. J. 1995. "A Double Jeopardy Analysis of the Medgar Evers Murder Case." *Journal of Criminal Justice* 23:41–51.

Hickman, M. J. 2003. "Tribal Law Enforcement, 2000." Bureau of Justice Statistics *Fact Sheet*, January. NCJ 197936.

Hickman, M. J., and B. A. Reaves. 2001. *Local Police Departments, 1999*. Washington, DC: Bureau of Justice Statistics, U.S. Government Printing Office.

———. 2003. *Local Police Departments, 2000*. Washington, DC: Bureau of Justice Statistics, U.S. Government Printing Office.

———. 2006. *Local Police Departments, 2003*. Washington, DC: Bureau of Justice Statistics, U.S. Government Printing Office.

Hicks, N. 2005. "Bill Aims to Gut Police Liability in High-Speed Chases." *Lincoln Journal Star*, February 6. http://www.journalstar.com.

Hicks, W. 2003. "Police Vehicular Pursuits: An Overview of Research and Legal Conceptualizations for Police Administrators." *Criminal Justice Policy Review* 14:75–95.

Hinduja, S. 2004. "Perceptions of Local and State Law Enforcement Concerning the Role of Computer Crime Investigative Teams." *Policing* 27:341–57.

———. 2007. "Neutralization Theory and Online Software Piracy: An Empirical Analysis." *Ethics and Information Technology* 9 (3): 187–204.

Hinduja, S., and J. W. Patchin. 2007. "Offline Consequences of Online Victimization: School Violence and Delinquency." *Journal of School Violence* 6 (3): 89–112.

———. 2009. *Bullying beyond the Schoolyard: Preventing and Responding to Cyberbullying*. Thousand Oaks, CA: Corwin Press.

Hinton, H. L., Jr. 2002. "Considerations for Investing Resources in Chemical and Biological Preparedness." In *Terrorism: Are We Ready?* ed. D. Miller. Huntington, NY: Nova Science, 21–31.

Hirsch, A. J. 1992. *The Rise of the Penitentiary*. New Haven, CT: Yale University Press.

Hirsch, M. 2007. "Midnight Run Re-Run: Bail Bondsmen, Bounty Hunters, and the Uniform Criminal Extradition Act." *University of Miami Law Review* 62:59–94.

Hirschel, D., and I. Hutchinson. 2003. "The Voices of Domestic Violence Victims: Predictors of Victim Preference for Arrest

and the Relationship between Preference for Arrest and Revictimization." *Crime and Delinquency* 49:313–36.

Hirschi, T. 1969. *Causes of Delinquency*. Berkeley: University of California Press.

Ho, N. T. 2000. "Domestic Violence in a Southern City: The Effects of a Mandatory Arrest Policy on Male-Versus-Female Aggravated Assault Incidents." *American Journal of Criminal Justice* 25:107–18.

Hoctor, M. 1997. "Domestic Violence as a Crime against the State." *California Law Review* 85 (May): 643–700.

Hoffman, M. 1999. "Abolish Peremptory Challenges." *Judicature* 82:202–4.

Hoge, R. D., N. G. Guerra, and P. Boxer. 2008. *Treating the Juvenile Offender*. New York: Guilford Press.

Holl, J. 2005. "How to Find the Gunman: By Listening for the Gunshot." *New York Times*, August 17. http://www.nytimes.com.

Holmes, M. D. 2000. "Minority Threat and Police Brutality: Determinants of Civil Rights Criminal Complaints in U.S. Municipalities." *Criminology* 38:343–67.

Holmes, M. D., H. M. Hosch, H. C. Daudistel, D. A. Perez, and J. B. Graves. 1996. "Ethnicity, Legal Resources, and Felony Dispositions in Two Southwestern Jurisdictions." *Justice Quarterly* 13:11–29.

Horne, P. 2006. "Policewomen: Their First Century and the New Era." *Police Chief* 73 (9). http://policechiefmagazine.org.

Houston, B., and J. Ewing. 1991. "Justice Jailed." *Hartford Courant*, June 16, p. A1.

Howard, J. 1929. *The State of Prisons in England and Wales*. London: J. M. Dent. (Original work published in 1777)

Howlett, D. 2004. "Chicago Plans Advanced Surveillance." *USA Today*, September 9. http://www.usatoday.com.

Huff, C. R. 2002. "Wrongful Conviction and Public Policy: The American Society of Criminology 2001 Presidential Address." *Criminology* 40:1–18.

Hughes, K. A. 2006. "Justice Expenditures and Employment in the United States, 2003." Bureau of Justice Statistics *Bulletin*, April. NCJ 212260.

Hurdle, J. 2008. "Police Beating of Suspects Is Taped by TV Station in Philadelphia." *New York Times*, May 8. http://www.nytimes.com.

Hurwitz, M. S., and D. N. Lanier. 2001. "Women and Minorities on State and Federal Appellate Benches, 1985 and 1999." *Judicature* 85:84–92.

Ill-Equipped: U.S. Prisons and Offenders with Mental Illness. 2003. New York: Human Rights Watch.

Internet Crime Complaint Center. 2008. *2007 Internet Crime Report*. Washington, DC: U.S. Department of Justice.

Iribarren, C. J., J. H. Markovitz, D. R. Jacobs, P. J. Schreiner, M. Daviglus, and J. R. Hibbeln. 2004. "Dietary Intake of n-3, n-6 Fatty Acids and Fish: Relationship with Hostility in Young Adults—the CARDIA

Study." *European Journal of Clinical Nutrition* 58:24–31.

Irwin, J. 1970. *The Felon*. Englewood Cliffs, NJ: Prentice-Hall.

———. 1980. *Prisons in Turmoil*. Boston: Little, Brown.

Irwin, J., and D. Cressey. 1962. "Thieves, Convicts, and the Inmate Culture." *Social Problems* 10:142–55.

Ith, I. 2001. "Taser Fails to Halt Man with Knife; Seattle Officer Kills 23-Year-Old." *Seattle Times*, November 28, p. A1.

Iyengar, R. 2008. "I'd Rather Be Hanged for a Sheep than a Lamb: The Unintended Consequences of 'Three-Strikes' Law." National Bureau of Economic Research Working Paper No. 13784.

Jacob, H. 1973. *Urban Justice*. Boston: Little, Brown.

Jacobs, J. B., and C. Panarella. 1998. "Organized Crime." In *The Handbook of Crime and Punishment*, ed. M. Tonry. New York: Oxford University Press, 159–77.

Jaksic, V. 2007. "Public Defenders, Prosecutors Face Crisis in Funding." *National Law Journal*, March 27. http://www.law.com.

Johnson, R. 2002. *Hard Time: Understanding and Reforming the Prison*. 3rd ed. Belmont, CA: Wadsworth.

Johnston, D. C. 2008. "Wesley Snipes Cleared of Serious Tax Charges." *New York Times*, February 2. http://www.nytimes.com.

Jordan, J. 2002. "Will Any Woman Do? Police, Gender and Rape Victims." *Policing* 25:319–44.

Juvenile Law Center. 2008. "JLC Argues Juvenile Adjudications Not a 'Strike' under California's Three Strikes Law." *Juvenile Law Center Newsletter*, May 10. http://www.jlc.org/newsletter/57/.

Kaczor, B. 2002. "King Brothers Will Return to Courtroom in 2003." *Naples* (FL) *Daily News*, December 27. http://www.naplesnews.com.

Kampeas, R. 2001. "Terror Attacks Bring Profound Changes in FBI Focus, Challenges for New Director." Associated Press News Service, October 27.

Kane, R. J. 2002. "The Social Ecology of Police Misconduct." *Criminology* 40:867–96.

———. 2005. "Compromised Police Legitimacy as a Predictor of Violent Crime in Structurally Disadvantaged Communities." *Criminology* 43:469–98.

Karmen, A. 2001. *Crime Victims*. 4th ed. Belmont, CA: Wadsworth.

Karnowski, C. E. A. 2008. "Setting Bail for Public Safety." *Berkeley Journal of Criminal Law* 13:1–30.

Kassebaum, G., and D. Okamoto. 2001. "The Drug Court as a Sentencing Model." *Journal of Contemporary Criminal Justice* 17:89–104.

Kelling, G. L. 1985. "Order Maintenance, the Quality of Urban Life, and Police: A Line of Argument." In *Police Leadership in America*, ed. W. A. Geller. New York: Praeger.

———. 1991. *Foot Patrol*. Washington, DC: National Institute of Justice, U.S. Government Printing Office.

Kelling, G. L., and C. M. Coles. 1996. *Fixing Broken Windows: Restoring and Reducing Crime in Our Communities.* New York: Free Press.

Kelling, G. L., and M. Moore. 1988. "The Evolving Strategy of Policing." In *Perspectives on Policing,* no. 13. Washington, DC: National Institute of Justice, U.S. Government Printing Office.

Kelling, G. L., T. Pate, D. Dieckman, and C. E. Brown. 1974. *The Kansas City Preventive Patrol Experiments: A Summary Report.* Washington, DC: Police Foundation.

Kennedy, R. 1997. *Race, Crime, and the Law.* New York: Pantheon.

Kenney, D. J., and J. O. Finckenauer. 1995. *Organized Crime in America.* Belmont, CA: Wadsworth.

Kerlikowske, R. G. 2004. "The End of Community Policing: Remembering the Lessons Learned," *FBI Law Enforcement Bulletin* 73:6–11.

Khanna, R., and L. Olsen. 2004. "1 in 3 Police Shootings Involve Unarmed People." *Houston Chronicle,* July 25. http://www.chron.com.

Kilgannon, C., and N. Cohen. 2009. "Cadets Trade the Trenches for Firewalls." *New York Times,* May 11. http://www.nytimes.com.

Kimber, K. 2008. "Mental Health Courts— Idaho's Best Kept Secret." *Idaho Law Review* 45:249–81.

Kimberly, J. 2003. "House Passes Crime Lab Bill." *Houston Chronicle,* May 2. http://www.houstonchronicle.com.

King, N. J., and S. Sherry. 2008. "Habeas Corpus and Sentencing Reform: A Story of Unintended Consequences." *Duke Law Journal* 58:1–67.

Kingsnorth, R., R. MacIntosh, and S. Sutherland. 2002. "Criminal Charge or Probation Violation? Prosecutorial Discretion and Implications for Research in Criminal Court Processing." *Criminology* 40:553–77.

Kirkpatrick, D. D. 2005. "In Secretly Taped Conversations, Glimpses of the Future President." *New York Times,* February 20. http://www.nytimes.com.

Klein, A. 2008. "D.C. Police to Carry Semiautomatic Rifles on Patrol." *Washington Post,* May 17, p. B1.

Klein, D. 1973. "The Etiology of Female Crime." *Issues in Criminology* 8 (2): 3–30.

Kleinknecht, W. 1996. *The New Ethnic Mobs: The Changing Face of Organized Crime in America.* New York: Free Press.

Klockars, C. B. 1985. "Order Maintenance, the Quality of Urban Life, and Police: A Different Line of Argument." *Police Leadership in America,* ed. W. A. Geller. New York: Praeger.

Klofas, J., and J. Yandrasits. 1989. "'Guilty but Mentally Ill' and the Jury Trial: A Case Study." *Criminal Law Bulletin* 24:423–43.

Knox, G. W. 2000. "A National Assessment of Gangs and Security Threat Groups (STGs) in Adult Correctional Institutions: Results of the 1999 Adult Corrections Survey." *Journal of Gang Research* 7:1–45.

Kolbert, E. 1999. "The Perils of Safety." *New Yorker,* March 22, p. 50.

Kotlowitz, A. 1994. "Their Crimes Don't Make Them Adults." *The New York Times Magazine,* February 13, p. 40.

———. 2008. "Blocking the Transmission of Violence." *The New York Times Magazine,* May 4. http://www.nytimes.com.

Kovaleski, S. F., and A. L. Cowan. 2009. "From Prep School to Murder Suspect at Wesleyan." *New York Times,* May 9. http://www.nytimes.com.

Kramer, G. P., and D. M. Koenig. 1990. "Do Jurors Understand Criminal Justice Instructions? Analyzing the Results of the Michigan Juror Comprehension Project." *University of Michigan Journal of Law Reform* 23:401–37.

Kramer, J. H., and J. T. Ulmer. 1996. "Sentencing Disparity and Departures from Guidelines." *Justice Quarterly* 13:81.

Krautt, P. 2002. "Location, Location, Location: Interdistrict and Intercircuit Variation in Sentencing Outputs for Federal Drug-Trafficking Offenses." *Justice Quarterly* 19:633–71.

Kridler, C. 1999. "Sergeant Friday, Where Are You?" *Newsweek,* May 17, p. 14.

Krimmel, J. T. 1996. "The Performance of College-Educated Police: A Study of Self-Rated Performance Measures." *American Journal of Policing* 15:85–96.

Kristof, N. D. 2005. "When Rapists Walk Free." *New York Times,* March 5. http://www.nytimes.com.

Kruttschnitt, C., and S. Krmpotich. 1990. "Aggressive Behavior among Female Inmates: An Exploratory Study." *Justice Quarterly* 7:371–89.

Kurbrin, C. E., and E. A. Stewart. 2006. "Predicting Who Reoffends: The Neglected Role of Neighborhood Context in Recidivism Studies." *Criminology* 44:165–97.

Kurlychek, M., and C. Kempinen. 2006. "Beyond Boot Camp: The Impact of Aftercare on Offender Re-entry." *Criminology and Public Policy* 5:363–88.

Kyckelhahn, T., and T. H. Cohen. 2008. "Felony Defendants in Large Urban Courts, 2004." Bureau of Justice Statistics *Bulletin,* April. NCJ 221152.

Laffey, M. 1998. "Cop Diary." *New Yorker,* August 10, pp. 36–39.

LaFraniere, S. 2009. "Facing Counterfeiting Crackdown, Beijing Vendors Fight Back." *New York Times,* March 2. http://www.nytimes.com.

Langworthy, R. H., T. Hughes, and B. Sanders. 1995. *Law Enforcement Recruitment Selection and Training: A Survey of Major Police Departments.* Highland Heights, IL: Academy of Criminal Justice Sciences.

Laub, J. H., and R. J. Sampson. 2003. *Shared Beginnings, Divergent Lives: Delinquent Boys to Age 70.* Cambridge, MA: Harvard University Press.

Lauritsen, J., J. Laub, and R. Sampson. 1992. "Conventional and Delinquent Activities:

Implications for the Prevention of Violent Victimization among Adolescents." *Violence and Victims* 7:91–102.

Lauritsen, J., and N. White. 2001. "Putting Violence in Its Place: The Influence of Race, Ethnicity, Gender, and Place on the Risk for Violence." *Criminology and Public Policy* 1:37–59.

Lave, T. R. 1998. "Equal before the Law." *Newsweek,* July 13, p. 14.

"Law Enforcement Solution." 2002. October 10. http://www.cisco.com.

Lear, E. T. 1995. "Contemplating the Successive Prosecution Phenomenon in the Federal System." *Journal of Criminal Law and Criminology* 85:625–75.

LeDuff, C., and S. Esparza. 2009. "Detroit Police Routinely Undercount Homicides." *Detroit News,* June 18. http://www.detnews.com.

Lee, J. 2009. "Study Questions Whether Cameras Cut Crime." *New York Times,* March 3. http://www.nytimes.com.

Lee, M. S., and J. T. Ulmer. 2000. "Fear of Crime among Korean Americans in Chicago Communities." *Criminology* 38:1173–206.

Leiber, M. J., and K. Y. Mack. 2003. "The Individual and Joint Effects of Race, Gender and Family Status on Juvenile Justice Decision-Making." *Journal of Research in Crime and Delinquency* 40:34–70.

Leo, R. A. 1996. "*Miranda's* Revenge: Police Interrogation as a Confidence Game." *Law and Society Review* 30:259–88.

Leonard, J. 2002. "Dropping 'Nonlethal' Beanbags as Too Dangerous." *Los Angeles Times,* June 3, p. 1.

Lersch, K. M. 2002. "Are Citizen Complaints Just Another Measure of Officer Productivity? An Analysis of Citizen Complaints and Officer Activity Measures." *Police Practices and Research* 3:135–47.

Lersch, K. M., and L. Kunzman. 2001. "Misconduct Allegations and Higher Education in a Southern Sheriff's Department." *American Journal of Criminal Justice* 25:161–72.

Levine, J. P. 1992. *Juries and Politics.* Belmont, CA: Wadsworth.

Levy, P. 2007. "4 Dead, 20 Missing after Dozens of Vehicles Plummet into River." *Minneapolis Star Tribune,* August 2. http://www.startribune.com.

Lewis, L. 2007. "Rethinking Miranda: Truth, Lies, and Videotapes." *Gonzaga Law Review* 43:199–238.

Lewis, N. A. 2009. "Stimulus Plan Has $1 Billion to Hire More Local Police." *New York Times,* February 5. http://www.nytimes.com.

Lichtblau, E. 2008a. "F.B.I. Made 'Blanket' Demands for Phone Records." *New York Times,* March 13. http://www.nytimes.com.

———. 2008b. "F.B.I. Says Records Demands Are Curbed." *New York Times,* March 6. http://www.nytimes.com.

Lichtblau, E., and J. Risen. 2009. "Officials Say U.S. Wiretaps Exceeded Law." *New York Times,* April 16. http://www.nytimes.com.

Lighty, T. 2005. "Prosecutors Boast of 'a Hit on the Mob.'" *Chicago Tribune*, April 25, p. 1.

Liptak, A. 2003. "County Says It's Too Poor to Defend the Poor." *New York Times,* April 15. http://www.nytimes.com.

———. 2008a. "Electrocution Is Banned in Last State to Rely on It." *New York Times.* February 9. http://www.nytimes.com.

———. 2008b. "Illegal Globally, Bail for Profit Remains in U.S." *New York Times*, January 29. http://www.nytimes.com.

———. 2009a. "Court Debates Strip Search of Student." *New York Times*, April 21. http://www.nytimes.com.

———. 2009b. "Justices Agree to Take up Sentencing for Young Offenders." *New York Times*, May 5. http://www.nytimes.com.

———. 2009c. "Supreme Court Steps Closer to Repeal of Evidence Ruling." *New York Times*, January 31. http://www.nytimes.com.

Liska, A. E., and S. F. Messner. 1999. *Perspectives on Crime and Deviance.* 3rd ed. Upper Saddle River, NJ: Prentice-Hall.

Lithwick, D., and J. Turner. 2003. "A Guide to the Patriot Act, Part 4." September 11. http://www.slate.msn.com.

Llana, S. M. 2006. "What's at Root of Boston's Rise in Murders?" *Christian Science Monitor,* May 10. http://www.csmonitor.com.

Lochner, T. 2002. "Strategic Behavior and Prosecutorial Agenda Setting in the United States Attorneys' Office." *Justice System Journal* 23:271–94.

Logan, C. 1993. "Criminal Justice Performance Measures in Prisons." In *Performance Measures for the Criminal Justice System.* Washington, DC: Bureau of Justice Statistics, U.S. Government Printing Office, 19–60.

Lombroso, C. 1968. *Crime: Its Causes and Remedies.* Montclair, NJ: Patterson Smith. (Original work published in 1912)

Lord, V. B., and P. Friday. 2003. "Choosing a Career in Police Work: A Comparative Study between Applications for Employment with a Large Police Department and Public High School Seniors." *Police Practices and Research* 4:63–78.

Loviglio, J. 2002. "Judge Reverses Himself, Will Allow Fingerprint-Analysis Testimony." Associated Press Wire Service, March 13. Lexis-Nexis.

Luginbuhl, J., and M. Burkhead. 1994. "Sources of Bias and Arbitrariness in the Capital Trial." *Journal of Social Issues* 7:103–12.

Lumb, R. C., and R. Breazeale. 2003. "Police Officer Attitudes and Community Policing Implementation: Developing Strategies for Durable Organizational Change." *Policing and Society* 13:91–106.

Lundman, R., and R. Kaufman. 2003. "Driving While Black: Effects of Race, Ethnicity, and Gender on Citizen Self-Reports of Traffic Stops and Police Actions." *Criminology* 41:195–220.

Lundy, S. 2009. "Judge Orders 2 Psychiatrists to Evaluate Lisa Nowak's Sanity." *Orlando Sentinel*, April 2. http://www.orlandosentinel.com

Lynch, D. 1999. "Perceived Judicial Hostility to Criminal Trials: Effects on Public Defenders in General and on Their Relationships with Clients and Prosecutors in Particular." *Criminal Justice and Behavior* 26:217–34.

Lynem, J. N. 2002. "Guards Call for Higher Wages, More Training: Industry Faces Annual Staff Turnover Rate of up to 300%." *San Francisco Chronicle,* August 22, p. B3.

Maag, C. 2008. "Police Shooting of Mother and Infant Exposes a City's Racial Tension." *New York Times*, January 30. http://www.nytimes.com.

MacArthur Foundation. 2007a. *The Changing Borders of Juvenile Justice: Transfer of Adolescents to Adult Criminal Court* (Issue Brief 5, MacArthur Foundation Research Network on Adolescent Development and Juvenile Justice). Philadelphia, PA: MacArthur Foundation.

———. 2007b. *Creating Turning Points for Serious Adolescent Offenders: Research on Pathways to Desistance* (Issue Brief 2, MacArthur Foundation Research Network on Adolescent Development and Juvenile Justice). Philadelphia, PA: MacArthur Foundation.

———. 2007c. *Less Guilty by Reason of Adolescence* (Issue Brief 3, MacArthur Foundation Research Network on Adolescent Development and Juvenile Justice). Philadelphia, PA: MacArthur Foundation.

Maitland, A. S., and R. D. Sluder. 1998. "Victimization and Youthful Prison Inmates: An Empirical Analysis." *Prison Journal* 78:55–73.

Mann, C. R. 1993. *Unequal Justice: A Question of Color.* Bloomington: Indiana University Press.

Marceau, J. F. 2008. "Un-Incorporating the Bill of Rights: The Tension between the Fourteenth Amendment and the Federalism Concerns of Modern Criminal Procedure Reforms." *Journal of Criminal Law and Criminology* 98:1231–1302.

Marciniak, L. M. 2000. "The Addition of Day Reporting Centers to Intensive Probation Supervision: A Comparison of Recidivism Rates." *Federal Probation* 58 (December): 34–39.

Margasak, L. 2006. "Security Agency's Security Hit." *Boston Globe,* March 7. http://www.boston.com.

———. 2007. "Ill-Trained, Underpaid Guard Terror Targets." Associated Press, May 29. http://news.aol.com.

Markoff, J. 2009. "Tracking Cyberspies through the Web Wilderness." *New York Times,* May 12. http://www.nytimes.com.

Marsh, J. R. 1994. "Performing Pretrial Services: A Challenge in the Federal Criminal Justice System." *Federal Probation* 58 (December): 3–10.

Martin, S. E. 1991. "The Effectiveness of Affirmative Action." *Justice Quarterly* 8:489–504.

———. 2005. "Women Officers on the Move." In *Critical Issues in Policing,* 5th ed., ed. R. G. Dunham and G. P. Alpert. Long Grove, IL: Waveland Press, 350–71.

Martinson, R. 1974. "What Works? Questions and Answers about Prison Reform." *The Public Interest,* Spring, p. 25.

Maruschak, L. 2008. *HIV in Prisons, 2006.* Washington, DC: Bureau of Justice Statistics, U.S. Government Printing Office.

Maschke, K. J. 1995. "Prosecutors as Crime Creators: The Case of Prenatal Drug Use." *Criminal Justice Review* 20:21–33.

Mastrofski, S. D., M. D. Reisig, and J. D. McCluskey. 2002. "Police Disrespect toward the Public: An Encounter-Based Analysis." *Criminology* 40:519–52.

Mastrofski, S. D., J. J. Willis, and J. B. Snipes. 2002. "Styles of Patrol in a Community Policing Context." In *The Move to Community Policing: Making Change Happen,* ed. M. Morash and J. Ford. Thousand Oaks, CA: Sage, 81–111.

Mauer, M., and M. Chesney-Lind, eds. 2002. *Invisible Punishment: The Collateral Consequences of Mass Imprisonment.* New York: The New Press.

Maxwell, S. R. 1999. "Examining the Congruence between Predictors of ROR and Failures to Appear." *Journal of Criminal Justice* 27:127–41.

Maxwell, S. R., and C. Maxwell. 2000. "Examining the 'Criminal Careers' of Prostitutes within the Nexus of Drug Use, Drug Selling, and Other Illicit Activities." *Criminology* 38:787–809.

Mayrack, B. 2008. "The Implications of *State ex rel. Thomas v. Schwarz* on Wisconsin Sentencing Policy after Truth-in-Sentencing II." *Wisconsin Law Review* 2008:181–223.

Mazerolle, L. D., D. Rogan, J. Frank, C. Famega, and J. Eck. 2003. "Managing Citizen Calls to the Police: The Impact of Baltimore's 3-1-1 Call System." *Criminology and Public Policy* 2:97–124.

McCall, M. A., M. M. McCall, and C. E. Smith. 2008a. "Criminal Justice and the 2006–2007 United States Supreme Court Term." *University of Missouri-Kansas City Law Review* 76:993–1043.

———. 2008b. "Criminal Justice and the U.S. Supreme Court 2007–2008 Term." *Southern University Law Review* 36:33–87.

McCormick, J. 2000. "Scene of the Crime." *Newsweek*, February 28, p. 60.

McCoy, C. 1986. "Policing the Homeless." *Criminal Law Bulletin* 22 (May–June): 263.

———. 1993. *Politics and Plea Bargaining: Victims' Rights in California.* Philadelphia: University of Pennsylvania Press.

———. 1995. "Is the Trial Penalty Inevitable?" Paper presented at the annual meeting of the Law and Society Association, Phoenix, AZ, June.

———. 2007. "Caleb Was Right: Pretrial Detention Mostly Determines Everything." *Berkeley Journal of Criminal Law* 12:135–48.

McDivitt, J., and R. Miliano. 1992. "Day Reporting Centers: An Innovative Concept in Intermediate Sanctions." In *Smart Sentencing: The Emergence of Intermediate Sanctions,* ed. J. M. Byrne, A. J. Lurigio, and J. Petersilia. Newbury Park, CA: Sage, 152–65.

McGarrell, E., S. Chermak, A. Weiss, and J. Wilson. 2001. "Reducing Firearms Violence through Directed Patrol." *Criminology and Public Policy* 1:119–48.

McGee, R. A., G. Warner, and N. Harlow. 1998. "The Special Management Inmate." In *Incarcerating Criminals*, ed. T. J. Flanagan, J. W. Marquart, and K. G. Adams. New York: Oxford University Press, 99–106.

McGeehan, P. 2007. "New York Plan for DNA Data in Most Crimes." *New York Times*, May 14. http://www.nytimes.com.

McGuire, D. 2004. "Study: Online Crime Costs Rising." *Washington Post*, May 25. http://www.washingtonpost.com.

McKee, T. A. 2007. "Judges as Umpires." *Hofstra Law Review* 35:1709–24.

McKelvey, B. 1977. *American Prisons*. Montclair, NJ: Patterson Smith.

McMahon, P. 2002. "311 Lightens Load for Swamped 911 Centers." *USA Today*, March 5. http://www.usatoday.com.

McNulty, T. L., and P. E. Bellair. 2003. "Explaining Racial and Ethnic Differences in Adolescent Violence: Structural Disadvantage, Family, Well-Being, and Social Capital." *Justice Quarterly* 20:1–31.

Mears, B. 2008. "Nebraska Court Bans the Electric Chair." February 8. http://www.cnn.com.

Meier, R. F., and T. D. Miethe. 1993. "Understanding Theories of Criminal Victimization." In *Crime and Justice: A Review of Research*, ed. M. Tonry. Chicago: University of Chicago Press.

Melde, C., F. Esbensen, and T. J. Taylor. 2009. "'May Piece Be with You': A Typological Examination of the Fear and Victimization Hypothesis of Adolescent Weapon Carrying." *Justice Quarterly* 26:348–76.

Melde, C., T. J. Taylor, and F. Esbensen. 2009. "'I Got Your Back': An Examination of the Protective Function of Gang Membership in Adolescence." *Criminology* 47:565–94.

Melekian, B. 1990. "Police and the Homeless." *FBI Law Enforcement Bulletin* 59:1–7.

Menard, S. 2000. "The 'Normality' of Repeat Victimization from Adolescence through Early Adulthood." *Justice Quarterly* 17:543–74.

Mentzer, A. 1996. "Policing in Indian Country: Understanding State Jurisdiction and Authority." *Law and Order* 44 (June): 24–29.

Messerschmidt, J. W. 1993. *Masculinities and Crime: Critique and Reconceptualization*. Lanham, MD: Rowman & Littlefield.

Messner, S. F., S. Galea, K. J. Tardiff, and M. Tracy. 2007. "Policing, Drugs, and the Homicide Decline in New York City in the 1990s." *Criminology* 45:385–413.

Messner, S. F., and R. Rosenfeld. 1994. *Crime and the American Dream*. Belmont, CA: Wadsworth.

Meyer, C., and T. Gorman. 2001. "Criminal Faces in the Crowd Still Elude Hidden ID Camera Security." *Los Angeles Times*, February 2, p. 1.

Miethe, T. D. 1995. "Fear and Withdrawal from Urban Life." *Annals of the American Academy of Political and Social Science* 539 (May): 14–27.

Mihm, S. 2006. "No Ordinary Counterfeit." *New York Times*, July 23. http://www.nytimes.com.

Miller, M. 2009. "LPD Cars Receive $24K Upgrade." *Lansing* (MI) *State Journal*, May 14, p. 4B.

Miller, M., and M. Guggenheim. 1990. "Pretrial Detention and Punishment." *Minnesota Law Review* 75:335–426.

Monkkonen, E. H. 1981. *Police in Urban America, 1869–1920*. Cambridge, England: Cambridge University Press.

———. 1992. "History of the Urban Police." In *Modern Policing*, ed. M. Tonry and N. Morris. Chicago: University of Chicago Press, 547–80.

Moore, M. 1992. "Problem-Solving and Community Policing." In *Modern Policing*, ed. M. Tonry and N. Morris. Chicago: University of Chicago Press, 99–158.

Moore, M., and G. L. Kelling. 1983. "To Serve and to Protect: Learning from Police History." *The Public Interest*, Winter, p. 55.

Moore, S. 2008. "$8 Billion Demand in California Prison Case." *New York Times*, August 14, p. A1.

———. 2009a. "Court Panel Orders California to Reduce Prison Population by 55,000 in 3 Years." *New York Times*, February 9. http://www.nytimes.com.

———. 2009b. "In a Lab, an Ever-Growing Database of DNA Profiles." *New York Times*, May 12. http://www.nytimes.com.

———. 2009c. "Science Found Wanting in Nation's Crime Labs." *New York Times*, February 5. http://www.nytimes.com.

———. 2009d. "Study Shows High Cost of Criminal Corrections, " *New York Times*, March 3, 2009, p. A1.

Moran, R. 2002. *Executioner's Current: Thomas Edison, George Westinghouse, and the Invention of the Electric Chair*. New York: Knopf.

Morash, M., and J. K. Ford, eds. 2002. *The Move to Community Policing: Making Change Happen*. Thousand Oaks, CA: Sage.

Morash, M., J. K. Ford, J. P. White, and J. G. Boles. 2002. "Directing the Future of Community-Policing Initiatives." In *The Move to Community Policing: Making Change Happen*, ed. M. Morash and J. Ford. Thousand Oaks, CA: Sage, 277–88.

Morash, M., R. N. Haarr, and L. Rucker. 1994. "A Comparison of Programming for Women and Men in the U.S. Prisons in the 1980s." *Crime and Delinquency* 40 (April): 197–221.

Morris, N., and M. Tonry. 1990. *Between Prison and Probation: Intermediate Punishments in a Rational Sentencing System*. New York: Oxford University Press.

Moses, P. 2005. "Corruption? It Figures: NY Police Department's Crime Stats and the Art of Manipulation." *Village Voice*, March 29. http://www.villagevoice.com.

Mosher, C., T. Miethe, and D. Phillips. 2002. *The Mismeasure of Crime*. Thousand Oaks, CA: Sage.

"The Most Stress Related Occupations." 2006. *Consumer Awareness Journal*, September. http://www.consumer-awareness-journal.com.

Mozingo, J. 2008. "L.A. Police Aggressively Target Hard-Core Gangs." *Los Angeles Times*, May 1. http://www.latimes.com.

Mueller, R. S. 2008. "Statement of FBI Director before the House Judiciary Committee." April 23. http://www.fbi.gov.

Murphy, P. V. 1992. "Organizing for Community Policing." In *Issues in Policing: New Perspectives*, ed. J. W. Bizzack. Lexington, KY: Autumn Press, 113–28.

Murray, J. 2008. "Transforming Juvenile Justice." *Indianapolis Star*, May 27. http://www.indystar.com.

Nagin, D. S. 1998. "Criminal Deterrence Research at the Outset of the Twenty-first Century." In *Crime and Justice*, vol. 23, ed. M. Tonry. Chicago: University of Chicago Press, 1–42.

Nagin, D. S., A. R. Piquero, E. S. Scott, and L. Steinberg. 2006. "Public Preferences for Rehabilitation versus Incarceration of Juvenile Offenders: Evidence from a Contingent Valuation Survey." *Criminology and Public Policy* 5:627–52.

Nalla, M. 2002. "Common Practices and Functions of Corporate Security: A Comparison of Chemical, Financial, Manufacturing, Service, and Utility Industries." *Journal of Security Administration* 25:33–46.

National Academy of Sciences. 2009. *Strengthening Forensic Sciences in the United States*. Washington, DC: Author.

"National Summits Help Federal Courts Prepare for Sentence Reduction Requests." 2008. *The Third Branch* 40 (no. 2, February): 1–3, 6. http://www.uscourts.gov.

Nava, M. 2008. "The Servant of All: Humility, Humanity, and Judicial Diversity." *Golden Gate University Law Review* 38:175–94.

New York Times. 2003. "Some Members of Congress Concerned over F.B.I. Shifts in Priorities." June 18. http://www.nytimes.com.

Newman, T. C. 1996. "Fair Cross-Section and Good Intention: Representation in Federal Juries." *Justice System Journal* 18:211–32.

Niesse, M. 2004. "Audit: Atlanta Hedged Crimes in '96 Bid." *Washington Post*, February 20. http://www.washingtonpost.com.

NIJ (National Institute of Justice). 1996. *Victim Costs and Consequences: A New Look*. Washington, DC: U.S. Government Printing Office.

———. 1997. *Research in Brief*, January.

———. 2003. *Correctional Boot Camps: Lessons from a Decade of Research*. Washington, DC: U.S. Government Printing Office.

Noble, R. K. 2006. "All Terrorism Is Local, Too." *New York Times*, August 13. http://www.nytimes.com.

Novak, V. 1999. "The Cost of Poor Advice." *Time*, July 5, p. 38.

Ogletree, C. J., Jr., M. Prosser, A. Smith, and W. Talley, Jr. 1995. *Beyond the Rodney King Story: An Investigation of Police Misconduct* in *Minority Communities*. Boston: Northeastern University Press.

O'Harrow, R. 2008. "Centers Tap into Personal Databases." *Washington Post*, April 2. http://www.washingtonpost.com.

O'Hear, M. M. 2006. "The End of *Bordenkircher*: Extending the Logic of *Apprendi* to Plea Bargaining." *Washington University Law Review* 84:835–49.

Oliver, W. M. 2002. "9–11, Federal Crime Control Policy, and Unintended Consequences." *ACJS Today* 22 (September–October): 1–6.

Orson, D. 2008. "White Sentenced in Police Corruption Trial." WNPR Connecticut Public Radio, April 29. http://www.cpbn.org.

Owen, B. 1998. *"In the Mix": Struggle and Survival in a Woman's Prison*. Albany: State University of New York Press.

Packer, H. L. 1968. *The Limits of the Criminal Sanction*. Stanford, CA: Stanford University Press.

Palmer, T. 1992. *The Re-emergence of Correctional Intervention*. Newbury Park, CA: Sage.

Patchin, J., and S. Hinduja. 2006. "Bullies Move beyond the Schoolyard: A Preliminary Look at Cyberbullying." *Youth Violence and Juvenile Justice* 4 (2): 148–69.

Paulson, T. 2004. "'Brain Fingerprinting' Touted as Truth Meter." *Seattle Post-Intelligencer*, March 1. http://www.brainwavescience.com.

Pennsylvania Prison Society. 2004. *Correctional Forum*, December.

Peoples, J. M. 1995. "Helping Pretrial Services Clients Find Jobs." *Federal Probation* 59 (March): 14–18.

"Perdue OKs Bill to Expand Use." 2008. *Augusta* (GA) *Chronicle*, May 8. http://chronicle.augusta.com.

Perkins, D. B., and J. D. Jamieson. 1995. "Judicial Probable Cause Determinations after *County of Riverside v. McLaughlin*." *Criminal Law Bulletin* 31:534–46.

Petersilia, J. 1990. "When Probation Becomes More Dreaded Than Prison." *Federal Probation*, March, p. 24.

———. 1996. "A Crime Control Rationale for Reinvesting in Community Corrections." *Perspectives* 20 (Spring): 21–29.

———. 1999. "Parole and Prisoner Reentry in the United States." In *Prisons*, ed. M. Tonry and J. Petersilia. Chicago: University of Chicago Press.

———. 2003. *When Prisoners Come Home: Parole and Prisoner Reentry*. New York: Oxford University Press.

Peterson, J. L., and M. J. Hickman. 2005. "Census of Publicly Funded Forensic Crime Laboratories, 2002." Bureau of Justice Statistics *Bulletin*, February, p. 1.

Pew Center on the States. 2008. *One in 100: Behind Bars in America 2008*. Washington, DC: Pew Trusts.

———. 2009. Press release, March 2. http://www.pewcenteronthestates.org/news_room_detail.aspx?id=49398. [Re: *One in 31:*

The Long Reach of American Corrections. Washington, DC: Pew Trusts, 2009.]

Phillips, S. 1977. *No Heroes, No Villains*. New York: Random House.

Pisciotta, A. W. 1994. *Benevolent Repression: Social Control and the American Reformatory-Prison Movement*. New York: New York University Press.

Pizarro, J. M., and R. E. Narag. 2008. "Supermax Prisons: What We Know, What We Do Not Know, and Where We Are Going." *Prison Journal* 88:99–110.

Pizarro, J. M., V. Stenius, and T. C. Pratt. 2006. "Supermax Prisons: Myths, Realities, and the Politics of Punishment in American Society." *Criminal Justice Policy Review* 17:6–21.

Platt, A. 1977. *The Child Savers*. 2nd ed. Chicago: University of Chicago Press.

Podlas, K. 2006. "The 'CSI Effect' and Other Forensic Fictions." *Loyola of Los Angeles Entertainment Law Review* 27:87–125.

Pollock, J. M. 1998. *Counseling Women in Prison*. Thousand Oaks, CA: Sage.

PR Newswire. 2001. "Ion Track Instruments Unveils New Technology to Aid in Fight against Terrorism and Drug Trafficking." March 22. Lexis-Nexis.

———. 2002. "As Homeland Security Bill Approaches House Vote, It Still Neglects Problems with Massive Private Security Industry." July 24. Lexis-Nexis.

Preston, J. 2005. "Rape Victims' Eyes Were Covered, but a Key Clue Survived." *New York Times*, April 28. http://www.nytimes.com.

Priehs, R. 1999. "Appointed Counsel for Indigent Criminal Appellants: Does Compensation Influence Effort?" *Justice System Journal* 21:57–79.

Propper, A. 1982. "Make Believe Families and Homosexuality among Imprisoned Girls." *Criminology* 20:127–39.

Protess, B. 2009. "The DNA Debacle: How the Federal Government Botched the DNA Backlog Crisis." May 5. http://www.propublica.org.

Provine, D. M. 1996. "Courts in the Political Process in France." In *Courts, Law, and Politics in Comparative Perspective*, ed. H. Jacob, E. Blankenburg, H. Kritzer, D. M. Provine, and J. Sanders. New Haven, CT: Yale University Press, 177–248.

Prussel, D., and K. Lonsway. 2001. "Recruiting Women Police Officers." *Law and Order* 49 (July): 91–96.

Purser, B. 2005. "Houston County, Georgia E-911 Able to Pinpoint Cell Phones." *Macon* (GA) *Telegraph*, February 10, p. 6.

Puzzanchera, C., and W. Kang. 2008. "Easy Access to the FBI's Supplementary Homicide Reports: 1980–2006." http://ojjdp.ncjrs.gov/ojstatbb/ezashr/.

Radelet, M. L. 2004. "Post-*Furman* Botched Executions." http://www.deathpenaltyinfor.org/article.php?scid=8&did=478.

Radelet, M. L., H. A. Bedau, and C. E. Putnam. 1992. *In Spite of Innocence*. Boston: Northeastern University Press.

Radelet, M. L., W. S. Lofquist, and H. A. Bedau. 1996. "Prisoners Released from Death Rows Since 1970 Because of Doubts about Their Guilt." *Thomas M. Cooley Law Review* 13:907–66.

Rafter, N. H. 1983. "Prisons for Women, 1790–1980." In *Crime and Justice*, 5th ed., ed. M. Tonry and N. Morris. Chicago: University of Chicago Press.

Rand, M. R. 2008. "Criminal Victimization, 2007." Bureau of Justice Statistics, *Bulletin*, December. NCJ 224390.

Randolph, E. D. 2001. "Inland Police Like New Weaponry." *Riverside* (CA) *Press-Enterprise*, November 24, p. B4.

Reaves, B. A. 1992. *State and Local Police Departments, 1990*. Washington, DC: Bureau of Justice Statistics, U.S. Government Printing Office.

———. 2006. "Federal Law Enforcement Officers, 2004." Bureau of Justice Statistics *Bulletin*, July. NCJ 212750.

Reaves, B. A., and T. C. Hart. 1999. *Felony Defendants in Large Urban Counties, 1996: State Court Case Processing Statistics*. Washington, DC: Bureau of Justice Statistics, U.S. Government Printing Office.

———. 2000. *Law Enforcement Management and Administrative Statistics, 1999*. Washington, DC: Bureau of Justice Statistics, U.S. Government Printing Office.

Reaves, B. A., and M. J. Hickman. 2002. "Police Departments in Large Cities, 1999–2000." Bureau of Justice Statistics *Special Report*, May.

———. 2004. *Law Enforcement Management and Administrative Statistics, 2000: Data for Individual State and Local Agencies with 100 or More Officers*. Washington, DC: Bureau of Justice Statistics, U.S. Government Printing Office, April.

Regoli, R. M., and J. D. Hewitt. 1994. *Criminal Justice*. Englewood Cliffs, NJ: Prentice-Hall.

Reibstein, L. 1997. "NYPD Black and Blue." *Newsweek*, June 2, p. 66.

Reichers, L. M., and R. R. Roberg. 1990. "Community Policing: A Critical Review of Underlying Assumptions." *Journal of Police Science and Administration* 17:105–14.

Reid, T. R. 2004. "Rape Case against Bryant Is Dropped." *Washington Post*, September 2. http://www.washingtonpost.com.

Reid, T. V. 1996. "PAC Participation in North Carolina Supreme Court Elections." *Judicature* 80:21–25.

———. 2000. "The Politicization of Judicial Retention Elections: The Defeat of Justices Lamphier and White." In *Research on Judicial Selection 1999*. Chicago: American Judicature Society, 45–72.

Reisig, M. D. 2002. "Citizen Input and Police Service: Moving beyond the 'Feel Good' Community Survey." In *The Move to Community Policing: Making Change Happen*, ed. M. Morash and J. Ford. Thousand Oaks, CA: Sage, 43–60.

Reisig, M. D., J. D. McCluskey, S. D. Mastrofski, and W. Terrill. 2004. "Suspect

Disrespect toward the Police." *Justice Quarterly* 21:241–68.

Reiss, A. J., Jr. 1988. *Private Employment of Public Police*. Washington, DC: National Institute of Justice, U.S. Government Printing Office.

———. 1992. "Police Organization in the Twentieth Century." In *Crime and Justice: A Review of Research*, vol. 15, ed. M. Tonry and N. Morris. Chicago: University of Chicago Press, 51–97.

Rennison, C. 2002. "Criminal Victimization 2001: Changes 2000–01 with Trends 1993–2001." Bureau of Justice Statistics *National Crime Victimization Survey*, September. NCJ 194610.

Reynolds, G. H., and B. P. Denning. 2008. "Heller's Future in the Lower Courts." *Northwestern University Law Review* 102:2035–44.

Richards, C. 2006. "Student Sent to TYC for Shoving Aide." *Paris* (TX) *News*, March 12. http://www.lamarcountyattorney.com.

Richburg, K. B. 2007. "N.J. Approves Abolition of Death Penalty; Corzine to Sign." *Washington Post*, December 14, p. A3.

Richburg, K. B., and A. Surdin. 2008. "Fiscal Pressures Lead Some States to Free Inmates Early." *Washington Post*, May 5, p. A01.

Richey, W. 2003. "Florida Fights over Death-Row Lawyers." *Christian Science Monitor*, February 20, p. 2.

———. 2006. "US Creates Terrorist Fingerprint Database." *Christian Science Monitor*, December 27, pp. 1, 4.

Richtel, M. 2002. "Credit Card Theft Thrives Online as Global Market." *New York Times*, May 13. http://www.nytimes.com.

Ring, W. 2005. "Backlogs in Labs Undercut DNA's Crime-Solving Value." *Lansing* (MI) *State Journal*, April 28, p. A3.

Roane, K. R., and D. Morrison. 2005. "The CSI Effect." *U.S. News and World Report*, April 25. http://www.usnews.com.

Robinson, A. L. 2000. "The Effect of a Domestic Violence Policy Change on Police Officers' Schemata." *Criminal Justice and Behavior* 27:600–24.

Rockwell, F. G. 2008. "The Chesterfield/Colonial Heights Drug Court: A Partnership between the Criminal Justice System and the Treatment Community." *University of Richmond Law Review* 43:5–17.

Rosen, L. 1995. "The Creation of the Uniform Crime Report: The Role of Social Science." *Social Science History* 19 (Summer): 215–38.

Rosenbaum, J. L. 1989. "Family Dysfunction and Female Delinquency." *Crime and Delinquency* 35:31–44.

Rosenfeld, R., R. Fornango, and E. Baumer. 2005. "Did *Ceasefire, Compstat,* and *Exile* Reduce Homicide?" *Criminology and Public Policy* 4:419–50.

Rosenfeld, R., R. Fornango, and A. F. Rengifo. 2007. "The Impact of Order-Maintenance Policing on New York City Homicide and Robbery Rates: 1988–2001. *Criminology* 45:355–83.

Rossi, P. H., and R. A. Berk. 1997. *Just Punishments: Federal Guidelines and Public Views Compared*. New York: Aldine DeGruyter.

Rothman, D. J. 1971. *The Discovery of the Asylum: Social Order and Disorder in the New Republic*. Boston: Little, Brown.

———. 1980. *Conscience and Convenience*. Boston: Little, Brown.

Rotman, E. 1995. "The Failure of Reform." In *Oxford History of the Prison*, ed. N. Morris and D. J. Rothman. New York: Oxford University Press.

Rousey, D. C. 1984. "Cops and Guns: Police Use of Deadly Force in Nineteenth-Century New Orleans." *American Journal of Legal History* 28:41–66.

Rudovsky, D. 2007. "Litigating Civil Rights Cases to Reform Racially Biased Criminal Justice Practices." *Columbia Human Rights Law Review* 39:97–122.

Sabo, D., T. A. Kupers, and W. London. 2001. "Gender and the Politics of Punishment." In *Prison Masculinities*, ed. D. Sabo, T. A. Kupers, and W. London. Philadelphia: Temple University Press.

St. Clair, S. 2008. "R. Kelly Verdict: Not Guilty." *Chicago Tribune*, June 13. http://www.chicagotribune.com.

Sampson, R. J., and J. H. Laub. 1990. "Crime and Deviance over the Life Course: The Salience of Adult Social Bonds." *American Sociological Review* 55:609–27.

———. 1993. *Crime in the Making: Pathways and Turning Points through Life*. Cambridge, MA: Harvard University Press.

Sampson, R., and S. Raudenbush. 2001. "Disorder in Urban Neighborhoods: Does It Lead to Crime?" National Institute of Justice *Research in Brief*, February, pp. 1–6.

Sampson, R. J., and W. J. Wilson. 1995. "Toward a Theory of Race, Crime and Urban Inequality." In *Crime and Inequality*, ed. J. Hagan and R. Peterson. Palo Alto, CA: Stanford University Press.

Sanchez, C. E., and M. Giordano. 2008. "Gang Activity in Suburbs Acknowledged." *Nashville Tennessean*, April 28. http://tennessean.com.

Sanger, D. E. and E. Lichtblau. 2006. "Administration Starts Weeklong Blitz in Defense of Eavesdropping Program." *New York Times*, January 24. http://www.nytimes.com

Santos, F. 2007. "'CSI Effect': Evidence from Bite Marks, It Turns Out, Is Not So Elementary." *New York Times*, January 28. http://www.nytimes.com.

Santos, M. 2004. *About Prison*. Belmont, CA: Wadsworth.

Saphire, R. B., and P. Moke. 2008. "The Ideologies of Judicial Selection: Empiricism and the Transformation of the Judicial Selection Debate." *University of Toledo Law Review* 39:551–90.

Sarche, J. 2005. "Kobe Case Settled." *Pasadena Star-News*, March 2. http://www.pasadenastarnews.com.

Saulny, S., and M. Davey. 2008. "Gunman Slays 6 at N. Illinois University." *New York Times*, February 15. http://www.nytimes.com.

Scalia, J. 2002. "Prisoners Petitions Filed in U.S. District Courts, 2000, with Trends 1980–2000." Bureau of Justice Statistics *Special Report*, January.

Schafer, J. A. 2002. "The Challenge of Effective Organizational Change: Lessons Learned in Community-Policing Implementation." In *The Move to Community Policing: Making Change Happen*, ed. M. Morash and J. Ford. Thousand Oaks, CA: Sage, 243–63.

Scheingold, S. A. 1995. *Politics, Public Policy, and Street Crime*. Philadelphia: Temple University Press.

Schlanger, M. 2008. "Jail Strip-Search Cases: Patterns and Participants." *Law and Contemporary Problems* 71: 65-88.

Schmitz, J., and M. Balingit. 2009. "Affidavit Outlines Shootings That Left Three Pittsburgh Police Officers Dead." *Pittsburgh Post-Gazette*, April 6. http://www.post-gazette.com.

Schultz, D. 2000. "No Joy in Mudville Tonight: The Impact of Three Strikes' Laws on State and Federal Corrections Policy, Resources, and Crime Control." *Cornell Journal of Law and Public Policy* 9:557–83.

Schwartz, J. 2003. "Acquitted Man Says Virus Put Pornography on Computer." *New York Times*, August 11. http://www.nytimes.com.

———. 2006. "All Smiles as Shuttle Ends a Nearly Perfect Mission." *New York Times*, July 18. http://www.nytimes.com.

———. 2007a. "Ex-Astronaut to Enter Plea of Insanity on Assault Charges." *New York Times*, August 29. http://www.nytimes.com.

———. 2007b. "From Spaceflight to Attempted Murder Charge." *New York Times*, February 7. http://www.nytimes.com.

———. 2009. "Mistrial by iPhone: Juries' Web Research Upends Trials." *New York Times*, March 18. http://www.nytimes.com.

Security Industry Association. 2000. "Economic Crime Cost Reaches $200 Billion in 2000." *Research Update*, January, p. 1.

Segal, D. 2009. "Financial Fraud Is Focus of Attack by Prosecutors." *New York Times*, March 12. http://www.nytimes.com.

Shane, S., and R. Nixon. 2007. "In Washington, Contractors Take on Biggest Role Ever." *New York Times*, February 4. http://www.nytimes.com.

Shapiro, B. 1997. "Sleeping Lawyer Syndrome." *The Nation*, April 7, pp. 27–29.

Sharkey, J. 2008. "Mistakes on Terrorist Watch List Affect Even Children." *New York Times*, September 9. http://www.nytimes.com.

Sheridan, M., and S. S. Hsu 2006. "Localities Operate Intelligence Centers to Pool Terror Data." *Washington Post*, December 31. http://www.washingtonpost.com.

Sherman, L. W. 1995. "The Police." In *Crime*, ed. J. Q. Wilson and J. Petersilia. San Francisco: ICS Press, 327–48.

———. 1998. "Police." In *Handbook of Crime and Punishment*, ed. M. Tonry. New York: Oxford University Press, 429–56.

Sherman, L. W., and R. A. Berk. 1984. "The Specific Effects of Arrest for Domestic Assault." *American Sociological Review* 49:261–72.

Sherman, L. W., P. R. Gartin, and M. E. Buerger. 1989. "Hot Spots of Predatory Crime: Routine Activities and the Criminology of Place." *Criminology* 27:27–55.

Sherman, L. W., J. D. Schmidt, D. P. Rogan, P. R. Gartin, E. G. Cohn, D. J. Collins, and A. R. Bacich. 1991. "From Initial Deterrence to Long-Term Escalation: Short Custody Arrest for Poverty Ghetto Domestic Violence." *Criminology* 29:821–50.

Sherman, L. W., and D. A. Weisburd. 1995. "General Deterrent Effects of Police Patrol in Crime 'Hot Spots': A Randomized Controlled Trial." *Justice Quarterly* 12:625–48.

Sichel, J. 1978. *Women on Patrol*. Washington, DC: U.S. Government Printing Office.

Sickmund, M. 2003. "Juveniles in Court." In *National Report Series Bulletin*. Washington, DC: Office of Juvenile Justice and Delinquency Prevention, June.

SignOnSanDiego.com. 2008. http://www .signonsandiego.com/news/metro/20080504-9999-In4de.

Silver, J. D. 2009. "Critical Error by 911 Worker Failed to Note Poplawski Owned Guns." *Pittsburgh Post-Gazette*, April 7. http://www.post-gazette.com.

Silverman, E. 1999. *NYPD Battles Crime*. Boston: Northeastern University Press.

Simon, R. 1975. *Women and Crime*. Lexington, MA: D.C. Heath.

Simons, K. W. 2008. "Self-Defense: Reasonable Belief or Reasonable Self-Control?" *New Criminal Law Review* 11:51–90.

Sims, B., B. Yost, and C. Abbott. 2005. "Use and Nonuse of Victim Services Programs: Implications from a Statewide Survey of Crime Victims." *Criminology and Public Policy* 4:361–84.

Skogan, W. G. 1990. *Disorder and Decline: Crime and the Spiral of Decay in America*. New York: Free Press.

———. 1995. "Crime and Racial Fears of White Americans." *Annals of the American Academy of Political and Social Science* 539 (May): 59–71.

Skolnick, J. H. 1966. *Justice without Trial: Law Enforcement in a Democratic Society*. New York: Wiley.

Skolnick, J. H., and D. H. Bayley. 1986. *The New Blue Line*. New York: Free Press.

Skolnick, J. H., and J. J. Fyfe. 1993. *Above the Law: Police and Excessive Use of Force*. New York: Free Press.

Slater, H. P., and M. Reiser. 1988. "A Comparative Study of Factors Influencing Police Recruitment." *Journal of Police Science and Administration* 16:160–75.

Smith, C. E. 1990. *United States Magistrates in the Federal Courts: Subordinate Judges*. New York: Praeger.

———. 1994. "Imagery, Politics, and Jury Reform." *Akron Law Review* 28:77–95.

———. 1995a. "The Constitution and Criminal Punishment: The Emerging Visions of Justices Scalia and Thomas." *Drake Law Review* 43:593–613.

———. 1995b. "Federal Habeas Corpus Reform: The State's Perspective." *Justice System Journal* 18:1–11.

———. 1995c. "Judicial Policy Making and Habeas Corpus Reform." *Criminal Justice Policy Review* 7:91–114.

———. 1997. *Courts, Politics, and the Judicial Process*. 2nd ed. Belmont, CA: Wadsworth.

———. 1999. "Criminal Justice and the 1997–98 U.S. Supreme Court Term." *Southern Illinois University Law Review* 23:443–67.

———. 2000a. "The Governance of Corrections: Implications of the Changing Interface of Courts and Corrections." In *Criminal Justice 2000*, vol. 2, *Boundary Changes in Criminal Justice Organizations*. Washington, DC: National Institute of Justice, 113–66.

———. 2000b. *Law and Contemporary Corrections*. Belmont, CA: Wadsworth.

———. 2003. *Criminal Procedure*. Belmont, CA: Wadsworth.

———. 2004. *Constitutional Rights: Myths and Realities*. Belmont, CA: Wadsworth.

———. 2007. "Prisoners' Rights and the Rehnquist Court Era." *Prison Journal* 87:457–76.

Smith, C. E., and J. A. Baugh. 2000. *The Real Clarence Thomas: Confirmation Veracity Meets Performance Reality*. New York: Peter Lang.

Smith, C. E., and H. Feldman. 2001. "Burdens of the Bench: State Supreme Courts' Non-Judicial Tasks." *Judicature* 84:304–9.

Smith, C. E., and J. Hurst. 1996. "Law and Police Agencies' Policies: Perceptions of the Relative Impact of Constitutional Law Decisions and Civil Liabilities Decisions." Paper given at the annual meeting of the American Society of Criminology, Chicago.

Smith, C. E., M. A. McCall, and M. M. McCall. 2009. "The Roberts Court and Criminal Justice at the Dawn of the 2008 Term." *Charleston Law Review* 3:265–87.

Smith, C. E., M. McCall, and C. Perez McCluskey. 2005. *Law and Criminal Justice: Emerging Issues in the Twenty-first Century*. New York: Peter Lang.

Smith, C. E., and R. Ochoa. 1996. "The Peremptory Challenge in the Eyes of the Trial Judge." *Judicature* 79:185–89.

Smith, S. K., and C. J. DeFrances. 1996. "Indigent Defense." Bureau of Justice Statistics *Bulletin*, February.

Snyder, H. N., and M. Sickmund. 2006. *Juvenile Offenders and Victims: 2006 National Report*. Washington, DC: U.S. Office of Juvenile Justice and Delinquency Prevention, March.

Sorensen, J. R., J. M. Marquart, and D. E. Brock. 1993. "Factors Related to Killings of Felons by Police Officers: A Test of the Community Violence and Conflict Hypotheses." *Justice Quarterly* 10:417–40.

Sorensen, J. R., and D. H. Wallace. 1999. "Prosecutorial Discretion in Seeking Death: An Analysis of Racial Disparity in the Pretrial Stages of Case Processing in a Midwestern County." *Justice Quarterly* 16:561–78.

Spangenberg Group. 2007. "Rates of Compensation Paid to Court-Appointed Counsel in Non-Capital Felony Cases at Trial: A State-by-State Overview." American Bar Association Information Program, June. http://www.abanet.org.

Spangenberg, R. L., and M. L. Beeman. 1995. "Indigent Defense Systems in the United States." *Law and Contemporary Problems* 58:31–49.

Sparrow, M. K., M. H. Moore, and D. M. Kennedy. 1990. *Beyond 911: A New Era for Policing*. New York: Basic Books.

Spears, J. W., and C. C. Spohn. 1997. "The Effect of Evidence Factors and Victim Characteristics on Prosecutors' Charging Decisions in Sexual Assault Cases." *Justice Quarterly* 14:501–24.

Spelman, W. G., and D. K. Brown. 1984. *Calling the Police: Citizen Reporting of Serious Crime*. Washington, DC: Police Executive Research Forum.

Spencer, C. 2000. "Nonlethal Weapons Aid Lawmen: Police Turn to Beanbag Guns, Pepper Spray to Save Lives of Defiant Suspects." *Arkansas Democrat-Gazette*, November 6, p. B1.

Spencer, M. 2009. "The Wrong Stephen Morgan's Photo Posted Online in Wesleyan Student's Death." *Hartford Courant*, May 8. http://www.courant.com.

Spitzer, S. 1975. "Toward a Marxian Theory of Deviance." *Social Problems* 22:638–51.

Spohn, C. 1992. "An Analysis of the 'Jury Trial Penalty' and Its Effect on Black and White Offenders." *Justice Professional* 7:93–97.

Spohn, C., and D. Holleran. 2000. "The Imprisonment Penalty Paid by Young, Unemployed Black and Hispanic Male Offenders." *Criminology* 38:281–306.

———. 2001. "Prosecuting Sexual Assault: A Comparison of Charging Decisions in Sexual Assault Cases Involving Strangers, Acquaintances, and Intimate Partners." *Justice Quarterly* 18:651–85.

Staba, D. 2007. "Killer of 3 Women in Buffalo Area Is Given a Life Term." *New York Times*, August 15. http://www.nytimes.com

Stahl, A. 2008a. *Drug Offense Cases in Juvenile Courts, 1985–2004*. Washington, DC: U.S. Department of Justice.

———. 2008b. *Petitioned Status Offense Cases in Juvenile Court*. OJJDP Fact Sheet #FS-200802. Washington, DC: U.S. Department of Justice.

Stahl, A., T. Finnegan, and W. Kang. 2007. *Easy Access to Juvenile Court Statistics: 1985–2004*. http://ojjdp.ncjrs.gov/ojstatbb/ezajcs.

Stafford, M. C., and M. Warr. 1993. "A Reconceptualization of General and Specific Deterrence." *Journal of Research in Crime and Delinquency* 30 (May): 123–35.

Standora, L. 2009. "Student Slain on Wesleyan Campus; Armed and Dangerous Suspect on the Loose." *New York Daily News*, May 7. http://www.nydailynews.com.

Stanko, E. 1988. "The Impact of Victim Assessment on Prosecutors' Screening Decisions: The Case of the New York District Attorney's Office." In *Criminal Justice: Law and Politics*, 5th ed., ed. G. F. Cole. Pacific Grove, CA: Brooks/Cole.

Stecklow, S., J. Singer, and A. O. Patrick. 2005. "Watch on the Thames." *Wall Street Journal*, July 8. http://www.wsj.com.

Steffensmeier, D., and S. Demuth. 2001. "Ethnicity and Judges' Sentencing Decisions: Hispanic-Black-White Comparisons." *Criminology* 39:145–78.

Steffensmeier, D., J. Kramer, and C. Streifel. 1993. "Gender and Imprisonment Decisions." *Criminology* 31:411–46.

Steffensmeier, D., J. Ulmer, and J. Kramer. 1998. "The Interaction of Race, Gender, and Age in Criminal Sentencing: The Punishment Cost of Being Young, Black, and Male." *Criminology* 36:763–97.

Steinberg, J. 1999. "The Coming Crime Wave Is Washed Up." *New York Times,* January 3, p. 4WK.

Steiner, B., C. Hemmens, and V. Bell. 2006. "Legislative Waiver Reconsidered: General Deterrent Effects of Statutory Exclusion Laws Enacted Post-1979." *Justice Quarterly* 23:34–59.

Steiner, B., and E. Wright. 2006. "Assessing the Relative Effects of State Direct File Waiver Laws on Violent Juvenile Crime: Deterrence or Irrelevance?" *Journal of Criminal Law and Criminology* 96:1451–77.

Stephens, M. 2008. "Ignoring Justice: Prosecutorial Discretion and the Ethics of Charging." *Northern Kentucky Law Review* 35:53–65.

Stephens, S. 2007. "The True Effect of Crime Scene Television on the Justice System: The 'CSI Effect' on Real Crime Labs." *New England Law Review* 41:591–607.

Steury, E., and N. Frank. 1990. "Gender Bias and Pretrial Release: More Pieces of the Puzzle." *Journal of Criminal Justice* 18:417–32.

Steward, D., and M. Totman. 2005. *Racial Profiling: Don't Mind If I Take a Look, Do Ya? An Examination of Consent Searches and Contraband Hits at Texas Traffic Stops.* Austin: Texas Justice Coalition.

Stickels, J. W., B. J. Michelsen, and A. Del Carmen. 2007. "Elected Texas District and County Attorneys' Perceptions of Crime Victim Involvement in Prosecution." *Texas Wesleyan Law Review* 14:1–25.

Stoddard, E. R. 1968. "The Informal 'Code' of Police Deviancy: A Group Approach to Blue-Coat Crime." *Journal of Criminal Law, Criminology, and Police Science* 59:204–11.

Stojkovic, S. 1990. "Accounts of Prison Work: Corrections Officers' Portrayals of Their Work Worlds." *Perspectives on Social Problems* 2:211–30.

Stolzenberg, L., and S. J. D'Alessio. 1994. "Sentencing and Unwarranted Disparity: An Empirical Assessment of the Long-Term Impact of Sentencing Guidelines in Minnesota." *Criminology* 32:301–10.

Strodtbeck, F., R. James, and G. Hawkins. 1957. "Social Status in Jury Deliberations." *American Sociological Review* 22:713–19.

Strom, K. J., and J. M. MacDonald. 2007. "The Influence of Social and Economic Disadvantage on Racial Patterns in Youth Homicide over Time." *Homicide Studies* 11:50–69.

Stroshine, M. S. 2005. "Information Technology Innovations in Policing." In *Critical Issues in Policing*, 5th ed., ed. R. G. Dunham and G. P. Alpert. Long Grove, IL: Waveland Press, 172–83.

Sullivan, J. 2009. "New Statewide Online Database Tracks Sex Offenders." *Seattle Times*, March 10. http://seattletimes .nwsource.com/html/localnews/2008833865_ offenderlist10m.html.

Sullivan, K. M. 2003. "Under a Watchful Eye: Incursions on Personal Privacy." In *The War on Our Freedoms: Civil Liberties in an Age of Terrorism*," ed. R. C. Leone and G. Anrig, Jr. New York: Public Affairs, 128–46.

"Survey Estimates Shoplifting Costs Retailers Billions." 2007. *Security Beat*, December 4. http://www.securitysolutions.com/news/ shoplifting-costs-billions-index.html.

Sutherland, E. H. 1947. *Criminology.* 4th ed. Philadelphia: Lippincott.

Swarns, R. L. 2004. "Senator? Terrorist? A Watch List Stops Kennedy at Airport." *New York Times*, August 20. http://www.nytimes.com.

Swarz, J. 2004. "Inmates vs. Outsourcing." *USA Today*, July 6, p. 1.

Sykes, G. M. 1958. *The Society of Captives.* Princeton, NJ: Princeton University Press.

Taifa, N. 2002. Testimony on Behalf of American Civil Liberties Union of the National Capital Area Concerning Proposed Use of Surveillance Cameras, before the Joint Public Oversight Hearing Committee on the Judiciary, Council of the District of Columbia, June 13. http://www.dcwatch.com.

Tashima, A. W. 2008. "The War on Terror and the Rule of Law." *Asian American Law Journal* 15:245–65.

Teeters, N. K., and J. D. Shearer. 1957. *The Prison at Philadelphia's Cherry Hill.* New York: Columbia University Press.

Terrill, W. 2005. "Police Use of Force: A Transactional Approach." *Justice Quarterly* 22:107–38.

Thomas, K. 2008. "For Leyritz, Future in Balance after a Fall." *New York Times*, November 3. http://www.nytimes.com.

Thomas, L. 2009. "Police Risked Their Lives to Rescue Downed Officer." *Pittsburgh Post-Gazette*, April 6. http://www.post-gazette.com.

Thompson, G. 2009. "Couple's Capital Ties Said to Veil Spying for Cuba." *New York Times,* June 19. http://www.nytimes.com.

Thompson, R. A. 2001. "Police Use of Force against Drug Suspects: Understanding

the Legal Need for Policy Development." *American Journal of Criminal Justice* 25:173–97.

Thurman, Q., J. Zhao, and A. Giacomazzi. 2001. *Community Policing in a Community Era.* Los Angeles: Roxbury.

Toch, H. 1976. *Peacekeeping: Police, Prisons, and Violence.* Lexington, MA: Lexington Books.

Tonry, M. 1993. "Sentencing Commissions and Their Guidelines." In *Crime and Justice,* vol. 17, ed. M. Tonry. Chicago: University of Chicago Press.

———. 1995. *Malign Neglect: Race, Crime, and Punishment in America.* New York: Oxford University Press.

———. 1998. "Intermediate Sanctions." In *Handbook of Crime and Punishment*, ed. M. Tonry. New York: Oxford University Press, 683–711.

———. 2008. "Learning from the Limitations of Deterrence Research." *Crime and Justice* 37:279–307.

Tonry, M., and M. Lynch. 1996. "Intermediate Sanctions." In *Crime and Justice*, vol. 20, ed. M. Tonry. Chicago: University of Chicago Press, 99–144.

Toobin, J. 2007. "The CSI Effect." *The New Yorker*, May 7. http://www.newyorker.com.

Travis, J. 2002. "Invisible Punishment: An Instrument of Social Exclusion." In *Invisible Punishment: The Collateral Consequences of Mass Imprisonment*, ed. M. Bauer and M. Chesney-Lind. New York: The New Press, 15–36.

Travis, J., and J. Petersilia. 2001. "Reentry Reconsidered: A New Look at an Old Question." *Crime and Delinquency* 47 (July): 291–313.

Trulson, C. R. 2005. "Victims' Rights and Services: Eligibility, Exclusion, and Victim Worth." *Criminology and Public Policy* 4:399–414.

Turley, J. 2002. "Detaining Liberty." *Lansing State Journal*, August 18, p. 11A.

Uchida, C. 2005. "The Development of the American Police: An Historical Overview." In *Critical Issues in Policing*, ed. R. G. Dunham and G. P. Alpert. Long Grove, IL: Waveland Press, 20–40.

Uchida, C., and T. Bynum. 1991. "Search Warrants, Motions to Suppress and 'Lost Cases': The Effects of the Exclusionary Rule in Seven Jurisdictions." *Journal of Criminal Law and Criminology* 81:1034–66.

Ugwuegbu, D. 1999. "Racial and Evidential Factors in Juror Attributions of Legal Responsibility." In *The Social Organization of Law*, 2nd ed., ed. M. P. Baumgartner. San Diego, CA: Academic Press.

Ullman, S. 2007. "A 10-Year Update of 'Review and Critique of Empirical Studies of Rape Avoidance.'" *Criminal Justice and Behavior* 34:411–29.

U.S. Department of Health and Human Services. 2005. *Results from the 2004 National Survey on Drug Use and Health: National Findings.* Washington, DC: Substance Abuse and

Mental Health Services Administration, U.S. Government Printing Office.

U.S. Department of Homeland Security. 2008. "State and Local Fusion Centers." http://www.dhs.gov/xinfoshare/programs/gc_1156877184684.shtm.

U.S. Department of Justice. 2008. "Foreign National Sentenced to Nine Years in Prison for Hotel Business Center Computer Fraud Scheme." Press release, April 11. http://www.usdoj.gov.

U.S. Department of State. 2008. *Country Reports on Human Rights Practices.* http://www.state.gov.

U.S. President's Commission on Law Enforcement and Administration of Justice. 1967. *The Challenge of Crime in a Free Society.* Washington, DC: U.S. Government Printing Office.

University of Pittsburgh Medical Center. 2005. "Lead in Environment Causes Violent Crime, Reports University of Pittsburgh Researcher at AAAS." *UPMC News Release,* February 18. http://newsbureau.upmc.com.

Unnever, J. D. 2008. "Two Worlds Far Apart: Black-White Differences in Beliefs about Why African-American Men Are Disproportionately Imprisoned." *Criminology* 46:511–38.

Urbina, I. 2009. "Citing Cost, States Consider End to Death Penalty." *New York Times,* February 25. http://www.nytimes.com.

Urbina, I., and S. D. Hamill. 2009. "Judges Plead Guilty in Scheme to Jail Youths for Profit." *New York Times,* February 13, p. A1.

Utz, P. 1978. *Settling the Facts.* Lexington, MA: Lexington Books.

Valencia-Martinez, A. 2006. "Futuristic Gadgets Arm LAPD Car." *Los Angeles Daily News,* July 31. http://www.dailynews.com.

Varano, S. P., J. D. McCluskey, J. W. Patchin, and T. S. Bynum. 2004. "Exploring the Drug-Homicide Connection." *Journal of Contemporary Criminal Justice* 20:369–92.

Vaughn, M. S. 2001. "Assessing the Legal Liabilities in Law Enforcement: Chiefs' Views." *Crime and Delinquency* 47:3–27.

Vicenti, C. N. 1995. "The Reemergence of Tribal Society and Traditional Justice Systems." *Judicature* 79:134–41.

Vidmar, N., and V. P. Hans. 2007. *American Juries: The Verdict.* New York: Prometheus Books.

Vila, B., and D. J. Kenney. 2002. "Tired Cops: The Prevalence and Potential Consequences of Police Fatigue." *National Institute of Justice Journal* 248:16–21.

Vitiello, M. 2008. "Punishing Sex Offenders: When Good Intentions Go Bad." *Arizona State Law Journal* 40:651–90.

Vives, R., and A. Blankstein. 2009. "A Mixed Reaction to a Use of Force." *Los Angeles Times,* May 15. http://www.latimes.com.

von Hirsch, A. 1976. *Doing Justice.* New York: Hill and Wang.

Wade, N. 2006. "Wider Use of DNA Lists Is Urged in Fighting Crime." *New York Times,* May 12. http://www.nytimes.com.

Wagner, J. 2009. "O'Malley Set to Move on as Death Penalty Repeal Sinks." *Washington Post,* March 5, p. B1.

Waldman, E. 2007. "Restorative Justice and the Pre-Condition for Grace: Taking Victims' Needs Seriously." *Cardozo Journal of Conflict Resolution* 9:91–108.

Walker, P. 1998. "Felony and Misdemeanor Defendants Filed in the U.S. District Courts during Fiscal Years 1990–95: An Analysis of the Filings of Each Offense Level." *Journal of Criminal Justice* 26:503–11.

Walker, R. N. 2006. "How the Malfunctioning Death Penalty Challenges the Criminal Justice System." *Judicature* 89 (5): 265–69.

Walker, S. 1984. "'Broken Windows' and Fractured History: The Use and Misuse of History in Recent Police Patrol Analysis." *Justice Quarterly* 1:88.

———. 1999. *The Police in America.* 3rd ed. New York: McGraw-Hill.

———. 2001. *Sense and Nonsense about Crime and Drugs: A Policy Guide.* 5th ed. Belmont, CA: Wadsworth.

Walker, S., C. Spohn, and M. DeLeone. 2007. *The Color of Justice: Race, Ethnicity, and Crime in America.* 4th ed. Belmont, CA: Wadsworth.

Walker, S., and K. B. Turner. 1992. "A Decade of Modest Progress: Employment of Black and Hispanic Police Officers, 1983–1992." Omaha: Department of Criminal Justice, University of Nebraska at Omaha.

Walker, S., and B. Wright. 1995. "Citizen Review of the Police, 1994: A National Survey." In *Fresh Perspectives.* Washington, DC: Police Executive Research Forum.

Walsh, W. F., and G. F. Vito. 2004. "The Meaning of Compstat." *Journal of Contemporary Criminal Justice* 20:51–69.

Warren, P., D. Tomaskovic-Devey, W. Smith, M. Zingraff and M. Mason. 2006. "Driving While Black: Bias Processes and Racial Disparity in Traffic Stops." *Criminology* 44:709–38.

Warren, R. 2007. "Evidence-Based Practices and State Sentencing Policy: Ten Policy Initiatives to Reduce Recidivism." *Indiana Law Journal* 82:1307–17.

Wasby, S. 2003. "The Work of the Circuit's Chief Judge." *Justice System Journal* 24:63–90.

Washburn, K. K. 2008. "Restoring the Grand Jury." *Fordham Law Review* 76:2333–88.

Wasserman, D. T. 1990. *A Sword for the Convicted: Representing Indigent Defendants on Appeal.* New York: Greenwood Press.

Watson, A., P. Hanrahan, D. Luchins, and A. Lurigio. 2001. "Mental Health Courts and the Complex Issue of Mentally Ill Offenders." *Psychiatric Services* 52:477–81.

Weinstein, H. 2001. "Georgia High Court Relegates Electric Chair to History." *Los Angeles Times,* October 6. http://www.latimes.com.

Weinstein, J. B. 1992. "A Trial Judge's Second Impression of the Federal Sentencing Guidelines." *Southern California Law Review* 66:357.

Weisburd, D., S. D. Mastrofski, A. M. McNally, R. Greenspan, and J. J. Willis. 2003. "Reforming to Preserve: Compstat and Strategic Problem Solving in American Policing." *Criminology and Public Policy* 2:421–56.

Weiser, B. 2008. "Police in Gun Searches Face Disbelief in Court." *New York Times,* May 12, p. 1.

Weiss, D. C. 2008. "New DOJ Rule Expands FBI Database to Include Arrestee DNA." *American Bar Association Journal,* December 12. http://abajournal.com.

———. 2009. "Calif. DA Dismisses Misdemeanor and Drug Charges in Exchange for DNA." *American Bar Association Journal,* April 15. http://abajournal.com.

Weisselberg, C. D. 2008. "Mourning Miranda." *California Law Review* 96:1519–1600.

Weitzer, R. 2002. "Incidents of Police Misconduct and Public Opinion." *Journal of Criminal Justice* 30:397–408.

Welch, M. 1994. "Jail Overcrowding: Social Sanitation and the Warehousing of the Urban Underclass." In *Critical Issues in Crime and Justice,* ed. A. Roberts. Thousand Oaks, CA: Sage, 249–74.

"Wesley Snipes Gets 3 Years for Not Filing Tax Returns." 2008. *New York Times.* April 25. http://www.nytimes.com.

West, H. C., and W. J. Sabol. 2009. *Prison Inmates at Midyear 2008—Statistical Tables.* Washington, DC: Bureau of Justice Statistics, March. NCJ 225619.

WFSB. 2007. "New Haven Detectives Plead Guilty: Men Charged with Stealing Money." October 5. http://www.wfsb.com.

White, J. 2004. *Defending the Homeland.* Belmont, CA: Thomson/Wadsworth.

White, M. D., J. Fyfe, S. Campbell, and J. Goldkamp. 2003. "The Police Role in Preventing Homicide: Considering the Impact of Problem-oriented Policing on the Prevalence of Murder." *Journal of Research in Crime and Delinquency* 40:194–225.

White, M. S. 1995. "The Nonverbal Behaviors in Jury Selection." *Criminal Law Bulletin* 31:414–45.

Widom, C. S. 1995. "Victims of Childhood Sexual Abuse—Later Criminal Consequences." National Institute of Justice *Research in Brief,* March. NCJ 151525

Wilbanks, W. 1987. *The Myth of a Racist Criminal Justice System.* Pacific Grove, CA: Brooks/Cole.

Williams, E. J. 2003. "Structuring in Community Policing: Institutionalizing Innovative Change." *Police Practice and Research* 4:119–29.

Williams, H., and P. V. Murphy. 1990. "The Evolving Strategy of Police: A Minority View." In *Perspectives on Policing,* no. 13. Washington, DC: National Institute of Justice, U.S. Government Printing Office.

Williams, H., and A. M. Pate. 1987. "Returning to First Principles: Reducing the Fear of Crime in Newark." *Crime and Delinquency* 33 (January): 53–59.

Williams. L. 2008. "Detroit-Area Man Gets 50 to 80 Years in Prison for Killing, Dismembering His Wife." *International Business Times*, February 21. http://ibtimes.com.

Williams, M. R., S. Demuth and J. E. Holcomb. 2007. "Understanding the Influence of Victim Gender in Death Penalty Cases: The Importance of Victim Race, Sex-Related Victimization, and Jury Decision Making." *Criminology* 45:865–91.

Williams, V., and M. Fish. 1974. *Convicts, Codes, and Contraband*. Cambridge, MA: Ballinger.

Willing, R. 2006. "FBI Cases Drop as It Focuses on Terror." *USA Today*, April 13. http://www.usatoday.com.

Willis, J. J., S. D. Mastrofski, and D. Weisburd. 2004. "Compstat and Bureaucracy: A Case Study of Challenges and Opportunities for Change." *Justice Quarterly* 21:463–96.

Wilson, J. Q. 1968. *Varieties of Police Behavior*. Cambridge, MA: Harvard University Press.

Wilson, J. Q., and R. Herrnstein. 1985. *Crime and Human Nature*. New York: Simon & Schuster.

Wilson, J. Q., and G. L. Kelling. 1982. "Broken Windows: The Police and Neighborhood Safety." *Atlantic Monthly*, March, pp. 29–38.

Winerip, M. 1999. "Bedlam in the Streets." *The New York Times Sunday Magazine*, May 23, p. 42.

Winkeljohn, M. 2002. "A Random Act of Hate: Duckett's Attack Linked to Racism." *Atlanta Journal and Constitution*, August 4, p. E1.

Wiseman, S. 2009. "Discrimination, Coercion, and the Bail Reform Act of 1984." *Fordham Urban Law Journal* 26:121–57.

Witt, H. 2007. "To Some in Paris, Sinister Past Is Back." *Chicago Tribune*, March 12. http://chicagotribune.com.

Wolf, A., B. E. Bloom, and B. A. Krisberg. 2008. "The Incarceration of Women in California." *University of San Francisco Law Review* 43:139–70.

Wolf, M. P. 2007. "Proving Race Discrimination in Criminal Cases." *Hastings Race and Poverty Law Journal* 4:395–427.

Wolfgang, M. E., and F. Ferracuti. 1967. *The Subculture of Violence*. London: Tavistock.

Wooldredge, J. D. 1998. "Inmate Lifestyles and Opportunities for Victimization." *Journal of Research on Crime and Delinquency* 35 (November): 489.

Worden, A. P. 1993. "The Attitudes of Women and Men in Policing: Testing Conventional and Contemporary Wisdom." *Criminology* 31:203–24.

———. 1994. "Counsel for the Poor: An Evaluation of Contracting for Indigent Criminal Defense." *Justice Quarterly* 10:613–37.

———. 1995. "The Judge's Role in Plea Bargaining: An Analysis of Judges' Agreement with Prosecutors' Sentencing Recommendations." *Justice Quarterly* 12:257–78.

Worth, R. F. 2001. "73 Tied to Genovese Family Are Indicted, Officials Say." *New York Times*, December 6, p. A27.

Wright, T. 2009. "Ex-Yankee Jim Leyritz Avoids Jail Pending Trial." *Miami Herald*, February 24. http://www.miamiherald.com.

Yang, S. S. 1990. "The Unique Treatment Needs of Female Substance Abusers: The Obligation of the Criminal Justice System to Provide Parity Services." *Medicine and Law* 9:1018–27.

Yardley, W. 2006. "DNA Samples Link 4 Murders in Connecticut." *New York Times*, June 8. http://www.nytimes.com.

Zagaris, B. 1998. "U.S. International Cooperation against Transnational Organized Crime." *Wayne Law Review* 44 (Fall): 1401–64.

Zalman, M., and B. W. Smith. 2007. "The Attitudes of Police Executives toward *Miranda* and Interrogation Policies." *Journal of Criminal Law and Criminology* 97:873–942.

Zedner, L. 1995. "Wayward Sisters." In *The Oxford History of Prisons*, ed. N. Morris and D. J. Rothman. New York: Oxford University Press, 329–61.

Zhao, J., C. Gibson, N. Lovrich, and M. Gaffney. 2002. "Participation in Community Crime Prevention: Are Volunteers More or Less Fearful of Crime?" *Journal of Crime and Justice* 25:41–61.

Zhao, J. S., N. P. He, N. Loverich, and J. Cancino. 2003. "Marital Status and Police Occupational Stress." *Journal of Crime and Justice* 26:23–46.

Zhao, J., M. Scheider, and Q. Thurman. 2003. "Funding Community Policing to Reduce Crime: Have COPS Grants Made a Difference?" *Criminology and Public Policy* 2:7–32.

Zimring, F. E. 2007. "Protect Individual Punishment Decisions from Mandatory Penalties." *Criminology and Public Policy* 6:881–86.

■ Cases Cited

Adams v. Williams, 407 U.S. 143 (1972).

Argersinger v. Hamlin, 407 U.S. 25 (1972).

Arizona v. Gant, 129 S. Ct. 1710 (2009).

Atkins v. Virginia, 122 S. Ct. 2242 (2002).

Austin v. United States, 61 LW 4811 (1993).

Barron v. Baltimore, 32 U.S. 243 (1833).

Batson v. Kentucky, 476 U.S. 79 (1986).

Baze v. Rees, 128 S. Ct. 1520 (2008).

Beard v. Banks, 524 U.S. 521 (2006).

Bell v. Wolfish, 441 U.S. 520 (1979).

Blackledge v. Allison, 431 U.S. 71 (1976).

Blake v. Los Angeles, 595 F.2d 1367 (1979).

Blakely v. Washington, 124 S. Ct. 2531 (2004).

Board of Education v. Earls, 536 U.S. 822 (2002).

Bordenkircher v. Hayes, 343 U.S. 357 (1978).

Boykin v. Alabama, 395 U.S. 238 (1969).

Breed v. Jones, 421 U.S. 519 (1975).

Brendlin v. California, 127 S. Ct. 2400 (2007).

Brewer v. Williams, 430 U.S. 387 (1977).

Brigham City, Utah v. Stuart, 126 S. Ct. 1943 (2006).

Brown v. Mississippi, 297 U.S. 281 (1936).

Bumper v. North Carolina, 391 U.S. 543 (1968).

Burch v. Louisiana, 441 U.S. 130 (1979).

California v. Acevedo, 500 U.S. 565 (1991).

Carroll v. United States, 267 U.S. 132 (1925).

Chandler v. Miller, 520 U.S. 305 (1997).

Chimel v. California, 395 U.S. 752 (1969).

City of Indianapolis v. Edmond, 531 U.S. 32 (2000).

Coolidge v. New Hampshire, 403 U.S. 443 (1971).

Cooper v. Pate, 378 U.S. 546 (1964).

Cupp v. Murphy, 412 U.S. 291 (1973).

Deck v. Missouri, 125 S. Ct. 2007 (2005).

Delaware v. Prouse, 440 U.S. 648 (1979).

Dickerson v. United States, 530 U.S. 428 (2000).

District Attorney's Office v. Osborne, 129 S. Ct. 2308 (2009).

District of Columbia v. Heller, 128 S. Ct. 2783 (2008).

Douglas v. California, 372 U.S. 353 (1963).

Durham v. United States, 214 F.2d 862 (D.C. Cir. 1954).

Eddings v. Oklahoma, 455 U.S. 104 (1982).

Escobedo v. Illinois, 378 U.S. 478 (1964).

Florida v. J. L., 529 U.S. 266 (2000).

Ford v. Wainwright, 477 U.S. 399 (1986).

Furman v. Georgia, 408 U.S. 238 (1972).

Gagnon v. Scarpelli, 411 U.S. 778 (1973).

Georgia v. Randolph, 126 S. Ct. 1515 (2006).

Gideon v. Wainwright, 372 U.S. 335 (1963).

Glover v. Johnson, 934 F.2d 703 (6th Cir. 1991).

Graham v. Connor, 490 U.S. 396 (1989).

Gregg v. Georgia, 428 U.S. 153 (1976).

Griggs v. Duke Power Company, 401 U.S. 424 (1971).

Griffin v. Wisconsin, 483 U.S. 868 (1987).

Hamdi v. Rumsfeld, 542 U.S. 507 (2004).

Heath v. Alabama, 474 U.S. 82 (1985).

Herring v. United States, 129 S. Ct. 695 (2009).

Hudson v. Palmer, 468 U.S. 517 (1984).

Illinois v. Caballes, 125 S. Ct. 834 (2005).

Illinois v. Gates, 462 U.S. 213 (1983).

Illinois v. Lidster, 540 U.S. 419 (2004).

Illinois v. Wardlow, 528 U.S. 119 (2000).

In re Gault, 387 U.S. 9 (1967).

In re Kemmler, 136 U.S. 436 (1890).

In re Winship, 397 U.S. 358 (1970).

Indiana v. Edwards, 128 S. Ct. 2379 (2008).

Irizarry v. United States, 128 S. Ct. 2198 (2008).

Johnson v. California, 543 U.S. 499 (2005).

Johnson v. Zerbst, 304 U.S. 458 (1938).

Kansas v. Hendricks, 117 S. Ct. 2072 (1997).

Kennedy v. Louisiana, 128 S. Ct. 2641 (2008).

Kent v. United States, 383 U.S. 541 (1966).

Knowles v. Iowa, 525 U.S. 113 (1998).

Kyllo v. United States, 533 U.S. 27 (2001).

Lawrence v. Texas, 539 U.S. 558 (2003).

Lee v. Washington, 390 U.S. 333 (1968).

Lewis v. United States, 518 U.S. 322 (1996).

Lockhart v. McCree, 476 U.S. 162 (1986).

Lockyer, Attorney General of California v. Andrade, 538 U.S. 63 (2003).

Mapp v. Ohio, 367 U.S. 643 (1961).

Maryland v. Wilson, 519 U.S. 408 (1997).

Massiah v. United States, 377 U.S. 201 (1964).

McCleskey v. Kemp, 478 U.S. 1019 (1987).

McKeiver v. Pennsylvania, 403 U.S. 528 (1971).

Medellin v. Dretke, 125 S. Ct. 2088 (2005).

Medellin v. Texas, 128 S. Ct. 1346 (2008).

Melendez-Diaz v. Massachusetts, 129 S. Ct. 2527 (2009).

Mempa v. Rhay, 389 U.S. 128 (1967).

Michigan Department of State Police v. Sitz, 496 U.S. 440 (1990).

Michigan v. Long, 463 U.S. 1032 (1983).

Miranda v. Arizona, 384 U.S. 436 (1966).

Missouri v. Seibert, 542 U.S. 600 (2004).

M'Naghten's Case, 8 Eng. Rep. 718 (1843).

Monell v. Department of Social Services of the City of New York, 436 U.S. 658 (1978).

Montana v. Egelhoff, 116 S. Ct. 2013 (1996).

Moran v. Burbine, 475 U.S. 412 (1986).

Morrissey v. Brewer, 408 U.S. 471 (1972).

Murray v. Giarratano, 492 U.S. 1 (1989).

New York v. Belton, 453 U.S. 454 (1981).

New York v. Class, 475 U.S. 321 (1986).

New York v. Quarles, 467 U.S. 649 (1984).

Nix v. Williams, 467 U.S. 431 (1984).

North Carolina v. Alford, 400 U.S. 25 (1970).

Oklahoma Publishing Co. v. District Court, 430 U.S. 308 (1977).

Pennsylvania Board of Pardons and Parole v. Scott, 524 U.S. 357 (1998).

People v. Nguyen, California Supreme Court, #07-416 (2008).

Powell v. Alabama, 287 U.S. 45 (1932).

Procunier v. Martinez, 416 U.S. 396 (1974).

The Queen v. Dudley and Stephens, 14 Q.B.D. 273 (1884).

Ricketts v. Adamson, 481 U.S. 1 (1987).

Robinson v. California, 370 U.S. 660 (1962).

Roe v. Wade, 410 U.S. 113 (1973).

Roper v. Simmons, 543 U.S. 551 (2005).

Ross v. Moffitt, 417 U.S. 660 (1974).

Rothgery v. Gillespie, 128 S. Ct. 2578 (2008).

Safford Unified School District #1 v. Redding, No. 08-479 (2009).

Samson v. California, 547 U.S. 843 (2006).

Santobello v. New York, 404 U.S. 260 (1971).

Schall v. Martin, 467 U.S. 253 (1984).

Scott v. Harris, 550 U.S. 372 (2007).

Scott v. Illinois, 440 U.S. 367 (1979).

Skinner v. Oklahoma, 316 U.S. 535 (1942).

Smith v. Daily Mail Publishing Co., 443 U.S. 97 (1979).

South Dakota v. Opperman, 428 U.S. 364 (1976).

Stanford v. Kentucky, 492 U.S. 361 (1989).

State v. Nowak, 1 So. 3d 215 (Fla. Dist. Ct. App. 5th Dist., 2008).

Strickland v. Washington, 466 U.S. 686 (1984).

Tennessee v. Garner, 471 U.S. 1 (1985).

Terry v. Ohio, 392 U.S. 1 (1968).

Thompson v. Oklahoma, 108 S. Ct. 1687 (1988).

Trop v. Dulles, 356 U.S. 86 (1958).

Turner v. Safley, 482 U.S. 78 (1987).

United States v. Bajakajian, 118 S. Ct. 2028 (1998).

United States v. Booker, 125 S. Ct. 738 (2005).

United States v. Brawner, 471 F.2d 969 (D.C. Cir. 1972).

United States v. Drayton, 122 S. Ct. 2105 (2002).

United States v. Jacobson, 503 U.S. 540 (1992).

United States v. Leon, 468 U.S. 897 (1984).

United States v. Robinson, 414 U.S. 218 (1973).

United States v. Salerno and Cafero, 481 U.S. 739 (1987).

United States v. Ursery, 116 S. Ct. 2135 (1996).

United States v. Wade, 388 U.S. 218 (1967).

Vernonia School District v. Acton, 515 U.S. 646 (1995).

Virginia v. Black, 538 U.S. 343 (2003).

Virginia v. Moore, 128 S. Ct. 1598 (2008).

Warden v. Hayden, 387 U.S. 294 (1967).

Weeks v. United States, 232 U.S. 383 (1914).

Whren v. United States, 517 U.S. 806 (1996).

Wiggins v. Smith, 539 U.S. 510 (2003).

Williams v. Florida, 399 U.S. 78 (1970).

Wilson v. Seiter, 501 U.S. 294 (1991).

Wisconsin v. Mitchell, 113 S. Ct. 2194 (1993).

Witherspoon v. Illinois, 391 U.S. 510 (1968).

Wolf v. Colorado, 338 U.S. 25 (1949).

Wolff v. McDonnell, 418 U.S. 539 (1974).

Wyoming v. Houghton, 526 U.S. 295 (1999).

Boldface page numbers refer to the pages on which the terms are defined.

Chapter 2. 50: Adapted from Robert F. Meier and Terance D. Miethe, "Understanding Theories of Criminal Victimization," Crime and Justice: A Review of Research, ed. Michael Tonry (Chicato: University of Chicago Press, 1993), 467. Reprinted by permission.

Chapter 5. 149: David Bayley, Forces of Order: Police Behavior in Japan and the United States (University of California Press, 1979), 33–34, 37, 41, 51–52. ©1979 The Regents of the University of California. Reprinted by permission.

Chapter 9. 267: From USA Today, Feb. 12, 1997. © 1997 USA Today. Reprinted by permission.

Chapter 10. 320: Timothy J. Flanagan, "Reform or Punish: Americans' Views of the Correctional System," in Americans View Crime and Justice, ed. Timothy J. Flanagan and Dennis R. Longmire (Thousand Oaks, Calif.: Sage, 1996), 88, 192. Reprinted by permission of Sage Publications, Inc. **321:** Brendan Kirby, "Prison Crowding Defies Easy Fixes," Mobile Register, Feb. 28, 2005.

Chapter 13. 377: Berlin, Leslie, "Running a Business After Doing Time," The New York Times, Sunday, Feb. 22, 2009, Business Section, p.3.

Chapter 14. 429: Table 1, p.11, in James M. Byrne, "The Best Laid Plans: An Assessment of the Varied Consequences of New Technologies for Crime and Social Control." Federal Probation 72(3): 10-21.

Chapter 15. 456: John Tierney, New York Times, April 13, 1993, pp. A1, B6. Copyright © 1993 by The New York Times Company. Reprinted by permission.